A HANDBOOK OF LATIN LITERATURE

A HANDBOOK OF LATIN LITERATURE

FROM THE EARLIEST TIMES TO THE DEATH OF ST. AUGUSTINE

By

H. J. ROSE

NEW YORK

E. P. DUTTON & CO., INC.

This paperback edition of
"A HANDBOOK OF LATIN LITERATURE"
Published 1960 by E. P. Dutton & Co., Inc.

HARVARDIANIS
PAVLLISPER COLLEGIS
SEMPER AMICIS MEIS
HVNC LIBRVM

PREFACE

LIKE its companion, my *Handbook of Greek Literature,* this volume claims no originality of matter or treatment, but is an attempt to put together, within a moderate compass, such things as are known or reasonably supposed concerning the classical and early post-classical writings in the Latin tongue. In one respect it differs from the other work. That excluded all Jewish and Christian authors as representing a spirit totally different from that of Greece and therefore needing to be treated separately. But Latin Christianity, so far as the author can perceive, is separated by no such gap from the main stream of Western literature. Greece originated both form and substance to an astonishing degree, and therefore a totally new tone was heard as soon as her language was used to express thoughts largely of Hebrew origin. Rome originated little, and far less change had to be made when her writers moved away from one set of foreign influences to another. Consequently the reader will find, in the last chapter, a sketch of those Christian writers whose interest for the non-theologian seemed greatest or their influence in any direction most important.

Many scholars, including not a few whom I have never seen, have helped me directly or indirectly. If an individual is to be singled out for thanks, I may mention Professor A. D. Nock, of Harvard University, to whose friendly criticism several of the following chapters owe much.

H. J. ROSE

ST. ANDREWS,
February, 1936

ADDENDA AND CORRIGENDA

p. 61, note 107, line 4. For ' differred ', read ' deferred '.

p. 91, line 2. For ' adopted ', read ' adoptive '.

p. 112, line 10 from bottom of text. For ' 747 ', read ' 748 ', and in the next line for ' six ' read ' seven '.

p. 114, line 7. After ' later ' insert a semi-colon.

p. 136, line 8 from end of text. For ' Catullus ', read ' Catullus' '.

p. 169, note 40. For ' had ' read ' has '.

p. 204, line 16. For ' 689/87 ' read ' 689/67 '.

p. 212, line 13 from end of text. For ' showed ' read ' shown '.

p. 239, note 17. Add at end ' See p. 294 '.

p. 243, note 31. Delete text of note and substitute ' See *Eclogues*, pp. 124–38 '.

p. 259, note 91. Add at end ' See p. 294 '.

p. 263, note 103. Delete everything after (61) and substitute ' . See p. 294 '.

p. 288, line 7 from end of text. For ' Kalends of March (The Matralia),' read ' first of March (the Matronalia),'

p. 294, For ' *Additional Note* ' read ' *Additional Notes* '. Add on last line (after ' xlviii, 8, 5.') ' For further observations on this Eclogue, see Rose in *Mnemosyne*, S. iv, Vol. vii (1954), pp. 57–68.'

Add below the following new paragraphs:

' P. 259. The whole question of authorship is magisterially dealt with by Ed. Fraenkel in *J.R.S.* xlii (1952), pp. 1–9.

P. 263. The epigram is discussed by R. E. H. Westendorp-Boerma in *Vt pictura poesis* (Leiden, Brill, 1955), pp. 215–26, who suggests that it is a joke and Musa was not dead but, as we say, dead drunk after a symposium.

P. 269, lines 6–8. Mr. D. C. C. Young tells me that gnats may continue to be troublesome quite late in the year, and therefore 714/40 remains a possible date.

P. 282. See further, Ed. Fraenkel, *Horace*, Oxford, 1957.

p. 305, note 44, lines 3 and 2 from end of note. For ' pede,' read ' pede ' and for ' acuto ' read ' acuta '.

p. 355, note 41, line 3. For ' abductis ' read ' abductus '.

p. 376, line 4 of small type. For ' note 79 ' read ' note 80 '.

p. 405, note 82. Add at end ' See p. 421 '.

p. 421. Add at end ' *Additional Note* (see p. 405, note 82). For an interesting and ingenious account of Juvenal's life and works, see Gilbert Highet, *Juvenal the Satirist*, Oxford University Press, 1954.'

p. 470, line 12. For 'Serapis' read 'Sarapis'

p. 481, note 34. Add at end 'See p. 533'.

p. 511, last line of large type. Delete ', 511'.

p. 533. Insert before note to p. 508. 'p. 481. Note 34. Marchesi's first edition having been largely destroyed in the late war, a second has appeared (same publisher, n.d.).'

p. 535, line 19. For '1887 and 1888' read '1897 and 1898'; line 10 from bottom. For 'books in' read 'books; in'

p. 536, line 17. For '4th edn. 1949' read '6th edn. 1958'. Delete last five lines and substitute 'A new critical edition of the Latin fathers is now appearing from the Abbey of St. Pierre, Steinbrugge, under the general title *Corpus Christianorum*. Of the authors mentioned in the above pages, there have so far been published two volumes of Tertullian (1, 2), six of Augustine (36, 38–40, 47–48) and one of Ambrose (14).'

p. 554. After 'Suetonius Tranquillus' read '449' instead of '429'.

CONTENTS

CHAPTER I

THE BACKGROUND

THE historian of Latin literature has a strange and fascinating story to tell. He must speak of a people capable indeed of civilization, but little better than barbarians when their history begins; he must relate how they adopted from strangers whom they at once despised and admired a growth foreign to themselves and finding little in the way of a native stock on to which it might be grafted; how the new plant flourished and spread and became a mighty tree; how in time it was made ready to send out those vigorous seedlings that have since grown into the literatures of Western Europe and of America. And this task he must accomplish from materials all too scanty, with little help from the early records of the people of whom he treats, and with the obligation of interpreting as best he may a long series of writings whereof but a fraction survives to our time, couched in a language presenting formidable difficulties to any modern, and not least to a native of more northerly climes.

If we try to estimate the condition of Italy at the date when Attic literature was raising its head and Greek lyric poetry was entering upon its final and most glorious stage—say, between the birth of Pindar, 522 or 518 B.C., and the Battle of Salamis, 480—we shall find a strange and varied picture, not very suggestive for the most part of literary or intellectual activity, present or future. The peninsula had been settled, first (about the middle of the third millennium B.C.) by neolithic Mediterranean peoples coming partly from the south, across the chain of islands, once a land-bridge, which took them over Sicily into Calabria, partly from the north, by way of Spain and the Riviera. These invaders, meeting little or no resistance from the sparse palaeolithic population, had occupied the whole country and held it till they were invaded by successive waves of new-comers who brought with them the Bronze and Iron cultures,[1] and those tongues, or the most important elements of them, from which sprung the chief Italian speeches of historical times, Latin, with its humbler relation Faliscan, and the Oscan and Umbrian languages. These peoples conquered the north of the country, and the west up to the Apennines, but not the south, and their arrival raised the standard of culture to that of a vigorous and progressive barbarism, feeling its way towards settled government, organized and advancing agriculture and trade, and the practice at all events of the simpler mechanical arts, with the beginnings of the fine arts also.[2] In turn, these invaders were invaded, and that from several quarters. From across the Adriatic came waves of Illyrians, barbarians like the inhabitants of Italy, and left traces of their speech and customs for future ages to note. Much more important, because far more civilized, were an Eastern people, the Etruscans, or, as they seem to have called themselves, the Rásna ; the Greeks knew them as Tyrsenoi or Tyrrhenoi, the Romans as Etrusci or later, Tusci, their country as Etruria. These began to immigrate, probably in small parties, seeking to found trading settlements rather than to conquer, perhaps about 820 B.C.[3] In no very long time they had become masters of a great portion of the peninsula, including not only the modern Tuscany but the fertile Campania, down to Naples. 500 B.C. is the approximate date of their greatest power, which was destined to be lessened, shattered and finally annihilated by successive blows from the Greeks (Battle of Cumae, 474), the Samnites, the principal Oscan-speaking people

[1] By ' culture ' is meant simply a mode of communal life characteristically human, *i.e.*, beyond the capacity of any beast. Refinement and civilization are not implied, though not excluded. Thus we may speak alike of the ' culture ' of the Australian blacks and of the modern French, distinguishing them as lower and higher respectively.

[2] A very brief account of these early movements will be found in *P.C.I.*, chap. i. For a fuller, but still brief, popular and very readable, treatment, see D. Randall-MacIver, *Italy before the Romans*, Oxford, 1928. On p. 13 of that work are listed three more detailed treatises, and these in turn give numerous references to the vast specialist literature, while more will be found in F. von Duhn, *Italische Gräberkunde*, Heidelberg, Winter, 1924–39.

[3] The old standard work on the Etruscans is K. O. Müller, *Die Etrusker*, Breslau, Max, 1828, revised and re-issued (Stuttgart, Heitz) in 1877 by W. Deecke and cited as Müller-Deecke. The older English work on the same subject, G. Dennis, *Cities and Cemeteries of Etruria* (third ed., London, Murray, 1883), is still of value and extremely readable. Later and excellent works are P. Ducati, *Etruria antica*, Torino, Paravia & Co., 1924 ; R.-MacIver, *The Etruscans*, Oxford, 1927 ; same, *Villanovans and Early Etruscans*, Oxford, 1924.

(Campania overrun, about 424), the Gauls (who invaded the region of the Po early in the fourth century) and the Latins, headed by the Romans (capture of Veii, 396, followed during about a century and a half by successive advances of Rome into Etruscan territory).

That all these peoples, or some of them, had at least the beginnings of literary activities is likely, and indeed some few facts may be adduced tending to prove it. As we shall see later (p. 12), the Oscans had developed a kind of drama in historical times, whereof the Roman writers made use: we may suspect Greek influence here. The Etruscans certainly had a sacral literature, whereof it is probable that one unintelligible document survives, the famous mummy-wrappings of the museum at Agram.[4] In addition, they had a mythology, for numerous Etruscan paintings show scenes in which gods and heroes take part, and some few of these agree with no known Greek story and therefore are probably not adaptations, but representations of native tales. They had also legends of their own past; for one of the few remnants which have come to us from the Etruscan learning of the Emperor Claudius (see p. 350) mentions one, and is confirmed, at least for the real existence of the legend, by Etruscan art. Servius Tullius, says the imperial antiquarian, if we may believe the Tuscans, was the faithful follower of Caelius Vibenna. At length, after many reverses of fortune, he led to Rome what was left of Caelius' army, settled there, named the Caelian hill after his old chief and, abandoning his Etruscan name of Mastarna, took his more familiar Latin appellation and became king.[5] Now one of the frescoes on the walls of the famous François tomb at Vulci[6] shows us two men, whereof one has his

[4] See M. Runes, *Der etruskische Text der agramer Mumienbinde*, Göttingen, Vanderhoeck u. Ruprecht, 1935 (= Forschungen z. griech. u. lat. Grammatik, 77 Heft).

[5] *C.I.L.*, xiii, 1668, col. i, 17 *sqq.*; Seruius Tullius . . . si Tuscos (sequimur), Caeli quondam Viuennae (*sic*) sodalis fidelissimus omnisque eius casus comes, postquam uaria fortuna exactus cum omnibus reliquis Caeliani exercitus Etruria excessit, montem Caelium occupauit et a duce suo Caelio ita appellita*uit* (appellitatus *the inscription*), mutatoque nomine, nam Tusce Mastarna ei nomen erat, ita appellatus est ut dixi, et regnum summa cum rei p(ublicae) utilitate optinuit. This is the famous bronze tablet of Lyons, preserved there since its discovery in 1528, containing the emperor's speech on bestowing the right to sit in the senate on inhabitants of Gallia Comata. I cite from the text of Fabia, *La table claudienne de Lyon*, Lyon, Audin, 1929.

[6] Reproduced, *e.g.*, by Martha, *L'art étrusque* (Paris, Firmin-Didot, 1889), p. 397; Fabia in his commentary, *op. cit.*, p. 73 *sqq.*, gives a sketch of the divergent views of critics as to the historicity of the story.

hands bound and the other is cutting the ropes to free him. The captive is labelled, after the fashion of such pictures, with the name *Caile Vipina* in Etruscan lettering; his deliverer is similarly named *Macstrna*. Thus the story is probably cited quite correctly from some Etruscan source, now totally lost to us; but the mere mention of it suggests that that most interesting people had historians of their own, very likely imitators of the Greeks, as the Roman writers were, and busied, after the fashion of their models, with collecting and systematizing the legends as well as the more authenticated facts of their nation's history.

The Romans themselves also had some literary monuments of ancient date. In the first place, there were traditional hymns going back to an epoch clearly remote, though not now to be fixed with any certainty. Of these we have one complete, though in a late copy, made by a stone-cutter who did not understand what he was carving and likely enough had anything but a correct text to guide him. This is the famous hymn of the Arval Brothers (*Fratres aruales*), a venerable priesthood said to have been founded by Romulus (*i.e.*, of unknown but ancient origin), revived by Augustus and still in existence under Elagabalus, in A.D. 218. By a fortunate chance we have a series of inscriptions containing a large part of their official records, and one of them gives the text of the hymn, in a description of one of their ceremonies in the above year.

As we have it, the words run thus: enos Lases iuuate (*three times*); neue luerue Marmar sins incurrere in pleores (*three times*); satur fu, fere Mars, limen sali, sta berber (*three times*); semunis alternei aduocapit conctos (*three times*); enos Marmor iuuato (*three times*); triumpe (*five times*). The division of the letters into words is conjectural and not always certain by any means; a very tentative rendering is as follows. 'O help us, ye Lares! Mars, let not destruction fall upon more. Be satisfied, fierce Mars; leap upon (?) the threshold; stay there, there (?). Call, either side (?) in turn, upon all the Semunes (spirits of sowing). Help us, Mars! Dance!' That the Arvals themselves understood it is most unlikely, and they sang it from written copies, not trusting their memories.[7]

We have also fragments of the hymn of another priesthood, the Salii or dancers, which we know consisted in large measure

[7] It should be understood that even this translation is made only by several times emending the letters of the inscription (*C.I.L.*, vi, 2104, 32 *sqq.*; Henzen, *Acta fratrum arualium*, Berlin, Reimer, 1874, p. cciv) and more than once guessing at the meaning. For a recent examination, see E. Norden, *Aus altrömischen Priesterbüchern* (Lund and Leipzig, 1939), p. 109 *sqq.* For a brief account of the corporation, see Wissowa, *R.K.R.*, p. 561 *sqq.*

of invocations to various deities, together with mentions of certain prominent men. These, however, have come down to us only in quotations, and the copyists of the authors citing them, excusably puzzled by compositions popularly attributed to Numa and next to unintelligible even to learned men in Augustus' day, have often corrupted them past certain restoration.[8] Even if we had authentic texts of the period when they, or the earliest of them, were composed, it would be no easy task for the most competent modern Latinist to produce a translation which should satisfy all his colleagues.

Next, we know that certain ancient ballads or lays once existed, for the elder Cato (p. 91 *sqq.*) had at least heard of them, and of the custom of having boys sing them at banquets. But they were lost before the time of Cicero, who vainly wishes that he could get hold of them. Their contents, according to Cato, were the praises of famous men,[9] *clarorum uirorum laudes*, which suggests some kind of narrative of their exploits, such as might have led, and in Greece did lead, in time to epic poetry.[10] Where Cato got his knowledge of them we cannot say.

The ingenious theory of Niebuhr, that the current legends of the Roman kings represent the contents of these and similar ballads, which was used by Macaulay for his *Lays of Ancient Rome*, was refuted by Schwegler in his *Römische Geschichte* (vol. i, Tübingen, 1853) and is now held by no scholar.[11]

In addition, there were some other ancient works which may have been in verse, for they are described as *carmina*. But it is a curious fact that Latin has no native word which means either 'poet' or 'poem'. *Vates* is properly a seer; *poeta* is a borrowing from Greek, and not very early; *carmen* means a formula, whether in verse or not. To this class belong such things as charms, prophecies, proverbs, prayers and other short compositions, which, in Latin as in other tongues, have a tendency to fall into a rhythmic, if not an actually versified form. We possess none that can be called very old, but several which may be comparatively late examples of old and native types.

[8] Horace, *epp.*, ii, 1, 86. The fragments and mentions of the hymn are collected by Maurenbrecher, in Fleckeisen's *Jahrbuch*, Supplement 21 (1894), p. 315. and before that by Zander, *Carminis Saliaris reliquiae*, Lund, 1888. See further, Schanz-Hosius, i. p. 18, and for the Salii, Wissowa, *op. cit.*, p. 554 *sqq.*

[9] Cato, p. 29, Jordan, where the references to Cicero are given.

[10] Achilles in Homer, Il. ix, 189, sings κλέα ἀνδρῶν, which is almost exactly *clarorum uirorum laudes* and may have suggested Cato's phrase.

[11] Brief account of the matter in Rose, *Myth.*, p. 305.

Thus, there is the jingling charm against gout quoted by Varro, *de re rustica*, i, 2, 27, *terra pestem teneto, salus hic maneto*; the weather-proverb, *hiberno puluere, uerno luto, grandia farra, camille, metes,* cited by Macrobius, *sat.*, v, 20, 18, as from a 'book of very old *carmina*', more ancient than anything in Latin literature—a statement which need not be taken seriously, for it seems to represent some one's endeavour to foist a collection of relatively late pieces on a public with a taste for antiquities; we know from Verrius Flaccus (see below, p. 444 *sq.*) [12] that it was from an old work on agriculture, supposed to be addressed by a father to his son, perhaps a sort of Latin equivalent of Tusser. There is the oracle cited by Livy concerning the draining of the Alban lake,[13] which is not, as we have it, in verse, yet seems to have a flavour of Saturnian metre about its short, rhythmical clauses. We need not pay attention to the alleged prophecies of Marcius the seer, whose two books were officially consulted, according to our authorities, in the darkest days of the Second Punic War, just before Cannae, for the extracts we have from him show Greek influence most patently; of his fellow-prophet Publicius we know next to nothing.[14] Yet the existence of such works may signify that in earlier days others not too unlike them were current.

There may have been, indeed probably were, other documents of early date in prose. Of these the chief were perhaps the laws, which are said to have been reduced to writing in the middle of the fifth century B.C. or even earlier (see p. 29 *sqq.*), and certainly were old and expressed in the language of a people not yet much accustomed to setting forth its thoughts. Other such monuments of early composition were the public official records, the later successors of which we have in the shape of lists of magistrates, triumphs and other notable events, chronicles, calendars and so forth, some of which at least indicate connexion, though hardly, at that date, direct, with Greek ideas of astronomy and the beginnings of historiography. To what extent the imperfect specimens we have go back to really ancient sources is, in the case of all the historical documents, a hotly contested point; certainly we have now none left which actually reproduce anything later than the records of classical republican days in Rome, for their language is but slightly more archaic, if at all, than that of the surviving literary works. Nor have we now any

[12] In Festus, p. 82, Lindsay.

[13] Livy, v, 16, 9–11, said to be a translation of a Greek oracle from Delphi. But it seems rather to have the flavour of an old piece of Latin verse paraphrased.

[14] For Publicius, see Cicero, *de diuin.*, i, 115, ii, 113, for Marcius, or the brothers Marcii, the same passages and also Livy, xxv, 12, 2; Macrobius, *saturn.*, i, 17, 25 and 28–30; more references in Schanz-Hosius, i, p. 24.

calendar which in itself is the work of an earlier period than that of Sulla [15]; but Roman conservatism has incorporated in the surviving documents traces of something much older, including a list of feast-days probably as old as the monarchy in Rome and picturesquely called by some moderns the 'calendar of Numa'.

For the historical records, the matter stands thus. According to Servius, the commentator on Vergil (see p. 455), who draws in some measure and by some route on Cicero, it was, apparently from time immemorial, the duty of the *pontifex maximus*, or head of the Roman state clergy, to keep by him a whitewashed board (*tabula dealbata*) upon which he inscribed the names of the magistrates for the year, adding any notable events which took place during their term of office; the whole would somewhat resemble one of those modern calendars which mention opposite each day any remarkable happening which has occurred on that date, except that the Roman documents would deal with strictly contemporary history. In time, the accumulated records were copied out into eighty book-rolls, known collectively as the Annales Maximi, or Very Great Chronicle; and on these, Dionysios of Halikarnassos adds, historians later drew.[16] That some sort of chronicle did exist we can hardly doubt, as it is mentioned, though in less detail, by several trustworthy and well-informed writers; modern attitudes towards its worth and ancientry have varied widely, from uncritical acceptance of whatever is cited from it as wholly veracious to almost total rejection of it as a late compilation from no authentic data.[17]

Besides these, we often hear of records of some kind, probably dealing rather with the technicalities of the various offices than with anything strictly historical, kept by the *pontifices*, augurs, Salii, the magistrates in general, the censors, a certain quaestor, by name Marcus Sergius, and, if we may trust the untrustworthy historian Licinius Macer (see p. 203) a number of old volumes written on linen (*libri lintei*) which contained useful historical data.[18] There were likewise

[15] For the surviving calendars, with the exception of the latest finds, see Wissowa, *R.K.R.*, pp. 2 *sqq.*, 20 *sqq.*, 434 *sqq.*; add, for important later discoveries, *Notizie degli Scavi*, 1921, p. 73 *sqq.*, and 1923, p. 194 *sqq.*; Wissowa in *Hermes*, lviii (1923), p. 369 *sqq.*; *cf.*, in general, M. P. Nilsson, in *Strena Philologica Upsaliensis* (1922), *Zur Frage von dem Alter des vorcäsarischen Kalenders*; Altheim, *R.R.*, i, p. 56 *sqq.*

[16] Servius auctus on *Aen.*, i, 373; cf. Cic., *de orat.*, ii, 52; Dion. Hal., *Antiquit.*, i, 73, 1. For more references, see Schanz-Hosius, i, p. 30.

[17] A list of some of the principal discussions in Schanz-Hosius, *ibid.*, p. 31 *sq.*; add M. Gelzer in *Hermes*, lxix (1934), pp. 46–55.

[18] For a full list of references to and citations from these documents, see Schanz-Hosius, *ibid.*, p. 27. Some of the principal passages are: *libri pontificii*, Varro, *de ling. Lat.*, v, 98; Cicero, *de re pub.*, ii, 54—elsewhere, as Cic., *de orat.*, i 193, they are called *libri pontificum*, or *pontificales*, as Seneca, *ep.*, 108, 31—*augurum* or *augurales libri*, Cic. and Sen.,

the *indigitamenta*, concerning whose much-disputed contents this much may be affirmed, that they included the correct formulae in which to address the numerous gods, small and great, of Roman worship.[19] Here again, though certainly an occasional brief fragment shows us the language in a somewhat more archaic condition than that of our earlier surviving authors, we have no proof that anything as ancient as, for instance, the first century of the republic was left in the hands of magistrates or priests of the days of Cicero and Varro. Indeed, Livy complains of the paucity of early records, which he attributes to the damage done by the Gauls when they burned the city in 390 B.C., while Cicero, and not he alone, has something to say of the interpolated and unreliable nature of such documents as were to be had.[20]

loc. cit., Festus, p. 298, 11 Lindsay; *libri Saliorum*, Varro, *op. cit.*, vi, 14; *libri* or *annales magistratuum* and *fasti*, Livy, iv, 7, 10 (apparently official records of past holders of offices, something like the surviving *fasti consulares*), 20, 8, which also mentions the *libri lintei* which *in aede repositos Monetae Macer Licinius citat identidem auctores; commentarium uetus anquisitionis M̄. Sergii Mani filii quaestoris*, Varro, *op. cit.*, vi, 90. Many of these authors use the term *commentarii* in speaking of priestly and magisterial records, with no indication that they mean a different set of works, although properly *commentarius* is rather a memorandum or rough draft than a regular book (*liber*), which was or might be intended for publication. The *libri* or *tabulae* of the censors, *i.e.*, the records of their activities, Gellius, ii, 10, 1, xvi, 13, 7, where it means the burgess-roll, Cic., *de leg. agr.*, i, 4, where a list of taxable property or property belonging to the state is meant. In many of these and similar cases there is no pretence that the documents were very old, *e.g.*, that in Cicero, *loc. cit.*, was a recent and still current record. See p. 19.

[19] On the *indigitamenta* and the *di indigetes* there is a huge literature. The chief works are Wissowa, *Ges. Abh.*, p. 175 *sqq.*; Peter in Roscher, ii, col. 132 *sqq.*; Richter in P.-W., ix, col. 1348 *sqq.*; C. Koch, *Gestirnverehrung im alten Italien*, Frankfurt a/M., Klostermann, 1933, p. 788 *sqq.* The earliest mention of the *indigetes* is in a passage, apparently iambic, from an unknown poet, possibly Ennius, in Diomedes, p. 476, 17 Keil; the *indigitamenta* were treated of by Granius Flaccus, cited by Censorinus, 3, 2 (p. 7, 4–6, Jahn), and by Verrius Flaccus, see Festus, p. 101, 15 Lindsay. The upshot of the discussion so far is, that the *indigetes* were an ancient class of gods, of whom nothing definite was known in classical times, and of whose name no wholly convincing explanation is now available; the verb *indigitare* means apparently 'to treat like an *indiges*', *i.e.*, to worship in due form; and the *indigitamenta* are the results of such treatment, *i.e.*, lists of officially recognized gods, with their titles and proper formulae of address. They were old, popularly supposed to go back to Numa, at least the earliest parts of them, see Arnobius, ii, 72 (p. 107, 26, Reifferscheid). See O.C.D., art. *Indigetes*.

[20] Livy, vi, 1, 2. Whether this is a *uera causa* or not is another matter. Apart from the intrinsic improbability, long ago pointed out by various critics, that the Gauls would burn a city which they were occupying and thus leave themselves without quarters, the archaeological data point to their having respected the few public buildings, including the temples,

From the purely literary point of view, the following facts are the most important. We have nothing, or practically nothing, now surviving which can be taken as an extract from a prose record of earlier date than about the third century B.C., so far at least as the language goes, whatever may be held regarding the contents. If we had, we may believe Cicero [21] when he says that the early documents were the driest of the dry, wholly without stylistic merit. But, whether or not the students of classical times in Italy had before them any writings from, say, the beginning of the republic or not, their constant testimony is that such records at all events had existed. We may therefore suppose that at that early date the Romans, and by implication the other Italians, many of whom were at least as civilized as their future masters, had at all events the beginnings of a habit of making records, in writing, in their own tongues but in a script adapted from that of the Greeks,[22] of such things as seemed to them worthy of permanent memorial. In other words, they were past the stage of illiterate barbarism and ready, if the impetus was given and sufficient leisure from immediate and pressing practical activities were obtained, to create some kind of literature.

We have so far been considering written records of one sort or another; it is to be noted that there existed in early, if not exactly dateable times, a sort of popular poetry which was probably unwritten, at least for the most part. We hear in our authors of Fescennine verses (*uersus Fescennini*) and of something called a *satura*, different from the literary compositions which afterwards went by that name. The former evidently were in some kind of metre, for they were sung at weddings and on other occasions of rejoicing; the latter in some cases at least were sung, and could and did, if our tradition is reliable, take on something like a dramatic form.

The evidence is briefly as follows. Vergil tells us that the Ausonii,

which were then standing, see Tenney Frank, *Roman Buildings of the Republic*, American Academy in Rome, 1924, pp. 83–4. That isolated fires broke out and did considerable damage is likely enough, of course, considering the undisciplined state of the Gaulish horde and the heat and dryness of an Italian summer. For Cicero's strictures, see *Brutus*, 62, on the false claims made by individual families to noteworthy exploits in the past, which Livy, viii, 40, 4–5 implies had vitiated the official records also.

[21] Cic., *de orat.*, ii, 53; *de legg.*, i, 6.

[22] All the Italian alphabets are either identical with or slightly modified from Greek characters of what is called the Western type, an outstanding feature of which is that X = ks, not kh.

i.e., the Italians, used to put on masks made of bark and sing rude verses; Tibullus gives the same account, but substitutes red dye (*minium*) on the mummers' faces for the masks. Horace adds that the verses sung on those or similar occasions were called Fescennine, and that they comprised *opprobria rustica*, countryside lampoons. The contemporary of these poets, Verrius Flaccus the antiquarian, had something to say about them in his lexicon (see p. 445), whereof there remains a brief statement, preserved by Paulus, that these verses were sung at weddings, and that they were named *ab urbe Fescennina*, *i.e.*, from the town of Fescennium, in Etruria; adding a much less likely, indeed a hardly possible explanation, that the name is derived from *fascinum* and that they were so called because they were supposed to avert the evil eye.[23] Concerning the *satura*, Livy tells us (see p. 22) that after the first introduction of Etruscan dramatic dancing, some of the young Romans took to singing *iocularia*, with appropriate gesticulations; and that later on, professional actors began to appear, who no longer 'interchanged rough extempore versified dialogue, like Fescennines', *Fescennino uersu similem incompositum temere ac rudem alternis iaciebant*, but replaced it by *impletas modis saturas descripto iam ad tibiam cantu*, *i.e.*, *saturae* fully set to music, with a written vocal part accompanied by wood-winds.[24] The question here is the trustworthiness of Livy's account, or rather that of the authors on whom he is here drawing. The whole tradition, including that of the three poets, savours more than a little of the Greek accounts which, from Aristotle onwards,[25] are given of the origin of Comedy. This may be interpreted in either of two ways. First, the Roman writers may be describing what really happened, and we must then conclude that the development of rustic merrymakings into at least the beginnings of a regular artistic performance was parallel in the two cultures; a thing nowise impossible, for not dissimilar phenomena are to be found elsewhere. Or, we may suppose that the Romans had no real idea of how Italian, at all events Roman drama began, and therefore put forward a theory in the guise of a fact, *viz.*, that its origins were much the same as those of Greece. In either case, the fact that no account is given of the origin of Roman Tragedy is understandable enough, for it was patent, to far less intelligent men than Livy and Horace, that this was a foreign art, never really popular in Rome. The former view I think to be the correct one; the latter, after being ingeniously maintained by Leo and afterwards by Hendrickson, was well answered by R. Reitzenstein.[26]

[23] Verg., *Georg.*, ii, 385 *sqq.*; Tib., ii, 1, 51 *sqq.*; Hor., *epp.*, ii, 1, 139 *sqq.*; Festus, p. 76, 6 Lindsay, *cf.* Catullus, lxi, 120.

[24] Livy, vii, 2, 4–7.

[25] For instance, Arist., *Poetics*, 1449ᵃ 11–13, and the various writers *de comoedia* collected in Dübner's edition of the scholia on Aristophanes (Paris, Didot, 1843).

[26] In *Göttinger Nachrichten*, 1918, pp. 233–58. For an account of writers on one side or the other of this discussion, see Schanz-Hosius, i, p. 21.

This much, however, may be reasonably conceded to the skeptics, that Latin writers, describing a phenomenon parallel to a Greek one, may have accentuated the resemblances by the use of language borrowed from the Greeks, much as the grammarians, when speaking of Latin accentuation, repeatedly use terms applicable only to that of Greek, often to the misleading of those moderns who cannot read between the lines.

It still remains to ask what exactly the *satura* was originally. Since Casaubon [27] proved that *satura* was not derived from Greek *σάτυρος* and had no connexion with the satyr-dramas of the Athenian stage, it has usually been held that the word means 'miscellany', from the *lanx satura*, or 'full plate', which, says Diomedes, 'was anciently offered to the gods, filled with various and numerous first-fruits'.[28] This is supported by the facts that *legem per saturam ferre* means to introduce many disparate topics into a motion proposed to the assembly, and that there was a kind of dish called *satura* consisting of a variety of ingredients; hence it is easy to see how the name came to be applied to miscellaneous compositions like those of Lucilius (p. 82 *sqq.*). But all this leaves somewhat out of count the plain implication of Livy that there was an element of dialogue in these early and popular performances, and so it may be well not to dismiss without consideration the ingenious, though as yet unproved, theory of K. Kerényi [29] that there existed in early days a cult of beings not unlike the Greek satyrs, namely certain *saturi*, full or lusty ones, whose worship among the country people might very easily involve a quasi-dramatic rite of singing, dancing and jesting, such as could develop into a sort of farce, and so into formless little plays like the 'interludes' of our medieval ancestors and also like the various *deikela*, *phlyakes* and so forth in Greece and Magna Graecia.[30]

From all this emerges the picture of a group of peoples, including the early Romans, not yet literary, but also not illiterate, since they could write, nor without some idea of imaginative compositions, at least in verse, since they were accustomed both to sing serious hymns to their gods and to jest in some kind of song. Given a strong enough stimulus, they or some of them would be likely to develop a language suited to literature and to find themes of various sorts worthy of being expressed in it. That stimulus was provided by an element of the mixed population which has hitherto been mentioned only in passing.

[27] Casaubon, *De Satyrica et Satira*, Paris, 1595.

[28] Festus, pp. 416, 13 and 417, 1 Linds.; Diomedes, p. 485, 35 *sq.* (in vol. i of Keil's *Grammatici Latini*).

[29] Kerényi in *Studi e Materiali di Storia delle Religioni* (Rome), ix (1933, xi), pp. 129–56.

[30] For these, see A. W. Pickard-Cambridge, *Dithyramb Tragedy and Comedy* (Oxford, Clar. Press, 1927), p. 225 *sqq.*

From a somewhat uncertain [31] but undoubtedly early date, Greek adventurers had been founding colonies along the coasts of Italy, as far north as Naples, and also in Sicily. Many of these had grown to considerable cities, having a rich civilization of their own, and maintaining relations, friendly or hostile, with the Italians, or, as they generally named them, the Ombrikoi, properly 'Umbrians'. To the Etruscans they were uniformly unfriendly, and a combined effort drove the allied Etruscan and Carthaginian fleets off the seas which wash Magna Graecia, as the part of the peninsula where the Greek colonies existed came to be called.[32] Later, when the Etruscan retreat from that part of the country made an end of the perpetual quarrels between them and the Greeks, the latter continued to take an interest in a people whose culture offered so many curious features, while trade relations, with them and with other inhabitants of the peninsula, were fairly regular, to judge by the widespread traces of Greek influence which the manufactured articles of the Italians show, to say nothing of the numerous objects of actual Greek workmanship found on Italian and Etruscan sites. One needs but to glance through any work on the art of the last-named people to realize how deeply both the technique of Hellenic craftsmen and the rich mythology of the nation had penetrated the consciousness of these adaptable and intelligent immigrants from Asia Minor. Greek influence was also to be found in large measure among the nearest Italians to them, whose principal language was Oscan. Thus the two most important masses of population existing in the sixth and early fifth centuries, the Oscan-speaking peoples to the south and the Etruscans, with the Umbrians among whom they had settled, more or less subduing them, to the north, were affected by the highest civilization then existing, not indeed to the point of losing their own characteristics, racial or linguistic, but enough to make them learn, imitate and adapt many of the arts of their more advanced neighbours. Of these one would seem to have been a form of drama, at least in the case of the Oscans; as we shall see later (p. 24), the *fabulae Atellanae* of early classical times were derived from Campania, and Campania in turn was most probably influenced by some such form of entertainment as the *phlyakes* of the Tarentines and the burlesques which, we have some reason to say,[33] were written by Campanian Greeks or Hellenized

[31] Traditional dates are, Syracuse 734, Naxos in Sicily a year earlier, Leontinoi and Katane 730, Sybaris 721, Kroton 710, Taras (Tarentum) 708.

[32] Battle of Kyme (Cumae), 474.

[33] See Rose, *H.G.L.*, p. 252.

Campanians, such as that Blaesus of whose existence we are only just aware. Greek became a language at least fairly well known outside the Greek cities, for it was already, and became more so, one of the international tongues used in diplomacy and commerce. Hence the way was open for Greek books sooner or later to be read by those who, as late as Plautus' time, still cheerfully accepted the epithet of 'barbarians' for themselves and the name 'Barbary' for their country.

Most important of all, the Greeks taught the Italians the art of writing, as is clear from the fact that no characters other than theirs are ever used to express any language of this whole region, even the most obscure and least cultural. The Etruscans indeed may have brought the alphabet with them; but the rest of the Italians seem rather to have learned direct from the Greeks themselves, the new art spreading through Campania. When they could get them, they probably used Greek writing materials, namely papyrus rolls of Egyptian manufacture inscribed with the handy Greek reed pen (which keeps its Greek name, *calamus*, in Latin), or tablets covered with a thin layer of wax, through which the characters could be scratched with a small pointed iron or bronze implement, in shape and size not unlike a modern steel knitting-needle of the ordinary pattern, and known to Latins as the *stilus*—the Greek *grapheion*, for the Greeks introduced the tablets (*codicilli*, *pugillares*, *tabellae*) also. But foreign materials for writing upon were not always to be had; so besides inscriptions on stone or metal and such crude notice-boards as we have already found the Roman officials using (p. 7), on whose whitened surface the letters were presumably written with ink and a brush, a substitute for papyrus-paper was found in bark,[34] doubtless prepared in some way, also, as mentioned in speaking of Roman records (p. 7), linen cloth. In time there grew up, in Italy as in Greece, a regular book-manufacture, corresponding on a much smaller scale to the activities of our printers and publishers; popular works were written out by professional scribes on rolls (*libri*, *uolumina*) of papyrus, provided with a round stick to roll them upon, often given a parchment cover, a dressing of cedar oil to keep insects away, and various decorations, corresponding to the taste and purse of the buyers. These were stored, a number of them together, in a case somewhat like a hat-box in shape, called a *capsa*. Books in our sense, *codices* (properly 'blocks'), as they are called in Latin, also existed; in late antiquity, they replaced the papyrus roll, and

[34] Hence the use of the word *liber*, properly bark, to mean a book or prepared roll of writing-paper; see Pliny, *N.H.*, xiii, 68.

were generally made of parchment. One of them would contain, for example, all Vergil (*i.e.*, seventeen rolls of the older fashion) or even Plautus (twenty-one rolls). Therefore a work as long as Livy's History originally was, 142 large book-rolls, each bulkier than that necessary for a book of Vergil or Ovid, took up a great deal of space and was expensive; it corresponded rather to one of our large works of reference, such as few private libraries can afford or find room for, than to even a long and elaborate historical treatise such as Gibbon's. Hence the tendency for such works to disappear, survive only in part (as much as would fill a *codex* or two), or be replaced by epitomes. It is exceptional, and to be explained by the universal interest aroused by its contents, that so large a composition as Pliny's *Natural History* (37 *libri*) has come down to us complete. Hence also the fact that all the longer surviving works are divided, usually by their authors, into a number of 'books', whereof a moderate-sized modern volume, in print large enough to be read easily and with the usual amount of margin, will contain anything from four or five, in the case of a historian, to a dozen or even more where the shorter books of a poet are concerned.[35] If we leave out Christian treatises, preserved as classics of the dominant religion, all that has come down to us of Latin literature from the first beginnings to the twilight can be contained in a few modern shelves. The rest has yielded to decay, barbarous negligence, occasionally hostility to the style or contents of a work, oftener to the more creditable attitude of mind which does not care to spend labour and money over books of second- or third-rate value. We may comfort ourselves with the thought that what has come down to us includes a large proportion of the best, though by no means all of it; yet when all is said and everything possible has been done to restore from fragments the general form of the lost works, it remains true that, for Latin as for Greek, we have not the materials for a complete literary history.[36]

The question now remains, what manner of language it was in which the Italians expressed themselves. The ancient speech, or more accurately the group of speeches, which had split off in prehistoric times from the Italo-Keltic stock and been carried by various waves of immigrants into the peninsula, was repre-

[35] In general, see, for the ancient methods of writing and publishing, Sir F. G. Kenyon, *Books and Readers in Ancient Greece and Rome*, Oxford, Clarendon Press, ed. 2, 1951 (contains references to larger treatises). Some of the Roman publishers will be mentioned later. It should be noted that a volume of poetry is often called a *libellus*, as being a smaller-sized roll than a 'book' of a history or other long prose work.

[36] *Cf.*, for Greek literature, Rose, *H.G.L.*, pp. 10–14.

sented by a number of dialects, whereof three, at the earliest date we can learn anything about, stood out above the rest and had possibilities of becoming the vehicle of literatures; the remainder all degenerated in time into local patois, and finally vanished. These three were Oscan, Umbrian and Latin. All had in common a system of inflections still rich, though showing signs of wearing down; none seems to have had a particularly large vocabulary, though here we cannot judge adequately of the first two, little being left of them. All had a certain roughness, such as might be expected from the tongues of peoples not yet fully civilized. But probably, if an observer of the year 500 B.C. or thereabouts had been asked which of them was the least likely ever to compete with Greek as the medium of cultured intercourse and eloquence, he would have named Latin. It was the language of one small region, Latium, where it had resulted from an admixture of the Sabine speech, a variety of Oscan, with another tongue, akin to that spoken by the barbarous pre-Greek natives of Sicily. Separated from the southern Greeks by the belt of Oscan-speaking Italians and for a time by the Etruscans in Campania, it had less chance of being refined by their more advanced culture. To the north, it touched Umbrians and Etruscans, whereof the former had not much to teach the Latins, for they themselves do not seem ever to have developed a literature of any account, while the latter used a speech so unlike any native Italian language that admixture was more likely to result in corruption than improvement. Yet Latin became the dominant tongue of Italy, drove out all other languages save Greek, which has never quite disappeared, and forms the chief, though not the only, foundation of modern Italian and of the cognate speeches of other countries, as France and Spain. The reasons for this were of course political; the Romans gradually conquering first Italy and then most of the then known world, the language of the conquerors became the speech, at least the second speech, of those of their subjects who were not either Greek or Hellenized, that is to say, of Western Europe, where to-day only some remnants of Keltic and the isolated and mysterious Basque tongue survive from the pre-Roman languages, while in Africa Latin has in turn yielded, not so much to the languages which were there before it, as to those of new arrivals, and particularly to those spoken by Mohammedans.

To judge by our earliest surviving monuments, Latin was undergoing a fairly rapid change, as is often the case with barbarous speeches, not yet given a standard literary form. Some of its inflections are completely lost by the time we meet with it; notably, the subjunctive mood of the verbs had almost entirely vanished, its place being taken by the optative, which is quaintly called the subjunctive in our grammars, influenced in this respect by the unscientific writings of ancient philologists. Final consonants were weakening or dropping; especially *—m* had almost disappeared in pronunciation,[37] while *—s* was so lightly pronounced that it was commonly dropped, or at best very faintly heard, if the next word did not begin with a vowel or diphthong. The accent was, like that of English, expiratory (stress), not, as in Greek, tonic (pitch)[38]; though probably lighter than ours, it was strong enough to cause a certain amount of slurring of the unaccented syllables.[39]. The diphthongs had a tendency to simplify into vowels, especially in the less careful speech of the country people; thus, we find that the literary word for a waggon, *plaustrum* (*au* like English *ow*) had a rustic form *plostrum*; the old diphthong *ou* (like English *oh-oo* pronounced quickly) is almost gone, even in most of our earliest documents,[40] reducing to *u* (like *oo* in *moon* or *foot*). But the

[37] Thus the epitaphs of the Scipios, which go back to the third and second centuries B.C., write *omne, urbe, Corsica*, &c., for *omnem, urbem, Corsicam*, though they also have *Loucanam, ingenium*; an interesting fact is that they occasionally have *-o* for *-um* (*duonoro optimo* = *bonorum optimum*) with a confusion of *u* and *o* very characteristic of Italian. The classical spelling restored the final *m* everywhere; to what extent this went with a restoration of it in pronouncing is uncertain, but it cannot have been very distinctly sounded, since it is regularly treated, before vowels, as if it did not exist. Final *s* can be neglected in scansion, *i.e., dabis supplicium* scanned like *dabi' supplicium*, up to the time of Catullus; after that it is always respected, as in Greek. Whether, in pronunciation, it was entirely dropped or weakened (as in Sanskrit) to something like *h* is not known.

For Latin generally see W. M. Lindsay, *The Latin Language* (1894; the standard work in English); for shorter accounts, his *Short Historical Latin Grammar*, 1915, R. S. Conway, *The Making of Latin* (London, Murray, 1923).

[38] This does not mean that Latin was pronounced in a monotone; it is, for instance, quite possible that the voice rose on the stressed syllables.

[39] Thus, a short *a* in a syllable originally unaccented appears as short *i*, as *incipio* from **incapio*; *periculum* is often pronounced *periclum*, and so forth. Most noteworthy, because largely affecting the scansion of the earlier poets, is the phenomenon known as iambic shortening or *breues breuiantes*. If a short but accented syllable is followed by one containing a long vowel, that vowel is commonly pronounced short, as *sciŏ* for *sciō*, *uàlĕtúdo* for *ualētudo*. By an extension of this, a preceding syllable is similarly affected, and also, a syllable containing a short vowel followed by two consonants is scanned as if it contained but one, *i.e.*, short. See Lindsay, *Capt.*, p. 30 *sqq.*; *Early Latin Verse*, p. 35 *sqq.*

[40] The epitaphs of the Scipios still have *Loucanam* (later *Luc-*), and the much older Forum cippus (see Platner-Ashby, art. *Sepulchrum Romuli*

language was far indeed from being degenerate ; it was sonorous, not difficult to pronounce nor harsh, supplied with a good stock of inflections, which were capable of being used to express fine shades of meaning, and gifted with a certain solid and manly quality, which often enabled a Roman to make up in dignity what he lacked in delicacy of expression. Compared to Greek, Latin, if properly used, was good ashlar masonry as against fine marble.

Since poetry forms an important part of every literature, and not least that of ancient Italy, it is necessary to realize what that careful and measured pronunciation of the language was like upon which all rhythm must depend. Latin, like Greek, and indeed like every European language, had some syllables longer (*i.e.*, taking more time to pronounce) than others ; therefore it was capable of creating a system of verse, like that of Greek, which should depend upon the regular recurrence of short and long syllables. But the Italians seem to have been far less conscious than the Greeks of this quality of their speech, a fact explicable enough when we remember that they certainly stressed some of their syllables, while we have no proof that the Greeks of classical times ever did so. Hence, as we shall see presently, accent was always a prominent feature in the verse of the earlier writers, and subtly used along with quantity in the poets of the best age. Hence it is not surprising that the only native metre of which we have any knowledge, the so-called Saturnian verse, shows no signs of being quantitative at all, and is, so far as we can make out from the scanty remnants at our disposal, accentual only.

There survive, besides a certain number of inscriptions [41] and a few other short specimens, 46 fragments of Livius Andronicus' translation of the Odyssey (see p. 21), mostly consisting of one line each ; also 74 fragments of Naevius' *Punic War* (see p. 26), all short. From an examination of these, the following facts emerge. No consistent and intelligible quantitative scheme can be got without wholesale emendation or the assumption of most extraordinary licences, which would make the verse next to unrecognizable as such ; modern theorists might have taken warning from their ancient confrères, who, trying to find an equivalent among the quantitative Greek metres for this kind of verse, could discover but one line—the much-quoted *dabunt malum Metelli Naeuio poetae*—which agreed with the norm they had laid down, and were obliged to seek other metres by

and *F.I.R.A.*[7], i, p. 14) gives *iouxmenta* = *iumenta*. Later, the diphthong was occasionally revived for rendering Keltic names, as Boudicca.

[41] Best known are the epitaphs of the Scipios (*C.I.L.*, i, 30 *sqq.* = i[2], p. 373 *sqq.*).

which to scan other lines.[42] But assuming accent and nothing else as the basis, we get the following results, easily and unforcedly, from almost every surviving verse. The verse falls into two halves, whereof the former has three, the latter two accents (unemphatic words, such as prepositions and most pronouns other than interrogatives, are counted as unaccented; a long word, such as *onerariae*, may have two stresses, as indeed it would have in common speech). Usually, at least one unaccented syllable separates each accent from the next, but occasionally two accented syllables come together. The former half of the line is normally longer by one or two syllables than the latter, but may be of the same length; the commonest proportions are 7 : 5, 7 : 7, 6 : 6, 7 : 6, 8 : 6, in about that order. As a sample we may take the following[43]:

námque núllum péius/mácerat homónem (humanum MS.)
quámde máre saéuom,/uís et quoi sunt mágnae
tópper cònfríngunt (?)/ímportunae úndae.

That there were other metres in native use, and that the Saturnian itself underwent changes during the century and a half or so in which we know of its existence, are highly likely propositions, but neitner can be called proved.

There remains one further remark to make. This book professes to deal with Latin literature, not Roman. The reason is, that the Romans themselves, even including under that name inhabitants of Latium outside the immediate territory of the City, had no leading or even very large share in the literature which centred about their capital. As Alexandria enticed in the days of her greatness, and London, since mediaeval English literature began, has attracted many men of talent or genius who were not natives of the place, or of its neighbourhood (one has but to recall Kallimachos, Theokritos and Herodas for the former, and for the latter, most of the great names of our literature, headed by Shakespere), so Latin was best handled by such men as Ennius of Rudiae, Plautus of Sarsina, Cicero of Arpinum, Livy of Patavium, Vergil of Mantua, Martial of Bilbilis, Augustine of Thagaste. Caesar, in this as in many other things, constitutes a rare exception. At the same time, the dialect of Rome, the *sermo urbanus* or speech of the City, became and remained the standard language for all these writers to use, as nearly as they could attain to it. To this day the same is largely

[42] See, for a list of participators in the long controversy, Schanz-Hosius, i, p. 16. The ancients referred to are Marius Victorinus, iii, 18, and Atilus Fortunatianus, i, 8. For some commonsense, see Lindsay, *Early Latin Verse*, pp. 9–10; *Am. J. Ph.* xiv, pp. 139 *sqq.*, 305 *sqq.*

[43] Preserved by Festus, p. 482, Lindsay.

true; for although modern Italian literature started with Tuscan, not Roman writers, and therefore the standard vocabulary and syntax come rather from the Arno than the Tiber, yet the pronunciation of the capital is that which all elegant speakers prefer; the ideal Italian is *lingua toscana in bocca romana*, the speech of Tuscany in a Roman mouth.

NOTE.—As it will be necessary to mention a number of proper names, a short account of the system of nomenclature may save the reader trouble. Romans and apparently all other Italians, including Etruscans, had regularly at least two names. (1) The *praenomen* or personal name. Of these not many were in use, hence they were commonly abbreviated, as A., Aulus; C., Gaius; Cn., Gnaeus (these two abbreviations are older than the letter G.); D., Decimus; K., Kaeso; L., Lucius; M., Marcus; M'., Manius; N., or Num., Numerius; P., Publius; Q., Quintus; Sex., Sextus; Sp., Spurius; T., Titus; Ti., Tiberius. The possession of such a name was a mark of Roman or at least some kind of Italian citizenship,[44] hence to address a person by it alone was not unduly familiar. (2) The *nomen*, indicating the *gens* or clan to which the individual belonged, as Tullius. This is written in full. (3) Frequently but not always, a third name, *cognomen*, originally a personal title or nickname, as Verrucosus, 'Warty', Crassus, 'Thick-set', Torquatus, 'wearer of a (Gaulish) neck ornament', the complimentary title of a branch of the Manlii in commemoration of an exploit of one of their ancestors (see p. 202). This would frequently pass to the man's descendants and thus become a family name. Highland nomenclature furnishes a fairly close parallel, *e.g.*, Iain Macdonald Mhor (John Macdonald the Big, *cf.* Cn. Pompeius Magnus). A freed slave regularly took the *praenomen* and *nomen* of his former master, adding his slave-name as a *cognomen*, as Marcus Tullius Tiro. A woman had properly only a *nomen*, of course in the feminine, as Tullia; though she might have a personal name, as Tertia, or be called in her own family by some affectionate diminutive, as Tulliola.

[44] This is the point of Persius v, 78 (a worthless slave becomes a respectable citizen by being set free and changing his name from Dama to Marcus); Horace, *sat.*, ii, 5, 32 (a man of doubtful social standing likes to be addressed as Quintus or Publius).

Additional Note.—Pp. 7–8, n. 18. See also G. Rohde, *Die Kultsatzungen der römischen Pontifices*, Berlin, Töpelmann, 1936 (*R.G.V.V.* xxv).

CHAPTER II

THE BEGINNINGS

WITH the successful war against Pyrrhos of Epeiros (B.C. 281–275, or 473–479 from the Varronian date of the foundation of Rome) [1] the Romans emerged from the position of a purely Italian power and began rapidly to find themselves playing a part in the greater affairs, at first of the western Mediterranean, then of the whole basin. In 490/264 the first of the Punic Wars broke out, and lasted till 513/241, to be succeeded by the second in 536/218–553/201. As early as 481/273 diplomatic relations with the Ptolemaic dynasty of Egypt were begun; in 526/228, with Greek states. By 586/168 Rome had conquered Macedonia, and in the same year Egypt became to all intents and purposes her protectorate; in 608/146 Carthage was destroyed and Greece made a province. One inevitable result of this was that Rome, now suddenly enriched, developed a leisured class, some of whom turned their attention seriously to literature; another was that Greek, the language of the whole eastern Mediterranean, became an indispensable language for a public man to know, and where the language went the thought and literature, already not unknown, were bound to follow. Rome in this period ceased to be Latin in mind, in religion, and in tastes, and became more and more obviously part of the Hellenistic world. She had, however, enough originality, to say nothing of her immense prestige, to stamp her large borrowings from the older culture with an impress of her own; and from that time onward it is proper to speak of Graeco-Roman culture as that participated in by the majority of civilized people down to the collapse of the ancient world.

Hence the paradox, as it seems at first sight, that the earliest

[1] For Varro's chronological studies, see p. 225. From now on, all dates will be given in double form, as 481/273, the former being the Varronian date, *i.e.*, the year counting from what we commonly call 753 B.C., the latter the year B.C. or A.D.

Roman poet whose name we know was a Greek from Tarentum, by name Andronikos. Captured during the war with Pyrrhos, he became the property of one of the Livii, and on being set free for his services in teaching his master's children, he followed the usual custom and took the name of his patron. Hence we know him as LIVIVS ANDRONICVS.[2] As a freedman with his living to earn, he continued to teach; and having evidently mastered Latin, he not only taught boys to read and write but composed a school-book for them. Now all Greek children learned to read out of Homer; there being no corresponding Latin poem, it was most natural that Livius should produce a Latin Homer for his classes. Hence his most famous work, a translation into Saturnians (see p. 17 *sq.*) of the Odyssey. This was still in use, despite its uncouth style, grown also unfamiliar with the passing of the centuries, in the schools of Horace's day.[3] From the little that survives, it would appear to have already caught the tone that was to be characteristic of Roman translations, for it was sometimes very literal, sometimes quite free.

Livius won, it would seem, public recognition as a professional poet, and this showed itself in a manner characteristically Roman. Twice during his lifetime the Romans had need of a solemn hymn to be sung to win back the favour of the gods. On one occasion at least, 547/207, Livius wrote it for them. He was therefore given his place as a craftsman, like any other skilled artisan, and allowed to found a gild of writers and actors, *scribae* and *histriones*, at the temple of Minerva, goddess of handicrafts, on the Aventine.[4]

[2] St. Jerome, *chron.* 1830 (see p. 492), says his master was Livius Salinator, *i.e.*, M. Livius Salinator, consul 535/219; but though the date of the poet's arrival in Rome is unknown, it must have been much earlier than this, when the future consul was probably a child. It may have been his father. Andronicus' praenomen was apparently Lucius (Gell., vi, 7, 11, and several other references); Jerome says Titus, by confusion with the historian. For his teaching, see Suetonius, *de gramm.*, 1.

[3] See Horace, *epp.*, ii, 1, 69–71, carmina Liui . . . memini quae plagosum mihi paruo Orbilium dictare. He does not say that he means the Odyssey, but it is likely. The fragments are perhaps most accessible in Morel, *F.P.L.*, p. 7 *sqq.*

[4] That the gild was founded is stated by Verrius Flaccus, see Festus, p. 446, 26 Lindsay. He says the hymn was composed in the second Punic War, and this fits well with Livy, xxvii, 37, 7, cum in Iouis Statoris aede discerent conditum ab Liuio poeta carmen, *ibid.*, 13, septem et uiginti uirgines . . . carmen in Iunonem Reginam canentes ibant, illa tempestate forsitan laudabile rudibus ingeniis, nunc abhorrens et inconditum si referatur. This was in connexion with certain ceremonies of expiation in 547/207. But he also, xxxi, 12, 14, says, in speaking of a similar ceremony, carmen, sicut patrum memoria Liuius, ita tum con-

As already stated, a sort of dramatic performance was not unknown to the Romans (see p. 11, and notes 27–30 there). According to Livy it had begun as follows.[5] In 390/364 a plague was raging in the City, and various methods of assuaging the divine wrath were tried; among them was the institution of a new kind of show for the entertainment of the gods, *ludi scaenici* or performances on the stage.

Certain players were summoned from Etruria. Without any singing or dramatic libretto, dancing to the accompaniment of wood-winds (*ad tibicinis modos*) they performed a pretty ballet enough after the Tuscan fashion. The young men then took to imitating them, at the same time exchanging versified badinage, and making gestures to suit it. This novelty won favour and was improved by much practice. . . . It was not till a good many years later that Livius, who was the first to venture on a regular play instead of the *saturae*, being himself the actor of his own plays, as was then the universal custom, found himself hoarse, so we are told, after repeated encores. He therefore, asking the permission of the audience, put up a slave to stand in front of the flute-player and sing, while he acted out the aria, rather more vigorously than before, as he was not hampered by having to use his voice. Thenceforward the practice began among actors of merely gesticulating their arias (*ad manum cantari*), using their voice only for the spoken dialogue.

Whatever view may be taken as to the historicity of this account, the last part of it can hardly be thought other than true. Livius, beginning, according to Cicero,[6] in 514/240, introduced plays on the Greek model, containing a large element of what we should consider operatic performance, with abundant solos for the chief actor, himself. That he had a chorus to assist him is not stated; Hellenistic actors often had not, but performed selections from plays rather than entire dramas. The

didit P. Licinius Tegula. Dukerus rightly notes that as the date of this is but seven years later, it is strange that Livy should use the phrase *patrum memoria*; and hence Cichorius, *Römische Studien* (Teubner, 1922), p. 1 *sqq.*, very plausibly suggests that the historian is referring to the secular games of 505/249, when we know a hymn of some kind was sung, see the ancient commentators (pseudo-Acro and the comment. Cruquii) on Horace, *carm. saec.*, *init.* K. Barwick, in *Philologus*, lxxxviii (1933), pp. 203–21, goes so far as to suppose that Livius wrote only the hymn for 249, and that the mentions of the later one are due to a confusion; see Gagé, pp. 41, 134, for recent comment. In any case, as the secular games were also called *ludi Tarentini* and in all probability the ritual was Tarentine, the Tarentine poet would be a very appropriate author.—Since Tegula wrote the hymn in 554/200, it is probable that Livius was by that time dead.

[5] Livy, vii, 2, 4 *sqq.*

[6] Cicero, *Brutus*, 72. His authority is Atticus, *ibid.*

plays themselves were his own composition, translations or adaptations from the Greek, and we have a few fragments of both comedies and tragedies ascribed to him, mostly the latter.[7] They are without exception in Greek metres, some fragments belonging to lyric passages (*cantica*) others to dialogue (*diuerbia*). Which kind of play it was in which his voice gave out, we are not told, but probably a comedy, for the whole passage deals mostly with comedies and farces, and tragedies were never so popular.

The same passage of the historian, however, tells us something of a native drama, developing side by side with this novelty from Tarentum. Livy says:

> After formless, if mirth-provoking jests were abandoned, thanks to this regular form of play, and the pastime gradually became an art, the amateurs left the production of dramas to the professional actors [*histriones*; according to Livy and several other authors, the word is not Latin, but derived from *ister* or *hister*, said to be Etruscan for a dancer or mime], and began, after the ancient manner, to exchange versified jokes among themselves, whence arose the farces later known as *exodia*,[8] which were put together into little plays mostly on the model of the Atellane pieces; this form of amusement had been taken over from the Oscans, and the amateurs kept to it and would not allow it to be defiled by the professionals, whence it became the established custom that actors in Atellane farces are not removed from the roll of their tribe,[9] and continue to perform military service as if they had no connexion with the stage.

The statement regarding actors refers to a somewhat curious provision of Roman law, explained by the later lawyers at some length.[10] A professional stage-player, that is to say one who appeared for money in a performance to which all and sundry were admitted, was *infamis*, or incapable of the full rights of a citizen, being thus on a level with those guilty of disgraceful occupations, such as keeping a disorderly house, of sundry crimes involving moral turpitude, and of such misconduct in the army as involved ignominious discharge. Whether the ultimate reason

[7] In O. Ribbeck, *Scaenicae Romanorum poesis fragmenta*, third ed. (hereafter cited as 'Ribb.'), two vols., Teubner, 1887 and 1888.

[8] Little pieces played at the end of the performance, just before the audience left, literally 'exits'. Despite their position, they corresponded somewhat to our 'curtain-raisers'.

[9] As to what is meant by removing a man from his tribe, *tribu mouere*, see P. Fraccaro in *Athenaeum* (Pavia), xi (1933/xi), pp. 150–72.

[10] *Digest*, iii, 2, 1 (Julianus, citing the praetor's edict), 2, 2, 5 (Ulpian, citing Labeo), 2, 3 and 4 (Gaius and Ulpian, explaining why certain persons were not *infames*).

for this was that the first actors were foreigners, and it was not for a Roman to engage in their occupation, or from the strong prejudice against making money by any display of one's physical capacities (*quaestum corpore facere*), as being too like the conduct of a harlot, the fact is certain. But amateurs were exempt from this ban, because they were merely amusing themselves and made nothing by their antics.

More complicated is the question what exactly the Atellane farces (*ludi Atellani* or *Osci*, *fabulae* or *fabellae Atellanae*) were. We have already seen that Livy supposed them to have come from the Oscans. In support of this we may cite the remark of Cicero to his correspondent Marcus Marius,[11] that the latter, who had stayed away from the shows given by Pompey in 699/55, had not missed much in failing to see the *ludi Osci*, 'since you can see Oscans in your own town council (at Arpinum), if you like'. We can hardly believe Strabo,[12] no great authority on Italian philology, when he tells us that in his own day the plays were actually composed and performed in the Oscan language at Rome; he probably had been deceived by their name. Much more probable, though later, is the statement of Diomedes the grammarian [13] that the *Atellana* was a sort of Roman drama, *i.e.*, Latin, like several other kinds which he enumerates. Certainly the fragments we have, though to be sure they are all much later than the early period we are now considering, are one and all in Latin; at most, we have traces of one or two names of characters which are Oscan in their origin, a fact proving nothing for the language of the rest of the play, any more than the name of Punch (Pulcinello) does for the familiar English puppet-show. We gather that the scene was laid in Italy, in a small town—hence possibly the name Atellana, for Atella is such a place, and in Oscan-speaking territory; but this may signify merely the original home, real or supposed, of this kind of drama. We hear of four stock characters, Maccus and Bucco, who were great fools,[14] Dossenus, perhaps also called Manducus, *i.e.*, Big-bellied Ben, whose greed, we may suppose, got him into absurd situations, and Pappus, a sort of Pantaloon or ridiculous old man, whose

[11] Cicero, *ad famil.*, vii, 1, 3.

[12] Strabo, v, 3, 6; for his date and writings, see Rose, *H.G.L.*, pp. 382–3.

[13] Diomedes, p. 482, 28 Keil.

[14] Apuleius, *Apol.*, 81, all those most celebrated for their cleverness in the past si cum hac una Rufini fallacia contendantur, Macci prorsus et Buccones uidebuntur; both names occur in the surviving fragments of Atellanae.

Oscan name was Casnar, according to Varro.[15] A traditional kind of farce, therefore, with stock characters like those of pantomime, is the meaning we may attach to the name.

Only to this extent can we speak of anything like a native Italian drama, for the *saturae* discussed in the last chapter contained at best dramatic elements. Hence, although both tragedies and comedies were written for some time after Livius, neither seems ever to have got much hold on the affections of the people in general. They became and remained regular features of public shows, including the elaborate entertainments given at the funerals of great men [16] (*ludi funebres*), until the beginning of the Empire and somewhat later; but one suspects that this was rather because the upper classes liked them and were glad to see something in their own country which might recall the glories of the Athenian stage than because the populace had much taste for such things. Certainly tragedies were never very popular,[17] although the skill of an individual actor, such as Cicero's acquaintance Roscius (see p. 173), or the finding of a political allusion in the manner of delivery of some ambiguous line [18] might now and then command success for a particular performance. Horace is not far wrong when he says [19] that the audience would ask for bear-baiting or a boxing-match in the middle of the arias, and we have the historic instance of one of Terence's most artistic productions, the *Hecyra* (see p. 74) being interrupted in just this way.[20] However, between the support of the educated and the popularity which one or two poets, notably Plautus,[21] contrived by sheer force of talent and native wit to wring from the crowds,

[15] Horace, criticizing Plautus (*epp.*, ii, 1, 173) says quantus sit Dossenus edacibus in parasitis, *i.e.*, apparently, his parasites (see p. 43) are not witty, but only vulgarly greedy; Varro, *de ling. Lat.*, vii, 95, manducari, a quo in Atellanis† ad obsenum† (Müller plausibly suggests *Dossenum*) uocant Manducum, and we know from Plautus, *Rudens*, 535, that in shows of some kind Manducus was represented with conspicuous teeth; his name clearly means Eater. Varro again, *ibid.*, 29, speaks of in Atellanis aliquot Pappum senem, quod Osci Casnar appellant.

[16] The *Hecyra* of Terence was produced for the second time at the funeral of Aemilius Paulus, see its didascalia.

[17] See, *e.g.*, Plautus, *Amph.*, 52: quid? contraxistis frontem quia tragoediam/dixi futuram hanc? deus sum, commutauero.

[18] See Cic., *ad Att.*, ii, 19, 3; some tragic lines were so delivered as to suggest that they were an attack on Pompey, who was then (695/59) unpopular. Significant emphasis on the word *magnus*, which happened to occur in one of them and was his surname, had much to do with it.

[19] Hor., *epp.*, ii, 1, 185–6.

[20] Ter., *Hec.*, 4, 33.

[21] See Plautus, *Casina*, 11–12, nos postquam populi rumore intelleximus/studiose expetere uos Plautinas fabulas.

the drama survived for nearly three centuries as a living art, and much longer as a form of literature intended to be read or declaimed, if not actually staged.

Livius' successor was a very remarkable man, GNAEVS NAEVIVS. He was probably a Campanian,[22] but spent a good part of his life in Rome. Having fought in the first Punic War,[23] he set himself to write the history of it in Saturnians, thus producing the first national epic Italy had ever known. Lampadio (see p. 442) divided it into seven books, which gives us some idea of its total length,[24] and its composition, or completion, furnished occupation for Naevius' old age.[25] Its loss is to be deplored, for it must have been an interesting linguistic and historical monument; but literature is little the poorer for it, to judge by the surviving fragments, which are of the most prosy and jejune imaginable. Only in the earlier part of his work did Naevius give his imagination much play. He seems to have begun by explaining why Rome and Carthage were enemies, and to have traced their strife from the days of their foundation. At all events, he mentioned the departure of Aeneas from Troy, spoke of Dido and Anna (see p. 251) and introduced some one asking Aeneas about his wanderings,[26] thus anticipating in some measure Vergil's handling of the story.

But his activity also extended to the stage, and here he seems to have done much better work. Tragedy he handled, if we may judge from the small number of titles (nine) and of fragments (62 lines, by no means all complete), with less zeal than comedy; in the latter he seems to have attained a deservedly high place. There survive to us over thirty titles and about 140 lines, enough to show a lively style, abundant vocabulary, and skill in handling the Greek metres in their Latin adaptation.

The quantitative metres were fitted to Latin by introducing as great an accentual element as possible without becoming too monotonous (as would be the case if accent always coincided with the 'rise' of the foot, *i.e.*, that part which in an English or German verse, though not in Greek, would bear the stress).[27] Sometimes a whole line can be scanned by accent, as 135 Ribbeck,

[22] His epitaph was *plenum superbiae Campanae*, Gellius, i, 24, 2; this may mean only that he was as proud as a Campanian (so Klussmann, p. 5), but it is much more pointed if he was one himself.

[23] So Varro *ap*. Gell., xvii, 21, 45, citing Naevius himself as his authority.

[24] Suetonius, *de gramm.*, 2.

[25] Cicero, *de senect.*, 50.

[26] See frags. 5 and 23, Morel.

[27] 'Rise' and 'fall' are the terms preferred by the present writer, as being unambiguous, which 'arsis' and 'thesis' unfortunately are not.

ingùrgitáuit úsque ad ímum gútturem,

and it is somewhat rare to have as much non-coincidence as 106,

patí necesse est multa mórtalés malá,

though the accent may not be that of classical Latin, but the old stress on the first syllable of every word, regardless of length, as 101,

sedens in cella circumtectus tégetibus.

On the other hand, since an unaccented syllable, not in the 'rise,' was less distinctly heard than an accented one, it was possible to have long syllables where Greek would not have tolerated them, for instance, 27,

qui decumas partis? quantum mi alieni fuit,

where the second foot—mas pár-, being a spondee, could not have come in a Greek trimeter, but apparently the accent on its second syllable made it sound but little different from an iambus to an Italian ear; in other words, – – could hardly be distinguished from ⏑–. Also, a phrase was often treated by Italians of that day as a single word, having but one accent [28]; hence, for instance, though the preposition *apud* had normally a stress on its first syllable, the phrase meaning *chez toi* was not pronounced *ápud te* but *apúd te*, and so it is in 21.

quís heri apúd te? Praènestíni et Lànuuíni hóspites.

In connexion perhaps with his plays, certainly with his hellenizing verse, he fell into a famous quarrel. He composed a line satirical of one of the greatest families in Rome, the Metelli:

fato Metelli Romae fiunt consules,

i.e., 'it is by fate (and not their own merits) that the Metelli become consuls'. One of the family, Q. Caecilius Metellus, consul 548/206, answered with a Saturnian,

dabunt malum Metelli Naeuio poetae

or 'Poet Naevius will catch it from the Metelli', and made good his words by having the comedian imprisoned.[29] In prison he

For a brief account of Latin metres in general, see W. R. Hardie, *Res Metrica* (Oxford, Clar. Press, 1920); for the adaptations of Greek metres to the Latin rhythms, see Lindsay, *Early Latin Verse*, p. 11 *sqq*.

[28] That this was the ordinary way to pronounce a common phrase is plain from modern Italian; *alla* (*valle*) is inexplicable phonetically unless the ancients said *ád illam* (*uállem*), not *ád íllam* nor *ad íllam*.

[29] The mere fact that he was imprisoned and left in prison for some considerable time is fairly good evidence that he was not a Roman citizen; it is hardly likely that, if he had been, he would have been dealt with in so summary a way. The offence with which he was charged was very possibly libel, a law against which had perhaps already made its way into Roman jurisprudence. The Twelve Tables (see p. 30) forbid

stayed for some time, indeed it is said that he composed two of his comedies there, *Hariolus* and *Leon*. Finally he was released by the action of the tribunes of the *plebs*, left Rome, and died in exile in either 550/204 or 553/201.[30] This is the first and last we hear of Roman comedy attacking contemporaries, at least if they were of any standing, always assuming that the offending line occurred in a play at all.[31]

Having thus spoken briefly of the first two Latin writers of any importance, it is worth mentioning that the first whose name we know was an older contemporary of Livius. The famous APPIVS CLAVDIVS CAECVS, consul in 447/307 and 458/296, who was still alive, though afflicted with the blindness which gave him his surname, during the war with Pyrrhos, seems to have published the speech by which, in 474/280, he persuaded the Senate to reject that king's terms of peace. At all events, Cicero mentions it as extant in his own day and as one of the oldest works he knows in Latin.[32] Appius is credited also with the authorship of a collection of maxims (*sententiae*), whereof three are cited by extant authors.[33] The work was in verse, though no quotation from it is exact enough for us to say with certainty what sort of verse.

Cicero,[34] who knew the literature of his country very well,

any one to make a *malum carmen* (viii, 1, *F.I.R.A.*), and there can be little doubt that this meant originally an evil spell; but as *carmen* is ambiguous, it could be taken to mean a poem intended to do hurt of some kind; so Horace interprets the words, with specific reference to legal opinion and procedure, *sat.*, ii, 1, 82, and so also many later authors. The fact of the imprisonment is first alluded to by Plautus, *mil. glor.*, 211, without mentioning the name of Naevius, whom he calls simply a *poeta barbarus*, *i.e.*, Italian; specific references to it in Gellius, iii, 3, 15 and in the commentator, wrongly called Asconius, on Cicero, *Verr.*, i, 29 (p. 140, Orelli); Cicero there half-quotes Naevius' verse, the commentator gives it verbatim.

[30] The former date (consulate of Cethegus and Tuditanus) is given by Cicero, *Brut.*, 60, who adds that Varro held Naevius to have lived longer than that; now Jerome mentions his exile and death *an. Abrah.* 1816 = 553/201, and he draws upon Suetonius, who may very well have used Varro. If it is true, as Jerome says, that he died in Utica, then the former date can hardly be right, since Utica is in Carthaginian territory and the war was not yet over at that time; but in any case it is strange that he should have gone so far.

[31] We might easily imagine a context; some one says that some inexplicable event must have been the work of fate, for fate can do anything, even to making a booby Metellus consul.

[32] Cicero, *Brut.*, 61, *de senect.*, 16.

[33] [Sallust], *ad Caes de r.p.*, i. 2—the famous *fabrum esse suae quemque fortunae*, which may be from Philemon, for its sense recurs in Plautus, *Trin.*, 363 (see p. 55); Priscian, p. 384, 4 Hertz; Festus, p. 418, 11 Lindsay.

[34] Cic., *Brutus*, 61.

could mention no old works in prose save the speech of Appius Claudius (see last paragraph) and some funeral orations, concerning whose veracity he had pungent things to say. But if all tales were true, we could claim that there existed in the days of Livius and Naevius a book in Latin prose which was already very old. Dionysios of Halikarnassos [35] declares that the fourth king of Rome, Ancus Marcius, collected the laws of Numa, particularly those relating to religious matters, and posted them up, written on oak tablets, for all to see. He adds that these became illegible in time, and that after the expulsion of the kings 'a pontiff, GNAEVS PAPIRIVS, chief of all the clergy' (*i.e.*, *pontifex maximus*) republished them. But Pomponius the jurist (see p. 463),[36] in a sketch of the history of Roman law from the earliest days, gives this Papirius a yet more venerable antiquity, for he puts him in the times of Tarquin the Elder, and adds that he reduced the laws to regular order and made a book of them, adding, however, nothing of his own, and that this book was called the *Ius ciuile Papirianum*. That such a book did exist is further indicated by the fact that Granius Flaccus, probably a contemporary of Julius Caesar, wrote a commentary on it.[37] But, though it existed and passed for genuinely old with Dionysios (an uncritical writer and an indifferent Latinist, but not a fool), there are grave reasons for doubting that it was much older than the date, 747/7, when he published his *Antiquities of Rome*. For Cicero,[38] in proving to his friend L. Papirius Paetus that the latter's family was originally patrician, mentions several Papirii who had held, as far back as 312/442, offices then open to patricians only. If he had heard, and a lawyer probably would have heard, of a law-book written by a Papirius who was *pontifex maximus*, and therefore a patrician, as far back as the beginning of the republic or even earlier, he assuredly would have cited him. That he does not is a decided hint that the book either did not exist or was known to be a forgery at the time, about 708/46, when the letter was written. The most we can claim

[35] *Antiquit.*, iii, 36, 4. For Dionysios, see Rose, *H.G.L.*, p. 399.

[36] In the *Digest*, i, 2, 2, 2, a confused passage enough, for he calls the Tarquin in question Superbus, which was the title of his son.

[37] *Digest*, 1, 16, 144, on a lexicographical point. Censorinus, 3, 2, cites a Granius Flaccus *in libro quem ad Caesarem de indigitamentis scriptum reliquit*. *Caesarem* can hardly be any one but Julius Caesar, a very appropriate person to whom to dedicate a book on religious matters, for he was himself *pontifex maximus*; this Flaccus was therefore probably an antiquarianizing grammarian of the school of Varro and so likely to be interested in the vocabulary of laws supposed to be very old.

[38] *Ad fam.*, ix, 21.

for it is that it may have contained some genuinely old material; we have still a few laws which have come down to us as 'royal', and the substance, if not the vocabulary, of some of them indicates a fairly high antiquity.

One collection of laws did undoubtedly exist, however. According to ancient tradition, Roman law was codified for the first time in 303/451 and the following year by the Commission of Ten (*Decemuiri*), set up to end the disputes which then distracted the state and were made worse by the fact that the law was not generally known but still in the condition of traditional 'dooms', living in the memories of the ruling class, the patricians, and not set forth in documents available to all. Three years earlier, commissioners had been sent to Greece to examine and report on the codes in use there, a story which we need not take too literally, but may still accept as true in a sense, for the idea of written and codified law had long been familiar to Greeks and may well have passed from them to the Romans. Nor has the early date of this codification passed unchallenged by modern critics, headed by Ettore Pais.[39] This much, however, is certain, that the code itself, the famous Twelve Tables (*duodecim tabulae*) was compiled somehow, if not at the date given by tradition, at all events early; for there survive fragments which, when we have the actual wording, show decidedly archaic Latin and an infantile style, obscure and ambiguous, suggesting something like a first attempt to express in writing the ancient maxims of jurisprudence of the nation.[40]

As an example we may take the first surviving passage (i, 1–3 F.I.R.A.) Si in ius uocat, ito. ni it, antestamino: igitur em capito. si caluitur pedemue struit, manum endo iacito. si morbus aeuitasue uitium escit, iumentum dato. si nolet, arceram ne sternito. Here, besides the archaic forms (*em* for the classical *eum*; *endo iacito* for *inicito*; *aeuitas* for *aetas*; *escit*; the imperative *antestamino*) and the words and phrases long obsolete in the classical tongue (*pedem struit*, 'runs away', *igitur*, 'thereupon' and others) we may note the stammering style, with its short phrases and its absence of defining words which the most ordinary writer of Cicero's day or our own would have added. The literal translation runs: 'If he summons before the court, let him go. If he does not go, let him call to witness; then let him arrest him. If he eludes or runs away, let him lay hand (on him). If disease or age is an impediment, let him provide a beast. If he does not wish, let him not make ready a waggon.' *I.e.*, if A has a complaint to make

[39] First in his *Storia critica di Roma durante i primi cinque secoli*, vol. i, Rome, Loescher, 1913, see his index under *Leges xii tabularum*. More references in Schanz-Hosius, i, p. 34.

[40] Perhaps most conveniently accessible in *F.I.R.A.*[7], i, pp. 15–40.

against B, B must obey his summons to appear before a court of law, and A may, first calling the bystanders to witness, lay hold of B if he will not come peaceably, and use force to compel him if necessary. If on the other hand B is old or infirm and cannot reasonably be expected to walk to the place where the suit is to be tried, A must provide a conveyance, if called upon to do so, but is not obliged to go to the expense and trouble of making ready a covered waggon with upholstery of some kind in it, such as old and ailing people seem to have used.

These, then, were the unpromising beginnings of Latin prose.

CHAPTER III

THE AGE OF ENNIUS

IN the epitaph which he is said to have composed for himself,[1] Naevius declares that since he is dead they have forgotten how to speak Latin at Rome. This is true in more senses than one. He may be regarded as the last of the old school who, for the most part, did what they could with the language almost as it was, apparently changing the native style and diction but little and certainly using the native metre to a considerable extent. He also, as we have seen, possessed an uncourtly outspokenness which brought him into conflict with the great men of his day. There now succeeds a literature almost wholly Greek in inspiration, favoured and protected by the most enlightened of the upper classes, the authors of which are busy converting the rude speech of Rome into a diction comparable for elegance and subtlety to that of Greece itself. This last task they and their successors never fully accomplished, for it was impossible; but they did make it a literary medium far superior to the unimproved idiom of the untaught Roman. By numerous and ever-multiplying devices of significant word-order, of combinations of words into telling phrases, of euphonic arrangement, they made the most of the small and inaccurate vocabulary (as compared, that is, with the huge stock of words with which a Greek writer could work if he wished), and added to it partly by loans from the richer language which all of them knew, partly by such compounds as Latin still had the power to form, made on the analogy of the simpler ones in Greek. Literary Latin became in time an idiom capable of expressing almost any shade of meaning of any idea; but in acquiring this power it always risked the disaster into which it finally fell, of separation from the living speech amounting to unintelligibility if the common people heard it and an accumulation of conven-

[1] Preserved by Gellius, i, 24, 2: immortales mortales si foret fas flere,/flerent diuae Camenae Naeuium poetam./itaque postquam est Orco traditus thensauro,/obliti sunt Romae loquier lingua Latina.

tional usages so great that to master them took years of study even for a native. Hence, incidentally, the great difficulty of Latin, as compared to Greek, for a modern, once the elementary matters of inflection and the like have been got by heart, and the scarcity of really competent Latinists as against the more numerous Grecians, though the number of those who have some smattering of the former tongue is by far greater. For the ancients whose task it was to write Latin rather than to consider how it had been and might be written, there was always one principal dilemma to face, namely that if they wrote as they spoke, they risked being as flat and harsh as the Twelve Tables themselves, while too great a departure from ordinary usage easily brought them into bombast and obscurities of all sorts. In time of course a modification of the written language became the daily speech of the more cultured, and doubtless this improvement filtered down to the lower orders; we cannot but assume that the mob in the Forum in Cicero's time could at least make out the sense of his public harangues; but evidence is only too abundant that after about the end of the Augustan Age the literary language either remained stable, and therefore lifeless, or else sought novelty by the fatal device of developing as it were *in uacuo*, without reference to contemporary usage, till by the end of antiquity a writer with any claims to elegance was bilingual, using one form of speech for the learned, another for everyday intercourse with common folk. That which befell Greek poetry from the Alexandrian period on was the fate of prose also as Latin advanced. For the present, however, we are concerned with the formation of a poetical style.

As with all literary movements, the periods here overlap; it has never been the case that the last of the old fashion dies and the first of the new then begins to write. But if we want a date around which to group our arrangement of the period, we cannot do better than to take the second Punic War as the boundary, following in that respect the example of the grammarian and poet Porcius Licinus (*cf.* p. 88).[2] Naevius, as already mentioned, fought in the first of the three struggles against Carthage; Ennius served in the second.[3]

QVINTVS ENNIVS, the Chaucer so to speak of Roman

[2] Cited by Gellius, xvii, 21, 45: Poenico bello secundo Musa pinnato gradu/intulit se bellicosam in Romuli gentem feram. By *Musa* he probably means Greek poetry.

[3] Silius Italicus, XII, 393 *sqq.*; it was in Sardinia (*ibid.*, 342–3) and he was a centurion (394–5), obviously of auxiliaries, for he was not then a Roman citizen.

literature, was born at Rudiae, a small town in Calabria, lying between Tarentum and Brundisium, but inland from them, in 515/239, and died at Rome in 585/169.[4] He fought, apparently as a centurion of auxiliaries, in Sardinia during the campaign of 539/215.[5] While in that island, presumably on garrison duty towards the end of the war, he somehow attracted the notice of Cato (see p. 91), then a quaestor, who, being on his way back from Africa to Rome, brought Ennius with him.[6] In Rome he won the friendship of several of the leading men of that day, notably Scipio Africanus himself,[7] also Marcus Fulvius Nobilior, who took him on his campaign against the Aetolians in 565/189, and his son Quintus, who five years later, when one of the commissioners for planting certain new colonies, got the poet a grant of Roman citizenship, apparently without obliging him to join the colonists, for we hear of him as living in Rome only.[8] Here he earned what seems to have been a modest living

[4] The facts are conveniently assembled by Vahlen, at the beginning of his *Ennianae poesis reliquiae*, ed. 2, Teubner, 1903. For Rudiae, see Strabo, vi, 3, 5–6 and Ennius himself, *Annal.*, 377 Vahlen, nos sumus Romani qui fuimus ante Rudini ; Cicero, *de orat.*, iii, 168, who preserves this fragment, explicitly cites it as an instance of plural used for singular, 'we' for 'I', therefore the poet means himself. Date of birth : Cicero, *Brut.*, 72, hic Liuius primus fabulam C. Claudio Caeci filio et M. Tuditano consulibus docuit, anno ipso ante quam ('just a year before') natus est Ennius, post Romam conditam autem quarto decimo et quingentensimo, ut hic (= Atticus) ait quem nos sequimur. Varro *ap.* Gellius, xvii, 21, 43, gives the same date. Jerome, *an. Abrah.* 1777 = 514/240 says Ennius was born in that year, and also puts his death a year too late. Death, Cic., *ibid.*, 78, Q. Marcio Cn. Seruilio coss., *i.e.*, 585/169.

[5] See note 3 ; the campaign is described in Livy, xxiii, 40–1, 7. Ennius may have spoken of his own share in it in the *Annales*.

[6] Nepos, *Cato*, 1, 4 ; the date of Cato's quaestorship is fixed by Cicero, *Brut.*, 60, *de senect.*, 10, as M. Cethego P. Tuditano coss., *i.e.*, 550/204.

[7] See Cicero, *pro Archia*, 22, for one of the many references to Ennius' relations with Scipio ; *ibid.*, 27, *Tusc. disp.*, i, 3, for the acquaintance with M. Fulvius ; *Brut.*, 79, for Q. Fulvius and the grant of Roman citizenship. The date is fixed by Livy, xxxix, 44, 10, who mentions the colonies and Q. Fulvius' position as *triumuir*, or member of a committee of three appointed to supervise the matter ; it occurs among the events of 570/184.

[8] Jerome, *an. Abrah.* 1777, says he lived on the Aventine, very modestly (parco admodum sumptu contentus) and had but one maidservant. The former statement may be a mere deduction from the gild of poets on the Aventine (see above, p. 21) ; the latter sounds very like a gloss on the story told by Cicero, *de orat.*, ii, 276, in which Scipio Nasica comes to visit Ennius and the *ancilla* answers the door. This, though it shows Ennius' household was not large, since he had no porter, certainly does not prove that he had no other slaves at all. But Cicero, *de senect.*, 14, vouches for his poverty (*paupertatem*, small means, not destitution).

enough, partly by teaching, as Livius had done,[9] partly by his poetry.

Ennius' native district was apparently Oscan in speech and Greek in culture; at any rate, he himself could speak both languages in addition to Latin. Plays continued to be in demand, and Ennius could at once suit his own tastes and please his patrons by translating or adapting Greek dramas, especially tragedies. His favourite model was Euripides, and of the twenty-two tragedies known to us [10] three are from surviving plays of that author, the *Hecuba*, the *Iphigenia* and the *Medea exsul.* Hence the tolerably numerous fragments give us some idea of Ennius' relation to his originals. He sometimes, especially in the *Medea*, translated pretty exactly, and he seems always to have kept the structure of the Greek play; but several passages which have no equivalents in Euripides' text show that he did not hesitate to use his own judgement in adapting, perhaps borrowing on occasion from some other tragedy what he thought suitable, as we think he did on occasion in comedy.[11] Once at least he went, not to Euripides, but to Aristarchos of Tegea [12]; and twice he wrote on a Roman subject (*fabula praetexta*, as it was technically called, from the Roman purple-edged dress which the chief characters would wear),[13] the subjects being *Ambracia*, presumably with reference to Marcus Nobilior's exploits in Aetolia, which included the capture of that town, and *Sabinae*, on the story, by this time accepted as a genuine Roman

[9] Suetonius, *de grammat.*, 1, Liuium et Ennium . . . quos utraque lingua domi forisque docuisse adnotatum est.

[10] The number is not quite certain, still less the assignment of the fragments to the plays; compare the editions of Ribbeck and Vahlen. For Ennius' languages, see the well-known passage of Gellius, xvii, 17, 1, Quintus Ennius tria corda (we should say ' three brains '; the heart was the seat of intelligence in popular Italian physiology) habere sese dicebat, quod loqui Graece et Osce et Latine sciebat. That he was a man of Hellenic culture is clear from the above passage of Suetonius (note 9), which classes him and Livius together as *semigraeci*; Festus, p. 374, 9 Lindsay, actually calls him a Greek.

[11] This is based on Terence, *Andria*, 18, qui quom hunc accusant (Terence, for running together two or more plays into one, *contaminatio*), Naeuium Plautum Ennium/accusant, quos hic noster auctores habet. Ennius therefore used this device in plays of some sort; if they were comedies, the argument is perhaps more forceful, but it is not meaningless if his tragedies are referred to.

[12] For this Aristarchos, see Rose, *H.G.L.*, p. 210. The *Achilles Aristarchi*, as it was called, see Plautus, *Poenulus*, 1, is the only tragedy not by one of the three great masters which we know to have been rendered into Latin.

[13] See Diomedes, p. 482, 28 Keil.

tradition, of how Romulus and his men, wanting wives, kidnapped the Sabine virgins.

He tried his hand also at comedy, but apparently without much success, for we know of but two titles and a very few fragments; tragedy occupied him almost literally to the day of his death, for his *Thyestes* was produced in 585/169, and we are told of this fact in connexion with his end in a way which suggests that this was sudden.[14]

His services to drama, however, were less important than those rendered to epic, of which he rather than Livius or Naevius is the founder in Rome. Like Naevius, and following a nearly contemporary Alexandrian fashion, he wrote a versified chronicle of Rome from the earliest days down to his own time, and considerable fragments of this have come down to us under the general title of *Annales*.[15] This work was definitely and explicitly of the modern school of that day—a whole-hearted imitation of Greek models, including the Greek metre, the Homeric hexameter, which from then on became the recognized medium of narrative verse in Latin, as it had long been in its native land.

It goes without saying that Ennius wrote this difficult measure clumsily. Verse after verse jars on an ear trained by Vergil; some are pieces of prose, scanning in that they have the correct number of syllables, but totally devoid of rhythm. A flagrant example of this is the bald statement

ciues Romani tunc facti sunt Campani,[16]

six spondees in a row, a theoretically possible verse, but theoretically possible only. Other lines are less atrocious than this, but offend the ear by too frequent coincidence of foot and word, such as

uires uitaque corpus meum nunc deserit omne,[17]

or too much of that favourite Latin ornament, alliteration, as

o Tite tute Tati tibi tanta, turanne, tulisti.[18]

More instances of bad verses would be easy to find; yet the fact remains that Ennius, with no model to guide him, did manage, in a surprisingly large number of cases, to adapt the new metre to Latin, and at the same time, again and again, to hit on a happy arrangement

[14] Cicero, *Brut.*, 78, cum Thyesten fabulam docuisset . . . mortem obiit Ennius.

[15] For the historical epics of Rhianos, who was a little older than Ennius, *cf.* Rose, *H.G.L.*, p. 344; for an earlier instance of the same kind of writing, *ibid.*, p. 315.

[16] *Annal.*, 169 Vahlen, perhaps not Ennius.

[17] *Annal.*, 38.

[18] *Annal.*, 109.

of words, rhythmical and expressive, such as was in the future to form the vocabulary of Latin poetry. Horace, who was no admirer of the earlier writers, had the good taste to point out that certain Ennian phrases were poetical in themselves, quite independently of metre; he instances [19]

> postquam Discordia taetra
> belli ferratos postes portasque refregit.

One might add many similar testimonies, notably some enthusiastic praise from Cicero, who was a conservative in such matters and therefore somewhat prejudiced in favour of the pioneers.[20] But with all allowance made for circumstances, we must recognize that it was not till some two centuries after Ennius' death that the rules of the Latin hexameter were fully worked out, *i.e.*, the means found of making it harmoniously varied, as a narrative metre must be. The chief lessons to be learned were, that too much coincidence of accent and ictus lead to a monotonous, sing-song effect, and therefore a certain amount of dissonance between the two must be deliberately retained; that, on the other hand, the last two feet should generally scan by accent as well as quantity, and therefore the best way of ending the line is with a word of two or three syllables; and that, for similar reasons and also to keep the line a whole and not break it up into smaller verses, the foot must not often coincide with the word.

The exact arrangement of Ennius' material is uncertain, since we have, for the most part, only short fragments; but there can be no doubt that the bulk of the poem simply related the events in chronological order, with one notable exception; the first Punic War was omitted entirely, apparently, because the newer poet scorned to enter the lists against Naevius.[21]

> 'Others', he says, 'have told the tale,
> In measures sung of old by bard and fairy,
> When none as yet had climbed the Muses' cliffs,
> Nor studied seemly phrase, until I came.'

[19] *Annal.*, 266–7: cited Horace, *sat.*, i, 4, 60, si soluas 'postquam . . . refregit' inuenias etiam disiecti membra poetae.

[20] See, for instance, Cic., *Tusc.*, iii, 45, o poetam egregium; quamquam ab his cantoribus Euphorionis contemnitur (*cf.* p. 145). Here he is speaking of Ennius generally, having just cited some verses from the tragedies. For the *Annals* specifically, see *pro Murena*, 30, where he is quoting *Ann.*, 268 *sqq.*, ingeniosus poeta et auctor ualde bonus.

[21] Cic., *Brut.*, 75, qui (Ennius) si illum (Naeuium) ut simulat contemneret, non omnia bella persequens primum illud Punicum acerrimum bellum reliquisset. The quotation in the text is made up from *Ann.*, 213–16 Vahlen, which seem all to belong to the same passage; for a discussion of textual and other difficulties, see O. Skutsch in *Class. Quart.* xlii (1948), pp. 94–6.

We have therefore his manifesto, the challenge of the new, completely hellenized school. As to the rest of the poem, it may have begun with what we know came near the commencement, a vision in which he saw the ghost of Homer and realized that he was himself Homer reincarnated.[22] It certainly went on to tell the story of Rome's beginnings, making Romulus the grandson of Aeneas,[23] and so through the whole history. The latest reference which can be dated is to the censorship of M. Lepidus and M. Fulvius, 575/179 [24]; the total number of books was eighteen; as we have some 600 lines left, we may perhaps say that approximately nineteen-twentieths of the work is lost.

This ambitious poem probably was the poet's chief occupation during his life in Rome [25]; but it left him time, not only for his plays, but for smaller works as well. He was not content to imitate the classics and be the Homer and the Euripides of the new literature, but gave attention to the moderns as well. After the example of Archestratos [26] and others, he wrote a *Hedyphagetica* or *Art of Dining* in hexameters; the fragment we have left explains where to get the best fish of various kinds, and no doubt the rest of the poem treated in similar fashion of other delicacies. Like most of the Alexandrians, he wrote epigrams, whereof there survive one intended to go under a portrait of himself, two apparently on Scipio Africanus (for two sides of a monument to him ?), and another on himself, proudly claiming

[22] *Ann.*, 6 Vahlen; the contents of the whole passage (an exposition of Pythagorean doctrine) is given by Lucretius, i, 112. That the passage came at the beginning of the *Annals* we are told by the scholiast on Persius, vi, 10; Persius himself there says of Ennius, postquam destertuit esse Maeonides, 'after he had got over his dream of being Homer', in quoting a passage from one of his other works, see Housman in *C.R.*, xlviii (1934), p. 50.

[23] Ilia, mother of Romulus, refers to Aeneas as her father, *Ann.*, 37, 44; see Servius on *Aen.*, vi, 777.

[24] Cicero, *de prouinc. cons.*, 20, assigned by Vahlen to Bk. xvii.

[25] Certainly it was not all published at the same time. In Book xii he mentioned that he was in his sixty-seventh year, Gellius, xvii, 21, 43; this, then, was in 581/173. After that he must have written Books xiii–xv as a sort of appendix, for in xii (see frag. vi Vahlen) he spoke of himself as an old race-horse which will run no more, *i.e.*, signified that his work was at an end; a second appendix followed in the shape of the remaining books, begun to celebrate the exploits of Titus Caecilius Teucer (?) and his brother, an otherwise unknown pair of worthies (see Pliny, *N.H.*, vii, 101), as the first appendix had been written to praise M. Fulvius Nobilior, and continued perhaps because Ennius was too fond of his task to leave it.

[26] See Rose, *H.G.L.*, p. 330.

eternal glory.[27] The style is far more reminiscent of the monumental dignity and simplicity of the older Greek masters than of even the best Alexandrian work, and these little pieces are among his happiest efforts. He wrote an encomium on Africanus, entitled *Scipio*, in a curious technique, for it was partly in hexameters, partly in trochaic tetrameters (the 'Locksley Hall' metre, which, under the name of 'square (*quadratus*) verse', was destined to become exceedingly popular in Rome, outlasting all the others and passing into accentual rhythms of the Middle Ages). He also dealt with philosophical themes, which as we have seen played some part even in the *Annals*, and we have a few scraps of a poem entitled *Epicharmus*,[28] giving an account of that comedian's views, or rather, it may be, of the theories and maxims which were fathered on him by Axiopistos and Chrysogonos, not long before Ennius' own day. More important in its consequences was his successful attempt to make Rome acquainted with the latest views on the history and genesis of religion, those of Euhemeros,[29] whose name gave the title to one of Ennius' most famous writings. It was presumably in verse; we know it through a prose summary in Lactantius (see p. 481) and a few references elsewhere; and the fact that its dry-as-dust resolution of the traditional gods into prehistoric kings aroused, apparently, no protests in pious Rome, shows as clearly as possible how divorced the native religion was from both theology and mythology, even in that age when it was becoming strongly hellenized and Greek stories were commonly known.[30] He even seems to have imitated Sotades,[31] though the little of the poem called *Sota* which has come down to us has indeed the unusual metre of its Greek model but, in our fragments at all events, not much of his indecency. Finally we may mention a kind of work destined to have a great future, the *Saturae* or Miscellanies. These were in verse of different kinds, and partly in dialogue

[27] The two concerning himself are preserved by Cicero, *Tusc.*, i, 34, save for a few words of the second, which, omitted by Cicero or the copyists, are supplied from *ibid.*, 117, and *de senect.*, 73. For that on Scipio, see Vahlen, p. 216.

[28] For Epicharmos and the various quasi-philosophical works issued under his name, see Rose, *H.G.L.*, pp. 250 *sq.*, 345 *sq.*

[29] For Euhemeros, see Rose, *op. cit.*, p. 368 *sq.* His book would be about fifty years old when Ennius was born.

[30] See for instance Plautus, *Cistell.*, 513 *sqq.*, where Alcesimarchus' blunders about the divine genealogies are made fun of; clearly, the audience was expected to know something of them. But they are purely Greek, Italian gods having no family relationships, although Latin names are used, Ops for example instead of Rhea.

[31] For Sotades, see Rose, *op. cit.*, p. 346.

form [32]; the fragments we have speak of morals, of the poet's own habits, of going out to dinner, and tell the fable of the Lark and her Young. There is nothing precisely like this in what we know of Greek literature, though moral discourses in verse are Cynic [33] and miscellanies are quite common, in prose at least. Here, then, we have the earliest known example of the one form of composition in which Rome, or rather Italy, definitely excelled Greece and set the model for future literatures.

While Ennius was enjoying a moderate amount of patronage from his aristocratic friends, a somewhat older man, likewise from outside Latium, was earning his living as best he could. This was TITVS MACCVS, or MACCIVS, PLAVTVS,[34] the one Italian of antiquity of whom we can certainly say that he possessed dramatic talent of a high order. He is not one of the highest type of dramatists, worthy to rank with Sophokles, for example, or Shakespere; his characters lack variety and depth, his construction is often careless and his exposition too hurried; he wears, as Horace said, the comic dress slovenly, *non astricto*

[32] In *sat.*, 6 Vahlen, some one, possibly a Muse, is addressing Ennius himself. The other passages referred to are 1 and 2; 64 (Ennius says he never writes poetry except when he has the gout, the disease of which he ultimately died, according to Jerome, *ann. Abrah.* 1839), 14 *sqq.*, and *incert. frag.*, ii = Gellius, ii, 29, 3–20. It is interesting that *sat. incert.* i mentions as one of his subjects the curiously mediaeval-sounding theme *contentio uitae et mortis*; such themes seem to be as old as Epicharmos, *cf.* Rose, *H.G.L.*, p. 251, and continued in the Atellanae, *cf.* below, p. 147.

[33] *Cf.* Rose, *H.G.L.*, pp. 344 *sq.*, 357 *sqq.*

[34] The true form of the name was first determined by Ritschl, see Schanz-Hosius, i, p. 56, for the controversy over it. (*a*) The best MS. of his plays, the Ambrosian palimpsest (A) has *T. Macci Plauti* at the end of the *Casina*; *Mercator* 10 and Accius, cited by Varro *ap.* Gellius, iii, 3, 9, both end a line with *Titi* when speaking of his authorship of a play. This determines the *praenomen*. (*b*) Besides the testimony of A, both the verses cited above have, before *Titi*, *m̄. actii* (*accii*)—so the MSS. of Gellius—or *mactici* (*mattici*)—so the MSS. of Plautus—for the two names. It is impossible that he should also have been called Marcus, for no one has two *praenomina*, and we have seen that he was called Titus. Remains therefore, to explain the variant, *Macci*, as given in A, above. Now this can be the genitive of Maccus or Maccius; the former is given in *Asin.*, 11. But *Titus Maccus Plautus* is an impossible Roman name, for the second member, the *nomen* proper, must end in *-ius*. Hence Ritschl decides for *Maccius*, and would emend *Asin.*, *loc. cit.*, accordingly. The other possibility is that he was called Titus Maccus, and that Plautus (= flat-foot) was a nickname only. Some confusion arose in antiquity, see Gellius, *loc. cit.*, 10, citing Varro, from the fact that there was a contemporary called PLAVTIVS, also a dramatist. As the genitive of both names is the same, *Plauti*, its occurrence in the title of a play would be ambiguous; in Cicero's time the less-known writer would probably have used the form *Plautii*, but that was not then employed.

percurrit pulpita socco. His plots are the conventional intrigues of New Comedy, the plays being confessed adaptations from the Greek. Yet when all this is freely admitted, the fact remains that Plautus' native wit and inexhaustible *verve* raise him above the level of his elegant, subtle, but languid models; that he finds tired Greeks whose best age is past, and turns them somehow into vigorous Italians, full of life and crude humanity. All the Greek names, Greek sentiments and Greek situations cannot make them otherwise. In like manner, Molière is never anything but French, and never more French than when, as in *L'Avare*, he borrows whole speeches and scenes from Plautus; Shakespere is always English, and not least so when he is taking what he needs unchanged or scarcely changed out of North's Plutarch. So far as our remains of ancient literature go, Plautus is the one author in whom there lives again something of the spirit of Aristophanes.[35]

Not a great deal is known of his life. He was born at Sarsina in Umbria, about 504/250, perhaps earlier; he died at Rome in 570/184.[36] Some time fairly early in his career he left his native place for Rome and there earned a certain amount of money by some sort of work for the stage, *in operis artificum scaenicorum*, says Varro.[37] With this as capital he engaged in trade, lost everything, and came back to Rome so poor as to be obliged, according to the same authority, to hire himself out to work a handmill for a baker. From this, which was little better than slave's work, his dramatic talents would seem to have set him free, and he made a name for himself, also some kind of living, by his writings. The dates of these, with few exceptions, are unknown or at best gathered from uncertain conjectures, but it is likely that they all lie between the last years of the second Punic War and the end of their author's life.

How many plays Plautus wrote was a disputed point in antiquity,

[35] Much has been written about his dramatic capabilities; see especially Ed. Fraenkel, *Plautinisches in Plautus*, Berlin, Weidmann, 1922 (= Philologische Untersuchungen, 28). There are some good, if brief remarks, in K. Westaway, *The Original Element in Plautus*, Cambridge, Univ. Press, 1917. A long list will be found in Schanz-Hosius, i, p. 78 *sqq*.

[36] Sarsina, Jerome, *ann. Abrah.* 1817 = 554/200, which by some blunder of his own or a scribe is given as the date of P.'s death. The real date is given by Cicero, *Brut.*, 60, as the consulate of P. Claudius and L. Porcius = 570/184. He was old when he wrote the *Pseudolus*, *de senect.*, 50; but a man was not *senex* till he was 60, and the *didascalia* of the Pseudolus, which survives, puts its performance in 563/191, therefore 503/251 is the latest possible birth-year. See note 86.

[37] Quoted by Gellius, iii, 3, 14.

for there were attributed to him some 130. Several ancient scholars made lists of those which they considered genuine; that which was finally accepted as canonical was Varro's, consisting of the twenty-one plays which still survive, entire or in fragments. But this consists solely of those which he thought quite indubitably genuine; there was a considerable class, perhaps numbering nineteen, of doubtful pieces, several of which Varro personally thought to be his, on stylistic grounds. The matter was complicated both by the confusion between Plautus and Plautius (see note 34) and by Plautus having worked over sundry older plays.[38]

Taking now the plays in alphabetical order,[39] we begin with the *Amphitruo* (the Plautine spelling of Amphitryon). This is described as a tragi-comedy, and indeed has a mingling of seriousness with its burlesque which is more like Elizabethan drama than what we know of ancient plays. It deals with the birth of Herakles (*Hercules* in Latin),[40] and in the first scene Zeus (*Iuppiter*), under the form of Amphitruo, is with Alkmene (*Alcumena*), while Hermes (*Mercurius*), disguised as the slave Sosia, keeps away intruders. When the real Sosia arrives with news of his master's return, and afterwards Amphitruo in person comes home from his wars, confusion of the most complicated sort ensues, and Amphitruo is nearly beside himself with bewilderment and jealousy; his wife, who retains her dignity throughout, is not only a sympathetic but a majestic figure in the midst of this comedy of errors. Finally, after the birth of her twins, Iuppiter in his true form appears and makes all plain.

The *Asinaria, i.e.* (*Comedy*) *of the Asses*,[41] is rollicking, almost slap-stick farce. It was adapted, surely in the freest manner, from a play of the New Comedy, the *Onagos* (*Ass-driver*) of Demophilos. Demaenetus, an old man whose wife Artemona keeps a tight hand on the purse-strings,[42] has a son Argyrippus, who appeals to him for aid to redeem his mistress, Philaenium,

[38] See Gellius, iii, 3, based on Varro, *de comoediis Plautinis*. Servius on the *Aeneid*, p. 4, 15 Thilo-Hagen, says there were lists of 21, 40 and 100 plays; the second might be Varro's 21 + 19 more.

[39] Approximately followed, with one aberration, in our MSS.

[40] For the story, see Rose, *Myth.*, p. 205 *sqq*.

[41] Whenever, as here, a title has an adjectival form, the word *fabula* (play) is to be supplied.

[42] Theoretically, a Greek woman could not hold property; her dowry was the property of her family and her husband had the usufruct, which might descend to her children. Practically, she no doubt often behaved very like Artemona. An attempt, on very insufficient grounds, to prove the play spurious has been made by L. Havet and A. Freté in their edition of it, Pseudo-Plaute, *Le Prix des ânes*, Paris, Les Belles Lettres, n.d.

from the clutches of a rascally old *lena*.[43] With the help of two slaves, at whose villanies father and son gladly connive, they manage to divert the money which should have been paid to Artemona's agent Saurea for a herd of asses. With this they buy Philaenium, before Argyrippus' rival Diabolus can do so. In a great rage, he sends a hanger-on (*parasitus*) [44] of his own to tell Artemona, who appears on the scene just as her husband and son are sitting down to supper with Philaenium, and drags the old man home. The *cantor* [45] ends the play by suggesting that she will be lenient with him if the audience applaud heartily.

The *Aulularia* (freely '*The Crock of Gold*') enjoys the distinction of having given Molière the idea of *L'Avare*. The plot is, however, somewhat different. Euclio, the miser of the piece, has discovered a treasure, thanks to the good offices of the Lar Familiaris or guardian deity of the household, whom his daughter Phaedria(?)[46] piously worships. Megadorus, a rich neighbour, who supposes from Euclio's manner of living that he is still miserably poor, proposes to marry his daughter without dowry, not knowing that his own nephew Lyconides has violated her. The preparations for the wedding, with the necessary invasion of professional caterers (*coqui*), make Euclio more terrified than ever for his pot of gold, and in the midst of his troubles two worse things happen; his daughter bears a child and the pot is stolen. Fortunately the thief is Lyconides' slave, and the young man explains matters to his uncle, gets the consent of all concerned to his marrying the girl himself, and restores Euclio's treasure to him.

The text of this excellent play is unfortunately incomplete, hence several details of the plot are obscure. We have, however, as usual in the case of Plautus, two summaries of the play in verse, one containing an acrostic of the title. This suggests that Euclio had lost something of his miserliness by the last scene, for it ends: illic (Lyconides) Euclioni rem refert./ab eo donatur auro uxore et filio. *I.e.*, Lyconides marries the daughter of Euclio, recognizes her baby as his, and gets the treasure, or part of it, by way of dowry.

[43] *Leno*, fem. *lena*, a white slaver', then a despised but not illegal occupation.

[44] A stock character of New Comedy, replacing the κόλαξ or flatterer of older works. He is regularly a poor but witty man, who picks up a living as hanger-on of a rich one, or of rich men generally. Properly the word means 'guest', see Rose, *H.G.L.*, pp. 227, 243.

[45] See below, p. 57.

[46] So the MSS., but this is a man's name, Φαιδρίας. Phaedra (Ussing) or Phaedrium (Leo, K. Schmidt) are possible corrections.

The *Bacchides* [47] has a rather complicated plot. The scene is laid in Athens. Mnesilochus and Pistoclerus are friends; the former has been sent by his father to Ephesos, on business. He has written to Pistoclerus to do what he can to get his mistress, Bacchis, free from a soldier who has hired her for the year; Pistoclerus, in carrying out this commission, falls in love with Bacchis' sister, who has the same name as herself. Mnesilochus' slave Chrysalus, returning with his master from abroad, has ready a plausible tale to deceive the former's father, Nicobulus, into thinking that the greater part of a large sum of money which his son was to fetch from Ephesos has had to be left there, and therefore into going abroad himself to fetch it back.[48] But Mnesilochus, hearing of Pistoclerus' love affair and confusing the two sisters, thinks his Bacchis unfaithful and his friend treacherous, and in consequence hands over the whole of the money to his father. Soon after, he learns the true state of affairs, and Chrysalus is once more pressed into service. Trading on his bad reputation with the old man, he suffers the news to be forced from him that Mnesilochus is in deadly peril; he is the lover of a married woman, and her husband has found it out. Nicobulus is easily persuaded to part with 200 gold *philippi*,[49] represented to him as the price of the husband's refraining from killing the seducer, really the fee which was to be returned to Bacchis' soldier-lover in the event of her refusing to leave Athens with him. Another ruse extracts another 200 *philippi* from him; but when he and Philoxenus, the good-natured father of Pistoclerus, find out the whole matter, the two women wheedle them into a reconciliation, and the play ends with general merry-making.

We can perhaps conjecture from what Greek original this merry

[47] By some accident, this play has been displaced in the Palatine MSS. of Plautus, and comes after the *Epidicus*, possibly a remnant of some attempt at chronological arrangement. Cf. n. 60.

[48] The elementary development of banking in Greece, and the rare and insecure commercial treaties between cities, often obliged principals and their agents to travel back and forth to fetch sums in specie which would nowadays be transmitted by banker's order or otherwise through the post.

[49] A *phìlippus* (always so accented in Plautus, and scanned with its second syllable short, by the workings of the law of iambic shortening, see p. 57) is a gold stater, originally of Philip II of Macedon, father of Alexander the Great, and having the same bullion value as an Attic stater, *i.e.*, about that of a napoleon (20 pre-war French francs = 16 shillings = $4, approximately), but of course much higher purchasing power, money being then a great deal scarcer than now.

play is taken. It cites Menander once, 816/17, quem di diligunt adulescens moritur = *ὃν οἱ θεοὶ φιλοῦσιν ἀποθνήσκει νέος*, and Ritschl draws attention to the fact that line and context occurred in the *Δὶς ἐξαπατῶν* (*Double Deceiver*). Hence it is far from an impossible idea that that was Plautus' model, for Chrysalus does in fact deceive Nicobulus twice. The *Bacchides* is later than the *Epidicus*, which it refers to, 214; efforts to fix an exact date for it rest on no real arguments.

The *Captiui* (*Prisoners of War*) Plautus boasts to be a moral play (*ad pudicos mores facta*) and not on a hackneyed theme. It is also one of his best works. Elis and Aetolia are at war; old Hegio, a respectable Aetolian,[50] has had two sons, but one disappeared while a small child, the other has been captured by the Eleans. The father therefore starts to buy Elean prisoners,[51] in hopes of exchanging one of them for his son. He purchases, among others, a young man called Philocrates and his slave Tyndarus. After some discussion it is agreed that the slave shall be sent under safe conduct to Elis to offer Philocrates in exchange for Hegio's son, Philopolemus. But master and slave have secretly plotted each to pretend to be the other; thus Philocrates gets away free, while Hegio, who is informed of the deception by one of the other prisoners, promptly sends Tyndarus to the quarries. Soon after, however, Philocrates returns, bringing Philopolemus with him, also a runaway slave of Hegio's, by name Stalagmus. This man confesses that he stole Hegio's other son, and that Tyndarus is he. The whole family is thus joyfully reunited.

No great concession to morality is made, however, in the *Casina*, one of the most amusing of the comedies. Casina is a pretty slave-girl, whose hand is sought by two of her fellow-slaves, Chalinus, the personal attendant of the son of the house, and Olympio, the *uilicus* or farm-bailiff; the latter has the support of their old master Lysidamus, who wants Casina for himself. The old man apparently gets his way, and Olympio's marriage with Casina is celebrated in due form.[52] Too late, he discovers that his bride is Chalinus disguised as a girl, who

[50] Plautus seems to imagine that Aetolia is a city and certainly does not realize that the Aetolians were much behind the Eleans in civilization, being little better than a people of brigands. For his commendations of the play, see 55 *sqq.*, 1029 *sqq.*

[51] Exchanges of prisoners between belligerent states occasionally took place in antiquity, but generally they were sold as slaves, and thus passed into the possession of private owners.

[52] The scene is in Athens, where such ceremonies seem not to have been uncommon, though strictly a slave could have no legal wife. See the prologue, 67 *sqq.*

improves the occasion by thrashing him soundly. Cleustrata, Lysidamus' wife, is privy to the whole plot, and triumphs gaily over her unfortunate husband. The play and her recriminations are alike cut short,[53] and the audience informed that Casina turns out to be free-born, the long-lost daughter of a neighbour, and will be married to Euthynicus, Lysidamus' son.

The prologue was written for a revival of unknown date, but within half a century or so of Plautus' death.[54] The original was the *Κληρούμενοι* of Diphilos.[55]

The *Cistellaria* (*Trinket-box*) takes its name from the case containing the ornaments (*crepundia*) [56] by which the heroine recognizes her long-lost parents. Demipho, while a young man, some eighteen years before the play begins, had violated a free-born girl in Sekyon (Sicyon, to give the place the Latin form of its name). Returning to his native Lemnos, he had married, and later been left a widower with one daughter. He has now revisited Sicyon and married his former victim, who had meanwhile borne a daughter and exposed her. The baby had passed into the hands of a courtesan, Melaenis, who had reared her as her own child. Now full-grown, Selenium, as she is called, has become the mistress of a young man, Alcesimarchus, who is obliged by his father to become engaged to Demipho's acknowledged daughter. Through the good offices of a slave, Lampadio, Selenium's origin is discovered; her mother reclaims her,[57] and she becomes Alcesi-

[53] *Cas.*, 1006, hanc ex longa longiorem ne faciamus fabulam. But it is not very long, 1018 lines (*Amph.* has 1146, with a considerable part lost, *Men.* 1162, *Merc.* 1026, *Mil.* 1437, *Most.* 1181, *Poen.* 1422, *Pseud.* 1334, *Rud.* 1423, *Trin.* 1189). Ours may be a 'cut' stage-copy.

[54] See prol., 14–15; the older but not the younger members of the audience have seen the play before.

[55] *Ibid.*, 32. *Cf.* Rose, *H.G.L.*, pp. 249–50.

[56] These trinkets, called in Greek *γνωρίσματα* or means of recognition, are a stock feature of New Comedy. It would appear that it really was the practice to put some kind of ornament on a child if exposed, for the reason given in Terence, *Heaut.*, 652, that if it died it might have its share (due to the dead and commonly buried with them) of the family property.

[57] Exposure was not tantamount to relinquishing parental rights, nor did the rearing of an exposed child by a stranger establish any claim, apparently, even to the repayment of expenses incurred. If relationship could be proved, the parents might automatically reclaim their offspring. Legally, the woman's husband, if she was married, would be the prime mover; if she was single, her natural or legal guardian (*e.g.*, her father or brother). Here, since the physical father of the child and the guardian of the woman are the same person, there are no legal complications, Demipho being quite willing to recognize and provide for his daughter.

marchus' wife. The plot is of the most conventional kind, and the treatment slight; the original is the *Συναριστῶσαι* of Menander, from whom two lines of the text are taken [58]—how much more, we cannot say. It probably is an early work,[59] and Plautus may have done little by way of alteration save the increase in the parts to be sung, which make it rather *opéra bouffe* than spoken drama.

The *Curculio* takes its title from the name, or rather nickname (the word means 'weevil') of a parasite who is its central character. A young man, Phaedromus, has fallen in love with a girl, Planesium, who is in the possession of a *leno*. He wishes to buy her, and sends Curculio to try and raise the money from a friend living in Karia. Curculio fails in this, but gets by a trick the signet-ring of a soldier who is also attracted by Planesium and has deposited her purchase-money with a banker at Epidauros, where the action takes place. A letter to the banker is easily forged, Planesium bought, under the guarantee that if she turns out to be free-born, the money shall be returned, and all is going as Phaedromus would have it when the soldier returns and sues the banker and *leno*. Suddenly, by means of his own ring and one which Planesium wears, he discovers that she is his sister, kidnapped years before. He recovers the money from the *leno* and agrees to Planesium's immediate marriage to Phaedromus.

Plautus' own favourite, the *Epidicus*,[60] has a complex plot, turning on the wiles of the slave after whom the play is named. Stratippocles, a young Athenian, has been absent on campaign, leaving instructions with Epidicus to buy for him a harp-girl, Acropolistis, who had caught his fancy. This Epidicus has contrived to do, or rather to induce Stratippocles' father, Periphanes, to do, by persuading the old man that the girl is his own illegitimate daughter. But meanwhile Stratippocles has fallen violently in love with a female prisoner and bought her with borrowed money. Epidicus, by a ruse, gets enough from Periphanes to settle this debt; he assures him that his son is wildly in love

[58] *Cist.*, 89–90 = Men., fgt. 558 Kock, *cf. Philologus* lxxxvii, p. 117.

[59] *Cist.*, 201–2, perdite perduellis, parite laudem et lauream, /ut uobis uicti Poeni poenas sufferant; since it is merely wished that the Carthaginians may be soundly beaten, the date can hardly be later than 552/202 (Battle of Zama), and of course may be earlier, *e.g.*, 550/204 (landing of Scipio in Africa).

[60] *Bacchid.*, 214, etiam Epidicum, quam ego fabulam aeque ac me ipsum amo. The speaker, Chrysalus, doubtless voices the author's own views. The date of the play and its Greek original are matters of somewhat futile conjecture.

with a harp-player, and advises him to buy her, keep her out of the young man's way, and sell her to a young officer who wants her for himself. Some woman has to be found to make this story plausible, and one is brought to the house, being told that she is needed to play during a religious service there.[61] But the inopportune arrival of the officer, the girl's own declaration that she is free, and the entry of Philippa, the mother of Periphanes' daughter, who naturally refuses to recognize Acropolistis, a complete stranger to her, as her own child, combine to unmask all Epidicus' plots. He is in despair when, by a device monotonously familiar in New Comedy, the woman Stratippocles had bought turns out to be the missing daughter. Periphanes promises Epidicus his freedom, and Stratippòcles is left, presumably, to console himself with Acropolistis.

Much more to the taste of a modern is the *Menaechmi*, which has the honour of having suggested to Shakespere the plot of the *Comedy of Errors*. The Latin play is much the simpler. The two Menaechmi, one of whom was originally called Sosicles, are identical twins, separated by an accident when they were seven years old. Menaechmus-Sosicles, searching all over the world for his brother, arrives in Epidamnus, and the two are comically mistaken one for the other (for the second Menaechmus had been carried thither and is now a substantial citizen) by the Epidamnian's wife, parasite, and mistress, and by Menaechmus-Sosicles' own slave. At last the two meet and the mystery is solved. Although Shakespere made the plot more complicated, and improved the play by adding a serious theme, the danger of the twins' father, even he could not intensify the farcical vigour of the successive confusions.

The *Mercator*, as its prologue informs us, is taken from the *Ἔμπορος* of Philemon.[62] The 'merchant' who gives it its title is a young Athenian, Charinus, whose father has sent him abroad to trade, by way of keeping him out of mischief at home. While away, however, he has fallen in love with and acquired a courtesan, Pasicompsa, whom he now brings home, pretending that she is a present to his mother. His father, Demipho, promptly falls in love with Pasicompsa himself, and, on the plausible excuse that she is much too pretty to be a waiting-maid in a quiet household, proposes to get rid of her. Charinus is afraid to object openly,

[61] Music of some sort, to drown ill-omened noises, was a regular accompaniment of sacrifice, public or private.

[62] *Merc.*, 9–10; for Philemon, see Rose, *H.G.L.*, p. 249. Both the words rendered 'merchant' mean one who travels for purposes of trade, whether on a large or small scale.

and Demipho manages to smuggle the girl into the house of his friend Lysimachus. However, the latter's wife at once becomes jealous, the whole plot is revealed, and Charinus, who was leaving Athens in disgust, is persuaded to stay at home and prosecute his love affair in peace.

One of Plautus' best plays is the *Miles Gloriosus* (*Braggart Captain*; *miles* is a soldier of any rank). The original was called *'Αλαζών, i.e., The Boaster, gloriosus*, as Plautus himself renders it,[63] and the central figure is a soldier of fortune, bearing the formidable name of Pyrgopolynices,[64] who has come back from the wars with full pockets, to enjoy himself at Ephesus, helped by his faithful hanger-on Artotrogus. The mistress of this Captain Bobadil, by name Philocomasium, has won the affections of a young civilian, Pleusicles, who plans to get possession of her, with her full consent. To begin with, she contrives to meet her lover in the next house, brazenly pretending, when seen there, to be her own twin sister. Next, Pyrgopolynices is assured that a lady of position is madly in love with him. He is easily persuaded to get rid of Philocomasium, paying her generous compensation for the shock to her feelings. While she and Pleusicles sail away to Athens, he prosecutes his intrigue with the supposed lady, who is a courtesan instructed for the purpose, and is caught and frightened out of his wits by Periplec(t)omenus, a merry old man who personates the girl's husband.[65]

The author of the Greek original is unknown; Menander and Philemon have been suggested, without any convincing proofs. Plautus may have composed his play early in his career as a dramatist, for in 211–212 he refers to the imprisonment of Naevius (*cf.* p. 27). This is more pointed if the event was recent, *i.e.*, if the play is not much later than about 550/204. Indeed, if we press the wording of the passage, Naevius might be supposed still in prison when Plautus

[63] *Miles*, 86–7; the ἀλαζὼν is a stock character in Greek comedy, see Rose, *op. cit.*, 243, and the professional soldier, home from one of the many campaigns of Alexander's successors, a common and usually ridiculous figure.

[64] He certainly was not called this in the original, such compounds belonging rather to Old than New Comedy; contrast the corresponding name in the *Eunuchus* of Terence (p. 75). It is a blend of πύργος, a fortified tower, with the mythological name Polyneikes (Much-strife). Artotrogus = Gnaw-loaf.

[65] The name Periplectomenus is, as it stands, impossible Greek; omitting one letter we get Periplecomenus, which is at least a legitimate word, περιπλεκόμενος, though its appropriateness is not very obvious. The soldier's terror is not altogether groundless, for if the old man had really been the woman's husband, as he pretends, he might legally have killed his wife's seducer.

wrote, for he uses the present tense in speaking of his warders (bini custodes . . . occubant).

Equally amusing is the *Mostellaria* (*Haunted House*, literally, play concerning the portent). An Athenian gentleman, Theopropides, has been away from home for some time. During his absence, his son Philolaches has been enjoying himself expensively, raising a large sum of money to buy and set free a girl of whom he is much enamoured. In the middle of a drinking-bout, he and his friends are startled by the news that Theopropides has returned. Tranio, Philolaches' confidential slave, takes command of the situation, hurries the revelers into the house, closes the street-door, and meets Theopropides with a gruesome story of hauntings by the ghost of a murdered man, which has insisted on all living men quitting the place. Now enters the money-lender from whom Philolaches had borrowed, demanding payment of what is due. Tranio is ready with another tale ; the money has been spent in buying an excellent house—he indicates the nearest—whose owner has met with reverses of fortune. This serves well enough for the moment ; but shortly afterwards, Theopropides learns the whole truth, and things look very black for Tranio, when, by one of those sudden changes of mood which in comedy take the place of a tragic *deus ex machina*, Theopropides relents at the plea of one of Philolaches' friends and forgives everyone.

Festus [66] calls this play the *Phasma, i.e.*, Apparition. Plays with this title are known to have been written by Menander and Philemon among the authors of New Comedy ; one or the other of these may therefore have been Plautus' model. There is no indication of its date.

The *Persa* (*Persian*) turns on the laws regarding slave-dealers. A rascally slave, Toxilus, during his master's absence from Athens, has bought a girl from a *leno*, and does not relish the idea of paying for her. The brilliant idea occurs to him of making the *leno* bear all the expense. He therefore induces Saturio, a poor man and a parasite, but an Athenian citizen, to offer his own daughter for sale to the *leno* as a prisoner of war from some distant region. A fellow-slave of Toxilus dresses in his idea of a Persian costume and poses as the girl's owner. The *leno* hands over a good price for such desirable wares, but hardly is the bargain concluded when Saturio enters, in righteous indignation, claiming the protection of the magistrates for his daughter. The

[66] Festus, p. 158, 33 Lindsay, citing *Most.* 240, and 394, 17, citing *Most.* 727, both times as 'Plautus in Phasmate'.

leno is obliged to forfeit the whole of the purchase-money, since he had been given no guarantee that the girl could lawfully be sold,[67] and the farce ends with Toxilus and his friends feasting merrily and plaguing the *leno* with ironical invitations to join them.

The text gives a fairly clear indication of the date. In 99–100 Saturio calls Toxilus his *Iuppiter terrestris* and himself a *coepulonus*. This is an obvious allusion to the officials known as *epulones*, whose duty it was to arrange a banquet, *epulum*, in honour of Iuppiter and in connexion with the Ludi Romani and Plebei.[68] But these officials were first instituted in 558/196; the play cannot therefore be earlier than that year. What its original was is wholly unknown; but the Persians are spoken of as taking a city in Arabia, *i.e.*, thought of as still an independent power, not yet conquered by Alexander.[69] This, if it is not Plautus' own invention, suggests a time earlier than the age of New Comedy, which may be taken as beginning about in the year of Alexander's death, and therefore, since Greek comedy in its political allusions regularly assumes a strictly contemporary situation, is a fairly good argument that for once he went to Middle Comedy for a plot. But the distinction between Middle and New Comedy is itself rather arbitrary,[70] and not much importance can be attached to this.

Numerous difficulties attend the *Poenulus* (*The Man from Carthage*; but Plautus himself called it *Patruos*, *i.e.*, *Uncle*),[71] for not only is its plot complicated but the text presents a number of remarkable variants, including two different versions of the last scene, which seem to indicate that our MSS. give us a mixture of two editions of the comedy.[72] The scene is laid in Kalydon, and the chief characters are all of Carthaginian extraction. Agorastocles, the central figure, was kidnapped from Carthage and sold to a woman-hater who freed him and adopted him as his son. His real and adopted fathers are both dead when the play begins, but his uncle, Hanno, is alive and searching for his two daughters, who have also been kidnapped and sold. This

[67] To sell a free-born person as a slave was not in itself illegal, especially in the case of prisoners of war; but if he or she was also a citizen of the state in which the sale took place, the bargain was invalid and penalties generally attended it.

[68] See Livy, xxxiii, 42, 1; Wissowa, *R.K.R.*², p. 518. For the literature on the *Persa*, see Schanz-Hosius, i, p. 70.

[69] *Pers.*, 506, Chrysopolim Persae cepere urbem in Arabia.

[70] Rose, *H.G.L.*, p. 242.

[71] *Poen.*, 53–4, Καρχηδόνιος uocatur haec comoedia;/Latine Plautus 'Patruos' Pultiphagonides. It is one of many oddities that the play keeps neither its Greek nor its Latin title.

[72] See, for the relevant literature, Schanz-Hosius, i, p. 69. A large-scale edition with full commentary is a desideratum.

man is the Carthaginian after whom the comedy is named, and he arrives at an interesting time. Agorastocles is deeply in love with Adelphasium, one of two sisters who are in the hands of Lycus, a particularly unamiable *leno*. Not being able to come to terms with him about the price of his sweetheart, Agorastocles, by the advice of his slave Milphio, plots to ruin him; he provides another of his slaves with money and sends him to represent himself to Lycus as a visitor to the city and deposit the money with him. Thus a charge of harbouring a runaway slave and stolen goods can be laid against the *leno*. Now Hanno arrives and at once is interested in the plot. Milphio suggests that he should pretend to recognize in Adelphasium and her sister his own lost daughters. He agrees, but almost immediately discovers that they really are so, and naturally presses the suit against Lycus with all the more zeal.[73] The play ends with the complete success of the two Carthaginians and the engagement of Agorastocles to Adelphasium.

There is a faint indication of date. In a nonsense-passage, 663 *sqq.* Agorastocles' disguised slave is said to have been a mercenary with Attalos of Pergamos in Sparta (about equivalent to serving with Wellington at Gettysburg); inde nunc aufugit, quoniam capitur oppidum. Now if this is Plautus' own nonsense, not that of his original (Menander and Alexis both wrote comedies called *Καρχηδόνιος*), the name of Sparta might have been suggested to him by the events of 562/192, when Nabis of Sparta was defeated by the Achaians and the city forced to join their league, and the play therefore written not long after, say in 564/190, when Manius Acilius Glabrio, just home from Greece, celebrated a triumph for his exploits against the Aitolians, and might thereby have drawn attention to recent Greek events.[74] But it is quite as arguable that the mention of Sparta is from the original, and that a city which notoriously never had been taken is chosen for the sake of a laugh.

One of the interesting things about the play, linguistically speaking, is that Hanno makes several remarks in his own language, or what is meant for it, and some of the other characters speak a few words of Punic also.

Another contest between lover and *leno* forms the plot of the *Pseudolus* (*i.e.*, Liar). Phoenicium, beloved by Calidorus son of

[73] It is to be supposed that some kind of treaty exists between Carthage and the people of Kalydon, whereby they respect the liberty of each other's citizens. Hanno, as a foreigner, would be represented in any legal matters by a citizen, in this case Agorastocles. Such at least would be the Athenian procedure, which may be assumed here, especially as Plautus once (370) forgets that the scene is not supposed to be Athens.

[74] Livy, xxxv, 27–30; xxxvii, 46, 2.

Simo, is owned by Ballio, who is quite willing to sell her if Calidorus will produce the money, twenty *minae*.[75] But another customer, a Macedonian soldier, is in the market, has already paid three-quarters of the price and is expected to send the rest on the very day when the play begins. Pseudolus, Calidorus' attendant, cheats the soldier's messenger Harpax into giving up the letter which authenticates him, and with the help of this and a strange slave disguised as a soldier, who is provided with five *minae* by a friend of Calidorus, gets possession of Phoenicium for his master. Ballio is thus doubly out of pocket; for the real Harpax demands and gets the return of the whole price on behalf of his master, while the *leno*, having fair warning of Pseudolus' reputation as a cheat, has bet Simo another twenty *minae* that he will not be cheated.[76]

We know the date of this play, for a fragment of the *didascalia* surviving in the Ambrosian palimpsest contains the words M. Iunio M. fil. pr(aetore) urb(ano), ac(ta) Me(galesiis). Now we are informed by Livy (xxxvi, 36, 3) that M. Iunius Brutus celebrated the Megalesia, or games in honour of the Mother of the Gods, on the occasion of the dedication of her temple, in 563/191.[77] It would appear that the performance was a brilliant one, Ballio's establishment parading on the stage handsomely dressed.[78]

While the *Pseudolus* is an excellent play, the *Rudens*, taken from one of Diphilos' comedies,[79] is even better, being very good romantic comedy with a certain freshness about it, as becomes a drama whose scene is laid on the sea-shore. Near Kyrene lives

[75] This would be equivalent to 2,000 drachmae, the drachma being worth, in bullion value, approximately a pre-war French franc, or about tenpence English = 20 cents American. In the surviving comedies, the purchase price of an attractive female slave varies greatly, though the originals all belong to about the same age. Probably such an article of luxury was subject to sudden and extensive fluctuations of price, much as pictures or jewellery are now.

[76] The law of this play is as curious as that of the *Merchant of Venice*; there is no assignable reason why Ballio should not sue Calidorus, or Simo, for the return of Phoenicium or the payment of her price, and less reason why he, represented throughout as a perjurer, should let himself be held to a perfectly informal promise to pay Simo twenty *minae* if Pseudolus succeeded.

[77] For this cult, see Wissowa, *R.K.R.*, p. 317 *sqq*.

[78] See Fraenkel, *op. cit.*, p. 149.

[79] See *Rud.*, 32–3, huic esse nomen urbi Diphilus/Cyrenas uoluit. But the title *Rudens* (rope) is puzzling; the only rope which plays any part is one attached to the net, 938. It may be that the *Vidularia* (see below) was already written, and the more appropriate name thus pre-empted. What Diphilos' play was called is unknown.

an amiable old gentleman, by name Daemones, who is childless, for his only daughter was lost years before. To him, on the morning after a storm, comes a young man, Plesidippus, asking for news of a *leno*, called Labrax, who had promised to meet him at the temple of Venus (*i.e.*, Aphrodite) near Daemones' house and hand over to him the object of his affections, Palaestra. But Labrax has repented of his bargain and set sail for Sicily, where his wares are likely to fetch better prices. His ship is wrecked, Palaestra and her attendant Ampelisca are washed ashore and take refuge in the temple; Labrax and his friend Charmides reach land a little farther along the beach. Labrax tries to reclaim Palaestra, but Daemones, hearing that she claims to be free-born and, like himself, of Athenian origin, protects her. Meanwhile his slave Gripus has been fishing, and has fetched up a wallet containing Labrax' ready cash and also Palaestra's *crepundia*.[80] This he agrees to restore to Labrax for a talent. But here Trachalio, Plesidippus' slave, intervenes, and finally the matter is referred to Daemones. On examining the contents, he recognizes the trinkets as belonging to his daughter. The *leno* is therefore obliged to surrender her, but gets his money, less the promised talent, half of which is returned to him on condition of setting Ampelisca free. Daemones keeps the rest, giving Gripus his freedom; Trachalio is likewise freed by his master, and marries Ampelisca, Palaestra of course being betrothed to Plesidippus.

Save that the play is assuredly the product of Plautus' maturity as an author, there is no sufficient indication of its date. The name of Daemones is puzzling, for it is a transliteration of no known Greek word. K. Schmidt suggests that we should read Demones, *i.e.*, Δημόνης, another form of the familiar Damon or Dēmon.[81]

A very odd production, rather of the nature of a *divertissement* than of a play, although it is taken from a comedy of Menander,[82] is the *Stichus*, which can hardly be said to have a plot at all. Two young Athenian wives have remained faithful to their long-absent husbands, though their father urges them to marry again.

[80] *Cf.* note 56. In this case, however, the *crepundia* are Palaestra's childish ornaments, for she had not been exposed.

[81] Schmidt in *Hermes*, xxxvii, p. 365; see the whole article for a scholarly and ingenious discussion of the significant names in Plautus.

[82] The Ἀδελφοί, or *Brothers*. This presumably had a plot, from which Plautus has taken just enough to make an excuse for the singing and dancing which constitute most of his play. The *didascalia* is preserved nearly complete in the Ambrosian MS. For the consuls of the year, see Livy, xxxi, 4, 4.

News is brought that the husbands are returned safe and prosperous, and the play continues and ends with the rejoicings of the two households, especially of the slave Stichus, after whom the piece is named. The date is given in the *didascalia* as the consulship of C. (*sic*) Sulpicius and C. Aurelius, *i.e.*, P. Sulpicius Galba and C. Aurelius Cotta, 554/200.

The *Θησαυρός* (*Treasure*) of Philemon [83] is the original of a somewhat dull play called the *Trinummus*. Charmides, an old Athenian, has occasion to go away from home for some time, and not trusting the discretion of his son Lesbonicus, he imparts to his friend Callicles the secret of a treasure which he has hidden away. Lesbonicus, who is a good-natured young rake, soon runs through all the available money, and even sells the house, which Callicles buys, to save it and the treasure from falling into the hands of strangers. Now an estimable young man, Lysiteles, proposes to marry Lesbonicus' sister. To save her from the disgrace of marrying without dowry, Lesbonicus intends to make over to her his only remaining property, a small estate near Athens. Callicles, realizing that this will leave him quite penniless, hires a hanger-on (hence the name of the play, for the man is paid three *nummi*, meaning presumably three drachmae, for his trouble) to pretend to be a messenger from Charmides and bring Lesbonicus a considerable sum of money, taken from the treasure. This well-meant endeavour has been preceded by an attempt on the part of Lesbonicus' slave to scare the father of Lysiteles from accepting the estate by representing it as extraordinarily unlucky. However, the return of Charmides puts an end to the necessity for further manœuvres, and the young man is provided by his father with that traditional remedy for dissipation, a wife.[84]

There is one slight indication of date. *Trin.*, 990, speaks of the ' new aediles '. As the position of aedile was not new in Plautus' day, this must mean the aediles recently entered upon office ; but they entered office, at that date, on March 15. Therefore the play was performed at some festival not long after March 15 ; and the only one which will answer this requirement is the Megalesia, April 4, for the Floralia, April 27, were not instituted till 581/173, after Plautus' death. Therefore the play is not earlier than 560/194, when the

[83] *Trin.*, 18–19, huic Graece nomen est Thensauro fabulae :/Philemo scripsit, Plautus uortit barbare.

[84] Lesbonicus, penitent and ready to fall in with his father's plans for his reform, here makes one of the best jokes of the play (1184) ; he is willing to marry ' her (the girl named to him, Callicles' daughter) and any one else his father wishes '.

Megalesia were first celebrated with dramatic performances (*ludi scaenici*).[85]

The *Truculentus* (*Boor*) is a work of Plautus' old age,[86] and suggests a soured outlook on life, for all the characters are singularly unamiable. The central figure is a courtesan, Phronesium, and three of her lovers constitute the other principal persons, all being drawn with skill and a kind of cynical relish. One is a man called Diniarchus, who has spent most of his fortune on Phronesium. She now has discarded him, as being no longer profitable, and is at present the mistress of a soldier, Stratophanes, who has been away from Athens, the scene of the play, on campaign. To increase her hold on him, she pretends to have borne a child, getting possession for this purpose of an ' unwanted ' baby. Meanwhile, she is intriguing with a third admirer, a country bumpkin called Strabax, whose slave, the ' boor ' of the title, is captivated by her waiting-maid, Astaphium, and so quite gives over his outspoken objection to his young master's misbehaviour. Finally, the child turns out to be the offspring of Diniarchus and a free-born girl whom he had violated; he consents to marry her, though in no way binding himself to give up his ruinous relations with Phronesium, and recognizes the child as his own.

These are all the plays we have complete, and several are sorely battered. The twenty-first, the *Vidularia* (*Wallet*) is preserved only in the Codex Ambrosianus, a palimpsest, *i.e.*, a MS. in which the original text, Plautus' comedies, has had written over it another document, part of the Latin Bible. This, together with unskilful use of chemicals to bring out the original text, has rendered much of it totally illegible, and when, as here, it is our only authority, we can but recover scraps of the text. But from these fragments we can see that the plot was very like that of the *Rudens*. See p. 53. Apparently a fisherman, Gorgines, played a part corresponding to that of Daemones, while the Plesidippus of the play, by name Nicodemus, had himself been wrecked and is heard offering his services for hire to a countryman named Dinia.

[85] See Mommsen, *Staatsrecht*, i^{3}, p. 599; ii^{3}, p. 470 *sqq*. (date of entering office and origin and functions of aediles): Wissowa, *R.K.R.*, pp. 318, 455 (dates of the festivals in question): Livy, xxxiv, 54, 3 (first Megalesia, 560/194, three years earlier than the games on the dedication of the temple, mentioned above, p. 53).

[86] Cicero, *de senect.*, 50: quam gaudebat Bello suo Punico Naeuius, quam Truculento Plautus, quam Pseudolo! all these being examples of the activity of old men. The latest edition of the *Truculentus* (P. J. Enk, Lugduni Batauorum [Leiden], Sijthoff, 1953, 2 vols.) suggests (Vol. i, p. 30) 565/189 as the most likely date for the play.

In addition, quotations in various authors give us a number of fragments from plays supposed with more or less likelihood to be works of Plautus. There are in all thirty-two titles, but in no case have we any means of reconstructing the plot.

The style of Plautus has been the subject of much study, partly from its intrinsic interest, partly because it is the only large specimen we have of the Latin of that day. To begin with its broader features, it is clear that he rearranged the Greek plays he handled so as greatly to increase the amount of singing. This was not an original thought of his, for we have seen that Livius already used a similar technique; that Plautus, like him, employed the device of letting the actual words be sung by some one in the wings, thus giving the actor more breath for the necessary dancing and gesticulation, is highly likely from the passages cited above (p. 22), and from the fact that Horace calls that actor who speaks the final *plaudite* the *cantor*.[87] But Plautus certainly used music very freely indeed. If we may trust the indications of our MSS., which append the letters DV (*diuerbia*, dialogue) to the spoken parts, C (*canticum*) to those sung, only iambic trimeters belong to the former, all other metres to the latter.[88] On the other hand, it does not follow that all other metres were arias, or that they were not delivered by the actor; indeed, we have clear evidence that some other metres were pronounced by the actor himself, though as it happens this is not directly witnessed for Plautus.[89] Moreover, if we examine the text of the plays, we shall find, on the one hand, a number of lively scenes, not indeed in trimeters, but in other metres of a sort which can be repeated indefinitely and do not tend to form stanzas, viz., the trochaic tetrameter, usually catalectic (*i.e.*, seven trochees, – ᴗ, or their equivalents, and one syllable more), the iambic tetrameter catalectic (ᴗ – seven times repeated and one syllable more), the anapaestic tetrameter (ᴗ ᴗ – seven times and one more syllable, Aristophanes' characteristic line)[90] or others differing but little from these; again, we shall find scenes in which the action does not progress at all, but one character, or it may be two, deliver what suggests an aria or duet from a modern opera rather than anything dramatic, even the soliloquy. Examining

[87] Horace, *ars poet.*, 155, donec cantor Vos plaudite dicat. The last word of a comedy is regularly *plaudite* or its equivalent, *e.g.*, *plausum date*, and our MSS. often head the speech in which this occurs GREX or CATERVA, *i.e.*, 'the troupe', or assign it to the actor who spoke last. Probably the practice varied.

[88] See Ussing's ed. of Plautus, vol. i, p. 171.

[89] Cicero, *Tusc.*, i, 107, after quoting two trochaic tetrameters: non intellego quid metuat cum tam bonos septenarios fundat ad tibiam. *Idem, de orat.*, ii, 193, introducing a quotation in the same metre: ut ex persona mihi ardere oculi hominis histrionis uiderentur . . . dicentis.

[90] All have their equivalents in English, respectively the metre of Tennyson's *Locksley Hall*, of the words of the *Vicar of Bray* and of the air of the latter. In Latin the first two are known as *septenarii* (seven-footers), for they counted iambi and trochees by feet, not by metra (groups of two feet each).

the metres of these, we see that they are lyrical, *i.e.*, that they consist of verses which, in Greek literature from about the seventh century on, are associated with songs, whether for one voice or for many. Of these Plautus has an enormous range.[91] It seems reasonable to conclude, therefore, that these scenes are arias or duets, sung to comparatively elaborate tunes and accompanied with lively dancing, probably of a pantomimic sort, to fit the sentiment of the words; while the simpler metres were delivered in a sort of recitative, with simple musical accompaniment (*ad tibiam*, says Cicero, see note 89), with no more gesture than would usually be thought necessary for proper dramatic utterance.

Concerning the prosody, something has already been said (p. 26) in dealing with Naevius. In Plautus we have an incomparably larger amount of material, and in him, if read aright, we can catch the very cadences of contemporary Roman speech. Careful attention to his verse delivers us from the thralldom of the single word, with which any one learning a language from books only has necessarily to struggle, and gives us instead the true unit of living speech, the phrase. For instance, the beginner, confronted with the commonest of curses, *i in malam crucem*, will rob it of all vitality by giving it four conscientious accents, much as if we were to say in English " Gó-tó-thé-dévil ". Plautus teaches us to read it as one word, *i'n malám-crucem*, or in the plural, with a slightly different rhythm, *ít'in málam-crucem.*[92] The most familiar endearment, *uoluptas mea*, finds its true cadence in his lines, *uolŭptás-mea.*[93] Even the inarticulate sounds, sobs, kisses, and so forth, are expressed in this marvellous prosody, for they fill hiatus, not once but many times: *o mi* (sob) *ocule, o mi* (sob) *anime*, says Philocomasium, taking leave of Pyrgopolynices.[94] The familiar

[91] For details, see Lindsay, *Early Latin Verse*, *passim*, which should also be consulted for a full account of the prosody. *Cf.* p. 69

[92] *Pseud.*, 839; *Rud.*, 1162.

[93] *Mil. Glor.*, 1346.

[94] *Ibid.*, 1330. For hiatus, see Lindsay, *op. cit.*, p. 211 *sqq.* But it is desirable to understand clearly the phenomenon known as elision, or, more correctly, as synaloepha, in Latin. If a Greek word ends in a short vowel, and the next begins with a vowel, the former seems to have been completely dropped in ordinary classical pronunciation; ἐκεῖνα ἔξεστι became ἐκεῖν' ἔξεστι, with no trace of the α remaining. But this was not quite the case in Latin. Nobis, says Cicero (*Orat.*, 152), ne si cupiamus quidem distrahere uoces conceditur, *i.e.*, final and initial vowels inevitably run together. In this case, as all Latin poetry shows, the former vowel ceased to count as a syllable; but we have clear evidence that it was not wholly dropped, but pronounced quickly, blending as far as possible with the following one. Gellius, xiii, 21 (20), 6, quotes the grammarian Valerius Probus as saying that Vergil wrote *turrim in praecipiti stantem* (*Aen.*, ii, 460), and not *turrem*, because it sounded better. This shows clearly that it was not pronounced *turr' in*, but enough was left of the ' elided ' syllable for an educated ear to detect the vowel-sound. Hence, if there was a pause, the possibility of hiatus, *i.e.*, of giving both syllables their full value, as if there had been a consonant between their vowels, was to be reckoned with.

clippings of words are echoed ; *obliuiscendi* is but four syllables long in the mouth of Palaestrio.[95] Such Latin becomes as real and human a language as its descendant Italian.

The vocabulary is remarkable, not only for the large range of Latin words, but for the number of Greek and half-Greek ones. Actual Greek phrases are quite common, and so intimately mixed with the Latin that it is clear Plautus was as familiar with one language as the other, and that the society he knew commonly used both.[96] Hybrids are not rare, for example *inanilogista* (*Pseud.*, 255), while such Graeco-Latin adverbs as *dulice* and *comoedice* abound. This rich store of words is arranged with constant regard for those ornaments which the popular Italian ear loved best, alliteration, rime and what is technically called *figura etymologica*, or the bringing together in one phrase of two or more words from the same stem. Thus, to take instances from the *Pseudolus* alone, we have such lines as

> *p*ietatem ergo istam am*p*lexator noctu *p*ro *P*hoenicio (292)
> *prae*sensit : nihil est *praedae praedatoribus* (426)
> stulti hau *scimus* frustra ut *simus* (683)
> *certa* mitt*imus* dum in*certa* pet*imus*, atque hoc euenit
> in lab*ore* atque in dol*ore*, ut mors obrepat interim (685–6)

Or, from another play, one of the daintiest turns in Plautus (*Merc.*, 508–9, Pasicompsa speaking),

> *n*amque *e*depol *e*quidem, mi senex, *n*on didici baiiol*are*
> *n*ec *p*ecua ruri *p*asc*ere* *n*ec *p*ueros *n*utric*are*.

Speaking generally, we may say that Plautus proves the existence of a native Italian literary style, doubtless influenced by Greek models, but not a mere imitation of them, since it employs as frequent and characteristic ornaments several devices, notably alliteration, which are neither so common nor so openly used in Greek.[97] Withal, he shows us a dramatic structure different from that of any surviving Greek play, tragic or comic ; but this we have no reason to call a native creation, but rather should look for its genesis in what we know of the history of

[95] *Mil. glor.*, 1359, muliebres mores discendi, oblîscendi stratiotici. It is the same stem as in Span. *olbidar*.

[96] That the Greek words are not untranslated remnants of his original is clear from the facts that they often occur in passages certainly original, and are often not Attic. A quaint example is *Pseud.*, 210–11, oliui *δύναμιν* domi habent maxumam, meaning uim habent maxumam, 'they own any amount of oil', a familiar use of *uis*, but unheard of for *δύναμις*.

[97] A random sample will illustrate this. In 100 lines of Sophokles, I count 47 instances of initial alliteration (two or more words in the same line or phrase beginning with the same sound). In 100 lines of Kallimachos, I find 39, in 100 of Plautus, 88. It is the exuberance of a young language.

Greek drama. Our research is much hampered by the scantiness of our material, for we have very little left, besides short fragments,[98] from any period but the fifth century, that is to say from a stage of the drama which Plautus certainly does not copy. But we can see that, as the fifth century went on, the chorus became less important, especially for Tragedy, while early in the fourth, Comedy was beginning to drop it also, and in Menander it is but a shadow of what it once was.[99] In Greek New Comedy, the upshot of this seems to have been that there was very little singing in the plays, except perhaps between acts. In Plautus too, there is extremely little, if any, choral singing,[100] but the plays are full of recitatives and arias, often demonstrably additions of the Latin poet. Now it is highly likely that a provincial writer, and all Latin writers of that date were, intellectually speaking, in the provinces, should look for guidance to the artistic and literary capital of the world, Alexandria. In that city we know that dramatic solos were to be heard, though our evidence is for their separate performance, not their occurrence in the plays which poets of that time and place still tried to write.[101] If this was so, then the Latin writers, Plautus especially, had done one of two things. Either they had taken the enterprising step of incorporating in plays what had previously been a separate entertainment, or else they had boldly transferred to comedies an ornament characteristic of the later (Euripidean) and fashionable type of tragedies such as the *Iphigenia in Aulide*,[102] namely the operatic aria. In either case, they restored to drama what the plays of Menander mostly lacked, the large musical element which Aristotle mentions as one of its essential parts.[103]

It is time now to say something of the exterior conditions under which Plautus and his contemporaries produced their plays.

[98] One complete tragedy, the pseudo-Euripidean *Rhesus*, and three incomplete Menandrean comedies.

[99] See, for the facts, Rose, *H.G.L.*, pp. 238, 239, 245; add Maidment in *C.Q.*, xxix (1935), p. 1 *sqq*.

[100] The *Rudens* has a chorus of fishers for one short passage, 290–324; their song may be a solo by their leader. The *Bacchides* has an *entr'acte*, after 108, perhaps however a solo dance.

[101] See Rose, *op. cit.*, p. 346.

[102] See Rose, *op. cit.*, p. 194.

[103] Arist., *Poet.*, 1450^a 10, 1450^b 15. This relates to Tragedy; but the Tractatus Coislinianus (see Rose, *op. cit.*, p. 400), which contains, if not actually Aristotelian, at least Peripatetic tradition, makes music (μέλος) one of the constituents of Comedy also, and so it is in the surviving examples of Old and Middle Comedy; the remains of Menander and his rivals show very little trace of it, otherwise than as an entr'acte.

The most extraordinary fact is that Rome possessed no theatre until Pompey the Great had one built in 699/55. The earlier plays were brought out in temporary wooden buildings, a sort of grandstand facing a raised platform (*proscaenium*) with a high wooden barrier behind it, the backscene or *scaena*. This was merely plain boards, with openings for the necessary entrances,[104] until 655/99, when C. Claudius Pulcher, aedile that year, followed the traditions of his innovating house and added to his own popularity by having it painted.[105] Before that, and before Pompey's erection, two attempts had been made at a permanent building at least for the actors, one in 575/179, the other five years later. What became of the first we do not know, but the second was destroyed by order of the boorish senate of that day, prompted by Scipio Nasica—the acquaintance of Ennius, and therefore sinning against the light—because it might damage public morals. The reform even went so far as to forbid the erection of seats of any kind for the spectators, but public feeling soon did away with this absurdity, as the mention of seats in the prologue of the *Pseudolus* shows [106]; in Plautus' own time they were in regular use.[107] The actors were professionals and some

[104] Usually, the back-scene shows two houses with a lane (*angiportus*) between them; it must therefore have had three openings or doors of some kind. The essential thing about the Roman theatre was the stage buildings; all the rest of the space was merely seating or standing accommodation for the audience. But the Greek theatre was essentially a circular dancing-place (*orchestra*), to which, in time, a stage and rows of seats were added. Hence it always kept approximately its old shape, whereas a Roman theatre, as appears from the very clear directions for tracing its ground-plan in Vitruvius (see p. 432), v, 6, 1, as well as from the surviving examples, was semicircular, the stage extending along the diameter of the circle, and the *orchestra* (Vitr., *ibid.*, 2) being used, like our stalls, for the best seats. For the wooden theatres, see Vitr., *ibid.*, v, 7; *cf.* the passages quoted in n. 105, below.

[105] See Pliny, *N.H.*, xxxv, 23, supported by Val. Max., ii, 4, 6, for the fact of the painting; Pliny, viii, 19 (from Fenestella, for whom see p. 313) for the date; and for Claudius' *praenomen*, *C.I.L.*, i², p. 200 = vi, 31586. The other mentions of him omit it.

[106] Exporgi melius lumbos atque exsurgier:/Plautina longa fabula in scaenam uenit. For the prologues in general, see next note. For the affair of the stone theatres, see Livy, xl, 51, 3; xli, 27, 5; *periocha*, xlviii (p. 57, 5 Rossbach); Val. Max., ii, 4, 2; *cf.* Tac., *ann.*, xiv, 20, 2–3.

[107] *Amph.*, 65; *Capt.*, 12; *Poen.*, 5, 20, all from prologues. Of the plays of Plautus as we have them, the following are without prologues: *Bacchides, Curculio, Epidicus, Mostellaria, Persa, Stichus.* The *Miles* and *Cistellaria* have differred prologues. The *Casina* has one, distinctly stated to have been written for a revival, after Plautus' death (13 *sqq.*). The prologue of the *Menaechmi* says (3) adporto uobis Plautum lingua, non manu, which is at least consistent with the poet being dead. The two

of them undoubtedly slaves,[108] though not all. The occasions on which the plays were acted were the various great festivals, the Ludi Romani, Plebei, Apollinares and Megalenses.[109] Extraordinary festivals, given, as the result of a vow, in honour of a god (*ludi uotiui*) and the funeral ceremonies of a great man (*ludi funebres*), occasionally other special occasions such as triumphs might be made an excuse for *ludi Graeci* or *Osci*, *i.e.*, respectively, plays of the sort Plautus, Ennius and the tragedians wrote and Atellanae (see p. 24).

That there were other comedians contemporary with Plautus we are assured by the prologue to the Casina: ea tempestate flos poetarum fuit,/qui nunc abierunt hinc in communem locum (18–19), *i.e.*, Plautus was the best of all the poets of that generation.[110] But who they were, if we except Ennius, Naevius and the obscure Plautius already mentioned (above, p. 40) we cannot tell; the other names seem all to belong to a later date.

While Comedy flourished, TRAGEDY also enjoyed a brief season of comparative prosperity, which, in the nature of things, could hardly last very long, because Roman Tragedy was at once

lines (quoted in n. 106) which survive of the prologue of the *Pseudolus* might well have been written for a revival. In *Cist.*, *Merc.* and *Mil.* the prologue is so woven into the structure of the play that it is absurd to suppose it anything but genuine; in the remainder, there is no real reason, though some have been alleged, for thinking them spurious. Their purpose is partly to get the audience quiet and good-humouredly attentive, partly to serve as a play-bill and explain what the action is about; the prologue of *Trimummus*, an allegorical dialogue between Prodigality and her daughter Want, draws attention to its own different technique (16–17, sed de argumento ne exspectetis fabulae,/senes qui huc uenient, i rem uobis aperient).

[108] See especially Plaut., *Cist.*, 784–5, speaking of what will happen to the troupe after the play: qui deliquit uabulabit, qui non deliquit bibet. But a freeman could not be thus beaten for a fault. *Cf.* Seneca, *epp.*, 80, 7, ille qui in scaena latus incedit et haec resupinus dicit (follows some tragic rant), seruus est . . . ille qui superbus atque impotens et fiducia uirium tumidus ait (more rant), diurnum accipit, in cenaculo dormit (*i.e.*, is a poor man hired by the day). Hence Plautus, *Asin.*, 3, wishes a blessing on the *grex* (troupe), the *domini* (of its various members) and the *conductores* (contractors, who provide the actors, properties and other necessaries for the performance). The wardrobe-master was called by the old name of *choragus* (*cf.* Rose, *H.G.L.*, p. 146), see *Persa*, 159–60, πόθεν ornamenta (costume)?—abs chorago sumito,/dare debet; praebenda aediles locauerunt (contracted with him to provide it).

[109] See Wissowa, *R.K.R.*, p. 451 *sqq.*

[110] It is just possible to construe this 'in those days there was a choice lot of poets', but the explanation in the text is more consistent with the metaphorical use of *flos* elsewhere.

too good and not good enough. To judge by what we have left of it, neither Ennius (see p. 35) nor his successors wrote anything so excellent that it could make its way in face of unpopularity; but on the other hand, serious plays dealing with lofty themes, having no comic relief to liven them and indulging in a considerable amount of philosophizing, needed an audience of some culture, and that was not to be had among the crowd which the Plautine prologues cajoled into listening more or less attentively. 'You frowned when I mentioned tragedy' says Mercurius,[111] it was, at best, an imported thing, like grand opera in England, and the enthusiasm of a few members of the small class which was really educated to an appreciation of the fine arts could not make up for lack of popular support. Rome had nothing corresponding to the small playhouses, holding perhaps a thousand people or so, which in modern times have often nursed a type of drama still unknown to and unliked by the majority; a play of any kind must at least be fairly popular with a holiday-making mob running into tens of thousands, for there seems to have been no way of exhibiting intermediate between that and the mere reading of it in a lecture-room, if even this form of semi-publication, the *recitatio* of later times, had then been thought of.

Hence, having spoken already of Naevius and Ennius, we have but two names left before coming to the closet-drama of Imperial days. The first of these is MARCVS PACVVIVS or PACVIVS.[112]. He again was not of Latin birth; the son of Ennius' sister, he was born in Brundisium (the modern Brindisi), about 534/220.[113] He came to Rome, where he seems to have been both painter and poet and to have lived till over eighty years old. He then retired to Tarentum, probably in hopes that his native climate would suit his enfeebled health, and died there about 624/130.[114] Of all his works, there remain to us thirteen titles and about 500 lines of fragments, many of them single

[111] Plaut., *Amphit.*, 52.

[112] Pācŭuius in Horace (cited in n. 115), and this is the ordinary Latin form of this Oscan name; Pacui (gen.) is a spondee in the couplet in Varro, *sat. Menip.*, frag. 356 Buecheler; Pacuies (nom.) in the Oscan inscr., Conway, *Italic Dialects*, 253.

[113] He was eighty years old when Accius was thirty, Cic., *Brut.*, 229; for Accius' dates, see p. 65. Son of Ennius' sister, Pliny, *N.H.*, xxxv, 19, which also mentions his stay in Rome and his painting; Jerome, *an. Abrah.* 1863 (= 600/154) says he was *clarus* then and calls him the grandson of Ennius, no doubt confusing the two senses of *nepos*.

[114] Pliny and Jerome, *ll. cc.*; Gellius, xiii, 2, 2. Jerome says he was *prope nonagenarius* when he died.

verses or half-verses. It is therefore impossible to form an adequate notion of his merits. Various ancient critics inform us that he was considered learned, with a copious style but too great fondness for uncouth compounds, against the genius of the language.[115] It is clear also from what remains that he liked philosophical speculation and not infrequently put remarks bearing on it into the mouths of his characters.[116] To what extent he possessed any qualities of a dramatist, we are quite ignorant; all his plots except one were Greek, the exception being the *praetexta* (see p. 35) *Paullus*, whereof so little remains that we cannot even tell what Paullus is meant, though the consul Lucius Aemilius Paullus who was killed at Cannae naturally suggests himself. It also cannot be determined what Greek author he chiefly followed, though it is reasonable to suppose that, like Ennius, he owed much to Euripides, and certainly some of his plays were taken from him.

We have the following titles: *Antiopa*, which seems to have followed at least the plot of Euripides' *Antiope*[117]; *Armorum Iudicium*[118]; *Atalanta*, a title which he shares with Aeschylus, but there is nothing to show whether Pacuvius imitated him; *Chryses*, a Sophoklean title[119]; *Dulorestes, i.e., Slave-Orestes*, an unknown version of the legend, in which presumably Orestes disguised himself as a slave to accomplish his vengeance; *Hermiona*, which suggests the *Andromache* of Euripides without being able to show us from its few fragments whether that was in any sense the model; *Iliona*, containing a famous scene in which a murdered child appeared in a vision to his mother, Iliona daughter of Priam[120]; *Medus*, dealing with Medeia's son, in all probability from a Greek model of some kind[121]; *Niptra, i.e., The Foot-Washing* (of Odysseus, by his old nurse), which seems to be

[115] Cicero, *Brut.*, 258, definitely says his Latin was bad. Persius, i, 78, quotes *luctificabile* (' dolorific ') as occurring in the *Antiopa* and laughed at by the critics of his day; Quintilian cites (i, 5, 67), frag. xliv Ribbeck, Nerei repandirostrum incuruiceruicum pecus. Horace (*epp.*, ii, 1, 56) indicates that *doctus* was the stock epithet to use of him in his time. Gellius, vi (vii), 14, 6, cites the opinion of Varro that P. was the best Latin example of *ubertas*.

[116] For instance, 88 *sqq.*, 366 *sqq.* Ribbeck.

[117] See Rose, *H.G.L.*, p. 201 *sq.*

[118] *Cf.* chap. ii, note 14.

[119] Rose, *op. cit.*, p. 176.

[120] There is a story about this Iliona or Ilionea in Hyginus, *fab.*, cix, taken from some Greek poem ultimately; this may represent the plot of a Greek play which Pacuvius adapted.

[121] Hygin., *fab.*, xxvii, has a story concerning Medos and Medeia with which the fragments of Pacuvius' play agree well enough, but it is not known whence it comes.

from Sophokles[122]; *Pentheus*, perhaps from the *Bacchae* of Euripides; [123] *Periboea*, the title of which suggests that it may have treated the same story as the *Hipponus* of Sophokles, how Hipponoos of Olenos in Achaia, finding his daughter Periboia with child, sent her to Oineus of Kalydon to be put to death, and how Oineus married her instead.[124] But the fragments do not help us. The *Teucer* dealt with the return of Teukros, the greater Aias' bastard half-brother, from Troy and his expulsion from Salamis by old Telamon, their father, because he had not saved Aias alive. There are also several fragments which, fitting none of these themes, suggest others, probably handled in plays of which we have no knowledge.

A younger man by fifty years, as we have already noted, was LVCIVS ACCIVS.[125] Born in 584/170, he lived well into the last century B.C., for Cicero, when old enough to take an interest in literary matters, saw and spoke with him, apparently on several occasions.[126] He was of humble origin, his family belonging to the class of *libertini*, *i.e.*, ex-slaves and their descendants.[127] Of his life we know very little. He was perhaps a native of Pisaurum,[128] but he lived for the most part in Rome, where he was on familiar terms with many men of high rank, as Julius

[122] This is definitely stated by Cicero, *Tusc.*, ii, 48, in citing frag. ix Ribbeck of the play. The plot seems to have included the return of Odysseus (see Rose, *H.G.L.*, pp. 28, 174) and his death (*ibid.*, p. 51), a remarkably long series of incidents for one tragedy, suggesting a contamination by Pacuvius of two plays.

[123] See Rose, *op. cit.*, p. 196 *sq.*, and in *Class. Quart.*, xx (1926), p. 204.

[124] See Rose, *op. cit.*, p. 173.

[125] This seems to be the true spelling of the name, often written Attius in our MSS.

[126] Jerome, *an. Abrah.* 1878, says he was natus Mancino et Serrano consulibus (A. Hostius Mancinus and A. Atilius Serranus, coss 584/170). Cicero, *Brut.*, 107, ut ex . . . L. Accio poeta sum audire solitus.

[127] Normally, a freed slave became a citizen of the country to which his master belonged, owed the latter and his kinsfolk certain obligations, and took their family name. He himself and his descendants continued to suffer under certain restrictions, although the most important privileges of a citizen remained theirs. Hence the existence of a class of *libertini*, *i.e.*, actual freedmen and their descendants. Some ancestor of Accius must thus have been the slave of a member of the gens Accia, a not particularly distinguished house. The authority for his origin is Jerome, *loc. cit.* (note 126), natus . . . parentibus libertinis.

[128] Jerome, *loc. cit.*, says an estate called the *fundus Accianus* near Pisaurum was named after the poet; more likely, for the colony of Pisaurum is fourteen years older than he, it was called after some other Accius; Cicero (*Brut.*, 271) says that his *pro Cluentio* (see p. 174) was in reply to a speech for the prosecution by a Titus Accius of Pisaurum, which indicates that some at least of the family itself, or of its freedmen, were settled there.

Caesar Strabo,[129] a poetaster and orator, whom we shall have occasion to mention later, D. Brutus Callaicus,[130] who especially befriended him, and naturally with members of the gild of poets. He won the acknowledged primacy in his own form of composition, and his seem to have been the only tragedies which continued to hold the stage for any considerable time after his death.[131] Like Pacuvius, he used Euripides largely, Sophokles to some extent as his model. We know of forty-five tragedies on Greek themes which he composed, also two *praetextae*, *Brutus*, on the expulsion of the Tarquins by the legendary ancestor of his patron, and *Decius*, otherwise *Aeneadae*, dealing with the heroic death of P. Decius Mus the younger, in 459/295.

The known titles are as follows. *Achilles*, which likely enough dealt with the main theme of the Iliad, the quarrel of Achilles and Agamemnon, and also may have been the same play as the *Myrmidones*. *Aegisthus* and *Agamemnonidae*, which, like the *Clutaemestra* and *Erigona*,[132] dealt with various parts of the blood-stained history of Pelops' descendants. *Alcestis*, of which we have almost nothing, and so cannot say how much or little it owed to Euripides. *Alcimeo* and *Alphesiboea*, which had to do with the history of Alkmeon.[133] *Amphitruo*, which has left us too few fragments to say definitely what part of that hero's story it handled, probably, however, not the birth of Herakles. The *Andromeda* handled the well-known legend treated by both Sophokles and Euripides.[134] The *Antenoridae* dealt with part of the Troy-saga. The *Antigona* has left us too little to judge of its merits or source. The *Armorum Iudicium* and *Astyanax* again went to the

[129] Of his relations with Accius it is said (Val. Max., iii, 7, 11) that when Caesar entered the *collegium poetarum* (presumably for one of its regular business or social meetings), Accius, conscious that he was the better poet, never showed him the courtesy, usual to a social superior, of rising when he came in.

[130] An officer of some distinction, whose surname was derived from the Callaeci, the natives of that part of Spain now called Galicia, among whom he had served in command of a Roman army. For his acquaintance with Accius, see especially Cicero, *pro Archia*, 27. Cicero there says that Brutus Acci . . . carminibus templorum ac monumentorum aditus ornauit suorum. This can hardly mean extracts from his plays; the *scholia Bob*. there (p. 359, Orelli) say the verses were Saturnians, that a book of them was extant, and that a number of them were inscribed over the entrance to a temple of Mars.

[131] Cicero in various passages (list in Schanz-Hosius, i, p. 134) mentions a number of his plays as being acted in his own time.

[132] For the relevant legends, see Rose, *Myth*., pp. 247, 86; the Erigone in question is not the Attic heroine, *ibid*., p. 154, but a daughter of Aigisthos, for whom see Hyginus, *fab*., 122, 3.

[133] See Rose, *op. cit*., p. 194; Alphesiboia is another name of Arsinoe, wife of Alkmeon.

[134] See Rose, *H.G.L*., pp. 172, 191.

Trojan cycle for their themes. The *Athamas* again is little but a title to us. The *Atreus* was famous in antiquity, and has left us one of the most familiar Latin tags, *oderint, dum metuant.* It was spoken by Atreus, who was apparently made as thoroughly hateful as the hideous legend demands.[135] What is left of the *Bacchae* suggests considerable use of Euripides.[136] The *Chrysippus* dealt, it may be supposed, with the sin of Laios.[137] The *Clutaemestra* has already been mentioned. *Deiphobus* and *Diomedes* had Trojan, *Epigoni* a Theban theme, *Epinausimache* (ἡ ἐπὶ ναυσὶ μάχη, the Battle at the Ships, the title of Iliad xiii) Trojan again; *Erigona* has been mentioned above, *Eriphyla* belonged to the Theban cycle, if it was not the same as *Epigoni*, *Eurysaces* and *Hecuba* to the Trojan; the former treated of the greater Aias' son. What the *Hellenes* was about and why it was not called simply *Graeci* are questions to which there is no answer. A doubtful reading in Priscian suggests that there was a play called *Io*, possibly another title for the *Prometheus*.[138] The *Medea* contained an interesting passage, in which a shepherd, never having seen a ship before, tried to describe the appearance of the Argo.[139] The play must have dealt with some incidents of the return voyage of the heroes from Kolchis. It is not clear with what the *Melanippus* dealt. The *Meleager* had probably much the same plot as Swinburne's *Atalanta in Calydon*; the subject had been handled by Euripides.[140] The *Minos* or *Minotaurus* has left us but one line, a mention of the Minotaur's monstrous shape. The *Myrmidones* has been mentioned above. The *Neoptolemus* had something to do with the coming of Achilles' son to Troy. The *Troades*, as also the *Nyctegresia* (*Night Alarm*) again dealt with the Trojan cycle. The *Oenomaus* has left us a fair number of fragments, but not enough to say how Accius handled the story of Oinomaos, his daughter Hippodameia, and the race for her hand. The *Pelopidae* may have told the tale of how Hippodameia brought about the murder of her husband's bastard son Chrysippos and afterwards killed herself in fear of his father's anger.[141]. Possibly the *Persidae* was the same as the *Amphitruo*, since that was the house to which Amphitryon belonged.

[135] It is quoted many times, including Cicero, *pro Sest.*, 102, along with some other lines taken, as the *schol. Bob.* there (p. 303 Orelli) explains, from the same poet, and probably the same play; *de off.*, i, 97, where he says the speaker is Atreus; Seneca, *de ira*, i, 20, 4, which says the words were written 'in Sulla's days', thus excluding Ennius and Pacuvius as the authors.

[136] See Rose, *H.G.L.*, p. 196.

[137] See Rose, *Myth.*, p. 187.

[138] Priscian, p. 210, 12 Hertz, the MSS. giving *ioe* (*Ione* editors).

[139] Cicero, *de. nat. deor.*, ii, 89, naming Accius; a citation of one line of the passage in Nonius, p. 90, 8 M., gives the name of the play, which Priscian, *de metr. Terent.*, 23, 9, p. 424 Hertz, calls *Argonautae*.

[140] See Rose, *H.G.L.*, p. 206.

[141] The legend is in Hyginus, *fab.*, 85, where see my notes; frag. vi, Ribbeck, of the play mentions some one's grief at the death of his wife, and this may be Pelops mourning for Hippodameia.

It is hard to say what was Accius' model, if any, for the *Philocteta*, seeing that all three of the great Athenian tragedians wrote on that theme.[142] The *Phinidae* perhaps had Sophokles for its original [143]; the *Phoenissae* certainly owed something to Euripides.[144] Not much can be made out of the two lines which are all we have left of the *Thebais*; it may well be an alternative title of the *Phoenissae*. There was a play called *Stasiastae, i.e.* presumably 'setters up', for the alternative title was *Tropaeum Liberi*, 'Dionysos' trophy'; but except that it must have had something to do with the myth of that god, we know nothing about it. The *Telephus* and the *Tereus* have respectively the names of well-known works of Euripides and Sophokles.

Besides being, by general consent, the best of the Roman tragedians, Accius tried his hand at other forms of literature, including literary history. We have no large fragments of any of these books, indeed it is anything but certain whether they were in prose, verse or a mixture of both; but we have sundry brief quotations of at least the substance, occasionally the wording, of them, under the titles *Didascalica* and *Sotadica*.[145] There are also a few scraps (the best known is the passage cited by Macrobius [146] on the Greek Kronia and their relation to the Roman Saturnalia) of a work called *Annales*, which seems to have dealt with the calendar—a sort of anticipation of Ovid's *Fasti* (see p. 335). The *Praxidicus* (or *Praxidica*, neut. plur) seems to have treated of astronomy, or astrology [147]; it is somewhat

[142] See Rose, *H.G.L.*, p. 169.

[143] *Ibid.*, p. 176.

[144] *Ibid.*, p. 192. Frag. i Ribbeck is a free rendering of the opening lines of Euripides' play.

[145] Gellius, iii, 11, 4, cites the first book of the *Didascalica*; Nonius has several references to the work and Charisius two, one of them (p. 220, 9 Keil) to the ninth book. It was then a treatise of some length. Gellius quotes in prose, but does not say that he is citing verbatim; the others quote what is apparently Sotadean verse (a peculiar line founded upon the *Ionicus a maiore*, – – ᴗ ᴗ, but with very free and erratic substitutions). The *Sotadica* therefore may be the same work under another name; it is quoted by Gellius and Priscian. Where more than a fragment of sense can be made out of these extracts (mostly given for the sake of some one rare word which they contain) they seem to deal with literary matters. This would suit the title *didascalica* well enough, lit., 'matters connected with the presentation of plays', *i.e.*, 'history of dramatic poetry'.

[146] Macrob., i, 7, 36. The work must have been on a large scale, whatever the subject, for Festus, p. 132, 14 Lindsay, quotes from Book xxvii.

[147] Pliny, *N.H.*, xviii, 200, cites from it some directions concerning the best position of the moon relative to the signs of the zodiac for sowing. It may of course have dealt with agriculture, though in that case it is somewhat remarkable that none of the surviving writers on that subject seem to have heard of it.

idle to conjecture what the *Pragmatica* and *Parerga* were about.[148] Somewhere, we do not know whether in one of these works or in a separate treatise, he seems to have proposed certain reforms in Latin spelling, to which occasional reference is made in later authors.[149]

We know that there were others who attempted tragedy, and that is practically the beginning and end of our knowledge here. GAIVS IVLIVS CAESAR STRABO was a public man of the second and early first centuries B.C.; he was killed in 667/87. Cicero says that he was personally delightful, witty, a pleasant speaker, not lacking force in his numerous orations; of his tragedies, whereof also Cicero had a moderately good opinion, there survive some four lines.[150] The verses of Varro cited in note 112 run: Pacui discipulus·dicor, porro is fuit Enni,/Ennius Musarum; POMPILIVS clueor, and Varro also cites one line of his work.[151] He must therefore have been about contemporary with Accius, perhaps rather older, but we know nothing about him. Not even one line survives of GAIVS TITIVS, a clever speaker, according to Cicero, whose tragedies had the defect of being witty in the wrong places.[152] The obscure grammarian SANTRA is twice cited for tragic fragments. This is the whole of our unsatisfactory acquaintance with tragedy of the Roman republican period.

148 The former mentioned dancing, or at least the name of a dance, Gell., xx, 3, 3, the latter (Nonius, p. 61, 19 M.) ploughing.

149 For example, Varro, *de ling. Lat.*, vii, 96, and a number of the later grammarians, some at least from Varro, or from an intervening author who had used Varro. He was in favour of writing a vowel double if it was long, as *Maarcus*, *g* instead of *n* if that letter had the sound it has in Eng. *sing*, *sink*, as *agceps* (for the usual *anceps*), apparently also *ae*, not *e*, to represent η in words derived from Greek.

150 Cicero, *Brut.*, 177; nemo unquam urbanitate, nemo lepore, nemo suauitate conditior. sunt eius aliquot orationes, ex quibus sicut in eiusdem tragoediis lenitas eius non sine neruis perspici potest. As elsewhere, *de orat.*, iii, 30, he says Caesar treated tragic matters *paene comice*, some would omit the *non* in the above passage from the *Brutus*; but neither gentleness nor a light touch implies absence of vigour. He may have had a fondness for happy endings.

151 Varro, *de ling. Lat.*, vii, 93. Nothing more is known of this man, not even the rest of his name.

152 Cicero, *Brut.*, 167, eiusdem fere temporis (as Crassus and Antonius the orators, see p. 105 *sqq*) fuit eques Romanus C. Titius . . . huius orationes tantum argutiarum, tantum exemplorum, tantum urbanitatis habent ut paene Attico stilo scriptae esse uideantur. easdem argutias in tragoedias satis ille quidem acute sed parum tragice transtulit.

Additional note. A number of difficulties of Plautine prosody (p. 58) are discussed in O. Skutsch, *Prosodische u. metrische Gesetze d. Iambenkürzung*, Göttingen, 1934.

CHAPTER IV

THE AFTERMATH

WHEN Ennius and Plautus had written, it could no longer be said that Rome had no literature, though not unfounded charges of crudity and undeveloped technique might have been brought against it. It was no longer remarkable that a few men somehow contrived to write books or plays in Latin, and the time was already ripe for the question what manner of books had best be written, and in what style. Hence it is not at all remarkable that we find, after the efforts of the great pioneers, several writers to whom the elder men are to some extent models, to an almost greater degree subjects of criticism, and in either case starting-points for further progress.

It must again be remembered that any division into periods, however convenient for study, is artificial, and that authors continually require our notice who might be classed indifferently with the older or the younger generation. Such a one, so far as it is possible to judge from fragments, was the author often known in antiquity and always in modern times as Caecilius,[1] in full CAECILIVS STATIVS or STATIVS CAECILIVS, his *praenomen* being unknown. Equally unknown is the date of his birth; but he was famous (*clarus habebatur*) in the year of Abraham 1838, in other words 575/179, according to Jerome, and died the year after Ennius, whose companion (*contubernalis*) he had been, therefore in 586/168.[2] He was not a Roman or even an Italian,

[1] To call him Statius in Cicero's time was unambiguous, for there was then no other writer of that name; to do so after the first century A.D. would invite confusion with the epic and occasional poet of Domitian's time, for whom see p. 391 *sqq*.

[2] So Jerome, presumably from Suetonius. Suetonius himself, *uit. Terenti*, p. 292 Roth, tells a story of Terence reading the *Andria* to him. As this was produced in 588/166 and presumably written not much earlier, Caecilius was alive and well some two years after the death-date given above. Hence either the anecdote is false or Jerome's scribes have miswritten, or himself misread, something like *anno iii* (or a larger number) *post mortem Ennii*, instead of *anno post*, &c., which now stands in his text.

but an Insubrian Gaul, according to some a native of Milan (Mediolanum). This perhaps was the reason why his Latin was not always of the purest.[3] The ancients rated him highly, above or equal to Terence[4]; we cannot judge of plays which do not survive, but the fragments show at least one clear characteristic of Plautus' technique, and therefore of the older, not the newer school of drama. This is the free use of lyric *cantica* where his Greek original, oftenest Menander, had a plain dialogue-metre.[5] Examples, also, of broad fun, resembling that of Plautus, are not hard to find. But on the other hand, whether or not we accept the story of his encouraging the young Terence,[6] he resembled him in a much closer adherence to his Greek models. For of the forty-two titles which we have of him, the greater part are Greek, not merely Greek proper names, which we should in any case expect, but Greek common nouns and even phrases, as *Hypobolimaeus* (*Ὑποβολιμαῖος, The Suppositious Child*), *Ex hautu hestos* (*ἐξ αὑτοῦ ἑστώς*, 'beside himself', *The Maniac*); Varro[7] praises him for his plots, the critics of Horace's day for his *grauitas*, serious handling of the subject, both suggesting Menander more than Plautus; and not a few sententious turns of phrase are preserved from him, suggesting the eminently quotable sayings of New Comedy, imitated by Terence later. It is not possible to reconstruct any of his plays.

The passage of Vulcacius Sedigitus quoted in note 4 professes to give a list of the Latin comedians in order of merit. They are, Caecilius, Plautus, Naevius, Licinius, Atilius, Terence, Turpilius, Trabea, Luscius, Ennius. Licinius is that P. LICINIVS TEGVLA (also called Licinius IMBREX,[8] both words meaning a roofing-tile; it was apparently a nickname, not yet become the regular *cognomen* of his family, if it ever did) whom we have already mentioned (p. 21 n. 4).

[3] He was *malus auctor Latinitatis*, Cicero, *ad Att.*, vii, 3, 10, *i.e.*, not necessarily a bad stylist, but not a final authority on a fine point of usage, such as is there discussed. Both he and Pacuvius spoke badly (*male locutos uidemus*), *Brutus*, 258; the context shows that this means 'not like native Romans'.

[4] Varro, *sat. Menip.*, frag. 399 Buecheler; Hor., *epp.*, ii, 1, 59; Volcacius Sedigitus *ap.* Gell., xv, 24.

[5] Frag. i of the *Plocium*, discussed and compared with its Menandrean original by Gellius, ii, 23, 9–10.

[6] Suetonius quoted in n. 2.

[7] Varro quoted in n. 4; Horace, quoted *ibid.* It has further been pointed out (see Schanz-Hosius, i, p. 102) that Terence never cites him as an authority for his own practice of running two plays into one (*contaminatio*), and therefore he perhaps kept fairly closely to one original at a time.

[8] Gellius, xiii, 23, 16.

Gellius cites from him one fragment of two lines, which he says is from a play called *Neaera* ; obviously nothing can be concluded from such scanty material. ATILIVS is but little better known ; Ribbeck assigns three fragments to him, one accompanied by a remark of Cicero that he was *durissimus, i.e.*, wholly lacking in attractiveness of style. Nothing is known of his date, and I am inclined to ask whether he is not the same as the AQUILIVS to whom two fragments are assigned, one from a play called *Boeotia*, which Varro declared to be by Plautus. The form of his name is not perfectly certain in either case.[9] SEXTVS TVRPILIVS, according to Jerome, died at Sinuessa in extreme old age (*senex admodum*), *ann. Abrahae* 1913, which is 650/104. Thirteen play-titles, all Greek, and some 215 lines of fragments survive, mostly in Nonius. A few of them show resemblances to surviving passages of Menander, and one (147) is very like a line of Terence (*Eunuchus* 1028). Of TRABEA there survive half a dozen lines and a faint indication that he was older than Atilius and Caecilius.[10] LVSCIVS LANVVINVS is known simply and solely from the fact that he was an unfriendly critic of Terence, who replied to him sharply, but without mentioning him by name. Hence the little that is to be found concerning him and his works is in the commentary of Donatus on the Terentian passages in question. We know the names and have a line or two of the writings of IVVENTIVS and VATRONIVS ; in the former case even the name is a little uncertain.[11]

The most remarkable figure of this period, one of the most remarkable in the history of letters, though he is not a writer of the first class, is PVBLIVS TERENTIVS AFER, known in English and French as Terence. We have in our own literature two men who may serve as a kind of parallel, Joseph Conrad, who though a Pole by birth, was master of a good English style, and Beckford, who chose to write his *Vathek* in French. But to get an exact equivalent we should have to imagine a Conrad or a Beckford who should serve as a model for the minutest elegances of the language to Englishmen or Frenchmen respectively. Terence, as his *cognomen* implies, came from Northern Africa. He was not a Carthaginian, though born in that city, for *Afer* is used only of the natives of Africa (approximately the same as the modern Berbers), not of the Carthaginians (*Poeni*). Somehow he lost, or never had, free status, and became the slave of a Roman senator, Terentius Lucanus, who educated him and set him free, being attracted by his personal beauty and his abilities. All

[9] See Schanz-Hosius, i, p. 125, for authorities.

[10] Varro *ap.* Charisius, p. 241, 28 Keil, mentions *Trabea Atilius Caecilius* ; since this order is not alphabetical it may be chronological.

[11] It is written clearly and without variant *Iuuentius* only in Charisius, p. 221, 16 Keil, according to Putsch ; Keil found the passage illegible, see his note.

this is but the common story of a clever and amiable slave getting his freedom from an indulgent or humane master. But the mysterious fact is that we now hear of him living on friendly terms with some of the noblest men in Rome, especially the younger Scipio Africanus and his friend Laelius, the heads in later times of the influential and cultured circle through whose efforts Greek thought and literature rapidly became fashionable. That he had by this time learned Latin well is not remarkable; what is astonishing is that he so perfectly reproduced the purest native style and idiom that it was commonly said his plays were really the work of Scipio and Laelius, or at least that they wrote some parts of them. Before he was twenty-five years old he had written six plays, the plots and titles of which, for they all survive complete, are given herewith.[12]

The *Girl from Andros* (*Andria*) was acted in 588/166.[13] The original was a play of Menander of the same title, combined with another, the *Perinthia*, which much resembled it.[14] A courtesan from Andros, since dead, has been kind to a friendless girl, by name Glycerium, who becomes the mistress of Pamphilus, son of Simo, an Athenian citizen; the scene is laid in Athens, as usual. Simo had arranged a marriage between his son and the daughter of a friend, Chremes; but Chremes, hearing of the young man's irregular union, has broken off the engagement. Hoping to put his son in the wrong, Simo tells him that the marriage is to take place immediately, but Davus, Pamphilus' slave, informs his master of this, and Simo is met by a dutiful agreement to his supposed arrangements. But Simo is resourceful; he brings Chremes to retract his refusal of his daughter's hand, and the sham arrangements for a marriage are in a fair way to become real. Davus has still a card to play, however; Glycerium has born a child, and he contrives to lay the baby down in front of Simo's house, where Chremes cannot but see it. He once more refuses his consent, and the strained relations between all parties are brought to an end only by the arrival of one Crito, who reveals that Glycerium is Chremes' own daughter,

[12] The above account is founded on the *Vita Terentii* of Suetonius (p. 510 *sqq.*), which in turn draws upon earlier antiquarians and historians, such as Fenestella (see p. 313), also, directly or indirectly, on the comedies and other verse of authors down to the time of Cicero and Caesar.

[13] The statements as to date rest in all cases upon the *didascaliae*, or short notes prefixed to each piece and giving the time and circumstances of its first production. For the *Andria* the *didascalia* itself is lost, but can be restored from the commentary of Donatus.

[14] So Terence himself says, *Andr.*, 9 *sqq.*

lost some years before. There is an underplot; Charinus, a friend of Pamphilus, is in love with Chremes' other daughter, and he and his well-meaning but stupid slave Burria play their part in a general comedy of cross-purposes. Charinus is now made happy by betrothal to the lady of his affections, while Glycerium, really Pasibula,[15] becomes the wife of her lover.

The *Mother-in-Law* (*Hecyra*), an adaptation of Apollodoros'[16] play of the same title, came out the next year and managed to get a hearing on its third presentation. It deserved a better fate, for though it lacks action, it has a moving plot and well-drawn characters. Pamphilus, a young Athenian, has been forced by his father to desert a mistress, Bacchis, and take to wife a very amiable girl called Philumena. During his absence from Athens, Philumena returns to her father's house. On his return, Pamphilus, who has come to love Philumena, discovers that in his absence she has born a son, who cannot be his, for it is much too soon after the marriage. His father meanwhile supposes that Sostrata, his own wife and the 'mother-in-law' of the title, has driven Philumena out of the house by her enmity towards her. The poor old lady makes pathetic attempts to reconcile her son and his wife, but Pamphilus, while keeping Philumena's secret, refuses flatly to live with her again. The situation is saved by Bacchis, who is in possession of part of the facts, while the usual lucky recognition of a ring makes the rest clear; Pamphilus is after all the father of the child, for he had violated Philumena at a nocturnal festival some time before the marriage. The play ends with general reconciliation.

The *Self-Punisher* (*Heauton timorumenos*, *i.e.*, Ἑαυτὸν τιμωρούμενος, from an original of Menander, apparently one of his earliest productions) appeared in 591/163, and though not so good as the *Hecyra* has its merits. It again is a quiet play, without lively action.[17] Chremes, an old Athenian, has a son

[15] Glycerium (Γλυκέριον, Dulcie) is a courtesan's name, given the girl by the people who had brought her up.

[16] Menander, according to the *didascalia*, but Donatus names Apollodoros, enough of whose play survives to show that it is the original. The mistake has probably arisen from the resemblance in plot to the Ἐπιτρέποντες of Menander, for which cf. Rose, *H.G.L.*, p. 247; for Apollodoros, *ibid.*, p. 250.

[17] This seems to be Terence's own opinion, for he calls the play *stataria*, 36. That it is a free adaptation, not a literal rendering of Menander, though certainly some lines of it are a close translation of surviving verses of the Greek, would seem to follow from the statement (line 6), duplex quae ex argumento facta est simplici, the natural interpretation of which is that Terence added something by way of subsidiary plot.

Clitipho who appears to him a model of respectability. Really, the young man is in love with Bacchis, a woman of expensive habits and extremely easy virtue. A neighbour, Menedemus, has driven his son, Clinia,[18] from home by keeping too tight a rein on him, and is since smitten with remorse and living a hard and laborious life by way of penance. Clinia now returns, not being able to keep away from his own love, Antiphila. He and Clitipho concoct a scheme. Menedemus can refuse nothing to the returned exile, and admits Bacchis, whom he supposes to be his own son's mistress, to his house, along with her maids, one of whom is Antiphila. But it very soon transpires that Bacchis' favours are going to Clitipho. On top of the recriminations and misunderstandings which this discovery produces comes a further revelation; Antiphila is Chremes' daughter, exposed years before. Clinia can therefore appear in the new character of an honourable suitor; he is betrothed to Antiphila, and Clitipho likewise provided with a wife to keep him out of further mischief. A rascally slave, Syrus, is in the thick of the intrigues and, as usual, forgiven in the last scene.

The year 593/161 saw the production of one of Terence's best works, the *Eunuch* (*Eunuchus*), derived from a play of Menander with the same title.[19] The plot turns on a double set of intrigues, closely connected. Thraso, a less farcical Pyrgopolynices (cf. p. 49), attended by a really humorous parasite, Gnatho, is in love with the courtesan Thais,[20] who has another and poorer admirer, Phaedria. Phaedria has a brother, Chaerea, who is desperately in love with Pamphila, a girl supposed to be Thais' sister, really one of her slave-women, given her by Thraso. Chaerea changes clothes with a eunuch whom his brother is giving to Thais, gets into the women's quarters and makes the most of his opportunities. Meanwhile Thais is giving Phaedria as much of her attention as she can, despite a promise to Thraso to admit him only to her society for the next two days. These manœuvres, largely contrived by a slave called Parmeno who acts as adviser to the two young men, lead to a series of most

[18] *Κλεινίας*, a common enough Athenian name.

[19] So Terence himself, *Eun.*, 20, adding (30 *sqq.*) that Thraso and Gnatho are taken from another play of Menander, the *Κόλαξ*, and that he has since discovered that this part of the material had already been used in a comedy of Naevius and another, apparently called *Colax*, ascribed to Plautus.

[20] Not of course the famous historical courtesan who was mistress of Alexander the Great, see Athenaios, 576 d *sqq.*, and many other passages both Greek and Latin. Dante, *Inferno*, confuses the two in xviii, 133–5, which is taken from *Eun.*, 391–2.

lively scenes. Thais and her household are loud in denunciation of the sham eunuch ; Phaedria nearly frightens the real one out of his wits with a string of questions and threats ; Thraso attempts to take Pamphila back by force, because Thais has played him false.[21] By this time, however, Thais has discovered that Pamphila is the sister of a certain Chremes,[22] an Athenian citizen, and therefore free-born. She and Chremes drive off Thraso, Pamphila is betrothed to Chaerea, and Thais becomes a client of Phaedria's father, and therefore readily accessible to Phaedria himself. Thus all except Thraso are satisfied.

In the same year the *Phormio* was produced. Apollodoros' *'Επιδικαζόμενος* was its original ; it is a good play, with a thoroughly amusing intrigue. A young Athenian, Antipho, during his father's absence, falls in love with a girl, of unknown parentage and very poor, but claiming to be Athenian also. Aided and abetted by his slave Geta he puts into operation a scheme for getting himself forced to marry her. A parasite, Phormio, is hired to claim acquaintance with her and, in accordance with the forms of Attic law,[23] to allege before the courts that Antipho is her next of kin and therefore should marry her. Antipho of course refutes none of Phormio's assertions, and therefore is found liable to carry out his supposed duty. Now his father returns and tries to get Phormio to withdraw his claim and take the girl off Antipho's hands. Phormio adopts an attitude of strong moral indignation and will not hear of playing fast and loose with a respectable young woman in this way. Geta meanwhile is besought by a cousin of Antipho, Phaedria, to raise thirty *minae* [24] for him to buy a flute-girl with whom he

[21] To students of English literature it is of interest that this scene is the original of the farcical attack on Cunstance's house by Ralph Roister-Doister in Udall's play of that name. Ralph and Matthew Merrygreeke are of the numerous offspring of Thraso and Gnatho.

[22] Here, exceptionally, the name of a young man ; it is so commonly that of an old man in New Comedy that Horace uses it practically = *senex* in *A.P.*, 94, iratusque Chremes tumido delitigat ore.

[23] That is, Phormio alleges that the girl is an *ἐπίκληρος*, an orphan without brothers, whose next of kin, being the natural heir to any estate which her father might have left, was obliged to marry her, even if it meant divorcing an existing wife, and thus provide for her. The comic irony of the play turns on Phormio's claim being almost exactly true, for Antipho and she are cousins, although they do not know it.

[24] An Attic *mina* (*μνᾶ*) was worth 100 silver drachmae, that is about £4 English or $20 American, in bullion value ; its purchasing power was of course very much higher, owing to the smaller amount of money then in circulation and the lower standard of living generally. Perhaps, if we think of Phormio's claim as about equivalent to £1,200 or $6,000, we shall not be far wrong.

is much in love. This Geta does by telling Antipho's father that Phormio will assent to his proposals for just this sum: he will not pay more than twenty, but his brother Chremes, Phaedria's father, subscribes the whole, because he wishes Antipho to marry his own daughter, the child of a woman he had married in Lemnos and then deserted years before, without the relationship getting to the ears of his Athenian wife, Nausistrata. It turns out, of course, that Antipho's wife is Chremes' daughter, of whom he had lost sight and whose mother is dead; Antipho is thus made happy, and also Phaedria, for Nausistrata, being told of her husband's double life by Phormio, thinks the information cheap at the price of the thirty *minae* which her son has already laid out, and is ready to forgive everybody, except the unhappy Chremes.

Terence's last play, the *Adelphi* (*'Αδελφοί, Brothers*; from an original by Menander, but not the same as that freely adapted by Plautus for the *Stichus*, with the addition of one scene from a play of Diphilos, the *Συναποθνήσκοντες, i.e., United in Death*),[25] came out in 594/160. Two brothers, Demea and Micio, are of strongly contrasted character, the former being frugal and strict, the latter easy-going. Demea has two sons, whereof one, Aeschinus, has been adopted by his uncle and indulgently reared; the other, Ctesipho, has remained with his father and been brought up to hard work in the country. Demea believes him a paragon of frugal virtue, and continually reproaches Micio with spoiling Aeschinus. The climax of his virtuous indignation has been reached when the play begins; Aeschinus has entered by violence the house of a *leno* and kidnapped one of its inmates,[26] but Micio still refuses to be seriously annoyed, though he feels privately that the young man has gone rather too far. As the play progresses, which it does in a lively manner enough, with amusing scenes in which the indignant *leno* appears, it turns out that Aeschinus was acting on Ctesipho's behalf, and has carried off a harp-girl with whom that young scion of virtue is violently in love. On

[25] See *Adelph.*, 6 *sqq.*, Sueton., *Vita Terentii*, p. 293 Roth. For Diphilos see Rose, *H.G.L.*, p. 249. The play was probably much less tragic in tone than its title would indicate; some such episode as a suicide pact which was afterwards abandoned would explain the name. A *Commorientes* was ascribed to Plautus and taken from Diphilos' work.

[26] Either this was in reality a characteristic prank of the rowdier young men of fashionable Athens, or it was near enough to their real escapades to be a plausible incident on the stage. The scenes in which the kidnapping of the harp-girl occurs are those borrowed from Diphilos (cf. n. 25), and the second mime of Herodas, which plainly owes much to New Comedy, has the same theme. Cf. Rose, *H.G.L.*, p. 340.

his own behalf, he has been carrying on an intrigue with a free-born girl, under promise of marriage. Now her relations begin to protest loudly against his supposed double-dealing, the more so as the girl is fallen in labour.[27] Micio, when he hears of the matter, promptly says that Aeschinus must marry her. Meanwhile Demea finds out what Ctesipho has been doing, and is beside himself with anger. Micio, however, succeeds in calming him. A good dinner and a little reflection lead him to see that he has been too strict, and in a most amusing scene, reminiscent of Scrooge's Christmas morning, he is shown practising affability to the slaves whom he meets, including his own son's personal attendant Syrus. In the end he has the better of it; for, preaching to Micio from the latter's own favourite maxims, he induces him to marry Aeschinus' newly made mother-in-law. So the play ends with the triumph of good-natured indulgence; Aeschinus has his wife and Ctesipho keeps his harp-girl.

All these plays have several features in common. They follow their originals closely, so far as surviving fragments allow us to judge, save for the *contaminatio*, or running of two plays into one, which Terence freely admits to be his practice. The scene is always Athens and the characters generally Athenians, unless the plot requires a foreigner. The metre is much simpler than that of Plautus, for lyric *cantica* are almost absent. The construction is always careful and adequate, the characters drawn with something of Menander's quiet humour and truth to life—no doubt this is largely an excellence at second hand—the tone Menandrean also, for Terence does not expect high virtue of ordinary human kind, but only good temper and moderation.[28] In fact, these are hyper-civilized dramas, and for that very reason not likely ever to be widely popular in a Rome still half barbarous. The last characteristic, and one which shows clearly to what an extent Terence had his eye on the educated, not the general public, is that most of the prologues [29] to the plays are literary

[27] Indicated in the usual manner; at 486 she is heard to cry out and call upon the birth-goddess (Iuno Lucina; in the original it would be Eileithyia).

[28] For the morals of Menander, and of New Comedy generally, see Rose, *op. cit.*, pp. 246, 250.

[29] An exception is that of the *Hecyra*, which is a plea for a quiet hearing. Evidently the *Andria* was given a prologue for its second performance, for it refers to criticisms of its author as already in circulation, which could not be so if he had as yet put nothing before the public. Several passages refer to the speaker as being one of the older actors, apparently L. Ambivius Turpio, a player of long experience, who had been Caecilius' star (*Hec.* 14). For a favourable estimate of Terence,

manifestos, defending his own method of constructing plays against ' ill-wishers ' (*maleuoli*) or the ' old poet who wishes him ill ' (*maleuolus uetus poeta*) [30] and on occasion carrying the war into the enemy's country by counter-criticisms. It is very plain that Greek art had not come to Rome unattended ; at least the beginnings of critical canons were already established there.[31]

Terence is the chief medium through which the art of constructing a play came to be known to modern Europe, and he, more than Plautus, is the ancestor of Comedy of Manners from the Revival of Letters on. One reason for this is that he was universally known, because used everywhere as a school-book, on account of his purity of style and easy simplicity of construction, from the end of the classical era [32] onwards, till modern teachers, presumably in fear for their pupils' morals, substituted for him the much more difficult Latinity of Caesar, one of the most unsuitable authors for a beginner that could be imagined.

How high Terence might have risen as a dramatic artist we can hardly estimate. His talents had little time to develop, for he was not yet twenty-five years old when he left Rome never to return. It is said that he meant to spend some time in Greece, and the confused and gossipy accounts of the manner of his death which Suetonius gives seem to contain this much solid fact, that he died either in that country or on the return journey, whether by disease or shipwreck. The date of his death was 595/159 ; Jerome, probably by a mere oversight, puts it a year later.

The above sketch will have made it plain that the plays of Terence were as pure Greek in tone as they were pure Latin in language. They were ' in Greek dress ', *palliatae*, an art foreign even to details of names and scenes. It is the more to be regretted that we have but fragmentary quotations of what seems an

see G. Norwood, *The Art of Terence* (Oxford, Blackwell, 1923). The present writer stands about half-way between the enthusiasm of Prof. Norwood and the position of those who allow the comedian only the merit of having written good Latin.

[30] *Andria*. 5–6. Luscius Lanuvinus is meant, cf. p. 72 ; that he is not named is due probably to a desire to avoid legal proceedings.

[31] Hence, for example, Atkins, ii, p. 5, rightly sees in Terence an early document of Roman literary criticism. Plautus had already made a few occasional remarks of a critical nature, see Atkins, *ibid.*, and no doubt discussions of such matters had been going on ever since Ennius at least.

[32] To take one example of many, Apollinaris Sidonius, *epp.*, ii, 2, 2, assumes that his friend Domitius will be reading Terence with his class ; exponere oscitabundus ordiris ' Samia mihi mater fuit ' (*Eun.*, 107). The corruptions in our MSS. are in very large measure nothing but teachers' notes on syntax, &c., incorporated in the text by copyists.

interesting attempt to naturalize this form of literature, the *comoedia togata*, represented for us by a few names and about 630 lines, nowhere forming a long continuous passage and generally single, often incomplete. There are three known names of poets, of whom one was possibly a little older than Terence, the others both perhaps and one certainly younger. With them the *togatae* seem to begin and end, unless we count Naevius as one of their group or include dilettante imitations of this *genre*, never intended to be acted.[33] So far as we can judge from such imperfect materials, these authors naturalized Greek comedy as the English writers after Ben Jonson did that of France, keeping the general tone and structure more or less well, but substituting Italian for Greek names and settings.

TITINIVS (we know no more of his name) was perhaps the oldest of the three[34] and Varro praises him for his character-drawing. However this may be, we should be glad to recover some of his work, for through the scanty and sometimes doubtful fragments of some fourteen plays which casual quotations preserve for us, we can catch tantalizing glimpses; a busy fuller's establishment,[35] a masterful wife,[36] another lady who apparently is her own lawyer,[37] a remark on the Hellenizing ways of Ferentinum [38] and the country speech of someplace else,[39] a thieveish slave-girl with a stolen hank of wool,[40]—all things which, if they were set forth with any tolerable skill, would restore to Italian life of that day not a little of the vividness which it now lacks for us.

T. QVINCTIVS ATTA is an extremely vague figure to us, though Horace had apparently read him,[41] and very little of his writing remains. Jerome says he died *ann. Abrah.* 1940 (= 677/77), at Rome. A dozen titles and a few stray lines do not suffice to

[33] Naevius wrote a play called *Tunicularia*, the one substantial fragment of which concerns a certain Theodotus at work behind a screen (*circumtectus tegetibus*) painting the Lares. Title and incident suggest an Italian setting. Juvenal, *sat.*, i, 3, mentions *togatae* among the new compositions which try his patience.

[34] Varro, *ap.* Charisius, p. 241, 27 Keil, says: ἤθη nullis aliis seruare conuenit quam Titinio Terentio Attae. The order of the names may be chronological, cf. n. 10.

[35] The *Fullonia*, especially frag. ix Ribb.

[36] This was apparently the theme of the *Gemina*.

[37] *Iurisperita* is one of the surviving titles.

[38] Ferentinatis populus res Graecas studet, 85 Ribb.

[39] Qui Obsce et Volsce fabulantur, nam Latine nesciunt, 104, 'Oscan is their speech, and Volscian, for of Latin they have none'.

[40] *Incert.*, xxi, Ribb.

[41] Hor., *epp.*, ii, 1, 79.

tell us how well justified was Varro's praise of his characters [42] or the opinion of Horace that his construction of a play was not beyond criticism.

LVCIVS AFRANIVS is better known to us. His exact dates are not recorded, but he lived about the same time as Pacuvius, Accius and Terence,[43] according to Velleius Paterculus. Possibly, since Cicero claims personal acquaintance with Accius (see p. 65) but says nothing of the sort concerning Afranius, the comedian was the older, or the shorter-lived. Two things are recorded of his manner, on good authority; one, that he made much use of Menander,[44] the other, that he often took unpleasant themes for his plots.[45] Of the two or three plays which we can make some attempt at reconstructing, none seems to have this fault. *The Divorce* (*Diuortium*) contained as one element of its story the interference of a father with his daughter's marriage. The *Exceptus* (perhaps *Saved from the Sea*) may have dealt with the misfortunes of a young man crossed in love who tried to drown himself, or fell into the water by some accident, was pulled out by an honest fisherman, one of the characters, and possibly softened the heart of his Neapolitan mistress in consequence. In the *Simulans* (*Pretender*) there seem to have been some episodes very familiar to sentimental drama of later date than Afranius—a husband who led a dissipated life, his wife's father who tried to frighten him into good behaviour by threatening to take his daughter back, and a child who intervened in a quarrel between the parents. But such reconstructions are of the most tentative nature. We are on more certain ground in saying that he, like Terence, discussed literary matters through the mouths of his prologues.[46] About forty titles in all of his plays and some 400 lines of his verse are known.

Of the Atellenae, which no doubt existed in this period along with the more regular plays, something has been said already (p. 24) and

[42] Varro and Horace cited in notes 34 and 41.

[43] Vell. Paterc., i, 17, 1, in Accio circaque eum Romana tragoedia est; dulcesque Latini leporis facetiae per Caecilium Terentiumque et Afranium suppari aetate nituerunt. ii, 9, 2, clara etiam per idem aeui spatium (the second century B.C.) fuere ingenia in togatis Afrani, in tragoediis Pacuui atque Acci.

[44] So he says himself, 25 Ribb. *sqq.* (from Macrobius, *sat.*, vi, 1, 4), besides references in later authors who could read and compare the two.

[45] Quintilian, x, i, 100: togatis excellit Afranius; utinam non inquinasset argumenta puerorum foedis amoribus ('with disgusting homosexual episodes').

[46] See the first two fragments of the *Compitalia*.

more will be said in a later chapter (p. 147); we cannot name a writer of this *genre* contemporary with Terence or Afranius.

Alongside of drama, an almost new art was coming into existence. Ennius had written a few miscellanies (*saturae*, see p. 39), but had not made that form of composition anything more than a side-line. In 574/180 was born at Suessa Aurunca a man of Latin, not Roman status (*socius nominis Latini*), GAIVS LVCILIVS.[47] He seems to have been the politically unambitious member of a rising family. A brother became not only a Roman citizen but a senator, married his daughter to a distinguished man, Cn. Pompeius Strabo, consul 665/89, and thus became the maternal grandfather of Cn. Pompeius Magnus, otherwise Pompey the Great.[48] But Gaius remained content with his comfortable fortune, his friendship with the younger Africanus and his circle, and the pleasures of reading and writing. For that he was far from poor is proved not only from his serving in the cavalry at Numantia,[49] but from the company he habitually kept, the many casual allusions in his works to possessions and activities of his own which would be quite beyond the reach of any one not in easy circumstances, and the fact that he lived in a house which the Senate had thought literally fit for a king, the young prince who became Antiochos IV, Epiphanes.[50] His one appearance as anything like a public figure did him credit. After the agrarian legislation of Tiberius Gracchus had been passed and the land

[47] The storehouse of information about him is the edition of his fragments by F. Marx (*C. Lucilii carminum reliquiae*, 2 vols., Teubner 1904 and 1905), to which reference is made in the following notes. That he was born at (Suessa) Aurunca we know from Juvenal, *sat.*, i, 20. That he never became a Roman citizen is likely, first from the absence of any mention of the fact, secondly from the circumstance that although he attacked many people by name in his writings, we hear nothing of any action being taken against him. But if he was an ally, not a Roman, it is probable that he would not be liable under a Roman law, cf. Macrobius, *saturn.*, iii, 17, 6. As to the date of his birth, Jerome gives *ann. Abrah.* 1869 (= 606/148). But this is absurd, for it would make him a lad of fifteen at Numantia (620/132), nineteen or so when Scipio died (625/129) and but middle-aged at his own death, whereas Horace says he lived to be old (*senex*), *serm.* ii, 1, 34. Jerome probably read that he was born in the consulate of Aulus Postumius Albinus and Gaius Calpurnius Piso, (574/180), and excusably confused them with Spurius Postumius Albinus and Lucius Calpurnius Piso, consuls in 606/148.

[48] Pedigree in Marx, vol. i, p. xix.

[49] Velleius Paterculus, ii, 9, 4.

[50] Asconius on Cicero, *in Pisonem*, p. 13 Clark, 12 Kiessling-Schoell. Presumably he bought it after Antiochos' younger brother Demetrios, who succeeded him as hostage, escaped in 592/162 (Polybios, xxxi, 11 *sqq.*, Büttner-Wobst).

commissioners set about the reclaiming from private possessors of the State domains, these worthies were most active among those least likely to resist their authority, the non-Roman allies. Scipio came forward as the champion of Italians generally against encroachments on what they regarded as their rights; and that Lucilius supported him is probable from the fact that when he died at Naples in 652/102 the town gave him a public funeral, as to a general benefactor.[51]

He was a ready and voluminous writer,[52] and embodied his views on a most miscellaneous selection of subjects in thirty books, composed in various metres.[53] Since his family was connected with that of Pompey and some at least of the grammarians who studied him were of Pompeian sympathies,[54] it might have been expected that the sentimental republicanism which was prominent in good society under the Empire would have preserved his works, or some part of them, for us to read, but we have only fragments, some 1,300 lines in all, no complete poem, nor even a long passage; the great majority of our quotations extend to no more than a line or two, and it is rare to have as many as six verses together. However, it is possible to get some idea both of his matter and his style. As regards the former, he was essentially a critic of life and letters. The first book contained, perhaps consisted of, a mock-heroic assembly of the gods to decide 'how and in what manner they could preserve the state and city of Rome any longer'.[55] The immediate cause of their deliberations was the

[51] Jerome, *ann. Abrah.* 1914.

[52] He could dictate two hundred lines in an hour without stopping for breath (*stans pede in uno*, literally, 'standing on one foot', clearly a proverbial expression), Hor., *serm.*, i, 4, 9–10.

[53] This arrangement is doubtless due to his editors, not himself, for so far as the chronology of the poems can be made out, it is quite independent of their order. See Marx, i, p. xxix *sqq.*, for conjectures as to dates. So far as can be seen from the remains, Books 1–20 and 30 were in hexameters, 22 in elegiacs (of 21 nothing at all can be recognized), 26–29 in various metres, largely trochaic tetrameters (the 'Locksley Hall' metre) and iambic trimeters. Twenty-three is represented by one line, a hexameter, 25 by two words, 24 is lost entirely, unless some of the unplaced fragments belong to it.

[54] Pompeius Lenaeus, who was a freedman of Pompey the Great; Valerius Cato, for whom see p. 131; Curtius Nicias, who was a Pompeian in politics. See Sueton., *de gramm.*, 2, 14 and 15.

[55] Quo populum atque urbem pacto seruare potisset amplius Romanam. The subject of *potisset* is not known, but very likely Iuppiter, acting as presiding magistrate of the divine senate. The next fragment in Marx' arrangement (lines 5–7) seems to continue the same question: si non amplius, at lustrum hoc protolleret unum; a god, probably the same one, is suggesting that at least Rome might be allowed to stand for a

death of a noted man, L. Cornelius Lentulus Lupus, *princeps senatus* at the time of his demise, which was in or near 629/125; Lupus, as Lucilius seems regularly to have called him, was a favourite target of his satire, and probably he was made to cut a sorry figure before the divine assembly. The third book described a journey from Rome to the Straits of Messina, via Capua. The fifth was an open letter to a friend. Some part at least of the ninth dealt with literature and grammar; our fragments range from the definition of 'poem' and 'poetry' to the correct spelling of Latin. The tenth, and also the second, seem to have been full of personal attacks; the latter of these had much to say of Titus Albucius, who according to the poet made himself ridiculous by affecting to talk Greek on all occasions.[56] The eleventh handled the quarrel between Scipio and the tribune of the plebs, Tiberius Claudius Asellus, who in 614/140 brought an accusation against him; Lucilius naturally took the part of his friend. The thirteenth dealt apparently with good living, at all events its fragments have something to say of various kinds of food. The sixteenth was known as *Collyra*, the name of Lucilius' real or feigned mistress; the seventeenth also had something to say about women, for two fragments deal respectively with Penelope and the personal beauty of epic heroines. Some part at least of the twenty-sixth treated of his own writings and of fit subjects for writing in general. In other books it is seldom possible to group all the fragments under any single subject; this is, of course, very likely due to the nature of the works themselves, which perhaps were called by their author *carmina* or *poemata per saturam*,[57] 'miscellanies in verse'. Certainly an author who

lustrum (five years) longer. The implication would seem to be that the wickedness of Lupus and his kind are more than divine patience can endure.

[56] Albucius accused Quintus Mucius Scaevola of extortion in 634/120 or the next year; perhaps the satire contained a humorous account of the proceedings; certainly one fragment (88–95) is an attack by Scaevola on Albucius' affectations. It is not to be supposed that Lucilius was a partisan of Scaevola, however, for we have the testimony of Persius that he attacked him too (secuit Lucilius urbem,/te, Lupe, te, Muci, et genuinum fregit in illis, i, 114–15). Perhaps the general tone of the piece was that it was a case of the pot calling the kettle black.

[57] Marx, i, p. x, gives good reasons for supposing that no such word as *satira* exists in Latin (if it does, why are no such forms as *satir* or *satirare* ever found?); it is an alternative spelling of *satyra*, a form which dates from about the third century A.D., probably under the influence of Gk. σάτυρος and its cognates. It is not till Persius that we find *saturae* regularly used as the title of poems of this kind (apparently his work never bore any other). Before that we hear of 'poems in the manner of Lucilius', 'familiar discourses' (*sermones*) or the like.

ranges from the distinction between *ei* and *i* in the spelling of words[58] to the concern of the gods in the morality of men was not likely to tie himself so very strictly to any one theme, even in a single poem, that he would admit no digressions. In the case of the twenty-second book there is some reason to suppose that it consisted of epigrams, perhaps epitaphs, on the author's own slaves; certainly it contained one such, which survives.[59]

The merits of Lucilius, by common consent of all who refer to him, even Horace, who disliked his careless style, were considerable. In vivid, direct, sometimes coarse language, he set forth his views concerning the world about him. He was, Horace declares, the successor of Old Comedy in this respect[60]; we may add that he was the inheritor of those writers who, like Kerkidas, Bion the Borysthenite, Menippos, and Timon of Phleius,[61] discoursed Greek ethics and popular philosophy in a fashion which could be appreciated by men of but moderate culture. Indeed, Lucilius himself says that it is not by great critics and scholars but by moderately learned men that he wishes to be read.[62] The later satirists all considered him their exemplar and the originator of their *genre*, with its familiar, serio-comic advice to mankind and its traditionally outspoken tone in dealing with vices and absurdities. His weakest point was his versification. Of the surviving lines, a great number scan, as it were, on sufferance; that is, the words are so arranged that they can be brought to give the requisite number of long and short syllables in the proper order, if allowance is made for the popular pronunciation of certain syllables. In this sense they form verses; but these are often so uncouth as to be painful to read. This is especially true of his hexameters, which have every fault of rhythm whereof that difficult metre is capable. The fact is that even after Ennius the art of writing them in Latin was a long way from being mastered, and especially the art of combining, in this

[58] Frag. 351 *sqq.*, Marx.

[59] It runs (579–80 Marx): seruos neque infidus domino neque inutili' quanquam/Lucili columella hic situst Metrophanes, 'here lies Metrophanes, who though but Lucilius' stand-by was a faithful servant to his master and a useful'.

[60] Horace, *serm.*, i, 4, 1 *sqq*.

[61] See Rose, *H.G.L.*, pp. 344, 357–9.

[62] 593 Marx; Persium non curo legere, Laelium Decumum uolo. Cicero (*de orat.*, ii, 25) quotes and explains this: Persius was counted the best scholar in Rome, Decimus Laelius was an honest and not uncultured man. 595, a passage loosely cited by Cicero (*de fin.*, i, 7), and therefore not to be restored with certainty, was to the same effect; here the reader he asks for is a certain Iunius Congus.

medium, ease and formal correctness. The other metres, having the experience of the comic poets behind him, Lucilius manages more successfully.

In or about this time several minor poets wrote. One was old enough for Lucilius [63] to mention his best-known work as enjoying popularity among some society, but what exactly the corrupt text of the fragment prevents us from learning. The work in question was the *Lex Tappula conuiuialis*, *i.e.*, the law put forward by Tappo for the better regulation of feasts. It was probably in verse [64]; but we have a badly damaged inscription in prose, set up in Imperial times, which bears the same title, and therefore is probably connected in some way with the older performance. It records, with mock gravity and in proper legal form, that it was passed on the motion of Tappo, son of Tappo,[65] by the advice and consent of his colleagues, Marcus Multivorus and Publius Properocius (Messrs. Bellyful and Bringitquick), and that the first vote cast in its favour was that of the *tribus Satureia* (about equivalent to the electors of Eatanswill). What its contents were we do not exactly know, but doubtless they were mock-solemn directions to eat and drink heartily. The author was called VALERIVS VALENTINVS, otherwise unknown save for having written a poem so scandalous that the reading of it in a court of law moved the jury to acquit an obviously guilty man accused by him.[66] He had Greek models for his comic legislature; serious rules for the regulation of feasts were written, or said to have been written, by several philosophers, including Aristotle, and Gnathaina, one of the most celebrated Athenian courtesans, wrote what seems to have been a parody on these

[63] Lucil., 1307, Tappulam rident legem . . . and the following words are corrupted past any plausible restoration. Marx' notes (vol. ii, p. 415) give conjectures and attempts at interpretation. Festus (p. 451 of Linday's *ed. mai.*, 496 of his Teubner text) says: Tappulam legem conuiualem ficto nomine conscripsit iocoso carmine Valerius Valentinus, cuius meminit Lucilius hoc modo, and then quotes the fragment. The cognomen Valentinus seems to mean that Valerius came from the town of Vibo Valentia in Bruttium.

[64] This is probable from Festus' use of *carmine*, see last note, though as above stated (p. 5) the word need mean no more than ' formula '. The inscription (text in *C.I.L.*, v, *supplem. Ital*, 898, Dessau, *Inscr. Lat. sel.*, 8761, and in several smaller collections, such as Bruns, ed. 7, p. 122) is certainly prose, and till we have further evidence, conjectures as to the relation between them are rather futile.

[65] This actually occurs as the name of a real person, *C.I.L.*, v, 4183, but in its origin is most likely a figure in some kind of farce, perhaps Greek; it has been suggested (Walde, *s.u.*) that it is = Θάπων, *i.e.*, ' gaper ', ' simpleton who wonders at everything '.

[66] See Valerius Maximus, viii, 1, 8. The poem bragged of its author's real or imaginary intrigues with persons of respectable family; possibly it was a deliberately coarse performance in imitation of Hipponax (Rose, *H.G.L.*, p. 92 *sq.*).

manuals of etiquette, for the guidance of her own lovers and those of her daughter.[67]

In 625/129 one of the consuls of that year, Gaius Sempronius Tuditanus, helped by one of the ablest officers of the day, Decimus Brutus Callaicus, waged successful war against the Iapydes, a troublesome people of Illyricum. This campaign may be called the second Istrian War,[68] and it was in all probability the subject of an epic poem, doubtless inspired by Ennius' *Annals*, known as the *Bellum Histricum*, whose author, so little known to us that we have not even a record of his full name, was called HOSTIVS. Of his work there survive less than ten lines [69]; one short passage it would seem that Vergil read and used.[70]

Another and perhaps more important epic poet was AVLVS FVRIVS of Antium (Furius Antias), a friend of the great Quintus Lutatius Catulus. As this means that he was alive and writing about the beginning of the first century B.C.,[71] it is not surprising that we find among his fragments verses of better craftsmanship than we have learned to expect from an Ennius or a Lucilius. His subject would appear to have been, like that of Ennius, the history of Rome; he called his work *Annales*, like that of the older poet, and it is in no way impossible that it was meant as a continuation of that poem. In any case, it extended to not fewer than eleven books.[72]

Didactic poetry seems also to have been represented during this period. QVINTVS VALERIVS of Sora (*Soranus*) comes late enough in Roman history to have been a friend of Cicero and Varro in their youth; he was tribune of the plebs in 672/82, in the last year of the wars between Marius and Sulla, of which struggle he was one of the many victims. In happier times he probably would have made a great name as scholar and writer, for he was very learned,[73] and the

[67] Athenaios, pp. 3 f and 585 b.

[68] It presumably was not the earlier campaign against the same people, in 586/178 and the following year, for that had been dealt with by Ennius.

[69] See *F.P.R.*, pp. 138–9/33–4.

[70] Frag. 5/3, from Macrobius, vi, 3, 6: nec si mihi linguae/centum atque ora sient totidem uocesque liquatae, imitated from Homer, Iliad ii, 489, who has ten, not a hundred; hence Vergil, *Aen.*, vi, 625, non mihi si linguae centum sint oraque centum,/ferrea uox.

[71] Cicero, *Brut.*, 132, speaks of a book which Catulus wrote and dedicated *ad A. Furium, familiarem suum.* This is the Catulus who was prominent in the campaigns against the Cimbri and Teutoni in 652/102 and the next year.

[72] See Gellius, xviii, 11. Macrobius, vi, 1, 31 *sqq.*, quotes several lines from a Furius who is probably this man, giving the numbers of the books and the title *Annales*; the highest number cited is xi.

[73] Cicero, *de orat.*, iii, 43, litteratissimum togatorum omnium, Q. Valerium Soranum; *Brut.*, 169, Q. D. Valerii Sorani, uicini et familiaris mei . . . docti et Graecis litteris et Latinis. For his death, see Oppius *ap.* Plutarch, *Pomp.*, 10; this is the Valerius Soranus of whom the story was told that he revealed the secret name of Rome's guardian deity,

scanty remnants of his work, most of which seems to have been in verse, indicate that he dealt with grammar, philosophy, and some other topic or topics, this last perhaps in iambics and in the form of a letter or address to one of the Scipios.[74] He also wrote a work, perhaps in prose, called *'Επόπτιδες*, whatever exactly that may mean,[75] which contained a novel feature in the shape of a table of contents.

Perhaps in the second century B.C. lived a certain Porcivs Licinvs, who wrote, in trochaic tetrameters, a work dealing with the Roman writers, at least to the time of Terence.[76] He also wrote epigrams, of which one is preserved, concerning a lover who could set the woods on fire by merely touching them, so strongly does his passion burn in him. Two other epigrammatists of about this age are known to us, one thought to be earlier than Licinus, the other later. They are Valerivs Aeditvvs, otherwise unknown, and Qvintvs Lvtativs Catvlvs, the great general. Of their surviving pieces, two, by Licinus and Catulus respectively, have known Greek originals,[77] and Aedituus is clearly attempting in elegiacs one of the most celebrated passages of Sappho's lyrics. The Pompilius mentioned as a minor tragedian on p. 69 may also be included among these epigrammatists.

Volcacivs Sedigitvs has already been mentioned in passing (above, note 4). The passage there cited from Gellius proves that he wrote a work *Concerning Poets*. Suetonius names him, among those who have given their opinion of Terence's worth, after Afranius and before Cicero, which is our one clue to his date.[78]

Plut., *quaest. Rom.*, 61, with my comments (*Roman Questions of Plutarch*, Clar. Press, 1924, pp. 37, 42, 196). Verrius Flaccus is the source. For his fragments, see *F.P.R.*, p. 272 *sq.* 40 *sq.*

[74] Frag. 1 Baehrens, as restored by him, runs uetus sat adagio est, o Publi Scipio.

[75] It is simply the feminine of ἐπόπτης, which means according to context ' overseer ', ' onlooker ', ' initiate '. Pliny, *N.H.*, *praefatio*, 32–3, says : quid singulis contineretur libris huic epistulae subiunxi . . . hoc ante me fecit in litteris nostris Valerius Soranus in libris quos *'Εποπτίδων* inscripsit.

[76] The only clue to his date (save that his verses are not good enough for the Empire) is Gellius' list of epigrammatists, xix, 9, 10, in the (chronological ?) order Aedituus, Licinus, Catulus. Apuleius, *Apologia*, 9, has the same order. On the other hand, there may have been a collection of epigrammatists, and there is no reason to suppose that this would arrange the names chronologically.

[77] The epigram in Gellius, *loc. cit.*, 11, by Aedituus, is from Sappho, frag. 2 Diehl (*Anthologia lyrica Graeca*) ; that of Licinus, *ibid.*, 13, mentioned above, somewhat resembles *Anth. Palat.*, ix, 15 ; that of Catulus, *ibid.*, 14, is not unlike Kallimachos, *epigr.* 42.

[78] *Vita Terenti*, end : hunc Afranius . . . Volcacius quoque . . . Cicero in Limone . . . item C. Caesar. Cf. Funaioli, pp. 82–4.

CHAPTER V

THE DEVELOPMENT OF PROSE

IF a serious student of our literature were provided with a damaged and imperfect copy of Chaucer, a Shakespere, Johnson's *Lives of the Poets* and his folio dictionary with its many quotations, and then bidden to compile an account of the chief writers down to the time of Burke, he might reasonably complain that his materials, while good as far as they went, were hopelessly inadequate. The historian of Latin literature before the age of Cicero is in little better case. He has Plautus and Terence, fairly numerous quotations from the other writers, and a charmingly written essay on the history of oratory, Cicero's *Brutus* (see p. 168). With these for guides, he must do what he can to tell the story of how Latin poetry and prose developed till they reached the classical style of what is traditionally called the Golden Age. With verse we have already dealt ; it remains to speak of prose.

In the natural course of things, verse comes first and prose later, for prose, as a literary medium, carefully written and having rules of its own, is apparently beyond the capacity of barbarous peoples, but some barbarians—our own Teutonic and Keltic ancestors for example—produce poems which are very far from contemptible and often show developed artistry. But a movement of foreign origin, such as the hellenizing literature of historical Rome, can and does introduce both media at once. In order therefore to tell the story of the coming of Ciceronian eloquence, we must once more go back to the first nameable Latin writer, APPIVS CLAVDIVS CAECVS (see p. 28). His speech on the war with Pyrrhos, though Cicero had apparently read it [1] and we have several accounts of its substance,[2] is completely lost, together with his legal writings, which had already perished

[1] Cicero, *de senect.*, 16, *Brut.*, 61. For the facts concerning Appius, see *O.R.F.*, p. 1 *sqq.*

[2] Ennius, in Cicero, *Brut.*, *loc. cit.*; Plutarch, *Pyrrh.*, 19; Appian, *Samnitica*, frag. 10, 2. Plutarch and Appian agree fairly well, and may therefore go back in some sense to the text of the actual speech.

when the authors wrote whose works are partly preserved in the *Digest* (p. 463).[3] That there were yet older orators who left no written monuments of their eloquence is the very reasonable supposition of Cicero, but it must remain a supposition. In general we may agree with his statement that oratory was early welcomed in Rome, at first the simple and untaught, later the learned kind.[4] But, learned or unlearned, we have but a scanty idea of its nature until we reach Cicero's own lifetime.

Of the funeral orations which Cicero mentions along with Appius' speech as the oldest surviving specimens of oratory, we can name three; one pronounced by QVINTVS FABIVS MAXIMVS VERRVCOSVS CVNCTATOR, who served with much distinction against Hannibal in the second Punic War and was five times consul between 521/233 and 545/209, over his son[5]; one, by MARCVS CLAVDIVS MARCELLVS the younger over his father, the conqueror of Syracuse, who was killed in a skirmish by Hannibal's men[6]; and a third, by QVINTVS CAECILIVS METELLVS son of Lucius, on the occasion of his father's funeral in 533/221.[7]

The great PVBLIVS CORNELIVS SCIPIO AFRICANVS MAIOR, the conqueror of Hannibal, was also a very tolerable speaker, according to Cicero.[8] He published nothing, but one famous saying of his has come down to us in two forms, one preserved by Gellius, the other in Livy. Being accused by the tribune Marcus Naevius of accepting bribes from the enemy to make peace on easy terms, he spoke briefly of his own services and then added, 'This is the anniversary of my victory over Hannibal. Let us leave this rascal to his own devices and go up to

[3] Pomponius in the *Dig.*, i, 2, 36: hunc (Appium Claudium) etiam actiones scripsisse traditum est, primum de usurpationibus, qui liber non exstat.

[4] Cic., *Brut.*, 53 *sqq.*; *Tusc.*, i, 5: oratorem celeriter complexi sumus, nec eum primo eruditum, aptum tamen ad dicendum, post autem eruditum. By *eruditus* he means trained in (Greek) rhetoric, with all that that training implied of literary culture.

[5] Cicero, *de senect.*, 12; Plut., *Fabius Maximus*, 1 and 24. The date of the son's death is unknown; it was apparently during the second Punic War and must have been after 541/213, when he was consul. So far as our authorities tell us, only this speech survived, possibly only this was written; but Fabius had some reputation in his own day as an orator, Cic., *Brut.*, 57.

[6] This speech survived long enough to be consulted by Coelius Antipater (cf. p. 117), to whom Livy, xxvii, 27, 13, seems to owe his knowledge of its contents. Possibly it had somehow perished in the meantime; at all events, no one else quotes it. Its date would be 546/208.

[7] *O.R.F.*, p. 10. No verbatim quotation survives; Pliny, *N.H.*, vii, 139–40, summarizes it. The dead man was that Metellus who, while *pontifex maximus*, lost his eyesight in saving the holy things from the burning temple of Vesta.

[8] *Brutus*, 77, ipsum Scipionem accepimus non infantem fuisse.

the Capitol to thank Iuppiter for all his goodness.'[9] His invalid son, the adopted father of Scipio Aemilianus, of whom we shall speak later, had some natural gift for eloquence and seems to have left a few rhetorical exercises, besides a historical work in Greek.[10]

Leaving these shadows of vanished reputations, we come to a solider figure. MARCVS PORCIVS CATO of Tusculum was one of the most noteworthy Romans of the third and second centuries B.C., and also one of the most original writers, so far as we can judge from the inadequate remains of his work. A member of a family previously undistinguished (*nouus homo*), he was born in 520/234; in 550/204 he held his first magistracy, the quaestorship, and continued in his political career till he attained the office of censor 570/184, when he distinguished himself for fearless and ruthless attacks on those whose way of life did not agree with his own somewhat old-fashioned and puritanical morality.[11] A born fighter and unimpeachably honest, he was perpetually at strife with some person or party; 'he never shrank from a quarrel on behalf of the commonwealth during all the eighty years or so which elapsed from his youth to his extreme old age' says Nepos.[12] But in his later years

[9] Cicero, *de off.*, iii, 4, says definitely that no work of his survived; yet *de orat.*, ii, 249, he cites as by Scipio a play on words, *quid hoc Naeuio ignauius* ('what a coward knave is this Naevius'; but the pun is so bad that Fleckeisen, followed by Wilkins, would read *Nauio*, in which case the saying need have nothing to do with this speech). It may be that some of his utterances were remembered, or recorded in a historical work (Cato's? *de off.*, iii, 1, quotes Cato for the assertion that Scipio declared he was 'never less alone than when alone', nunquam . . . minus solum quam cum solus esset). Gellius, iv, 3–4, who cites the speech, gives as his authority a written oration which was extant in his day, but of doubtful authenticity; Livy, xxxviii, 50, 7–11, puts into his mouth no defence at all, but only the invitation to leave the court and come with him to the Capitol. He may have used the same document as Gellius. The occasion was in 569/185, after the war with Antiochos of Syria.

[10] Cicero, *Brut.*, 77. See *O.R.F.*, p. 158, for more testimonies to the same effect. Nothing whatever is left of his writings.

[11] Cornelius Nepos wrote a life of Cato, which is unfortunately lost, but we have a short epitome of it, by Nepos himself, and Plutarch's life of him (usually cited as *Cato Maior*). Cicero's *de senectute*, in which Cato is the chief speaker, contains good information, although allowance must be made for rhetoric and idealization. There is in addition a character of him in Livy, xxxix, 40, and many mentions in other writers. His oratorical fragments are in *O.R.F.*, p. 11 *sqq.*, and all fragments of his lost works in H. Jordan, *M. Catonis praeter librum de re rustica quae extant*, Teubner, 1860, quoted as 'Jord'. His historical fragments are also in *H.R.F.*, p. 40 *sqq.*

[12] Nepos, *Cato*, 2, 4. This is, of course, exaggerated, since Cato's whole life lasted but eighty-five years; perhaps Nepos wrote *septuaginta*

he seems to have allowed himself some leisure, which he improved by getting a wider knowledge of Greek literature (although he never quite approved of Greeks and their ways) [13] and writing his historical work, besides revising his speeches for publication.[14] He died in 605/149,[15] active, it would seem, almost to his last day.

Since he was at once soldier, lawyer, historian, statesman and advocate, and always, when he had opportunity, a practical farmer as well, it is not to be supposed that any of his works showed very high polish; indeed, many must have been thrown off almost as fast as they could be written, with no opportunity for long meditation or extensive revision. It is quite possible to understand both the Roman enthusiasts who compared him to Lysias, for the remnants of his works have that force which comes from absolute sincerity and naturalness, and the doubts of Atticus and Plutarch about the comparison, for Cato wholly lacks grace and polish.[16] The fact is that, in style as in character, he was a typical intelligent peasant. He was shrewd, hard-working, frugal, honest, brave and sincere; but his stock of ideas was limited to a few practical maxims and rule-of-thumb techniques; he had the rustic's suspicion and fear of men of scientific knowledge [17]; and, lacking any real principles, as opposed to mere rules applicable to a narrow range of activities, he could neither give his materials any other form than that imposed by the subject itself nor behave with sympathy and humanity towards citizens or slaves, if their cases did not come

(LXX for LXXX). Pliny, *N.H.*, vii, 100, echoed by several other authors (see Jord., p. xcv), says he was accused forty-four times and always acquitted.

[13] Especially of their medicine: see the famous fragment, Jord., p. 77 (from Pliny, *N.H.*, xxix, 14), in which he informs his son that it is well to look into Greek literature, but not to be deep in it, because they are a race of rascals and quite incorrigible: et hoc puta uatem dixisse, quandoque ista gens suas litteras dedit, omnia corrumpet, tum etiam magis, si medicos suos huc mittet. iurarunt inter se barbaros necare omnis medicina, sed hoc ipsum mercede facient . . . nos quoque dictitant barbaros . . . interdixi tibi de medicis. For his late studies of Greek literature, see for instance Plut., *Cat. mai.*, 2. Hence the often repeated and nonsensical statement that he knew no Greek till late in life. No statesman of that time was without a knowledge of it, for it was the language of diplomacy everywhere but in Western Europe.

[14] Cicero, *de senect.*, 38. This specifies only causarum illustrium quascunque defendi . . . orationes; we do not know how and when the rest were published.

[15] Cicero, *Brut.*, 61.

[16] See Cicero, *Brut.*, 63; *ibid.*, 293; Plut., *Cat. maior*, 7.

[17] Cf. note 13.

under his limited stock of precedents and proverbs. Hence his waste of time, when censor, in restrictive measures against those who spent a little more than he thought proper on table-silver or clothing; hence also his heartless getting rid of worn-out slaves whose labours and meals he had himself shared while they were still able to work.[18] The paradoxical Greek maxim that slaves are human beings he probably regarded as outside the scope of a good Roman's interests. And to the same cause is due the utter formlessness of the one work of his which has come down complete to modern times. A speech imposes a certain order on the speaker; he must begin with an exordium of some kind, if only to let his audience know what he means to say, or, for Cato was very pious, to ask the blessing of heaven on his cause[19]; he must tell his story plainly and clearly, group his arguments, and try to end with a telling utterance. A history must have something like chronology; it is natural to mention the foundation of Rome first, the expulsion of the kings later. But as agriculture moves in the unending circle of the seasons and its activities at any one season are very varied, some literary skill and rhetorical training are necessary to compose a handbook for practical farmers which shall have a regular order and therefore be convenient for reference. Cato, who was an excellent farmer himself, wrote a sort of commonplace-book, having neither beginning, middle nor end, which has survived under the title, not always appropriate, of *de agri cultura*. It is full of interest, for it gives us an intimate view of the life of an old-fashioned landowner in that age and country. Further, it contains not a little welcome information on Roman cult and rustic folklore. It plainly was much valued and read by Cato's fellow-countrymen, for not only do the later writers on agriculture quote it, but it has come down to us with the language somewhat modernized, the result of frequent copying. Yet as literature, even as a piece of ordinary book-making, it is grotesque, the more so as the author hardly ever seems aware that his work lacks form and arrangement.[20]

This was apparently one of a series of technical works by Cato, of which the rest are lost. Pliny tells us that he mentions a monograph (*commentarius*) on medicine, containing an account of the methods by which he and his wife lived to a good old age and treated the

[18] Plutarch, *op. cit.*, 3 and 5; Plutarch strongly rebukes his inhumanity.

[19] Servius on Verg., *Aen.*, xi, 301, says: maiores nullam orationem nisi inuocatis numinibus incohabant, sicut sunt omnes orationes Catonis.

[20] The best edition is that of Keil, Teubner, 1884, along with Varro *de re rustica*.

ailments of their household; this seems to have survived to the encyclopaedist's own day.[21] Both he and his son wrote on law.[22] He was also the author of a treatise on tactics (*de re militari*), which extended to at least two books.[23] To give a complete list is not too easy, for he also wrote a kind of handbook of useful knowledge for his son, containing sections on medicine (apparently), agriculture and rhetoric. The last contained that oft-quoted and golden maxim, 'Get the matter and the words will come' (*rem tene, uerba sequentur*) and the equally famous definition of an orator as *uir bonus dicendi peritus*.[24] There may well have been sections on other matters likewise.

As an orator, Cato was prolific. Cicero knew of more than 150 speeches; Nepos says he began in his early youth to be a speaker, but if that is so, his earlier works have vanished utterly, perhaps were never written out or published in any form, for no fragment which we now have can be assigned to an earlier

[21] Pliny, *N.H.*, xxix, 15, after quoting Cato's diatribe against Greek medicine, cited in note 13, says: subicit enim qua medicina se et coniugem usque ad longam senectam perduxerit, iis ipsis scilicet quae nunc nos tractamus (the book from which this quotation comes is filled with traditional remedies), profiteturque esse commentarium sibi quo medeatur filio, seruis, familiaribus, quem nos per genera usus sui digerimus. The natural interpretation of this is that Pliny had a copy of this *commentarius* and takes some of his material from it. He does not, however, include Cato in the list of authorities for this book given in Bk. i.

[22] Cicero, *de orat.*, ii, 142, and iii, 135, mentions Cato's juristic works in language and also in a context which makes it unlikely that any but the elder Cato is meant. Festus, p. 144, 18, cites a passage from Cato in commentariis iuris ciuilis, which is also probably from the elder Cato. Gellius, xiii, 20 (19), 9, speaks of Cato's son, qui praetor designatus patre uiuo mortuus est et egregios de iuris disciplina libros reliquit. Paulus, in the *Digest*, xlv, 1, 4, 1, cites a passage from 'Cato libro quinto decimo', meaning probably the younger man; but many citations have simply the name Cato, in contexts which make it difficult or impossible to determine which is meant. The full name of the younger writer was MARCVS PORCIVS CATO LICINIANVS.

[23] It is several times mentioned and quoted by various writers; but Vegetius, *de re militari*, i, 15 (cf. p. 467), says definitely Cato in libris de disciplina militari, which indicates a work of some length, at least two books, and not a section in the compendium of knowledge addressed to his son.

[24] The general title seems to have been *ad Marcum filium*, meaning no doubt the man mentioned in note 22, not his half-brother, Marcus Porcius Cato Salonianus, the offspring of Cato's second marriage (Gellius, xiii, 20 (19), 8). It is generally quoted simply as *Cato ad filium*. See the fragments and testimonia, Jordan, p. 77 *sqq*. The genealogy of the family is given by Gellius in the chapter already quoted. Cato's elder son, Licinianus, had a son, also called Marcus, who was an orator of some repute and ability, became consul in 636/118, and during his term of office died in Africa. He is generally known simply as MARCVS CATO MARCI FILIVS MARCI NEPOS. His son died in Gaul after having held the

date than the year when he was consul, 559/195.[25]. Jordan reckons at eighty in all the orations which can be named and to which any fragments can be assigned; the number is not certain, for we have to allow for the possibility of one speech being quoted by more than one title: But at best, we have lost the very names of about half his performances, which is to be regretted, for not only would they be of interest to the philologist and the historian, but it is evident from what little is left that they contained many shrewd and witty sayings and much sarcastic criticism of his contemporaries. There is a delightful passage, for example, preserved by Fronto,[26] in which Cato explains how, having occasion to use the notes of a speech in which he had dealt with his own and his ancestors' public services, he thought it advisable to delete all mention of his having behaved honestly towards citizens and allies, lest reminders of conduct so unusual and so unlike their own should offend his audience. It is also from Cato that we have the pretty tale of how a senator's son who, according to the ancient custom, had been present when his father attended a meeting of the Senate, met his mother's curious inquiries as to what had happened by gravely assuring her that the subject of discussion was whether it would be better to allow every man two wives, or every wife two husbands.[27]

In his old age Cato set about writing a considerable historical work, the *Origines*, in seven books.[28] The title, as was so often the case in antiquity, did not describe the contents fully. The first three books dealt with Rome under the kings (and therefore also with the foundation of the city by Romulus) and the beginnings of the other Italian cities; [29] the other four brought down the history of Rome to the writer's own day. The style

offices of curule aedile and praetor. Salonianus had two sons, Lucius and Marcus, whereof the latter became the father of that Cato who by his suicide at Utica became the hero of all sentimental Stoics and republicans, and is commonly called either Cato the Younger (*minor*) or Cato of Utica (*Vticensis*).

[25] Nepos, *Cato*, 3, 3, ab adulescentia confecit orationes; Jord., p. lxiii. Cicero, *Brut.*, 65, orationes amplius centum quinquaginta, quas quidem adhuc inuenerim et legerim.

[26] Fronto, *ad Anton.*, i, 2, 9 (vol. ii, p. 44 of the Loeb ed.); Jord., p. 37.

[27] Gellius, i, 23.

[28] Nepos, *Cato*, 3, 3, confirmed by other authorities, see Jord., p. xix *sqq.* This is, of course, not the little text-book which he wrote in large letters for his young son, Plut., *Cat. mai.*, 20, though Plutarch seems to imagine it was.

[29] This is clear from the fragments.

was, as might have been expected, somewhat uncouth and rugged, but not without vividness, in the more lively descriptive parts at least. After the Greek fashion, speeches were inserted here and there; one of them was an actual oration of his own.[30]

There remain a few lesser works to be mentioned. One was the *carmen de moribus*, whereof we have a few remains cited by Gellius in a prose paraphrase by some unknown hand.[31] They include what seems to be the ancestor of our own saying that it is better to wear out than rust out.[32] Of a similar nature was probably the collection of good sayings which Cato put together; but much more famous than this, also very much better known to us, was a collection made by some unknown person of Cato's own dicta. It is tolerably evident that Plutarch,[33] or his authority, made use of this, and the numerous samples of the old man's wit which we find in various writers may in large measure come from the same source, though some of them may be from his published works. Some of his letters were also preserved in later times; the only one of whose contents we know anything was to his son, defining the status of a discharged soldier.[34]

TIBERIVS SEMPRONIVS GRACCHVS, father of the two famous tribunes, was an orator of some merit, and had sufficient command of Greek to address the people of Rhodes in their own language on one occasion.[35] A speech of his on behalf of Scipio Africanus survived at least long enough for Livy to be acquainted with its contents.[36] Gracchus was born about 534/220, was consul in 577/177 and 591/163, and held the

[30] In Bk. vii, see Jord., p. 27.

[31] Gellius, xi, 2; Jord., pp. 82–3.

[32] Frag. 3 Jord.; nam uita humana prope uti ferrum est. si exerceas, conteritur; si non exerceas, tamen robigo interficit. item homines exercendo uidemus conteri, si nihil exerceas, inertia atque torpedo plus detrimenti facit quam exercitio.

[33] Cicero, *de orat.*, ii, 271, for Cato's collection; for his own sayings, see especially Plut., *op. cit.*, 8–9.

[34] Preserved by Cicero, *de off.*, i, 37, Plutarch, *quaest. Rom.*, 39 (273, e–f). Cato held that, unless he got permission of the commanding officer, *i.e.*, renewed his military oath (*sacramentum*), he might not do any act of war against an enemy. See the remarks of Warde Fowler, cited in Rose, *Rom. Quest. of Plutarch*, p. 186 *sqq*.

[35] For his fragments and the facts concerning him, see *O.R.F.*, p. 151 *sqq*. The Rhodian oration is known from Cicero, *Brut.*, 79, and the occasion of it was probably an embassy to Asia Minor in 590/164, of which Gracchus was a member, since he and his colleagues spent some time in Rhodes (Polybios, xxvii, 3, 2, Büttner-Wobst). It seems to have been extant in Cicero's day.

[36] Livy, xxxviii, 56, 5 *sqq*., has seen the speech, but is neither satisfied that it is genuine nor at all sure on what occasion it was delivered.

censorship in 585/169. No verbatim quotations of his speeches are known. About contemporary with him was LVCIVS PAPIRIVS of Fregellae, who is known to have delivered a speech in the senate on behalf of his native place and the Latin colonies, but the work is totally lost and even the occasion of it uncertain.[37] The famous general and statesman LVCIVS AEMILIVS PAVLLVS, surnamed Macedonicus for his victory over Perseus in the third Macedonian War, left at least one speech, an account of his services in the campaign, delivered shortly after his triumph in 587/167. We have the substance of its most famous passage; commenting on the recent death of two of his sons, he declared that he had prayed that any impending misfortune might fall on himself and not on the state, and therefore accepted his bereavement as an answer to his petition.[38] Another prominent man of those times, QVINTVS CAECILIVS METELLVS MACEDONICVS, son of that Metellus whose oratory has already been mentioned (p. 90), defended Lucius Aurelius Cotta against the younger Africanus, who in 623/131 accused him of extortion, opposed Tiberius Gracchus in 621/133, and in 623/131, being then censor along with Quintus Pompeius, delivered a very famous discourse on the duty of increasing the population by raising the birth-rate (*de prole augenda*), which much later won the approval of Augustus, then at grips with the same problem in an acuter form, and so survived long enough for some fragments of it to have come down to us.[39] Another opponent of the elder Gracchus, TITVS ANNIVS LVSCVS, had the reputation of being personally a rascal, but a clever debater, and by chance one taunt of his against Gracchus has survived.[40] A speaker of considerable ability, the first Latin, according to Cicero, to give oratory its proper ornaments of digression, appeals to the emotions of the audience, and skilful use of commonplaces, was SERVIVS SVLPICIVS GALBA, consul 610/144, three of whose speeches survived at least to the Augustan age, probably later. Two of them were in his own defence when impeached for an act of foul treachery, as his enemies represented it, or drastic precaution against treachery, according to his own account, which had resulted in the killing of a number of the

[37] See *O.R.F.*, p. 154 *sq.*; Cicero, *Brut.*, 170.

[38] Valerius Maximus, v, 10, 2, gives what purports to be a verbatim quotation of this passage; Livy, xlv, 40, 8, embodies an eloquent paraphrase of it in the speech which he puts into Paullus' mouth. See *O.R.F.*, p. 155 *sqq*.

[39] *O.R.F.*, p. 159 *sqq.*; the fragments are in Gellius, i, 6, 2 and 8, who says the author was Metellus Numidicus (see p. 103), a blunder which can be corrected by the attribution of the speech to Metellus Macedonicus in other authors. It is interesting to notice that Metellus uses a Greek commonplace: quoniam ita natura tradidit ut nec cum illis (*sc.*, mulieribus) satis commode nec sine illis ullo modo uiui possit. Cf. Aristophanes, *Lysistrata*, 1039, *οὔτε σὺν πανωλέθροισιν οὔτ' ἄνευ πανωλέθρων* ('Neither with the women—blast 'em—nor without them can we live'), see the commentators *ad loc.*

[40] *O.R.F.*, p. 162 *sqq.* The fragment is in Festus, p. 416, 20 Lindsay.

natives of Spain.[41] The third was on behalf of a company of tax-farmers (*publicani*) who were allegedly implicated in a murder.[42]

Two much better-known figures than these are the younger Africanus (PVBLIVS CORNELIVS SCIPIO AEMILIANVS AFRICANVS MINOR) and his friend GAIVS LAELIVS SAPIENS. They were the centre of what we commonly know as the Scipionic circle, the most important element in Roman society of that day, so far as literature and thought are concerned. We have already spoken of their relations to Terence and Lucilius (pp. 73, 82); a few words are necessary concerning themselves. Scipio, or, to give him his original name, Publius Aemilius, was the son of a not uncultured man, whose services against the Greek-speaking Macedonians resulted in his son's improved knowledge of Greek literature. Of the spoils of the war, which he brought to a successful conclusion in the autumn of 586/168, the general claimed for his sons one important item, the library of the defeated king Perseus,[43] which we may suppose to have been well furnished, since the Macedonian dynasty had cultivated Greek literature and learning even to the point of ostentation ever since the days of Archelaos, the patron of Euripides.[44] His sons had therefore what must have still been somewhat uncommon in the Rome of those days, a really good selection of the best classical literature. Nor was this all. The young Publius, who by adoption passed into another family of culture, that of the Cornelii Scipiones, sought the companionship of living Greek scholars and thinkers. Panaitios the Stoic philosopher and Polybios the historian [45] were his inseparable companions; he must have spoken Greek with something like perfection, and his favourite book was Xenophon's curious moral romance, the

[41] See *O.R.F.*, p. 164 *sqq.* The reference to Cicero is *Brut.*, 82. He goes on to say that Galba's speeches had nevertheless a more antiquated flavour than those of Scipio and Laelius or even Cato. The three speeches are mentioned in the epitome of Livy's forty-ninth book, which also describes the affair in Spain. The victims of Galba's, or their own, treachery were Lusitanians, *i.e.*, inhabitants of what is now Portugal, Estremadura and Toledo.

[42] See Cicero, *Brut.*, 85–8, who says he had the story from a younger contemporary of Galba, P. Rutilius Rufus. Galba took over the case from Laelius at a day's notice and handled it admirably, securing the acquittal of the accused.

[43] Plutarch, *Aem. Paullus*, 28.

[44] See Rose, *H.G.L.*, p. 195.

[45] See *ibid.*, pp. 361, 371; Polyb., xxxi, 23 *sqq.* (Büttner-Wobst; in other eds., xxxii, 9 *sqq.*); Cicero, *Tusc.*, i, 81, and many other passages; more refs. in Schanz-Hosius, i, p. 214.

Education of Cyrus (*Cyropaedia*),[46] that long-winded and dull account of the means by which a leading position in the state may be gained and kept. Scipio had no ambition to make himself king of Rome; but consciously or not he was tending towards principles which logically resulted in the overthrow of the republican constitution and the creation of a monarchy. For the present, so far as we can judge, the ideal was that the worthiest man of the time should be *princeps*—not the holder of any extraordinary office, but the one whose authority, willingly recognized by his fellow-citizens, should beneficently guide the councils of the rest in peace and war. Hence his interest in the philosopher and the philosophic historian; for while Plato's dream of the philosopher-king[47] remained unrealized, then as now, ever since Plato it had been unthinkable that the good ruler of a good state should not have some tincture of philosophy, and treatises on kingship, discussions of the best form of constitution, and essays on the theory of jurisprudence were among the commonest products of philosophical activity.

Around Scipio there gathered a little group of men including some of the most intelligent then living in Italy. The nearest to him was Laelius; of the rest of the *grex* (' troupe ') as Cicero calls it[48] we can make a fairly complete list by noting the names of the speakers in his *de re publica*. They are, Quintus Aelius Tubero, son of Scipio's sister Aemilia; Lucius Furius Philus; Publius Sulpicius Rufus; Spurius Mummius, brother of the conqueror of Greece; Gaius Fannius, the husband of Laelius' daughter; Quintus Mucius Scaevola, of whom more will be said later; and Manius Manilius, the jurist. Doubtless there were other members less known, for Scipio had a genius for friendship[49] and could make the humblest feel at his ease. All seem to have had in common earnestness, interest in cultural studies, and sympathy with what seemed to them best and most ennobling in the Greek tradition; and all or most of them were writers.

Concerning Scipio himself we have to trust almost entirely to the opinions of ancient authors, for we have preserved very little of his eloquence, and there is no sign of his having composed anything except speeches for various important occasions in his active career (he was born about 569/185, served in various capacities, military and civil, always with credit, between 603/151

[46] Rose, *op. cit.*, p. 307 *sq.*

[47] Plato, *Rep.*, 499 b, 540 d.

[48] *De amic.*, 69, in nostro, ut ita dicam, grege (Laelius is supposed to be speaking of Scipio).

[49] See the passage quoted in the last note.

and 622/132, and died, probably by violence, in 625/129). Of these we have ten titles and a few quotations. One goes to show that he owed none of his great popularity to flattering the city mob, for when a remark of his displeased the audience he replied to their hoots with, 'Be quiet, you stepsons of Italy!' and added, 'You shall not make me fear you unbound whom I brought hither in bonds.'[50] If he was capable of reminding newly-made citizens that they were freed slaves, he was no more ready to pass over the defects of his own order, since another fragment is a most bitter indictment of the corrupting influences to which children of good families were subjected.[51]

Laelius was generally reckoned the more eloquent of the two friends,[52] but to us he is represented by six titles and next to no fragments. His most celebrated utterance seems to have been a funeral oration over Scipio, whom he long survived. We get a far more vivid idea of him from the sympathetic portrait (how true to life, we have no means of discovering) drawn by Cicero in the *de amicitia*.

Once more we find a number of names which are hardly more than that to us. Cicero tells us that MARCVS AEMILIVS LEPIDVS PORCINA was the first Latin orator to handle the period well; he was consul in 617/137 and a few mentions of his speeches survive.[53] LVCIVS SCRIBONIVS LIBO, tribune of the plebs in 605/149, was, still according to Cicero, 'a very fair speaker, as may be seen from his orations,'[54] but not a word of these has come down to us. We have seen that SPVRIVS MVMMIVS was a member of the Scipionic circle; both he and his brother, LVCIVS MVMMIVS ACHAICVS, were second-rate orators; Spurius also wrote epistles in verse, as we know from a casual mention of them in Cicero.[55] SPVRIVS POSTVMIVS ALBINVS, as was natural in a man who rose to be consul (606/148), was able to express himself, and composed a considerable number of speeches, whereof nothing is left to us.[56] Of LVCIVS AVRELIVS ORESTES and his brother GAIVS, whereof the former was consul in 628/136 and the latter praetor four years earlier, we barely know that speeches of theirs

[50] Val. Max., vi, 2, 3; see *O.R.F.*, p. 190.

[51] Macrobius, *Sat.*, iii, 14, 7.

[52] Cicero, *Brut.*, 83; he does not agree. The funeral oration was written for Q. Tubero, Scipio's nephew, Cic., *de orat.*, ii, 341; see *O.R.F.*, p. 174 *sq.*, which cites the evidence (*schol. Bob.* on Cic., *pro Mil.*, p. 283 Orelli) that Laelius wrote a second speech for this occasion, delivered by Quintus Fabius Maximus.

[53] Cic., *Brut.*, 95–6; *O.R.F.*, p. 193 *sqq.*

[54] Cic., *op. cit.*, 90; *O.R.F.*, p. 196.

[55] Cic., *op. cit.*, 94; *ad Att.*, xiii, 6a (= 6, 4); *O.R.F.*, p. 196 *sq.*

[56] Pliny, however, preserves a good story at Albinus' expense. When aedile, in 597/157, he was moved, whether by malice or superstition, to accuse a prosperous farmer, one Gaius Furius Cresimus, a freedman, of

existed in Cicero's day.[57] About contemporary were QVINTVS POMPEIVS, consul 613/141 and afterwards censor, 'a not despicable orator', says Cicero, and, if we may accept a plausible conjecture in Cicero's text, another member of the same family, SEXTVS, who produced speeches somewhat old-fashioned in style, but full of good sense.[58] An opponent of Gaius Gracchus, GAIVS FANNIVS, who was consul the year that Gracchus was first tribune (632/122), seems to have delivered a speech against him, but whether he composed it or its real author was the scholarly GAIVS PERSIVS was doubted among Roman critics.[59] A hero of the second Punic War, MARCVS SERGIVS SILVS, delivered an oration in 557/197 which at least had an interesting subject, for it was a reply to his colleagues (he was then praetor) who were objecting to his taking part in the sacred rites which a Roman magistrate must needs perform, on the ground that his services in the wars had left him mutilated.[60] GAIVS TITIVS, whose date and public career are not very exactly known, save that he was contemporary with Lucilius and Crassus and Antonius the orators, had a bitter tongue, to judge from the unsparing description of the idleness and intemperance of Roman exquisites which is the only specimen of his work we have left.[61] A somewhat similar attack on the *gourmets* of his time is the one relic which preserves from oblivion the name of the otherwise unknown FAVONIVS.[62] A friend and colleague of Tiberius Gracchus, GAIVS PAPIRIVS CARBO, who ended a stormy career by suicide in 635/119, was, like Gracchus, a student of the eloquence of Aemilius Lepidus Porcina, already mentioned, and some few of his political speeches survived to later times, but are totally lost to us.[63]

Much more conspicuous figures, though here again we have

having attracted his neighbours' crops to his own land by sorcery. The defendant brought into court his efficient farm implements and well-fed labourers and oxen, pointed to them as being the charms he had used, and was unanimously acquitted. See Pliny, *N.H.*, xviii, 41–3; Cicero, *Brut.*, 94; *O.R.F.*, p. 197.

[57] Cicero, *ibid.*; *O.R.F.*, p. 198.

[58] Cicero, *Brut.*, 96 (non contemptus orator); *ibid.*, 97, after discussing several others, he continues, according to the MSS., sed Pompei sunt scripta nec nimis extenuata, quamquam ueterum est similis, et plena prudentiae, which is an awkward resumption of a subject he seemed to have finished. Madvig is therefore in all probability right in changing one letter and reading *Sex.* for *sed.* See *O.R.F.*, p. 198.

[59] Cic., *Brut.*, 99–100. For this Persius, cf. chap. iv, note 62.

[60] See Pliny, *N.H.*, vii, 104–6; *O.R.F.*, p. 202. Technically, Sergius' opponents were right, for both the victim and the priest should be physically perfect for an acceptable sacrifice.

[61] See *O.R.F.*, p. 203 *sqq.*; Macrobius, *sat.*, iii, 16, 15–16.

[62] In Gellius, xv, 8. *O.R.F.*, p. 207, gives the name as Favorinus, from the older editions of Gellius, but rightly points out that this is quite impossible.

[63] *O.R.F.*, p. 211 *sqq.*; the chief passage concerning him is Cic., *Brut.*, 103 *sqq.*

little left of their works, are the GRACCHI themselves. Of these, TIBERIVS, the elder, seems to have had the purer style and the greater power of exciting pity; GAIVS was a much more vigorous orator, ornate as ornateness went in those still early days, and extremely effective, before a popular audience at least.[64] Since he was one of the chief models of young speakers before the time of Cicero, and still continued to be read long after his date, it is the more to be regretted that we have nothing of his but a couple of stories, briefly and vigorously told, of the cruelty of Roman magistrates towards Italian allies,[65] together with a few scraps of other speeches, quite as often cited because they contain some obsolete word or idiom as for any merit they have as rhetoric. A prominent contemporary of the two reformers, MARCVS AEMILIVS SCAVRVS, born 591/163, consul 639/115 and 647/107, was less of an orator than they were, but had at least matter, if not style, to commend his utterances.[66] A determined opponent of his in politics, PVBLIVS RVTILIVS RVFVS, was not superior to him in eloquence, but apparently a good lawyer and fond of introducing Stoic moralities into his speeches.[67]

The age was fertile in speakers of tolerable abilities, such as MARCVS IVNIVS BRVTVS, who had apparently no political ambitions but, in the general opinion of later times at least, disgraced his respectable family by specializing in accusations, whereas the right-thinking orator sought all possible opportunities to extend his influence by defending some illustrious or at least notorious person, whose gratitude might be of use to him in his career.[68] Galba, mentioned already (p. 97), had a son, GAIVS SVLPICIVS GALBA SERVI FILIVS, whose career came to an abrupt end in 644/110, when he fell a victim, justly or otherwise, to the general indignation aroused by the gross mismanagement of the war against Jugurtha. His defence on this occasion had a peroration still admired and studied in Cicero's boyhood.[69] That turbulent politician, GAIVS FLAVIVS FIMBRIA, consul 650/104, was a vigorous speaker.[70] Lucilius' butt (cf. p. 84), TITVS ALBVCIVS, perhaps tried his hand at satire, but also, until he was condemned for extortion while

[64] *O.R.F.*, pp. 215 *sqq.*, 224 *sqq.* The chief discussions of their styles are Cic., *Brut.*, 104, 126; Plutarch, *Ti. Gracch.*, 2, the latter probably from some good Latin source.

[65] Preserved by Gellius, x, 3, 3, 5, 17.

[66] Cicero, *Brut.*, 110 *sqq.*; *O.R.F.*, p. 253 *sqq.* He also wrote an autobiography, for the fragments of which see *H.R.F.*, pp. 118–20.

[67] Cicero, *Brut.*, 113–14; *O.R.F.*, p. 263 *sqq.* Rufus was born about 600/154, and was still alive in 676/78, living quietly in Smyrna, Cic., *Brut.*, 85, cf. n. 42 above.

[68] Cicero, *Brut.*, 130; *O.R.F.*, p. 261 *sqq.*

[69] *O.R.F.*, p. 262; Cicero, *Brut.*, 127.

[70] *O.R.F.*, p. 268 *sq.*; Cicero, *Brut.*, 129.

governor of Sardinia, appeared occasionally as an orator of no great merit.[71] CATVLVS has already been mentioned (p. 88) as a minor poet; he was also no bad speaker, and gained some reputation for the purity of his style and the euphonious collocation of his words. Furthermore, he was something of a historian, having to his credit an account of the stirring events of his consulship.[72] QVINTVS CAECILIVS METELLVS NVMIDICVS, who won his surname honourably from services in Numidia against Jugurtha during his consulship (652/102), had some repute as a correct and dignified orator.[73] GAIVS MEMMIVS and his brother LVCIVS are said by Cicero to have been indifferent speakers but keen and bitter prosecutors. The former, who was murdered in 654/100 while a candidate for the consulship, left some orations which were occasionally studied in later times, but nothing which has reached us save one insignificant quotation.[74]

The general impression gathered from our very scanty records of the lost orators of the second century is that most of them were about as good as the average public man of to-day, able to set forth a case or a policy in orderly fashion, with a reasonable amount of attention to style; but that on the whole the loss of their works is to be deplored rather by the historian, to whom they would be most valuable documents, than by the student of literature. We now come to a group of speakers whose literary merits, to judge by the high opinion which Cicero had of them, must have been considerable. In other words, we pass from the type of speaker who is used to making an audience listen to him with some attention and does not become confused because the occasion is important or the crowd inclined to be unruly, to the artist who is striving for the maximum of immediate effect combined with the greatest possible lasting beauty. Many of the earlier speakers seldom or never troubled to make permanent records of what they had said; those whom we have now to discuss did so far more usually. Two outstanding features

[71] *O.R.F.*, p. 269 *sq.*; Cicero, *Brut.*, 131; Varro, *de re rust.*, iii, 2, 17, but the mention of Albucius is not certain; the MSS. have L. ABVCCIVS, homo, ut scitis, adprime doctus, cuius Luciliano charactere sunt libelli. That L. is a slip, of Varro himself or a copyist, for T. and Abuccius a miswriting of Albucius are no more than tolerably likely conjectures, and the name Abuccius appears again in the same book, 6, 6.

[72] *O.R.F.*, p. 270 *sqq.*; the chief passage relating to his works and style is Cicero, *Brut.*, 132–3. The fragments of his *liber de consulatu et de rebus gestis suis*, as Cicero calls it, are in Peter, *H.R.F.*, pp. 124–5; they all come from Plutarch's life of Marius, 25–7.

[73] *O.R.F.*, p. 272 *sqq.*; Cicero, *Brut.*, 135.

[74] *O.R.F.*, p. 277 *sqq.*; Cicero, *Brut.*, 136; but Sallust, *Iugurtha*, 30, 4, says (C.) Memmi facundia clara pollensque fuit. This, however, is probably no more than an advertisement of the speech, nominally by Memmius, really Sallust's own, which follows in the next chapter.

characterize the period which leads up to Cicero. Rhetoric was almost universally studied, and its precepts supplemented practical experience, ultimately displacing it to a great extent. Owing partly to this and partly to the growth of a reading public before whom a written speech could be laid as a sort of political pamphlet, the writing out and publishing of a speech delivered on some important occasion became quite common, and with this went naturally the careful revision of what had been said. The actual delivery, however, was and continued to be made without the help of a manuscript to read from; the speaker, if he had written out what he wished to say, committed his work more or less exactly to memory and recited it to his audience, with such deviations from the original text as might be necessary or desirable in view of interruptions, the inspiration of the moment or any of the numerous happenings which, then as now, combine to make a speech a different thing from an essay.

There were, naturally, all manner of compromises between the toilsome business of learning a long speech word for word and the risky attempt to speak *ex tempore*. Cicero was acquainted with a speech of Crassus (see below) in which several sections were not fully developed, showing that the orator had said more than he wrote, and with another which was 'not a speech but a sort of outline or memorandum for a speaker, somewhat fuller than usual'.[75] He also tells the story of a third-rate advocate who had all his emotional appeals written out beforehand, with disastrous results, for when bidding the jury 'turn their eyes upon his client's grey hairs' he happened to look that way himself, just in time to see the subject of all his eloquence sneaking out of court.[76] Quintilian, who cites this story as a terrible warning against trusting too much to paper-work, adds some very choice specimens of the same sort of thing.[77] Occasionally we hear, as so often at Athens, of a professional speech-writer; a celebrated one was LVCIVS AELIVS PRAECONINVS STILO, a native of Lanuvium, of equestrian rank, whose two *cognomina* were derived from his father's occupation as a crier (*praeco*) and his own readiness with the pen (*stilus*). This man died about 664/90, living long enough to number Cicero and Varro among his pupils, for he was (besides his antiquarian knowledge, of which more will be said on p. 442), a teacher of literature and rhetoric. He never appeared in person as an orator.[78]

[75] Cicero, *Brut.*, 164; contrast 328, where he notes, as if it were something rather unusual, that one of Hortensius' speeches in the written copy agreed exactly with what he had really said.

[76] Cicero, *pro Cluentio*, 58.

[77] Quintilian, *instit.*, vi, 1, 41 *sqq*.

[78] Cicero, *Brut.*, 205–7; Suetonius, *de gramm.*, 23; *O.R.F.*, p. 336 *sq*. For Athenian speech-writers, see Rose, *H.G.L.*, pp. 280, 283, 285, 286, 287 *sqq*., 295.

Of some of the chief orators of the generation before his own, Cicero has given us a brilliant sketch in his most important work on rhetoric, the *De Oratore*, besides frequent mentions of them elsewhere. A reputation which hardly outlasted his own life-time and the memories of those who had heard him was the portion of MARCVS ANTONIVS, father of Cicero's worthless colleague in the consulship and grandfather, through another son, of that famous bearer of the same name whom we commonly Anglicize as Mark Antony. For Antonius, although one of the best speakers of his age,[79] and particularly happy in his delivery and in the air of unstudied, almost casual arrangement of his words which hid considerable, though unacknowledged, theoretical training and very thorough preparation to assist his native quickness of wit, would never publish anything, nor, if he could help it, let himself be regarded as any but a 'plain blunt man'[80] The occasions of nine of his speeches are known. One was a defence of himself, when, in 640/114, three of the Vestal Virgins were condemned for unchastity and Antonius was accused of being the lover of one of them.[81] In another, the defence of a probably guilty man, Manius Aquillius, consul in 653/101, on a charge of

[79] Cicero, *Tusc.*, v, 55; *Brut.*, 139 *sqq.*; *O.R.F.*, p. 280 *sqq.*; Wilkins, pp. 13–17 of his edition of the *de oratore* (Oxford 1892).

[80] The Shakesperean tag (*Julius Caesar*, iii, 2, 222) is not used at random; I think it highly likely that Shakespere confused the grandfather and grandson. He would know of Antonius' attitude, for he was a tolerable Latinist, to say nothing of his friendship with the very erudite Ben Jonson, from such passages as Cicero, *de orat.*, ii, 55 *sqq.*, in which Antonius, humorously and probably with substantial truth, is made almost in the same breath to declare that his knowledge of all things Greek is scanty and to show considerable acquaintance with Greek literature and rhetoric. Cicero would know that such a pose was a likely one to assume before a Roman court; we shall see later (p. 164) that he did it, on occasion, himself, and much later than his day, we find Tiberius trying to exclude from Roman parlance on official occasions even the most necessary Greek words, Suetonius, *Tib.*, 71. For his writing nothing, cf. Cicero, *orator*, 132; that some knowledge of his speeches, possibly from notes taken down during their delivery, survived is fairly plain from Diomedes, p. 472, 4–7, who says, confessedly at second hand it is true, that he was apt to end his sentences with such unbecoming rhythms as – ⏑ ⏑ – – – : ⏑ ⏑ ⏑ ⏑ ⏑ : – ⏑ ⏑ ⏑ ⏑ – : and other combinations which he stigmatizes as *delumbis, fluxa, mollis*. This agrees not too ill with Cicero's remark, *Brut.*, 140, that Antonius' *sententiae* were better than his choice and combination of words. One short and unfinished work of his got abroad, an essay on oratory (*de ratione dicendi*), apparently never intended for publication. See Cicero, *de orat.*, i, 94; *orator*, 18; *Brut.*, 163; Quintilian, iii, 1, 19 and 6, 45.

[81] Authorities in *O.R.F.*, p. 282.

extortion when governor of Sicily, he saved his client by a variant of the gesture by which Hypereides exposed the beauty of Phryne to an Athenian jury. Laying hold of Aquillius, he tore away the clothing from his chest, showing scars honourably got in battle, and so aroused the sympathy of the court as to secure an acquittal.[82] Antonius was born in 611/143, and fell a victim to the proscription under Marius in 667/87.

With Antonius Cicero couples Lvcivs Licinivs Crassvs, a man some three years younger, who also died earlier, in 663/91. Like Antonius, he was an active politician and held every important magistracy, including the post of censor (in the year before his death; Antonius had been one of the censors next preceding, in 657/97). Against Antonius' vehemence and air of rough-and-ready fluency, he had an artistic and pure style, 'most impressive', says Cicero,[83] 'combining with its impressiveness a refined humour, suitable to an orator, not a buffoon, and a careful and choice, but unpedantic, correctness of language'. His delivery was quiet, his gestures few, his wits quick, never deserting him when an argument with his opponent broke out. His preference was for short, well-balanced sentences rather than long and sonorous periods, and while Antonius was perhaps even more effective before a jury, Crassus could hold the attention of a political meeting most admirably. Cicero wishes he had committed more of his work to writing; we may well wish that something of what he did write had survived to us, and we were not reduced to second-hand appreciation of an orator who seems to have been of no common abilities. We have, unfortunately, no more than a few short scraps of his eloquence, quite insufficient for any independent judgement.[84] Among the speeches which he delivered (we know of some fourteen) one raised a very curious point of law, a matter with which Crassus was well qualified to deal, for he was a competent jurist. A certain man, named apparently Coponius, had left a will naming as his heir the son

[82] Cicero, *in Verrem*, ii, 5, 3. The defendant's name is a little doubtful, the spelling varying between Aquilius and Aquillius. For the incident of Hypereides and Phryne, see Rose, *H.G.L.*, p. 294.

[83] Cicero, *Brut.*, 143. See, for this and many other accounts of Crassus' eloquence, *O.R.F.*, p. 291 *sqq*.

[84] One is of some interest, as showing his care for rhythm and order of words. It is cited by Cicero, *de orat.*, i, 225, from some unknown speech: eripite nos ex miseriis (⏑ ⏑ ⏑ – – ⏑ ⏑ ⏑ ⏓), eripite ex faucibus (– ⏑ ⏑ – – ⏑ –) eorum quorum crudelitas (– – – – ⏑ –) nostro sanguine non potest expleri (– ⏑ – – – –); nolite sinere nos cuiquam seruire (– – – – ⏑) nisi uobis uniuersis, quibus et possumus et debemus. (I am inclined to emend debemus et possumus, – ⏑ – – ⏑ –, a good and effective final cadence). Cf. p. 163, for prose rhythm in general.

whom at the time he expected his wife to bring into the world, but if that son should die before his majority, the estate was to go to one Manius Curius. The testator died and his widow never bore a child at all. Curius therefore claimed the estate and was opposed by Marcus Coponius, presumably the dead man's next of kin. Crassus appeared for Curius.[85]

His opponent on this occasion was a contemporary whom Cicero twice calls the most eloquent of lawyers, as Crassus was the best lawyer among the eloquent,[86] QVINTVS MVCIVS SCAEVOLA, generally surnamed Pontifex Maximus, to distinguish him from his elder kinsman and namesake the Augur, Crassus' father-in-law and the son-in-law of Laelius. What his style was like we may gather from Cicero, who speaks of him [87] as conducting a case 'after his usual fashion, with no elaboration, plainly and perspicuously'. He was of about the same age as Crassus, was his colleague in the consulship (659/95) and survived him by nine years, being murdered in 672/82, by Marius' orders. But his chief fame in after times rested on what he wrote, not on any of his orations; for he was the first codifier of Roman law, unless we reckon the shadowy authors of the Twelve Tables (p. 30). In eighteen books he set forth the whole of the *ius ciuile, i.e.*, the common law of Rome, as opposed to the *ius sacrum*, or canon law, to give the phrase its nearest modern equivalent. It would appear that he also wrote a short treatise in one book, called *Ὅροι*, or *Definitions*, presumably a sort of law-lexicon; it is remarkable, as showing the influence of Stoic legal theory on practical Roman jurisprudence, that the title was in Greek and consisted of a technical term of philosophy. A few scraps of his work are quoted in the *Digest*—whether any of them come from the *Ὅροι* is uncertain—and he had successors and disciples; but in the next generation he and they were overshadowed by the fame of Servius Sulpicius, of whom more will be said in discussing the Ciceronian circle.[88]

[85] Cicero, *Brut.*, 194 *sqq.*; more references to this celebrated case are collected in *O.R.F.*, p. 303 *sqq.*

[86] Cicero, *Brut.*, 145, ut eloquentium iuris peritissimus Crassus, iuris peritorum eloquentissimus Scaeuola putaretur. In *de orat.*, i, 180, Cicero puts into Crassus' mouth the variant that Scaevola was iuris peritorum eloquentissimus, eloquentium iuris peritissimus, and makes him prefix it with ut ego soleo dicere; Crassus may therefore really be the author of the epigram.

[87] Cicero, *de orat.*, 229. For the little that is left of Scaevola's speeches, see *O.R.F.*, pp. 317–20.

[88] Cicero says more than once (*e.g.*, *Brut.*, 145) that he was a very able lawyer; the account of his works in the text is founded upon Pomponius

Crassus had likewise a younger adherent, PVBLIVS SVLPICIVS RVFVS, born in 630/124 and killed by Sulla's party in 666/88, being then a tribune of the plebs. He was an eloquent speaker, and as such is one of the characters in the *de oratore*, but left nothing in writing.[89] Another character, and an amiable one, is GAIVS AVRELIVS COTTA, in style a rather inferior copy of his model Antonius,[90] in his life attractively honest in an age which saw many rascals. He was born the same year as Sulpicius; in 662/92 he defended his uncle Rutilius Rufus, who, having incurred the hatred of the *equites* by defending the provincials of Asia against the outrageous demands of the tax-farmers (*publicani*), was found guilty of the very abuses which he had tried to prevent and retired to pass the rest of his life in exile among his alleged victims, loved and honoured by them. Cotta himself soon followed his uncle into exile, being impeached under the *lex Varia*, a measure which threw upon his party, the *optimates*, the onus of the recent Social War. Leaving Rome in 664/90, he returned when Sulla triumphed, and so came into contact with Cicero, who won a case against him (see p. 171). Cotta was never Sulla's creature, but retained to his death in 679/75 a certain measure of independence and a leaning towards moderate and constitutional reforms, though he lacked both physical strength and moral courage to be a very vigorous opponent of those in power. He also left nothing in writing, and some of his utterances were composed for him by Aelius (cf. p. 104).[91]

Two other orators, considered inferior to Antonius and Crassus but better than Sulpicius and Cotta, were LVCIVS MARCIVS PHILIPPVS and GAIVS IVLIVS CAESAR STRABO VOPISCVS; these six were the principal members of what may be loosely called the

in the *Digest*, i, 2, 2, 41, together with the Greek list of works used in compiling the *Digest*, known as the *Index Florentinus* from its occurrence in the Florentine MS. which is the best authority for that work. See further Schanz-Hosius, i, pp. 239–40.

[89] Cicero, *Brut.*, 205; some speeches attributed to him were in circulation, but they were really the compositions of Cicero's contemporary PVBLIVS CANNVTIVS, *ibid.* See further *O.R.F.*, p. 343 *sqq.*; Wilkins, 1892, p. 17 *sqq.*

[90] See in general *O.R.F.*, p. 338 *sqq.*; for the relation of Cotta to Antonius, see Cicero, *Brut.*, 203; the whole passage is a considered criticism and comparison of him with Sulpicius.

[91] Here as elsewhere, it is assumed that the reader has access to some good history of Rome, Mommsen's or another. That he wrote nothing is stated by Cicero, *orat.*, 132; that he let some short and unimportant works of Aelius pass for his own, *Brut.*, 207; Aelius wrote his defence when he was tried under the lex Varia, *ibid.*, 205.

Roman bar[92] of that day. Philippus was consul in 663/91, censor in 668/86. He was, says Cicero, much inferior to the two leading lights, and in particular, he had a habit of rising to speak without knowing exactly how he was to begin; his own defence of his methods was that he could not fight till his arm was warmed.[93] He and Crassus had one vehement and public political debate, when the former, in his consulship, arraigned the senate for its inactivity and declared he must seek another advisory body (*consilium*), since that one was useless. Crassus replied with a speech generally acknowledged his masterpiece, and in a sharp exchange of reproaches which followed, went so far as to say that if Philippus considered him no senator, he refused to consider him a consul.[94] It need hardly be said that the two were of opposite parties, Crassus being of the *optimates*, Philippus of the *populares*. He was especially esteemed for his witty rejoinders in debate; the few examples which have come down to us are not of the highest order of humour, but the ancients were more tolerant of bad puns than our generation; hence it seems to have taken the popular fancy when Philippus, requesting leave to cross-question a witness of dwarfish stature and being told not to be too long about it, replied meekly, 'I will ask only a very little one'[95]; and a few other witticisms of the same kind are recorded of him. Caesar's dates were 623/131, or a little later, to 667/87, when he was killed by the

[92] See Cicero, *Brut.*, 207. There was in Rome no profession or status exactly corresponding to that of a barrister; but it was the traditional duty of a Roman of position to watch over the interests of his retainers (*clientes*) in every way, including the pleading of their causes in court. Hence by an easy extension of this custom, a man of ability as speaker or lawyer would often widen his influence and connexions by speaking on behalf of, or less commonly accusing, those who found themselves parties to a suit, especially one of political importance, for this was a recognized way of bringing oneself before the public. Hence the common modern use of 'client', which descends from classical Latin, see Horace, *epp.*, i, 5, 31; Persius, iii, 75.

For Philippus, see *O.R.F.*, p. 323 *sqq.*; for Caesar, *ibid.*, p. 330 *sqq.*

[93] Cicero, *de orat.*, ii, 316. For Cicero's opinion of his relative merit, see *Brut.*, 173, Crasso et Antonio L. Philippus proximus accedebat, sed longo interuallo tamen proximus.

[94] Cicero, *de orat.*, iii, 1 *sqq.*, tells the story admirably. It was Crassus' swan-song; he had symptoms of pleurisy on him as he spoke and returned home with a high temperature, to die in a week's time of pleuro-pneumonia. His retort to Philippus is recorded by Quintilian (viii, 3, 89; xi, 1, 37) and one or two others. It is to be remembered that theoretically the senate was not a legislative body but purely advisory (*consilium*), hence Philippus' taunt.

[95] *Perpusillum rogabo*, Cicero, *de orat.*, ii, 245.

Marians; his tragedies have already been mentioned (p. 69). While Cicero tells us[96] that his wit, which he sedulously cultivated, did not prevent his speeches from carrying weight, all that we have of him is a couple of rather personal jokes. On one occasion, when debating with Curio, the father of the better-known politician who became a supporter of Caesar the dictator, he asked, in allusion to his opponent's bad habit of shifting from one foot to the other as he spoke, who that was who was talking from a boat; on another, when opposed by Helvius Mancia, he promised to describe him, and on being challenged to do so, merely pointed to a shield hung up within sight of the audience, which showed a Gaulish warrior with a ridiculously distorted face.[97] The general impression gathered from such stories is that the Roman standard of wit was at that time neither high nor delicate.

This HELVIVS MANCIA was a native of Formiae, and belonged to the class of freedmen (*libertini*). He is remembered chiefly for one piece of grim rhetoric which he produced in his old age. In 699/55 he accused Lucius Scribonius Libo before the censors of that year. Pompey, who was then consul for the second time, appeared as Libo's advocate, and called Helvius an accuser from the lower world (*ab inferis*). Helvius answered that he had indeed come from the underworld, and had there seen the blood-stained ghosts of those whom Pompey, in his younger days when he was Sulla's partisan, had put to untimely and unjust deaths.[98]

Another minor orator of those times was QVINTVS SERVILIVS CAEPIO, *quaestor urbanus* in 654/100; on occasion he had recourse to Aelius for his speeches, but apparently was capable of composing for himself. He was one of the *populares*, and his most celebrated appearance was in an affair of accusation and counter-accusation with Aemilius Scaurus (p. 102),[99] who was of the opposite faction. One of those with whom he came into contact was TITVS BETVCIVS BARRVS of Asculum, whom Cicero declares to be the best speaker of those living outside Rome. Nothing at all is left of his speeches.[100] Finally, mention should be made of the oratorical activities of GAIVS SCRIBONIVS CVRIO, already spoken of in connexion with Caesar Strabo. Several speeches of his are known by title, and he was still active in

[96] Cicero, *de orat.*, iii, 30. For the titles, &c., of his known speeches, see *O.R.F.*, p. 330 *sqq*.

[97] Cicero, *Brut.*, 216 (hence Quintilian, xi, 3, 129); *de orat.*, ii, 266, where Wilkins' note gives some variants of the story.

[98] *O.R.F.*, p. 327 *sqq.*; the passage cited above is preserved, though hardly in Helvius' own words, by Valerius Maximus, vi, 2, 8.

[99] See *O.R.F.*, p. 320 *sqq*.

[100] Cicero, *Brut.*, 169.

the days of Cicero, against whom he defended Clodius in 692/62. His dates are 630/124 (approximately)—701/53.[101]

Having thus brought down our account of oratory to the age of Cicero, it is time to turn to the writers of history, which now begins to be of some importance as a branch of literature. It is necessary to realize that it had long had that position in Greece, and in particular, that since Isokrates (436–338 B.C.) and his immediate pupils, Ephoros, Theopompos and the rest,[102] it had been an important department of that serious and moralizing type of rhetoric which his school taught with such acceptance. Disinterested and purely scientific research into the past was not the ideal of any Greek writer after Herodotos, not even Thucydides, who combined with his passion for accuracy a pedagogic purpose, to set on record what had happened in his own generation for the instruction of posterity. The later and poorer historians copied him in the latter, but not the former characteristic. To teach ethics and politics by practical examples was an object never far from their minds, and it was rare for any of them to resist the temptation to sacrifice fact to rhetoric or effective sermonizing; Polybios, who was as fond of moralizing as any of them, is honourably distinguished for his scrupulously accurate researches into every source which could enlighten him. The rest probably did not often wilfully and deliberately distort the truth; but when a writer, however honest of purpose, is thinking of edification rather than of pure science, and is a rhetorician in the first place, a researcher in the second only, the pressure on him is very strong to see perfect and exemplary villains and heroes in the worse and better characters of his story, and to paint them accordingly; while the march of events is apt to be similarly accounted for, such dull things as pressure of population and other economic factors giving place to the virtues and vices of peoples as causes for their rise and fall. Such temptations are not weakened when the historian's subject is the conflicts through which his own nation or his own party has recently passed. Hence it is that Roman historiography had before it from the beginning models which, while not worthless (Livy in antiquity, Macaulay in modern times, are both products of this school), were not the best nor the most likely to lead to the production of works both reliable in content and agreeable in style.

It is characteristic of their dependence upon Greek models

[101] *O.R.F.*, p. 347 *sqq.*

[102] For Isokrates, see Rose, *H.G.L.*, p. 284 *sqq.*; for Ephoros and Theopompos, *ibid.*, p. 310.

that the first of the Romans to attempt something less skeletonic than the Annales Maximi (see p. 7) did not use his own language for the purpose. QVINTVS FABIVS PICTOR, who took an active part in the second Punic War, wrote in Greek a history of Rome down to his own day. His was a family of quite unusual culture for that nation and age, for it is recorded that one of its members was a painter, apparently of some merit; whence the surname.[103] His history was apparently Greek in spirit as well as in language, or rather Hellenistic; for it began with an account of the foundation of Rome, following an obscure Greek writer, Diokles of Peparethos.[104] This was quite in accordance with the taste of that age for combining mythology with history, and gave scope for sheer romancing, it being understood that the legends of early times were not to be taken too seriously; hence Fabius did not scruple to insert a story of a dream wherein Aeneas saw all that was to befall him, and the familiar tales of the white sow and her farrow, the adventures of Romulus and Remus, and so forth, filled a part of his work.[105] That it was mostly foreign and artificial pseudo-saga he apparently never realized. Chronology, another favourite study of that date, was also a matter to which he gave some attention, and he was of opinion, on what precise grounds we do not know, that Rome had been founded in the first year of the eighth olympiad, 747 B.C. of our reckoning and six years later than Varro's computation. Coming down to later times, he included the events in which he had himself taken part; at what year he stopped we do not know, but he is cited for the events of 537/217.[106] As to his merits as a historian, good witnesses testify to his honesty of purpose and freedom from absurd exaggerations; Polybios warns us that he was violently prejudiced in favour of his own people, a defect neither unique nor surprising. His style was apparently plain to baldness.[107]

[103] Cicero, *Tusc.*, i, 4; Pliny, *N.H.*, xxxv, 19. He painted the walls of the temple of Salus, in 450/304.

[104] See frag. 5a in *H.R.F.* = Plutarch, *Rom.*, 3. Plutarch's use of Fabius is the reason why we have disproportionately much of this part of the work, which was quite summary (*κεφαλαιωδῶς ἐπέδραμεν*, Dion. Hal., i, 6, 2).

[105] Frags. 1–12, largely from Plutarch and Dionysios.

[106] By Livy, xxii, 7, 4 (battle of Lake Trasumene). He very likely came down to the end of the war. For his estimate of the age of Rome, see Dion. Hal., i, 74, 1.

[107] See note 109; if the Latin version was so wanting in ornament, the Greek original can hardly have been florid. For his trustworthiness, see, *e.g.*, Livy (in n. 106); prejudice, Polybios, i, 14, 1–3, which at the same time acquits him of any deliberate falsehood.

That there was a Latin version of his work we are assured by several writers; as to its author we are not informed, for the fact that it is quoted under such formulae as *Fabius rerum gestarum libro primo* [108] and the statement of Cicero that its style was dry and poor [109] tell us merely that it was a translation of his history and of fairly early date. That he wrote it himself there is nothing at all to prove.

A Fabius, whom certainly some later writers took to be the same as this one, wrote a work *de iure pontificio*.[110] But it is as least as likely that the real author was QVINTVS FABIVS MAXIMVS SERVILIANVS, consul 612/142, who is known to have written on that subject.[111] When we hear of *Seruilianus historiarum scriptor*,[112] it is not easy to say whether this is the opposite confusion or the later writer did also compose a historical work of some kind.

Fabius Pictor having shown the way, there were not wanting imitators, even in his own time. The plan of the historical work composed by his contemporary LVCIVS CINCIVS ALIMENTVS, who was for a while Hannibal's prisoner, seems to have been much the same as his, for the scanty citations from it range from the doings of Euandros (Evander) before the foundation of Rome to the numbers of the Carthaginian army. He also had notions of chronology, and placed the date of the foundation of Rome at olympiad 12,4 (= 729 B.C.). That he was less esteemed than Fabius is evident from the small number of references to him [113]; that this adverse opinion was not without justification seems probable, not so much from the fact that Dionysios finds his version of the death of Sp. Maelius lacking in plausibility, but from Livy's testimony that he made poor use of good information.[114]

The historical essay of the elder Africanus' son has been mentioned already, p. 91. Another follower of Fabius Pictor's methods was GAIVS ACILIVS. Half a dozen references tell us that he began, like the others, with the earliest history and legends, that he came down to his own days (he is cited for an event of 570/184), that he wrote in Greek,

[108] Nonius, p. 518, 34. For the fragments, see *H.R.F.*, p. 74 *sq.*

[109] Cicero, *de orat.*, ii, 51; *de legg.*, i, 6.

[110] *E.g.*, Nonius, *loc. cit.*, idem (Fabius) iuris pontificii libro III.

[111] Macrob., *sat.*, i, 16, 25.

[112] Scholia Veronensia on Vergil, p. 409, 14 Hagen. See further Schanz-Hosius, i, p. 171 *sqq.*

[113] In *H.R.F.* there are but seven, while Fabius Pictor has in all 34, including those from the Latin version, Cato 143, Cassius Hemina 40.

[114] Dion Hal., xii, 4, 2–5; Livy, xxi, 38, 3, who says he would follow Cincius regarding the strength of Hannibal's force when he reached Italy but that he reckons in the local levies of Gauls and Ligurians, and so does not give any clear idea of the Spanish and African strengths; this although he had spoken to Hannibal himself on the subject.

but was Latinized by some one called CLAVDIVS, and possibly, for the reading is uncertain, that he composed his history about 512/142.[115] Except that he was a senator in 599/155, and therefore had probably held some magistracy before that date,[116] we know nothing whatever of his life.

Of AVLVS POSTVMIVS ALBINVS we are rather better informed. He was praetor in 599/155, and consul four years later in 608/146 he formed one of the commission of ten who were sent to organize Greece as a Roman province. The Greeks seem to have liked him, and he returned the compliment by using their tongue for his history and apologizing for any inelegancies of which he might be guilty. It would appear that he also wrote a poem in Greek. Personally he was a talkative man, with an excellent opinion of himself.[117]

Omitting Cato, of whose historical writings an account has already been given (p. 95), we pass to a group of writers who, imitating him, used Latin for their annals; it can hardly be said that they, any more than Fabius and his imitators, succeeded in writing histories. Of these, the earliest seems to be LVCIVS CASSIVS HEMINA, who was alive in 608/146. His work seems to have treated the antiquities of the country on a large scale, comparatively at least, for it was not till the second book that he came to the foundation of Rome.[118] He, like the Greek-using historians, seems to have brought down his work to his own

[115] Livy, *epit.*, 53, says, according to the MSS., C. Iulius senator Graece res Romanas scribit; but no Iulius of anything like the right date (about 610/142) is known. Probably therefore we should read C. Acilius (Madvig) or simply Acilius (Hertz, Rossbach). For Claudius, see Livy, xxv, 39, 12, Claudius, qui annales Acilianos ex Graeco in Latinum sermonem uertit; xxxv, 14, 5, Claudius, secutus Graecos Acilianos libros. It may be conjectured that the *Κλώδιός τις* whom Plutarch cites (*Numa*, 1) as having written a work on chronology and expressed no high opinion of the trustworthiness of early Roman annals is this same man; but the name is very common. See below, p. 118.

[116] He acted as interpreter to the famous embassy of the three philosophers, Gellius, vi, 14, 9; it was not the law until Sulla's time that a senator must be an ex-magistrate, but it was the usual custom to recruit the senate in that manner.

[117] The chief account of him and his works now surviving is Polybios, xxxix, 1, 1 *sqq.*; more in *H.R.F.*, pp. 37–9. Macrobius (*sat.*, iii, 20, 5) quotes a few words in Latin as from Albinus, whence it has been conjectured that some one translated his history; but there is no other indication of this.

[118] See his fragments, *H.R.F.*, pp. 68–74. The cognomen Hemina suggests that either he or some ancestor was not distinguished for sobriety. It is the name of a liquid measure, equivalent to 0·2736 of a litre (Hultsch, *Metrologie*, p. 704), and therefore exactly corresponding to *κοτύλη* (' Halfpint '), the nickname of the drunken rascal who insulted the Roman embassy to Tarentum, Dion. Hal., xix, 5, 2.

generation. His style was dry and unadorned, his method apparently little better than an annalistic enumeration of events, brief and rapid once the mythological period was finished, for the second book began with Romulus and ended not earlier than 365/389.[119] At least his interests were fairly wide, for one or two of the statements for which he is quoted deal with matters of cultural importance, including the first coming of Greek physicians to Rome.[120]

About the same time lived a politician of some note, LVCIVS CALPVRNIVS PISO, said to have been the first of his family to bear the honourable surname of FRVGI (Honest). He was also occasionally surnamed CENSORIVS, as he held that office in 634/120. Cicero briefly describes his literary output as 'speeches, which have now disappeared, and annals, very jejunely written'.[121] So far as we know, the latter work was in seven books, and it ended not earlier than the secular games of 608/146.[122] Two characteristics at least it had; one was very creditable to its author's zeal, if not his ability, for it would seem that he had a good deal to say of the religion of his country and tried to throw light on difficult points by etymologies; the other was much less suitable to a sober historian, since it consisted in a fondness for little anecdotes, not only of historical persons, but of so legendary a figure as Romulus, some of whose table-talk Piso professed to know.[123] Both are borrowings from Hellenistic literature. Piso was roughly contemporary with Apollodoros of Athens,[124] who besides his other services to antiquarian lore wrote twenty-four books *On the Gods*, and Apollodoros was by no means alone in his taste for researches into the history and science of religion, as then understood. Anecdote was a frequent ornament of Greek history (Timaios for instance is often quoted

[119] Frag. 20. For his style, which is ranked with those of Cato, Piso and Fabius Pictor, none of whom sought for any virtue beyond intelligibility and brevity, see Cicero, *de orat.*, ii, 51–3.

[120] Frag. 37 (= Pliny, *N.H.*, xiii, 84). Nonius, p. 346, 24, quotes: Cassius Hemina lib. II de censoribus; 'et in area in Capitolio signa quae erant demoliunt'. This somewhat suggests that Cassius wrote a work called *de censoribus*, in two or more books; but as no one else seems to have heard of it, it seems more natural to take Nonius as meaning, 'in Book II (of the *Annals*), speaking of the censors'.

[121] Cicero, *Brut.*, 106.

[122] See frag. 39 (*H.R.F.*, p. 86).

[123] Frags. 4, 7, 10, 11, 12, 13, 14, 25, 36, 39 all deal with religious matters; 33 is the anecdote about Spurius Albinus told in n. 56; 27 and 8 are again anecdotes, the latter dealing with an edifying remark of Romulus.

[124] Rose, *H.G.L.*, p. 392.

for good stories),[125] and was the chief stock-in-trade of the biographers who flourished among the followers of Aristotle especially.[126] The general impression conveyed by the fragments is of an ingenious and chattily entertaining writer, fonder of saying something new and interesting than of very profound search after historical truth.

Several minor writers were of about the same date as Piso. GAIVS FANNIVS, Laelius' son-in-law, has already been mentioned (p. 101). He wrote a history in tolerably good style (*non ineleganter*), says Cicero,[127] who has some difficulty in distinguishing between this man and another of the same name; the truth of the matter seems to be that the historian was the better-known Fannius, who besides his relations with Laelius was first the friend and later the opponent of Gaius Gracchus. Precisely what period his work covered is not known, for the fragments are rather scanty. The highest-numbered book cited is the eighth, and certainly the third Punic War and the tribunate of Tiberius Gracchus were among the events recorded.[128] Sallust was of opinion that Fannius was a very trustworthy writer,[129] a testimony which would carry more weight if its author's own standard of veracity had been higher (cf. p. 219). Brutus, the assassin of Julius Caesar, made an epitome of Fannius' work, which, like the original, has perished.[130]

A very obscure name is that of VENNONIVS (his praenomen is unknown, also his cognomen, if he had one), whom Dionysios quotes once for a detail of Servius Tullius' constitution and Cicero regrets not having access to for some unknown literary purpose and elsewhere criticizes for his dry style.[131]

Better known, and also, if we may trust Cicero, a better stylist was GAIVS SEMPRONIVS TVDITANVS. He was praetor in 622/132, consul three years later, and in that capacity fought the Iapydes, as already mentioned on p. 87. He found time to write two considerable works, one a history which began with the earliest times and came down at

[125] Rose, *H.G.L.*, p. 370.

[126] *Ibid.*, p. 357.

[127] Cicero, *Brut.*, 101. In this passage he distinguishes (99) between C. Fannius C.f., qui consul cum Domitio fuit (632/122) and (100) C. Fannius M.f., C. Laeli gener. But *ad Att.*, xii, 5, 3, he is in the thick of a controversy with Atticus and Brutus as to the identities of the two men. It so happens that an inscription (*C.I.L.*, i², 658) records that Fannius the consul was son of Marcus, not of Gaius; it is therefore likely enough that he is also the historian, and certain that he is Laelius' son-in-law. Of the other Fannius nothing seems to be known. See Schanz-Hosius, i, p. 199.

[128] Frags. 2, 3.

[129] Sallust, *Hist.*, i, p. 4 Mauernbrecher.

[130] Cicero, *ad Att.*, xii, 5, 3 (= 50).

[131] Dion. Hal., iv, 15, 1; Cicero, *ad Att.*, xii, 3, 1; *de legg.*, i, 6.

least to the end of the second Macedonian War in 560/194,[132] the other a treatise on the functions of Roman magistrates (*libri magistratuum*), extending to at least thirteen books.[133]

The date of GNAEVS GELLIVS is not known, unless he was that Gellius who was a contemporary of Cato.[134] As a historian he seems to have been somewhat voluminous; the fragments cite books numbered as high as 33, the first of which would seem to have contained mythological disquisitions not always very obviously connected with Rome or Italy; the third found him still occupied with Romulus and his successors, and even the thirty-third had got no further down than 538/216, whereas we know that he mentioned the Secular Games of 608/146.[135] That his repute was not of the highest would seem to follow from the fact that our fragments of him amount to but 34 in all, counting a number which are merely citations of the strange forms of words in which he seems to have indulged.

All the above writers, so far as we know the contents of their works, wrote histories of Rome from the beginning to at least a date near their own. We now come to a somewhat different class, whose compositions dealt with a single period. The first and best known of these is LVCIVS COELIVS ANTIPATER, whose work, apparently in seven books, recounted the second Punic War only. He thus handled the subject a little more briefly than Livy, who devotes ten books (xxi-xxx) to the same matter. Coelius' date is known approximately from his having been Crassus' teacher of rhetoric and from his mentioning the tribunate of Gaius Gracchus (631/123 and the next two years).[136] In style he was more ornate than his predecessors, and seems to have discussed it in a somewhat naïve fashion in the preface of his work; but he was not a finished master of language.[137] In

[132] Fragments in *H.R.F.*, p. 89 *sqq*.

[133] Macrobius, *sat.*, i, 13, 21, cites the third book, Messalla in Gellius, xiii, 15, 4, the thirteenth.

[134] Gellius, xiv, 2, 21; Cicero, *de diuin.*, i, 55, mentions him in passing between Fabius and Coelius.

[135] Frag. 28, from a book of unknown number, but presumably after the thirty-third.

[136] Cicero, *Brut.*, 102. Here as in several citations in various authors the MSS. call him Caelius; but the weight of authority, including the majority of the best MSS. of Livy in most places where the name occurs, is for the form Coelius. As the tribunate of Gracchus (Cicero, *de diuin.*, i, 56 = frag. 50) has nothing whatsoever to do with the Punic Wars and Coelius' work is cited under more than one title, a plausible theory has several times been put forward (see Schanz-Hosius, i, p. 201) that he wrote two histories, dealing with different periods. But this is unnecessary, though it cannot be disproved; Coelius may have digressed occasionally.

[137] Cicero, *Brut.*, 102; *de legg.*, i, 6; *de orat.*, ii, 5; *orator*, 230.

matter he seems to have shown an undue fondness for marvels, especially dreams and portents. He seems to have been at some pains to get his facts, for he used not only Roman sources, but also the Greek history of Seilenos, one of two men (the other being Sosylos the Lakedaimonian) who accompanied and recorded Hannibal's campaigns. Sometimes at least he gave different accounts of the same event, with a note of his sources,[138] a method which Livy often uses. Perhaps his worst fault, both as historian and stylist, was a fondness for puerile exaggerations (*e.g.*, the army with which Scipio invaded Africa was so huge that Italy and Sicily appeared depopulated, and the birds fell to the ground when the men shouted).[139]

He was something of a lawyer, being a pupil of Scaevola (cf. p. 107), but apparently his work in this field was not very important.[140] In any case, nothing survives. Lost also is the epitome of his work which Brutus made.[141]

Cicero mentions several other writers as coming after Coelius but not nearly so good as he. The name of one of these appears in the MSS. as *belli clodius*[142]; obviously this is corrupt, but the second part of the name may be that of the obscure CLODIVS whom we have already heard of in passing as possibly the translator of Acilius (see note 115). At all events, we know from Plutarch, cited there, that a Clodius wrote a work called ἔλεγχος χρόνων (approximately, 'critical chronology'), while Appian mentions a Paulus Claudius as the author of a similar work. If these last two are the same, this author must have lived sometime after 647/107, since it is for an event of that year that Appian cites him.[143]

Less obscure, for at least we know that he served under the younger Africanus at Numantia and wrote an account of the campaign, was SEMPRONIVS ASELLIO (his praenomen is not recorded). The few fragments tell us enough of him to show that he was not without an idea of how history should be written; he stated his intention to set down not merely events but the ends which their actors had in view, for the encouragement, it would seem, of good citizens and the admonition of the unpatriotic.[144] In this he showed that he had learned his lesson well, for this is the tone of Greek history from at least the time of Thucydides. His work was on a not inconsiderable scale; our quota-

[138] Three accounts of the death of Marcellus, Livy, xxvii, 37, 13, with a statement of his own preference for one of them.

[139] Livy, xxix, 25, 3–4 (= Coelius, frag. 39).

[140] Pomponius in the *Digest*, i, 2, 40.

[141] Cicero, *ad Att.*, xiii, 8.

[142] Cicero, *de legg.*, i, 6.

[143] Appian, *de rebus Gallicis*, i, 3 (ὡς ἐν χρονικαῖς συντάξεσι δοκεῖ Παύλῳ τῷ Κλαυδίῳ).

[144] Gellius, v, 18, 8 *sqq*.

tions include one from the fourteenth book, relating probably to the assassination of Livius Drusus in 663/91.[145]

Elsewhere, Cicero speaks of a blind man, GNAEVS AVFIDIVS, who among other activities composed a history in Greek ; nothing more is known of it.[146]

Of the orators already dealt with, some wrote, if not exactly history, at least memoirs. MARCVS AEMILIVS SCAVRVS (p. 102) composed an autobiography in three books, which nobody, says Cicero, troubled to read, although it was an improving work.[147] The scantiness of quotations from it in later authors seems to confirm Cicero's remark as to its unpopularity. Its object was perhaps to secure its author's reputation with posterity, or with his own younger contemporaries, since neither his personal character nor his public actions seem to have been wholly commendable. PVBLIVS RVTILIVS RVFVS (p. 102), besides speeches, composed, probably while in exile, a history of Rome, written in Greek, and an autobiography in not fewer than five books.[148] Of CATVLVS' autobiographical work something has already been said (p. 103).

[145] In Gellius, xiii, 22 (21), 8. Charisius, p. 195, 18 Keil, professes to cite Bk. 40, which seems an impossibly high number ; possibly xi (Cortius) should be read for xl.

[146] Cicero, *Tusc.*, v, 112 ; Aufidius was alive in Cicero's boyhood.

[147] Cicero, *Brut.*, 112. Scaurus was a sapiens homo et rectus, according to him (*ibid.*, 111) ; a clever hypocrite, if we believe Sallust, *Iug.*, 15, 4.

[148] Speeches, Cicero, *ibid.*, 114 ; he was a better lawyer than orator. Greek history, Athenaios, 168d, 274c. Autobiography, frags. in *H.R.F.*, p. 123 ; they all, by an odd chance, are due to Charisius the grammarian, save one from Isidore of Seville.

CHAPTER VI

LUCRETIUS AND THE NEW POETS

THE turmoil of the last two centuries B.C., during which Rome rose from an Italian to a world-power and then to the only first-rate power in Europe, while her constitution, evolved to meet the needs of a small and compact state, proved every day more hopelessly inadequate for an empire, had political consequences far too wide-reaching to be even sketched in a work of this kind. More pertinent, for us, is a comparatively small incidental result. As Rome became larger and richer, and her antagonists one by one disappeared or sank to the level of provinces and vassal states, the need for the services of each of her citizens became rapidly less urgent. Instead of calling upon every able-bodied man to pass a very large part of his life either in military service or in legislation, the abler and more active combining both functions, she could now be sufficiently well protected and her numerous dependencies governed after a fashion by a comparatively small portion of her citizens. The insensate civil wars which brought the republic to a disastrous end and made the empire not merely a desirable change but the one way to prevent utter collapse did indeed constitute a new drain on her man-power ; but even at their worst, despite the horrors of massacres and proscriptions which attended each fresh victory of one party or the other, there was a certain amount of room for the moderate man, not politically conspicuous, to earn his safety by timely submission or merely by keeping quiet ; while even the most active politicians had by now begun to feel the spirit of the age in which they lived and have some interests outside politics or, what remained important to the typical hard-headed Roman, the betterment of their own material fortunes. Under the double influence of a higher standard of living, at least for the wealthier, and the growing contact with Greek thought, there was fast developing, not merely an occasional cultured circle like that which we have seen gathered about the younger Africanus (p. 98), but a cultured class, not confined to any one district or rank, whose members were by no means always active in public life. An interest, not merely in a practical art such as oratory, with its adjunct, rhetorical study, or in popular exhibitions like those of the theatre, but in literature generally, and not least in poetry, was becoming a quite common thing, affecting the persons most highly thought of by the general public, and therefore something respectable, not a Greek eccentricity to be ridiculed, denounced or excused as a little weakness of some one otherwise useful to the state and of good character. The poets had henceforth two possible encouragements for their talents. A rich and prominent man might come forward as a patron of literature, not merely the friend of a particular poet who could be useful to him, or a philosopher whose advice he valued; and writers on other things than politics, or history capable of supplying politicians with examples to follow or quote, might count on a reading public, probably never large as compared with modern standards,[1] but not confined to one small circle of Roman gentry.

In this age therefore we find a man whose one title to fame is that he wrote a single poem, not intended for public performance nor capable of flattering national or individual vanity, although it was addressed to one who seems to have been in some sense the author's patron, but consisting of the exposition of a philosophical system in exalted and ornate language, and of exhortations to follow that system and attain to happiness. TITVS LVCRETIVS CARVS, so far as we know, took no part in public life; indeed, we know almost nothing about him, apart from his literary activity, save two dates (his birth, in 660/94; his death, Oct. 15, 699/55),[2] a curious statement regarding the publication

[1] Much later than this, the younger Pliny (see p. 417 *sqq.*) implies (*epp.*, iv, 7, 2) that 1,000 copies is a large edition and is surprised to hear (*epp.*, ix, 11, 2) that there are book-shops in Lugudunum (Lyons) and his own works are on sale there. This would be about equivalent to a popular English writer of to-day being astonished to learn that he had readers in Montreal or Cape Town.

[2] Jerome, *an. Abr.* 1923 (= 660/94): Titus Lucretius poeta nascitur, qui postea amatorio poculo in furorem uersus, cum aliquot libros per interualla insaniae conscripsisset quos postea Cicero emendauit, propria se manu interfecit anno aetatis xliiii (*i.e.*, in 704/50). Donatus, *Vit. Verg.*, 6, initia aetatis Cremonae egit usque ad uirilem togam, quam XV anno natali suo accepit isdem illis consulibus iterum duobus quibus erat natus, euenitque ut eo ipso die Lucretius poeta decederet. Vergil was born Oct. 15, *coss. Pompeio et Crasso, ibid.*, i, cf. p. 236; their second consulship was in 699/55. Both these notices, past all reasonable doubt, come ultimately from Suetonius (cf. p. 511); the second is the likelier to be correct as to the date of Lucretius' death because in 700/54 we find the two Ciceros corresponding about his poem, Cicero *ad Q. fratrem*,

of his poem, and an utterly worthless anecdote. We cannot even be sure of his family; the Lucretii were indeed an ancient patrician *gens*, or clan, but their cognomen, so far as we know, was Tricipitinus,[3] and we have no record of any of them adding or substituting that of Carus. The tone of the poet's addresses to the not very distinguished Memmius is that of a social inferior,

ii, 9, 3: Lucreti poemata, ut scribis, ita sunt, multis luminibus ingeni, multae tamen et artis. sed cum ueneris; 'As to Lucretius' poetry, I agree with you that it shows many flashes of genius; there is, however, much art in it as well. But more of this when you come.' This, so far as it goes, suggests that the work was in their hands, and as it was never finished and therefore never published by its author (see n. 11), it is at least consistent both with the poet being dead and with one of the brothers (almost certainly Marcus, for Quintus was just then busy in Gaul and Britain with Caesar, and Marcus infinitely the better-known man of letters and therefore far more likely to be entrusted with such a task) having been asked to edit the poem; cf. Munro, vol. ii, p. 2 *sqq*. The story of the editing, therefore, need not be doubted; it may be added that Cicero's own philosophic works show what may at least be interpreted as a knowledge of Lucretius, *e.g.*, *Tusc.*, i, 48, on the attitude of Epicureans towards their master might very well be derived from Lucr., iii, 1–30, ii, 55–61, 1090 *sqq*., i, 120 and the whole passage in which that line occurs, v, 8. Such knowledge could readily be got by Cicero from having carefully read the poem through from Lucretius' own MS.; more than this and a little rather hurried arranging of detached passages, plus handing the work to a scribe to copy out fair, the 'editing' can hardly have amounted to. The astonishing fact, on any theory, is that Cicero, save for the letter above quoted, never mentions Lucretius at all.

But the tale of Lucretius having written his poem in the intervals of insanity is a bit of spiteful gossip from some one who did not like Epicureans. There are, of course, examples of authors who have gone mad (Nathaniel Lee), or written in the intervals of a recurrent insanity (Mary Lamb), or been all their lives eccentric to the verge of madness (Nietzsche); but none of these wrote, and no such person is ever likely to write, a closely reasoned philosophic work embodying no eccentricity of style or matter but breathing calm sanity from every page. 'Of insanity of any type,' says the late Sir Wm. Osler (*Brit. Med. Journ.*, for July 5, 1919, p. 5a), 'that leaves a mind capable in lucid intervals of writing such verses as *De Rerum Natura* we [physicians] know nothing. The sole value of the myth is its casual association with the poem of Tennyson. Only exsuccous dons who have never known the wiles and ways of the younger Aphrodite would take the intensity of the feeling in Book IV as witness to anything but an accident which might happen to the wisest of the wise, when enthralled by Vivien or some dark lady of the Sonnets.' The story of the poet's suicide is hardly better, when we recall his general courageous attitude to life and especially his contempt for weaklings who kill themselves, as being merely another instance of cowards' fear of death, iii, 79 *sqq*. It is far more probable that his early death and absence from all public activity were alike due to weak health or some chronic illness which did not affect his mind.

[3] These facts are to be found in Munro's edition of Lucretius, London, Bell, 1905, *loc. cit.*: see also C. Bailey's edition, Oxford, 1947 (3 vols.).

although a self-respecting one. We may therefore fairly suppose that his was some junior branch of the house, sprung perhaps from a client or freedman of old or recent date. We have no evidence that he was either rich or very poor. Nor can we tell why he chose to address his work to Memmius in particular, or to what extent, if any, Memmius was his patron or friend. Two men of that name, both called Gaius and both *Luci filius*, were contemporary with the poet; the one was tribune of the plebs in 700/54, the other was praetor four years earlier, governed Bithynia in 697/57, supported Pompey for a while, deserted him for Caesar, was a candidate for the consulship in 700/54, but was found guilty of corrupt practices (*ambitus*) and exiled.[4] He went to Athens, and further distinguished himself by acquiring the land on which Epicurus' house had stood, planning to pull down what was left of that memorable building, and afterwards refusing, at least for a time, to let the Epicureans of the day have what they regarded as holy ground.[5] This man, who smattered poetry a little, is probably the addressee of Lucretius' poem, *De rerum natura* (*Concerning Nature*).[6] It is an exposition of the somewhat naïve Epicurean philosophy, and from that material, not the most promising for a great work of literature, Lucretius constructs the finest didactic poem now extant in any language.

Didactic poetry had its origin, so far at least as Europe is concerned, in that era of Greek literature which verse was well developed, prose hardly yet thought of as a serious literary medium.[7] In the Alexandrian age it revived, owing presumably to the anxiety of the writers of that time to find something on which to employ their skill, the usual themes of imaginative literature having reached a stage of such over-development as to make them hackneyed. But no Alexandrian didactic poem ever rose to a high level in anything but linguistic finish and smoothness of versification; the reason being that none of their poets hit on a theme capable of arousing his own intense emotion, and without this there can be no great poetry. Lucretius was more fortunate, for in Epicureanism he found a gospel which his essentially religious mind accepted and proclaimed with the enthusiasm of a Bunyan or an Augustine.

Epicurus (*'Επίκουρος*, 341–270 B.C.) was the author of a

[4] See Schanz-Hosius, i, pp. 310–11 and 276; cf. *infra*, p. 138.

[5] Cicero, *ad fam.*, xiii, 1, is an attempt to win Memmius from this churlish attitude; whether it succeeded or not is unknown.

[6] The title is no doubt taken from the various Greek works *περὶ φύσεως*. The addition of *rerum*, a very vague word ('existents', 'real objects'), gives the required generality.

[7] See Rose, *H.G.L.*, pp. 57 *sqq.*, 253, 326 *sqq.*

system taken over largely from the atomic materialism of Demokritos, with some alterations of his own. He held that both this and the innumerable other universes which he supposed to exist are the result of fortuitous conglomerations of atoms, which are of all shapes and different, but very minute, sizes and fall eternally through space.[8] As they fall, they swerve somewhat, in an erratic way which makes their motions not fully predictable; by this curious device he avoided the conception of a world in which everything happens by absolutely rigid law, and therefore every action of man is predetermined by an infinite series of events over which he has no sort of control. Nothing is immaterial, although some things, such as the soul, are the result of combinations of comparatively few and very fine and mobile atoms, and thus are much more tenuous than others. As all things are thus more or less accidental compounds, all things are capable of dissolution, save the atoms themselves, which are too small to be broken into anything smaller and also are perfectly solid, the void, which being nothing cannot be injured, and—a curious and rather illogical exception—the bodies of the gods, which are also composed of atoms and void, but protected from harm by their living in no universe but in the spaces between them, where nothing can collide with and so break them. As all things are material, not only sense-impressions but ideas also consist of matter; everything is continually throwing off thin outer shells of atoms, which, travelling in straight lines through space, often impinge either upon the organs of sense or on the mind itself. Hence all ideas are in some way true; if we now and then conceive of impossible things, such as centaurs, it is because our mind has received fragments of emanations from disparate objects and has combined them. The gods exist, because we have ideas of them, and even of their appearance, which are simply emanations from their bodies. Man therefore has nothing to fear from death, which is merely dissolution followed by complete absence of all consciousness, since that which is not cannot feel. His one good is pleasure; this is not to be found in over-indulgence of physical desires, for experience teaches us that this results in an overplus of pain, and not of pleasure. The right course is to satisfy the bodily wants in the simplest possible ways, hunger for example by a reasonable amount of plain food, and concentrate on gratifying and pleasing the mind, which has such resources as memory and hope and can be made quiet and peaceful (a pleasurable state in itself) by reflection on the true nature of

[8] It is typical of his unscientific mind that he conceived them as falling, *i.e.*, supposed that infinite space has an 'up' and 'down'.

the world and avoidance of the mental disturbances brought about by ambition, inordinate desire, and especially by an insensate fear of death, which does not concern us, since it and we can never coexist, and an equally foolish and superstitious terror of the gods. For the gods do not concern themselves with us or with the world. Being perfectly happy, they cannot have any such painful activities as the government of matter or the entertaining of angry and revengeful thoughts ; all natural phenomena are capable of a purely material explanation, without any necessity for supposing divine activity past or present. We may well venerate them, because all that is excellent is worthy of veneration [9] ; but to fear them is absurd. The good Epicurean will, remembering and jealously preserving these doctrines, live a quiet life, withholding himself from public employment and from all that would mar his tranquillity and devoting much time to philosophic reflection and study.

It is obvious that such a system has many flaws, which its opponents did not fail to point out, such as the wholly inadequate treatment of the problem of pain, for which Epicurus had no remedy but the trite and unsatisfactory reflection that if very violent it brings its own relief by causing death, while if long-lasting it cannot be unendurable. It is clear also that it would find favour neither with the highest natures nor with the coarsest part of mankind, who, if they had any relation to it, made it an excuse for looseness and evil living, as such persons are apt to do with any materialistic system. But there is an intermediate type of character, sensitive, intellectual without being very profound, and apt to be troubled with fears other than material. Such a one is in danger of running into aimless melancholy, morbid religiosity or mere superstition unless he finds some system, religious or philosophical, which he can comprehend and use as a guide for practical conduct and a source of comfort against

[9] It would presumably be on such lines as these that the followers of Epicurus justified their own cult of their master after his death. Bailey has well pointed out (see his *Phases in the Religion of Ancient Rome*, Oxford Univ. Press, 1932, p. 224 *sqq.*) that this system leaves room for a sort of contemplative worship of a type far from degraded. The Epicurean, fixing his attention on the nature of the gods, was exposing himself to the influences from their persons, corpore quae sancto simulacra feruntur (Lucr., vi, 76), which of themselves, without any will of their originals, could beneficially affect him (*τὰς γοῦν βελτίονας ἀποῤῥοίας αὐτῶν φασι τοῖς μετασχοῦσι μεγάλων ἀγαθῶν παραιτίας γίνεσθαι*, is the Epicurean statement of it cited in Eusebios, *praep. euang.*, xv, 5, 9) in the highest way, giving him a certain likeness, as we may suppose, to their entirely blessed nature.

dread of the unknown in this life or another. It is to this type of intelligence and conscience that Epicureanism seems particularly to have appealed; of that type also the recurrent statements of Lucretius are probably true concerning the prevalence of the two fears, of death and of the supernatural, for deliverance from which he is above all grateful to Epicurus.[10] Men and women of such a nature lack the self-confidence to make discoveries of their own, and are eager for some all-explaining orthodoxy supported by arguments which convince them; having found it, they become faithful adherents, often showing the zeal of a missionary or a martyr on behalf of the system. What they cannot bear is uncertainty. This is neither a low nor a stupid type (Cardinal Newman belonged to it), and there is no reason why representatives of it should not show subtlety in philosophic or theological discussion, or, as was the case with Lucretius, poetical genius.

The great work in which he sets forth his master's system with far more eloquence than his master either had or wished for is divided into six books, whether by the author or the editor matters little. After an address, of haunting beauty, to Venus, he gives as his aim the freeing of men from besetting fears by means of a philosophy which has nothing impious in it, but rather delivers us from the impieties of superstition. Book I then proceeds, after laying down the fundamental principle that nothing can come from or pass into nothing, to state the atomic theory of matter as understood by Epicureans. Book II, after a proem in praise of philosophy, continues the subject and states the doctrine of the 'swerve', already mentioned. Book III, which commences with a laudation of Epicurus, explains the nature of the soul. There are two parts, the *animus* or *mens*, situated in the chest, with which we think and feel, and the *anima* or soul proper, dispersed throughout the body. Both are composed of several sorts of very minute atoms, and both are mortal, passing out and dispersing at death. Death therefore is nothing to be dreaded, for it and we cannot coexist. The legendary tortures of the other world are nothing more than allegories of the woes

[10] This is the author's solution of the difficulty often raised by commentators on Lucretius or exponents of Epicureanism, that we have no evidence that fear of the gods, death, or the after-life was very prevalent. For instance, a much-quoted passage of Cicero (*Tusc.*, i, 48) asks what old woman is so doating as to believe in the mythical terrors of hell. I am ready to suppose, with Dr. Bailey (*op. cit.*, p. 220), that Lucretius exaggerated the prevalence of these fears; but I would hold that they really were widespread, not in any particular class, but among persons of the type above described, and occasionally among others, if weakened by age or illness, like Plato's Kephalos (*Rep.*, i, 330 d, e).

which beset the foolish in this life. Book IV has no proem,[11] one of many indications that the work was never finally revised. It explains the Epicurean theory of perception by the impingement of thin outer shells (*simulacra*) from all objects on the organs of sense and also directly on the mind. From this it passes to a discussion of sexual passion, explained as set up by stimuli from without upon a system already suffering from an inward disturbance. Recognition of its purely physical nature, and of the non-supernatural causes for such things as barrenness, will guard us against the miseries of extravagant lovers and of the superstitious. Book V, again having for its prologue an eloquent laudation of Epicurus, is one of the most interesting of the whole poem, for it gives the school's theory of the history of the universe and of man. The former is neither perfect, everlasting nor divinely governed, and will have an end as surely as it had a beginning. All its phenomena, such as sunrise and sunset, have perfectly natural explanations. Men and other animals were originally born directly from the earth, which was once capable of producing all kinds of creatures, also of feeding them with a sort of milk; she is now past her prime and rapidly losing her fertility, like an aging woman. Primitive man was sturdy, able to endure his hard life; little by little he has learned the various arts and sciences and developed a system of government. Book VI, the most plainly unfinished of all, after another encomium of Epicurus, passes to a somewhat miscellaneous series of discussions, first of celestial and meteoric phenomena, then of remarkable things on the surface of the earth (Mount Aetna,[12] the inundation of the Nile, the loadstone, and other curiosities, less well founded on fact), and finally to the causes of disease, which is explained as largely due to unwholesome or even unfamiliar air, driven from one part to another of the surface of the earth. By way of peroration, the poem concludes with a free rendering in verse of Thucydides' account of the plague at Athens.

The above jejune summary does no sort of justice to the excellence of the *De rerum Natura*. This is principally of two sorts; firstly, the ingenuity and command of language which

[11] IV, 1–25 are merely i, 926–50 repeated. This is but one of several passages whose final place in the poem was never determined by the author, while the editor seems to have dealt with them somewhat capriciously, being in doubt as to where to put them. To the same cause are due sundry repetitions, in thought though not in words, of parts of the argument; they probably are no more than alternative forms of the same passage.

[12] He discusses Aetna, not volcanoes in general, because no other active volcano was then known.

enable the poet throughout to be interesting and lucid, even when explaining dry and abstruse matters; secondly, the splendour and eloquence of the many passages of moral reflection, descriptions of nature (for whose beauties Lucretius evidently had an open eye), satirical expositions of vices and follies and panegyrics on the wisdom and goodness of Epicurus. The chief formal defect of the work, a certain tendency to ramble, is beyond doubt the result of it having been composed, perhaps under stress of illness, certainly in no very great time (since the author was not forty years old when he died and no part of the poem suggests the immature utterances of a beginner, however ingenious) and never finally revised for publication. If we ask for the reason of its outstanding merit, we must put first its author's own genius. In the second place, as a subsidiary cause only, we have to reckon his not inconsiderable learning in his own language and in Greek.

It is clear that he knew and loved the older Latin poets, and especially Ennius. Of him he speaks with affectionate admiration, as having brought from Helikon an unfading crown, and as the author of immortal verse[13]; and it is clear that his own hexameters are largely, though by no means slavishly, modelled on those of the older writer, and hence must have sounded rather archaic to his contemporaries. To take but two or three points, he frequently elides the final *s* before a consonant, as *e fontibu' magnis* (i, 412); he ends many lines with words of more than three syllables, as *quo referentes* (i, 424), *exiguusque* (i, 435), *frugiferentis* (i, 3), and many more with one or two monosyllables, as *dum sit* (i, 434), *faciet quid* (i, 440), *per se* (i, 445); he is careless about the rhythm of the first two feet, allowing the second to end with the end of a word inelegantly often, as *aduentu manet* (i, 457), *permanat calor* (i, 494); even letting the verse sometimes fall into three parts, almost without caesura, as *irreuocabilis/abstulerit iam/praeterita aetas* (i, 468). Thus the rhythm is archaically rugged; in addition, the language, while most pure and choice Latin, has a savour of the preceding century, occasionally allowing an old form, such as the genitive in *āī* of the first declension (*materiai* often), a compound of a sort going rapidly out of fashion in his day, as *terriloquos* (*terriloquis uictus dictis*, i, 103) or *circumcaesura*, a too literal adaptation of the Greek περικοπή (*extima membrorum circumcaesura*, iii, 219, iv, 647). His syntax, also, has now and then the freedom of the earlier writers, who had not yet so fixed a grammar as prevailed among Cicero's contemporaries for the most part; Cicero would hardly have said *primum quidquid* instead of *primum quidque* for 'each

[13] Lucr., i, 117 *sqq*. He also knew the tragedians and Naevius; see Munro, ii, p. 8. It is remarkable that he had carefully read and clearly admired Cicero's *Aratea* (see p. 145), Munro, *ibid*., 9.

successive top layer' (v, 264),[14] nor *perfunctus praemia* (for *praemiis*), iii, 956. His ear allowed him still to make very free use, freer than was in fashion among his contemporaries, of alliteration and assonance of the most patent kind, as *ualidi uerrentes aequora uenti*, v, 266; *domi domitos*, v, 1334. The innovations and experiments of his own time left him wholly untouched.

Of Greek it must be said that he had a good reading knowledge enough, doubtless also could speak the language of that day fluently; but he had not a scholar's accuracy, as is seen, for example, from several rather elementary mistakes in his rendering of Thucydides, above mentioned (see Munro's and Bailey's commentaries). He has been shown to have had more or less acquaintance with Homer, Euripides, Empedokles, the philosophic writers, especially those of later date, such as Epicurus' contemporaries, and here and there the best of the Alexandrians.[15] In short, he had the wide knowledge of the best models for his purpose which was becoming characteristic of the leading writers of that day, and he had absorbed what they could teach him and made it his own after a manner possible only to writers of genius, then or at any other time.

One point remains to be considered, which, although small, has given rise to much discussion. Why does Lucretius, whose attitude towards the conventional gods we have described, open his poem with so glowing an invocation of one of them, Venus? The answer is most probably to be sought in the digression in Book II, 600 *sqq*. Having explained that the poetical descriptions of the earth as the Mother of the Gods are nothing but fables, he adds (652 *sqq*.), 'If any one is determined to call the sea Neptune, the fruits of the earth Ceres, and had rather use the title of Bacchus out of its meaning than pronounce the true name of the liquid, let us grant him also to call the globe of earth Mother of the Gods, provided only that he himself is careful not really to pollute his mind with foul superstition.' If, therefore, the poet's serious beliefs were sound, he might indulge in such verbal fancies as he thought fit. This license Lucretius uses more than once, as when, in the sixth book (92–5) he invokes Kalliope to guide him, or in the fifth (737 *sqq*.) animates a pageant of the seasons with the names of Venus, Zephyrus, Flora, Ceres and Euhius. Hence to pray, 'Grant, Venus, that Mars may leave the world in peace while I sing', was no more than a legitimate poetic equivalent of the more prosy 'May the

[14] He does indeed use *quidquid* by itself in the sense of *quidque*, see Madvig on de fin., v, 24. Historically, the words are one and the same, like Gk. ὅστις and ὅστε; so Oscan says *putreìpid*, Umbrian *putureìpe*, for Lat. *utrumque*.

[15] Thus, iv, 181–2, paruus ut est cycni melior canor ille gruum quam/clamor in aetheriis dispersus nubibus austri, has a distinct resemblance to Kallimachos, Frag. 1 Pfeiffer, 13–14, which, being part of the *Aitia*, is a more likely model than the less-known Antipatros of Sidon, whose epigram, itself probably imitated from Kallimachos, Munro quotes *ad loc*.

course of events be such as to leave us time for poetry and philosophy '. If the result is high poetry and not hackneyed rhetoric, the poet's own genius may be thanked for that, and especially his deep sense of the wonder and beauty of the process of growth and reproduction which, for him, is symbolized by the traditional name of the goddess.[16]

Before taking leave of Lucretius, it should be mentioned that there was another didactic poet of about that date, whose work was likewise called *de rerum natura*. His name was EGNATIVS ; he is twice mentioned after Accius and once before Lucretius by Macrobius,[17] who at that point is giving examples of how Vergil borrowed words from older writers, and regularly arranges his quotations from the latter in chronological order. Hence his date may be somewhere in the generation preceding Lucretius' death, and this fits the fact that Macrobius cites from him two quite pretty lines, one of which has the old-fashioned dropping of a final *s* (*labentibu' Phoebe*). We know no more of him.

Except Lucretius himself, every poet of any importance in that age was more or less decidedly a modernist. To explain the influences under which they worked, it is well to digress for a moment and consider what sort of education was then available to Romans of good social position.[18] In the old days, no regular provision had been made for this ; a father taught his sons and a mother her daughters at home, chiefly, though no doubt such things as small elementary schools may have existed from fairly early times to propagate the widely known arts of reading and writing.[19] Cato very likely was following a practice still surviving in other old-fashioned households than his own when he took the teaching of his son into his own hands and would not let a slave give him instruction.[20] Later, if the father was a man of any distinction, the boy would get practical instruction from him, not so much by any formal lessons as by seeing and hearing him transact business, for it was the custom that father and son should be continually together.[21] If more was wanted, the young man would be attached to the personal following of some dis-

[16] Not a little has been written on this proem, see Schanz-Hosius, i, p. 276 ; and for more of the bulky literature on Lucretius, *ibid.*, pp. 272–84, which also give references to the ancient mentions of him.

[17] Macrob., *sat.*, vi, 5, 2 and 12.

[18] There is a handy short account by A. S. Wilkins, *Roman Education*, Cambridge, Univ. Press, 1905.

[19] If we knew how old the story of Verginia is, we might speak more definitely ; Livy, iii, 44, 6, represents Appius Claudius as having her arrested on her way to school.

[20] See Plutarch, *Cat. mai.*, 20 ; cf. *sup.*, p. 95, n. 28.

[21] As when the father was dining out, Plut., *quaest. Rom.*, 33, or at the senate, *sup.*, p. 95.

tinguished statesman, whom he would attend in public, accompanying him, for example, to the courts when he was to plead there,[22] and so enjoy the advantage of a good model for the performance of public business. This practical education had obvious advantages for producing a useful citizen, brought up under those influences considered most wholesome by public opinion; it made no provision for culture. Greek influence not only made additions to it, but in time quite altered its central features; for Greece had for centuries valued theoretical and literary knowledge, sometimes to an exaggerated extent. By the age of which we are speaking, Rome had had, besides the elementary schools already mentioned (*ludi litterarii*; *ludus* is a clumsy attempt to translate σχολή, properly 'leisure', a word and an idea foreign to the native Romans; the master was called *litterator*) places of higher education, presided over by men often of considerable culture, whether natives or foreigners.[23] They were called by the Greek name of *grammatici*, and after the Greek fashion they expounded to their pupils the most notable authors, Greek or Latin, especially the poets. *Grammaticus* means much more than simply 'grammarian', although grammar was one of the subjects studied; 'philologist' would translate it more nearly. By their side were to be found, in small numbers at first but afterwards more and more commonly, two other representatives of the higher culture, the teacher of rhetoric (*rhetor*) and the philosopher. All these enterprises were private, the state doing nothing except now and then to object to philosophy, or to some particular school thereof, and the teachers being paid directly by their pupils. Not infrequently the teacher was an educated slave, whose earnings went to swell his owner's revenues. It was thus possible, and actually happened, that a group of young men, trained by an unusually able *grammaticus*, would become a school in the literary sense of the word, a body of conscious artists in language, having certain principles in common. Such a group formed around the leading *grammaticus* of the period we are discussing, VALERIVS CATO.[24] This man was himself a writer of some repute, mostly using verse as his medium.[25] But his chief

[22] This was called *tirocinium fori*; the young speakers in the *de oratore* (*sup.*, p. 108) stand in that relation to Antonius and Crassus.

[23] For an account of some of these men, see below, p. 441 *sqq*.

[24] Our chief source of information is Suetonius, *de grammaticis*, 11.

[25] Suetonius says that he wrote a *libellus* (which might be either a book of verse or a small prose pamphlet) called *Indignatio*, in which he rebutted the charge that he was a freedman from Gaul; also certain other *libelli*, this time certainly in prose, on points of scholarship. Of these works nothing is left.

claim to our interest is that he gathered about him most of the young poets of the day, Cinna, Furius Bibaculus, Ticidas, possibly Catullus also, and seems to have inspired them with his own keen interest in the technique of poetry and the lessons to be learned from the careful and conscious art of the Alexandrians. The result was that all these men are distinguished by their small, carefully finished output, full of learning on occasion, often having an erotic theme, and using those metres which were most in favour in Alexandria, viz., besides the hexameter, which they brought to a state near perfection, the elegiac couplet and some of the simpler lyric metres.

Neither interest in metre nor study of Alexandrian models was unheard of. Besides what the earlier poets had done along these lines, we may point to the name of LAEVIVS—he is so little known that we cannot tell what his praenomen was nor if he had a cognomen—who seems to have lived about 653/100, though the indications are somewhat vague and he is mentioned only by much later writers.[26] This man wrote some very curious little works, apparently known by the general title of *Erotopaegnia*, approximately 'amatory trifles', marked especially by two features, great variety of metre and fantastic language; we learn that he called the dawn 'shame-coloured' (*pudoricolor*) and Nestor a 'triple-century-sire' (*trisaeclisenex*), while his adverse critics were crushed under the weight of a compound more suggestive of Attic comedy than of the Alexandrians, *subductisupercilicarptores*, 'brow-knitting-detractors'.[27]

It is a question whether or not any work of Valerius Cato survives. We know he wrote a poem called *Lydia*, and also that he was left an orphan in the days of Sulla and in consequence lost all his property. Now there are two little poems, falsely attributed to Vergil, whose subjects

[26] The one indication of date is in frag. 23 (*F.P.R.*, p. 292, 60), which mentions a *lex Licinia*. This, as we know from Gellius (ii, 24, 9), who cites the passage, means the sumptuary law introduced by P. Licinius Crassus Diues, who was consul in 657/97. But we do not know the date of his measure, save that it was some time before Sulla's dictatorship (672/82), Gellius, *ibid.*, 11, legibus istis situ atque senio oblitteratis, and before the death of Lucilius (652/102), who also mentioned it (Gell., *ibid.*, 10). If we suppose him a contemporary of Lucilius' later years who survived him for some time, this fits well with the greater skill he shows in handling Greek metres.

[27] This is not certain; our authorities often cite Laevius by that title only, but also quite frequently by what seem to be the titles of other poems, as *Adonis*, *Alcestis*, *Centauri*, but never under any which might not be the name of a work dealing with love or a love-story. It is therefore admissible to suppose that *Erotopaegnia* was the general name of a collection, *Adonis*, &c., those of individual poems within it. The list of strange words cited in the text is from Gellius, xix, 7, 3 *sqq.*, who gives several more.

would suit these indications well enough. One invokes a succession of vehement curses on a soldier, who, thanks to the injustices which follow in the train of civil war, possesses the poet's estate. This might conceivably be Cato abusing some follower of Sulla. On the other hand, it fits the proscriptions and confiscations of Octavian's time quite as well (cf. p. 238), which was no doubt the reason why it came to be thought Vergil's. The style, moreover, is tolerably mature, while it would appear that Cato, when he lost his property, was no more than a child, whereas, if he wrote this poem many years afterwards, the matter was somewhat out of date. Following this work, which is appropriately known as *Dirae*, or *The Curses*, is another, which the editors style *Lydia*, a lament for its author's separation from a woman of that name, who is also mentioned in the *Dirae*.[28] The controversy as to who really wrote these trifles is by no means settled, for the material is scanty ; a total of 180 lines, which is their combined length, does not yield very abundant internal evidence, especially as the text is very corrupt, rendering minute examination of the metre and language more uncertain than usual in its results.

All that we know of Cato shows us a very amiable man, covetous of nothing but learning, poor but apparently contented to the end of his days. Suetonius cites from Furius Bibaculus two pleasant little epigrams, in one of which the author wonders how Cato contrives to attain to such wisdom on ' three cabbages, half a pound of coarse grain and two bunches of grapes, under a single roof-tile ',[29] and another which alludes punningly to his financial difficulties. An unnamed admirer called him ' the Siren

[28] Suetonius (*loc. cit.* in n. 40) reports Cato as saying, ingenuum se natum et pupillum relictum eoque facilius licentia Sullani temporis exutum patrimonio, and quotes from Ticidas the pentameter, Lydia doctorum maxima cura liber, obviously from a context which made it clear that he meant Cato's work. Of a third poem, called *Diana*, Cinna wrote, saecula permaneat nostri Dictynna Catonis, but nothing seems to have survived from it. It is not unworthy of note that all the known or alleged subjects of Cato's poetry have close Alexandrian parallels, the *Dirae* in the *Ibis* of Kallimachos or the *'Ἀραί* of Euphorion (Rose, *H.G.L.*, p. 325, 344 n. 101), the *Lydia* in the *Lyde* of Antimachos (*ibid.*, p. 315) or the *Leontion* of Hermesianax (*ibid.*, p. 342), the *Diana* perhaps in Kallimachos' Hymn to Artemis. The text of the two poems will be found in editions of the minor pieces ascribed to Vergil, *e.g.*, R. Ellis' *Appendix Vergiliana*, in the O.C.T.

[29] Suet., *loc. cit.*, ut auctor est Bibaculus : si quis forte mei domum Catonis/depictas minio assulas et illos/custodis uidet hortulos Priapi, /miratur quibus ille disciplinis/tantam sit sapientiam assecutus,/quem tres cauliculi, selibra farris,/racemi duo tegula sub una/ad summam prope nutriant senectam. The words *illos hortulos* suggest that Cato had described his garden in some poem ; perhaps he had written Priapea (cf. p. 348). *Tegula sub una*, of course, means that his lodging was so small as to need but one tile to roof it over.

of Latium, the only reader and maker of poets'.[30] Whatever his own works may have been like, he certainly had it in him to rouse literary enthusiasm on the part of his pupils and friends.

It is therefore to be regretted that there survive only small fragments of the work of this circle, with one great exception. We know at least a few names. GAIVS LICINIVS CALVVS MACER [31] was celebrated, in his own day and also later, both as an orator and a poet. In the former capacity, we know that Cicero, who disliked his style, was fair-minded enough to allow him great abilities, only weakened by too much fastidiousness; we know also that some later critics ranked him very much higher than this.[32] His greatest speech, so far as we can judge from what others say of it,[33] was delivered in 698/56 or the year following, and was one of a series of accusations directed against Vatinius, by no means the most admirable of the partisans of Caesar. The charge was corrupt practices at an election, and it was perhaps during the delivery of this speech that Vatinius rose and asked whether he was to be condemned merely because Calvus was eloquent. This and other evidence suggests that, although Cicero may have found his speeches not very exciting reading, at least his manner of delivery did not lack vigour.[34]

As a poet, he is coupled with Catullus in a way which suggests that he was thought little or not at all inferior to him.[35] If this is so, we have much reason to regret the loss of all his works, for the few lines which survive in quotations give us no idea of his powers; some of them are graceful, one or two indicate learning of the usual recondite Alexandrian sort, two or three contain

[30] Suet, *ibid.*, Cato grammaticus, Latina Siren,/qui solus legit ac facit poetas. It is to be remembered that the Sirens of the Odyssey (xii, 188) promise not only delight but increase of knowledge to those who will listen to them.

[31] He is called as a rule simply Calvus; C. Licinius Calvus by Cicero, *Brut.*, 280; but his father was Licinius Macer the historian (cf. p. 203), Valerius Maximus, ix, 12, 7, C. Licinius Macer . . . Calui pater. Hence also Cicero, *ad Q. fratrem*, ii, 4, 1, names him Macer Licinius. To have two cognomina was not rare.

[32] Cicero, *Brut.*, 283 (Calvus was an Atticist, cf. p. 162); Quintilian, x, 1, 115, says some preferred Calvus to all others. More passages are cited, *O.R.F.*, p. 470 *sqq.* He and Cicero were on terms of friendly correspondence (fragments of it at the end of vol. iii of Cicero's letters, O.C.T.).

[33] See Tacitus, *Dial.*, 21, 4, in hominum studiosorum manibus uersantur accusationes quae in Vatinium inscribuntur, ac praecipue secunda ex eis oratio. It would seem (Schanz-Hosius, i, p. 393) that Calvus also accused Vatinius in 696/58 and a third time in 600/54.

[34] Seneca rhetor, *controu.*, vii, 4, 6; cf. Catullus, 53.

[35] As by Horace, *sat.*, i, 10, 19; Propertius, ii, 25 4, and other writers.

biting personal attacks on men of the day; all are consistent with his having been an excellent poet, but far from sufficient to prove that he was. Of his subjects, we know that he wrote a poem on the legend of Io,[36] at least one epithalamium or marriage hymn, a lament on the death of a lady called Quintilia, who perhaps was his wife,[37] and some epigrams and other light pieces. Probably the total was not large; as he was born on May 28, 672/82, and was dead by 707/47, no great output of poetry could be expected from one who took an active part in politics and wrote and published some twenty-one speeches.[38] The above facts are practically all we know of him, save that he was of low stature.[39]

FVRIVS BIBACVLVS [40] is a somewhat puzzling figure. We hear of him mostly as a writer of lampoons, *iambi* [41]; but of the few lines surviving from his works, the tender and humorous verses on Cato, already mentioned, compose the greater part. However, we are assured on good authority that Julius and Augustus Caesar treated him and Catullus with forbearance [42]; as we know the former was assailed by Catullus, it seems reasonable to suppose that Bibaculus attacked the latter, or perhaps vented his spite on both. We have also a fragment from a letter of Messalla (see p. 305), who remarks with poorly disguised pique that he wants nothing to do with 'Furius Bibaculus, nor with Ticidas

[36] There survive some half-dozen lines from it. The subject might be taken from Kallimachos, who wrote an *Arrival of Io* (presumably in Egypt), for which see Suidas *s.u.* *Καλλίμαχος*.

[37] Mentioned by Propertius, ii, 34, 89–90, haec etiam docti confessa est pagina Calui/cum caneret miserae funera Quintiliae; cf. Catullus, xcvi, 5–6. We know Calvus was married, for Diomedes, p. 37, 1 Keil, quotes from a letter of his *ad uxorem*. Still, Propertius is giving a list of poems written in celebration of mistresses, not wives (Quintilia comes between Catullus' Lesbia and Gallus' Lycoris), so the conjecture is far from certain.

[38] Birth, Pliny, *N.H.*, vii, 165; death, deduced from Cicero, *ad fam.*, xv, 21, 4, which was written in 707/47 or not much later and throughout speaks of Calvus in historical tenses, indicating that he is dead. Number of speeches, Tacitus, *dial.*, 21, 3, and Gudemann's notes thereon. Some one called Calvus wrote a work, apparently medical, *de aquae frigidae usu*, see Martial, xiv, 196: I see no reason to assume that it was this Calvus.

[39] See the passages cited in n. 34.

[40] Also written Vivaculus; *b* and *v* are much alike in many medieval hands, and our MSS. therefore constantly confuse them. Bibaculus ('little toper') seems the likelier word; many cognomina were once nicknames.

[41] As by Quintilian, x, 1, 96; Diomedes, p. 485, 17 Kiel.

[42] Tacitus, *Ann.*, iv, 34, 8.

either, nor that elementary school-teacher Cato '.[43] Catullus himself addressed four poems,[44] two friendly and two abusive, to some one called Furius, in whom there is no real difficulty in recognizing Bibaculus. Finally, Bibaculus speaks of Orbilius, who lived long enough to teach Horace, in terms which suggest that he is dead.[45]

All this suggests a man of about Catullus' own age, though probably longer-lived ; it will hardly agree with the statement of Jerome that in the year of Abraham 1914 (= 651/103), ' Marcus Furius the poet, surnamed Bibaculus ', was born at Cremona, for this makes him some twenty years older than Catullus. Nor is it very consistent with his repute as a composer of scandalous *vers d'occasion* that we have attributed to him one or two lines of what seems to have been a silly and ill-written epic. As the Furius mentioned above, p. 87, must have been a good deal older than this and was called Aulus, not Marcus, we apparently must distinguish three writers of the same clan, Aulus Furius the friend of Catulus, MARCVS FVRIVS BIBACVLVS (?),[46] whose one claim to remembrance is that Horace made fun of him, and Furius Bibaculus (praenomen unknown) Catullus' contemporary, possibly the son or nephew of the poetaster.

Another member of Catullus, own circle was a poet, apparently of some merit, called GAIVS HELVIVS CINNA, whose chief work was an *epyllion* or miniature epic in the Alexandrian style dealing with the misfortunes of Smyrna, otherwise Myrrha.[47] The immortality which Catullus promised it has not been its portion ; we have three lines and one stray word left. Another poem was one of good wishes to Asinius Pollio (p. 307) (*Propempticon*) [48] when the latter was setting out on a journey to Greece, perhaps

[43] Suet, *op. cit.*, 4, non esse sibi dicens rem cum Furio Bibaculo, ne cum Ticida quidem aut litteratore Catone. Suetonius, who tries to make out that *litterator* here means *litteratus* (= *grammaticus*), spoils the effect of a taunt which recurs in a different context, Catullus, xiv, 9, where see Ellis.

[44] Catullus, xi and xxvi (friendly), xvi and xxii (abusive).

[45] Frag. 4/3, F.P.L., Orbilius ubinam est, litterarum obliuio ? It need not, of course, mean that he is dead, but might refer to an absence.

[46] Horace, *sat.*, ii, 5, 41, Furius hibernas cana niue conspuet Alpis ; the ancient commentators there say he is alluding to an absurd verse of Furius, Iuppiter . . . conspuit, &c., ' Jove bespews the wintry Alps with snow.' Jerome may be wrong as to the cognomen, owing to a confusion with the iambographer.

[47] Best known from Catullus, xcv, who says it took nine years to write and will be ' thumbed by hoary centuries ' (Zmyrnam cana diu saecula peruoluent). See commentators there ; the story is in Rose, *H.G.M.*, p. 124 *sq.* For epyllia, see Rose, *H.G.L.*, p. 321.

[48] Pollio was in Greece then, as appears from Cicero, *ad fam.*, i, 6, 1, written at that time.

in 698/56. Both were very obscure poems, designedly so, which is again a feature of some of the Alexandrians, and both had learned commentaries written on their difficulties, respectively mythological and geographical, the former by Lucius Crassicius, the latter by Julius Hyginus (see pp. 422, 445).[49] Unlike most of his circle, Cinna became a supporter of Caesar, and was tribune of the plebs the year of his leader's assassination. Then befell that event which has made him one of the best known of Roman writers to the average English reader, for he was that 'Cinna the poet' whom the mob killed at Caesar's funeral by mistake for Cinna the conspirator.[50] His reputation outlived him, for not only did Vergil, in 717/37, think him a model too high for himself yet to equal, but he had his fervid admirers in Martial's time.[51]

Of the same school and age were a few others, scarcely known to us by more than their names. We have already had occasion to mention TICIDAS, or TICIDA, but must confess we do not know who he was; the name he used can hardly have been his own. We learn from Appuleius that he wrote love-poetry addressed to a certain Metella, whom he called Perilla[52]; it is therefore possible, but no more, that he is that son of Aesopus the actor (in which case Claudius Aesopus was his real name) who, according to Horace, also loved a Metella and was extravagant in his demonstrations of affection.[53] Of the public career of QVINTVS CORNIFICIVS, or CORNVFICIVS, we know rather more; he was praetor in 707/47 or 709/45, held several posts in the provinces, won some distinction as a soldier, left the Caesarian for the senatorial party in

[49] Suetonius, *op. cit.*, 18, names Crassicius; Charisius, p. 134, 12 Keil, quotes Hyginus.

[50] Shakespere, *Julius Caesar*, iii, 3, derived from Plutarch, *Caesar*, 68, and *Brutus*, 19, cf. Appian, *de bell. ciu.*, ii, 147, Suetonius, *Iulius*, 85. The text assumes, what is not certain, that the reading in Plutarch is sound.

[51] Verg., *Ecl.*, ix, 35–6; Martial, x, 21, 3–4 (to an affectedly obscure writer), non lectore tuis opus est, sed Apolline libris;/iudice te maior Cinna Marone fuit (because Cinna was obscure, Vergil comparatively easy to understand).

[52] Apul., *Apol.*, 10: eadem igitur opera accusent C. Catullum, quod Lesbiam pro Clodia nominarit, et Ticidam similiter, quod quae Metella erat Perillam scripserit, et Propertium, qui Cynthiam dicat, Hostiam dissimulet, et Tibullum, quo ei sit Plania in animo, Delia in uorsu. Cf. Ovid, *trist.*, ii, 433 *sqq.*

[53] Horace, *sat.*, ii, 3, 239: filius Aesopi detractam ex aure Metellae, /scilicet ut decies solidum absorberet, aceto/diluit insignem bacam. The suggestion that this is Ticidas' Metella is due to Tenney Frank in *Class. Rev.*, xxxiv (1920), pp. 91–3. This Metella was a notorious figure of the Roman 'smart set' of the day, a woman of good family and apparently no moral sense whatever. Claudius Aesopus was a thorough-going spendthrift of whom various stories were told.

710/44, being then governor of one of the African provinces, and two years later was deserted by his soldiers and killed in hostilities with the governor of the neighbouring province, who supported the triumvirs.[54] But of his poetry we know very little. Catullus mentions him as a friend,[55] several later writers speak of his verse, and we have left one line and part of another. Jerome says that he had a sister who made a name for herself as a writer of epigrams.[56] Another friend of Catullus was CAECILIVS, of whom we know, on Catullus' testimony, three facts, that he lived in Comum, that he began (we do not even know if he finished it) a poem about Kybele, and that an unnamed girl much admired him.[57] That Memmius dabbled in verse has already been mentioned (p. 123).

After so many lost poets, we come to one of the greatest names in Latin literature, despite his small bulk. A fortunate discovery, early in the fourteenth century, of a MS. whereof we have several more or less good copies, has put us in possession of what seems to be nearly the whole work of GAIVS VALERIVS CATVLLVS,[58]

[54] References in Schanz-Hosius, i, p. 309.

[55] Catullus, xxxviii, is addressed to him.

[56] Jerome on *an. Abr.* 1976 (= 713/41) : Cornificius poeta a militibus desertus interiit quos saepe fugientes galeatos lepores appellarat ; huius soror CORNIFICIA cuius insignia exstant epigrammata. A probable reading in Ovid, *trist.*, ii, 436, makes him mention *leue Cornifici opus*.

[57] Catullus, xxxv ; lxvii is a humorous dialogue between Catullus and the door of a house into which Caecilius has recently moved.

[58] It is not certain that his name was Gaius ; a respectable MS. tradition in Pliny, *N.H.*, xxxvii, 81, calls him Q. Catullus ; some of the least bad of his own MSS. agree ; and a very doubtful passage in one of his poems, lxvii, 12, in which the door of Caecilius' new house is addressing him, would be helped out if we could suppose, with Scaliger, that the true reading is *ianua, Quinte, facit*, for the meaningless *qui te* of the MSS. On the other hand, the MSS. of Pliny are divided, many giving simply *Catullus*, not *Q. Catullus* (one has *n̄ Catulus*). Not much can be argued from the MSS. of Catullus himself, especially as before their archetype was written there had been time enough to confuse the poet with Quintus Catulus the general. We may add that St. Jerome's MSS. write out *Gaius* in full (one has the obvious corruption *Gallus*), and as the word comes between *quendam* and *Valerius* there is no question of this being an expansion of an accidentally repeated *c*, whereas Pliny's *Q.* might well be nothing but the preceding word, *quem* (written abbreviatedly), copied twice by mistake. It is of less importance that Apuleius, *Apol.*, 10 (cited in n. 52), calls him *C. Catullus*, for a like mistake is very easy here. On the whole, the balance of probability is in favour of Gaius, chiefly because that is not the *praenomen* of Catulus, with whom Catullus is frequently confused in writing.

For the MS. tradition, see the introductions to the modern editions of C., as Ellis or Kroll. The literature concerning him is large, and lists of some of the principal books and articles will be found in Schanz-Hosius, i, p. 292 *sqq*. The reason for supposing that we have nearly all that he wrote, apart from the unlikelihood of his having pro-

116 poems of lengths varying from two to 408 lines. These are enough to show that he, above all others of Latin tongue, had mastered the best lesson of the Alexandrians, the art of exquisitely expressing personal feeling. That he was able to profit by this to an extent which his masters never did, rivalling thereby the Aiolic lyricists and obtaining for himself a supreme place in that form of poetry so far as Latin literature is concerned, and a very high one even if the greatest masters of self-revelation in all countries are matched against him, is due a little to his not having confined himself to even the best of the Alexandrians, but gone also to Sappho for inspiration. It is due in much greater measure to a circumstance such as no historian of literature can account for, his own possession by intense emotion, quickened with the impulse to make it known in an artistic form.

Catullus had no public life; his contribution to politics was simply that he, like Furius Bibaculus (p. 135), lampooned Caesar and the Caesarians. Of his private career we know this much. He was born, according to Jerome, *an. Abr.* 1930, *i.e.*, 667/87,[59] and died in his thirtieth year, in 696/58. But this latter date cannot be correct, for Catullus himself mentions events later, though not much later, than that year.[60] His native place was Verona in Cisalpine Gaul, which fact has given rise to much speculation as to the effect which Keltic blood, a perfectly possible

duced much more in his short life, is that we have very few citations from him which cannot be readily assigned to the existing poems (one or two may be from passages lost in our MSS., which certainly present gaps in several places).

[59] Or a year earlier; the assignment of events to dates is not always perfectly certain in Jerome, and the MSS. vary a little here.

[60] In lii, 2, Nonius (probably tribune of the plebs in 698/56) sits *sella in curuli*, therefore has gone on to some other magistracy, perhaps the aedileship. (Nothing can be made of the next line, per consulatum peierat Vatinius; V. was indeed consul in 707/47, but he might easily have sworn *ita consul fiam* before that, cf. Plautus, *Poen.*, 420, perque tuam leibertatem 'by your hopes of enfranchisement'; Cicero, *ad Att.*, xvi, 15, 3, Octavian swears ita sibi parentis honores consequi liceat; Statius, *Theb.*, xi, 708, felicia per te/regna, verende Creon, which must mean 'by your hopes of a prosperous reign', since Kreon has been king but a few days; pseudo-Kallisthenes, ii, 9, 7, p. 75, 26 Kroll, Alexander swears by *τὴν ἐπάνοδον τὴν ἐν Μακεδονίᾳ γινομένην μοι*, *i.e.*, by his hopes of a safe return.) In lv, 6, C. looks for a friend *in Magni ambulatione*, meaning the portico of Pompey, erected in 699/55, see Platner-Ashby, p. 428; cxiii, 2, Pompey is consul for the second time (same year); xi, 12 and xxix, 4, allusions to Caesar's British campaigns point, at the very earliest, to the end of the same year. Common sense suggests that some one, either Suetonius or an authority on whom he drew, had said that Catullus was *about* thirty when he died, and chronologizing zeal made the rough estimate into the semblance of an exact one.

thing in that district, may have had on his temperament and genius.[61] He was poor, according to himself.[62] Leaving Verona, we do not know when but can guess that the reason was to join in the intellectual and literary life of the capital, he made the acquaintance of Cato's circle, perhaps studied under Cato himself.[63] At least equally important was another acquaintance, with the woman whom he calls Lesbia. There can be little doubt that this is Clodia, sister of P. Clodius, Cicero's enemy.[64] She was one of the most brilliant and fascinating women of that day, and also one of the most completely unscrupulous and immoral. How they first met, what attracted her in Catullus, and how long the affair lasted are controversial points among those who love to research into the unknowable; in 697/57 he was sufficiently heart-whole to leave Rome and go to Bithynia, then governed by Memmius (cf. p. 123), in hopes of mending his fortunes. In this he was disappointed, for Memmius apparently kept what plunder there was to be got from the unfortunate provincials in his own hands and those of his immediate staff.[65] While in the Levant, Catullus went on a sad errand to the Troad, where his brother, apparently but lately dead, was buried.[66] He sailed home, it would appear, in a yacht (*phaselus*), which he immortalized in an exquisite little poem, dedicating it to the patrons of seafarers, Castor and Pollux.[67] How much longer he lived, and

[61] That he was born in Verona is certain, as there are several mentions of it, the earliest in Ovid, *amores*, iii, 15, 7. In the present state of ethnological knowledge, I prefer not to go into speculations concerning the effect of Keltic descent.

[62] See xiii, 7, tui Catulli/plenus sacculus est araneorum; xxvi, his country cottage (*uillula*) is mortgaged. This is not to be taken as signifying real poverty. He owned the *uillula*, lived usually in Rome (lxviii, 34), whether in his own house or a hired one, had a good-sized library (*ibid.*, 36) in an age when books were dear, and sailed home in his own yacht, see n. 67. The fact probably is that he had been left master of a moderate fortune and lived consistently beyond his income.

[63] Some one called Cato is addressed, lvi, 1, 3, and bidden to laugh at an exceedingly improper story. This is most likely Valerius Cato, though conceivably it is an attempt to shock the very moral Cato of Utica. No mention of studying under any one occurs, nor is Cato the addressee of any other poem.

[64] This is definitely asserted by Apuleius (cf. n. 52) and supported by cogent parallels between what C. says of Lesbia and what is known of Clodia in Ellis, vol. ii, pp. lxiii–lxxii.

[65] This one may gather from Catullus xxviii.

[66] This is the subject of that most beautiful little lament, No. 101 of Catullus' poems.

[67] Catullus, iv, further distinguished by being written in pure iambics, a great *tour de force* in such a language as Latin, which abounds in long syllables.

if he saw anything more of Clodia, is not known; certainly his love for her had turned into disgust and hatred by the time the intrigue was over. It may be that his grief for her utter unworthiness shortened his life. Some time, probably towards the end of his days, he published his poems, or a part of them,[68] with a graceful dedication to Cornelius Nepos (p. 208) the historian.

As we have them, whoever may have arranged them, his poems fall into three groups. The first, which is lyrical, contains the greater part of his addresses to Lesbia-Clodia. It is at least very likely that No. 51 comes early in this series; it is an imitation of one of Sappho's surviving odes and consists of a description of the poet's almost fainting rapture at the sight of the beloved. Nos. 2 and 3 are playful trifles, one an ode to a *passer* (conventionally called a sparrow, but 'throstle' is more nearly correct) which was Lesbia's pet, the other, No. 3, a lament for its death. No. 36 is also playful; he and Lesbia are reconciled after a quarrel, and, in gratitude, she is making a novel sacrifice to Venus, of the works of the worst poet she knows; Catullus calls him Volusius. Nos. 5 and 7 are outbursts of wild amorous passion; Catullus is obviously Lesbia's favoured lover. Several poems attack her; the affair may have survived such assaults as No. 8, in which he is resolved to leave her, but certainly not No. 58, in which he calls her a street-walker, and that in the coarsest of language.

In the second division of poems come all the longest compositions. No. 61 is a most lovely epithalamium, Greek in metre and spirit but describing the Roman ritual of weddings and therefore sometimes called the 'Latin epithalamium' to distinguish it from the next poem, which is in hexameters, implies the Greek rite, and seems to be wholly a work of the imagination, certainly owing something to Sappho,[69] whereas the other, which is in a lyric metre, glyconics grouped into short stanzas, each ending with a pherecratic,[70] celebrates the wedding of real persons, the

[68] The first poem refers to the collection as a *libellus*, which is a small word for a volume containing 2,276 lines (not counting the passages, of unknown length, which have been lost), and its contents as *nugae*; but the *Peleus and Thetis* (No. 64) is hardly a trifle. Both words would fit the short lyrics (in all 809 lines, say 900 at most originally, and probably less than that) far better.

[69] Certainly the lovely description of virginity in lxii, 39–47 (the original of Gay's song, 'Virgins are like the fair flower', in the *Beggar's Opera*), has a flavour of Sappho; cf. her frags. 116, 117 in Diehl, *Anthologia Lyrica*.

[70] A glyconic line consists of two syllables of indeterminate quantity (never, however, both short in Catullus, while in Horace they are both invariably long) forming the so-called Aeolic base, followed by a choriam-

bridegroom being called Mallius, the bride Iunia Aurunculeia. They are unknown to us, but manifestly friends of Catullus. No. 63 is a most extraordinary and brilliant performance; it tells the story of Attis' self-mutilation,[71] in a metre extremely difficult to handle, especially in Latin, which is deficient in the short syllables it requires, known as the galliambic, after the Galli, or eunuch priests of Kybele.[72] No. 64 is an epyllion, having for its framework the nuptials of Peleus and Thetis, but for its main episode a different story altogether, the tale of Theseus and Ariadne, which occupies 214 lines out of 408 and is introduced in a manner somewhat novel, by making it the subject of a tapestry in Peleus' house.[73]

The third part of the collection consists of poems in elegiacs, a metre in which Catullus shows less mastery than in any other, though his powers of language and poetical phraseology seem little hampered by this defect; perhaps, indeed probably, he was himself unaware of it, since it was left to the Augustans to fit this very subtle measure perfectly to Latin cadences. Most of the elegies are brief, some consisting of but one couplet, and therefore rather to be called epigrams. Some of these concern Lesbia, one of the very finest, No. 76, being a prayer that he may forget her, and another, 85, summing up the whole of his heartbreak in two lines which have nothing to distinguish them from prose save their metre and their supreme poetry.[74] One, No. 68, obviously dating from an early stage of the intrigue, is a poetical letter of thanks to a friend, Allius, who had lent his house for a meeting of the lovers. This is one of his longest poems (160 lines), and contains perhaps his most unfortunate excursion into mythology, for he elaborately compares Clodia to

bus (– ᴗ ᴗ –) and an iambus (ᴗ –), as *non diu remoratus es*; *qui uostri numerare uolt*. A pherecratic is the same, but lacking the second syllable of the iambus, as *compararier ausit*; *Hymen o Hymenaee*.

[71] See, for the legend, Rose, *H.G.M.*, p. 170.

[72] The fundamental foot is the *ionicus a minore* (ᴗ ᴗ – –). But this is freely modified, not only by the common licences of putting two short syllables for one long, or one long for two short, but also by anaclasis, a curious irregularity by which the long final syllable of one ionic and the short initial one of the next change places, thus, ᴗ ᴗ – ᴗ – ᴗ – –. Hence we get lines so apparently different as *face cuncta mugienti fremitu loca retonent* and *iam iam dolet quod egi, iam iamque paenitet*.

[73] Greek furnishes us with something like a parallel, the epyllion of *Herakles the Lion-slayer*, No. 25 in the Theokritean collection; its authorship is doubtful. In this, Herakles, arriving at the country of Augeas, meets the latter's son, Phyleus, and in reply to a question from him tells the story of how he killed the Nemean lion.

[74] It runs: Odi et amo: quare id faciam, fortasse requiris./nescio, sed fieri sentio et excrucior.

Laodamia, of all inappropriate heroines, the light-of-love to the most faithful and affectionate of wives.[75] Another effort of some importance, dating from after Catullus' return from the East, as the poem (No. 65) which serves as a sort of covering letter to it, shows, is No. 66, a fairly close translation, to judge by what we have left of the original, of Kallimachos' *Lock of Berenike.*[76]

The above are the subjects of some of the most important poems; there are also scurrilous lampoons, political, as 57, or directed against private enemies of the poet, as 69; there are merry little jests, as 84, the famous account of a man, most appropriately called Arrius, who misplaced his h's; there are exquisite trifles, as 45, the description of a love-scene between Septimius, clearly an acquaintance of the poet, and his mistress Acme.[77] And there are a few scraps of unmixed filth, sometimes excused, if it is ever excusable for such a master of polished invective to stoop so low, by the obvious fact that Catullus was very angry when he wrote them. It may be mentioned in conclusion that, whereas Lucretius keeps much of his dignity and eloquence in a good translation, no one has yet succeeded in making anything like an adequate version of Catullus into any other language.

Much though his most fervent admirers regretted the fact and his adverse critics made capital of it, a not unimportant name among the verse-makers of this age is that of CICERO, whose prose works will be handled later (p. 156 *sqq.*). It may be said briefly that he had all the technical qualifications necessary for a good poet, wide reading, metrical skill, perfect mastery of language and a generally faultless ear. What he lacked was simply the higher gifts which differentiate the poet from the versifier.[78] In particular, he never was able to see the profound difference between poetry and vigorous, impassioned rhetoric, and the result was that when he attempted flights beyond the scope of prose, his taste deserted him and he wrote flat or bombastic nonsense. Still, if we may trust Plutarch,[79] he had for a time the reputation

[75] For her legend, cf. Rose, *H.G.M.*, p. 233.

[76] For this, cf. Rose, *H.G.L.*, p. 321; E. A. Barber in *Greek Poetry and Life* (Oxford, 1936), pp. 343–63; Kallimachos, frag. 110 Pfeiffer.

[77] For elucidation, see Rose in *Harvard Studies*, vol. xlvii, p. 1 *sq.*

[78] The most famous criticism of his verses is that of Juvenal, x, 122 *sqq.*: 'o fortunatam natam me consule Romam';/Antoni gladios potuit contemnere, si sic/omnia dixisset. The allusion in *gladios contemnere* is to the admirable peroration of the second Philippic, 118, contempsi Catilinae gladios, non pertimescam tuos. The first verse is probably from the *de consulatu*. For more examples, see Schanz-Hosius, i, p. 538.

[79] Plutarch, *Cicero*, 2, *οὐ μόνον ῥήτωρ ἀλλὰ καὶ ποιητὴς ἄριστος εἶναι Ῥωμαίων.*

of the best poet of his day. He began young with a mythological subject, *Glaukos of the Sea* (*Glaucus Pontius*; the story is in Ovid) [80] and followed it with others, from one of which, *The Halcyons* (again Ovid was to tell the tale later and no doubt much better),[81] there survives a pretty fragment, in hexameters; another, whose title is doubtfully restored as *Thalia maesta* (*The Grief of Thalia*),[82] was in elegiacs. The life of his great fellow-townsman Marius provided him with a theme for a historical poem named after that excellent soldier and ruinously bad politician[83]; and in an evil hour, he put his own exploits into verse, in two books *On my Consulship* (*de consulatu meo*) and a poem called apparently *de temporibus meis*. The passage from the former which his own vanity has preserved for us [84] inspires no great sorrow that the rest is lost, together with its companion piece and a separate poem on Caesar's British campaign of 700/54, whereof nothing seems to have survived.[85] Perhaps rather more to be regretted is his *Limon*, *i.e.*, *Λειμών*, 'the Meadow',[86] which, to judge from the one fragment we have of it, a criticism of Terence, was a review of Latin poetry, or Latin literature generally. Yet all these works seem to have been, from the purely metrical point of view, that is to say regarded simply

[80] Plut., *loc. cit.*, *καί τι καὶ ποιημάτιον ἔτι παιδὸς αὐτοῦ διασώζεται Πόντιος Γλαῦκος, ἐν τετραμέτρῳ πεποιημένον* (written in trochaic tetrameters). The titles of his other mythological pieces are rather obscure, and I have given only those of which quotations survive or which are named by good authors. The *Historia Augusta* (see p. 514) says that the emperor Gordian I in his youth poemata scripsit, quae omnia exstant, et quidem cuncta illa quae Cicero, id est Marium et Aratum et Halcyonas et Vxorium et Nilum (*Hist. Aug.*, xx, 3, 2); but I should hesitate to make any positive statement on an obscure point with no better authority. For the story of Glaukos, the fisherman who was turned into a merman, see Ovid., *Met.*, xiii, 905 *sqq*.

[81] Frag. 1, F.P.L., preserved by Nonius, p. 65, 8: Cicero Alcyonibus; hunc genuit claris delapsus ab astris/praeuius Aurorae, solis noctisque satelles. See Ovid, *Met.*, xi, 270 *sqq.*; Rose, *H.G.M.*, p. 257.

[82] Frag. 21/3; Servius on Verg., Ecl., i, 57, Cicero in elegia quae talia masta (talia in asta, talamasta) inscribitur. There have been several conjectures as to the title.

[83] The chief fragment, 19/7, is quoted by Cicero himself, *de diuin.*, i, 106.

[84] Frag. 3/11, also from the *de diuin.*, i, 17–22. For the other poem, see especially *ad Q. fratrem*, iii, 1, 24, mirificum embolium excogito in secundum librum meorum temporum ('an admirable episode to insert into Book 2 of my *de temporibus*').

[85] He mentions it several times in letters to his brother, then serving with Caesar: see *ad Q. fratrem*, ii, 13, 2; iii, 1, 11; 8, 3; 9, 6.

[86] This was a not uncommon Greek title for a miscellaneous work; see Pliny, *N.H.*, i, *praef.*, 23.

as an arrangement of Latin words in harmonious verse, very far from contemptible, marking a distinct advance in the technique of the hexameter; we have not enough of his elegiacs to pronounce on them. Therefore it is not surprising to learn that when he had to find words and verses only, not ideas, his performances were of some value. In his youth, he translated part of the inexplicably popular poem of Aratos [87] on the celestial and meteoric phenomena, and of this a good deal survives to us, generally called *Aratea* (*carmina*). The remainder of the work, dealing with weather-signs and sometimes printed under a separate title in modern editions, he apparently rendered into Latin a good deal later, in or about 694/60,[88] under the title *Prognostica*. Of this we have merely a few quotations. A comparison of the remains with the original Greek suggests that in his schoolboy effort he omitted some things which he did not fully understand and felt at liberty slightly to modify others, while his more mature work departed so far from Aratos as to be more a paraphrase than a translation.[89] The various renderings of shorter passages from Greek poets which occur in sundry of his prose works generally have merit as free and spirited representations of the original, though not always very correct. There existed also in antiquity a collection of epigrams by Cicero, the surviving specimens of which do not give a high opinion of his capabilities in a medium demanding a lighter touch than his.[90]

All the group of poets just described, both Cicero and those whom he contemptuously classed as 'singers of Euphorion',[91] were influenced by one school of Alexandrians, that of which Kallimachos was the centre. Since, however, this was not the only Alexandrian group, it is not surprising that Kallimachos'

[87] For Aratos and his work, see Rose, *H.G.L.*, p. 326 *sqq*. Cicero's youthful version is mentioned and quoted from *de nat. deor.*, ii, 104.

[88] See *ad Att.*, ii, 1, 11, Prognostica mea . . . propediem expecta (June 694/60); the only natural explanation seems to be that he is just finishing it and will send Atticus a copy.

[89] If we compare, *e.g.*, *Arat.*, 47 (281)–54(288) (C. F. W. Müller's numbering, in the last vol. of his Teubner edition of Cicero, which collects all the poetical fragments very conveniently) with the original, Aratos 274–81, it is apparent that Aratos 278, a pretty but difficult line, is not represented. For the *Prognostica*, if the fragment preserved in *de diuin.*, i, 13–15, is put beside Aratos, especially 946 *sqq.*, we find Cicero tacitly correcting a rather silly expression in the original, by calling frogs *aquai dulcis alumnae*, where Aratos could think of nothing better than πατέρες γυρίνων, 'fathers of tadpoles'.

[90] The remains are in Müller, *op. cit.*, pp. 414–15.

[91] *Cantores Euphorionis*, Cicero, *Tusc.*, iii, 45. For Apollonios and his controversy with Kallimachos, see Rose, *H.G.L.*, p. 323 *sqq*.

opponent, Apollonios of Rhodes, also found a Latin imitator, apparently a very tolerable writer. This was PVBLIVS TERENTIVS VARRO of Atax in the province of Gallia Narbonensis (the modern Provence), usually called after his birthplace Atacinus, to distinguish him from the better-known Varro of Reate (p. 220 *sqq.*). He was born in 672/82,[92] and tried his hand at several kinds of composition. As an author of satires, he met with little success, according to Horace[93]; he wrote a poem of geographical content, called *Chorographia*, to which ten fragments are with more or less certainty referred[94]; an isolated mention of a work called *Epimenides* has raised doubts as to whether the title was not really *Ephemeris* and also which of the Varros wrote it[95]; Propertius and Ovid say that he wrote elegies in honour of a mistress called Leucadia, apparently fairly late in his career, and Priscian cites a hexameter from a work of his called *Bellum Sequanicum*, apparently a chronicle-epic after Ennius' manner[96]; but the poem of which we are least ignorant was a translation, apparently free and in good verses, of the *Argonautica* of Apollonios. Of this there remain about a dozen quotations, including three or four exceedingly good lines.[97] It is to be regretted that we have no more of him.

[92] Jerome on *an. Abr.* 1935, P. Terentius Varro uico Atace in prouincia Narbonensi nascitur qui postea xxxv annum agens Graecas litteras cum summo studio didicit. That he knew no Greek till he was thirty-five is most unlikely, but the statement may rest on evidence that he translated Apollonios at that age.

[93] Horace, *sat.*, i, 10, 46–7: hoc (satire) erat, experto frustra Varrone Atacino/atque quibusdam aliis, melius quod scribere possem.

[94] Charisius quotes a line describing the boundaries of some district in Africa: cingitur Oceano, Libyco mare, flumine Nilo (p. 61, 9 Keil); and that there was a work by him called *Chorographia* is indicated by Priscian, ii, p. 100, 14 Keil, Varro in chorographia; but his MSS. agree only in *-graphia* (or *-grafia*) and leave the first two syllables very doubtful. Frags. in *P.L.F.*, pp. 334–5/93–9.

[95] In the *breuis expositio Vergilii Georgicorum* included in the last volume of Thilo and Hagen's Servius (see Bibliography), p. 265, 3; Varro in Epimenide: nubes sicut uellera lanae constabunt. It is easy to make this into verse by reading *ceu* (Baehrens), or *ut*, for *sicut*. For conjectures as to what the title really was and which Varro wrote the work, see Hagen's critical note *ad loc.* and Schanz-Hosius, i, p. 313.

[96] Propertius, ii, 34, 85: haec quoque perfecto ludebat Iasone Varro, /Varro Leucadiae maxima flamma suae; *i.e.*, he wrote elegies after he had finished his translation of Apollonios. Ovid also mentions him, *trist.*, ii, 449, among amatory writers. Priscian, ii, p. 497, 10 Keil: P. Varro belli Sequanici libro II; deinde ubi pellicuit dulcis leuis unda sapores.

[97] See F.P.L., p. 332 *sqq.*/93 *sqq.* The original passages are generally easily recognized.

There is just a trace of the influence of Theokritos and his imitators, which was to be much more important in later times. Macrobius has heard of some one called SVEIVS, author of what he calls an idyll, entitled *Moretum* (*The Salad*; cf. p. 264). He cites eight clumsy hexameters,[98] which, after directing some one to add walnuts (*Persicae nuces*) to his other ingredients, go on to explain why they are called Persian. A series of not improbable conjectures, which substitute his name for some meaningless letters, would make this Sueius the author also of a poem in trochaic tetrameters dealing with fowls and entitled *Pulli*. Such works might be the result of a not very happy attempt to combine sketches of country life with miscellaneous information.[99] Finally either Sueius or some one with a name resembling his [100] is cited twice for epic phrases.

Two or three very minor names remain to be mentioned. Among the murderers of Caesar was a certain CASSIVS PARMENSIS, not to be confused with the better-known Cassius, who wrote elegies and epigrams.[101] One line is casually quoted by a grammarian from an otherwise unknown VOLVMNIVS.[102] Another name or two can be collected from inscriptions, but mean nothing to us.

Meanwhile the stage, though past its great days, was not dead but merely degenerate. While tragedies and comedies were apparently no longer written, or composed only as closet-dramas,[103] the old Atellane farces enjoyed popularity and found exponents of some ability. LVCIVS POMPONIVS of Bononia (the modern Bologna; hence he is called Bononiensis) has left us titles of some seventy farces, whereof some contain the names of the old stock

[98] Macrobius, *sat.*, iii, 18, 10.

[99] Nonius, p. 139, 27 (where the MSS. have *suis*), 513, 20 (*ueius* the MSS.), 72, 24 (MSS. *uaeius*).

[100] Macrobius, *sat.*, vi, 1, 37 (*sueuius* MS.), 5, 15 (MS. *sue*jus*).

[101] Horace, *epp.*, i, 4, 3; the ancient commentators there give some particulars of his life and writings.

[102] In Keil's *Grammatici Latini*, vol. v, p. 574, 1. It is a hendecasyllable, stridentis dabitur patella cymae. It seems just conceivable that this Volumnius, of whom absolutely nothing is known, is the same as the Volusius of Catullus, xxxvi and xcv, 7, who informs us that he was a very bad poet, from the district of the Po, who had written a poem called *Annales*, fit only for wrapping-paper or even less dignified uses. He may have tried his hand at lighter verse also, and the names are sufficiently alike for confusion to be possible; but this is mere conjecture.

[103] The Horatian scholiasts quoted in n. 101 say that when Cassius Parmensis was put to death by Varius (see p. 340) the latter found a tragedy, *Thyestes*, among his papers and passed it off for his own. This is but one of several indications that plays, or at least poems in dramatic form, were written in that age; but that any of them were acted there is no proof.

figures, Maccus, Pappus, Dossennus, Bucco (cf. p. 24), others those of trades or regions (*Fullones*, the Fullers; *Galli Transalpini*, and others), one or two suggest mock-heroics (*Armorum Iudicium*; the language of the one surviving fragment would suit such a theme, for it runs

> tum prae se portant ascendibilem semitam
> quam scalam uocitant.

> 'And in their hands they bear a climbing way
> Which men step-ladder call.')

Another has a title suggestive of New Comedy, *Synephebi* (*Young Friends*); another is called frankly *The Brothel* (*Prostibulum*), and what survives of it contains language not distinguished for delicacy. What we know of his life is not much. He was famous (*clarus habetur*) in *an. Abr.* 1928, or 665/89, according to Jerome, which agrees well enough with Cicero's mention of him, in 710/44, as *Pomponius noster*,[104] suggesting that he knew or had known him. Velleius Paterculus [105] says that he had little stylistic merit but his wit was good and he was the inventor of his *genre*. This is certainly not literally true; but it is quite possible that Pomponius was the first to write out these farces in full and set his actors to learn them, instead of sketching a scenario and leaving the rest to the players' own inspiration, as with the *improvisatori* of a much later date. He is also accused of having invented some kind of punning, apparently like the modern 'back-chat' in which one speaker uses a word and the other takes it in a wrong meaning; it is added that Laberius (see p. 151) imitated him, and so Cicero picked it up and made it into an excellence instead of a defect.[106] Another and obscurer name is that of NOVIVS. Either Cicero commits an anachronism when he cites him in the *de oratore*, the dramatic date of which is 665/91, or this man was already writing somewhat before the year at which Pomponius became famous.[107] At all events, there

[104] Cicero, *ad fam.*, vii, 31, 2.

[105] Vell. Pat., ii, 9, 3: Pomponium sensibus celebrem, uerbis rudem et nouitate inuenti a se operis commendabilem.

[106] Seneca Rhetor, *contr.*, vii, 3, 9: auctorem huius uiti quod ex captione unius uerbi plura significantis aiebat (Cassius Seuerus) Pomponium Atellanarum scriptorem fuisse. There are such jokes in Pomponius, as frag. 10 Ribbeck; Bucco, puriter ('holily' or 'cleanly')/fac ut rem tractes.—laui iamdudum manus. But they are common enough in Plautus.

[107] He is quoted, *de orat.*, ii, 255, 279, 285, for examples of various humorous turns of phrase; but an anachronism of a few years in a dialogue would not be surprising, Plato himself being a notable offender in this kind.

is no reason to suppose that there was much difference between them in time. Of Novius we have some forty-five titles, and the remains of the plays suggest that in plots, manner and style he was not unlike Pomponius.

We hear of a few other writers of Atellanae. Athenaios has read that SVLLA wrote 'satyr-comedies in his native tongue', which if it is not a misunderstanding of some reference to his having attempted satire might possibly mean something like Atellanae.[108] Some one whose name the MSS. give in the improbable form APRISSIVS is cited by Varro for a line in which Bucco is mentioned; this would suit an Atellane very well. Finally, Macrobius says that MVMMIVS (otherwise unknown to us) revived this form of composition after it had been long neglected, therefore presumably under the Empire and quite possibly as a mere literary pastime, not intended to be acted.[109]

A more novel form of drama was the mime (*mimus*; the word means both the play and the player). As the name denotes, this is a Greek invention, and Greek literature contains some notable examples of it, besides others which now are unhappily lost to us; the chief names are Sophron, in the fifth century B.C., and Herodas in the third.[110] We know also that there were some Italian writers of it. It signifies, in Greek literary usage, a sketch in dramatic form, portraying some scene of everyday life. In Rome, it would appear that it was regularly a little play, which may well have been its original form, for there is some evidence of stage-mimes not only at Alexandria[111] but on the Greek mainland,[112] besides the literary works already mentioned, which may not have been intended for public performance. These

[108] Athen., 261 c, among the evidences of Sulla's fondness for the ridiculous are *αἱ ὑπ' αὐτοῦ γραφεῖσαι σατυρικαὶ κωμῳδίαι τῇ πατρίῳ φωνῇ*. The phrase is so odd in itself that it sounds like an attempt on the part of Athenaios' authority, Nikolaos of Damascus, to render something in Latin which he did not understand. It seems to recur only in Iohannes Lydus, *de magistr.*, i, 41, in which passage that late and puzzle-headed writer is trying to give an account of satire from Lucilius onward. I am not convinced by the remarks of Kerényi, *Studi e materiali*, 1933/xi, p. 148.

[109] Macrobius, *sat.*, i, 10, 3. In Varro (*de ling. Lat.*, vi, 68), Aprissius ait: Io Bucco! the name has been suspected and variously emended by a number of scholars.

[110] For these writers, see Rose, *H.G.L.*, pp. 252, 339 *sq.*

[111] For a surviving example, see *op. cit.*, p. 347. It is, of course, not certain that the curious little farce there described would be called a mime by the Alexandrians.

[112] A terra-cotta lamp, of date earlier than 200 B.C., found at Athens, has on it three unmasked figures, with an inscription running as follows, if we neglect some misspellings: *μιμολόγοι. ἡ ὑπόθεσις, ἑκυρά*, *i.e.*, 'Performers of a mime; theme, "His wife's mother".' Clearly they

plays were farcical, very commonly indecent, and had two outstanding peculiarities, one that the actors were unmasked, the other that the female parts were taken by women.[113] It is in this period that we first hear of them, and the names of two notable composers of such plays are recorded. The better known is PVBLILIVS SYRVS, *i.e.*, Publilius the Syrian, a freedman, as his Roman name shows, who came from his native country, perhaps from Antioch, at an unknown date, but early enough to be in high favour in 711/43.[114] This man seems to have kept to the old-fashioned type of mime, which was improvised and depended for its effect on the broad wit and clever acting of the players; the manager—author he can scarcely be called—contributed apparently some kind of sketch of the plot. Publilius, however, is remembered especially as the author of a number of sage proverbial sayings, whereof a collection has come down to us; it has suffered the usual fate of all such collections, having been added to and subtracted from, but some 700 lines of the original selection remain.[115] Perhaps its most famous line is that which

are about to act an extempore farce, since it is said that they have a 'theme' only, not a play. See Schanz-Hosius, p. 255, for literature on this curious little record.

[113] Hence *mimus*, alone of words signifying an actor, has a feminine, *mima*. The reputation of these actresses was of the lowest. Horace puts *mimae* along with *meretrices* among the companions of a rake, *sat.*, i, 2, 58; the notorious Cytheris, Mark Antony's mistress (Cicero, *Phil.*, ii, 58, from which it appears that her real name was Volumnia, she being a freedwoman of Volumnius Eutrapelus, as may be gathered from Cic., *ad fam.*, ix, 26, 2), was a *mima*; and indeed it would be hard to find women of respectable character to take part in the sort of performances described below, p. 152.

[114] Pliny, *N.H.*, xxxv, 199, says he came to Italy in the same ship as Manilius of Antioch, his cousin (*consobrinus*), the founder of astronomy in Rome; he may therefore well have been an Antiochene himself, and the probably corrupt words of Pliny's MSS., Publilium Lochium mimicae scaenae conditorem, should be emended, as suggested by Otto Jahn, to *Publilium Antiochium*. As to the date, Jerome says, *an. Abr.* 1974 (= 711/43), Publilius mimografus natione Syrus Romae scenam tenet, and this fits very well both with his relations to Laberius and with the fact that Cicero, writing to Atticus (*ad Att.*, xiv, 2, 1) in March, 710/44, acknowledges the receipt from him of some news about *theatrum Publiliumque*. His unfree status (apart from the fact that a Syrian of undistinguished birth, as he seems to have been, could hardly have got Roman citizenship and a Roman name in any other way) is clear from Macrobius, *sat.*, ii, 7, 6, which mentions his introduction *ad patronum domini*; he had therefore been bought by an ex-slave of some one called Publilius.

[115] The standard edition (there have been literally hundreds) is that of W. Meyer, Leipzig, 1880; for an outline of the complicated MS. tradition and some of the modern literature on the *sententiae*, as they are called, see Schanz-Hosius, i, p. 261 *sq.*

was long the motto of the *Edinburgh Review, iudex damnatur cum nocens absoluitur,* ' a rogue acquitted is a judge condemned '.

Alongside this low-born, clever entertainer appeared a man of very different status. DECIMVS LABERIVS, a Roman knight, either to amuse himself or for profit, wrote mimes, whereof there survive over forty titles and upwards of a hundred quotations, including some witty phrases and one magnificent passage. In 708/46 Julius Caesar did one of the few cruel things of his career, and forced Laberius, who was then an old man, to contend against Publilius in an extempore performance. Publilius, as might be expected, did better than his opponent, who had never actually played in a mime before, but had kept his rank (cf. p. 23). But the prologue which Laberius delivered was not extempore, and it has fortunately come down to us.[116] In good verses it combines bitter irony, manly regrets for the disgrace which has overtaken its author, and a proud disclaimer of any baseness up to that day, when ' having left my house a Roman knight, I must return to it a stageplayer '. Caesar was great enough to value this splendid protest, and then and there, by his absolute power, restored Laberius to his position and gave him a handsome indemnity on which to support it. Laberius outlived Caesar, dying at Puteoli nine months after the dictator's assassination.[117]

Of the circumstances under which mimes were produced, we know this much. During the pauses in a dramatic performance it was only natural that a ' turn ' of some kind should be introduced, whether music, dancing, or some other entertainment, especially as it meant a *uitium* or religious defect, which might need a repetition of the whole festival to make it good, if the performance was not continuously carried out.[118] It became the practice, how early we do not know, to hang a plain cloth curtain (*siparium*) [119] across the stage and let the mime or mimes act before it ; in such a case the performance was often called an

[116] It was recorded by Gellius, viii, 15 ; of this chapter only the heading is left, the text being lost, but Macrobius, *sat.*, ii, 7, 2 *sqq.*, has copied it.

[117] Jerome on *an. Abr.* 1974 = 711/43.

[118] Any interruption of a rite in honour of a god, and all the games (*ludi*) were such, constituted a *uitium*. Thus we can understand the story in Festus, pp. 436–8 Lindsay, how in 543/211 the *ludi Apollinares* were interrupted by an alarm of an attack, the audience left the theatre, but returned later and found an old *mimus* had been dancing all the while, whence a proverb arose, salua res est dum saltat senex. See, for parallels, p. 419 of Lindsay's *ed. maior*.

[119] See Juvenal, viii, 185 *sqq.*, speaking of two impoverished ' bloods ' : consumptis opibus uocem, Damasippe, locasti/sipario, clamosum ageres ut Phasma Catulli./Laureolum uelox etiam bene Lentulus egit,/iudice me dignus uera cruce. See Mayor's notes there, and the scholia.

embolium or *entr'acte.* It may very well have been the case that at first there was but one performer, dancing, singing, or mimicking, much like one of our music-hall comedians; then two or three combining in a little sketch, finally something like a short play; it is not to be wondered at that the composition of these trifles was often loose, a character in difficulties for instance often saving himself and bringing the performance to an end by merely running off the stage.[120] In course of time it became customary also to have a mime as an after-piece to a more serious play; hence it is often called *exodium*, properly 'exit-piece'.[121] Finally, after the annual games in honour of Flora (*ludi Florales*) were introduced in 581/173,[122] the mime was raised to a yet higher place, being the only stage performance on these occasions; it gained nothing in decency thereby, for it was the regular custom for the actresses, at the call of the audience, to strip completely,[123] a thing so alien to the general decorousness of Roman cult that it cannot be otherwise explained than as a foreign custom, though we cannot point to the place from which it was imported.

Besides the two mime-writers already mentioned, there were several others of whom we hear a little. Cicero mentions a friend called VALERIVS, probably LVCIVS VALERIVS, known as an authority on law,[124] as likely to introduce a new figure to the stage, the jurisconsult from Britain (*Britannicus iure consultus*) if Trebatius, his correspondent and himself a famous lawyer, stays there much longer with Caesar. There is one line surviving of a play called *Phormio* by some one named Valerius; whether the same man, is not certain, nor is it definitely known if the play was a mime or not.[125] He also speaks of a follower of Antony,

[120] Cicero, *pro Caelio*, 65, mimi est exitus, non fabulae (regular play), in quo cum clausula non inuenitur, fugit aliquis e manibus, dein scabilla concrepant, aulaeum tollitur. Mimes then were not always acted before a *siparium*, but sometimes on a regular stage with a curtain which could be dropped below stage-level when the performance began, then raised on some apparatus of wheels or rollers (*scabilla*) to hide the scene when the piece was over.

[121] It is simply the diminutive of Gk. ἔξοδος.

[122] See Wissowa, *R.K.R.*², p. 197.

[123] Valerius Maximus, ii, 10, 8. Lactantius, *inst.*, i, 20, 10, says they were not regular *mimae*, but meretrices, quae tunc mimarum funguntur officio. But from what we hear of the morals of Cytheris and her kind, it is doubtful if such a substitution was necessary.

[124] Cicero, *ad fam.*, vii, 11, 2: si diutius frustra afueris, non modo Laberium sed etiam sodalem nostrum Valerium pertimesco; mira enim persona induci potest Britannici iure consulti (written in January, 701/53).

[125] Priscian, vol. ii, p. 200, 1 Keil, Valerius in Phormione: quid hic cum tragicis uersis et syrma facis? The distinctly vulgar form, *syrma*

NVCVLA, as composing mimes.[126] In Imperial times this form of composition survived, and we know of a writer called CATVLLVS, two of whose plays were the *Laureolus*, in which the hero, a brigand of that name, apparently was crucified on the stage,[127] and the *Phasma*, or *Apparition*.[128] Tertullian has heard of two more mime-writers, by name LENTVLVS and HOSTILIVS, S. Jerome also of a third, PHILISTION ; we cannot fix their dates, but know that a fourth, MARVLLVS, was contemporary with Marcus Aurelius (914/161–933/180).[129]. Finally, we hear several times of a popular mime known as *The Bean*, but have no indication of its author ; the same is true of another piece, *The Guardian* (*Tutor*), which was an old play in Cicero's time and, in his opinion, very funny.[130] Probably of about the time of Nero was yet another of these, to us, anonymous productions, *The Silphium-vendor* (*Laserpiciarius*).[131]

Imitation of Greek literary mimes was not a thing unknown ;

for *syrmate* (abl.), coupled with *uersis* for *uersibus*, strongly suggests that Valerius, whether Cicero's friend or not, was imitating common speech to an extent which would fit a mime much better than *comoedia palliata*.

[126] Cicero, *Philip.*, xi, 13.

[127] See Juvenal, cited in n. 119. That the *Laureolus* was by Catullus is stated by Tertullian, *adu. Valent.*, 14. A horrible production of it was seen in the arena in Martial's time, *spect.*, 7 ; a criminal was substituted for the actor, crucified in earnest and torn in pieces by a bear. If this sort of thing was not only tolerated but liked by the public, it is not to be wondered at if legitimate drama did not flourish. Cf. Schanz-Hosius, ii, pp. 564–5.

[128] See Juvenal, *ibid.* We do not know what the play was about; for the title, cf. p. 56.

[129] Tertullian, *de pallio*, 4, pugil Cleomachus . . . incredibili mutatu de masculo fluxisset . . . inter Fullones iam Nouianos (cf. p. 148) coronandus, meritoque mimographo Lentulo in Catiensibus commemoratus. *Apolog.*, 15, dispicite Lentulorum et Hostiliorum uenustates, utrum mimos an deos uestros in iocis et strophis rideatis, moechum Anubin et masculum Lunam et Dianam flagellatam et Iouis mortui testamentum recitatum et tres Hercules famelicos inrisos. Hence we learn that burlesque mythology formed part of the mimes' stock-in-trade. Jerome, *adu. Rufinum*, ii, 20 (vol. ii, p. 514, B, Vallarsius), quasi mimum Philistionis uel Lentuli ac Marulli stropham eleganti sermone confictam. There are one or two more mentions of Philistion, all in patristic writers (see Vallarsius' note *ad loc.*), which possibly indicate that he was late. Marullus' date is clear from *hist. Aug.*, iv, 8, 1, Marcus Aurelius and Verus showed great moderation, cum eos Marullus, sui temporis mimografus, cauillando impune perstringeret. This was after the death of Antonius Pius, 914/161, and before that of Verus, 922/169.

[130] Cicero, *ad Att.*, i, 16, 13 (written in 693/61), consulatum illum nostrum. . . . Fabam mimum futurum. *De orat.*, ii, 259, Tutor, mimus uetus, oppido ridiculus.

[131] In Petronius, *sat.*, 35, 6, one of Trimalchio's slaves sings de Laserpiciario mimo canticum.

a learned man called Gnaevs Mativs [132] wrote *mimiambi*, probably in imitation of Herodas, though no translations from him exist in the few fragments we have, and likewise a version of the Iliad in hexameters. The former work had at all events this characteristic of Herodas, that its metre was the scazon, or limping iambic trimeter.[133] We do not know exactly when he lived, but Varro had read him.

Two minor poets lived about this time. A certain Ninnivs Crassvs is cited four times by grammarians, who give as the title of his work either *Cypria Ilias* or simply *Ilias*.[134] Of these passages, one only might be from Homer: it runs *o socii, nunc fite uiri*, and translates well enough the recurrent ἀνέρες ἔστε, φίλοι, of the *Iliad*. It seems reasonable to suppose that Ninnius imitated the cyclic epic known as the *Kypria*; he cannot simply have translated it, for it was but eleven books long, and one citation of Ninnius is from his twenty-fourth book. The fact that he uses *fite*, which had quite gone out of Augustan Latin, seems to indicate that he is of the republican period. A small number of references, in some of which the name is none too certain, point to the varied activities of Manilivs—his praenomen was perhaps Lvcivs—a senator, self-taught, who is recognized as very learned by Pliny, no bad judge of such things.[135] He was alive and writing in 657/97; his subjects included the phoenix, the story of Leto and her twins, the legend of Europa, and other curious and interesting matters, possibly a sort of mythological geography or guide-book. The only verbatim quotations we have are in iambic trimeters, suggesting that he may have imitated the Alexandrian scholars who used this metre for such things as geographical and chronological works.[136] There is also an epigram, likewise in iambics, cited from him by Varro, and his

[132] He was earlier than Varro, or at least not later, for he is cited, *de ling. Lat.*, vii, 95; for his learning, see Gellius, xx, 9, 1, Cn. Matii, hominis eruditi. Frags., *F.P.R.*, pp. 281–3/48–51, and at the end of the Teubner ed. of Herodas (Crusius).

[133] *I.e.*, iambic trimeters with a spondee for an iambus in the last foot.

[134] Frags. in *F.P.R.*, p. 283/51–2. But some of the citations are ascribed to 'N(a)euius'. If this is not mere scribal blundering, we have another obscure name, for it cannot be Cn. Naevius (p. 26 *sqq.*).

[135] Pliny, *N.H.*, x, 4 *sqq.*, which gives us most of our information. The date is fixed by Pliny's statement there that Manilius mentioned the consulship of P. Licinius and Cn. Cornelius, which was 657/97, as being the 215th of the period between the birth of one phoenix and the next. That his praenomen was Lucius is suggested by the remark of Dionysios of Halikarnassos, i, 19, 3, that a man of some distinction called *Λεύκιος Μάμιος* (so the MSS.; editors mostly read *Μάλλιος*) gave some interesting information about an inscription he had seen at Dodona; this may be our Manilius.

[136] Fragments in *F.P.R.*, p. 283 *sqq.* Works in iambics on scientific subjects, see Rose, *op. cit.*, p. 392 (Apollodoros' chronology), 284 (the so-called Skymnos on geography).

opinion on matters connected with Roman religion is occasionally quoted, suggesting, unless his book of legends and curiosities was very miscellaneous, another work, likely in prose.[137]

[137] A Manilius is certainly quoted on the subject of the *di nouensiles* by Arnobius, *adu. nat.*, iii, 38 (p. 136, 24 Reifferscheid), and the name is restored with considerable probability in a mutilated passage of Festus, p. 450, 23 Lindsay, in a discussion of the Argei. It is, of course, not certain that this is the same man.

CHAPTER VII

CICERO

IT now and then happens that a single writer is of such importance as to sum up in himself all the tendencies of the age and people in which he lives. Such a claim can be made for MARCVS TVLLIVS CICERO, the man who, more than any other with the possible exception of Vergil, transmitted to later generations the best of what Rome had to teach. Whenever and wherever he had been born, his varied talents would have won him a high place in his native country and, supposing his people advanced beyond illiterate barbarism, have secured his memory with posterity. But as he was an Italian and a Roman citizen, in an age when Rome was fast displacing Greece and even Alexandria as the centre of culture, besides having achieved the leading position among the states of the then known world, he was not only a distinguished man then but a model and a teacher for the following centuries, whose influence is unconsciously felt to this day among people who may never have heard his name nor read a line that he wrote. Greece, whose chief spokesman in this respect was Isokrates, created the art of seemly and dignified, yet flexible style in writing and speech ; Rome handed on that doctrine to the rest of Europe, and its high priest among the Romans was Cicero.

The facts of his life, which are very well known from his own writings and those of others,[1] are briefly these. He was born at Arpinum, a small town, distinguished for nothing else than having been the birthplace of Marius, on January 3, 648/106,

[1] There is an ancient biography by Plutarch, but the chief source of information is Cicero himself, especially the letters, but also numerous autobiographical details in other works. Modern accounts of him are innumerable ; a few, chosen almost at random, are Gaston Boissier, *Cicéron et ses amis*, Paris, 1865, and thereafter many times reprinted ; J. L. Strachan-Davidson, *Cicero and the Fall of the Roman Republic*, New York and London, Putnam's Sons, 1903 ; E. J. Sihler, *Cicero of Arpinum*, Oxford and New Haven, 1914 ; and for his significance in later times, Th. Zielinski, *Cicero in Wandel der Jahrhunderte*, Leipzig, Teubner, 1912 (3rd ed.). Many more works in Schanz-Hosius, i, p. 402 *sqq*.

while Marius was serving in Africa against Jugurtha.[2] He was thus a few months older than Cn. Pompeius Magnus (Pompey the Great), who was born on the last day of September that same year. His father, whose name was the same as his own, and his mother Helvia, were, to use modern terminology, respectable middle-class provincials; the elder Cicero belonged to the equestrian order, the second rank in the state. He had never taken any prominent part in public affairs, certainly not at Rome, nor had any member of the family; young Marcus, if he was to rise high, must do so by his own talents, for he had neither wealth nor influence behind him. During the troublous times of his early life, the boy was given a good education, which he afterwards supplemented by continual studies, both by himself and under the guidance of the best available teachers in various branches. His father had himself literary tastes,[3] though it does not appear that he ever wrote anything, and no doubt was well pleased at his son's rapid progress. Meanwhile a second son, Quintus, was born in 652/102; the two brothers, though differing widely in temperament, for Quintus was at once more violent and less able than Marcus, remained on friendly terms all their lives. In 663/91 the sixteen-year-old lad assumed the garb of manhood (*toga uirilis*) and was attached to Q. Mucius Scaevola the Augur (cf. p. 107); two years later he began the military service compulsory on every able-bodied citizen, under the command of Q. Pompeius Strabo, in the Social or Marsian War against the rebellious Italian allies.[4] During the next few years he lived in Rome, studying rhetoric, partly under Apollonios Molon of Rhodes, one of the best teachers of the subject then living, also philosophy under Phaidros, an Epicurean, afterwards under Diodotos, a Stoic, and Philon, head of the Academy, the school of thought which traced its origin to Plato, but was then the vehicle of a moderate skepticism, in some respects not unlike the Pragmatism of modern times, which denied the possibility of certain knowledge (since it is possible to argue for and against any conceivable proposition), but allowed its followers to assume for practical purposes such principles as seemed reasonable to them, especially in matters of conduct. So far as one of his unphilosophic race could be called a philosopher at all,

[2] Year, Cicero, *Brut.*, 161; place, *de legg.*, ii, 3, 5; day, *ad Att.*, vii, 5, 3; xiii, 42, 3; cf. Gellius, xv, 28, 3. Mother, Plutarch, *Cic.*, 1, who also gives (*ibid.*, 2) a legend or two about his birth.

[3] Cic., *de legg.*, ii, 3, uillam (at Arpinum) . . . lautius aedificatam patris nostri studio, qui quom esset infirma ualetudine, hic fere aetatem egit in litteris.

[4] Cic., *Phil.*, xii, 27; *de amic.*, 1.

Cicero was an Academic in theory, a moderate Stoic in practice; for Epicureanism, despite his friendship with some exponents of it, he always professed considerable contempt.[5] During these years Cicero made the acquaintance of several young men destined to be important later; one of them was Pompey, and the two engaged together in the extremely elaborate exercises required of those who had any ambition to become orators.[6] Scaevola had died in 666/88, and Cicero had attached himself to his namesake the Pontiff (see p. 107). In 673/81 he made his first known public speech, that for P. Quinctius (see p. 171). The next year he became so prominent for his courageous defence of Sextus Roscius that it was advisable for him to leave Italy altogether for a while and betake himself to surroundings less directly visible to Sulla and his immediate followers. He spent some time in Athens, playing with the idea of becoming a scholarly recluse in what was practically a university town; he visited Asia Minor and studied under several masters of the Asianic school of rhetoric; then went to Rhodes, where he took more lessons from Molon and also attended the philosophic lectures of Poseidonios.[7] Meanwhile (675/79 and 676/78) Sulla retired, and shortly afterwards died. The reaction against his too conservative legislation began to set in directly his strong hand was removed from the helm, and Cicero's friends urged him to return. He did so in 677/77, married Terentia, a woman of strong and ambitious character, and re-entered public life by the natural avenue for a man of his abilities, the courts of law. He soon became well known, was elected quaestor in the *comitia* of 678/76, and spent the next year in Sicily, being stationed at Lilybaeum as what we might call deputy-governor.[8] That he behaved with honesty and discretion in his post we have but his own assurance,[9] but that is enough; for Cicero, while his

[5] Molon, *Brut.*, 312 (the mention of him in 307 can hardly be genuine). Phaidros, *ad fam.*, xiii, 1, 2. Diodotos, *Brut.*, 309. Philon, *ibid.*, 306. The Mithridatic War had driven him and other men of learning from Athens.

[6] *Brut.*, 310.

[7] Particulars of these studies are given by Cicero himself; *Brut.*, 315, 316; cf. Plut., *Cic.*, 4.

[8] *In Verr.*, ii, 5, 35; *pro Plancio*, 65; cf. *ad fam.*, xiii, 34.

[9] Cf. the passages cited in the last note, especially that from the *pro Plancio*. In this connexion Cicero tells a good story against himself. On returning, he expected to find his reputation had preceded him; but the first person he met and talked with wanted to know where he had been, and on his answering that he was just home from a province, said he supposed it was Africa, while a second corrected him and said *tu nescis hunc quaestorem Syracusis fuisse?*

most unpleasant fault was a peacock vanity, never boasted without some cause.[10] Besides, he had the old-fashioned and provincial virtues of frugality, clean living and a palm which did not itch. His temperament was in many ways very suitable for a statesman, since besides honesty he had ability of many kinds, great industry, considerable shrewdness, a certain amount of tact and a genuine devotion to the public weal. Had he lived at a time when all the main currents of opinion set in one direction, he might have been successful and happy in some great post; for example, if he had been born in Europe in the Middle Ages, long enough before the Reformation not to be troubled by the counter-claims of the new and the old faiths, we might know of him as the saintly but prudent and genial head of a powerful religious order, or as a cardinal or even Pope celebrated for his eloquent defence of orthodox doctrine against Jews and Saracens and for the wisdom with which he governed the Church. Unhappily for him, his was an age of strongly opposed tendencies, republican and monarchical, and he was too good a lawyer not to see that a case could be made out, not only for the old order, which he upheld and idealized, but for the new, championed by Caesar, whose merits and abilities he perceived as clearly as any. Hence it is that, while, if confronted with a situation which left but one course of action for a patriot, such as that created by Catiline's plot in 691/63, he behaved with discretion and courage, finally crowning his long career with what might be called martyrdom after the last struggle against Antony, in face of such a crisis as the opposition between Caesar and Pompey, when both sides had claims upon him, he behaved with a vacillation so great as to give the impression of a hopelessly undecided, even cowardly character. The age was a hard one, and needed, to grapple with it, a man like Caesar, who could aim at one good thing and sacrifice, if need

[10] Seneca, *dial.*, x, 5, 1, sums the matter up with his usual neatness and unusual accuracy when he calls Cicero's highest magistracy illum consulatum non sine causa sed sine fine laudatum. He seems never to miss an opportunity for praising himself, though usually making some decent show of citing the opinions of others, or using a little rhetorical modesty. Caesar seems on occasion to have found an impish pleasure in seeing how much flattery Cicero would accept; for we hear (*ad Q. fratrem*, ii, 15, 5) that he had gravely assured him that the first part of a poem (the *de temporibus* ?) was as fine as anything he had ever read, even in Greek (prima sic ut neget se ne Graeca quidem meliora legisse); that Caesar went on with a little mild criticism of the rest of the poem much perturbs the author, who asks his brother to tell him exactly what it is that Caesar does not like, adding nihil est quod uereare; ego enim ne pilo quidem minus me amabo.

were, other goods to it. Cicero's policy was amiable but impracticable, to preserve all that was good (*i.e.* consistent with his own ideal of the true Roman state, as it had never been save in the beliefs of such men as he) in all the political elements of that chaotic whirlpool. But for the present, events were in Cicero's favour. He could conscientiously support the party represented by Pompey and Crassus, the consuls of 684/70, and won one of his greatest early triumphs by his impeachment of C. Verres in that year. His dreams of a *concordia ordinum*, or understanding between the equestrian order into which he had been born and the senatorial to which he now belonged by virtue of his having held curule office, did not look too unsubstantial. He was aedile in 685/69, and about that time probably made the acquaintance of Titus Pomponius Atticus, who for the rest of his life was to be his confidential adviser, unpaid man of business, and the recipient of all his hopes and fears.[11] In 688/66 he was praetor, consul in 691/63, and stood at the height of his reputation as a patriot-statesman, *pater patriae.* The decline then set in. Caesar was every day becoming more powerful, and little though he wished to offend or harm Cicero, he found him too intractable and procured his banishment in 696/58. Recalled in 697/57, Cicero remained prominent in public life, though definitely not the leader of the state's policy, until the civil war broke out. He was in Cilicia the year before (July 703/51 to July 704/50), where he governed the province ably and with his usual honesty and humanity. Returning, he made some attempts to negotiate between the two great rivals, followed Pompey to Greece in 705/49, but was not present at the battle of Pharsalus the next year. He made his peace easily enough with Caesar when the war was over, but took no prominent share, indeed for the most part none at all, in public matters during the dictatorship which followed. Unmolested by those in power and generally respected by all parties, he was left to his studies and his private affairs. He divorced Terentia about the end of 708/46, and a little later made an unsuccessful experiment at a second marriage, with a lady named Publilia, much younger than himself, who was his ward.[12] Soon after this, his

[11] The correspondence begins in 686/68, and even the earliest surviving letters are written as no one would write to any but a close and trusted friend.

[12] Quintilian, vi, 3, 75; Plutarch, *Cic.*, 41, largely from Tiro; Cicero, *ad fam.*, iv, 14, 3; *ad Att.*, xiii, 32, 1; Cassius Dio, xlvi, 18, 3. The business, of course, gave rise to spiteful gossip; it may well be that the charge brought against Cicero of marrying Publilia to use her estate for the payment of his own debts had something in it.

daughter Tullia died. She had been his favourite child, for his son Marcus (born 690/64) was a not over-amiable young man of very mediocre abilities. Cicero was for a time half-mad with grief at her loss, and played for a while with the idea, extravagant for a Roman, of building a temple to her memory, in other words declaring her a goddess. He found more lasting consolation in study ; to this period are due nearly all his philosophical and some of his rhetorical treatises. His studies were interrupted by the renewed disorders following on the death of Caesar ; abandoning a journey from Italy into Greece, he entered public life for the last time, and from the middle of 710/44 till the autumn of the next year, when Octavian deserted the senatorial party and made overtures to Antony and Lepidus, Cicero was the head of the Roman government, in fact, though he held no office of state. The triumvirate making a clean sweep of all personal and political enemies, Cicero fell a victim to the rancour of Antony, and was put to death by his emissaries on December 7.

Being thus not quite sixty-four years old when he died, never robust,[13] and occupied during the greater part of his maturity by public business and the many cases in which he appeared as an advocate, usually for the defence, it is clear that he must have had very unusual powers of concentrated, yet rapid, work to achieve any outstanding position as a stylist. That he became the great exemplar of Latin prose for his own and subsequent generations [14] indicates that he possessed, not talent only, but genius, though not of the highest kind ; he had no creative powers, but simply an extraordinary ability for expression, given something to express. This he had sedulously improved by constant and unremitting study on every possible opportunity, including moments of leisure snatched in the midst of business. The merits and defects of his verse compositions have been dealt with (p. 143) ; his prose cannot be fully studied in a book of this kind,[15] which has room but for a sketch of its outstanding features and a list of the known works.

In Cicero's time, two principal tendencies seem to have been active in Rome, so far as compositions in prose, and above all speeches, were concerned. One was the Asianic movement, which afterwards fell into such disrepute with the Greeks that we are at a loss to find anything like sufficient examples of its manner to form our own opinion ; it would appear, however,

[13] Plut., *Cic.*, 8.

[14] Despite the anti-Ciceronian movements to be described later.

[15] A recent and good work is L. Laurand, *Étude sur le style des discours de Cicéron*, 2nd ed., Paris, Les Belles-Lettres, 3 vols., 1925–7.

that Seneca represents a survival of it in Latin after it had disappeared in Greek.[16] Its chief characteristics were short, highly rhythmical clauses, often riming, seldom forming a period of any length, and containing the maximum of ingenious turns of thought or phrase, what the Romans called *sententiae*, together with a choice of words which approached poetical diction in the avoidance of commonplace, everyday speech. It is evident that to the Italians of that day, who had no aversion to ornateness and used a prose style of necessity somewhat artificial, this manner was bound to make a strong appeal. But it had a danger, indeed a vice, which was that it could not be quite natural and was extremely apt to degenerate into a wholly artificial medium, unlike any real form of human expression, too intent on its own elaborate cleverness to have any feeling left for actuality or even for what was appropriate to the subject in hand. The other tendency was to Atticize. In the case of Greek writers, this meant imitating not only the manner but the dialect, now long obsolete, of Demosthenes and his contemporaries. The Romans, having no classical period of prose style in their history, were not then tempted seriously to archaize ; and the Atticists' principles of using the speech of every day, though in a form refined by careful choice of words, and avoiding all extravagance and over-elaborateness of phraseology, were in themselves good. Unfortunately, the Latin language, if not handled with some freedom of departure from everyday idiom and arrangement, was apt to be harsh, jejune and dull ; it quite lacked the natural grace of Attic, which had behind it, before its first prose author began, some generations of poetical tradition, inducing a habit of careful and pleasing collocation of words and providing a very large vocabulary and a supply of happy turns of phrase from which the intending writer might choose. Hence neither manner was quite satisfactory, since one tended to be extremely affected, the other lifeless and dull. Cicero, with fine taste, took a middle course, doubtless affected in his choice, though we cannot say to what extent, since materials are lacking, by the precepts of his Rhodian teacher. He had in common with the Atticists insistence on purity of vocabulary and correctness of idiom. In his speeches especially, we find

[16] See Rose, *H.G.L.*, p. 362 *sqq*. Cicero himself says (*orat.*, 231) that some of the best Asianists were *minime contemnendi*, though they lacked variety in their effects, the worst fault in an orator (*ibid.*, 213). He distinguishes two kinds (*Brut.*, 325), one *sententiosum et argutum*, the other *uerbis uolucre atque incitatum*. He parodies the style of Hegesias, one of the principal Asianists, *ad Att.*, xii, 6, 1, by a series of jerkily short sentences which scan almost like verse.

him most sedulously avoiding foreign or unusual words; and there are occasional interesting discussions of points of grammar and usage [17] in his correspondence. With them also he shares the ability to speak in a perfectly plain and straightforward style when it is appropriate to do so, that is, in passages which belong to the *genus tenue* or simple manner of oratory; the speech *pro Caelio* is a model of that very good rhetoric which never seems rhetorical. But he differed from them in holding that on occasion, when something lofty is attempted, ornament and avoidance of a commonplace tone are peremptorily called for by the principles of good oratory.[18] Here the Asianic elaborations helped him, though he is never immoderate in his use of them. In particular, he adopted from them and extended to every part of his speeches one of their most outstanding adornments, well-marked rhythm, especially before a pause in the sense.

Thanks to the immense industry of Zielinski,[19] the principles which Cicero followed half-unconsciously (for his own attempts to explain what constitutes prose rhythm are inadequate) [20] are now clear. Every sentence ends with a trochaic cadence (– ᴗ, – ᴗ –, or – ᴗ – ᴗ), which is preceded by a cretic (– ᴗ –) or molossus (– – –). This simple formula, without any licences, accounts for 60·3 per cent. of all final rhythms in the speeches. Hence Zielinski calls these the *clausulae uerae*. But a variety of these, allowing two short syllables to be substituted for one long, is common (26·5 per cent.), and comprises a sub-class which has a choriambus or an epitrite (– ᴗ ᴗ – or – ᴗ – –) in place of the cretic. Hence, while the first class is represented by such terminations as *pati)entia nostra, mul)to iucundissimus, audeat iudicare*, the second is more varied, containing such forms as the famous *esse uideatur* (– ᴗ ᴗ ᴗ – ᴗ, *i.e.*, – ᴗ – – ᴗ, with two short syllables instead of the second long), *genus honoris tributum est*, which is the third of the *clausulae uerae* (V3, in Zielinski's notation) with two short syllables in place of its first long; and many others. To this class belong also those clausulae which, taking no other liberties, have a run of five syllables at the end, *e.g.*, *spiritum pertimescerem*. These are known as *clausulae licitae*. Anything departing still further from the norm is a *clausula mala*, or even *pessima*, the degree of inferiority being determined by statistical methods and not by any preconceived ideas, and the percentages of *malae* and *pessimae* being respectively

[17] *E.g.*, *ad Att.*, vii, 3, 10 (ought one to say *in Piraeum* or simply *Piraeum* for 'to the Peiraieus'?); *ibid.*, xiii, 21, 3 (does *inhibere remos* mean 'easy' or 'back water'?). It is characteristic of Cicero's healthy regard for usage that he consulted no grammarian on the latter point, but listened to a ship's officer.

[18] See, *e.g.*, *Brut.*, 234 *sqq.*

[19] *Clauselgesetz* (see Bibl.).

[20] See *orator*, 212 *sqq.*

6·1 and 1·4; there is, however, a small class of *selectae*, produced by substituting spondees for the trochees of the *uerae* (as *carcerem condemnati*). These account for but 5·2 per cent. of all the clausulae; but the passages in which they occur are so free from any suspicion of careless composition, and so often meant to be impressive—in which attempt they regularly succeed—that it seems an inevitable conclusion that these heavy rhythms are there on purpose, meant to strike upon the ear and draw attention. Further analysis shows that these same rhythms are still present, although with some loss to the *uerae* and gain to the other classes, as the lighter pauses in the sense.[21]

In the philosophical and rhetorical treatises he allows himself more liberty in vocabulary, for he is addressing a more restricted and more cultured audience. It is the difference between good journalism and technical or purely literary writing for a cultivated public only.[22] In particular, he is careful to express everything in a purely Latin diction when he speaks to the general public; he even makes quaint pretences of knowing little or nothing of anything Greek.[23] In the treatises he rather displays his Greek knowledge, which was very considerable, and addresses himself to the task of meeting and rivalling these masters of literature and thought on their own ground. One of his chief preoccupations is to find or make Latin equivalents for the numerous technicalities, scientific and philosophical, which centuries of discussion had added to the Hellenic vocabulary. In this he had great success, adding largely to the meagre store of Latin abstract nouns and other special instruments of the most highly civilized diction. Thus it is in no small measure to him that the greater part of modern Europe owes the words, of Latin derivation, which it uses for the discussion of scientific and philosophical matters.

In his letters, the style naturally varies very much. Several of them are manifestos in letter form; many more are formal productions, dealing with official business. These perforce differ but little in vocabulary or structure from speeches. In them, and in the treatises, we also find the rhythms observed in the

[21] Zielinski, *Con. Rhyth.*

[22] Laurand, *op. cit.*, gives elaborate comparative vocabularies (see especially p. 363 *sqq.*) which illustrate this very well.

[23] The *locus classicus* for this is *in Verr.*, ii, 4, especially 4, where he pretends to have learned the names of the most celebrated Greek artists specially for the occasion; 5, where he feigns to have forgotten the name of Polykleitos and thanks some imaginary person in the audience for reminding him. As a matter of fact, he was much interested in Greek art, and often asks Atticus to procure him statues and other works, or thanks him for having done so.

orations, though this matter has not been so thoroughly studied. In them also, as in the larger works, the period is freely used; that is to say, the long and frequently involved type of sentence, needing skill to handle it properly, in which the construction begun with the first word is not completed till the last. Abundant illustrations of this may be found in the famous 'letter to Lentulus', *ad famil.*, i, 9, obviously intended for circulation among his and the recipient's friends, for it contains a reasoned and clever defence of Cicero's political attitude.[24] Others have a less formal tone, while others again, especially those written to Atticus on private affairs, have no stylistic pretensions at all, but consist of short, elliptic sentences, packed with idiomatic phrases, tags of Greek from various authors, mostly classical and not Hellenistic, single Greek words, sometimes a whole sentence in that language.[25] It may be added that no compositions of Cicero's are more obviously his than these hurried notes, often written or dictated two or three in the same day. This, more perhaps than anything else, shows the essential soundness of his style; it was not an artificial dialect for the use of literary men, but the speech of his own people, purified, carefully arranged, and made more flexible and expressive.

Taking now the various groups of his writings, in the order they usually have in our printed editions, we begin with the rhetorical treatises. The first of these, the two books *de inuentione* (on the choice and arrangement of subject-matter), are the work of his school-days. They are, he says, unfinished and rough performances, which got abroad from his note-books,[26] and their contents bear this out. They are the unoriginal work of a very clever boy who has got together precepts and examples from the approved text-books of his day, mostly Greek, and given them a sort of literary form by grouping them under the proper headings and writing short prologues. That he never carried out his task thoroughly is fairly obvious, for many parts of the subject are handled inadequately, or not at all.

[24] Of course, neither this nor any other work consists wholly of periods, which would give a most monotonous and ponderous effect.

[25] For a discussion of his Greek, see Rose in *J.H.S.*, xli (1921), p. 91 *sqq.*, and the works there quoted.

[26] *De orat.*, i, 5, quae pueris aut adulescentibus nobis ex commentariolis nostris incohata ac rudia exciderunt. He was, then, not more than twenty or so at the oldest when he wrote; this would put the date not after 668/86, hardly late enough for the *ad Herennium*. What, if anything, he called his work we do not know; Quintilian cites it as *rhetorici* (*libri*), ii, 15, 6, cf. iii, 1, 20, as does Jerome, *adu. Ruf.*, i, 16 (vol. ii, p. 471 c, Vall.).

There are many resemblances, strongly suggesting that Cicero had used it, to an anonymous work generally called *ad Herennium*. It is in four books, addressed to a certain Gaius Herennius, and its author says that he is more interested in philosophy than rhetoric, intends to write on grammar, and has some thoughts of composing treatises on tactics and government.[27] Who he was, is quite uncertain. In later antiquity, and also for a while after the Revival of Letters,[28] it was imagined that Cicero had written it; but it is the work of a mature scholar, master of his subject, which he handles excellently, and not of a young beginner. It has been suggested [29] that it was composed by that CORNIFICIVS whom Quintilian cites several times, and certainly there are decided resemblances between what Quintilian says Cornificius teaches and what the *auctor ad Herennium*, to give him his usual modern title, really says. The chief objection to this is that Cornificius the rhetorician, according to Quintilian himself, wrote on figures of style,[30] apparently not on rhetoric in general, whereas our work is a complete, though brief, handbook. Of its date we can get a fairly good idea from some of the examples the author uses. In iv, 68, to show how one may be brief, he sketches in hardly more than twenty words the career of some one who is pretty obviously Marius, down to his seventh consulate, in 668/86; in iv, 47, he is explaining how a speaker may appeal to the passions of various classes in his audience, and illustrates by an attack on an imaginary person whose conduct has offended not

[27] *Ad Herenn.*, i, 1, etsi negotiis familiaribus impediti uix satis otium studio suppeditare possumus et id ipsum quod datur oti libentius in philosophia consumere consueuimus. This is evidently not a young man nor a leisured student speaking. *Ibid.*, iv, 17, haec . . . in arte grammatica dilucide dicemus. iii, 3, magis idoneo tempore loquemur si quando de re militari aut de administratione rei publicae scribere uolemus.

[28] Jerome, *loc. cit.*, lege ad Herennium Tullii libros; cf. *comm. in Abdiam prophetâm, praef.* (vol. vi, p. 361–2 Vall.). The first modern to show that Cicero could not have been the author was Raphael Regius, in 1491.

[29] First, apparently, by Kayser in 1852. See Schanz-Hosius, i, p. 589. Some of the relevant passages are as follows. Quint., v, 10, 2, Cornificius calls one kind of enthymeme *contrarium*; *ad Her.*, iv, 25, uses *contrarium* in that sense. Quint., ix, 3, 70, cites as an example of a play on words the phrase *ăuium dulcedo ad āuium ducit*, and mentions Cornificius in that context; *ad Her.*, iv, 29, has the same example. Quint., ix, 3, 88, discusses the figure *dubitatio*, in which the speaker affects to be uncertain which of two words to use, and gives as an example, siue me malitiam siue stultitiam dicere oportet; *ad Her.*, iv, 40, speaks of *dubitatio*, and gives the same example, almost in the same words.

[30] Quint., *ibid.*, 89, mentions several authors of monographs on figures of language or thought, Cornificius among them, and seems never to quote him unless figures are being discussed. It is, of course, possible that Cornificius, of whom we really know nothing, was the author also of such a monograph, but at least equally possible that the resemblances between Quintilian's Cornificius and the *ad Her.* arise from both drawing on a common source.

only the senators but those who wish for the prosperity of the equestrian order, thus suggesting that that class was not yet in the depressed condition in which Sulla left it; again in iv, 68, another example of brevity is a description of some one's operations on the coast of Thrace and near the Dardanelles, which may be a reference to the services of Lucullus, in 670/84.[31] All this points to some one, probably a Marian, who was writing his treatise between 668/86 and the triumph of Sulla's faction in 672/82.

A very different work is that which Cicero wrote as a sort of corrective to his juvenile essay, the three books *de oratore*. This was composed in 699/55, thus obeying the general rule that his compositions, other than speeches and letters, are the fruits of his political inactivity, or comparative inactivity.[32] It explicitly leaves behind the rules taught in the class-rooms of rhetoric,[33] and sets itself to answering the question how the perfect orator may be produced. Every one was agreed that he must have five qualities, ability to choose the right material (*inuentio*), skill in arranging it (*dispositio*), power of expression (*elocutio*), a good memory (*memoria*) and finally the capability to deliver his compositions in a fitting manner (*pronuntiatio*). Cicero, following the practice of Aristotle in his philosophical dialogues,[34] sets up two principal spokesmen to deal with these matters and give their opinions how they may best be acquired; these are the orators Antonius and Crassus (cf. pp. 105–7). After they and the other characters have spent the first book in discussing the necessity of the higher education to an orator (Antonius denies this and Crassus affirms it), each is given his

[31] The suggestion was made by W. Warde Fowler, *Roman Essays and Interpretations*, Oxford, 1920, p. 91 *sqq*. He seems also to have been the first to dispose of the suggestion that the person mentioned in the same passage as having been lately made consul was Sulla and not Marius; *Journal of Philology*, 1882, p. 197 *sqq*.

[32] The date is given by Cicero, *ad Att.*, iv, 13, 2, fixed by contemporary events to which reference is made at about the middle of November, 699/55: de libris oratoriis factum est a me diligenter (= I have put my best work into the *de oratore*). diu multumque in manibus fuerunt (this need not mean more than a few months' work; Cicero composed very rapidly). describas licet (sc., for publication; Atticus seems to have been in some sense Cicero's publisher). Ten years later, *ad Att.*, xiii, 19, 4, he says: sunt etiam de oratore nostri tres mihi uehementer probati.

[33] *De orat.*, i, 23.

[34] Cicero, *ad fam.*, i, 9, 23 (to Lentulus, Dec. 700/54): scripsi igitur Aristotelio more, quem ad modum quidem uolui, tris libros in disputatione ac dialogo de oratore. Cf. *ad Att.*, xiii, 19, 4, where he mentions that Herakleides of Pontos used a similar method. In contrast to most of the Platonic dialogues, such works are not conversations, but debates in set speeches.

own strongest points to dilate upon, Antonius, in Book II, treating of *inuentio, dispositio* and *memoria,* while Crassus spends the third book over the remaining qualities. It is an admirable example of the good and bad qualities of a first-rate Roman mind. On the one hand, it never really deals with the fundamental problems either of style in general or of rhetoric in particular; one has but to contrast it with such different works as the *Gorgias* of Plato and the *Rhetoric* of Aristotle to perceive this. On the other, it is in close touch with practical realities, and, assuming that stylistic perfection may exist and that it is morally justifiable to use rhetorical persuasion, at least in a good cause, it gives on every page fresh insight into the means by which a Cicero, and by implication other moulders of public opinion, can attain their ends.[35]

At an unknown date, reasonably conjectured to be about 701/53,[36] Cicero composed a little catechism of rhetoric, for the instruction of his son Marcus and his nephew Quintus. It is called *Partitiones oratoriae, i.e., The Orator's divisions* or *classification,* a title which is ancient and seems derived from the questions near the beginning. 'Into how many parts should the whole theory of speech be divided?—Three.—Name them. —First, the powers of the orator themselves; next, the speech; third, the point under discussion.' And, a little later, 'How many parts has a speech?—Four. Two of them aim at giving information, narrative and proof; the other two at exciting feeling, exordium and peroration.' Cicero himself never seems to have attached any importance to this little book, or to refer to it in any later work; by his own account of it, he has merely made an abstract of Academic teaching.[37]

A much more important work is the *Brutus,* which has been so constantly quoted, especially in the notes to Chapter V, that I may almost claim to have dealt with it already. Its framework, however, is not merely that of a literary history. In form it is a dialogue; Cicero, returning from his province at the end of 704/50, hears of the death of Hortensius (cf. p. 198). A while

[35] For Cicero as a literary critic, cf. Atkins, vol. ii, chap. i.

[36] Cicero, *ad Q. frat.*, iii, 3, 4 (written in 700/54), says he hears young Quintus is making good progress with his rhetoric, but would like to get him away to the country and give him some further instruction himself. The two speakers in the *part. orat.* are Cicero and his son, not his nephew. It may be therefore that Cicero carried out his plan and gave his own son the benefit of his expert coaching at the same time, writing this little work as a manual for both pupils. But this is no more than an intelligent guess.

[37] Title, Quintilian, iii, 3, 7; Academic teaching, *part. orat.*, 139.

afterwards, he is visited by Brutus and Atticus, and falls into a discussion of oratory, which results in his giving a sketch of its development both in Greece and Rome. Here, by his own account, he is largely indebted for his facts to Atticus' historical researches (see p. 207), save for those orators whom he himself remembered. But all this leads up to a discussion of his own development, the process by which he equalled and outshone Hortensius, and the moral to be drawn therefrom, which is, briefly, that Asianism is not a style which wears well, especially when its practitioner lacks that unremitting diligence without which no speaker can remain at his best.[38] But this is not to be taken as meaning that Cicero approves of Atticism, as he makes clear by an interesting digression occasioned by a mention of Calvus [39] (cf. p. 134). As to when the work was written, we have no exact information. The dramatic date, *i.e.*, the time when the dialogue is supposed to take place, is early in 708/46 [40]; we have no definite proof whether or not Cicero wrote it at the time thus fixed, but the probabilities are that he did, for he refers to it in the *Orator*, which was finished and in the copyists' hands by November of that year.[41]

The *Orator* was sent as a sort of open letter to Brutus, then in Gaul, and labours to convince him and those who think with him that their view of Atticism is much too narrow. The true orator must be master of all forms of style, the simple, *humile*,[42] the more florid medium style (*modicum et temperatum*), and the grand (*ille amplus copiosus, grauis ornatus*),[43] and use them all in the proper places. He must therefore understand what forms of ornament and what choice of language are appropriate to each. In this connexion Cicero has much that is highly interesting to say about the details of style, often handling quite minute questions of pronunciation, collocation of words, rhythm

[38] *Brut.*, 15 (use of Atticus); *ibid.*, 319 (quoniam omnis hic sermo noster non solum enumerationem oratorum uerum etiam praecepta quaedam desiderat); follows the sketch of Hortensius' career.

[39] *Brut.*, 284 *sqq.*

[40] Brutus had not left for Gaul, but is still in Italy; he left in 708/46. The campaign in Africa has begun, *Brut.*, 266 (praeteritorum recordatio est acerba—clearly the campaign of Pharsalus—et acerbior expectatio reliquorum—this can be nothing but the African operations), but the battle of Thapsus has not taken place, for Cato, who killed himself a very short time after it, is spoken of in the present tense, 118 *sq.*

[41] *Orat.*, 23, in illo sermone nostro qui est expositus in Bruto (the title, then, is Cicero's own). *Ad Att.*, xii, 6, 3, Atticus has the *Orator*, and Cicero asks him to substitute *ab Aristophane poeta* for *ab Eupoli* in 29.

[42] *Orat.*, 91.

[43] *Orat.*, 98; 97.

and other technical points, such as would involve a long treatment if this were a work on linguistics.

By way of a *pièce justificative*, Cicero proceeded, probably not long after the completion of the *Orator*, to translate two of the greatest Attic speeches, the indictment of Ktesiphon by Aischines and Demosthenes' reply thereto, the so-called *De Corona*. These translations have completely disappeared, but we have the preface, known since the early Empire at latest as *de optimo genere oratorum*.[44] Its keynote is that there is really but one kind of oratory, the perfect, whose exponent can 'instruct, delight and move' his audience.[45]

One more short work on rhetoric was begun to satisfy the curiosity of a friend and finished in a few days, during a voyage, from memory, with no books at hand. Certainly, Cicero practised what he preached in regard to the necessity for an orator of cultivating his memory; but the subject was one very familiar to him. His friend Gaius Trebatius, visiting him at his villa at Tusculum, was turning over books with him in the library when he happened on a copy of Aristotle's *Topica*. Being a jurist and not a rhetorician, he asked Cicero what it was about, and was told that it was Aristotle's classification of proofs. This interested Trebatius, who wanted more details, and after vainly seeking them from a professor of rhetoric to whom Cicero referred him, or from the very obscure Greek of Aristotle himself, he once more fell back on his friend's expert knowledge. Having occasion, in August 710/44, to sail from Velia, where he met Trebatius once more, to Rhegium, Cicero good-naturedly occupied the journey in writing out a kind of synopsis of the bulky Aristotelian work, charmingly expressed and beautifully clear, with illustrations from Roman law. It was sent to Trebatius from Rhegium.[46]

Turning now to the speeches,[47] in which Cicero shows his mastery of his art most completely, we begin with the very few which survive from the period before his departure from Rome

[44] So called by Asconius, *in Milon.*, p. 30 Clark (p. 26 Kiessling-Schoell). For the speeches in question, see Rose, *H.G.L.*, p. 292.

[45] *De opt. gen.*, 3, optimus est enim orator qui dicendo animos audientium et docet et delectat et permouet.

[46] The whole story is told in *Top.*, 1–5, cf. *ad fam.*, vii, 19. For Aristotle's work, see Rose, *H.G.L.*, p. 274. Like all Aristotle's major works, this is of the nature of lecture notes, very condensed and crabbed in style; hence Trebatius' inability to make it out for himself.

[47] There survive fifty-eight speeches more or less complete, and we have some forty-seven names and, in seventeen cases, fragments of others. See Schanz-Hosius, i, pp. 404, 444.

to Athens. The earliest is the *pro Quinctio*, which, although immature as compared with the later masterpieces, already shows many of the qualities of Cicero's style, and in particular, has his characteristic rhythms. It was a complicated suit, arising out of the business relations of Quinctius' dead brother with a certain Sextus Naevius. The counsel for the other party was Hortensius. The result of the proceedings is not known. The date is 673/81.[48] In the next year he had a much more important case, needing not only eloquence but courage. Sextus Roscius of Ameria in Umbria had committed the grave offence of being heir to a very considerable fortune. His father had illegally (if anything in that connexion could be considered more illegal than another) been included in the list of the proscribed, put to death, and his estate confiscated and bought for a trifle by Chrysogonus, a creature of the all-powerful Sulla. Roscius seems to have been a man of some spirit, likely to make an attempt to get back his property ; hence a person named Erucius was put up to accuse him of having murdered his father. Cicero had at once to make it clear that his client was innocent and to avoid offending Sulla ; he performed the task admirably and Roscius was acquitted.[49]

It must have been about this time that Cicero found himself opposed to Cotta (see p. 108) on a legal point, namely whether a certain woman of Arretium—we do not even know her name—could be regarded as free-born, when her town was alleged to have lost its rights of citizenship in the troubles. Cicero took the line that citizenship is not a thing of which any one can be legally deprived, and won his case, he says, *contra dicente Cotta et Sulla uiuo*.[50]

Returning from his visit to Greece, Cicero came before his public a better orator, cured of his bad habit of shouting all his more emphatic passages, and a healthier man than when he went away.[51] We have but one speech, and that very fragmentary, from the six years following his reappearance ; in 682/72 or the year following he defended a namesake of his, Marcus Tullius of Thurii, who had got into a dispute over the boundaries of his estate with an apparently violent and unscrupulous neighbour.[52]

[48] Gellius, xv, 28, 3.

[49] Gellius, *ibid.* ; schol. Gronou., in the argument of the speech (p. 424, 22 Orelli) ; Plutarch, *Cic.*, 3 (κατορθώσας ἐθαυμάσθη).

[50] Cicero, *pro Caecina*, 97. The speech is usually dated 675/79, for it was before Cicero left for Greece, but may have been somewhat earlier.

[51] See Plut., *Cic.*, 4 ; Cic., *Brut.*, 313–4.

[52] The date is approximately fixed by the mention, *pro Tullio*, 39, of Metellus as the praetor who had directed the proceedings. Now there are but two of that name who were praetors at any likely date, Quintus Metellus Creticus in 682/72 and his brother Lucius the next year.

But in 684/70 he had much more important business on hand. The government of the provinces had got into an abominable state of corruption, for the magistrates entrusted with it, ex-consuls and ex-praetors, had no check upon them save the possibility of an accusation for extortion (*res repetundae*, literally property which should be reclaimed) on their return. But they would be tried before a jury of their own, the senatorial, order, and most shameless bribery was in use to secure acquittals. Gaius Verres, a particularly atrocious product of this bad system, had crowned an active career of fraud by plundering the Sicilians on a magnificent scale. Cicero was asked to undertake his accusation, and had a case so clear that if it came to a straightforward trial, the most prejudiced or corrupt tribunal could hardly do otherwise than convict. Verres' confederates knew this perfectly well, and did their best for him. The date of the trial was fixed late in the year, so that it might be completed, not under Pompey and Crassus, the consuls of 684/70, who were reformers and of the anti-senatorial faction,[53] but under the magistrates of the next year, who would be more amenable to Verres' arguments. Cicero, after getting rid of a dummy accuser, Quintus Caecilius, who was put up to take his place and mishandle the prosecution,[54] hurried on his preparations, got his witnesses together, and then, after a short opening speech, abstained from all further displays of oratory and overwhelmed Verres and his advocate Hortensius by sheer weight of testimonies from all quarters; for, Roman procedure not confining an accuser to the particular charge he had brought, but allowing him to review the defendant's previous career, Cicero had collected information covering Verres' whole political life. When the defendant had anticipated the verdict by going into voluntary exile,[55] Cicero published the speeches he

[53] They were, of course, senators themselves, being magistrates; the opinion of their faction was, not that the senate should be abolished, but that the too exclusive powers given to its members by the Sullan constitution should be shared with the *equites*.

[54] The speech on this occasion, *diuinatio in Q. Caecilium*, is preserved and belongs to the preliminary proceedings (*diuinatio*) instituted by Roman usage, when more than one person came forward as an accuser, to determine who had the better claim. There was no official corresponding to the Public Prosecutor or a District Attorney.

[55] This course was regularly open to a defendant, up to the moment when the last juryman had voted and the result was declared. Being unguarded, he had but to leave the court and make for some territory technically outside Roman jurisdiction, such as that of an allied state. Hence exile is not strictly a legal punishment, though outlawry (*aqua atque igni interdictio*) and, under the Empire, confinement to some particular place (*relegatio*) are.

would have delivered if the trial had run its normal course. They were no doubt intended as political pamphlets, awful warnings of the results of the existing system of appointing governors and of the iniquities of the less reputable members of the senatorial order. They constitute perhaps the most damning review of any one's life that ever was given to any public. While making full use of what the ancient critics called δείνωσις, the rhetorical emphasizing of the facts (in this case of course the setting of Verres' crimes in the worst possible light), Cicero does not indulge in mere vulgar abuse, but maintains a high and serious tone throughout the five speeches known collectively as the *Second Action against Verres.*[56] The only adverse criticism that can be made is that at times the list of misdeeds grows so unrelievedly appalling as to create a doubt in the reader's mind whether any human being was ever such a monster of lust, cruelty and cynical dishonesty.

About 685/69 (the exact date is not certain), Cicero defended Marcus Fonteius on the same charge as that which he had himself brought against Verres. Fonteius had been governor of Gaul (at that date about = Provence) and had not been blameless in his office. Indutiomarus, chief of the Allobroges, had complained, and to judge by what we have left of the speech, never published in full, Cicero made what he could of a bad case.[57] Somewhere about this time came the case, arising out of a dispute over a piece of land, in which Cicero delivered the speech known as *pro A. Caecina.* It turned on a number of subtle legal points, and its author was well pleased with it.[58] Perhaps also to this period belongs another speech whereof we have a large fragment, that *pro Roscio comoedo.* This is the celebrated actor Roscius, who was a personal friend of Cicero. He had undertaken to train for the stage a slave belonging to a C. Fannius Chaerea, and had done so. He had marked talents, so that his earnings, which Chaerea and Roscius divided, were considerable, but was murdered, and the killer offered compensation to Roscius. Difficulties had arisen about the proper division of the compensation between the two partners, and this suit was the result.[59]

[56] They are entitled: *de praetura urbana; de praetura Siciliensi; de frumento; de signis; de suppliciis.* See p. 533.

[57] *Pro Font.*, 1, the *lex Valeria* is in force; its date is 684/70. *Ibid.*, 20, several headings are set down (*de crimine uinario, &c.*) with no corresponding text. Cf. p. 104.

[58] See his own remarks on it, *Orator*, 102.

[59] The appropriate date is arrived at thus. *Pro Rosc.*, 33, the value of an estate has increased greatly since the time when property was insecure; that time (37) was fifteen years ago. A likely date for the insecurity is the Sullan proscriptions of 672/82–673/81; add 15 and we get 687/67 or the following year.

By this time Cicero was a thorough-going supporter of Pompey. When therefore the tribune C. Manilius introduced a bill giving Pompey extraordinary powers to deal with the Mithridatic War, Cicero, in 688/66, spoke warmly before the popular assembly in favour of the measure. The speech is, in its author's opinion, a good specimen of the middle, or florid, style of oratory, very appropriate to the occasion [60]; the subject-matter is not so much a reasoned presentation of the legal aspects of the bill or of the military position in the East as a skilful panegyric on Pompey as a thoroughly honest man and capable officer, which indeed he was, and also, a curious item to the modern reader, as eminently possessed of the quality of good luck without which no general is complete.

The same year produced a masterpiece in a different style, the oration *pro Cluentio*. Aulus Cluentius Habitus, a man distinguished for nothing but his connexion with this case, had secured the condemnation of his stepfather, Oppianicus, on a charge of attempted poisoning. Oppianicus had died in exile, and Cluentius' mother now accused her son of having poisoned him. This may have been untrue, but was complicated by the subsidiary charge that he had secured Oppianicus' condemnation by bribing the jury, which was very likely the case.[61] Cicero, by a speech composed of clever handling of the matter of bribery, indignant and scornful repudiation of the accusation of poisoning, and abuse of the prosecutors,[62] whose character indeed seems to have been vile enough, got his client off without having himself any delusions as to his moral worth.[63]

About this time Cicero also pled the causes of several clients the speeches for whom have been lost. One of these was C. Cornelius, tribune of the plebs in 687/67, who, having been very active in introduc-

[60] See *orat.*, 102, fuit ornandus in Manilia lege Pompeius: temperata oratione (in the 'middle' style of oratory, cf. *ibid.*, 98) ornandi copiam persecuti sumus. Old editions call the speech *pro lege Manilia*, but *pro* should mean 'on behalf of' a client, not a measure. Hence later editors name it *de imperio Cn. Pompei*. I should be inclined to take a hint from the above passage of the *orat.* and call it *de Manilia lege*.

[61] Oppianicus was condemned by the *iudicium Iunianum*, the notoriously corrupt court presided over by the praetor Junius, who was tried and found guilty. The speech is dated by 147, mea (quaestio) de repetundis. If Cicero was hearing cases of extortion, he must have been praetor, which office he held in 688/66.

[62] Cluentius' mother naturally, being a woman, could not herself conduct the case.

[63] He said afterwards that he had thrown dust in the eyes of the jury (*tenebras offudisse iudicibus*), Quint., ii, 17, 21.

ing anti-senatorial legislation, though of a moderate type, had made himself unpopular with that body and was accused of treason (*maiestas*). The case, after interruptions due to riots, was tried in 639/65, and we have some fragments of Cicero's two speeches, mostly preserved by Asconius, whose commentary also gives us the date. The occasion was one of some political importance, and it increased his popularity, as did also a speech in defence of Manilius, the tribune for whose act to give Pompey special powers Cicero had already spoken (p. 174).[64] Of two other cases we know very little, except that they helped to gain him useful friends; the defendants for whom he spoke were C. Fundanus, Q. Gallius, and C. Orcivius.[65] We have also some fragments of his electioneering eloquence in what little is left of the speech *in toga candida*, when, in 690/64, he was a candidate for the consulship.[66]

Once become consul, he was active in spreading his views on public affairs, and we have a group of three speeches, collectively known as *de lege agraria*; a fourth is lost. Of these the second now surviving begins by thanking the people for his election; the date of the whole group therefore is 690/64–691/63. The first which we have, a part of which is lost, is addressed to the senate. The chief subject discussed was a vote-catching scheme of the tribune P. Servilius Rullus, to appoint a board which should sell sundry state domains, mostly outside Italy, buy land in Italy with the money, and settle colonies of the poorer citizens on it. It was a device to provide members of his party, the rapidly developing faction adverse to Pompey and the moderates, with influential posts, and Cicero headed the successful opposition to it. Another speech countered a manœuvre of Caesar's; Titus Labienus, afterwards one of Caesar's best officers, and then tribune, brought a charge of treason (*perduellio*, a graver word than *maiestas*, which is approximately 'conduct calculated to bring the Government into contempt') against a senator, C. Rabirius, who twenty-seven years before had had a share in the death of the turbulent tribune Saturninus. After much creaking of obsolete machinery, the charge turned into a more ordinary suit involving a money fine; Cicero and Hortensius defended Rabirius, who was apparently acquitted.[67] The whole business was meant as

[64] See Q. Cicero, *comm. petit.*, 51.

[65] Q. Cicero, *ibid.*, 19.

[66] Preserved by Asconius, p. 82 *sqq.*, Clark (p. 73 *sqq.*, Kiessling-Schoell). In general, for the fragments of speeches, where any exist, see the last vol. of C. F. W. Müller's (Teubner) edition of Cicero, p. 231 *sqq.*

[67] Rabirius, by a procedure of immemorial antiquity, was first solemnly found guilty and sentenced by a commission of two chosen for the purpose; then appealed to the people; then was tried before them; then the proceedings were interrupted by striking the flag on the Ianiculum,

a warning to those in power against disposing too directly of troublesome revolutionaries ; Cicero was soon after to show that he had the spirit and courage to disregard it. The discovery of Catiline's long-suspected conspiracy moved him to action as energetic as it was tactful. He got rid of Catiline himself by telling him, in detail, before the whole senate, what he knew of the plot. This is the first speech *in Catilinam.* The next day he delivered the second oration of this series, to the assembled citizens in the Forum, explaining the situation to them. The third was again addressed to the people, and set forth the information given by the Allobrogian envoys to the government, which had put all the most important facts in his hands. The fourth speech was his contribution to the discussion in the senate as to what they should do with the arrested confederates of Catiline. All of these are preserved, doubtless not exactly as they were delivered, but in the form in which Cicero afterwards sent them to Atticus for publication.[68]

The rest of what Cicero regarded as his consular orations are lost. They were, a speech *de Othone,* as he himself calls it, while the grammarians gave it the clumsy title *cum a ludis contionem auocauit.*[69] M. Roscius Otho, then praetor, had passed his famous law reserving the best seats in the theatre for the senators and *equites.* The lower orders were annoyed at this, and hissed him when he appeared. Cicero at once summoned all present to a meeting (*contio*) at the temple of Bellona,[70] and put the case for Roscius' innovations so persuasively

the ancient signal that an enemy was attacking Rome and all citizens must arm at once ; finally Labienus brought the suit to which Cicero's speech (preserved only in part) belongs. See Cassius Dio, xxxvii, 27, 1, for the most complete ancient account of the business, which has been discussed in all the modern histories of the time.

[68] *Ad Att.,* ii, 1, 3, a list of the speeches in question. The passage has been strangely suspected by critics. But if it is a spurious addition, either it is a gloss accidentally incorporated in the text from the margin, and the glossator would not use the first person (*Catilinam emisi*), but the third ; or it is a forgery, and one can hardly imagine a forger posing as Cicero who should be able to refrain from rhetorical flourishes in such a context, whereas the language is as perfectly simple and straightforward as a mere list ought to be.

[69] See Plut., *Cic.,* 13. There is but one small fragment preserved, see p. 269 of the ed. cited in n. 66.

[70] Probably, then, the games were in the Theatre of Flaminius, in the Campus Martius ; the temple would be the nearest convenient place for a meeting. See Platner-Ashby, *s. uu.* Circus Flaminius and Bellona. The meeting would, of course, be held in the open space in front of the temple, not in the building itself, where there would be no room for a large number. A modern would have addressed the people where they sat ; a Roman could not do so, as it would amount to an interruption of a ceremony; cf. p. 151.

that all objection ceased. He also addressed the senate in opposition to a motion for repealing Sulla's law excluding the children of the proscribed from holding office. Before the assembly he made a speech on the occasion of his resigning his claim to a provincial governorship after his year of office as consul.

While still consul he appeared as advocate, but in a suit of public interest and in the place of honour, for he spoke last of the counsel for the defence. Lucius Murena, consul-elect for the next year, was impeached by one of the defeated candidates, Servius Sulpicius, the jurist, under a law which bore Cicero's own name, the *lex Tullia de ambitu*, for corrupt practices (*ambitus*) in the election. Cicero contributed largely to Murena's acquittal by a speech in which he made gentle fun of Sulpicius' legal studies, exalted Murena, who had served creditably in the operations against Mithridates, and gave the doctrinaire Cato, who was associated with the prosecution, some practical advice as to tact. Two younger accusers were disposed of in terms which the orator did not think worth writing out for publication.[71]

Next year Cicero was again busy with the defence of an aspirant for the consulate, this time P. Cornelius Sulla, who had been convicted of *ambitus* after the elections of 688/66, and was now further accused of having been privy to the plots of Catiline. Whether his conduct in that matter had been so irreproachable as Cicero would have the jury believe is doubtful; but presumably the appearance on his behalf of Catiline's arch-enemy carried weight with the jury, and Sulla was acquitted.[72] In the same year Cicero had the pleasure of winning a case before a court presided over by his own brother, who was then praetor.[73] Aulus Licinius Archias, a Greek of considerable poetical, or at least versifying ability, found his claims to Roman citizenship disputed. Cicero, if we may judge by the speech as it stands, said little on the matters of law and fact involved, but read the jury a charming essay on literature, with special mention of Archias' services thereto. That the resulting oration, the *pro Archia poeta*, is not

[71] *Pro Mur.*, 57, ends with the note de Postumi criminibus, de Serui adulescentis (= accusations brought by Postumus and the younger Servius). He has just said respondebo igitur Postumo, and the next paragraph begins uenio nunc ad M. Catonem.

[72] This is not directly vouched for, but we find that Sulla's political career continued beyond that date, which it could not have done had he been convicted of treason.

[73] This fact is furnished by the schol. Bob., p. 175, 23 St., and serves also to date the speech. The acquittal of Archias is also not directly testified, but is an easy deduction from the confident tone of the whole piece. For the question of its authenticity, see Schanz-Hosius, i, p. 426.

a genuine production is an idea not worth refuting, though a few inferior scholars of the last century put it forward; that it was revised for publication by leaving out a good deal of dry detail, necessary before the court, is likely enough.

In that same year, Cicero answered an attack on his and the senate's policy towards the Catilinarian conspirators by the tribune Metellus Nepos; the speech was published with some additions, but only a few fragments are preserved.[74] In the next, a wrangle with Clodius, the brother of Catullus' mistress, led to a speech in the senate, which also is lost,[75] as are all his senatorial utterances up to the time of his banishment, together with the Greek work on his consulship which he composed and on which he was flattered to the top of his bent.[76]

One speech survives from the year 695/59, that *pro Flacco*. L. Valerius Flaccus had governed the province of Asia and apparently lined his own pockets at the expense of the provincials. Cicero was under some obligation to him, for he had been praetor in 691/63 and helped to put down the conspiracy; therefore he joined Hortensius in defending him. Part of the speech is lost; from the rest it appears that Cicero, having no case, devoted himself to praising his client and proving to the jury that the witnesses against him, being Greeks, were of necessity liars.[77]

[74] Cic., *ad Att.*, i, 13, 5: in illam orationem Metellinam addidi quaedam. Fragments in C. F. W. Müller, *op. cit.*, pp. 269–70.

[75] The Bobiensian scholiast preserves us some fragments of a work called *in P. Clodium et C. Curionem* which he says Cicero wrote quoniam habuerat in senatu quandam iurgiosam decertationem. Now Cicero himself tells Atticus (*ad Att.*, i, 16, 8 *sqq.*) that he had 'smashed' Clodius in the senate cum oratione perpetua plenissima grauitatis tum altercatione, and gives some samples of his telling replies. Here he does not mention Curio. *Ibid.*, iii, 12, 2, writing from exile, he is horrified that a speech which he never intended to publish has got abroad: scripsi olim equidem ei (= Clodio) iratus. Then, *ibid.*, 15, 3, he says: sed quid Curio? an illam orationem non legit? quae unde sit praelata nescio. All these passages may well refer to one and the same work.

[76] Cicero, *ad Att.*, i, 19, 10, sends Atticus commentarium consulatus mei Graece compositum, asking for stylistic criticisms. *Ibid.*, ii, 1, 1–2, Atticus has now sent him a work of his own on the same subject, also in Greek; Cicero has sent his own book to Poseidonios in Rhodes (meaning the celebrated philosopher and historian, for whom see Rose, *H.G.L.*, p. 361 *sq.*), who declares that having read it, he dare not attempt the subject himself.

[77] In 695/59, Cicero mentions to Atticus (*ad Att.*, ii, 25, 1) the complimentary way in which Hortensius had spoken of him cum de Flacci praetura et de illo tempore Allobrogum diceret. This can hardly be anything but his speech in defence of Flaccus, and would not be mentioned in a familiar letter unless it were fresh news; hence 695/59 is the date of the trial of Flaccus.

On his return from exile in 697/57, Cicero had recovered his self-confidence and his vanity with it. The two speeches of thanks, *cum senatui gratias egit* and *cum populo gratias egit*, which he then delivered,[78] while showing his usual mastery of language, are so wearisomely full of the virtues of his supporters and himself and the black villainy of his enemies that no one would wish them longer. The same tone pervades the much more interesting orations *de domo sua ad pontifices* (on the restoration of his house in Rome, which Clodius had demolished and consecrated its site to Liberty; Cicero, of course, took the line that the consecration was irregular and invalid) and *de haruspicum responso* (an earthquake had been interpreted by the Etruscan specialists usually consulted about such ominous things as meaning that 'consecrated and holy places had been treated as profane'; Clodius declared this meant the restoration of Cicero's house, and Cicero made short work of his sudden zeal for religion). This speech was delivered the year after his return, by which time he had got back into full activity again. Besides two or three speeches of which the text is lost,[79] he repaid a debt of gratitude by appearing as the advocate of Publius Sestius, who had been tribune of the plebs the year before and had exerted himself to secure Cicero's return. Attacked by Clodius and his bodyguard of roughs, he had surrounded himself with a similar following, and was now accused by his opponent of violence (*de ui*). Cicero enjoyed himself in rebutting the allegations of this scrupulous champion of law and order, for it gave him an opportunity [80] of defending his own conduct in 696/58 and eulogizing himself and his supporters. He also made the most of the appearance of Publius Vatinius, one of his especial aversions, as a witness against Sestius. Roman procedure allowed counsel almost boundless liberty in their questions to witnesses and comments on what they said; Cicero, having Vatinius thus at his mercy, treated him to a flood of invective remarkable even for Latin, and afterwards published

[78] They are also known as the *oratio post reditum in senatu habita* and *oratio post reditum ad Quirites habita*.

[79] He mentions (*ad Q. frat.*, ii, 3, 6) that he had defended, on February 11 of that year, Bestia, one of Sestius' supporters, on a charge of *ambitus*. It would be about this time that he defended M. Cispius, probably on the same charge, without success, for the matter is mentioned in the *pro Plancio*, 75, obviously as a recent happening; also P. Asicius (*pro Caelio*, 24), whose acquittal he secured on a charge of *uis*.

[80] At least, the published speech uses such opportunities. It is always to be remembered that speeches of this kind took the place of the political pamphlets of later ages, and Cicero was fighting for his position as a leading statesman.

it, or the substance of it, in what has come down to us as the *interrogatio in P. Vatinium testem.* It may be conjectured that the strength of the expressions used did not evaporate while the author wrote them down.

Another action *de ui* produced one of Cicero's most interesting speeches, also belonging to 698/56, the *pro Caelio.* M. Caelius Rufus, of whom more will be said later (p. 200), was accused by L. Sempronius Atratinus, whose father Caelius had accused once and meant to accuse again; one of Sempronius' supporters was Clodius. The accusation was complicated, and one of the charges was that Caelius had tried to poison Clodia, among whose lovers he had formerly been. Cicero devoted himself to this point and those most closely associated with it, and produced a speech whose chief interest is its brilliantly hostile picture of Clodia and her circle; the style shows what he could do when abstaining from all the more ambitious and high-flown rhetorical affects and confining himself almost to the *genus tenue.* Caelius was acquitted.[81]

Still in this year came Cicero's reconciliation with, or rather surrender to the real power in the Roman state, the coalition of Pompey, Caesar and Crassus. Having had it made clear to him that resistance to them was futile for him and the senatorial opposition to their schemes was neither strong nor honest enough to support him, he enlisted with a fairly good grace in their service, and on their behalf delivered two speeches, one in the senate, *de prouinciis consularibus*, opposing an arrangement of provincial governorships which would have robbed Caesar of his command in Gaul, and the other the *pro Balbo*, in defence of the claims of L. Cornelius Balbus (see p. 190) to be a Roman citizen, and therefore on behalf of Pompey, who had got him his citizenship and was thus indirectly attacked through him.[82]

Next year (699/55) he was able to indulge himself in at least one unprompted and thoroughly sincere speech.[83] A result of

[81] This is not directly testified; but if he had been condemned he would have gone into exile, whereas we find him at Rome and again attacked by the Clodii in 700/54, Cicero, *ad Q. frat.*, ii, 11, 2.

[82] Neither of these speeches, however, is the recantation (παλινῳδία) which Cicero tells Atticus (*ad Att.*, iv, 4, 1) that he must make, much against his will. That that was a letter, in all probability to Pompey, has been made clear by chronological and other arguments by T. Rice Holmes in *Class. Quart.*, xiv (1920), p. 39 *sqq.*; cf. C. Saunders in *Class. Phil.*, xiv (1919), No. 3.

[83] It was not so with all his speeches: Cicero complains, *ad fam.*, vii, 1, 4, of the trouble he has had (dirupui me paene) in defending Gallius Caninus on some unknown charge.

the senate's action concerning the provinces was that L. Calpurnius Piso, one of the consuls of 696/58 and therefore one of Cicero's bitterest enemies, was recalled from Macedonia.[84] He therefore attacked Cicero in the senate, an unwise action, for the reply was a long speech (*in Pisonem*) of vitriolic invective, mingled with some self-laudation. The abuse was the more effective because it contained elements of truth ; Piso may not have been the runaway slave, filth, fiend, drunkard and other things which Cicero calls him in the large portion of the speech which we have left (the beginning is lost), but he seems to have been a far from admirable character, occupied in getting as much benefit as he could from the marriage of his daughter Calpurnia to Caesar.

The next year (700/54) must have been a singularly bitter one for Cicero. Aulus Gabinius, Piso's colleague in the consulship, returned from his province, was accused, no doubt with perfect justice, of extortion (*res repetundae*), and condemned. His advocate, by a request of Pompey which amounted to a command, was Cicero, who probably felt some satisfaction in his want of success.[85] Less painful than this was his appearance as advocate for Vatinius, which happened at least once, if not twice.[86] Growing out of the condemnation of Gabinius was another case, that of C. Rabirius Postumus, adopted son of that Rabirius whom Cicero had defended in the year of his consulate. This man had been involved in some extremely shady transactions of Gabinius in Egypt, and as Gabinius was unable to pay the damages in which he had been cast, Rabirius, by the terms of the Julian law concerning extortion of the year 695/59, was liable, as having shared his principal's illegal gains. Cicero, in a speech (*pro Rabirio Postumo*) which still survives, apparently succeeded in securing his acquittal. Another case under the laws of extortion was that of M. Aemilius Scaurus, ex-governor of Sardinia ; Cicero was one of six advocates who defended Scaurus, and the prosecution, which was chiefly a manœuvre to prevent him standing for the consulship, failed. The speech is represented, for us, by a number of fragments, large and small.[87] Fully preserved is another defence of the same year, the oration *pro Plancio* ; Gnaeus

[84] The date is given by Asconius, p. 1.

[85] The speech has not been preserved, although it existed in antiquity. See Quint., xi, 1, 73 ; Jerome, *adu. Ruf.*, i, 1 (vol. ii, p. 459 a–b Vall.) ; Cicero, *ad Q. frat.*, iii, 1, 15 ; 5 (6), 5 ; *pro Rab. Post.*, *passim.*

[86] Cicero, *ad fam.*, i, 9, 19 ; ad *Q. frat.*, ii, 15, 3 ; Val. Max., iv, 2, 4, which makes the unsupported statement, (Cicero) P. Vatinium . . . duobus publicis iudiciis tutatus est.

[87] A good deal of information is contained in the commentary of Asconius, which survives ; two palimpsests preserve most of the text.

Plancius had befriended Cicero in his exile, and Cicero in turn pled his cause when an unsuccessful competitor accused him of having been elected aedile by means of unlawful associations (*sodalicia*).[88]

From the next year, no speech of Cicero's survives; in 702/52 came one of his few failures. Clodius and an equally ruffianly character of opposite political sympathies, T. Annius Milo, were candidates for the consulship; bribery and violence were unprecedentedly rampant, and a fight between Clodius and Milo resulted in the death of the former. Cicero defended Milo, when accused *de ui*; but the combination of an obviously guilty client and the military guard which Pompey, not without reason, had placed around the court broke his nerve; he spoke feebly, Milo was condemned and went into exile, and Cicero consoled himself by writing the speech he should have delivered, the wholly admirable *pro Milone*, the perusal of which half-persuades an unwary reader that its subject, instead of being a fit companion for the worst 'gunmen' of modern Chicago, was a high-souled patriot, the victim of most unscrupulous machinations.[89]

Shortly afterwards, Cicero had better success in defending one of Milo's confederates, by name M. Saufeius, who had led the final assault on Clodius. He and Caelius between them secured his acquittal by the odd vote. A second trial on a different charge resulted in Saufeius' acquittal by a larger majority; Cicero was again one of his defenders.[90]

After this year there comes a period in which Cicero made no speeches; it is the time of his provincial governorship and the civil war. In 708/46, when something approaching tranquillity had returned under Caesar's government, Cicero began to make himself heard once more. To this year and the next belongs the

[88] *Sodalicia* seem to have been regarded as a particular case of *ambitus*; see *pro Plan.*, 36: hoc igitur sensimus; cuiuscunque tribus largitor est, et per hanc consensionem quae magis honeste quam uere sodalitas nominaretur quam quisque tribum turpi largitione corrumperet, eum, &c. It was then an organization for purposes of bribery and corruption at elections.

[89] The facts concerning the trial of Milo are known chiefly from Asconius' commentary and Plut., *Cic.*, 35. Milo's comment on the written speech is famous: 'How lucky that Cicero did not deliver this speech! I should never have known the taste of these excellent Massiliote mullets' (Cassius Dio, xl, 54, 3; Milo had retired to Marseilles).

Cicero had already defended Milo successfully earlier in the consular campaign, when Clodius had sought to prove him an ineligible candidate on the ground of his heavy debts; see the fragments of the *interrogatio de aere alieno Milonis*, in Müller, *op. cit.*, p. 276 *sqq*.

[90] Asconius *in Milon.*, p. 54, 22 *sqq.*, Clark (p. 48, Kiessling-Schoell).

little group known as the Caesarian orations, because addressed to Caesar on behalf of three of his opponents. M. Claudius Marcellus was in exile; Caesar, on the entreaty of his brother, pardoned him, and Cicero would appear (for the genuineness of the speech, generally called *pro Marcello*, which we have is not quite above suspicion)[91] to have taken part in the chorus of thanks and laudation which followed. In contrast with this feeble performance is a little masterpiece of tactful petitioning, in which delicate flattery is blended with clever rebuttal of a charge, the speech *pro Ligario*. This man had been in Africa when the war broke out, and was certainly a supporter of Pompey; Caesar had spared his life when he fell into his hands, and Cicero, in order to secure his recall, set himself to minimize the part he had played in the hostilities, against the objections of Q. Tubero, who seems to have opposed his reinstatement on the grounds that he had been a dangerous enemy. Cicero, who was supported by Caesar's adherent C. Pansa, was successful in his plea, making good use of the fact that Tubero himself had served against Caesar at Pharsalus. The third speech was delivered the next year, and was a defence of Deiotarus, tetrarch of Galatia and notoriously a supporter of Pompey, like the other petty Asiatic kings, against a charge of having tried to poison Caesar. The proceedings were perhaps adjourned and their resumption hindered by Caesar's assassination.

After this event Cicero for a while took no prominent part in public affairs. When, however, the opposition to Antony began to take definite shape, he was urgently sent for, and for the last time found himself at the head of a Roman government. In imitation of Demosthenes, he called the speeches which he delivered on successive occasions against Antony the *Philippics*[92]; it is as much to their violent attacks on his opponent as to anything in the Demosthenic orations of that title that the word owes its modern meaning of an invective. The first of the series was delivered in the senate on September 2, 710/44. To outspoken criticism of Antony and his methods is joined a moving appeal to him to return to constitutional ways (34–8). Antony, who had not been present at the meeting, took violent offence

[91] For literature on the question of its authenticity, see Schanz-Hosius, i, p. 438. The clausulae seem to be those of a genuine speech, see Zielinski, *Clauselges.*, pp. 219–20.

[92] *Ad Brut.*, ii, 3, 4 (Brutus to Cicero): legi orationes duas tuas (*Phil.* i and ii, as appears from the context) . . . iam concedo ut uel Philippici uocentur, quod tu quadam epistula iocans scripsisti. *Ibid.*, 4, 2 (Cicero's reply): quoniam te uideo delectari Philippicis nostris. Both letters are dated in April, 711/43.

and answered Cicero, who in his turn was absent for prudential reasons, in a furious invective, when the senate met again on September 19. To this Cicero answered in the pamphlet known as the Second Philippic, in form a speech supposed to be delivered in reply to Antony's, and by the consensus of ancient opinion [93] one of his greatest works, which indeed it is, although the element of personal abuse in it is not to modern taste; ancient notions of propriety were different on this head. Antony was now out of Rome, on his way to get by fair means or foul the province of Cisalpine Gaul from its then governor, Decimus Brutus.[94] The result was the campaign of Mutina, to which all the remaining speeches have reference in one way or another. The last of the series was delivered on the Parilia (April 21), 711/43. There is a certain appropriateness—an ancient Greek might have said a *κληδών* or unintentionally significant utterance,—in the fact that this great oration, delivered on the day considered to be the Birthday of Rome, dealing with the honours to be decreed to the soldiers who had fallen in a victorious battle with Antony, ends: si uiui uicissent qui morte uicerunt, 'If they had been conquerors in life who are conquerors in death', which are thus the last words in public of Cicero, so far at least as they are recorded. October saw the end of all hopes for the constitutional party, and December 7 Cicero's murder.

If now we turn to the philosophic works, we are confronted with the strange paradox that one who was not a philosopher nor capable of original thought in that or any other branch of learning has exercised through them an amount of influence on subsequent European opinion comparable to that of Plato or Aristotle. Their value is best summed up by their author: 'just copies, and all the easier to write; I supply nothing but words, and I have plenty of those'.[95] It must be added that they are by no means always accurate copies, for Cicero was quite capable of misquoting and misunderstanding his authorities, the Greek philosophers of his own and earlier generations. Yet, such as they are, aided by their charm of style and unquestionable moral earnestness, they have served to convey some of the leading ethical ideas (on other branches of philosophy they have less to say) through the centuries, till modern Europe became once more capable of original thought and not of mere recording and interpreting. They have but lately ceased, if indeed they have yet quite ceased, to be the

[93] See Mayor on Juvenal x, 125.

[94] The 'Decius Brutus' of *Julius Caesar*.

[95] *Ad Att.*, xii, 52, 3: ἀπόγραφα sunt, minore labore fiunt; uerba tantum adfero, quibus abundo.

handbooks and guides of some gentle and thoughtful souls; the author was once acquainted with a charming old man who read the *de officiis* every year for his own edification.

Cicero began to show his interest in such things quite early, for in his youth he translated the *Oeconomicus* of Xenophon.[96] This may well have been no more than a stylistic exercise, as Jerome suggests,[97] but it found readers, as the fairly numerous fragments show. Less is known of another translation which he made of the *Protagoras* of Plato, perhaps also a youthful exercise; but his interest in Plato was deep and real, and his knowledge of him considerable.[98] The first important work was Platonic in title, though differing very much from Plato's treatise with the same name. This is the six books *de re publica*, begun in Cicero's villa near Cumae in 700/54 and finished, after some hesitation as to the form it should take, about three years later.[99] It is a discussion, supposed to occupy three days, between the younger Africanus and several other members of his circle (see p. 99). Its subject is not, as in Plato, justice as illustrated by the perfect state, but the state itself, its best constitution and government. From the fragmentary condition in which the work has come down to us, not all the details of the argument can be followed; but it is clear enough that Cicero's Utopia, as expounded chiefly by his idealized Africanus, was an idealized Rome, guided by the wisdom and patriotism of her leading man.

[96] Fragments in Müller, *op. cit.*, p. 306 *sqq.* For the original, cf. Rose, *H.G.L.*, p. 308.

[97] *Chron.*, praef. *init.*, unde et noster Tullius Platonis integros libros ad uerbum interpretatus est, et . . . in Xenofontis Oeconomico lusit.

[98] Jerome, *loc. cit.*, and Quint., x, 5, 2, say generally that he translated some works of Plato; Priscian, vol. ii, p. 182, 3 Keil, and in several other passages quotes specifically from *Cicero in Protagora*. Cicero himself, *de fin.*, i, 7, says: si plane sic uerterem Platonem et Aristotelem ut uerterunt nostri poetae fabulas, male, credo, mererer de meis ciuibus . . . sed id neque feci adhuc nec mihi tamen ne faciam interdictum puto, which seems to say that in 709/45 he had not yet translated the *Protagoras*; but I suggest that he means 'if I translated them as badly as our poets do Greek plays, which so far I have not done, though I suppose I have as good a right as any to do so', and not that he had not translated any such works at all.

[99] He is starting it, *ad Q. frat.*, ii, 12, 1 (scribebam illa quae dixeram *πολιτικά*, spissum sane opus et operosum). iii, 5, 1, acting on Sallust's advice, he is going to change the whole plan of the work, making it a dialogue between himself and Quintus. These letters are respectively of May and November, 700/54. *Ad fam.*, viii, 1, 4, Caelius (about the beginning of June, 703/51) writes to Cicero: tui politici libri omnibus uigent. This can mean no other work than the *de r.p.*, which therefore by that time had been published, perhaps just before Cicero left for his province, where he arrived on the last day of June.

The end of the work is its most celebrated part, for it long survived alone. Still following Plato, Cicero ends with a vision of the other world; Scipio has a dream in which he is shown the heavenly habitation of great and righteous souls and bidden to prepare himself for such a dwelling when his career on earth is ended. This eschatological passage was greatly to the taste of the fourth century A.D., the more so as it reproduced, not pure Stoicism nor any other of the later views, but Platonizing Stoicism, of the type made popular by Poseidonios, and therefore not very much out of tune with the neo-Platonic speculations of that age. Hence Macrobius (see p. 459) wrote an elaborate commentary on it, which, together with the text, has come down to us in several MSS.; for the rest of the work we have to depend on a damaged palimpsest and some quotations.

Related to this work in subject and date alike is the treatise in three books entitled *de legibus*. Unfortunately, it has not come down to us complete, for there were at least two books more.[100] What there is is most interesting both for what it tells us about legal theory of that date and for its information concerning the actual law of Rome at this comparatively early period. After a preliminary book devoted to the proposition that law is a natural thing, a function as it were of morality, and not a mere convention changing from state to state (a Stoic doctrine, going back ultimately to Plato), Cicero proceeds in the second book to treat of sacral law, in the third of the machinery of government. In both he gives the text of the statutes as he would have them, borrowing a good deal from contemporary law and making use of its archaic phraseology, and then comments on them. The speakers are himself, Atticus and Quintus; apparently he had taken Sallust's advice to heart, though he had not been able to bring himself to re-write the *de re publica* in accordance with it.[101]

There is no exact indication of the date. In ii, 42, there is a clear reference to the death of Clodius; hence the work is not earlier than January, 702/52. There is no certain reference to any later event; hence it is unlikely that it was written much after that time. For some doubtful speculations of various scholars, see Schanz-Hosius, i, p. 498.

Cicero was always favourably inclined towards Stoicism, although he never agreed with either its excessively dogmatic

[100] Macrobius, *sat.*, vi, 4, 8, cites *Cicero in quinto de legibus*. The surviving books have several gaps.

[101] See n. 99.

teachings or the extremes to which some of its followers went in applying them. Shortly after writing the *Brutus*, about the spring of that same year, it would seem,[102] he sent Brutus a work half philosophical, half rhetorical, explicitly as an example of how he would handle Stoic dicta, in contrast to their own dry and too theoretical manner.[103] It is called the *Paradoxa*, and consists of applications, suitable for delivery before a popular audience, of some of the most famous Stoic maxims, as 'that only the sage is rich', 'that virtue is alone sufficient for happiness'. It gives us an interesting glimpse of Cicero's own method of practising rhetoric, which seems regularly to have been related to actual circumstances, not to purely imaginary cases. Thus, the declamation on the maxim 'that every unwise person is mad' becomes an assault upon Clodius, who is plainly alluded to. The philosophical value of the little treatise is *nil*.

During this period of comparative political inactivity, Cicero's philosophic interests occupied him largely. In the next year, 709/45, he set himself to explain, in dialogue form, the tenets of his own Academic school. The work extended to two books, and the chief speakers were Lucullus, the general who commanded the Roman forces during a great part of the Mithridatic war, Catulus, son of that Catulus already mentioned (pp. 88, 103), and in subsidiary parts Cicero himself and Hortensius. He then heard that Varro (see p. 220) was anxious to be mentioned in one of his works; in deference to him, he re-wrote the *Academica*, as his treatise was called, dividing it this time into four books, giving Varro a leading part, and introducing Cato and Brutus as speakers.[104] Both editions survived; but by an odd chance, we have the second book of the earlier treatise (the *Academica Priora*) and the first book of the later (*Academica Posteriora*).

Much more important is the *de finibus* (in full, *de finibus bonorum et malorum*), written also in 709/45; Cicero's rapidity of composition is amazing, for while the philosophical content of all these works is, as has been said, second-hand and by no means free from mistakes, there is nothing slovenly or hurried about the style. The subject of this treatise is, as the title suggests,

[102] *Parad.*, 5: accipies igitur hoc paruum opusculum lucubratum his iam contractioribus noctibus, quoniam illud maiorum uigiliarum munus in tuo nomine apparuit (the *Brutus*), et degustabis genus exercitationum earum quibus uti consueui, cum ea quae dicuntur in scholis θετικῶς ad nostrum hoc oratorium transfero dicendi genus.

[103] θετικῶς, see the last note.

[104] See *ad Att.*, xii, 44, 4; xiii, 32, 2; 12, 3; 13, 1; 14, 2; 16, 1; 19, 3. All these letters are of June, 709/45.

the extremes or furthest boundaries of good and evil.[105] It is divided into five books, and is again in dialogue form. In Book I, Lucius Manlius Torquatus expounds the Epicurean doctrine of good and evil; Cicero criticizes his views in Book II. The third book is a similar exposition of Stoicism, by Cato; again Cicero answers, in the fourth. In the fifth, M. Pupius Piso sets out ideas with which Cicero had much sympathy, those of Antiochos, the somewhat heretical Academic whose lectures he had attended while at Athens. This man had departed from the skeptical attitude of his school and tended rather towards Aristotelianism. Against this Cicero has some few criticisms to make, but ends on a note of quasi-agreement. Indeed his whole attitude of mind in these works seems to be that he would like some positive doctrine which he might follow whole-heartedly, in ethical matters especially, but is too honest with himself not to see that every view, at least in so far as he could understand it, leaves a strong possibility of its being wrong; a good advocate can make out a plausible case against as well as for it.

The date of the next work, the *Tusculan Disputations*, can be fixed with considerable accuracy. That he wrote it after the *de finibus* we know, by his own testimony.[106] On May 29 of the same year he asks Atticus to lend him some works of Dikaiarchos because 'they will come in useful for something I have in mind'.[107] Dikaiarchos is cited, for his views on the soul, in Book I of the *Tusculans*. He had begun thinking of the subject, then, before completing the *de finibus*. Less than a year later,[108] Atticus is reading the *Tusculans* and recommending a friend to do the same. Many accepted the advice and the work was widely

[105] *Ad Att.*, xiii, 32, 3 (May 29, 709/45): Torquatus (= *de fin.*, i) Romae est; misi ut tibi daretur. In March (xii, 12, 2) he has been discussing Epicurus with Atticus, suggesting that he was then writing or thinking of that book. In 19, 4, written on the last day of June, he says: confeci quinque libros περὶ τελῶν. About three months, then, sufficed for the whole.

[106] *De diuin.*, ii, 2, after mentioning the *de finibus*: totidem subsecuti libri Tusculanarum disputationum . . . primus enim est de contemnenda morte, secundus de tolerando dolore, de aegritudine lenienda tertius, quartus de reliquis animi perturbationibus, quintus . . . docet . . . ad beate uiuendum uirtutem se ipsa esse contentam.

[107] *Ad Att.*, xiii, 32, 2, Dicaearchi περὶ ψυχῆς utrosque uelim mittas et καταβάσεως. Τριπολιτικὸν non inuenio et epistulam eius quam ad Aristoxenum misit. tris eos libros maxime nunc uellem; apti essent ad id quod cogito. Cf. the mentions of these works, *ibid.*, 31, 2 and 33, 2; in the latter, he has received the books, or some of them, for the text is uncertain. For the use of them, cf. *Tusc.*, i, 21 and 77; for Dikaiarchos, Rose, *H.G.L.*, p. 355 *sq*.

[108] *Ad Att.*, xv, 2, 4 and 4, 2 and 3.

popular, then and afterwards. Apart from its style, the doctrines that death is not to be feared, whether the soul is immortal or not, that pain is endurable, grief can be overcome, the other disturbances of the mind alleviated, and that virtue is sufficient to happiness, were comforting ideas for honest men in troubled times, even if the proofs are often better rhetoric than logic.

Before the *Tusculans*, Cicero had written a work very famous in antiquity, though lost to us, the *Consolatio*. It was his attempt to comfort himself for the death of Tullia, and with an odd return of his usual vanity in the midst of his very genuine sorrow, he points out to Atticus that no one else had yet written a consolation to himself. It has been conjectured that much of the material in *Tusc*. I is taken over from it; we may be reasonably certain that it owed much to a famous Greek work, the essay of Krantor on a similar theme. How a Greek handled such a subject we know from the work falsely ascribed to Plutarch, the *Consolatio ad Apollonium*, which contains many passages closely resembling the first *Tusculan* in matter and arrangement.[109] Another work, also of the early months of that crowded year, we may well regret having lost, for it was clearly very suited to Cicero's powers, being an exhortation to the study of philosophy. It was called *Hortensius*, because that orator was given the part of an opponent of philosophy, whose objections were then disposed of by the other speakers, this also being a dialogue. Perhaps its greatest title to remembrance above all other works of that popular type is that it first turned the attention of St. Augustine to serious things.[110]

[109] For conjectures on the relation between the *Consolatio* and the Tusculans, see Schanz-Hosius, i, p. 522. Krantor (of Soloi, a pupil of Xenokrates, Plato's successor) was famous for his work on this subject, which Cicero elsewhere calls a golden book (*Acad*., ii, 135) and says Panaitios advised learning by heart. It is mentioned several times in the *Tusculans*. The *cons. ad Apollonium* is published in all editions of Plutarch, *Moralia*. An ingenious forgery of Cicero's lost work, thought to have been written by Carlo Sigonio, deceived the unwary for some time; see Farrer, p. 5 *sqq*.

[110] It was of the kind called protreptic, προτρεπτικοὶ λόγοι, exhortations to various studies and so forth. We know that works of the sort were written at least as early as Aristotle, and we have specimens by Galen (*Protrepticus*, an exhortation to the study of medicine) and Clement of Alexandria (same title, an invitation to embrace Christianity). Cicero mentions it several times, particularly *de diuin*., ii, 1, at the beginning of his (chronological) list of his philosophic works. It is therefore earlier than the *Academica*, *i.e.*, than June (see n. 104). But all his interest in philosophy, other than political theory, dates from his inactivity after the dictatorship of Caesar, *i.e.*, after 707/47, and after the rhetorical works of 708/46; there is no reason to suppose the *Hortensius* was an exception. The fragments are in Müller, *op. cit*., p. 312 *sqq*.; the reference to St. Augustine is *Conf*., iv, 4/7, from which it appears that it was part of the regular reading course for students of rhetoric (usitato iam discendi ordine perueneram in librum); cf. *de beata uita*, 4 (p. 299 a, ed. Bened.).

At some uncertain time, but after the *Academica*, to which it refers, Cicero composed a work, or started to compose one, for in the fragmentary state in which we have it it cannot be determined whether or not he ever finished it, known to us as the *Timaeus*, because it consists chiefly of extracts from Plato's dialogue of that name, turned into Latin. But there was an introduction,[111] which may have simply led up to the translation, but also may have been meant to preface some longer and more elaborate discourse on Plato's doctrines. If this was so, Cicero had undertaken a task beyond his powers, and possibly realized it and abandoned his project.

A treatise of no small interest, despite its inaccuracies and some signs of haste in its composition, is the dialogue in three books *On the Nature of the Gods*. Cicero was not a profound theologian, indeed no Roman of that or any other date ever was ; it is not without significance that the great doctors of the Latin Church whom we shall have occasion to discuss later came from distant provinces. But he had knowledge of some interesting speculations of Greek writers now lost to us, and when these were set forth in his inimitable style, they made good reading enough. The work begins, after an introduction to bring the characters together, with a sketch of the history of the subject and an account of Epicurean theology by C. Velleius, who belonged to that school ; C. Aurelius Cotta, who supports the Academic view throughout, then criticizes Velleius. In the next book, Balbus speaks for Stoicism ; in the third, or what we have left of it, for a great deal has been lost, Cotta gives expression to the Academic doubts concerning theism. Here we are able to point definitely to Cicero's source ; he used a treatise of Kleitomachos of Carthage, a pupil of the great Academician Karneades, who became head of the New Academy after his master and handed on the latter's teachings, which were oral only, to posterity.[112] This man was an acquaintance of Lucilius, and on friendly terms with several other Romans ; doubtless his views were familiar

[111] It is this which gives the date, at least the *terminus post quem*, for it begins : multa sunt a nobis et in Academicis conscripta, &c., goes on to speak of Nigidius Figulus (died 709/45) in historical tenses (fuit ille uir), and begins to describe a meeting with him.

[112] For a discussion of this man and his relations to Cicero's treatise, see the introduction to vol. iii of J. B. Mayor's edition of the *de nat. deor.* (Cambridge, Univ. Press, 1880–5), p. lx *sqq*. That practically everything in all the philosophical works is from some Greek source is undoubted, see Cicero's own remark (in n. 95) ; but the assignment of what he says to particular works or authors is usually a matter of uncertainty, owing to the loss of so much Greek philosophical literature.

to many of Cicero's countrymen as well as to himself. The work was written, hurriedly, as inconsistencies and loose construction show, after the *Tusculans* and before the death of Caesar. Part of it was composed in August, 709/45.[113]

Still, before the murder of Caesar, but probably not much before, Cicero wrote one of his most charming and popular works, the little treatise *On Old Age* (*de senectute*; but his own title for it was *Cato maior*).[114] The scheme is very simple; Cato is visited by Scipio and Laelius, and in answer to their inquiries, sets forth his reasons for finding old age no burden, but rather pleasant. It was meant to comfort Atticus, and incidentally himself, and it succeeded, at least so far as the former was concerned.

Just after Caesar's assassination, Cicero produced yet another work of a quasi-theological nature, the two books *de diuinatione*.[115] The plan is the simplest possible; in Book I, Quintus Cicero defends, on Stoic lines, the proposition that the science of divination and also the revelations of inspired prophets and of oracles are realities. In Book II, his brother replies with the Academic arguments against this position. The interest lies largely in the fact that neither disputant shows any originality, and therefore the book gives us, in an eminently readable form, illustrated here and there with choice anecdotes, the stock arguments of that age for and against the possibility of foretelling the future either by human science or divine intervention. A sort of appendix to this work is the *de fato*, part of which has come down to us; it was to have been on the same plan as the longer work, but for some reason which Cicero does not particularize it was changed in form; as we have it, Hirtius, one of the consuls for 711/43, visits him at his villa near Puteoli and asks to hear him discuss a philosophic theme. The one chosen is the question whether or not our actions are all regulated by fate or predestination. Cicero for a while uses ideas borrowed from Poseidonios and then goes

[113] After the *Tusculans*, *de diuin.*, ii, 2; before Caesar's death, *de nat. deor.*, i, 7; in August, see *ad Att.*, xiii, 38, 1 and 39, 2; *ibid.*, xiii, 8, asks for the loan of Panaitios *On Providence*, doubtless for this work; the letter was written on June 8.

[114] See *ad Att.*, xiv, 21, 3 (May 11, 710/44), xvi, 3, 1 (July 16, same year). In *de diuin.*, *loc. cit.*, 3, he says it was written *nuper*; but it nowhere hints at Caesar's death.

[115] A very elaborate and complete commentary, with critical text, by A. S. Pease, University of Illinois Studies, Urbana, Ill., 1920 and 1923, is now the chief repository of information. Caesar's death is mentioned, i, 119 and ii, 23 and 99; yet i, 11 and ii, 142 say that Cicero is without any public or forensic occupation. Probably he began the work before the Ides of March and revised or otherwise finished it after.

on to arguments derived from Chrysippos.[116] The work clearly was composed after the elections of 710/44 and before January, 711/43, for he describes Hirtius as consul designate [117]; as he speaks of disturbances and renewed strife as threatening but still hopes to avoid them, it cannot be very late in the year, perhaps about May or June. This impression is strengthened when we find him occupied with other philosophic works that same year.

At a date earlier than the *de officiis*, about July, 710/44, he composed two books *de gloria*, obviously in great haste, for he not only made an elementary mistake, which, as Gellius rightly says, any one who had read the seventh book of the *Iliad* could detect,[118] but provided the work with a proem which he had already used. We have but a few fragments and references.

The next work of this kind is again short and excellent reading, the little treatise *de amicitia*, otherwise known as *Laelius*, from its principal character. Laelius, after Scipio's death, is introduced speaking to Gaius Fannius and Mucius Scaevola the augur, first briefly of his dead friend and then at more length of friendship in general. We shall probably not be far wrong if we accept the criticism of Gellius,[119] that Cicero adapted to his own purposes the monograph of Theophrastos on friendship, omitting most of its thorniest part, the discussion of the conflicting claims of private affection and public duty. The precise date when this essay was written cannot be determined, but it mentions the *de senectute* and is itself mentioned in the *de officiis* [120]; it must therefore have been composed between about March and October, 710/44.

The last philosophical work of any importance is the treatise on duties, *de officiis*, addressed to his son. He had completed the first two books, which were based on a work of Panaitios, by November; later in the same month he had secured the material he wanted for the third, a sketch or outline of an essay

[116] *De fato*, 7.

[117] *Ibid.*, 2.

[118] Gellius, xv, 6; Cicero has transferred to Aias words which belong to Hektor. Cicero, *ad Att.*, xv, 27, 2 (July 3), librum tibi celeriter mittam de gloria. *Ibid.*, xvi, 2, 6, de gloria misi tibi (July 12): 6, 4, the matter of the prologue. *De off.*, ii, 31: nunc dicamus de gloria, quamquam ea quoque de re duo sunt nostri libri.

[119] Gellius, i, 3, 10 *sqq.* Of Theophrastos' work we have but fragments; for his characteristics in general, see Rose, *H.G.L.*, p. 351 *sqq.*

[120] *De amic.*, 4: in Catone maiore qui est scriptus ad te de senectute. The *de amicitia* is likewise addressed to Atticus. *De off.*, ii, 31: sed de amicitia alio libro dictum est, qui inscribitur Laelius. This, then, was his own title for it.

of Poseidonios on conflicts between duty and interest.[121] Thus the whole work is Stoic in its inspiration ; in other words, it draws on the system of dogmatic ethics then most in vogue, which Cicero, as an Academic, felt himself at liberty to adopt, as it were provisionally, pending further enlightenment.[122] The arrangement is simple in the extreme, no dialogue or other literary device being employed beyond a short introduction to each book.

It would appear that he wrote a sort of pendant to it, known as *de uirtutibus*. St. Jerome knew of it, and it is possible that Petrarch had seen a copy[123]; at present, pending possible discoveries in some neglected corner of a library, it must be regarded as lost.

Cicero was, in addition to his formal works, a great letter-writer. As already mentioned (p. 164), the epistles from his pen vary from formal dispatches and pamphlets to hurried notes. It is especially from the latter that we learn what Latin as spoken ordinarily by men of culture was like in that age ; one of the most outstanding features, here as in the works of Lucilius, is the immense amount of Greek in common use for everyday things, besides the masses of technical terms employed as required. Into the linguistic questions, however, we cannot go, any more than the great historical value of the correspondence[124] can be discussed here. There remain to us, out of a number originally much larger, two great collections, with two smaller ones. First and most important, because most intimate and freest from all formalities, is the correspondence with Atticus (cf. p. 165). This begins not long before the consulate of Cicero, the earliest letter we have being of about the beginning of 687/67, and continues down to within a few months of his death, the latest taking us into December, 710/44.[125] There are naturally gaps, due not

[121] *Ad Att.*, xv, 13, 6 (October) ; xvi, 11, 4 ; 14, 4.

[122] *De off.*, ii, 7.

[123] Jerome, *comment. in Zachariam* (on Zach., i, 18–19), vol. vi, p. 792 a–b Vallarsi : quattuor scilicet uirtutes . . . de quibus plenissime in officiorum libris Tullius disputat, scribens proprium quoque de quattuor uirtutibus librum. This is confirmed by Charisius, who quotes (p. 208, 15) : idem (sc., Cicero) in commentario de uirtutibus. For Petrarch, see Schanz-Hosius, i, p. 526.

[124] The fullest and best edition from the historical point of view, though the text has since been bettered in many places, is that of Tyrrell and Purser, Dublin and London, various dates from 1897 to 1914, under the general title *The Correspondence of Cicero*. This arranges the letters in their chronological order, known or conjectured, and provides a commentary and introductions.

[125] *Ad Att.*, i, 5 ; xvi, 15.

only to loss of some of the correspondence but also to the periods when the two friends were together. Cicero had intended to edit a selection of letters himself,[126] but never did so; Atticus kept those he received, but apparently no copies of his own answers, which perhaps were not documents he regarded it as safe to have extant. Nepos saw several rolls of them in his library, and some one, quite unknown to us, but presumably in possession of Atticus' material, put together and gave to the world the sixteen books we have, in order generally chronological, some time about the principate of Nero.[127]

The other large collection which we have is generally known by the modern and rather inappropriate title of *ad familiares*.[128] It consists also of sixteen books of letters (suggesting that the editor of one of the two series had the length of the other in mind) and contains, not only Cicero's own letters to all manner of people on all sorts of subjects, but also a large number of their replies, whence and how collected we do not know, though the most likely explanation seems to be that either Cicero or Tiro kept them, together with copies of Cicero's own. Certainly Tiro had the idea, in 709/45, of getting out a collection in more than one book of Cicero's and his correspondents' letters.[129] We do not know of our collection, or even any of the letters contained in it, being published earlier than Claudius' time, when the persons who might have taken offence at the many outspoken statements contained therein were all dead.[130] Thus the neighbourhood of 794/41 (accession of Claudius) is the earliest reasonably likely date, while anything later down almost to the end of antiquity is possible for the complete collection, if indeed it

[126] *Ad Att.*, xvi, 5, 5: mearum epistularum nulla est συναγωγή; sed habet Tiro (his freedman and secretary) instar septuaginta, et quidem sunt a te quaedam sumendae. eas oportet perspiciam, corrigam; tum denique edentur.

[127] Nepos, *Atticus*, 16, 3; for xi, Aldus and, following him, Winstedt read xvi, very plausibly. Asconius could not have known the *ad Att.*, or he would certainly have quoted i, 2, 1 when (p. 86, 15 *sqq.*, Clark) he is questioning Fenestella's statement that Cicero once defended Catiline. Therefore the collection is later than his work, *i.e.*, than about 808/55.

[128] This dates only from Stephanus, and is inadequate in view of the facts that Cicero was not on terms of close friendship with all his correspondents and many of the most famous letters (as that from Servius Sulpicius on the death of Tullia, v, 5) are not from but to Cicero.

[129] Cic., *ad fam.*, xvi, 17, 1 (to Tiro, June 28, 709/45): uideo quid agas; tuas quoque epistulas uis referri in uolumina. There were therefore to be more books than one, and the collection was not to be confined to Cicero's own letters.

[130] Seneca Rhetor (see p. 317), *suas.*, i, 5, cites *ad fam.*, xv, 19, 3.

is a collection and not several rolled into one. However this may be, the letters are arranged under the correspondents addressed, all those to Cicero's wife, for instance, occupying the fourteenth book, while ix, 15–26 is a series of communications to L. Papirius Paetus, and v, 9–11 a most amusing interchange of letters with Vatinius, who among other things reproaches Cicero with asking pardon for one Catilius. 'Drat you and our friend Sextus Servilius! . . . How can you undertake such clients and such cases? The most cruel brute on earth, the murderer, kidnapper and ruiner of so many free-born persons, respectable married women, Roman citizens, and layer waste of whole districts! The fellow is an ape, not worth a cracked farthing; he levied war on me, and I beat him and took him prisoner.'[131] This, some eleven years after the *interrogatio in Vatinium* and ten after Cicero's defence of him, combines with numerous expressions of apparently genuine affection from the adventurer to the orator to throw a new light on their relations; and it is but a random sample of what we find in this rich collection.

Of the two smaller collections, one consists wholly of letters to Quintus Cicero. The first is rather of the nature of a short tractate, which, under cover of a panegyric on Quintus' management of his province of Asia, gives good advice on how the country should be governed and on the duty of restraining a naturally hot temper. The rest of the three books contain less formal communications, though the two brothers never seem to have been as familiar with one another as the elder was with Atticus. The collection extends over but six years, 694/60–700/54. Another collection, in two books, contains letters from Cicero to Brutus and from Brutus to Cicero (one, however, is to Atticus), all dating from the last year of Cicero's life.[132]

These are all the complete letters we have. The ancients mention many more, however, and some few fragments are preserved. The ones which perhaps it would be most interesting to have are those addressed to a lady named Caerellia, a good deal older than Cicero, apparently highly educated and on friendly terms with him.[133] Quota-

[131] *Ad fam.*, v, 10 (= No. 696 Tyrrell-Purser), 1.

[132] For a while, doubts were entertained as to the genuineness of the correspondence with Brutus, which now, however, is universally considered to be entirely or almost entirely authentic. See Schanz-Hosius, i, p. 475 *sq*.

[133] Cicero, *ad Att.*, xiii, 21a, 2 (21, 5); Caerellia has got hold of Atticus' copy of the *de finibus* and is making one from it. *Ad fam.*, xiii, 72 (recommends some affairs of Caerellia's in Asia to P. Servilius; evidently she had a considerable estate). Quint., vi, 3, 112; Cassius Dio, xlvi,

tions from and references to letters to Pompey, Julius Caesar and Octavian, Hirtius, Pansa, Quintus Axius (a friend of Varro, who takes part in the conversation in the latter's *de re rustica*, cf. p. 221), Marcus Cicero the younger, Calvus, Nepos, Marcus Titinius the rhetorician, Cato, Hostilius, and some Greek correspondents are also extant; several of these refer to collections in more than one book. That all these were genuine cannot be guaranteed; we still have an obviously spurious letter, the exercise of some rhetorician, supposed to be addressed to Octavian after he had formed his coalition with Antony and Lepidus and overthrown the senatorial party.[134]

It may be mentioned that QVINTVS CICERO was not without literary ambitions, and the letters to him often speak of his writings. However, nothing of his has come down to us except a long letter of advice to his brother on the art of canvassing (known as the *commentariolum petitionis consulatus*) and a scrap of verse dealing with the signs of the zodiac.[135]

A few lost works of Cicero may be conveniently mentioned here, as they do not fall exactly into any of the above classes of composition. Akin to his speeches are a few panegyrics (*laudationes*) on persons recently dead, whereof by far the most famous was that on Cato, after his suicide at Utica in 708/46.[136] It is well known that Caesar was displeased with the tone of this, as being in effect an attack upon himself; but, with his usual moderation, he merely replied in writing with a somewhat bulky work entitled *Anticato*.[137] Another *laudatio* was pronounced over the body of Porcia, Brutus' wife.[138] Cicero also occasionally wrote a speech for some one else to deliver; he names one himself, Quintilian two others, implying that there were still more.[139]

Unlike many great authors, he was but little imitated by forgers. We have only two speeches which are certainly spurious, one *pridie quam in exsilium iret*, and the other *in C. Sallustium Crispum controuersia*, the latter one of a pair whereof the other is supposed to be an attack upon him by Sallust. Both these pieces of declama-

18, 4 (Caerellia's age, and some scandal about the relationship); Ausonius, *cent. nupt., ad fin.* (in epistulis ad Caerelliam subesse petulantiam); Boissier, *op. cit.*, pp. 94–5.

[134] Usually printed at the end of the genuine correspondence: for all these matters, see Schanz-Hosius, i, p. 477 *sqq.*

[135] The *commentariolum*, usually printed with the letters; the verses, Müller, *op. cit.*, p. 405.

[136] Fragments and references, Müller, *op. cit.*, p. 327 *sqq.*

[137] That it was bulky seems to follow from Juvenal, vi, 338.

[138] The 'Portia' of *Julius Caesar*. See Cic., *ad Att.*, xiii, 37, 3; 48, 2.

[139] Cic., *ad Q. frat.*, iii, 8, 5; Quintilian, iii, 8, 50: Cicero cum scriberet Cn. Pompeio et cum T. Ampio ceterisue . . . ut melius quidem sed tamen ipsi dicere uiderentur.

tion are printed in the principal editions of Cicero (end of the last vol. of C. F. W. Müller's, for example), the latter in some editions of Sallust. Very little is heard of the existence of spurious speeches in antiquity; see Schanz-Hosius, i, p. 447.

One interesting project was to write a work on jurisprudence, although he seems to have abandoned it before it was finished. Our fragments are so scanty that we cannot tell whether the title, *de iure ciuili in artem redigendo*, implied merely a dissertation on the advisability of codifying the law in accordance with intelligible principles (to be borrowed, we may conjecture, from the Stoic jurists) or an actual attempt to do something of the kind.[140] He also wrote *de auguriis*. It is tempting to suppose that this was in 703/53, when after the death of the younger Crassus he was elected to the place thus left vacant in the college of augurs; but the only possible allusion to such a work anywhere in Cicero is too ambiguous to found anything upon.[141] Finally, we hear of the existence of a work on geography, *Chorographia*,[142] a collection of wonders, *Admiranda*, apparently consisting of real or alleged freaks of nature,[143] and a pasquinade against Clodius in the form of an imaginary official notice, *edictum Luci Racili tribuni plebi*.[144] A more serious defence of himself was a pamphlet, *expositio consiliorum suorum*, *i.e.*, a statement of his political principles.[145]

[140] Gellius, i, 22, 7: M. autem Cicero in libro qui inscriptus est De iure ciuili in artem redigendo. Quintil., xii, 3, 10: et M. Tullius non modo inter agendum nunquam est destitutus scientia iuris sed etiam componere aliqua de eo coeperat.

[141] The few quotations, all late, are in Müller, *op. cit.*, p. 312. Cicero, *de diuin.*, ii, 76, after mentioning augury, says: sed de hoc loco plura in aliis. This might be a reference to an existing work (supply *scripsi*), but quite as readily understandable of one to be written (*sc. scribam*). For his augurate, see *Phil.*, ii, 4; *Brut.*, 1; Plut., *Cic.*, 36.

[142] Cic., *ad Att.*, ii, 4, 3; 6, 1; 7, 1, mentions a geographical work on which he is engaged. Priscian, vol. ii, p. 267, 5 Keil, cites from Cicero in chorographia, which would seem to be the same work.

[143] Fragments in Müller, *ibid.*, p. 340 *sq.*; they are mostly from the elder Pliny. Books of this sort were very popular in the Hellenistic period, see Rose, *H.G.L.*, p. 369.

[144] Schol. Bob., on *pro Planc.*, 77, p. 145, 26 *sqq.* Hildebrandt. This Racilius was a real person, see Cic., *ad Q. frat.*, ii, 1, 3, and the scholiast, *ibid.*

[145] Fragments in Müller, *ibid.*, p. 338 *sq.* As the date was during the First Triumvirate, before the death of Crassus in 703/53, it is a not unplausible conjecture, often made, that the ἀνέκδοτα which he will read to none but Atticus (*ad Att.*, ii, 6, 2, written in 695/59) are this work or a draft of it.

CHAPTER VIII

PROSE OF CICERO'S TIME

WHILE Cicero, for us and to a considerable extent for his contemporaries also, was so outstanding a figure as to dominate the fields of oratory, rhetorical study, and what passed for philosophy, there were other authors of merit in some of those branches during his lifetime, and others again busy in departments of literature and scholarly activity to which he made no important contribution, although they interested him.[1]

Of contemporary orators, most belonged, as already indicated (p. 162), to the Asianic school, until the Atticizing movement made itself felt. Perhaps the greatest name of the age, next to Cicero's own, is that of QVINTVS HORTENSIVS HORTALVS, generally known as Hortensius simply. He was eight years older than Cicero, being born in 640/114,[2] and was the undisputed leader of the Roman bar when the younger man began to make his name as a pleader. Owing, however, partly to the fact that his speeches were much more effective to hear than to read, partly to the triumph for the time being of the Ciceronian and Attic styles, his reputation almost died with him, and we have next to no verbal quotations from the fairly numerous orations of which the names or occasions are known.[3] His style, says Cicero,[4] was well enough in his youth, but ill suited to an elderly man who had held high office in the state; furthermore, he did not practise enough, and consequently deteriorated and lost the fluency which was one of his strong points. Besides his speeches,

[1] He had thoughts of writing a history of Rome, Plut., *Cic.*, 41, and remarks on historical, grammatical, antiquarian and other matters are common in his works.

[2] Cicero, *Brut.*, 229: is L. Crasso Q. Scaeuola consulibus (659/95) primum in foro dixit . . . undeuiginti annos natus erat eo tempore, est autem L. Paullo C. Marcello consulibus mortuus (704/50).

[3] Remains in *O.R.F.*, p. 361 *sqq.*

[4] Cic., *Brut.*, 325–7, 320 *sqq.*

he was the author of a historical work [5] whereof we know far too little to criticize it, and also dabbled in poetry, apparently erotic, without much success.[6] He died in 704/50.[7]

One of the few women prominent in Latin literature was his daughter HORTENSIA. She made her name by one famous speech, actually delivered, against all precedent, by herself, in 712/42, in protest against a proposed levy by the triumvirs on the property of wealthy women to pay for the war against Brutus and Cassius. No man dared plead their cause; but she entered the forum, spoke with her father's eloquence, was protected by the crowd against attempts to silence her, and won her case.[8]

A famous name among the speakers of the time is that of ANTONY (MARCVS ANTONIVS), who is said to have been an adherent of the Asianic school; but unless his orations were much superior in style to his letters, of which a few are preserved in the correspondence of Cicero, he was hardly able even to express himself in respectable Latin.[9]

There are a number of other persons, some of them very well known, who are mentioned as having spoken on occasions, or even as possessing a certain oratorical ability; these include POMPEY (GNAEVS POMPEIVS MAGNVS), MARCVS LICINIVS CRASSVS, his colleague in the consulship and in the first triumvirate, LVCIVS SERGIVS CATILINA (CATILINE) and many more. Their names, dates, and references to their utterances will be found in *oratorum Romanorum fragmenta*; but, as practically nothing is left of anything they said, and the existence of some of their letters in the Ciceronian corpus is hardly reason enough for allotting them space in a book of this size, further mention of them is omitted. Some at least of them were probably of the Asianic school.

Their rivals, the Atticists, included a number of the younger men. We have already dealt with Calvus (p. 134). The most famous name is that of MARCVS IVNIVS BRVTVS, the assassin of

[5] See *H.R.F.*, p. 205 *sq.* Cicero, *ad Att.*, xii, 5b (= 5, 3), says he was a *bonus auctor*, *i.e.*, a reliable historian, and Velleius, ii, 16, 3, that he wrote *dilucide* on events of the Social War. Cicero seems to be in accord with the general opinion when he remarks (*orat.*, 132) that he spoke better than he wrote.

[6] Catullus addresses the 65th poem to him; Ovid (*trist.*, ii, 441) classes him among lascivious poets; Gellius (xix, 9, 7) cites the opinion of unnamed critics of his own day that his poems were *inuenusta*.

[7] See n. 2.

[8] Appian, *Bell. ciu.*, iv, 32–4. Whether the words which he there puts into Hortensia's mouth owe anything to the actual speech (extant and read *non tantum in sexus honorem* in Quintilian's time, *inst. orat.*, i, 1, 6) we do not know.

[9] See especially *ad Att.*, xiv, 13 a, b (letter from Antony and Cicero's reply, full of tacit corrections of its bad style).

Caesar. His life is too well known for any details to be necessary here; he was born in 669/85 and died by his own hand in 712/42. His interests were wide and his literary activity considerable; it is not mere flattery when Cicero credits him with 'recondite learning and unparalleled diligence'.[10] Nothing has survived of his speeches[11]; of his other works we know from Cicero, Seneca and Diomedes[12] that he wrote *On Virtue*, *On Duty* and *On Patience*, from Cicero and Plutarch that he epitomized various historical works,[13] and from Tacitus and Pliny the Younger[14] that he tried his hand at verse. Of his style when he composed carefully we know that in avoiding Asianic ornaments he ran into the opposite extreme of inharmonious collocations of words and loose structure of the whole work.[15]

An interesting case of a vanished reputation, fit to warn us how little we know of the literature of that time, is that of MARCVS CALIDIVS, the earliest, apparently, of the Atticists.[16] According to Cicero, he was possessed of every oratorical virtue except the power to excite his audience; he was much too calm at moments when a show of emotion would have been most in place. Probably a more northerly audience would have appreciated him more. He was a Caesarian, and died during the civil war; his public career was but moderately distinguished, for although twice a candidate for the consulship, he was never elected.[17] His dates are 657/97–706/48.

Two well-known names in the politics of the time are those of GAIVS SCRIBONIVS CVRIO and MARCVS CAELIVS RVFVS; both apparently had considerable ability as speakers, and to judge by the company they kept, for both ultimately were Caesarians, they may have been Atticists. The former, whose actions as tribune of the plebs in 704/50 set the match to the train which started the civil war, was the son and grandson of more or less able speakers, and distinguished himself by his natural eloquence rather than by any great diligence in study. The latter, whose career was cut short in 706/48, when he was killed in trying

[10] *Brut.*, 22. [11] See *O.R.F.*, p. 443 *sqq.*

[12] Cic., *Tusc.*, v, 1; Sen., *ep.*, xlv, 45, who gives a Greek title, περὶ καθήκοντος, but certainly the text was in Latin, as some quotations in grammarians show. Diomedes, i, p. 383, 8 Keil.

[13] See chap. v, notes 130 and 141; add Plut., *Brut.*, 4.

[14] Tac., *Dial.*, 21, 11; Pliny, *epp.*, v, 3, 5.

[15] Tacitus, *op. cit.*, 18, 9, Cicero called him otiosum atque diiunctum, 'careless and formless'; Quint., ix, 4, 7, he deliberately used bad rhythm.

[16] See Cicero, *Brut.*, 274–8. His fragments are in *O.R.F.*, p. 434 *sqq.* His teacher, Apollodoros of Pergamon, must have had a long career, for he also taught Augustus, see Jerome, *an. Abr.* 1953 = 690/64.

[17] For this and other biographical details, see *O.R.F.*, *loc. cit.*

to create a revolt against his leader, had likewise much readiness in speech and a polished wit which made him effective especially in political harangues and in accusations; as counsel for the defence he was never so good. Of his share in the suit which occasioned Cicero's speech *pro Caelio* something has already been said (p. 180).[18]

Passing over a number of men of whom it is recorded that they were more or less able orators, we come to an important branch of the literature of that time, history. For some reason, the age of Sulla was fertile in attempts to record the earlier history of Rome; we sometimes speak of the Sullan annalists. The earliest of them was QVINTVS CLAVDIVS QVADRIGARIVS. Apart from his somewhat doubtful claims to be considered the Latinizer of the work of Acilius (see p. 113 and n. 115 there), he was the author of a history (*annales*) in at least twenty-three books, which began, not with the earliest times, but after the Gaulish invasion,[19] and came down to his own day, apparently devoting more space to the more recent events. In this he at

[18] Cicero, *Brut.*, 213 *sqq.* (Curio pater), 280 (Curio filius), 273 (Caelius). More details, and fragments, *O.R.F.*, pp. 252 *sqq.*, 458 *sqq.*, 481 *sqq.*

[19] The facts concerning the historian, or historians, are as follows: (1) *Claudius Quadrigarius* is cited by several authors (frags. in *H.R.F.*, p. 136 *sqq.*), with or without his cognomen. The quotations from Book I of his *annales* deal with the year 364/390; consequently his work began at that date, or at most had prefixed to it a very brief sketch of earlier events. As the number of the books grows higher, the events assignable to each of them become fewer and nearer together; consequently the later part of the work was on a larger scale. There is therefore no reasonable doubt that the Claudius whom Livy cites in several passages from his sixth book on is Claudius Quadrigarius. (2) As stated in chap. v, n. 115, Livy also has references to a Claudius who translated the Greek annals of Acilius. He nowhere mentions his cognomen, nor do the other authorities throw any light on this matter. Hence the translator of Acilius may or may not be the same man; recent opinion tends to identify them (Schanz-Hosius, i, p. 316 *sq.*) but really cogent evidence one way or the other is wanting. (3) Plutarch's *Κλώδιος* (chap. v, n. 115), who says in his *ἔλεγχος χρόνων* that the earlier Roman records were all destroyed in the Gaulish invasion, might again be Claudius Quadrigarius, if we suppose that the Greek title is a rather poor translation of *annales*; such a remark would be in place in a preface justifying the author for beginning comparatively late. But this leaves unexplained why Plutarch, who was not ill-informed about Roman matters, calls him by the plebeian form of the name, Clodius instead of Claudius, and plainly does not know who he was (*Κλώδιός τις*), whereas he had plenty of Roman friends who could have told him about Claudius Quadrigarius if his own reading had not done so. The date of Claudius Quadrigarius is approximately given by Velleius, ii, 9, 6, who says that he and Valerius Antias (p. 202) were contemporary with Sisenna (p. 204); Sisenna was praetor in 676/78.

least showed some attention to the primary duty of a historian to document his work. The style of the existing fragments is plain and homely, but not bad; for example, the duel between Manlius and the Gaul from whose neck-ornament he got his surname of Torquatus [20] is good straightforward narrative, with no misplaced attempts at cleverness to interfere with its interesting matter. The remark of Fronto that Quadrigarius used unaffected, pure, almost everyday colloquial Latin seems to be justified.[21] As to matter, his worst fault seems to have been a patriotic exaggeration of the damage done by the Romans to their various enemies [22]; he had a flair for what would attract his readers, for he tells some very interesting tales of courage, ingenuity and kindness.[23]

Contemporary with him was VALERIVS of ANTIVM (VALERIVS ANTIAS), a man gifted with more imagination than veracity. Livy, who is not critical, occasionally finds his statistics of those killed in various obscure battles hard of belief,[24] and no historical doubts prevented him spending at least two of his seventy-five books on the legends of the kings, some of which he told in considerable detail.[25] Obviously he worked on a large scale; his chronological limits were the foundation of Rome, apparently, and his own times or some date very near them; the latest event which we definitely know that he mentioned is the death of L. Crassus the orator in 663/91.[26] The bulk of his work, combined with an unattractive style,[27] no doubt made it easy for him to be superseded by Livy, who seems to have been the last person, apart from word-hunters and antiquarians, to read him.[28]

[20] Frag. 10, from Gellius, ix, 13, 7–19.

[21] Fronto *ap*. Gell., xiii, 29, 2, uir modesti atque puri ac prope cotidiani sermonis.

[22] So, frag. 66 (= Livy, xxxviii, 23, 6), he makes Cn. Manlius kill 40,000 Gauls, where even Valerius was content with 10,000, at the battle on the Mysian Olympos in 565/189.

[23] See for examples frags. 69 (valour of a Lusitanian horseman), 80 (two slaves by a stratagem rescue their mistress), 81 (ingenuity of the defenders at the siege of Athens in 667/87–668/86).

[24] *E.g.*, Livy, xxx, 19, 11; xxxiii, 10, 8; xxxviii, 23, 8.

[25] It is to him, for example, that we owe one of the fullest accounts of the dealings of Numa with Iuppiter Elicius, frag. 6.

[26] Frag. 64, from Pliny, *N.H.*, xxxiv, 14. The death of Sulla may have been his stopping-place.

[27] So at least Fronto judged, *ad Verum*, i, 1, 2 (vol. ii, p. 48, Loeb ed.): historiam quoque scripsere Sallustius stricte, Pictor incondite, Claudius lepide, Antias inuenuste.

[28] Plutarch cites him four times by name, always to contrast his statements with another's, thus suggesting that the other writer (Juba, in *Rom.*, 14; Livy, xxxix, 43, 1, in *T. Flam.*, 18) may have been his source.

Concerning GAIVS LICINIVS MACER (tribune of the plebs in 681/73, committed suicide in 688/66) opinions differ widely. He asserted that he had read and used certain ancient records written on linen (*libri lintei*), and on the strength of them he several times gave information which, if true, is interesting concerning early events in the history of Rome. Either this was an important and neglected discovery or else an impudent lie. The historians of the last two or three generations, including Mommsen, declared for the latter alternative; before them Niebuhr and of late Beloch incline towards the former.[29] Personally, I hold rather strongly to Mommsen's opinion, although it is a subject on which I cannot speak as a specialist. Macer was a man of little learning and great impudence; he occupied no very high position in public life, but had some repute as an advocate not of the highest class[30]; it is hard to see how he would have opportunity to make out-of-the-way researches through the public archives and find among them treasures of which neither Varro nor Atticus was aware. On the other hand, even the uncritical Livy caught him lying in the interests of his family,[31] and that he should tell another lie to the enhancement of his own reputation is in no way improbable. Posterity seems not to have regarded him much; Livy and Dionysios of Halikarnassos used him, and his name appears in the elder Pliny's omnivorous bibliography; otherwise we scarcely hear of him and do not know how far down he brought his history (the latest datable event the fragments mention is in 326/428) nor of how many books it consisted.

LVCIVS AELIVS TVBERO and his son QVINTVS were fairly prominent supporters of Pompey against Caesar, but were reconciled to the latter after Pharsalus. The father seems to have set about writing a history,[32] but we have no evidence that it was ever published, unless the work of his son was the completion of it. Quintus certainly won himself some repute as a

[29] For the controversy, see Schanz-Hosius, i, p. 321.

[30] Cicero, *de legg.*, ii, 7: nam quid Macrum nominem? cuius loquacitas habet aliquid argutiarum, nec id tamen ex illa erudita Graecorum copia sed ex librariolis Latinis. *Brut.*, 238, speaking of his oratorical abilities: in inueniendis componendisque rebus mira accuratio, ut non facile in ullo diligentiorem maioremque cognouerim, sed eam ut citius ueteratoriam quam oratoriam diceres. It is to be noted that the former passage is put into the mouth of Atticus, with whose views Cicero would be well acquainted.

[31] Livy, vii, 9, 5; for the *libri lintei* see iv, 7, 12; 20, 5 *sqq.*; 23, 2–3 (Tubero also mentions them—at second hand from Macer?).

[32] Cicero, *ad Q. frat.*, i, 1, 10 (Tubero is Quintus Cicero's *legatus* and is writing a history; the date is 694/60, too early for the son).

jurist after the failure of his accusation of Ligarius (see p. 183); that he and not his father wrote the annalistic work of which we hear is well testified.[33] When it was begun we do not know; it consisted of not fewer than thirteen books and came down to the writer's own day, mentioning some incidents in the youth of Julius Caesar, if nothing later.[34] As usual, its starting-point was the foundation of Rome, including the story of Aeneas.[35]

Two obscure writers of about this time were PROCILIVS, of whom we know nothing save that his work included some matters of Roman topography and cultural history,[36] and LIBO, perhaps SCRIBONIVS LIBO, father-in-law of Pompey, whose work was extant in 709/45 and known to Cicero.[37]

An author of some little importance was LVCIVS CORNELIVS SISENNA. This man was city praetor and also *praetor inter peregrinos* in 678/76, one of Verres' defenders against Cicero (p. 172), and died in Crete in 689/87, being sent on a mission to Metellus from Pompey, whose *legatus* he then was.[38] He was, says Cicero, a man of learning, versed in public affairs, witty, but no great pleader and an indifferent stylist, although his familiar speech was correct.[39] He was born about 634/120, and seems to have taken an interest in history while still fairly young,

[33] Livy, iv, 23, 1: Valerius Antias et Q. Tubero (no variant of any significance in the names). Suetonius, *diu. Iul.*, 83; Quintus Tubero tradit. For his legal writings, see Pomponius in Dig., i, 2, 46: Tubero . . . transiit a causis agendis ad ius ciuile, maxime postquam Quintum Ligarium accusauit nec obtinuit apud Gaium Caesarem. . . . Tubero doctissimus quidem habitus est iuris publici et priuati et complures utriusque operis libros reliquit: sermone etiam antiquo usus affectauit scribere et ideo parum libri eius grati habentur.

[34] Frag. 10a.

[35] Frag. 2.

[36] See the fragments in *H.R.F.*, p. 198.

[37] Cic., *ad Att.*, xiii, 30, 2 (3); 32, 3; Appian, *bell. ciu.*, iii, 77, seems to cite him, but it is for events of 708/46, only a year before Cicero's letters above quoted; probably therefore the *Λίβωνι* in his text is a scribal error for *Λιβίωι*, cf. Livy, *epit.*, 124. An entirely unknown writer is SVLPICIVS BLITHO, cited by Nepos, *Han.*, 13, 1.

[38] Praetorship, SC de Asclepiade (C.I.L., i², 588 + I.G. xiv, 951 = *F.I.R.A.*, No. 41), 2, *στρατηγοῦ δὲ κατὰ πόλιν καὶ ἐπὶ τῶν ξένων Λευκίου Κορνηλίο[υ . . . υἱοῦ] Σισέννα* (this also preserves his praenomen, apparently not recorded elsewhere); Verres, Cicero, *in Verr.*, ii, 4, 43; death, Cassius Dio, xxxvi, 19, 1.

[39] Cic., *Brut.*, 228; *de legg.*, i, 7, which says S., though better than any who preceded him, is still very far from a really good historical style and seems to have read nobody but Kleitarchos (see Rose, *H.G.L.*, p. 365; K. was of the Asianic school, and therefore it would seem that S.'s style was of the same kind; Cicero, *ibid.*, says puerile quiddam consectatur).

though the bulk at least of his work was composed towards the end of his life.[40] It was called *historiae*, or at least is always cited under that title when any is given, and dealt with his own age, the period of civil wars up to and including the days of Sulla. Its length is doubtfully estimated at about twenty-three books, certainly at least half that.[41] He also translated the Milesian Tales of Aristeides.[42]

Some one called Sisenna also wrote a commentary on Plautus several times quoted by grammarians, but this was certainly a later author, although his exact date is not known, for he once at least quoted Vergil.[43]

Several other writers gave an account of their own times. The best known of these was LVCIVS LICINIVS LVCVLLVS, the general and statesman. If we may believe Plutarch,[44] his attempts in this direction were the result of a kind of bet; Hortensius and Sisenna challenged him to take the Social War for his subject and draw lots to see whether he should use Latin or Greek, verse or prose as his medium; chance decided for Greek prose, and he wrote accordingly, purposely making a few stylistic and grammatical errors, says Cicero,[45] to show that he was a Roman. TANVSIVS GEMINVS wrote a long and apparently dull work which included some account of Caesar.[46]

[40] Velleius, ii, 9, 5; historiarum auctor iam tum (*i.e.*, about the time of the fall of Numantia, in 621/133; but Sisenna was older than Sulpicius and younger than Hortensius, Cic., *Brut.*, 228, therefore born between 630/124 and 640/114) Sisenna erat iuuenis, sed opus belli ciuilis Sullanique post aliquot annos ab eo seniore editum est.

[41] Nonius, p. 127, 32, cites *Sisenna ab urbe condita*, which can hardly be anything but a confusion with Livy's title; elsewhere, always *historiae*. There is one quotation from Book xxiii, but it refers to an event of 672/82, and we have the happenings of 666/88 spoken of in one from Book vi (see frags. 125, 132). He can hardly have spent seventeen books over six years. Apart from this, the highest-numbered citation is from Book xii.

[42] Ovid, *trist.*, ii, 443: uertit Aristiden Sisenna, nec offuit illi/historiae turpis inseruisse iocos. For Aristeides, see Rose, *op. cit.*, p. 415. By historiae . . . iocos, Ovid of course means, not that S. enlivened his *historiae* with Milesian tales, but that he occupied himself with such things in the intervals of his graver researches.

[43] Charisius, i, p. 229, 9 Keil: tractim Plautus in Amphitryone, ubi Sisenna, 'pro lente', inquit, 'non ut Maro georgicon iiii, "tractimque susurrit", inquit'. Either the first or the second *inquit* should probably be deleted.

[44] Plut., *Lucull.*, 1.

[45] Cic., *ad Att.*, i, 19, 10: non dicam tibi quod, ut opinor, Panhormi Lucullus de suis historiis dixit, se quo facilius illas probaret Romani hominis esse idcirco barbara quaedam et σόλοικα dispersisse. How genuine this excuse of Lucullus was, is matter of opinion.

[46] Seneca, *epp.*, xciii, 11: annales Tanusii scis quam ponderosi sint et quid uocentur. hoc est uita quorundam longa, et quod Tanusii sequitur annales. We do not know what Tanusius' *annales* were called, but it is an old conjecture (Muretus) that Catullus' annales Volusi, cacata carta

Others wrote biographical works and memoirs. LVCIVS CORNELIVS SVLLA produced the most celebrated of these, an autobiography, though he did not live to finish it and it was edited for publication by his freeman CORNELIVS EPICADVS. It was dedicated to Lucullus.[47] The fragments show that its loss is to be regretted, not so much as a trustworthy historical document, for its author was capable of amazing lies,[48] but as throwing a light on one of the most extraordinary characters in history, a blend of ruthless and single-minded efficiency with a confidence in his own good fortune which amounted to gross superstition. A rhetorician whose name is rather doubtful, perhaps LVCIVS VOLTACILIVS PITHOLAVS,[49] numbered Pompey among his pupils and wrote a long biography of him, which has not survived.

A much more remarkable figure was Cicero's friend, TITVS POMPONIVS ATTICVS, one of the most completely self-consistent Epicureans in history, and a notable example for any one to use who would argue that enlightened and far-seeing self-interest combined with lack of too strong attachments or emotions can

(36, 1) alludes to them under a disguised name (cf. p. 141). But this involves supposing that they were in verse, or that he wrote two historical works, one in verse and the other in prose, for Catullus here and elsewhere (95, 7) implies that Volusius was a versifier, but the quotations from Tanusius, or Tanusius Geminus (it is not even certain that the two were the same) which we have (*H.R.F.*, p. 239 *sq.*) give no indications of being taken from other than a prose work. He is cited by Suetonius, *diu. Iul.*, 9, and Plut., *Caes.*, 22, for events of 688/66 and 699/55 respectively.

A completely lost historian of this period is LVCIVS LVCCEIVS, to whom Cicero wrote in 698/56 (*ad fam.*, v, 12), asking that, as he had nearly finished a work on the civil wars and was going to write more, he would treat of Cicero's consulship and not be too strictly bound by the facts in praising it.

[47] Plut., *Lucull.*, 1; Sueton., *de gramm.*, 12.

[48] He would, for example, have his readers believe that at the battle of Sacriportus he lost but 23 men and the enemy 20,000 killed and 8,000 prisoners, frag. 19 (*H.R.F.*, p. 134) = Plut., *Sulla*, 28; the surviving fragments are full likewise of supernatural events, especially divine warnings.

[49] The MSS. of Suet., *de rhet.*, 3, agree on the *praenomen* L., vary between Oltacilius, Octacilius and Otacilius for the *nomen*, and give Pilutus (with small variants) as the *cognomen*. Jerome, who speaks of the same man, *an. Abr.* 1936 = 673/81, calls him Vultacilius Plotus, Plautus, Plutus or Plocius, according to various MSS. But there was some one called M. Votacilius Pytholaus, according to the MSS. of Macrobius, *sat.*, ii, 2, 13, who lived about the same time, to judge by the anecdote there told of him. The majority of these divergent testimonies can be satisfied if, as Hertz has suggested (*Rhein. Mus.*, xliii, 1888, p. 312 *sqq.*), we suppose that there was one person, Voltacilius Pitholaus, with a *praenomen* which may have been either Lucius or Marcus; but the matter is far from certain.

produce a character not only successful but generally useful.[50] Born in 645/109, he was heir to a very considerable estate, which he afterwards augmented by his skill in business and also by his own great popularity, resulting in the receipt of numerous legacies. His family were connected with the tribune P. Sulpicius Rufus, and during the troubles which followed the latter's murder (see p. 108) he judged it wise to leave Italy for Athens, where he spent some years and gained his *cognomen* of Atticus. He consistently kept out of politics, attended to his own affairs, lived simply but comfortably, and used his increasing wealth to succour the necessities of men of all parties. His list of friends included, besides Cicero, Sulla, Hortensius, Cato, Antony and Octavian, and later M. Vipsanius Agrippa, who married his daughter (his sister had become the wife of Quintus Cicero, brother of the orator). Agrippa's daughter Vipsania Agrippina was the first wife of Ti. Claudius Nero, better known as the emperor Tiberius, and thus Atticus became the great-grandfather of the elder Drusus. When a severe intestinal disorder impelled him to suicide in 722/32, his very simple funeral seems to have been respectfully followed by half Rome. His great interest, apart from personal relationships, was the history of his country, and, in verse or in prose, all that he wrote was on this theme. Chronology had apparently been rather neglected; Atticus produced a single volume which, starting from the foundation of Rome (this he computed at the third year of the sixth Olympiad, which we call 753 B.C.),[51] gave a table

[50] The chief authority for his life, besides numerous references in Cicero, is Nepos' *Atticus*. From this the facts in the text are taken. Nepos, 22, 3, says he died on March 31, Cn. Domitio C. Sosio consulibus, *i.e.*, 722/32, and that he had completed his seventy-seventh year (*ibid.*, 21, 1) when his last illness began and lasted some three months. Strictly speaking, his name for the latter part of his life was Q. Caecilius Q. f. Pomponianus Atticus, for his uncle Q. Caecilius adopted him by will, *ibid.*, 5, 2, in 696/58, see Cicero, *ad Att.*, iii, 20, 1.

[51] This detail is from Solinus (cf. p. 438), i, 27. Strictly, Olymp. 6, 3 is B.C. 754–3; but an Olympiad begins in late summer, whereas Atticus may naturally be supposed to have reckoned either from Jan. 1 or Mar. 1, the latter, which is the old Roman New Year, being much the more probable. Thus his first year would come in the latter part of the Olympiadic year, and so in 753. Solinus there gives the other computations: Cincius (Alimentus) supposed it to have been in the twelfth Olympiad (B.C. 733/2–729/8); Pictor (Fabius) in the eighth; 'M. Tullius' (a mistake of writer or copyist for M. Terentius, *i.e.*, Varro) agrees with Atticus, while Nepos and Lutatius (Daphnis, cf. p. 442) put it in the second year of the seventh. Solinus' authority would put it at the beginning of Olymp. 7, *i.e.*, the end of 753 B.C. By what process such nearly agreeing results were arrived at is not known.

of the chief events, the magistrates, the authors and so forth of every year down to his own times or some date near them (it is not certain when it ended). The title was *liber annalis*, ' the Book of Years '. He also produced essays on the family history of the Claudii Marcelli, the Fabii and the Aemilii, all by request of individuals interested. His one incursion into modern history was a Greek monograph on Cicero's consulship.[52]

Atticus was also a publisher, at least incidentally. His household consisted of literates, down to his foot-boy,[53] and, being an excellent man of business, it is not likely that he failed to turn their useful accomplishments to profit. Apparently there was as yet no publishing house in Rome; for his acquaintances, at least, it would seem that Atticus filled this gap. Certainly he was, as has already been noticed (*e.g.*, p. 176), Cicero's publisher; and there is some evidence, not conclusive but fairly strong, that he also dealt in Greek books, a natural activity for a man who spoke that language like a native.[54]

His biographer, CORNELIVS NEPOS (his *praenomen* is unknown), wrote a number of historical books, the fruits of reading apparently wide, if not very critical, whereof the most are lost to us and the principal surviving performance has come down with a false name attached to it, though its attribution to Nepos is hardly doubted to-day. This is the *liber de excellentibus ducibus exterarum gentium*,[55] twenty-two short biographies of notable

[52] See Nepos, *Att.*, 18. The verses were a series of tetrastichs intended to be inscribed under portraits of distinguished Romans and giving a brief account of the career of each. The few actual references to the *liber annalis* are in *H.R.F.*, p. 215 *sqq.*; its influence may be suspected in numerous chronological passages, and Cicero's frequent appeals to Atticus show how wide was the scope of his friend's researches. For the account of the consulship, see also Cic., *ad Att.*, ii, 1, 1.

[53] Nepos, *ibid.*, 13, 3.

[54] We have occasional references (the earliest seems to be in Harpokration, *s.u.* ἀργᾶς, and therefore probably of the second century A.D., see Rose, *H.G.L.*, p. 398) to certain Ἀττικιανά, sc. ἀπόγραφα, which must mean copies (of classical Greek authors) made by or somehow connected with some one called Atticus. The suffix of the word is of Latin type. If this is not our Atticus, it is a very curious coincidence that there existed another man of that name, with Latin connexions, having sufficient critical knowledge of Greek for copies bearing his name to be cited as authorities for textual questions. For Atticus' perfect Greek, cf. Nepos, *op. cit.*, 4, 1; Cicero often jokingly calls him a Greek, and continually asks his opinion on matters of Greek style.

[55] The work has come down to us in MSS. which bear the superscription *liber Aemilii Probi de laudibus exterarum gentium*, or *Emilius Probus de laudibus ducum exterarum gentium*, and end with a few very bad verses, in which Probus, whoever he was, commends to Theodosius (either the first emperor of that name, 1132/379–1148/395, or the second, 1162/409–

leaders, all Greeks except Datames the Persian and two Carthaginians, Hamilcar Barca and Hannibal, together with an excursus on kings who have also been generals, which implies that there is a separate group of their biographies also. The last words of the collection introduce a companion book of Roman generals, which is lost. There also remain the biographies of Cato and Atticus, already cited (pp. 91, 207), which are said by our MSS. to be excerpted from a work *de historicis Latinis*; that this also had a companion dealing with Greek historians seems likely enough. Other references to Nepos testify that he wrote on poets, rhetoricians, grammarians and generally *de uiris illustribus*[56]; the impression is conveyed that he covered ground not unlike that of Plutarch's *Parallel Lives*, but with a wider scope, less detail, and incomparably less charm. For it must be admitted that the style is poor and dull, though it has the merit of being readily understood, and the Latinity much less choice than one would expect from a friend of Atticus and Cicero. This doubtless accounts for the absence of his name from Quintilian's review (cf. p. 400) of Latin literature, the loss of most of his works, and the scantiness of our knowledge about him.[57] He knew Catullus (cf. p. 141), who compliments him on his Universal History, in three books; it seems to have been called simply *Chronica*, and may very well, being so short, have been more like Atticus' *liber annalis* than a history proper, but of larger scope.[58] He himself wrote some verse, apparently erotic;

1203/450) a collection of poems (*carmina nuda*) by himself, his father and grandfather. But the biographies are not in verse, are addressed to Atticus, speak of events and conditions prevailing at the end of the republic, and certainly are not in fourth- or fifth-century Latin. After the lives of the generals come one or the other of the remaining biographies, and two MSS. have headings testifying that these are by Nepos. Stylistically, all the biographies are much alike; hence it is the general opinion that Nepos wrote them all and that Probus' name has wandered to the wrong place by some blunder of a scribe presumably copying out a large MS. of very miscellaneous content. See Schanz-Hosius, i, p. 355, for literature on this matter. I conjecture (but it is a conjecture only) that Probus and his versifying ancestors may have turned the substance of Nepos' book into metre and so paved the way for the confusion.

[56] Jerome, *de uir. ill.*, praef. (vol. ii, col. 807, Vallarsi); but he is speaking only of men illustrious in letters; Nepos had a wider range.

[57] Besides what he tells us himself, we know only that he was born in the region of the Po (Pliny, *N.H.*, iii, 127, cf. Pliny the Younger, *epp.*, iv, 28, 1). It is evident that he outlived Atticus, and so must have attained a considerable age, for his *Chronica* was written before 700/54, see next note.

[58] Catullus, i, 5–7: iam tum cum ausus es unus Italorum/omne aeuum tribus explicare cartis/doctis, Iuppiter, et laboriosis. The work was not, therefore, quite new when Catullus collected his poems. Exactly how

we also hear of a work called *Exempla*, which, to judge by the fragments, contained not only remarkable actions, good or bad, like the work of Valerius Maximus (cf. p. 356), but also such things as the dates of introduction of various luxuries into Rome. We have his own word for it that he wrote a separate and fuller life of Cato the Elder, and several quotations testify to his having written a life of Cicero.[59]

It may conveniently be mentioned here that Cicero's freedman and confidential secretary, MARCVS TVLLIVS TIRO, paid a tribute to his patron's memory by writing a biography of him. He had a long and not inactive life, surviving his old master more than forty years.[60] There is evidence of various value for what is probable enough in itself, that he edited Cicero's works, especially the speeches, together with a collection of his notes for those orations which were never written out in full.[61] He also published, or was supposed to have done so,[62] a collection of Cicero's good sayings, from which doubtless many of the remarks attributed to him by Plutarch and others are taken. On his own account, he wrote a work on Latin style (*de usu atque ratione linguae Latinae*), a miscellany (*Πανδέκτης*, 'the universal receiver'), and certain letters, probably essays in epistolary form, on literary questions.[63] He would seem also to have tried his hand at drama.[64] In addition to all this, he contributed largely to the invention of a

much is meant by *omne aeuum* we do not know; the fragments mostly deal with Italian matters. The title is given several times, *e.g.*, by Gellius, xvii, 213, Cornelius Nepos in primo chronico.

[59] Verses, Pliny, *epp.*, v, 3, 6. *Exempla*, fragments in *H.R.F.*, p. 224 *sqq*. Separate life of Cato, Nep., *Cato*, 3, 5. Life of Cicero, Gellius, xv, 28, 2: in librorum primo quos de uita illius (=Ciceronis) composuit. Fragments, *H.R.F.*, p. 223 *sq.*; he also had something to say of him in the group of lives of Roman historians, *ibid.*, frag. 18.

[60] Jerome, *an. Abr.* 2013 (= 750/4): M. Tullius Tiro Ciceronis libertus qui primus notas commentus est in Puteolano praedio usque ad centesimum annum consenescit. There is some confusion, for if Tiro was 100 years old then, he must have been born in 650/104; but he was *adulescens* in 704/50, Cicero, *ad Att.*, vi, 7, 2; vii, 2, 3, which would put his birth in the neighbourhood of 684/70. However, all the passage of Jerome need mean is that he was growing old in 750/4 and that he lived to be a hundred; Suetonius may have learned that from some mention of him, but been unable to find any trace of what he was doing at a later date than the one given. If this is so, he died about 774/21. Fragments of the biography (the highest-numbered book cited is the fourth, which however dealt apparently with the events of 702/52 and therefore was not the last) in *H.R.F.*, p. 212.

[61] Gellius, i, 7, 1, and elsewhere (Verrines); a number of subscriptions in MSS., for which see Schanz-Hosius, i, p. 548; Quintilian, x, 7, 31.

[62] Quintilian, vi, 3, 5. The collected dicta of Cicero will be found in the last volume of Müller's Teubner edition, p. 341 *sqq*.

[63] Gellius, xiii, 9, 1–4; vi (vii), 3, 8; x, 1, 7.

[64] Cicero to Tiro, *ad fam.*, xvi, 18, 3: an pangis aliquid Sophocleum?

system of shorthand, the *notae Tironianae*, which continued in use, though with additions and modifications for which he was not responsible, till the twelfth century.[65]

Another freedman of Cicero, TVLLIVS LAVREA, was a poet in a small way. We have a Latin epigram of his, also a few in Greek.[66]

Since the greatest name of that age was that of GAIVS IVLIVS CAESAR, it is remarkable that we have comparatively little left of what he wrote.[67] Besides some juvenile works, an encomium on Herakles and a tragedy on the well-worn theme of Oidipus, which Augustus very rightly suppressed,[68] and a collection of good sayings, somewhat later in date, which apparently the Emperor also objected to, probably as too trifling for his adopted father's great reputation,[69] he found time to compose a work on grammar, *de analogia*, which he wrote on his way across the Alps back to his province, perhaps in 700/54, and dedicated to Cicero.[70] As already noted (p. 196), he answered Cicero's *Cato* with an *Anticato*, in two books (hence the title is sometimes in the plural, *Anticatones*). Finally, while on his way to Spain for the final struggle with the Pompeians, in 708/46, he beguiled the journey by what would seem to have been a versified account of it, *Iter*.[71] According to Tacitus,[72] he was no better than Cicero as a poet, but he seems to have been fond of writing verse; there survive a few hexameters of his concerning Terence, obviously part of a longer work in which criticisms of various Latin authors occurred.[73] He also had no small repute as an

[65] Jerome, cited in n. 60; Isidore, *etymol.*, i, 22, 1; sketch of the subject in Schanz-Hosius, i, pp. 590–93.

[66] The Latin is in Pliny, *N.H.*, xxxi, 8 (*F.P.R.*, p. 316–17/80); the Greek in the *Anthology*, vii, 17; 294; xii, 24. In content, style and metre they are very feeble performances.

[67] It is, however, to be noted that his reputation with posterity was rather as a statesman and the founder of the empire than a stylist.

[68] Suetonius, *diu. Iul.*, 56.

[69] Suet., *ibid.*; Cicero, *ad fam.*, ix, 16, 4.

[70] Suet., *ibid.* By analogy is meant the principle that a language should follow uniform rules, while the anomalists held that usage was the sole guide.

That Caesar wrote it during his governorship of Gaul is manifest; that the date was 700/54, *i.e.*, after Cicero's *de oratore* (cf. p. 167), is not unlikely, see Hendrickson in *Class. Phil.*, i (1906), p. 97 *sqq.* The grammatical fragments are in Funaioli, pp. 145–57.

[71] Suet., *ibid.*

[72] Tacitus, *dial.*, 21, 11: fecerunt enim (Caesar et M. Brutus) et carmina et in bibliothecas rettulerunt, non melius quam Cicero sed felicius, quia illos fecisse pauciores sciunt.

[73] They are preserved in Suetonius' life of Terence; see L. A. Post in *Trans. Am. Ph. Ass.*, lxii, 1931, p. 203 *sqq.*

orator, beginning from his impeachment of Cn. Dolabella in 676/78 and continuing in a manner which won Cicero's admiration.[74] But of all these works next to nothing is left. 'Caesar', to the modern schoolboy, means one or both of the two writings which their author called modestly *Commentarii belli Gallici* and *belli ciuilis, i.e.*, Notes for a history of the Gaulish and Civil Wars. No one in antiquity seems to have taken up the implied challenge and ornamented what Caesar had left plain.

The *Bellum Gallicum* is in seven books, with an eighth added by Hirtius. The first deals with the campaigns of 696/58, against the Helvetians, who had tried to invade Gaul and seize land there for their own use, and Ariovistus, a German raider who had taken possession of territory of the Sequani and was governing it according to his own fashion. The second handles the operations of the following year, consisting of the Belgian revolt and the desperate fighting which was necessary to crush it. The third tells of two less important campaigns, Caesar's own against the Veneti and that of his lieutenant, P. Crassus, in Aquitania. The fourth and fifth are sometimes called the *Bellum Britannicum*, since they contain an account of Caesar's two invasions of Britain; the former, however, has in addition the story of the demonstration (it can hardly be called a campaign) across the Rhine in the early summer of 699/55 and the latter recounts the serious rising which took place in Gaul while Caesar was in Britain, the annihilation of fifteen cohorts, and the courage and presence of mind showed by Q. Cicero when besieged with his detachment. The sixth book describes a further demonstration against Germany and the crushing of the rebellion of Ambiorix. The seventh deals with the great rising under Vercingetorix and its overthrow.

The *Bellum ciuile* has but three books, but the third is of much greater length than any of the *Gallic War*, even the long seventh (112 chapters against 90). Book I brings the story down to the end of the brief campaign against Pompey's Spanish forces in 705/49, Book II describes the fall of Massilia and the destruction of Curio's army in Africa; Book III deals with the events of 706/48 down to the death of Pompey after Pharsalus and the arrival of Caesar in Alexandria.[75]

[74] Cicero, *Brut.*, 252; Suet., *ibid.*, 55. For the orations, see further, *O.R.F.*, p. 404 *sqq.*; the fragments of all the lost works are in Nipperdey's larger ed. of Caesar.

[75] This departure from the arrangement of the *Bellum Gallicum* is to be explained by the fact that Caesar never finished the *Bellum ciuile*, and so cannot be held responsible for the division into books, no doubt made

The matter of these treatises is for a historian rather than a writer on literature to deal with. It is enough to say here that Caesar neither attained nor sought perfect impartiality, such as one or two of the greatest historians have achieved. He was not writing purely to record facts, but to put before a public torn between his claims and those of his opponents the story of his own services to the state and the ingratitude with which he had been repaid. Hence his frequent insistence on his own moderation and clemency, qualities which he really possessed and also saw the value of in a nation which remembered Sulla's massacres. Hence also the fair colours in which he paints the somewhat wild adventure into Britain and other operations which were less complete successes than he would have them believed. Of actual fiction there may be none and certainly is not much; of skilful arrangement and probably also judicious omission there is a good deal. The quality of the information must of necessity vary somewhat, according as Caesar relies on his own first-hand knowledge, or memoranda of operations, &c., made at the time, or upon reports from his officers, who doubtless were not all as accurate as he. But the general impression, after many centuries of criticism,[76] is of trustworthiness; the most questionable part is perhaps the excursus on German habits and customs in the *Gallic War*.[77]

The style is like nothing else in Latin, save the imitations of it in the continuations to be dealt with presently. If it is to be called anything but Caesarian, it is Attic in tendency, and its peculiarities of diction are very many [78]; it is unfortunate that most young students of Latin are introduced to it early and thus get the mistaken impression that it is normal writing

by some one after his death. Book III plainly is meant to lead up to what Caesar never wrote, the operations in Alexandria. The beginning of Book I is lost.

[76] Since the time of Asinius Pollio (see p. 307), who declared (Suet., *diu. Iul.*, 56) that Caesar would have revised them if he had lived, for they were carelessly written and contained many errors of fact, due to lapses of memory, wrong information uncritically accepted, and perhaps deliberate misstatements.

[77] *B.G.*, vi, 21–8, especially the statement (21, 2) that they worship only the sun, moon and fire, which is nothing but current theory of the day about barbarian cults and has no resemblance to the facts of early German religion; some of the natural history of the fauna of the Hercynian Forest (26–8) is fabulous and probably derived from travellers' tales, written or oral.

[78] *E.g.*, the monotonous frequency with which the verb ends the sentence, and some very loose uses of the ablative absolute, as *B.G.*, v, 44, 6.

of that time. That it is good Latin we have Cicero's assurance,[79] to leave out of account that of every later critic who deals with it; but nothing more unlike Cicero's own style, even at its plainest, could well be imagined; it differs from his simplicity more than the most characteristic parts of Jane Austen differ from Addison.

As to the time when these works were composed, we are not exactly informed, but may arrive at a fairly close estimate. The *Gallic War* was written at high speed,[80] probably after the seventh campaign was over, in the winter of 702/52–703/51, certainly not much later, for it nowhere implies that Caesar has broken with Pompey. The *Civil War* must have been written after 706/48, and as it seems to be incomplete, we may suppose that its date is nearly 710/44.

Caesar's officers and supporters imitated his example of writing the events they had seen. AVLVS HIRTIVS, consul in 711/43, meant to work up the *Commentaries* with supplements of his own into a continuous history from the beginning of the Gallic campaigns to the death of his chief. If he ever did this,[81] and his own life was prolonged but thirteen months after that event, during which he had plenty of public affairs to occupy him, his work is mostly lost. We have, however, at least one book of his writing, the eighth of the *Gallic War*, which gives an account of the operations in 703/51 and 704/50, with the events leading up to the Civil War. This is plainly and straightforwardly expressed, in a style not altogether unlike Caesar's own, which no doubt Hirtius imitated. Then, continuing the *Civil War*, comes a work in similar style, the *Bellum Alexandrinum*, which takes the story down to the return of Caesar to Italy. If this is Hirtius' writing, that much at all events of his plan was completed; but

[79] Cicero, *Brut.*, 262: nudi enim sunt (commentarii), recti et uenusti. Cf. Hirtius, *B.G.*, viii, praef. 4–6.

[80] Hirtius, *ibid.*, 6. If any parts were written earlier, it is very strange that Cicero says nothing of them in his correspondence with Quintus while the latter was in Gaul.

[81] His own words, *loc. cit.*, 1–2, are: rem difficillimam suscepi. Caesaris nostri commentarios rerum gestarum Galliae, non comparantibus superioribus atque insequentibus eius scriptis, contexui, nouissimumque imperfectum ab rebus gestis Alexandreae confeci usque ad exitum non quidem ciuilis belli, cuius finem nullum uidemus, sed uitae Caesaris. This is not as clear as it might be, but the sense is that Hirtius, since he can find no works of Caesar's own which introduce or continue the *Commentaries* (I suspect *Galliae* of being a mistaken gloss), has filled the gaps himself. But as no trace of any works by Hirtius save this one and perhaps the *Bellum Alexandrinum* is to be found, it is likely that the perfect tenses are anticipations which remained unrealized.

in antiquity doubts were expressed as to this, some suggesting that the author was Oppius.[82] Now comes another book which also some ancient opinions credited to Hirtius or Oppius; but it is certainly not by the former, for it is pretty obviously the work of some one who served in the African campaign of 708/46, in which Hirtius took no part; moreover, the style is different and not nearly so good. What Oppius' historical style was like we cannot say, but he also was absent from that theatre of war, and so is not the author.[83] Finally, we have a most wretched piece of writing, *de bello Hispaniensi*, by some half-educated man trying to be eloquent. Its only merit is that its author shared the campaign of Munda, 709/45, and so has some idea of what he is saying, though none of how to say it.

But another Caesarian tried higher flights and acquired a reputation, far from undeserved, as an eloquent historian. This was GAIVS SALLVSTIVS CRISPVS, commonly known to us as SALLUST. He was born at Amiternum, in the Sabine territory, in 668/86, and died in 719/35.[84] His public life was active but not particularly respectable or distinguished. In 702/52 he was tribune of the plebs and very vocal against Milo, with some mention of Cicero also.[85] In 704/50 Appius Claudius, then censor with Piso and a strong Pompeian, struck his name from the roll of the senate, chiefly no doubt for political reasons, but probably with good excuses based upon Sallust's private life. In the general assignment of rewards to Caesarians, he was not forgotten; his leader, at the beginning of hostilities, had procured him the office of quaestor and so restored him to senatorial rank[86]; he then was given command of part of a force which unsuccessfully tried to save Illyricum from the Pompeians in 705/49[87]; during

[82] Suet., *op. cit.*, 56.

[83] Cicero, *ad Att.*, xii, 29, 2 (April, 709/45); 44, 3 (May); xiii, 19, 2 (July); 50, 1 (August), all indicate that Oppius was in Italy; xii, 2, 1 (April, 708/46) says that *Hirtius et isti omnes*, which would naturally include Oppius, are at Praeneste.

[84] Jerome, *ann. Abr.*, 1931 (= 668/86) and 1981 (= 718/36; but he says it was *quadrennio ante Actiacum bellum, i.e.*, 719/35, hence probably the notice has been affixed to the wrong year).

[85] Ascon., *in Milon.*, p. 37, 18, Clark (p. 33 Kiessling-Schoell).

[86] Pseudo-Cic., *inuect. in Sall.*, 6, 17: idem Sallustius, qui in pace ne senator quidem manserat (the facts are in Cassius Dio, xl, 63, 4), postea quam res publica armis oppressa est (but surely it was before he was entrusted with his various posts!), idem a uictore . . . in senatum per quaesturam reductus est. He had been the lover of Milo's wife, Gell., xvii, 18, citing Varro.

[87] Orosius, vi, 15, 8. Sallust was later in danger from the mutiny in Campania, Cassius Dio, xlii, 52, 2; Appian, *bell. ciu.*, ii, 92.

the African war he held an important subordinate post,[88] and at the close of it, he was made governor of Juba's old kingdom, now become a province. From this office he returned a wealthy man, by the usual methods of unsupervised governors,[89] bought land and houses,[90] and devoted the rest of his days to elegant retirement and the composition of his chief works.

His principal composition was a *History*, now lost.[91] It began from the consulship of M. Lepidus and Q. Catulus, in 676/78, told the eventful story of the next twelve years,[92] and so came down to the command of Pompey against Mithridates, or the events just before that. Whether the writer's intention was to trace the steps which brought Caesar's great rival to the fore, or the work was interrupted by his death, is not known. In any case, the size of the treatise was modest, five books only. Of its style and object we may form a tolerable conjecture from the two surviving works.

His first attempt at history was the monograph on the Conspiracy of Catiline (*de Catilinae coniuratione*).[93] The facts were well enough known, and if they had not been, Sallust was not the man to throw new light upon them by researches. His work is really a most skilful political pamphlet. A preface of grave moralizing sketches the growing depravity of Rome from the time when her conquests put an end to the honest and patriotic poverty of the old days. Sallust, in disgust at the corruption he sees around him, has withdrawn from politics and, as he cannot approve of an idle life, will choose out remarkable incidents in Roman history to set forth with the impartiality of one who has nothing to fear or hope and belongs to no faction.[94] Then follows an effectively written account of the conspiracy and its detection and suppression, beginning with the early career of Catiline and ending with his death. The principal figures are not, as one would expect, Cicero, but rather Caesar and Cato. The speeches of these two in the senate when the fate of the arrested conspirators is under debate are the most elaborate in the book, and form, with the sketches of their characters which

[88] *Bell. Afr.*, 8, 3; 34, 1; 97, 1. [89] Dio, xliii, 9, 2–3.

[90] Especially the famous *horti Sallustiani*, see Platner-Ashby *s.u.*

[91] The fragments are best collected by B. Maurenbrecher, Teubner, 1891–3.

[92] Fr. 1 Maur., and his *prolegomena*, p. 8.

[93] This is how Sallust himself speaks of it, see next note. The MSS. and a number of later writers from Quintilian on call it, rather absurdly, *bellum Catilinae*, or *Catilinarium*.

[94] *Catil.*, 4, 2: a clear enough indication that it is the first of his historical works.

follow, a kind of central feature, to and from which the rest lead, as in a good picture.[95] Cicero is throughout damned with cleverly faint praise; he is an honest man enough, if not very courageous nor always very scrupulous, who cannot be induced to descend to the utter baseness of accusing Caesar of any part in Catiline's intrigues.[96] The impression the reader is obviously meant to bear away with him is that in those evil days the moderation, humanity and profound insight of Caesar shone forth all the clearer for their surroundings; there was one other notable example of virtue, Cato, and we are left to draw the conclusion which Sallust is too clever to state for us. Cato's too severe righteousness led to nothing but his own unsought and barren renown; Caesar rose to the position of a beneficent and enlightened ruler, careless of himself and a blessing to all about him.[97]

The memory of Marius was cherished by the Caesarian party, as it had been by the *populares*, out of whom that party had grown. The horrors of Sulla's dictatorship had apparently done much to obliterate the memory of the older man's excesses and those of his supporters, while the recollection of his great services to the state in war was still active. Hence to glorify Marius was a piece of orthodox Caesarianism in Sallust's time, as it had been correct democratic language in Cicero's day. This easily explains the choice of subject for his second monograph, that on the war with Jugurtha, the *Bellum Iugurthinum*.[98] It was the more effective as the African campaigns of 643/111–650/106 had in truth been shockingly ill-managed by the successive generals, save only Metellus, while the decisive operations were carried out under Marius' command. We find therefore something of the same formula as in the *Catiline*; Sallust's hero is to be pitted against a strong antagonist, and shown the superior, not of some worthless specimen of the ruling class, but of one of their best men, whose portrait must therefore be drawn in fairly flattering colours. Metellus' defect is haughtiness, 'the chronic vice of a nobility'.[99] A second foil to the blunt soldierliness of Marius is Sulla, who is presented as the veriest demagogue.[100] He also does excellently in bringing about the final capture of Jugurtha,

[95] *Catil.*, 51–4. [96] *Catil.*, 31, 6; 48, 8–9; 49, 1.

[97] *Catil.*, 53, 6–54.

[98] So it is called by Quintilian, iii, 8, 9 (in bello Iugurthino et Catilinae; the second title is presumably by analogy with the first), and by the best MS.

[99] *Bell. Iug.*, 64, 1: cui quamquam uirtus gloria atque alia optanda bonis superabant, tamen inerat contemptor animus et superbia, commune nobilitatis malum.

[100] *Bell. Iug.*, 96.

but Sallust quietly but effectively and at exactly the right times reminds the reader that he was but carrying out Marius' orders.[101]

Thus in both the monographs Sallust had preached party politics under a cloak of grave and philosophic impartiality. We can therefore guess with some confidence what the tone of the *Historiae* must have been. It doubtless pointed the moral at every turn in the story, never obtruding it but never letting it drop quite out of the reader's mind. We may also be fairly sure that he never resorted to the vulgar and ineffective method of making his heroes angels and their opponents devils. As his Marius has faults, doubtless his anti-Sullan reformers had, and their antagonists were allowed credit for their virtues with every appearance of scrupulous fairness. Doubtless also, the general impression to be gained from the work was that only in the methods of Caesar and Octavian was salvation to be hoped for in public matters. For assuredly Sallust, although not a great speaker and though slow in composition,[102] was a very great advocate with his pen.

He was also a great stylist, with an originality not common among writers of Latin. While laying under contribution for ideas, and sometimes for whole passages fairly literally translated, a number of the best Greek writers, especially Thucydides, and on occasion plundering the older Latin authors as well,[103] he gave what he took a form of his own. His style is modelled, so far as it is not his own creation, upon that of Thucydides, and attains to the faults of the original, especially obscurity from over-compression, but by no means without having a share in its virtues as well. He is never feeble; his rhetoric is highly coloured, and most carefully finished under its superficial air of ruggedness; an archaic tinge in the language fits excellently with the didactic tone and gives the impression that the wisdom and virtue of the past speak through him. Perhaps his most obvious characteristic is his ability to present vigorous action, the very words seeming to hurry and stumble when his theme

[101] *Bell. Iug.*, 102, 2; 104, 1; 105, 2; 113, 6.

[102] Seneca rhet., *contr.*, iii, praef., 8: orationes Sallustii in honorem historiarum leguntur. Quint., x, 3, 8: sic (with leisurely and careful revision) scripsisse Sallustium accepimus, et sane manifestus est etiam ex opere ipso labor.

[103] For literature on this subject, see Schanz-Hosius, i, p. 375 *sq.* Known models include, besides Thucydides, Demosthenes, especially *orat.* iii, ix, xviii and the spurious x; Xenophon; Plato, *Menex.* and *ep.* vii. Quintilian, x, 1, 101, says: nec opponere Thucydidi Sallustium uerear; *ibid.*, 102: diuinam illam Sallustii uelocitatem. Many more criticisms, ancient and modern, in Schanz-Hosius, *ibid.*

is a hard-fought battle, like those against Jugurtha's Numidians. Scarcely less good, however, is the skill with which he catches the atmosphere of a heated debate. For the first time, history is provided, in Latin, with an eloquence befitting it.

It must be added that eloquence is almost his sole contribution. In the light of our conception of history as a science, indeed of the ancient ideas of that kind, he is hardly a historian at all. Except for what he may have heard from actors in the events he describes,[104] his working library, we are credibly informed, consisted of an epitome of Roman history, no doubt good of its kind, made for him by Ateius Philologus (p. 443).[105] There is much truth in the dictum quoted by Granius Licinianus (p. 514), that he should be read not as a historian but as an orator.[106]

We do not know exactly when the various works were written; but as the order is probably *Catiline*, *Jugurtha*, *Histories*, and the first of these implies that Caesar is dead, we get the period 710/44–719/35 for them all. This means less than a book-roll a year, and agrees with what Quintilian says (note 102) about his leisurely composition; something like 711/43 or a little later, 713/41 and the year of the author's death would be not impossible dates.

Hitherto we have been dealing with his undoubted compositions; we have under his name one performance which is not his and two which are doubtful. He certainly did not write the *inuectiua in M. Tullium*, the most astonishing thing about which is that it befooled Quintilian into thinking it genuine Sallust.[107] The real Sallust would make a plausible attack, with studied moderation of language; this silly product of some rhetorician is in the phraseology of the gutter. Its author shows a very fair knowledge of Cicero's speeches and the events of his life, however. Less certainly spurious are two pamphlets, as they seem to be, a speech and a letter *de re publica*, supposed to be addressed to Caesar. The second presupposes the situation just after Caesar's return from Gaul; the former, that after his victory over Pompey. Opinions have differed, and continue to differ, as to whether Sallust wrote either or both of them; I personally feel certain that at least the letter is spurious, from its opening sentence,

[104] He several times refers to such information, *e.g.*, *Catil.*, 48, 9.

[105] Suetonius, *de gramm.*, 10.

[106] Gran. Licin., xxxvi, p. 33, 9 Flemisch: nam Sallustium non ut historicum aiunt sed ut oratorem legendum.

[107] Quint., iv, 1, 68; ix, 3, 89. For the history of the controversy over all three works, see Schanz-Hosius, i, p. 370 *sqq*.

which implies,[108] in a way hardly possible at the supposed date, that Caesar is something very like an absolute king, an aspect of his ambitions which the real Caesar and his followers were careful to keep in the background just then. Nor is this an unguarded statement in a private letter, for the whole tone and style show that it is a document intended for more eyes than those of the supposed addressee.

The last notable writer of this period is one whom, save that he lacked the Scot's charm of style, we might call a Roman Andrew Lang: MARCVS TERENTIVS VARRO. He had a long life, (638/116–727/27),[109] which he seems to have enjoyed and certainly filled up with the most varied activities. He was a landowner on a large scale, like most of his, the senatorial, class; he served under Pompey with distinction in the war with the pirates, when he was awarded the *corona naualis*, and with discretion in Spain, where he surrendered to Caesar with little delay and without useless bloodshed.[110] He was proscribed in 711/43, but rescued by the good offices of Fufius Calenus from Antony's killers. With Augustus he had no quarrel, and seems to have spent the rest of his days very peaceably among his books. There is no doubt that he was the greatest scholar Rome ever produced; a remarkable fact is that he was not a dry pedant, but one whose works included witty and lively sketches of life, side by side with long and very erudite treatises. His interests seem to have been as wide as learning itself, with the exception one must always make in the case of a Roman, that he was no mathematician.[111] With all this scholarship went not only taste but a measure of originality.

Though the bulk of his works are lost, we have a catalogue of a large number of them, handed down by a curiously indirect route. St. Jerome, *de uir. ill.*, 54 (vol. ii, p. 879 Vall.), says that he had drawn up a list of Origen's works in uoluminibus epistularum quas ad Paulam scripsimus, in quadam epistula contra Varronis opera conferens. This

[108] *Ad Caes.*, ii, 1: scio ego quam difficile atque asperum factu sit consilium dare regi aut imperatori, postremo quoiquam mortali quoius opes in excelso sunt.

[109] Jerome, *ann. Abr.* 1901 and 1989.

[110] Pliny, *N.H.*, vii, 115; Caesar, *bell. ciu.*, 20, 6–8, who is careful to show that Varro surrendered without dishonour, being in a hopeless position, and behaved honestly (*cum fide*) afterwards. Varro was reconciled to his conqueror, to whom he dedicated part of the *Antiquitates* and who meant to put him in charge of his project for a public library, Suet., *diu. Iul.*, 44.

[111] His work *de principiis numerorum* does not disprove this: it was philosophic and not properly mathematical.

letter is lost ; but Rufinus quoted it in his controversy with Jerome [112] and borrowed the catalogue from it in the preface to his translation of Origen's homilies on Genesis, where it is preserved in three MSS. It contains lists of both Varro's and Origen's writings ; the former comprises titles of either forty-eight or forty-nine works, most of them being in several books. They are : *Antiquitates*, 45 books ; *de uita populi Romani*, 4 ; *imagines*, 15 ; *λογιστορικοί*, 76 ; *de lingua Latina*, 25 ; *disciplinae*, 9 ; *de sermone Latino*, 5 ; *quaestiones Plautinae* 5 ; *annales*, 3 ; *de origine linguae Latinae*, 3 ; *de poematis*, 3 ; *de originibus scaenicis*, 3 ; *de scaenicis actionibus*, 3 ; *de actis scaenicis*, 3 ; *de descriptionibus*, 3 ; *de proprietate scriptorum*, 3 ; *de bibliothecis*, 3 ; *de lectionibus*, 3 ; *de similitudine uerborum*, 3 ; *legationes*, 3 ; *suasiones*, 3 ; *de Pompeio*, 3 ; *libri singulares*, 10 ; *de personis*, 3 ; *de iure ciuili*, 15 ; *ἐπιτομὴ antiquitatum*, 9 ; *ἐπιτομὴ ex imaginum libris*, 4 ; *ἐπιτομὴ de lingua Latina*, 9 ; *de principiis numerorum*, 9 ; *res rusticae*, 3 ; *de ualetudine tuenda*, 1 ; *de sua uita*, 3 ; *de forma philosophiae*, 3 ; *res urbanae*, 3 ; *saturae Menippeae*, 150 ; *poemata*, 10 ; *orationes*, 22 ; *pseudotragoediae*, 6 ; *saturae*, 4. Here Rufinus breaks off ; uix medium descripsi indicem et legentibus fastidium est, is his comment. The list is clearly from a well-informed source, either Varro himself [113] or some one acquainted with his work and probably not far from him in time. The only difficulty which arises is whether the book *de ualetudine tuenda* may not be the same as one of the *λογιστορικοί*, which we know was called *Messalla de ualetudine tuenda*. It lends substance to the remark which Gellius quotes from Varro that he was entering, as he wrote the *Hebdomades*, on his twelfth 'week' of years and had so far written seventy times seven books.[114]

Of all this mass of literature, there remains to us one complete work, a part of another, and sufficient fragments of the rest to give us an idea of their character and reconstruct the general outline of a few. The three books *de re rustica* are preserved except for a few words at the beginning. They were written, Varro himself tells us, in his eightieth year.[115] The form of the work is the Aristotelian dialogue, like the philosophic and other discourses of Cicero ; but here the resemblance to Cicero ends. The style is chattily slipshod, and the writer's learning so abundant that it pours out suddenly, at the most unexpected points, not only in the short prefaces (that of Book I to his wife Fundania, on the occasion of her buying an estate ; that of Book II to his friend Turranius Niger ; Book III is addressed to his neighbour Pinnius) but in the midst of the sound and practical directions for managing a farm (Book I), a stock-ranch (Book II) and the

[112] Rufin., *Inuect.*, ii, 19 (vol. ii, p. 646 *sqq.*, Vall.).

[113] For discussion of the list, see especially Ritschl, *opuscula*, vol. iii, pp. 419 *sqq.*, 524 *sqq.*

[114] Varro, *ap.* Gell., iii, 10, 17.

[115] *R.R.*, i, 1, 1.

various minor sources of revenue such as poultry-run, aviary and herb-garden (Book III). While giving interesting information on the state of agriculture at that time, it is withal a pleasantly discursive book, the work of a garrulously entertaining old scholar.

Of the *de lingua Latina* there are left Books V–X fairly complete. They are dedicated, apparently all, to Cicero, and this helps to fix the date of their completion, between the middle of 711/45 and the end of 713/43.[116] The plan of the whole can be made out from various references. There was one book of introduction; then followed three, addressed to Publius Septimius, which dealt with etymology in general. Books V–VII treat of the etymologies of particular classes of words; it hardly need be said that Varro does not group them as a modern philologist would, and has no idea of the immutable or nearly immutable phonetic laws which govern the development of speech. There follow three books on declension, which includes the formation of words by the additions of suffixes and the like. There were three more on this topic, and then twelve (XIII–XXV) on syntax. Each of these major divisions began with the more general and theoretical aspects of the subject and went on from that to the particulars. Within this framework, however, to judge by what we have left, the arrangement of the lesser parts was rather haphazard. The style is plain to the point of crabbedness. With all its faults and its incompleteness, however, the work is of much importance in the history of linguistic study, and incidentally is crammed with fragments of welcome information on a great variety of topics.

This was Varro's principal work on language. Ancilliary to it were a number of others, mostly mentioned in the catalogue given on p. 221. They are represented, for us, only by stray quotations, and we are not always sure of what they treated. The *de sermone Latino* dealt with the question what constitutes good Latin. The *de similitudine uerborum* and a book or books (they may have been three, to balance the three of its companion piece; Varro loved triads) *de utilitate sermonis* [117] treated of the conflict between anomaly and analogy. The

[116] Obviously before Cicero's death; after June, 711/45, because Cicero then writes (*ad Att.*, xiii, 12, 3) that Varro had promised two years before to dedicate an important work to him, but nothing has yet come of it. Everything from Book V on is dedicated to him, although vii, 109, speaks of but three books, because quotations from more than one of the later books call them (*de lingua Latina*) *ad Ciceronem*.

[117] Fragments of all these and several other works bearing on linguistic and literary subjects are conveniently assembled at the end of the *de lingua Latina* in Goetz and Schoell's edition of that work (Teubner, 1910). The *de utilitate* is represented for us by one citation in Charisius,

subject-matter of the work περὶ χαρακτήρων is uncertain.[118] There was a history of the alphabet, *de antiquitate litterarum*, in not less than two books.[119] The *de origine linguae Latinae*, to judge by the very little that is left, had much to say of foreign words, real or supposed, in the vocabulary.

The heaviest loss to us of all Varro's works is his *Antiquitates*. In his grammatical writings, his out-of-date etymologies and pre-occupation with controversies of interest to his contemporaries, but not to us, become somewhat wearisome to any but a specialist. But in the *Antiquitates rerum humanarum et diuinarum* Varro had collected a great reservoir of facts on subjects of the utmost historical interest, the past of his own nation and its customs. We benefit, as it is, to no small extent by his researches, for his historical encyclopaedia—it was hardly less—was drawn upon by a series of lesser scholars in later times, and through them, by one channel or another, a good deal has trickled down to us. We know from St. Augustine that the work fell into two great divisions.[120] The first twenty-five books dealt with human affairs, 'not those of the world at large, but merely those of Rome'. The following sixteen [121] treated of *res diuinae*, meaning, not abstract theology, but rather matters of cult, a systematic discussion of Roman religion, which Varro, who was a Stoic, held to be the setting forth of philosophical truths in a manner suited to the general understanding.[122] The subdivisions were as follows: Books II–VII, *de hominibus*; VIII–XIII, *de locis*; XIV–XIX, *de temporibus*; XX–XXV, *de rebus*. Book I was a general introduction. In the second section, Books XXVI–XXXVIII again treated *de hominibus, de locis, de temporibus*, three to each subject; XXXIX–XLI had for their subject rites (*sacra*), and these were handled according to the nature of the gods addressed. This division was purely subjective, for Varro divided the gods into *certi*, those whose nature he felt he could definitely explain,

p. 123, 3 Keil, who draws on Varro through Pliny. This, however, is enough to show that he was there defending forms which are against analogy, if protected by usage.

118 There is but one citation, Charisius, p. 189, 25, which tells us only that there were at least three books and that something was said about adverbs.

119 Priscian, ii, p. 8, 2 Keil: Varro in II de antiquitate litterarum (follows a remark about the Chaldean alphabet).

120 Aug., *de ciuit. Dei*, vi, 3. Probably Augustine came by his information at second hand.

121 Evidently the catalogue is in error as to the number of books, see p. 221.

122 See August., *ibid.*, 5.

incerti, those who raised problems as to their origin and functions, and finally *selecti*, who were also *praecipui*, outstanding deities who for one reason or another needed special treatment. The whole arrangement was a piece of Stoic logic; everything that is done must have a doer, and therefore he began by dealing with men; the act must be done somewhere and somewhen, hence the sections on places and times; and finally, the something which is done must be described and discussed. For example, in the second part, the men concerned were the Roman clergy, pontiffs, augurs and so forth; the places were the chapels, temples and *loca religiosa*, or spots which, while not exactly consecrated, were felt unsuited for profane use; the times were the holy days of the calendar. The amount of information to be had under these heads from a man like Varro was plainly enormous; its remnants are among our most valued materials for the study of Roman religion, and if only some one had taken as vigorous exception to his views on secular matters as the Christian apologists did to his religious opinions, doubtless an equally useful store of facts concerning the organization of the Roman State would be at our disposal.[123]

Varro seems to have composed a number of smaller works dealing with details of this subject or related matters, possibly in imitation of the groups of books on related subjects written by Aristotle.[124] We know of several such. The catalogue gives us *de uita populi Romani*, the title of which at once suggests a work of Dikaiarchos, famous in its day, the Βίος Ἑλλάδος, or *Manner of Life in Greece*.[125] It was dedicated to Atticus, and its subject was the manner of life in Rome at different periods, in other words a history of Roman culture. The four books *de gente populi Romani* dealt with what we now call pre- and proto-history. We happen to know that they were written in 711/43 [126] and they had naturally much to say of the chronology

[123] A selection of the bulky literature on his work in Schanz-Hosius, i, p. 565 *sq.*; for the other antiquarian treatises, see *ibid.*

[124] For the grouping of Aristotle's works, see Rose, *H.G.L.*, p. 271 *sqq.*

[125] See Rose, *op. cit.*, p. 355. There was another work with the same title, doubtfully ascribed to a contemporary of Varro, Jason of Nysa, see Suidas, *s.u.* Ἰάσων Μενεκράτους. This may have given Varro the idea.

[126] Arnobius, *adu. nat.*, v, 8, p. 181, 14 *sqq.* Reifferscheid: Varro . . . in librorum quattuor primo quos de gente conscriptos Romani populi dereliquit curiosis computationibus edocet, ab diluuii tempore . . . ad usque Hirti consulatum et Pansae annorum esse milia nondum duo. Augustine, *de ciuit. Dei*, xviii, 13, says the second book ended with the Trojan War, and (*ibid.*, 2) that Varro handled in order the Sekyonians, the Athenians and the Romans. He also mentions in several places a distinction of Varro's between really historical and other data; this is illustrated by and serves to place the extract from Varro in Censorinus,

of the earliest times. The fragments indicate that their end was the beginning of the historical period, in other words the time when it might be said that such a *gens* or people as the *populus Romanus*, the Roman commonwealth, existed. Perhaps as a sort of continuation of this came the works entitled *de familiis Troianis*, mentioned by Servius,[127] dealing apparently with those Roman houses which claimed Trojan ancestry; *tribuum liber*,[128] which would seem to have treated of the thirty-five tribes into which the citizen body was divided; the *res urbanae*, of which we have but one fragment, mentioning Spartacus,[129] and therefore cannot say whether it was a history of the city itself, a topographical work, or on some other subject; the *annales*, which may have been a chronological table like that of Atticus, though doubtless on a larger scale [130]; the *augurum libri*, if indeed this is not merely part of the *antiquitates* mistaken for a separate work [131]; the *aetia*, *i.e.*, *αἴτια*, the 'reasons for' sundry customs; the title is taken from Kallimachos and was afterwards used by Plutarch, with how much of the contents we do not know [132]; the autobiography (*de sua uita*), from which it may very well be that the catalogue comes [133]; also a work apparently biographical, *de Pompeio*, and a sort of letter of advice to him, *isagocicus ad Pompeium*, which had the misfortune to die before its author; it was a memorandum of the proper procedure to

21, that he distinguished three periods, the obscure (ἄδηλος), down to the deluge of Ogygos, the fabulous (μυθικὸς), to the first Olympiad, and the historical (ἱστορικὸς), from then to his own day. Clearly this extract is from the *de gente*, not, as Ideler supposed (*Hdb. d. Chronologie*, ii, p. 152, n. 3), from the *antiquitates*.

127 Servius on Verg., *Aen.*, v, 704: quod etiam Varro docet in libris quos de familiis Troianis scripsit. The work must therefore have been at least two books long.

128 Varro, *de ling. Lat.*, v, 56: ab his rebus quibus in tribuum libros (*libro* or *libris* ?) scripsi.

129 Charisius, p. 133, 23 Keil: Varro de rebus urbanis III, 'Spartaco innocente coniecto ad gladiatorium'.

130 The famous Varronian computation of the date of the foundation of Rome (753 B.C., cf. p. 20) may well have been in this work, though Censorinus (see n. 126) suggests that it was also in the *de gente*. He proceeds: sed hoc quodcunque caliginis (the doubt as to when Rome was founded) Varro discussit . . . lucemque ostendit per quam numerus certus non annorum modo sed et dierum perspici possit. secundum quam rationem nisi fallor hic annus, cuius uelut index et titulus est Vlpii et Pontiani consulatus (A.D. 238), ab olympiade prima millensimus est et quartus decimus . . . a Roma autem condita nongentensimus nonagensimus primus.

131 Macrobius, *sat.*, i, 16, 19, is our only reference to it, and he does not seem to have used Varro directly (cf. p. 459).

132 Kallimachos, see Rose, *H.G.L.*, p. 320; Plutarch's work in question is the *Αἴτια Ῥωμαϊκά*, usually called in modern times the *quaestiones Romanae*. For some discussion of its relations to Varro, see Rose, *Roman Questions of Plutarch* (Oxford, Clar. Press, 1924), Introd., chap. i.

133 The catalogue itself calls this work *de suauitate*, a mere mechanical blunder, long since corrected from Charisius, p. 89, 28 Keil.

adopt in dealing with the senate in his capacity of consul, in 684/70.[134] The *legationes* obviously dealt with embassies of some sort, but what, is unknown.

Varro was also interested in the literary history of Rome, although he wrote no one large work on that topic. He wrote a treatise *de poetis*, however, the first book of which had got down as far as the death of Plautus,[135] and a monograph on Plautus himself, the *quaestiones Plautinae*, concerning which a damaged [136] gloss survives to tell us that it dealt with Plautus' life, while two quotations make it clear that it handled his vocabulary as well. That he took a great interest in matters pertaining to the stage is clear from the three titles *de scaenicis originibus*, *de actionibus scaenicis*, *de actis scaenicis*, which are conjectured to have been respectively a kind of history of drama, a work on dramatic productions, and a record, like the *διδασκαλίαι* of Greek authors, of the occasions on which various plays were put on. The *de comoediis Plautinis* was perhaps merely another name for the *quaestiones Plautinae* [137]; the three books *de personis* probably dealt with the masks used by actors, not with persons in the legal sense. Literary criticism of a more general kind may have been the contents of the treatises *de poematis* and *de proprietate scriptorum* (probably ' on the characteristic features of writers ', some sort of comparative review of various authors). The three books *de lectionibus*, it is conjectured, may have dealt with what the next age called recitations and found a growing nuisance, namely the practice of inviting an author's acquaintance to a preliminary hearing of his new work, read by himself, a sort of literary equivalent of a ' private view '. What the *de descriptionibus* was about is not known ; the title suggests a rough Latin equivalent of the equally unknown *περὶ χαρακτήρων*, since to describe a thing (if that is what *descriptio* here means) and put a distinguishing mark (*χαρακτήρ*) on it are much the same. But that such a polymath as Varro, at a time when public libraries were being planned,[138] should write a treatise *de bibliothecis* is perfectly intelligible. Of a nature partly historical,

[134] See Gellius, xiv, 7, 1–3.

[135] See Gellius, i, 24, 3.

[136] *C.G.L.*, v, p. 234, 12 : Plautinarum ; Plauti auctoris re(s) gestas. This fragmentary note (for which see Lindsay in *C.R.*, xxxv, 1921, p. 67) can hardly be an explanation of anything but Varro's title. On the other hand, the two actual quotations we have from the book are glosses of Plautine words. The title might easily cover a miscellaneous work.

[137] We hear of the existence of this work in but one passage, Gellius, iii, 3, 9.

[138] Cf. n. 110.

partly literary, was the great work *de imaginibus*, also called *hebdomades*, *The Sevens*.[139] The fifteen books probably consisted, first, of an introduction, then of fourteen books (2 × 7), containing in all 700 pictures of men famous in different capacities, arranged in seven departments, fifty Greeks and fifty Romans in each, every picture having attached to it a short descriptive epigram. It was thus a sort of illustrated biographical dictionary.

While the *imagines* much suggest certain types of popular modern work, the *disciplinae* seems to look forward to the Middle Ages. Each of the nine books having this common title discussed a branch of learning; of these, seven, probably the first seven, were identical with the seven liberal arts of later times, Grammar, Dialectic, Rhetoric, Geometry, Arithmetic, Astronomy, Music; the other two dealt with Medicine and Architecture.[140]

That he wrote *de iure ciuili* we know only from the catalogue; that he was the author of a geographical work, *de ora maritima*, appears from a few quotations. He himself mentions as his own a book *de aestuariis* [141]; two or three other works are known from citations to have existed.

Like other writers of his time, he had a lively correspondence, and it appears that he or some one for him published it in two parts, one of Greek and the other of Latin letters [142]; besides these, he put forth a work called *epistolicae quaestiones*, to all appearance informal discussions, in the manner of familiar letters, on various topics.[143]

Such an array of learning might have sufficed even for a man of Varro's gigantic powers of work; but in addition he made numerous contributions to pure literature. Of the books of speeches and poems mentioned in the catalogue of his works we

[139] This is partly conjectural, but the following facts are certain. The two titles are given in Gellius, iii, 10, 1; the rest of the chapter outlines the fanciful reasons, derived from Pythagoreanism, for making the number seven prominent. Pliny, *N.H.*, xxxv, 11, gives the total number of pictures. Several mentions attest the presence of both Greek and Roman worthies: Ausonius, *Mosella*, 306, indicates that Book X contained a heptad of famous architects. The epitome in four books perhaps omitted the illustrations.

[140] See, for what is known of this work, Schanz-Hosius, i, p. 188 *sq.*; Varro also wrote separate works on several of these subjects (*de forma philosophiae*, *rhetoricorum libri*, cited by Priscian, ii, p. 489, 2 Keil, *de mensuris*, Priscian, *ibid.*, p. 420, 15, and *de principiis numerorum*, cf. n. 109).

[141] *De ling. Lat.*, ix, 26; the words quoted deal with tides.

[142] Inferred from the fact that Nonius cites from *epistula Latina* or *epistulae Latinae*, implying that there were also Greek ones.

[143] Gellius, xiv, 7, 3, cites the fourth book.

can say nothing, for they have vanished; but more is known of a series of writings whose loss is to be regretted for more reasons than one. Menippos of Gadara, the Cynic philosopher,[144] had introduced a new type of popular ethical discourse, which we know as the Menippean satire. It was in prose, but freely interspersed with poetry, whether his own or another's. Varro imitated him, and of the 159 specimens of this kind of composition which he found time to produce, we have fragments of some 90, and even in that condition they are worth study.[145] They form a humorous commentary on life as Varro saw it, expressed in all manner of quaint forms. One, for example, the *Eumenides*, seems to have upheld the Stoic paradox that all except the sage are mad—mad as Orestes in the legend when the Furies pursued him. This gave rise to a series of vivid scenes, in which the observer met all sorts of madmen, including a mob of male and female slaves who insisted that he was mad himself. Another, the *Manius*, drew a picture of old-fashioned rustic industry and hospitality. A third, the *Sexagesis*, introduced a Rip Van Winkle, who after sleeping for fifty years came back to find a totally unrecognizable Rome. The vocabulary is very large, including a great amount of Greek, and the tone varies from serious philosophical rhetoric in verse, not unworthy of Lucretius himself[146]; or a bitter lament for civil strife, clearly written after Thapsus,[147] through the quest for the ideal woman on the part of one Chrysosandalus, who commissions Prometheus[148] to make him 'a girl of milk and Tarentine wax', to the reasonable protest of a boxer, whose audience complain of his lack of spirit,[149]

'Gentlemen, since you think me a poor creature for being beaten, if the other fellow should scrape off my eyebrows with his glove, will any of you give me his?'

We know less of the *logistorici*, but they were discussions (*λόγοι*) on various matters, such as the education of children, piety, health and so forth, enlivened by anecdotes or historical

[144] See Rose, *H.G.L.*, p. 358.

[145] Best collection by Buecheler, at the end of his text of Petronius, ed. 4, Berlin, Weidmann, 1904.

[146] Frag. 36 Buecheler.

[147] Frag. 225 Bue.

[148] Frag. 432: Chrysosandalus locat sibi amiculam de lacte et cera Tarentina quam apes Milesiae coegerint ex omnibus floribus libantes, sine osse et neruis, sine pelle, sine pilis puram putam proceram candidam teneram formosam.

[149] Frag. 89: dicat pugilis; spectatores qui miserum putatis uinci, quaero a uobis, si aduersarius supercilia mihi caestis descobinarit, numquis uestrum sua mihi est daturus?

examples (ἱστορίαι), and bearing each a double title, first the name of a person, apparently the acquaintance to whom it was addressed, then the theme, as *Pius de pace*, *Gallus Fundanius de admirandis*. Of the other literary works we know practically nothing.

One other name of a scholar from that age deserves mention here.[150] This is the erudite mystic PVBLIVS NIGIDIVS FIGVLVS.[151] A friend of Cicero, he took a line very different from his in matters of religion. So far as we know, he is the reviver, at least in Italy, of Pythagorean doctrine, one of the founders of what is known as the neo-Pythagorean movement in philosophy, and therefore, since it was as much a cult as a dogma, in worship also. This revived Pythagoreanism, known only from books to begin with, for its oral tradition was long extinct, received elements from the dominant Stoic philosophy. Perhaps the most important of these was belief in astrology, which at that date and for many centuries afterwards, indeed down to the general acceptance of the Copernican theory, remained a dominant force in the intellectual world, however much a number of authorities, not least among which was the Church, might denounce it as false, immoral, or diabolical. But a belief in astrology necessarily involved more or less consistent determinism. This in turn led to one of two main consequences among men of serious mind. Those who, like the great saints and doctors of Stoicism, held firmly to the dogma of the infinite wisdom and goodness of God, Whose will is expressed in or identical with fate, found it a comforting doctrine: but to the majority, it was hateful, a kind of eternal slavery in which mankind was fast bound. A way out was therefore sought and promised, and this in two main forms. The gods were beyond fate, for that is the centripetal influence of the stars, which are below the sphere in which they live. Therefore, man can overcome fate by becoming a god himself, or by compelling the gods to do his will. The former method was that of the so-called mystery-religions, which promised one form or another of deification to the true votary; the latter was that of magic, with its formulae and actions intended to compel the obedience of anything in heaven or on earth. In practice, the two methods no doubt were often combined and perhaps

[150] Others are discussed in Chap. XIV.

[151] Cicero never calls him anything but Nigidius, with or without the *praenomen*; Lucan, i, 639, is the first to use the *cognomen*, and a story accounting for it (he was called 'the potter' because he said the heavens turned as fast as a potter's wheel) is told by schol. Lucan., *loc. cit.*, Augustine, *de ciuit. Dei*, v, 3.

oftener said to be; hence it is no surprise to hear Nigidius spoken of as a Pythagorean and a magician.[152] Certainly, some of the Pythagorean circle, including that model of devout asceticism Vatinius, were said to practise necromancy, human sacrifice, and other more than doubtfully lawful arts.[153]

Nigidius, however, by no means confined his attention to mysticism, but was in Gellius' opinion the greatest scholar next to Varro.[154] His writings [155] may be classed under three heads, grammatical (in the widest sense of that word), theological and biological. Of the first, one was called *commentarii grammatici*,[156] or approximately 'philological notes'; parts at least seem to have been lacking in finish and even clearness of expression. One outstanding fact about the work was that it maintained the doctrine (favoured by the Stoics, and Pythagorean also) [157] that words have a natural affinity to the things they signify, and are not merely conventional symbols. Akin to this verbal study is oratory, and Nigidius is known to have written a work *de gestu*, *i.e.*, concerning action or delivery, part of which at least dealt with the costume of orators.[158] His principal theological work was entitled simply *de dis*, and certainly a part of it dealt rather with theology in the ancient than in the modern sense,[159] for we

[152] Jerome on *an. Abr.*, 1972 (= 709/45) says: Nigidius Figulus Pythagoricus et magus in exilio moritur. As he was praetor in 696/58 (Cicero, *ad Q. frat.*, i, 2, 16, written in 695/59 and giving a list of the magistrates for the next year), he must have been at least forty years old then (Mommsen, *Staatsrecht*, i, 3rd ed., p. 568 *sqq.*), and therefore was born not after 656/98 and was at least fifty-three when he died. As to his magic, we may cite Apuleius, *apol.*, 42, who says on the authority of Varro that Nigidius, being consulted about some stolen money, recited a charm over certain boys, who then told exactly what had become of it; a form of clairvoyance by means of a hypnotized subject which is still familiar, especially in the East.

[153] See Cicero, *interr. in P. Vatin.*, 14. A more respectable practitioner of curious arts was Appius Claudius Pulcher, consul 700/54, elder brother of Clodius; see Cicero, *Tusc.*, i, 37, *de diuin.*, i, 132.

[154] Gellius, iv, 9, 1: Nigidius Figulus, homo, ut ego arbitror, iuxta M. Varronem doctissimus.

[155] The fragments have been collected by A. Swoboda, *P. Nigidii Figuli operum reliquiae*, Vindobonae 1889.

[156] Gellius, x, 4, who cites an ingenious argument of Nigidius on this matter.

[157] Gellius, xvii, 7, 4 *sqq.*, who goes on to give an example which shows that Nigidius, obscure or not, was on the verge of noticing a fact not yet familiar to all Latinists, namely, that the participles in *-tus* have of themselves no reference to past time.

[158] Quintilian, xi, 3, 143.

[159] *Theologia* includes what we call mythology, also such matters as the origin and development of cults.

find him inquiring whether the Penates publici of the Roman state were the same as Apollo and Poseidon and had been brought to Italy by Aeneas.[160] This work was in nineteen books at least.[161] Lesser treatises seem to have been those on divination, on individual taking of omens (*de augurio priuato*), *de extis* (on those parts of animals which were sacrificed and could be consulted, to ascertain the will of the gods, by the form of divination known as haruspicy), and perhaps [162] on dreams and their significance. With these works on divination we may class his astrological writings. We know that he described the *sphaera Graecanica* and also the *sphaera barbarica*, in other words the star-map according to the Greek astronomers and also according to the non-Greek (originally Babylonian) observers, who had different arrangements and names for some of the constellations. Probably both were discussed in the same work, but details are lacking as to its arrangement.[163] John of Lydia (Iohannes Lydus), a writer of the sixth century A.D., who smattered a little Latin and professed to draw largely on Italian writers, includes in his work *de ostentis*, a silly fortune-telling book, what he declares is 'a literal translation of the lunar calendar of observations from thunder (ἐφημερὶς βροντοσκοπία) of Figulus the Roman, taken from the works of Tages' (the mythical founder of Etruscan divination).[164] What he gives is a list of the significances to be attached to a peal of thunder on every day of the lunar month from the first new moon of June, with which he begins, to the last old moon of May. This is certainly not Etruscan fulgural divination, of which we know something from other sources (see p. 368), and whether any remnant of Nigidius' work is to be found in it is a doubtful point. Gellius mentions a work *de uento*, which must have had at least two books, since he quotes from the second [165];

[160] Macrobius, *sat.*, iii, 4, 6: Nigidius etiam de dis libro nono decimo requirit num di Penates sint Troianorum Apollo et Neptunus, qui muros eis fecisse dicuntur, et num eos in Italiam Aeneas aduexerit.

[161] The citation in the last note is the highest-numbered.

[162] Our evidence is nothing better than Iohannes Lydus, *de ostent.*, 45, ὁ Νιγίδιος ἐν τῇ τῶν ὀνείρων ἐπισκέψει (says that to dream of lightning is a good sign). Lydus is a most unreliable author, and even supposing him to be telling the truth, the ὀνείρων ἐπίσκεψις may be only some passage in one of Nigidius' other works in which he discussed dreams.

[163] Servius, on the *Georgics* of Vergil, cites both, the former in the fuller form (known as Daniel's Servius, or *Seruius auctus*) of the note on i, 43 (p. 143, 4 Thilo), and again on 218 (p. 183, 4); the latter on i, 19 (p. 136, 25).

[164] Lydus, *de ostentis*, 27–36. It is one of a series of 'literal translations' from Latin writers.

[165] Gell., ii, 22, 31.

Servius has an extract from the fourth book of a treatise *de hominum naturalibus*,[166] and Macrobiu cites the fourth book of another, *de animalibus*. Nigidius may perhaps have written a treatise *concerning the earth*, but the evidence is doubtful.[167]

[166] Servius on *Aen.*, i, 177. It is not very clear what *naturalibus* meant ('natural functions'?).

[167] Servius on *Aen.*, xi, 715, has, according to the MSS. of the fuller text, *Nigidius de terras*, which has been variously emended to *de terris*, *de terra* and *de sphaera*.

CHAPTER IX

VERGIL AND AUGUSTAN POETRY

UNDER the Republic, a small ruling class enjoyed freedom in a sense in which the word was never again to be understood. Personal liberty was the possession in large measure of every law-abiding citizen; but to the men among whom the offices of state passed from hand to hand, the laws were a thing partly of their own creation (the sovran people had become little more than an urban mob, to be bribed or cajoled into voting the right way), partly a check from which they might hope to escape for no inconsiderable part of their public careers; for a provincial governor was an absolute despot during his term of office and within the bounds of his allotted sphere of action. For such enviable rewards it is no wonder that a great supply of public servants was always available, many more candidates coming forward year by year than there were places to fill; and the indispensable tool of all public men in an age practically without newspapers,[1] the ability to sway by speech the reason of a judicious audience or, still more important, the passions and prejudices of a less intelligent one, was zealously studied and frequently mastered. Rhetoric was the most prominent feature in the education of every lad of promise whose family was or might be of senatorial rank; for the two direct roads to prominence, power and licence to do good or evil were that and military prowess. Under the Empire all this was changed. A share in the government was indeed available to men far below Imperial rank; the best of the emperors were anxious that the senate should take on itself a reasonable part of their immense burden of administration; posts, both advisory and administrative, were multiplied, and the old

[1] Corresponding somewhat to our press were such things as the published copies of new laws, the reports (*acta*) of transactions in the senate and the assembly and other written documents available to the public, while published speeches fulfilled part of the function of our editorial comments; but the reading public was never so important as the audience, and the spoken word was of more political account than the written.

magistracies retained their names and at least a part of their functions under the new régime. Provinces there continued to be, and even opportunities to plunder them, if on a less magnificent scale than that of a Verres, when the thief was influential or the central government negligent. But the old absolute power was in the hands of one man, if he chose to exercise it, and not of a class; the mightiest subject was still a subject, and had no hopes of being anything more, at least by constitutional means. And to win the favour of a single man and get delegated power from him called for other arts than those potent to sway an election or dazzle a jury. The powerful pleader did not automatically become a leading statesman, for his advancement was not now in the hands of those who had been or might be his clients. Yet the popularity of rhetoric was as great as ever; we have seen that to make Latin more than a rustic dialect some adornment had been necessary (p. 32), and the instinct to adorn speech and make it effective was now too deep-seated for the loss of one incentive, even the greatest, to uproot it.

For the man of speech-craft there were now three main opportunities for activity. He might turn to the courts of law, with hopes of making his way thence into the senate and gaining, in that usually ineffective and often grossly disloyal body, such prominence and influence as he could. He might pursue rhetoric for its own sake, a course which, as we shall see later, appealed to an astonishingly large number. Or, and this is the possibility with which we are most interested, he might turn his attention, like Cicero when out of place, to literature, in verse or in prose. For this last purpose, he required an inspiring subject, if he was to produce work of anything like the first order; and the tragedy of the later literature, in Rome as in Greece, was that the supply of subjects which appealed to serious candidates for literary fame was narrowly limited and soon gave out, taking with it all opportunity of creating new masterpieces.

For the present, however, subjects were not lacking. Apart from the happy circumstances that sundry recognized branches of literature, notably history and several departments of poetry, were still in process of being conquered by Roman littérateurs, there lay to hand a most fruitful field, the praises of the new order of things as fulfilling the highest destinies of Rome. Augustus was fully alive to the possibilities of propaganda, and missed no opportunity of getting himself well reputed among that wide public which, then as now, could be reached by the eloquent stating of a case, orally or on paper. Directly and through his confidential ministers he encouraged poets to make him and his doings their theme, not in gross and vulgar flattery, which he did not much like and his subjects were too shrewd to be much impressed by, but rather in favourable interpretations of his actions, his motives, and still more, his nature and position in the world. Officially, he was an extraordinary magistrate, a survivor of the Commission of Three to regulate public affairs (*tresuiri rei publicae constituendae*), of whom the other two, Antony and Lepidus, had fallen by the wayside. Semi-officially, in the East, he was a kind of god, in receipt of worship by the various states, and this spread to many parts of the West also, though Augustus himself would never let it go beyond reasonable limits, for divine honours and titles had been showered upon all manner of rulers from Greece eastwards, and by no means all of them were desirable associates for the head of a community such as Rome. But in Italy, where he was careful to allow no public worship of himself, but only of his guardian spirit or *genius*,[2] which, being divine, might without offence be adored by any one, as the *genius* of every householder was by himself and his family, it was well that one of two opinions should be held, according to the individual's tastes and beliefs. One was, that the Emperor was the *princeps*, the leading man and patriot statesman, after whom such writers as Cicero had aspired; a man, if one chose to believe in Providence, providentially appointed to help the sorely tried state. The other, which again was nothing revolutionary, but only an application of a respectable philosophic doctrine vouched for especially by some of the Stoics, was that he had in him something more than ordinary human nature, being a chosen soul, destined in life to high things and after death to something like divine status. The latter was in time to come much the more important and popular doctrine, for with the arrival of the Empire there came also a general tendency towards belief in the supernatural, not only among the lower classes, who appear to have been extremely superstitious, but in higher circles. Nigidius Figulus (p. 229) was a forerunner of many who found philosophy and learning perfectly compatible with transcendental doctrines appealing much more to the imagination and the feelings than to dry reason.[3]

[2] Whatever the ultimate origin of the *genius* may have been, there is no doubt that this is how it was conceived by the time of Augustus. The influence of the Greek doctrine, philosophical and popular, of the personal *δαίμων*, something not unlike a guardian angel, was strong here.

[3] This fact, the implications of which are much too far-reaching to discuss here, has been repeatedly noticed, for example, by Gaston Boissier in the preface to his work *La religion romaine d'Auguste aux Antonins*, Paris, Hachette, 1874, and by many writers since. The revival of religion,

Clearly, there was much room for poetical expression here. For an official document to declare that the Emperor was providentially appointed, still more that he was divine, was sure to arouse opposition. But to let a poet say so might be taken as mere poetic licence, gratitude or flattery, and, after all, was no more than Lucretius had said of Epicurus.[4] Again, it would have been inviting criticism for the Emperor and his officials to inform the world that he was the very man whom Cicero had unwittingly foreshadowed in his idealizing picture of Scipio (cf. p. 185); the objection was ready to hand that Cicero himself had died in defence of the old system of government against the new. But to allow men of letters, well acquainted with the Republican authors, to paint the portrait of an ideal and unselfish ruler and imply delicately that Augustus was such a man was a very different matter, and at least as good propaganda, provided that the portrait was a good work of art, and also recognizable. The merits of the work would win it readers, and its doctrines, rather hinted at than bluntly expressed, would remain in the minds of those who had felt the charm of the style.

This, very briefly, by way of explaining why a man of inconspicuous birth, retiring temperament, and no political ambitions became one of the most important and influential authors of that age, cherished by the highest in the Empire, including its head, purely because he was a poet. PVBLIVS VERGILIVS MARO[5] was born on October 15, 684/70, at Andes, a village in the Mantuan territory, whose site has never been quite satisfactorily determined.[6] His family appears to have been of some local

which was part of Augustus' policy, was not a mere device to strengthen his position in the eyes of the vulgar, but a response to a genuine sentiment, whether or not he himself shared it. The problem of the deification or quasi-deification of emperors is not yet fully solved; the facts are well known, but the proportions of genuine belief, flattery, and official expressions of loyalty have yet to be determined. For a recent study of the matter, see L. R. Taylor, *The Divinity of the Roman Emperor*, Middletown, Conn., Amer. Phil. Ass., 1931.

[4] For example, Lucr., v, 8.

[5] There is no such name as Virgilius, consequently to call the poet Virgil is nonsense; the correct English form is Vergil. It may be conjectured that his name, which has no very clear etymology and is not borne by any other well-known person, was altered in post-classical times to fit the story (Donatus, *uit. Verg.*, 5) that a slip (*uirga*) was planted in commemoration of his birth and grew at an astonishing rate.

[6] That it was probably not far from the modern towns of Carpenedolo and Calvisano was the view of the late Professor Conway, which I too held for a time, but later abandoned. It has against it the tradition of ancient scholarship that his birthplace was *non procul* from Mantua itself (Donatus, 2), *milia passuum tria* (Probus, *init.*) according to one

importance[7]; his mother, Polla Magia,[8] would seem to have belonged to a *gens* fairly widespread in Italy and, so far as we can tell, reasonably prosperous. At all events, his parents gave him a good education, probably hoping that he would make his way, as Cicero did, by his eloquence. He studied successively at Cremona, Milan and Rome, and actually appeared once before a jury as pleader; but the experiment was not repeated. His shyness and awkward manner stood in his way, and he seems to have abandoned all thoughts of a career at the bar, probably without much regret, and turned to philosophy and poetry.[9] In the former, his only known teacher was Siron the Epicurean, but there are good grounds for supposing[10] that he came to feel Epicureanism an unsatisfactory explanation of the world and of life, though he always retained a great admiration for its poet; Lucretius was an author whom he seems to have known practically by heart, and imitations of him are scattered throughout his works. Vergil was well read in Latin poetry, from Ennius to Catullus; of the Greeks, Theokritos and Apollonios of Rhodes seem to have been favourites of his, of course after the great masters, especially Homer.

That he began early to try his own hand at poetry is asserted by the biographers, but their material seems to be simply the

reading, and the local tradition that Andes is Pietole, about three Roman miles from Mantua, and therefore in flat, marshy country. Favouring it is the variant in Probus, *milia passuum xxx*, and, far more important, the scenery of the *Eclogues*, which is perfectly accurate if one assumes a hilly region, with sufficient differences of altitude for a dweller in it to be acquainted with the flora and lesser fauna corresponding to the climatic changes experienced in climbing any considerable height. In addition to this, the neighbourhood of Calvisano would lie so near the territory of Cremona that the confiscation of the poet's estate becomes much more intelligible. See, for discussion in some detail and references to recent literature, the present author's *Eclogues of Vergil* (Berkeley and Los Angeles, 1942), pp. 45–68, 228–33. This book is hereinafter quoted as *Eclogues*.

One of the primary sources for the facts of Vergil's life is the ancient biographies, conveniently collected in No. 72 of Lietzmann's *Kleine Texte* (Bonn, Weber, 1911). They are cited by their authors, real or supposed (Donatus, Donatus auctus, Focas, Servius, Probus, Filargyrius, and three anonymous lives, the Bernensis, the Monacensis and the Noricensis). Their chief source is Suetonius, cf. p. 511.

[7] See M. L. Gordon in *Journ. Rom. Stud.*, 1934, pp. 1–12, and the literature there quoted.

[8] Polla (*i.e.*, Paulla) was probably her pet-name ('baby'); see Gordon, p. 7.

[9] See the Donatan life, 27.

[10] Siron, Focas, 63, and, if genuine, *catalept.* 5. For the signs that he deserted Epicureanism, see below, p. 253.

minor poems supposed to be his, hence our attitude on this point must be determined partly by our views as to their genuineness. In itself it is more than likely that he wrote a good deal in his formative years, for the technical skill of the earliest certainly Vergilian works is far too great to have been attained otherwise than by long, diligent practice. But be this as it may, his quiet life of study was broken by the civil wars. In that between Caesar and Pompey we have no evidence that he took any part; the later contests, first between the triumvirs and Brutus and Cassius, then between Octavian and the partisans of Antony, brought him and his family dangerously near to ruin. The demobilization of the large armies employed meant, according to the methods of that day, finding land for the men to settle upon, and that in Italy, for colonization overseas would have been unpopular and also impolitic, considering how often already time-expired men had been hastily recalled to the colours when a new struggle was imminent. After Philippi,[11] Octavian seized upon the territory of Cremona, on some excuse of unfriendliness towards his party, and settled his veterans there. But, this not being enough, he proceeded, on no excuse save necessity, to confiscate a large part of the Mantuan territory also. In this was included Vergil's own estate.[12] What happened is not exactly known, for we must depend on interpretations, ancient and modern, of the *Eclogues* (see below). In the first of these, to which Vergil clearly meant to draw attention by putting it where it stands in the collection, a certain slave called Tityrus has managed after many years to earn his freedom, and finds himself also confirmed in the possession of a plot of ground, large enough for his needs, when his neighbours are being turned out of their holdings on all sides. The conventional interpretation is that Tityrus is Vergil, and that the *deus* who bade him have no fear for his land is Octavian intervening on Vergil's behalf. In the ninth poem of the same collection, Menalcas, a farmer and poet, has vainly appealed to Alfenus Varus, the commissioner charged with the appropriation of the land of Mantua, to exempt him; he is now absent on some unstated business, probably another appeal, and his farm is to be lost to him. Again the ordinary interpretation is that

[11] So Donatus 19 (30); the schol. Bern. on *ecl.*, 8, 7 say Perusia (714/40), but it does not appear that any considerable demobilization took place then, and most of the commentators Actium, a chronological impossibility.

[12] This at least may be regarded as certain, for we never find Vergil living anywhere near Mantua again, but always in Naples, or Rome itself, where he had a rarely used house on the Esquiline (Donatus, 14, cf. 11).

Menalcas is Vergil, and that this represents an earlier stage of the business—earlier, because the first poem, with its note of enthusiastic gratitude and tone of security, may be taken as representing the latest stage, which the poet wished to stress. But this leaves quite unsolved the difficulty of Vergil calling himself by two different names, in the one case that of a freeman and in the other that of a slave; that he should use a conventional name taken from Greek pastoral poetry is quite in keeping with the traditions of the *genre*, but two allegories are one too many.[13] What we may assert with confidence, for it cannot have been derived by any ingenuity of interpretation from the poems themselves and so must come from another source, is that Vergil's farm was assigned to a soldier who turned him out by violence and with some danger to his life.[14] On the whole, the most reasonable supposition is that Vergil is not hinting at his own experiences in the first Eclogue at all; Tityrus and his friend Meliboeus are simply two typical small-holders; the scene is a mountain pasture [15] in early spring,[16] somewhere in the highlands above the actual territory of Mantua; Meliboeus has collected his flock and is driving it away, to sell it, presumably, before emigrating,[17] while Tityrus, who had been to

[13] That one name should throughout the *Bucolics* denote one person only is the very reasonable assumption on which L. Herrmann founds his theories (in themselves often fanciful and incapable of proof, for we really know far too little of the minor events of this period to catch the many allusions which doubtless were there) in his book *Les masques et les figures dans les Bucoliques de Virgile*, Travaux de la Faculté de Philosophie et Lettres de l'Université de Bruxelles, I, 1930. For the disguise of contemporaries under pastoral names, cf. Theokritos, *idyll* vii (Rose, *H.G.L.*, p. 332).

[14] Servius, *comm. in Bucol.*, *prooem.*, p. 3, 3 *sqq.* Probus, *praef.*, p. 328, 2 *sqq.*, Thilo-Hagen; the others agree in substance.

[15] *Ecl.*, i, 1, Tityrus lies sub tegmine fagi; the beech is not a tree of the hot lowlands. *Ibid.*, 82–3, et iam summa procul uillarum culmina fumant, /maioresque cadunt altis de montibus umbrae; the speakers therefore are in a place where they can see several steadings and get a clear view of the long shadows from the higher hills. Some spot well up in the foothills would satisfy the conditions; there is no reason to suppose that shepherds in search of summer pasture regarded local boundaries any more than Varro did when he sent his cattle to Apulia for the winter and kept them about Reate for the summer, *de r.r.*, ii, 2, 9; the revenue authorities kept track of such movements, *ibid.*, i, 16.

[16] Because the she-goats are just dropping their kids, and Meliboeus has lost two already through having to move his flock, 14–15. Cf. Pliny, *N.H.*, viii, 200.

[17] He says *nos patriam fugimus*, 4, which might mean only leaving the Mantuan territory; but 64–6, he says the exiles will leave Italy altogether for distant countries, perhaps outside the Empire (Scythiam et rapidum cretae ueniemus Oaxen).

Rome to see his master and give him the money he had saved to buy his own freedom,[18] is one of the luckier holders who own or occupy land near the town itself, probably on the Mincio.[19] The ninth poem may quite well refer to Vergil and some unsuccessful effort which he made to induce Alfenus Varus to spare the Mantuans as much as possible. Varus, so far from doing anything of the sort, had taken all the land of any value,[20] and it may be that this was remedied to a certain extent by Octavian, and that was the good news which Tityrus heard in Rome.[21] But I confess to having almost as little faith in this very conjectural restoration of the lost details of an obscure injustice as in the many other attempts, ancient and modern, ingenious or merely perverse, which have been made to extract from Vergil's surviving words a meaning probably never intended to be too plain, though intelligible to those of his contemporaries who knew the local circumstances in a way they never can be known to us, and were not to the later commentators.

However we interpret them, the *Bucolics*, or *Eclogues* (*Bucolica*, *Eclogae*; *i.e.*, *Poems of the Pastures* or *Select Poems*), established Vergil's reputation, and attracted the attention of Maecenas (see p. 304), who seems to have been (unofficially, for he had no wish for titles) Octavian's Minister for Propaganda, a post which fitted well with his own love for literature. Vergil soon became one of the distinguished writers grouped around this patron whose very name has become a common noun, in Latin and in modern languages, for an encourager of literature or art.[22] The *Eclogues* number ten in all, whereof we have sufficiently considered the first and ninth. The second, a lovely piece of verse, lyric in quality though its form is the dactylic hexameter

[18] *Ibid.*, 27 *sqq.*

[19] Not only because it is swampy land overgrown in places with riverweed, 48, but because that was the region actually left to the Mantuans, see n. 20. See p. 294.

[20] Menalcas, *ecl.*, ix, 26, had left unfinished a poetical address to Varus (for whom see Daniel's Servius on *ecl.*, vi, 6 and ix, 10, 27, and the Berne scholia on ix, *praefatio*, and on viii, 6). Varus was appointed commissioner after Asinius Pollio, who according to the commentators was friendly and helpful to Vergil. That he took all the land of Mantua except the swamps is a statement supported by an extract, preserved in Daniel's Servius on *ecl.*, ix, 10, from a speech of Cornelius Gallus in which he denounced Varus' action. Cf. *O.R.F.*, p. 514 *sq.*

[21] Tityrus hears the *iuuenis* whom he will henceforth regard as a god say in answer to his petition: pascite, ut ante, boues, pueri, summittite tauros, *ecl.*, i, 42 *sqq.* This might possibly be a poetical version of Octavian's response to complaints, voiced by Gallus, of Varus' proceedings.

[22] Sint Maecenates, non deerunt, Flacce, Marones, is Martial's way of saying (*epigr.*, viii, 55 [56], 5) that good patrons make good poets.

used with a grace and variety hitherto unattained, tells of the woes of an imaginary [23] Corydon, in love with his master's favourite, Alexis. To solace himself he sings a medley of love-songs, partly suggested by those of the love-lorn Cyclops in Theokritos' eleventh idyll, of which Vergil was particularly fond, to judge by the frequency with which he imitates it. By way of marking the indebtedness, he puts into the mouth of his shepherd a Cyclops-song (19–27), which has greatly worried some literal-minded commentators. The third is a singing-contest between two rival shepherd-boys, judged by another. This is again Theokritean, suggested by such pieces as his fifth idyll, or the very pretty imitation of his style which is generally printed with his works as the eighth of the series. These two pieces we know to be early.[24] The fourth, perhaps the most discussed of all Vergil's writings, announces itself in its opening lines [25] as attempting a higher strain than ordinary pastoral. It dates itself; it is dedicated to Pollio, when consul, *i.e.*, in 714/40, and so was written at or shortly before the beginning of his term of office. The year was a memorable one in several ways, for not only did the fall of Perusia and the death of Antony's turbulent wife Fulvia occur in it, but also the Peace of Brundisium between the two great rivals, confirmed by the marriage of Octavian's sister Octavia to Antony. It was therefore a time when all men of good will would naturally be anxious for the future, but hopes of a peaceful settlement of the points at issue between the masters of the eastern and western halves of the Empire were not absurd. How long beforehand hints of the possibility of Antony's new marriage were current, it is of course quite impossible to say; certainly, in January, 714/40, or, for he was a slow composer,[26] as early as 713/41, while Fulvia was alive and powerful and the rebellion which she and Lucius Antonius hatched was either not yet actually begun or not yet crushed, Vergil could have had no inkling of its possibility. Antony was living openly with Kleopatra VII of Egypt, and it probably was common knowledge that the East regarded them as married. Octavian was married to his second wife, Scribonia.

[23] The ancient commentators, of course, declared that Corydon was Vergil. We need not spend time over this wholly gratuitous supposition.

[24] They are both mentioned, by their opening lines, in *ecl.*, v, 85–7, which contains also the one definite identification of Vergil with one of his pastoral characters, Menalcas.

[25] To give a full list of the literature on this poem is impossible. Schanz-Hosius, vol. ii, p. 47 *sqq.*, has an account of it up to 1935. Add Kerényi in *Klio*, xxix (1936), pp. 1–35.

[26] Donatus, *uita*, 22, confirmed by Quint., x, 3, 8, who cites Varius as his authority.

Hence to say that a marvellous child [27] was to be born before long to a father who had pacified or would pacify the world would inevitably be taken, according to the reader's sympathies, as a compliment to one or the other of the two chief men of the whole earth. The poem, in imagery chiefly Greek but certainly showing some Oriental influence,[28] declares that the new age of the world is at hand; a child will soon be born during whose lifetime the ages will run quickly back (as Plato had declared time occasionally did when God set His hand to the helm of the universe)[29] until, passing through the Heroic Age with its wars, we shall arrive once more at the Golden Age, and all shall once more be peace and innocent prosperity. This Vergil hopes he may live to see in his latter years.

The fifth poem of the series is more nearly ordinary pastoral. Menalcas and Mopsus meet on the hillside, and after some exchange of compliments, the latter, who is the younger of the

[27] The chief guesses as to this child's identity are (1) Pollio's son, Asinius Gallus, who may have been born in the year of his father's consulship. He himself claimed this distinction, Serv. Dan. on *ecl.*, iv, 11; but his alleged brother Saloninus was also named by some as the child. It is extraordinary that this view should have found supporters in modern times; the inevitable and cogent objections to it are briefly stated by F. Skutsch, *Aus Vergils Frühzeit* (Teubner, 1901), p. 154 *sqq*. Pollio is quite sufficiently honoured by being told that the restorer of the Golden Age will be born in his consulate, without being given the position of his father and assured (17) that his virtues have brought or at least will bring peace to the world, a statement as impolitic as untrue. (2) Octavia's son by her first husband, Marcellus. This is less impossible, in view of Octavia's relationship to Octavian; but again it meets the insuperable difficulty that it gives the child far too undistinguished a father, and in any case, Marcellus the younger was in all probability born in 712/42. See, however, Garrod in *Class. Rev.*, xxii (1908), p. 150 *sqq*. (3) No one in particular, a sort of incarnation of the coming age (Norden). This depends on Norden's theory, according to which the child is to be a divine king, a son of the supreme god as the Pharaohs were. (4) A son of Antony and Octavia (Tarn), see *Journ. Rom. Stud.*, xxii (1932), p. 135 *sqq*. This certainly gives him a sufficiently distinguished father, but involves a late date, October, 714/40, for the composition of the poem. Despite the ingenuity of Mr. Tarn's plea, I do not think this has been got over. (5) A son of Octavian (? by Scribonia). This I think the only view consistent with Vergil's admiring attitude towards Octavian, though I also think that he was purposely a little indefinite in his language. He could not be expected, at that date, to foresee Actium. See further, *Eclogues*, chap. viii.

[28] Hardly, as has been suggested (*e.g.*, by T. F. Royds, *Virgil and Isaiah*, Oxford, Basil Blackwell, 1918) from the Hebrew Scriptures; but Vergil himself mentions the Sibyl (4), in whose alleged prophecies there was at least some oriental material, and more may be contained, indeed almost certainly is, in the doctrine of world-ages which he implies, perhaps elsewhere as well.

[29] Plato, *Polit.*, 269 c; cf. Rose in *Class. Quart.*, xviii (1924), p. 113 *sqq*.

wo, sings his companion a lament for Daphnis. Menalcas eplies with a song of triumph ; Daphnis is not dead, but becomes god, and will watch over his faithful followers in the country-ide. That Daphnis is Julius Caesar is the opinion of some ncients [30] and of very many moderns [31] ; and indeed it is not asy to see of what other recently dead man Vergil could have aid that he was become a great deity without being ridiculous r offensive. Caesar had been officially deified, and to praise im in such a manner was quite in order. The sixth Eclogue s addressed to Varus, possibly at his suggestion or request.[32] Two young shepherds catch Seilenos asleep and bind him ; awak-ng, he bids them let him loose and sings them a number of ongs, beginning with the creation of the world and ending uriously with a meeting of Gallus with the Muses, in plain llusion to one of his poems.[33] The exact point of this has ever been satisfactorily explained, but that does not seriously amper our enjoyment of an exceedingly pretty poem. The eventh is a singing-contest between Corydon and Thyrsis, judged y Meliboeus and Daphnis. The framework is much like that f Theokritos' fifth idyll, for in both pieces the shepherd who ings first is declared the winner. In the eighth, as in the fifth nd in Theokritos' sixth, there is no contest or wager, but only friendly rivalry in song. Damon and Alphesiboeus sing each long solo ; the former chooses for his theme the complaint of lover whose sweetheart is wedded to his rival, and, despite he wide difference of ancient and modern form, attains a tone ften reminiscent of Heine's lyrics. The latter replies with a ree imitation of Theokritos' second poem, which describes a irl vainly trying by magic to win back an inconstant lover. Vergil's shepherd gives the charms a more favourable outcome, or they break off suddenly as the young witch hears the lover's ootfall outside her house. Of the ninth poem something has lready been said ; the framework, taken from the seventh of he Theokritean collection, is a noonday walk, but the contents re very different, save that in both poems there is some allusive alk of literary matters. Vergil's speakers are Moeris, a slave

[30] See Servius on 20.

[31] See, however, Tenney Frank in *Class. Rev.*, xxxiv (1920), p. 49 *sqq*.

[32] vi, 9, non iniussa cano. But see *Eclogues*, p. 88.

[33] F. Skutsch, p. 28 *sqq*., starting from our positive knowledge (*ecl.*, i, 64 *sqq*., and Serv. Dan. on 72) that a poem of Gallus, on the Gryneian rove, is alluded to, ingeniously suggests that the whole song of Seilenos s similarly made up ; a curious thing, if true, in a work not dedicated o him. In any case, the poem seems early, before the confiscation of he Mantuan territory and its sequels.

of the dispossessed Menalcas, and a friend, Lycidas—the name is Theokritean. The tenth poem announces itself as the last of the series.[34] It is extraordinarily pretty, a compliment from one poet to another in the setting of a conventional Arkadia.[35] Gallus, broken-hearted at his desertion by his mistress, Lycoris (see p. 284), is dying amid a sympathetic audience of woodland and pastoral personages, with Apollo at their head, the poets' god giving good advice to a faithful servant. Gallus answers with a lament which very possibly [36] contains a series of allusions to his own poetry, ending with a resolve to ' sing on the Sicilian shepherd's pipe the strains I reared in Chalkidian measures ', meaning apparently that he intends to write pastoral poems; Euphorion of Chalkis had been his model hitherto for poems of a learned Alexandrian type.[37] The last paragraph is spoken in Vergil's own person and constitutes his formal farewell to pastoral poetry. No doubt he already was planning the *Georgics*, the last lines of which refer back to the *Eclogues*.[38]

The precise date when the *Eclogues* were written is not determinable, but it can be approximately fixed. The so-called Probus twice tells us, on the authority of Asconius, that Vergil wrote, or published, them when he was twenty-eight years old.[39] As it stands, this is absurd; Vergil's twenty-eighth year was 712/42, and we have seen that the fourth Eclogue refers to events of 714/40. ' Probus ' must have misunderstood Asconius, and the latter doubtless meant that the work was begun in that year. This is reasonable enough, and if we add Donatus' statement that the composition occupied three years in all,[40] we get the limits 712/42–715/39 for the writing and publication of the series, which manifestly, from the careful arrangement of it, the leave-taking which ends, not the tenth poem only, but the whole

[34] *Ecl.*, x, 1, extremum hunc, Arethusa (= pastoral poetry in the Theokritean manner; from Arethusa, the famous fountain at Syracuse), mihi concede laborem. The poem takes its framework from Theokr., i, and in turn is imitated in Milton's *Lycidas*.

[35] The real Arkadia was known chiefly, in earlier times, as a recruiting ground for mercenaries; in later, as a district famous for its breed of asses.

[36] So Skutsch, *op. cit.*, p. 2 *sqq*.

[37] Lines 50–1.

[38] *Georg.*, iv, 566, Tityre, te patulae cecini sub tegmine fagi: *Ecl.*, i, 1, Tityre, tu patulae recubans sub tegmine fagi.

[39] Probus, p. 329, 5, Hagen, cum certum sit, eum, ut Asconius Pedianus dicit, xxviii annos natum Bucolica edidisse. P. 323, 13: scripsit Bucolica annos natus viii et xx.

[40] Donatus, *uita*, 25 (40): Bucolica triennio, Georgica vii, Aeneida xi perfecit annis.

collection, and the poet's own allusion to the book by citation of part of its first line,[41] was not put together by any editor but by the author, though no doubt individual poems circulated among his acquaintance earlier. It established his reputation among good critics, and his next work was in a manner the result of an official commission; he himself says that Maecenas asked him to write the *Georgics*, which is tantamount to saying that it was, for all its extreme beauty as poetry, or rather because beautiful poetry was wanted in the service of the government, a piece of propaganda.

Octavian was far too shrewd not to realize that the depopulation of the countryside which had already been seen and lamented by the elder Gracchus a century earlier [42] was a source of weakness to Italy and the Empire such as no government could afford to neglect. To discuss his imperfectly known measures for getting the free population back on the land is outside our scope; the literary side of the endeavour is represented, for us, by Vergil's didactic poem on farming, with its title taken from Nikandros, its contents influenced by Hesiod, Aratos and Lucretius, to name no others, and its metre and manner purely Vergil's own. Its four books constitute the second finest work of this kind which the Latin genius produced, only the *de rerum natura* excelling it. A poorer poet would probably have spent much effort in laudations of the agricultural policy of the new government; Vergil, though he has not a little to say in praise of Octavian,[43] devotes his space to describing agriculture, as seen through the eyes of one country-bred and not only loving but knowing the simple, hardy life of a farmer or stock-breeder. The first book treats of crops and then gives an account, taken mostly from Aratos, of the signs of fair and foul weather.[44] The second discusses the vine and olive, the third stock-breeding, the last bee-keeping, which was a far more important industry then than now, as the ancients had no other form of sugar available, and concludes with a mythological episode nearly three hundred lines long, the tale of how

[41] In the last line of the *Georgics*, see n. 38.

[42] See especially Plutarch, *Ti. Gracchus*, 8.

[43] Especially i, 498 *sqq*., an impassioned prayer to the gods of Rome to spare Octavian and allow him to save the almost ruined state; iii, 10 *sqq*., evidently one of the latest passages in the poem, in which Vergil erects an imaginary temple in the Emperor's honour.

[44] This is Vergil's own summary of Book i: ii, 1, hactenus aruorum cultus et sidera caeli. It goes without saying that Hesiod is laid under contribution for many passages; what, if anything besides the title, is taken from Nikandros cannot be known, as his poem is lost.

Aristaios was the cause of Eurydike's death, and was afflicted by the nymphs her sisters with the loss of all his bees; how he consulted his mother Kyrene and was sent from her to Proteus, heard from him the reason for his loss, appeased the nymphs and was given a new swarm from the rotting bodies of oxen he had sacrificed to them.[45] Throughout the poem, the art of the poet somehow contrives to make living and full of interest the plainest passages describing the most ordinary operations of ploughing, planting, making beehives and so forth. Here and there, in digressions never of undue length and never dragged in, we catch a higher note; the famous praise of country life and country piety in the second book, the dying ox in the description of the great cattle-plague in the Noric Alps which concludes Book III (it ranks with the death of Odysseus' dog Argos, in Homer,[46] among the very few passages throughout literature in which a beast is made a wholly pathetic figure without the least touch of sentimentality), Orpheus' visit to Hades in quest of Eurydike, in Book IV. But the whole work is, as has a hundred times been said, pure poetry, such as only an artist of the first rank could have produced.

[45] The ancients believed that bees could be bred from the flesh of an ox, and Vergil himself (*georg.*, iv, 295–314), besides many other authors, describes the process. The foundation for the belief is the fact that *eristalis tenax*, a fly very like a honey-bee in general appearance, lays its eggs in carrion, whence they hatch out. See, for the first full statement of the facts with examination of the relevant data, ancient and modern, C. R. Osten Sacken, *On the Oxen-born Bees of the Ancients*, Heidelberg, 1894.

It is to be wished, but scarcely hoped, owing to the slowness with which cogent evidence is seen to be such, that we may soon have heard the last of a silly tale in Servius (on *ecl.*, x, p. 117, 6–9; *georg.*, iv, 1), that Vergil originally filled the second half of the fourth Georgic with a panegyric on Gallus, and that on the disgrace and death of the latter he was ordered by Augustus to alter it. This involves the suppositions (*a*) That after *georg.*, iv, 314, or thereabouts, having said that the process for breeding bees from oxen is Egyptian, Vergil went on to speak of Gallus' doings in Egypt without mentioning Octavian's recent conquest of that country, and had the temerity and bad taste to read this aloud to the Emperor. (*b*) That this version was afterwards suppressed with such unexampled thoroughness that not a copy remained, nor so much as a line is ever quoted by the many writers who dealt with Vergil long after Augustus was dead; and this despite the fact that Gallus was a poet of considerable reputation, and also a speaker of sufficient importance for one at least of his orations to be preserved for some time after his death (see n. 20). This falsehood, after imposing on such men as Skutsch and Hosius, was exposed independently by W. B. Anderson (*Class. Quart.*, xxvii, 1933, pp. 36–45, 73) and E. Norden (*Berlin. Sitzungsber.*, 1934, p. 627 *sqq.*).

[46] Odyssey, xvii, 290 *sqq.*

The work bears some traces of the seven years during which it was in Vergil's hands [47]; for instance, at the end of Book I he almost despairs of the state and of civilization, whereas in Book III Octavian is hailed as the victor over the East and the praises showered on him sound almost too extravagant for good taste until we remember from what a gulf of distress and anxiety the world had been raised by that victory. The date can be got closely enough. Vergil had the poem ready when Octavian came back from the East,[48] and he and Maecenas took turns to read it aloud to the Emperor; he had therefore begun it in or before 718/36. This, of course, does not exclude the possibility of revisions, partial publications and so forth; what we have is Vergil's own definitive edition, authenticated by the poetical signature in the concluding lines.[49]

Vergil had early experimented with heroic poetry,[50] though at the time nothing came of it and he suppressed anything he may have written. But a heroic poem, an epic on the grand scale, was badly wanted by Augustus and his supporters. Rome had nothing to set against Homer except Ennius, and however much some critics might praise him,[51] he was too rude and old-fashioned for the taste of the new age, refined by the 'neoteric' poets of the school of Catullus and taught by Vergil how magnificent a serious theme treated in Latin hexameters could be. The project of writing a national epic on some subject connected with Augustus' achievements seems to have been brought to the notice of every poet of any ability [52]; only one had either the will or the power to respond to the suggestion.

[47] Cf. n. 40.

[48] Donatus, *uita*, 27 (42). Octavian reached Italy not long after the beginning of 725/29; of course the poem may have been finished some little while before that, as indeed the epilogue suggests.

[49] *Georg.*, iv, 559 *sqq.* Such signatures are not unexampled; Statius has something similar, though without his actual name, at the end of the *Thebais*, and an unknown hand has added one to the Fourth Gospel.

[50] Cum canerem reges et proelia, *ecl.*, vi, 3. Donatus, *uita*, 19 (30), says he tried to write on Roman history, but did not like the subject and so gave it up; Servius, *ad loc.*, that it was the gesta regum Albanorum, and that he dropped it nominum asperitate deterritus. Whether these statements are anything more than the ingenuity of commentators we do not know.

[51] Sapiens et fortis et alter Homerus was the correct thing to say about him, Horace, *epp.*, ii, 1, 50, quoting unnamed *critici*.

[52] Traces of such hints are to be found in Horace, *sat.*, ii, 1, 10–12; Propertius, ii, 1, 17 *sqq.*; perhaps Tibullus, ii, 4, 16; Ovid, *A.A.*, i, 205.

Vergil spent the last eleven years of his life, 724/30–Sept. 21, 735/19, in composing the *Aeneid*. We are fairly well informed as to the stages of the work. He first sketched it in prose,[53] and then began to turn it into verse, taking now this part and now that, as he felt inclined. He did not feel tied to any particular order of the books he had outlined, for there are reasons for supposing that what is now Book III, and part of Aeneas' own story of his adventures during six years of wandering, was originally meant for the first book, and therefore was told in the third person, not the first.[54] Composing slowly, he did not always remember precisely what he had written, and so we find an occasional inconsistency between one part of the story and another; in Book II, Aeneas is plainly told by the ghost of his wife that he is to settle in Italy, while in Book III he does not know where his wanderings are to end. These and other similar irregularities, together with the presence of a number of incomplete lines (a phenomenon recurring in the *Metamorphoses* of Ovid, also an unfinished poem, see p. 332), are witnesses to the truth of the account given by our authorities,[55] that he never lived to give his work the finishing touches, and was so little satisfied with it that he asked on his deathbed that it should be burned, and on finding that this request would not be granted, inserted a clause in his will appointing Varius and Tucca his literary executors and asking them not to publish anything left unpublished by himself. A wise compromise was reached by order of Augustus; the *Aeneid* was published, but with no attempt at extensive revision. We know of one passage which the ancient editors omitted, though it is, past reasonable doubt, genuinely Vergilian work. The modern editors quarrel

[53] Donatus, *uita*, 23 (34) *sq*.

[54] Donatus, *uita*, 42 (60): Nisus grammaticus audisse se a senioribus aiebat Varium duorum librorum ordinem commutasse et qui nunc secundus sit in tertium locum transtulisse, etiam primi libri correxisse principium, his uersibus demptis, 'ille ego', &c. The prefaratory verses are certainly not Vergil's, among other things because they contain the construction *coegi ut parerent*, which he never uses; they probably were the inscription under a portrait prefixed to an edition of the *Aeneid*, as suggested by Marx, *Lucilius*, i, p. li, and independently by E. Brandt, *Philologus*, 1928, p. 331 *sqq*. That a transposition of Bks. i and iii was made by Varius is quite incredible, but that it was a revision of Vergil's own is in no way unlikely; for a list of modern works dealing with his methods of composition, see Schanz-Hosius, ii, p. 65 *sqq*.

[55] Donatus, *uita*, 30(45)–42(60); Servius, *praef. ad Aen.*, p. 2, 10 *sqq*., Thilo-Hagen; Probus, p. 324, 1 *sqq*., Hagen. Vergil had gone on a journey to Greece; while there, he contracted an illness, grew worse on the voyage back to Italy, landed at Brundisium in a very serious condition, and died on September 21, 735/19.

with their taste in this respect, and it appears in our printed copies.[56]

The revision which the poet would have given his work had he lived to bestow on it the further three years' attention he had in mind [57] would certainly have been no more than a re-arrangement and polishing in detail, for the story is complete and the handling such as no one but Vergil could have given it. The material is the legend of Aeneas' arrival in the West and his settlement there, by that time fully developed and old enough to be accepted by Romans as the genuine Roman tradition it certainly was not.[58] It had the advantage of a slight historical foundation, the settlement of Mount Eryx in Sicily by Easterners who may well have been of the Trojan clan of the Aineiadai, known to Homer as a ruling family there.[59] The central figure is of necessity Aeneas himself, and he labours under a heavy disability. He must be more than an ordinary epic hero, for he is not merely Aeneas, but Rome, and in a sense Augustus as well, the embodiment of the aspirations and the destiny of the greatest ancient power. Since the worst weakness of Vergil was a certain lack of ability to understand men of action (his gentle and almost effeminate nature made him a better painter of women), his Aeneas does not emerge very successfully from his trying ordeal. He is apt to be brutal instead of strong, and then inconsistently kindly and scrupulous ; his own words and actions do not always fit the immense admiration which his followers and even his enemies express towards him ; and in bringing a love-interest into the story, the meeting of Aeneas with Dido, Vergil is so hampered by the exigencies of his plot that he is constrained to make his hero behave like a brute towards a woman sympathetically drawn. No doubt it was partly his own consciousness of these defects that made so delicate an artist dissatisfied with a poem which seems to have been more than good enough for almost every one else in Rome and the Latin-reading world, and to have fulfilled, for his admirers, even the vast expectations of Propertius that ' something greater than the Iliad was coming into being '.[60] Whether he would have suc-

[56] *Aen.*, ii, 567–588 ; see below.

[57] Donatus, *loc. cit.*, 35.

[58] See Rose, *H.G.M.*, p. 307 *sqq.*, but cf. next note.

[59] This is the result of the very ingenious re-examination of the evidence by L. Malten, in *Arch. f. Religionswissenschaft*, xxix (1931), p. 23 *sqq.* It is to be noted that the geography of the legend is good ; the newcomers arrive up the west coast of Italy and settle in the one promising region not dominated by the Etruscans.

[60] Nescio quid maius nascitur Iliade, Prop., iii, 34, 66.

ceeded, even with another three years of his maturest work, in making 'Aeneas the Good'[61] all that he would have had him be, is a vain speculation now; we must content ourselves with understanding what, though manifestly faulty, is equally clearly a masterpiece. In order to do so, it is well to remember that to compare it with Homer is futile, despite external details in which the Latin imitates the Greek. Homer composed for an audience who knew no other form of composition on a large scale than epic; he meant his work to be heard, not read or minutely studied; his society, though very far from primitive, was relatively simple, a nobility not unlike the feudal barons of our own Middle Ages. Vergil lived in a community as complex as ours, and wrote for readers quite as much as hearers—readers who included the most scholarly men of the day as well as the usual more or less educated public. For him, there was no possibility of winning favour by merely telling a story, even a good one told well. The manner of the telling must include a thousand delicate strokes of art, subtle allusions and reminiscences of works become classical, hints of underlying meaning never degenerating into mere allegory, unostentatious displays of learning; and throughout, his real hero must be the Roman ideal, as a thing worth living and dying for, with the implication, not too much stressed and yet unmistakable, that Augustus was the leader under whom, by Heaven's especial grace, this ideal was to be realized. To use Homer as a standard by which to measure such work is as unreasonable as to praise or blame a poet of to-day because he does not much resemble Chaucer or the *Nibelungenlied*.

The following is a sketch of the twelve books into which the author himself[62] meant his poem to be divided. In Book I, Aeneas is introduced on his way from Sicily towards the Italian coast. Iuno, who is implacably his enemy, persuades the wind-god Aeolus to raise a storm and scatter his fleet, which is driven helpless towards the treacherous coast of Africa. Neptune, however, hears the disturbance and quells it; three of the ships are sunk, the rest land their crews safely, but not all at the same spot. Next day Aeneas makes his way inland, accompanied by his faithful retainer Achates,[63] and arrives at the site of Carthage. Meeting on the way with his mother Venus, he is warned by her

[61] *Pius Aeneas*; in Homeric fashion he is given a standing epithet. The word is untranslatable, for though it includes it is not coextensive with its modern derivatives. A man is *pius* if he displays, in all relations both human and divine, a strong sense of duty vivified by strong affection.

[62] Cf. n. 53.

[63] His standing epithet is *fidus*, and he has become proverbial in modern times.

that the leader of the new settlement is the widowed Tyrian princess Dido, who has left her native city after the murder of her husband and is seeking a new kingdom at the head of a powerful band of followers.[64] Dido welcomes him hospitably, and also his missing consorts, who have likewise found their way to her city. At a banquet that night she asks Aeneas to tell her the story of his wanderings. Meanwhile Venus has stolen away Aeneas' son Ascanius, or Iulus,[65] and substituted Cupid for him, to make Dido love Aeneas.

Book II. Aeneas begins his narrative. When Troy fell, he was warned by Venus to make his escape, taking with him the other members of his family and the household gods (*Penates*).[66] He succeeded in doing so, but on the way was separated from his wife Creusa. Searching for her, he met her ghost, and was told that he was destined to settle in Italy.[67]

Book III continues the story. Aeneas, with a number of refugees, constructs a fleet and sails away in the spring of the next year. They go to the neighbouring coast of Thrace, but are warned away by the voice of Aeneas' murdered kinsman Polydorus, heard from his grave. They next visit Delos, where they are told by the oracle of Apollo to 'seek their ancient mother'. Anchises, Aeneas' father, interprets this as meaning Crete. But on attempting to settle there, they are visited by a plague, and the Penates, appearing by night to Aeneas, warn him that Italy, and not Crete, is meant. Anchises confirms the statement. They therefore set out; a storm drives the fleet to the Strophades, where the Harpies encounter them, and, being attacked by the Trojans, depart with the prophecy from their leader Celaeno that Aeneas will never find an abiding-place until hunger compels him and his followers to eat the tables from which they feed. Leaving the islands, they land on the coast of Epeiros, where they meet Helenus, now reigning there and married to Andromache.[68] Inspired by Apollo, Helenus bids

[64] We have seen (cf. p. 26) that probably some version of this story was as old as Naevius; the question of its origin cannot be discussed here. Usually, Rome and Carthage are represented as of the same age.

[65] Ascanius, Ἀσκάνιος, is a royal Trojan name, found in Homer; Iulus, Ἴουλος, 'Curly-head' is good Greek, and has a genealogical significance; the Iulii claimed to be his descendants.

[66] That the *penates publici*, originally the divine guardians of the king's store-chamber, were identical with the Samothracian gods and had been brought to Italy by Aeneas was a popular theory; cf. chap. viii, n. 160, and further, Wissowa, *Gesammelte Abhandlungen* (Munich, Beck, 1904), pp. 95–128.

[67] For the inconsistency here, cf. above, p. 248.

[68] For the legends of these subsidiary figures, see any dictionary of mythology, or Rose, *H.G.M.* (references in index under the names).

them go around Sicily and make for the west coast of Italy; on arrival, they are to consult the Sibyl at Cumae and propitiate Iuno. Taking his advice, they coast along the south-eastern portion of the peninsula, then along the shore of Sicily, where they see the Cyclops Polyphemus and pick up one of Odysseus' men who had been left behind there.[69] Arriving finally at the western extremity of the island (they are hospitably received by Acestes, Aeneas' kinsman, and spend the winter there, during which) [70] Anchises dies.

Book IV. Dido falls more and more deeply in love with Aeneas, and finally they are united in what she regards as a regular marriage. This is the outcome of an intrigue of Venus, who persuades Iuno to consent to it as a means of reconciling their differences.[71] Iuppiter sends Mercury to warn Aeneas that Africa is not his destined abode and that he must leave Dido at once. He tries to depart secretly, but the queen discovers his intentions, and vainly tries to induce him to remain. Finally, in despair, under pretence of a magical ceremony, she commits suicide. Aeneas (Book V) sees the gleam of her funeral pyre as he sails away. He returns to Acestes, and there celebrates the anniversary of his father's death with funeral games, which are elaborately described.[72] In the course of these, Iuno appears in human form and persuades the Trojan women to burn his ships. Four are destroyed; Aeneas leaves behind the weakest of his followers to found a town of their own in Sicily, to be called Acesta after their host. He himself sets sail, losing one man on the way, his pilot Palinurus, who, in accordance with a pact between Venus and Neptune, pays with his life for the safety of all the rest; he is supernaturally overcome with sleep, and so falls overboard.

[69] See Odyssey, ix, 105 *sqq*. The incident of the abandoned man is probably Vergil's own invention, but that the Homeric land of the Kyklopes was Sicily was a popular Greek idea, found, *e.g.*, in Theokritos and apparently set going by a local tale of giants.

[70] Aeneas says nothing about this, but the rest of the poem presupposes it; here, then, we have another mark of the poem's unfinished state.

[71] The utterly heartless way in which Venus sacrifices Dido is the result of her being rather a piece of conventional epic machinery than a character. See further the introduction to Pease's edition (Bibliography).

[72] This episode was inevitable. An epic poet must be Homeric, and Homer devotes the twenty-third book of the Iliad to the funeral games over Patroklos. Vergil, who is not at his best in describing athletics, since he knew little about them, varies the imitation by introducing a race between Aeneas' ships and the military spectacle known as the *ludus Troiae* (a sort of 'musical ride' by young men), which was actually to form part of the Augustan secular games of 737/17.

In Book VI, Aeneas, in obedience to Helenus and to the shade of Anchises, who in the last book had bidden him descend to the lower world and there consult him, goes to seek the Sibyl of Cumae. She passes into a prophetic frenzy, foretells that he will wage wars in Italy for the sake of a new Helen [73] and find help from a Greek city. She then tells him that to descend into the nether world he must find the golden bough which is the one passport for the living thither. This he succeeds in doing; the Sibyl in person conducts him across the Styx,[74] past the way which leads to Tartarus, and finally to the Elysian Fields, where he meets with the beatified spirit of his father and is shown a pageant of the souls of future Romans awaiting reincarnation. These, as might be expected, include Augustus himself and his nephew Marcellus, over whose virtues and too brief life are pronounced some of the most affecting lines in all Vergil.[75]

In this connexion we get an interesting light thrown upon the poet's own religion, which appears now to have left Epicureanism far behind, for the framework of this book is no mere epic machinery and its language everywhere suggests at least a measure of personal belief. Anchises expounds to Aeneas a cosmology which contains a strong element of Pythagoreanism. There is a spirit animating all the world and found also in every living thing. Though divine, it is hampered by the coarser material surroundings in which it finds itself, and thus man is capable of evil passions. The soul thus polluted must be cleansed again, and therefore undergoes a painful purification in a sort of Purgatory. A few choice spirits (*pauci* 744) are so freed from all guilt that their wanderings are at an end, and they abide, like Anchises himself, permanently in Elysium.[76] But for the most part there remains a fresh trial. They pass into new bodies on earth, first drinking the water of Lethe, which makes them forget all that has passed. Of this kind, which may include very exalted spirits, like those of the heroes of Roman history, are the throng now in Elysium and awaiting rebirth.

[73] *Externique iterum thalami*, 94; *i.e.*, as the Trojan War was fought over Helen, so the new war of the Trojans must be for Lavinia.

[74] The way to the underworld, when Aeneas has made the necessary sacrifices to the infernal powers and purified himself and his following by finding and burying his trumpeter Misenus, who has been drowned in the meantime, is through the volcanic clefts about Lake Avernus, renowned in Italian belief as a hellmouth.

[75] 860–886; for the interpretation of part of the passage, see Rose in *Class. Rev.*, xlv, 1931, p. 51 *sq*.

[76] For Vergil's religion in general, see C. Bailey, *Religion in Virgil* (Oxford, Clar. Press, 1935); for the many difficulties in this book, see especially E. Norden's commentary on it (*Buch VI der Aeneis*, 3rd ed., Teubner, 1926).

With this book, a glorious adaptation of the visit of Odysseus to Hades in the eleventh book of the Odyssey, ends that part of the poem which its author seems to have regarded as most nearly finished. The second half, if perhaps less polished, has in it much that must have been written as a labour of love, for Vergil was a thoroughly patriotic Italian, author of perhaps the noblest panegyric ever pronounced on his country [77]; while there is also a great deal, the battle-scenes inevitable in an epic, in which he shows to advantage only in details, pathetic deaths or brilliant similes, for the actual carnage was clearly little to his taste and he never describes it well. Book VII brings Aeneas at last to the scene of his future settlement, and on landing, his followers accidentally fulfil the Harpy's prophecy by using cakes of bread, which they afterwards eat, as platters. Latinus, ruler of Latium, has a daughter Lavinia, of whom it has been told him that he must not marry her to a native of the country. Turnus, prince of the Rutuli, claims that he is the destined bridegroom, for he is of partly foreign stock; but on the arrival of the Trojans, who send an embassy and ask the king's leave to settle in the country, he perceives that the true mate for his daughter is Aeneas. His queen, Amata, favours Turnus, and Iuno brings on strife through the agency of a Fury. A pet stag is unwittingly killed by Ascanius while hunting; blows are exchanged between his following and the country people, and the whole kingdom is up in arms against the invaders. Latinus is reluctantly forced to approve, and the book ends with a magnificent catalogue of the Italian forces.[78]

In Book VIII, Aeneas visits Rome itself, or rather the site of the future city. The god of the Tiber, appearing to him in a dream, tells him that Euander the Arkadian has settled there and that Aeneas should seek his help. He will know that the dream is true by seeing on the shore a white sow with thirty white farrow. On finding her, Aeneas knows that the omens are favourable to him and his vision no empty phantasm; he sets out upstream and reaches Rome during a festival of Hercules at the site of the Ara Maxima, outside the settlement on the Palatine which was the primitive Rome. Euander and his son Pallas

[77] *Georg.*, ii, 136 *sqq.*

[78] This, like the visit to Hades and the funeral games, is an almost inevitable feature of an epic poem, because of the Catalogue of the Ships in Iliad II. How excellently and with what knowledge of the country Vergil has handled it is made clear in W. Warde Fowler, *Virgil's Gathering of the Clans* (Oxford, Blackwell, 1916). For archaeological commentary on his knowledge, see Catherine Saunders, *Vergil's Primitive Italy*, New York and Oxford (Univ. Press), 1930.

welcome him ; he joins in the rite, is told the story of how Hercules overcame the monster Cacus, and spends the night with his host. Venus meanwhile cajoles her husband Vulcan into making Aeneas celestial armour, and brings it when ready to her son. On the shield is wrought a prophetic series of scenes from Roman history, ending with the battle of Actium.

Thus Vergil introduces a parallel picture to Homer's description of the arms of Achilles in the eighteenth book of the Iliad ; the older poet, however, leads up to the scene more naturally, for his Achilles has lost his armour and his Hephaistos is appealed to by a goddess to whom he owes a debt of gratitude, not coaxed by a faithless wife into helping the offspring of her irregular amours. Alexandrian epic, with its much too human gods, had come between Vergil and his great model ; it says much for him that his Venus does not become merely an intriguing woman in her conjugal scene with Vulcan, but retains something of Roman *grauitas* in her appealing speech to him.[79] The fire-god also is rather more than the operatic figure of fun who sings *Au bruit des lourds marteaux d'airain* on the modern stage.

Book IX tells of the happenings during Aeneas' absence. Turnus, whom Iuno had sent Iris to warn that his opportunity had come, attacks the Trojan camp and is nearly successful. He sets the ships on fire at their moorings, but, owing to the intercession of Kybele, on whose sacred mountain of Ida they had been built from the trees growing there, Neptune turns them into sea-nymphs. The Trojans, acting on instructions left by Aeneas, remain within their walls. During the night, however, Nisus and his young friend Euryalus make a sortie, with the object of getting through the Rutulian lines to let Aeneas know the state of affairs. After doing much damage in the sleeping and ill-patrolled camp, they are finally discovered and killed, and next day the attack is renewed more vigorously than before ; Turnus succeeds in making his way inside the walls, but is cut off from his following and escapes with difficulty.[80]

[79] *Aen.*, viii, 374 *sqq*. For excellent comment on the book as a whole see W. Warde Fowler, *Aeneas at the Site of Rome*, Oxford, Basil Blackwell, ed. 2, 1918. For Euandros (Euander), see Rose, *H.G.M.*, pp. 309, 311, 327.

[80] This book therefore corresponds partly to Iliad X (the sortie of Odysseus and Diomedes by night to spy out the Trojan camp), partly to the great attack on the Greek camp, led by Hektor, in Iliad XII *sqq*. Vergil introduces a non-Homeric feature ; the two men who set out from Aeneas' camp are lover and loved (ἐραστής and ἐρώμενος), the sentimental relation characteristic especially of the warlike Dorian nobility, which thence became fashionable throughout Greece, considerably later than Homer's day. In the adventure of Turnus also he has no Homeric prototype, though he may have found one in later epic, of which we know nothing.

Book X opens with a council of the gods. Iuppiter, after a stormy debate between Iuno and Venus, declares that the issue of the war must be left to fate. Meanwhile fighting is going vigorously on. Aeneas, on Euander's advice, has offered himself as leader to an Etruscan army which has rebelled against its tyrannical king Mezentius but is at present impotent because it is foretold that it cannot hope for success save under the command of a foreigner. With this strong reinforcement, and a contingent led by Pallas from his father's people, he arrives to the rescue of his hard-pressed men. A furious battle results in the defeat of the Rutulians, who lose Mezentius and his son Lausus, the latter killed unwillingly by Aeneas while trying to cover the retreat of his wounded father, the former also by Aeneas, whom he attacks with javelins from horseback. Pallas is killed by Turnus earlier in the battle.[81]

Book XI opens with a truce for the burial of the dead on both sides; Drances, the leader of the peace party among the Latins, heads an embassy to Aeneas, who offers to settle the war by a single combat between himself and Turnus.[82] The body of Pallas is sent home and mourned over by Euander. A second embassy from Latinus to ask help of Diomedes, now settled in Italy, returns unsuccessful. A stormy council of war results in determination to accept Turnus' advice and try another battle. This is again a victory for the Trojans and their allies, despite the valour of an Amazonian heroine, Camilla (apparently Vergil's own invention), who is killed with an arrow after greatly distinguishing herself.[83] The beaten Latins retreat in disorder to their city.[84]

Book XII begins with another truce, involving acceptance of Aeneas' offer, which Turnus now agrees to despite the opposition

[81] The divine council and its decision are both Homeric (Iliad VIII, 5 *sqq.*); the death of Pallas corresponds to the death of Patroklos in Homer, and, like that, provides a motive for the killing of his slayer. Lausus on the other hand is a post-Homeric figure, corresponding to Antilochos in the *Aithiopis*, one of the Cyclic epics (cf. Rose, *H.G.L.*, p. 49), who is killed by Memnon as he covers the retreat of his father Nestor.

[82] This is again Homeric; Paris, Iliad III, 67 *sqq.*, offers to settle the war by a duel with Menelaos; the offer is accepted, a truce arranged, and after Paris has been defeated by Menelaos and rescued by Aphrodite, Athena stirs up Pandaros to shoot at Menelaos, thus breaking the truce.

[83] Camilla corresponds, not to any Homeric figure, but to Penthesileia, queen of the Amazons, who comes to the help of Priam and the Trojans in the *Aithiopis*.

[84] At this point the poem is most plainly unfinished. In x, 833, the fighting is going on more fiercely than ever, and the killer of Camilla is himself shot down by the nymph Opis, 836–867; then, for no assignable reason, in 868 the whole force begins to run, led by Camilla's following.

of Queen Amata. Turnus' sister, however, the nymph Iuturna,[85] rouses the Rutuli to prevent the duel by violating the truce. Aeneas is treacherously wounded by an arrow just as an irregular fight begins, in his efforts to stop it; Venus comes invisibly to the aid of his physician Iapyx and heals the wound; Aeneas re-enters the battle and routs the Latins; the queen kills herself. Turnus is kept out of his way by Iuturna, who takes the form of his charioteer. At last he insists on meeting Aeneas, and a duel with a good deal of divine interference on both sides results in his being disabled. He asks for life, which Aeneas is disposed to grant him till he sees that he is wearing Pallas' belt; this so enrages him that he kills Turnus at once.[86]

Some idea has been given in the notes on the above synopsis of the use made by Vergil of Greek models. This, however, does not begin to illustrate the vast learning which united with poetical genius in framing this great epic. In the first place, Vergil had taken ideas from the entire literature of Greece, not merely from the older (Homeric and Cyclic) epic. Alexandria contributed, for the credit of being the first to introduce into epic poetry not only a love-motive but a psychologically interesting heroine seems to belong to Apollonios of Rhodes; different though Vergil's Dido is from his Medeia, the fundamental idea is derived from the Greek poet.[87] The legend on which the poem is based seems to be almost entirely a Greek creation; the ornaments are everywhere Greek in colouring, though they also bear everywhere the unmistakable mark of Vergil's own work, which (like that of Milton, the most Vergilian of English poets) is never more truly original than when it is most plainly derivative. But besides all this foreign learning, Vergil was remarkably well informed concerning his own nation. His procession of Roman souls in the sixth book and the epitome of Roman history in the eighth could not have been written but by a man who had saturated himself in all the available historical knowledge of his time. His many references and allusions to the traditional religious practices of his people are as remarkable for their accuracy as for the deep feeling which makes them expressions of piety and not only of antiquarianism. His philosophy is that of one who has thought for himself. It is an exaggeration to make him, as later readers from Macrobius to

[85] A real deity, with a cult in the Roman forum and elsewhere; a legend of Greek pattern had been found for her.

[86] For comment on this book, see W. Warde Fowler, *The Death of Turnus*, Oxford, Blackwell, 1919.

[87] For Apollonios, see Rose, *H.G.L.*, p. 324, and the literature there cited.

Dante were prone to do, an epitome of all human learning; but the exaggeration is of something already considerable.

We have now considered all the poems which are by universal consent and on irrefragable grounds ascribed to Vergil. His name, however, is associated likewise with a number of compositions in verse generally known collectively as the minor poems, or the Appendix Vergiliana. We may conveniently begin with the list given by Donatus.[88]

He made his first acquaintance with poetical composition while yet a child, with a couplet on Ballista, a school-teacher and a notorious bandit, who had therefore been buried under a heap of stones:

> monte sub hoc lapidum tegitur Ballista sepultus;
>   nocte die tutum carpe, uiator, iter.

> 'Beneath this cairn Ballista's corpse is laid;
> By day or night pass, traveller, unafraid.'

He then wrote the *Catalepton, Priapea, Epigrams, Dirae, Ciris* and *Culex*, being at that time sixteen years old. . . . He also wrote, but there is some doubt about this, the *Aetna*.

In addition to this, we have two other poems quoted as his and of a style and content which does not make the attribution manifestly ridiculous,[89] the *Copa* and the *Moretum*. If we now consider all these in turn, no time need be lost over the epitaph of Ballista; it is a correct elegiac couplet, such as doubtless the child Vergil could have produced, and doubtless also hundreds of other children old enough to have learned the elementary rules of prosody in their own language. We need not spend much thought over the *Aetna*; it is so manifestly of the Silver Age that it is better to consider it there (see p. 384). More examination is necessary for the *Culex*, or *Gnat*. In this curious production, a shepherd is lying asleep when a gnat awakes him with its bite.

[88] Donatus, *uita*, 17–18 (28–29).

[89] Among the absurdities we may reckon the famous *sic uos non uobis* (Donatus auctus, 69–70). A bright day on which games were to be held followed a rainy night; Vergil posted up the couplet: nocte pluit tota, redeunt spectacula mane;/diuisum imperium cum Ioue Caesar habet. An impostor said the verses were his; Vergil said nothing, but posted up another couplet, this time incomplete: hos ego uersiculos feci, tulit alter honores;/sic uos non uobis. . . . This no one could complete, and Vergil proved it to be his own by adding four different conclusions, *nidificatis aues, uellera fertis oues, mellificatis apes, fertis aratra boues*. The lateness of the authority and the post-Augustan verbs *nidificatis* and *mellificatis* would prove it apocryphal if proof were needed. A few more trifles are included in R. Ellis' *App. Vergiliana* (O.C.T.).

He kills it, and sees that it has saved him from a snake which had crept near while he slept. Killing the snake also, he goes home and that night is visited in his dreams by the ghost of the gnat, which reproaches him with ingratitude, gives him an account of the nether world, and asks to be remembered. Next day he makes it a little tomb surrounded with flowers. The poem is addressed to an Octavius who is called *sancte puer*. It is hard to see what Octavius can be meant other than the one better known as Octavian and still better as Augustus ; yet harder to explain why he should be ' holy ' except in the eyes of one who knew his future greatness, which certainly Vergil did not while Octavius was still a boy and himself therefore a bigger boy or a young man ; there were seven years between them. The scheme of the poem is a disguised lesson in mythology, history and tree- and plant-names given by the sage to the future emperor, and this alone is quite enough to show that the author is not Vergil but some foolish pedant with a certain knack of turning verse. The final proof of the poem's lateness is that its metre is most definitely post-Ovidian.

Latin poetry, as it grew older, became more and more sensitive to elisions. Whereas in Greek real elision takes place, as already explained (p. 58), the fact that in Latin the first of the two vowels which come in contact was never quite dropped in pronunciation meant a certain retarding of the tempo at that point ; a line like

Corneli et factum me esse puta Harpocratem

must have taken longer to pronounce than

cuius sit penitus nota fides animi.[90]

Therefore all but the easiest elisions, for example that of a short final *e*, came to be more and more avoided by careful writers, Ovid setting the example.[91] Now in the *Culex* all the harsher elisions are very rare, and no elision is common ; a final long never elides before a short, nor is any monosyllable elided. Furthermore, it contains stylistic peculiarities and conventions which are elsewhere found only in post-Augustan times, and sheer vulgarisms in the Latin. That Vergil in his youth should have written a silly poem is understandable ; it is no

[90] Catullus, 102, 4 and 2.

[91] In the first hundred lines of Ovid's *Metamorphoses* there are 25 elisions, or possibly 27, the reading being twice doubtful. Of these, 14 or 15 are of short final *e*, 7 of other short final vowels, 3 of final vowel + m, only 1, or 2, of a long final vowel, and that never before a short initial vowel. Vergil, *Aen.*, i, 1–100, has 49 elisions, 10 being of long final vowels, whereof two occur in iambic words (a scansion usually avoided). See, for the style of the *Culex*, W. A. Baehrens in *Philologus*, lxxxi (= N.F. xxxv), p. 364 *sqq.* ; for an attempt to prove it Vergilian, D. L. Drew, *Culex*, Oxford, B. Blackwell, 1925.

sillier than *Queen Mab* ; but this kind of silly poem is conceivable only in a forger pretending to be the young Vergil. The most astonishing thing is that it imposed not only on Martial, who was no great authority on the history of Latin literature,[92] but even Lucan [93] imagined it to be Vergil's.

The *Ciris* is a much better poem, and presents a harder problem. Its subject is the legend of Skylla of Megara, who stole from the head of her father Nisos the magic lock of hair which was the luck of the city, and so enabled Minos to take it. Minos would have none of her, but in disgust at her unnatural teachery hung her from the stern of his ship, where Amphitrite took pity on her and changed her into the bird called *ciris* (*κεῖρις*, not identified). Her father became a sea-eagle, which still pursues the *ciris* relentlessly. The author of the poem tells us a good deal about himself, but not his name. He is no longer young ; he has dabbled in politics and is ill-satisfied with the fruits of his labours there ; he is something of a philosopher, apparently (his expression is somewhat obscure and the copyists have made the passage obscurer) an Epicurean ; he has now and then written light verse ; he would like to compose a Lucretian poem *de rerum natura*, but feels too diffident of his own powers ; he has spent a considerable time over the *Ciris* ; and he dedicates it to ' the most learned of the younger men ' (*iuuenum doctissime*), Messalla.[94] It remains to ask, then, who he was.

In the first place, he was not Vergil, who never had anything to do with politics, was associated with Maecenas, not Messalla, and, by the age which the poet of the *Ciris* had reached, was busy with a very different type of composition.[95] But he must have

[92] Mart., *epigr.*, viii, 55 (56), 19–20 ; xiv, 185. But for Martial's imperfect knowledge, cf. iv, 14, 14, where he imagines Vergil already *magnus* and well known when Catullus was writing the sparrow-poems.

[93] Suetonius, *de poetis*, p. 299 Roth : ut . . . (Lucanus) ausus sit dicere, Et quantum mihi restat/ad Culicem ? *I.e.*, he accepted the *Culex* as an early work of Vergil, and asked if he had not got as far as that already, implying that with more mature powers he would equal the *Aeneid*.

[94] *Ciris*, 2, irritaque expertum fallacis praemia uulgi. *I.e.*, he had held or been a candidate for some sort of office. If this means a curule magistracy, the lowest of these, the quaestorship, could not be held till a man was thirty-seven, see Mommsen, *Staatsrecht*, 3, p. 568. If this is so, we may abandon the theory that the *Ciris* is by Gallus immediately. He was born in 685/69, and therefore was thirty-seven in 722/32 ; but the *Ciris* is earlier than the *Eclogues* or else later than the *Aeneid* (see above), not of a date between *Ecl.* and *Geor.* *Ibid.*, 3 *sqq.*, interest in philosophy ; 36 *sqq.*, desire to write a philosophic poem ; 19–20, his earlier writings in verse ; 36 also, Messalla as *iuuenis*.

[95] See n. 98.

some relation to Vergil, for one of them has copied the other more than once: for example, lines 430 and 474 of the *Ciris* are identical, respectively, with Vergil, *ecl.*, viii, 41, and *Aen.*, iii, 74. In these and a number of other passages one poet has, not plagiarized from the other, but complimented him by a quotation. Either, then, the author of the *Ciris* is earlier than even the earliest of Vergil's publications or else he is later than his death, as he must have read the *Aeneid* if he is not quoted in it.

The former is the theory of Skutsch,[96] who argues very persuasively that the *Ciris* was written by Gallus. Briefly, his position is this. Vergil undoubtedly was on friendly terms with Gallus, therefore it is not improbable that he should seek to keep his memory green by reminiscences of his poetry in his own. Gallus was a statesman, though in that capacity he cut no very glorious figure; he was a poet, and apparently a fairly good one, who might quite possibly have written this epyllion. It is likely enough that he would imitate Catullus, which the author of the *Ciris* certainly does several times. His metre should be less ultra-refined than that of the Ovidian school; that of the *Ciris* shows the characteristics of Vergil's own hexameters in several respects. In an age when every one smattered philosophy, he might claim some little proficiency in that subject with as good right as any other. Some of the parallels between the *Ciris* and Vergil are of such a nature that the *Ciris* seems to make the better use of the words,[97] as the author, not an adapter, might be expected to do.

But there is much to be said on the other side. In the first place, Gallus never did withdraw from public life till his final disgrace and death (see p. 284). Our poet speaks as if he were considerably older than Messalla, but Gallus and M. Valerius Messalla Corvinus were of about the same age, the former's five years of seniority being of no great account when both were mature.[98] The *Ciris* is not particularly obscure, save here and

[96] It was not original with him, but his is the best-known defence of it, *Aus Vergils Frühzeit*, p. 61 *sqq.*; *Gallus und Vergil* (Teubner, 1906), *passim*. Earlier upholders of the theory, p. 62 of the former work.

[97] The most interesting example, which makes the best argument for the priority of the *Ciris*, is line 280. Skylla tells her nurse that she will either kill herself or cut the fatal lock with a dagger which she suddenly produces (aut ferro hoc; aperit ferrum quod ueste latebat). The parallel in Vergil is *Aen.*, vi, 406, where the Sibyl shows Charon the Golden Bough (at ramum hunc; aperit ramum qui ueste latebat). There is certainly more point in Skylla hiding her weapon than in the Sibyl keeping her own and Aeneas' passport to Hades out of sight.

[98] Messalla is *iuuenis*, 36; the poet has his *iuuenes anni* behind him apparently, 45.

there, nor so reconditely learned as one would expect the composition of a follower of Euphorion to be; it shows a good knowledge of ordinary mythology, but no more. As to the imitations, while Vergil never scruples to use expressions from another poet, he does not elsewhere quote so largely as he is supposed to do from the *Ciris*. On the whole, then, it is perhaps rather more likely than not that we have to do with a work written after, though assuredly not long after, Vergil's death than with a performance of about the years when he was composing, or contemplating, the *Eclogues*. In the former case, the Messalla addressed would be Messallinus, born about 712/42.

The *Catalepton* [99] is an interesting little collection of short poems, written in various metres and for various occasions, real or feigned. The last four lines, which form a separate epigram, are evidently by the editor, and state that the rest of the book is by Vergil in his youth. If we look at these trifles separately, we shall find that the attribution to Vergil, presumably made on some kind of evidence, good or bad, cannot be called certain and is in some cases unlikely. The first three pieces are the *Priapea* mentioned by Donatus; they are variants, in three several metres, on the theme, 'Priapos is given different offerings at different seasons.' If we assume that one of them is Vergil's, and even this has nothing to prove it, then probably the other two are not, for we have but to glance at the Greek *Anthology* to find many examples of an epigram by one author followed by an imitation by another, sometimes two or three imitations.[100] Of the *Catalepton* proper, the first poem is an address apparently to Tucca, about a love-affair between him and an unnamed woman; there is no particular reason to suppose it a forgery of later date. The second is an attack on an affected rhetorician, Annius Cimber, who was accused of having murdered his brother; the author declares that the murder was committed with a decoction of the extraordinary words which Cimber affected, and Quintilian cites it explicitly as Vergil's own.[101] This, then, we

[99] *I.e.*, *κατὰ λεπτόν*, 'in small parcels'. The title had been used by Aratos for a collection of short poems, see Rose, *H.G.L.*, p. 328.

[100] For example, *Anth. Pal.*, v, 82 and 83 (both anonymous); 89 and 90 (same); 141 and 142 (anonymous; Meleagros); 143 (said to be Meleagros also, a more elaborate working out of the same theme); 171 and 172 (said to be both of Meleagros, but one is clearly an imitation of the other).

[101] Quintilian, viii, 3, 27–9. We have seen that Quintilian is not infallible in such matters (p. 219), but here, where the subject is one which would be known to Vergil, the tone (objection to archaisms) quite in keeping with the usual opinion of his time, and nothing of weight can be urged against the genuineness of the little poem, there is no reason why we should not subscribe to his opinion.

may with some confidence declare genuine. The third is a little poem, apparently on a quite imaginary person, who was on the point of conquering the world, Rome included, when he was suddenly overthrown and exiled.[102] No. 4 is an affectionate address to Octavius Musa (see p. 314), who is also the subject of No. 11, a half-serious reflection on his death, which, following an epigram of Kallimachos, the poet declares was not due to heavy drinking.[103] No. 5, in scazons (cf. p. 154), professes to be Vergil's farewell to other and vainer pursuits (except that poetry may now and again visit him) as he turns to philosophy under Siron's guidance; there is no sufficient ground for supposing it other than a tribute of the young student to his new teacher. No. 6, which quotes Catullus and is in one of his metres, pure iambic trimeters, is an attack on some one whom the author calls Noctuinus and assails again in No. 12. They have the air of being merely exercises in Catullan abuse, very likely of some one wholly imaginary, and there is simply no evidence to prove that they are or are not experiments of Vergil's own. Nos. 7 and 8 are very probably his; the former is a jocular quatrain to Varius, the latter an address to a little country-house (*uillula*), once the property of Siron, in which the poet is taking refuge with his father and others of his immediate circle during the troubles arising out of the confiscation of the Mantuan land, further particulars of which he is anxiously awaiting (line 4, *si quid de patria tristius audiero*). Everything points to this being really Vergilian. Everything points to the next poem being by some one else. It is a congratulatory address to Messalla, in sixty-four lines of good pre-Ovidian elegiacs.[104] Messalla has come back bearing 'the rude ensigns of barbarian warfare' with him (5); this would be in 727/27, when he celebrated a triumph over the Aquitani. The

[102] Why it should be commonly assumed that Alexander the Great is meant I do not know. The eighth line of the epigram, corruit ex patria pulsus in exsilium, makes any such idea absurd, for Alexander was never an exile and his conquests were stopped by his death only. It is true that Horace uses *exsilium* of death, but with qualification, *aeternum exsilium*, *carm.*, ii, 3, 27–8; and in any case, Alexander was a long way from home when he died. I think it just possible that Mithridates of Pontos may be the subject: line 4, hic reges Asiae fregerat, hic populos, would fit him well enough; 5, hic graue seruitium tibi iam, tibi, Roma, ferebat could represent some exaggerated war-time rumour of his ambitions, and the fact that the last stages of the war saw him in constant flight, or that he fell back upon Armenia, could at a pinch be called exile.

[103] The model is Kallimachos, *epigr.* 62 (61) = *Anth. Pal.*, vii, 725.

[104] That is, the last word of the pentameter may consist of any number of syllables, though oftenest of two. Cf. p. 329.

poet has no desire for warlike renown and its perils; he hopes to make a Latin version of some elegant Greek poems by his hero (59 *sqq.*). Vergil, at that date, had something much better to do. No. 10 is an amusing parody of Catullus' poem to his yacht (p. 140), lampooning Sabinus, otherwise Ventidius Bassus, *consul suffectus* in 711/43. Sabinus, or Bassus, had according to the poet been a muleteer in his earlier days, and knew all the muddy roads of (Cisalpine) Gaul; now he dedicates his whip and curry-comb to the gods of bypaths (*semitalibus deis*) and sits comfortably in his ivory chair of office. Since this is the work of a clever metrician who knew his Catullus and seems to have had northern Italian connexions (he mentions Cremona in line 12), again there is no real reason against supposing that Vergil wrote it, though also no sort of proof that he did. No. 13 is curious; it is in the same kind of metre (alternating iambic trimeters and dimeters) which Horace uses in several of the *Epodes*. Its subject is an exceedingly coarse lampoon on a fellow of very immoral life, who is styled Lucius. If Vergil wrote it as an exercise in this style and metre, it did him no great credit and he never seems to have repeated the experiment; if, as has been conjectured, Lucius' other name was Noctuinus, the style of the poem is like enough to that of 6 and 12 for all to be by the same author. 13a, as it is numbered by Ellis,[105] is absent from some MSS. of the *Catalepton*; it is an epitaph on a learned Roman who had died in Athens and was buried within sight of the Akropolis; who he was and who wrote the epitaph we do not know, but in all probability the dead man is imaginary. A real epitaph would naturally contain his name, or at least be accompanied by a prose inscription which gave it. The fourteenth piece is a pretty little prayer to Venus to help Vergil with the composition of the *Aeneid*, and strongly suggests that it was written for him after the poem had been published. It seems not at all unlikely that its author was the editor who wrote the neat little tail-piece to the whole collection.

That poem which one would most willingly attribute to Vergil on its merits is the most weakly attested of all the more important pieces. Its title is *Moretum*, the name of a kind of salad made of cheese and herbs finely pounded and kneaded into a ball. This relish is made by a cottar before going off to his day's work in the fields; the poem has no other content than this, together with his rising, grinding a little corn, and baking, with the help

[105] The numbering of the *Catalepton*, annoyingly for readers, is not the same in all editions. The *O.C.T.* edition being the most easily available in this country, it has been followed in this respect.

of an old negress who comprises his entire household, a large bannock. The *genre* is one which may be traced to the *Hekale* of Kallimachos, and thence to Leonidas of Tarentum; the man's simple and honest life is described with sympathy, tinged with a little quiet humour, shown in several phrases of good-natured mock-heroic. The date, as was pointed out long ago by Scaliger, is given approximately by line 76, which implies that lettuce was eaten at the end of a dinner; now Martial mentions that in his time it was eaten at the beginning, but had been eaten at the end 'in our grandfathers' days'. Therefore the *Moretum* mentions a habit of the early Empire, and consequently, so far as that goes, might be Vergil's. But the only external evidence is medieval, and the style quite unlike his; in particular, it is hardly likely that Vergil would have composed 124 hexameters with but 5 elisions. We have therefore the work of an unknown but quite respectable poet.[106]

The *Copa* is better attested; although it is not in Donatus' list, *i.e.*, not recognized by Suetonius, it is mentioned as Vergilian by Servius. It is a delightful little work, a sketch of a wayside tavern, whose hostess (*copa*), with her bagpipes tucked under her arm, dances and sings an invitation to wayfarers to turn in at her door and enjoy themselves in the little garden behind. The metre (pre-Ovidian elegiacs) suggests Vergil's age, the style sounds quite unlike his.[107]

The next great name of Augustan poetry is that of HORACE (QVINTVS HORATIVS FLACCVS). Though he loved and admired Vergil,[108] he was like him only in one feature of character, amiability. He was a man of the world, though not ambitious for public distinctions, entirely lacked the depth of thought and tinge of profound melancholy which marked the Mantuan poet, had studied philosophy and was well enough versed in current religious ideas, but mostly took his own shrewd common sense for his guide. Before all else, however, he was a man of letters, whose chief interest was the improvement and reform of Latin poetry. Like every one else of his generation, his mental diet at school (his master was Orbilius, see p. 443) had been the earlier Latin poets, from Livius Andronicus on, and his close acquaintance with

[106] See Rose, *H.G.L.*, pp. 321, 349; Mart., xiii, 13: cludere quae cenas lactuca solebat auorum,/dic mihi, cur nostras incohat illa dapes?

[107] Servius on *Aen.*, i, *praef.*, p. 1, 13 Thilo-Hagen; cf. Charisius, i, p. 63, 11 Keil; *Copa*, 4, ad cubitum raucos excutiens calamos. That these are bagpipes and not castanets (which are neither *rauci* nor played with the elbow) is pointed out by Housman, vol. v, p. 123 of his edition of Manilius.

[108] See especially *carm.*, i, 3, 8; *sat.*, i, 5, 40–2; 10, 44–5.

the best Greek models, combined with a good but somewhat narrow sense of what constitutes classically perfect expression, led him to condemn them all as falling much too far below the standard which he set for himself and proposed to all who would listen to his advice. Hence his output was small, his range of tones not wide, but his finish exquisite. Like Pope, he tried to give the world ' what oft was thought, but ne'er so well expressed ', and his success was such that within his limits, self-imposed and never exceeded, his is again and again the final expression. He is, if we like, the poet of sanity.

The facts of his life are pretty well known, thanks chiefly to his own references to them.[109] He was born on December 8, 689/65, of parents who stood high neither socially nor economically; his father had been an auctioneer's clerk (*coactor*) and apparently had retired to live on his savings and the produce of a little farm at Venusia, on the borders of Lucania and Apulia. Either, however, ambition to lift his family above his own position in the freedman class (*libertini*) or insight into the character and ability of his son moved him to give the young Quintus the best possible education. He took him to Rome, where he himself performed the functions of a *paedagogus* and watched over the youth's behaviour[110]; thence he managed to send him to Athens. While there, the young Horace was caught up by the civil wars; Brutus was looking for recruits, Horace joined his army and was given the rank of *tribunus*, or staff officer attached to a legion. According to himself—but we do not know how much of this is fact and how much a mixture of poetic convention, inherited from Archilochos and Alkaios,[111] with a desire to prove that he had never been a very formidable opponent of the Imperial régime—he distinguished himself chiefly by the speed with which he ran away at Philippi. At all events, he made his way back to Rome poor and friendless, and there took to such occupation as he could find. Apparently his peace with the government was easily

[109] Besides a life by Suetonius, preserved in the scholia on Horace, we have the dates of his birth and death in St. Jerome, *ann. Abr.* 1952 (689/65) and 2009 (746/8), confirmed and given more exactly by Suetonius. More important are the following passages of Horace: *sat.*, ii, 1, 34–5, his birthplace; *epod.*, 13, 6, birth; *sat.*, i, 6, 45 *sqq.*, his early education and his father; his introduction to Maecenas; 4, 105 *sqq.*, more details concerning his father; *epp.*, ii, 2, 41 *sqq.*, his education, military service and fortunes after the war; *carm.*, ii, 7, 9 *sqq.*, his conduct at Philippi.

[110] Horace, *sat.*, i, 6, 81 *sqq.*, cf. 4, 105 *sqq.* The *paedagogus* was a confidential slave detailed to supervise his young master's conduct and keep him from dangers, especially moral.

[111] See Rose, *H.G.L.*, pp. 90, 99; Horace, *carm.*, ii, 7, 10.

made, but he lost [112] what was left of his father's little estate; probably by this time his parents were dead. He got a small post in what then corresponded to the Civil Service, that of a *scriba quaestorius*, a sort of treasury clerk. Thus kept from starvation, but probably not much more, he turned his hand to writing, and it is no doubt to this period that the earliest *Epodes* belong. They take their title from the fact that almost all of them are written in a metre consisting of a longer line followed by a shorter, the latter being technically known as an 'after-song', ἐπῳδή. Their subjects vary a good deal, but it may be said generally that their inspiration is Archilochos.

The first ten are in a simple form enough; the odd-numbered lines are iambic trimeters, but not like the trimeters of the dramatists; the Greek rules are strictly observed, for the spondee is admitted only in the odd-numbered feet and resolutions are rare. The even-numbered lines are dimeters, *i.e.*, each consists of four iambi with the allowable substitutions. The others are in various metres, but of types known to have been used by Archilochos. No. 11 has trimeters for its odd-numbered lines, the even-numbered being iambelegi, *i.e.*, – ⏑ ⏑ – ⏑ ⏑ –/⏑ – ⏑ – ⏑ – ⏑ – . No. 12 alternates hexameters with iambic dimeters; No. 15 does the same; No. 16 has trimeters (pure, *i.e.*, having no foot but the iambus anywhere in the line) instead of dimeters; No. 17, quite exceptionally, is written in trimeters throughout.

The collection, which Horace himself seems to have called simply *iambi* and put together at the instance of Maecenas,[113] is plainly the work of a long period during which his fortunes and sentiments varied. Nos. 4, 6, 10 and 12 are all of the nature of lampoons; the first attacks an upstart who has contrived to become a military tribute though he was born a slave, No. 6, a writer, real or imaginary, of libels, No. 10, a real and notorious person, Mevius the versifier (cf. p. 345), No. 12, a lustful woman who would have Horace be her lover. Nos. 5 and 17 deal with a witch, Canidia, whose name occurs also in more than one passage of the *Satires*, whence it would seem that she is either a real person or Horace's poetical disguise for one. In the former poem she is drawn with horrible vigour in the act of murdering a boy by starvation to get his liver and marrow to make a love-potion; in the latter, Horace represents himself as vainly trying to make his peace with her. To date any of these is not easy, nor is there any very definite dating to be had for Nos. 11 (a complaint to a

[112] Like Vergil's, his land was seized, along with much besides in that neighbourhood, to provide allotments for demobilized soldiers.

[113] *Epod.*, 14, 6–8.

friend, Pettius, that Horace is too love-sick to write), 13 (invitation to another acquaintance, Amicius,[114] to spend a cold and stormy winter day in good cheer), and 15 (complaint of the unfaithfulness of a certain Neaera and a threat to be revenged on her). But some of them have the air of being purely metrical and stylistic exercises, and so may represent the poet's own selection from his earliest attempts. Nos. 7 and 16 can be dated by their political references. Both mourn that Rome is on the verge of another civil war; the second of these, which is one of the longest and best of the collection, declares that there is no hope left and the one possibility is to emigrate and find some new and happy land elsewhere.[115] Clearly both these date from not very long before the final struggle, but to find the exact year is another matter; they may represent the apprehensions which were allayed for the time being by the Treaty of Brundisium in 714/40. Nos. 3 and 14 must have been written not immediately after the introduction to Maecenas which took place through the good offices of Vergil and Varius,[116] for both address him familiarly. We may therefore suppose that the introduction, and with it the end of Horace's days of poverty, was effected some little time before Actium; for No. 1 addresses Maecenas as *amice* and mentions his intended departure for the front; it also thanks him for making Horace 'rich enough and to spare'. No. 9 was written when the first news of the victory had come to Rome, but before the capture of Alexandria and the deaths of Antony and Klecpatra. Finally, No. 2, an amusing mock-serious rhapsody on the delights of the country, turns out in the last few lines to be the resolution, lasting exactly a fortnight, of a money-lender to turn farmer.

The impression that Horace had been put, some time before Actium, in a position safe from want and indeed as comfortable and prosperous as a man of his modest tastes cared for, is fully confirmed by the other early works. The first book of his familiar talks (*sermones*, Horace's own title) or miscellanies (*saturae*) must have come out in the neighbourhood of 721/35, for they refer to nothing later than that and to a good deal that is earlier. No doubt they had been in circulation individually before that; thus, in 10, 1 *sqq.*, he answers some one's objections to what he

[114] *Epod.*, 13, 3. As the name occurs in the voc., it has generally been taken for the plural of *amicus*, but the verbs which follow are in the sing.; Housman restored the correct spelling with an initial capital.

[115] Horace's Utopia and Vergil's Golden Age in *ecl.* iv are manifestly much alike; which was written first is a question whereon no agreement has yet been reached, but certainly one poet imitated the other.

[116] *Sat.*, i, 6, 54 *sqq.*

had said in 4, 8, concerning the defects of Lucilius.[117] Of the collection, No. 1 is an address to Maecenas, on the foolish discontents of mankind; it probably was written for the position it now holds, to introduce this book of free-and-easy moralizing. No. 5 amusingly tells the story of a journey from Rome to Brundisium. This cannot be in 714/40 (Treaty of Brundisium) for that was in October, this is spring or early summer (gnats are troublesome, 14). However, the circumstance that one of Horace's fellow-travellers, Fonteius, mentioned in line 33, has the fact that he is a great friend of Antony recorded among his good qualities proves the satire was published before the breach between the latter and Octavian had become clearly inevitable, that is, before 722/32. Also, the second book, which appears to be later than anything in the first, itself contains work as old as 721/33 (see below), thus making the date suggested a reasonable one enough for the first, especially for a writer like Horace, who seems always to have composed slowly.

The ten pieces of which the book is composed are arranged on no very obvious principle. No. 1 is followed by a dissertation on the extremes into which fools run, especially in sexual matters. The next, No. 3, preaches the duty of preserving a sense of proportion, especially with regard to others' faults; the Stoics, who say that all misdeeds are equally bad, are merely absurd, as much so as when they claim that their sages are *ipso facto* the repository of every possible form of excellence and efficiency. No. 4 is a sort of apologia for the poet's manner both of life and writing. Greek Comedy and its heir Lucilius lashed vice; such works, while hardly poetry, have their place, are in no wise to be confounded with slander and backbiting, but rather resemble the sort of practical counsels, with illustrations from real life, which Horace's good father used to give him. No. 5, which we have already discussed, has of course a Lucilian model (see p. 84). No. 6, together with a complimentary address to Maecenas which skilfully avoids falling into mere adulation, draws a picture of the contented and moderate man, Horace himself, who knows his place and is as well off as if he were of higher station. No. 7 is simply an anecdote of a small affair which took place in Asia while Brutus was there, in 711/43; it looks like an early attempt, an imitation of the anecdotes in verse which Lucilius wrote on

[117] Not regularly published, see 4, 71 (no works of Horace are on sale), but read to friends (*ibid.*, 73), and doubtless shown to Maecenas, who would hardly have been at the expense of mending the poet's fortunes if it were not understood that he was going to publish some time. Title, *epp.*, i, 4, 1: nostrorum Sermonum candide iudex.

occasion. No. 8 is also a comic story, put into the mouth of a statue of Priapus on the Esquiline, of how it frightened away Canidia and her associates. It dates itself; unfortunately, the indication is one which we cannot exactly interpret. The incident which Priapus tells happened before Maecenas turned the old pauper burial-ground of the Esquiline into a park, but at the time of writing (*nunc*) the park has been made and the place is habitable.[118] But as it is not now known when Maecenas did this, we are little the wiser. The slightness of the work suggests that it is early. No. 9 is the famous Encounter with the Bore; Horace is overtaken by a talkative fellow who cannot take a hint and will not be snubbed, and suffers under his endless flow of words and boundlessly good opinion of himself until a lucky chance at last relieves him. No. 10 is a further defence of himself, his style of composition and his literary opinions. It was written for its present place.[119]

These compositions, not yet containing Horace's best work, nevertheless were good enough to be deservedly popular when at last they saw the full light of day. Nothing nearly so good in that vein had been written since Lucilius, unless it was Varro's Menippeans (see p. 228), and the style of those was old-fashioned, not in line with the taste of the newer generation. Horace was now a poet to be reckoned with, and before long gave the public another similar collection. This time he tried a slightly different technique, also Lucilian, the dialogue; Book I had consisted wholly of monologues, which with one exception were in his own person. It would seem that the date of the new book was about 724/30, for the last datable allusion is to Augustus' actions in the East after Actium; he is 'a terror to the Parthians', the correct and loyal way of mentioning the diplomacy by which, in that year, he took advantage of dynastic quarrels in Armenia to establish his influence in those parts without the risks of an actual war.[120] The earliest work is about three years earlier than this; we may therefore allow about that space of time for the composition of the whole.[121] In No. 1, manifestly a sort of preface, he introduces himself talking to Trebatius the great jurist, who, after carefully weighing the reasons for and against writing satire,

[118] Line 74.

[119] The last line is: i puer atque meo citus haec subscribe libello.

[120] Iuuenis Parthis metuendus, 5, 62.

[121] In 3, 185, one of the kinds of madness denounced is that of the man who ruins himself to be applauded like Agrippa. This is clearly M. Vipsanius Agrippa, who was aedile in 721/33 and distinguished himself by the magnificence of his shows, of course a move to gain popularity for the government just when it needed support with a war impending.

tells him that if he really cannot compose epic or panegyrics on Caesar, at least no jury would convict him for attacking what deserves to be attacked, always with the approval of Caesar and keeping clear of the law of libel. No. 2 is a sermon on frugal living (a thing in which Horace seems really to have believed, for he himself led a quiet and unostentatious life, well within his means; but at the same time doctrine very acceptable to the Imperial government, which was making well-meant efforts to bring the upper classes especially back to saner and more moral ways). It is put into the mouth of an old farmer, Ofellus, who has always lived plainly, is now the tenant of the land he once owned, the proprietorship having passed to a veteran, and remains perfectly content, healthy and cheerful. The third is an address to Horace himself from a certain Damasippus, who, having become bankrupt, was saved from suicide and converted to Stoicism by one of that school, and now finds contentment in spreading the good news that all men, including Horace, are mad. At this point the discourse is broken off by the poet looking about for a stone to throw at his monitor. No. 4 has lost something of its point for us, but it is a kind of humour which was in favour from about the fourth century B.C., the handling of gastronomy with mock solemnity.[122] Horace improves on the formula by making the speaker, a certain Catius, really take the matter quite seriously and declare that the string of recipes which he pours forth is wisdom far above that of the philosophers. No. 5 is a piece of social satire in the form of burlesqued mythology; Odysseus, after interviewing the shade of Teiresias, remembers that there is another thing to ask him, viz., how to become rich. The prophet obliges with a set of instructions which, if properly followed up, will make him a complete legacy-hunter, a sort of rascal apparently very common in Imperial Rome, for the usual result of a too high civilization was in evidence there; marriage and its responsibilities were avoided, childless rich men and women were not uncommon, and to find a place in their wills was the ambition of numerous parasites.[123] The sixth satire is simply a description of Horace's own daily life in Rome, with his trials at the hands of people who insist on believing that he has enormous influence and knows exactly what the government will do next; by way

[122] The mock-heroic *Ἡδυπάθεια,* or Art of Good Living, of Archestratos of Gela (or Syracuse), see Rose, *H.G.L.*, p. 330; cf. *sup.*, p. 38.

[123] Mock-mythology for satirical purposes is a common Greek form from about Timon the sillographer (Rose, *op. cit.*, p. 358) on. Horace's ultimate source is the eleventh book of the Odyssey, in which the hero goes to Hades to get Teiresias' advice as to his return.

of contrast, he sketches an evening at his little country estate, the famous Sabine farm which Maecenas had given him, and a rustic supper at which one of the guests tells the fable of the Town and the Country Mouse. No. 7 is again a Stoic sermon, handled lightly; Davus, supposed to be one of Horace's own slaves, takes advantage of the freedom of speech allowed at the Saturnalia to prove to his master that he too is a slave, to his own folly and unruly desires. As in the third satire, the discourse is brought to a sudden end, and thus saved from becoming tedious, by an explosion of temper. The eighth and last of this book is once more a piece of humour which we cannot perfectly appreciate. The narrator tells how he and certain others, including Maecenas, were entertained by a rich and would-be magnificent person called Nasidienus. The host obviously is committing every possible breach of etiquette and good taste, but the point of some of his blunders is lost owing to our imperfect knowledge of how the best society then behaved.

Meanwhile, Horace was trying his hand at something never attempted seriously and on a large scale by any Latin hitherto. Lyric metres had been used, as we have seen, occasionally and for trifling works by a number of poets, and some of their performances had been of great merit. Now the world was to be given a collection of Latin lyrics on a large range of subjects, in the metres of the Aiolic school.[124]

Speaking very broadly, the Aiolian poets, Sappho and Alkaios, had written mostly for soloists, not for choruses, in simple style and in metres which either repeated one verse indefinitely or fell into short and easily remembered stanzas. The principle of all their verses may be interpreted as follows. The most fundamental foot was the choriambus, – ◡ ◡ –, introduced and followed by shorter rhythms, such as the iambus and trochee; the line often began with the Aiolic base, two syllables of indeterminate quantity. How to adapt this charming style of composition to Latin was a question not easily settled. We have seen that simplicity without baldness or rusticity was a virtue which hardly any one but Catullus ever attained, and he not for long at a time. The natural rhythm of the language was different from that of Greek, principally because of the different kind of accent, cf. p. 16. Hence, to produce effects as artistic as theirs in another tongue, it was necessary to make a thousand delicate adjustments of metre and of speech, sacrificing much of the Greeks' naturalness and substituting for it Horace's own 'combination of happy knack and careful finish' (*curiosa felicitas*),[125] which must at the same time avoid sounding too artificial. Whether the majority of his odes were really

[124] For the lives and works of these writers, see Rose, *op. cit.*, p. 93 *sqq*.
[125] Petronius, 118, 5.

meant to be sung or simply recited is a question to which we can give no certain answer; this much is certain, that he found it necessary to come to a series of most subtle compromises between the beat of the metrical foot and the native stress of the accented syllables.

Horace must have spent fully seven years in composing his collection of lyrics (*Odes*, as we usually call them; *carmina* is the ancient title), which, when published, filled three book-rolls of moderate size. The arrangement of these, as of the *Satires*, is clearly his own; it is not chronological, except that the earlier books contain the earlier works, and a certain development of the metre can be traced, some slight licences occurring in the first book, for instance, which are not to be found in the third.[126] Book I begins with nine odes in nine different metres, all but two (the fourth and seventh, which are reminiscent rather of Archilochos) in measures of the Aiolic school. The rest of the book introduces further varieties. The subjects vary greatly. The first is a preface, assuring Maecenas that his approbation will make the poet happy. The second is a lament on the signs of the times and a prayer that Caesar may be granted grace to make all well. The third is an address to the ship which carried Vergil to Greece, not, however, on what proved his last journey, for that must have been about 734/20, but on some unknown occasion; the fourth is a pretty trifle, a spring song ending in a reflection on the brevity of life; the fifth, the exquisite and quite untranslatable ode to Pyrrha, best taken as Horace's comment on some scene of love-making, observed or imagined.[127] The sixth is his apology to Agrippa for not celebrating his exploits; his talents do not lie that way, and he must confine himself to lighter and merrier matters, leaving the serious themes to Varius. No. 7 is a celebration of the beauty of Tibur (Tivoli), turning suddenly into an exhortation, reinforced by a story from mythology, to let good cheer lighten one's sorrows. No. 8 is again erotic; a girl, Lydia, is reproached for occupying her lover's whole attention, to the ruin of his mind and body. No. 9 is a winter scene; Soracte is white with snow, the rivers frozen; therefore it is well to pile up the fire and make merry. And so the collection goes on, changing subject with every ode and very often metre as well;

[126] For example, in Book i he occasionally divides a word between the third and fourth lines of a Sapphic stanza, as labitur ripa Ioue non probante u/xorius amnis. This is still allowed in Book ii (16, 8), but not in iii nor iv. In the higher-numbered books, also, he is increasingly averse to ending a line and beginning the next with a vowel (neglect of synapheia), see *Class. Rev.*, xxxvii, 1923, p. 113.

[127] See Mackail in *Class. Rev.*, xxxv, 1921, p. 2 *sqq.*

for example, the thirty-seventh ode of the first book celebrates the good news of the fall of Alexandria, while the thirty-eighth and last is a merry little drinking-song. Book II consists chiefly of odes in Sapphics and Alcaics,[128] but the twelfth is in Asclepiadics,[128] the eighteenth in alternating trochaic and iambic lines. It is the shortest book of the three and ends with one of Horace's very few departures from perfect taste. He foretells his own immortality, an allowable poetic conceit in itself, but must needs explain in most unconvincing detail that he will turn into a swan, Apollo's sacred bird. It is the more unimpressive when we remember that he was a fat little man, prematurely grey, and most unswanlike in appearance.[129] But there are enough good odes among the twenty which comprise this book to make up for this unhappy thought. The seventh and fifteenth are subtle pieces of propaganda. The former is an address to an old comrade in Brutus' army, Pompeius Varus, who has come home safely from his adventures; the government, then, shows liberal clemency even to those who were its avowed enemies. The latter laments the decay of the countryside under the influence of selfish luxury; it thus says a poetical Amen to the *Georgics*. Book III preaches the Augustan doctrine most openly and on its strongest side, in the so-called Roman Odes (Nos. 1–6) with which it begins. They are all in Alcaics, Horace's most solemn metre, and open with a prelude of their own in which the poet claims to be the priest and prophet of the younger generation (*Musarum sacerdos/ uirginibus puerisque canto*).[130] Clearly, he was by this time something like a poet laureate. In this capacity, he recommends in serious and moving fashion the traditional virtues of the race, moderation (No. 1), frugality combined with valour (No. 2), justice and *grauitas* (No. 3), patriotism (No. 5), piety (No. 6). No. 4 is a sort of poetical profession of faith and loyalty; the Muses, who have cherished Horace, cherish Augustus also, and therefore he, like the gods when the Giants attacked them, must

[128] The Sapphic stanza has been naturalized by Swinburne ('All the night sleep came not upon my eyelids', in *Poems and Ballads*) and occasionally attempted by other English poets. The best-known English Alcaic stanza is Tennyson's 'O mighty-mouthed inventor of harmonies'. The Asclepiadic metres are various combinations of the Lesser Asclepiadic (–– – ∪ ∪ – – ∪ ∪ – ∪ –) with the glyconic (see p. 141); one might represent the former in English by 'Nay, our flesh is as grass, flowers of the field are we'.

[129] Habitu corporis fuit breuis atque obesus, Suetonius, *uita*, appealing to the *Satires* (he means the *Epistles*, i, 4, 15 and 20, 24) and to a letter of Augustus which says tibi statura deest, corpusculum non deest. The grey hair is mentioned in the second passage from the *Epistles*, above.

[130] *Carm.*, iii, 1, 3–4.

overcome his enemies by good counsel opposed to brute force. No. 3 also has a very curious episode, in which Iuno proclaims the prosperity of Rome so long as Troy remains in ruins. It is not in point to recall an idle rumour [131] that Julius Caesar had some thoughts of making Troy his capital; Troy stands simply for the East, and the meaning is that, to be great, Rome should remain a Western power, not giving way to the Orientalizing dreams of an Antony. The other twenty-four odes of this book, which forms the finest part of the whole collection, are in a variety of metres corresponding to an equally great variety of themes, sometimes humorous, sometimes grave; the book closes with a proud declaration that Horace has raised a memorial 'more lasting than bronze, loftier than the mouldering pyramids of the Pharaohs' [132] and will therefore not wholly die.

The indications as to date are briefly as follows. In *Epp.*, i, 13, Horace gives directions to a messenger how he is to deliver the poet's *uolumina* (plural, therefore not the one *uolumen* of *Epistles*, which has its own tail-piece, No. 20) to Augustus. The Emperor is some distance away, but the journey can be made by land. Therefore he is not in the East, whither he went in 732/22, at the end of the year, via Sicily. No movements of his much earlier than this need concern us, for the *Epistles* were published about 734/20 (see below). Looking at the Odes themselves, we find that Marcellus is praised (i, 12, 46) in terms which imply that he is alive (crescit . . . fama Marcelli); he died at the end of 731/23. Again, L. Licinius Murena is mentioned in congratulatory phrases (iii, 19, 10–11) and has an ode addressed to him (ii, 10); he came to a sudden end in 731/23 also, having conspired against Augustus. Quintilius Varus is dead (i, 24, 5), and Jerome gives the date as 731/23, or perhaps a year earlier.[133] On the other hand, no passage implies a situation earlier than the time immediately after Actium (i, 37, the earliest datable ode). We therefore conclude that Horace began to write these poems about 724/30 and completed the collection in 731/23, some time before the middle of summer, since Murena's conspiracy was in the second half of the year.

Having shown what he could do in the manner of Lucilius modernized, Horace composed a number of other pieces in the

[131] Suetonius, *diu. Iul.*, 79: quin etiam uaria fama percrebruit migraturum Alexandream *uel Ilium*, translatis simul opibus imperii. Caesar was a practical statesman, not an antiquarian.

[132] Exegi monumentum aere perennius,/regalique situ (' mould ', not ' erection ') pyramidum altius . . . non omnis moriar, *carm.*, iii, 30, 1 *sqq.* The metre is the same as that of i, 1.

[133] Jerome, *an. Aur.* 1994 = 731/23; but a few MSS. place it a year earlier. This is not the Varus who was killed in Germany (762/9), but a literary man, a good critic (Horace, *A.P.*, 338 *sqq.*) and a friend of Horace and Vergil.

same vein and in a form Lucilius had used, the familiar letter. He ranges, as might be expected, from real letters (there is no reason why we should doubt that such a little gem of a commendatory epistle as *epp.*, i. 9 was actually sent to its addressee, the future emperor Ti.Claudius Nero) to discourses on various subjects with the name of some acquaintance at the head. So in No. 1 of the collection of twenty such *epistulae*, which appeared in or very shortly after 734/20,[134] he once more addresses Maecenas, with affectionate gratitude, and describes his own personal philosophy; as before, it is not of the schools, though he knows the chief systems of the day and values the good advice they give, but rather quiet good sense, avoiding such follies as the mad lust after wealth which neglects both ease and honour. No. 2 is in appearance an adaptation to his own purposes of a familiar philosophic, and especially Stoic doctrine, that deep ethical lessons were to be discovered in Homer. A few lines of this, however, soon bring Horace to his own theme, the stupidity of neglecting the effort necessary for moral self-improvement. No. 3 is a letter to a friend abroad, Iulius Florus, then absent with Tiberius; it consists of questions about other acquaintances on the same staff, especially concerning their literary activities. No. 4 is a few lines of pure friendship and admiration, addressed to Tibullus (see p. 285). No. 5 is an invitation to dinner; No. 6, a lay sermon on the text 'Marvel at nothing' (*nil admirari*). No. 7, in the form of an address of thanks to Maecenas for his bounty, sketches not only the ideal giver but, by implication and in the form of a humorous story, the right type of recipient also. No. 8 is again a letter to a member of Tiberius' *entourage*, by name Celsus Albinovanus. Of No. 9 we have already spoken. No. 10, to Aristius Fuscus, is on the delights of country life, and thence on the contented mind. No. 11, to a friend on his travels, has the moral that happiness is to be found everywhere, if we bring a mind capable of it. No. 13 has also been spoken of; it is addressed to one Vinius Asina, who is to carry the presentation copy of the Odes to Augustus. No. 14, in the form of a letter of instructions to his farm-bailiff, once again takes the tone of a sermon on contentment; it is extraordinary with what ingenuity

[134] The chief indications of date are in Nos. 12 and 20. In the former, 25–9, he gives the latest Italian news to a friend in Africa: Agrippa has been successful in Spain, Tiberius in Armenia. These campaigns were concluded in 734/20 and the next year; we would therefore think of 735/19 as the date of publication, but that Horace says, 20, 27, that he has completed his forty-fourth December; the book came out, therefore, late (for the harvest is all in, 12, 28–9) in 734/20, Horace's forty-fifth year, but before December.

Horace contrives so to vary his favourite theme that no two of these little diatribes are alike, and he finds fresh illustrations and new turns for each. No. 15 is still on the same topic, the occasion being a letter of inquiry concerning conditions at Velia, which the court physician, Antonius Musa, has advised him to visit for a cure. This time the key-note is a Latin equivalent of Burns' ' contented wi' little an' canty wi' mair '. No. 16 is a description of the Sabine Farm, accurate enough for its position to be determinable. It again philosophizes, on the nature of true virtue and the self-sufficiency of its possessor. No. 17 is a letter of advice to a young man who intends to advance his fortunes as a frequenter of great houses ; No. 18 is a more elaborate and detailed handling of the same topic. No. 19 is a sketch of his own literary career ; No. 20 is a clever series of double meanings, for, addressing his book and crediting it with a desire to leave his desk, he finds phrases which would equally well apply to a spoilt young slave who wanted to be sold out of a quiet household into one where his personal beauty and wit might gain him advancement. The tone of both these last works suggests that Horace, for the moment at least, felt that his work was done and he had no more to say.

However, his career was not yet over, in view of his usefulness to the government and to the many who read and delighted in him. But he was evidently aging ; his descriptions of his way of life all indicate that his health was delicate ; it is noteworthy that he says nothing of the death of Vergil, which quite possibly was too deep a grief for him to express in such a calm and unexcited medium as his poetry. When forty-four years old, he was already talking as if he might not live much longer,[135] and a shock of that kind may have had ill effects on a constitution already by no means robust. At all events, for some two years after the first book of the *Epistles*, we have no evidence that he wrote at all. But Augustus, who had a great personal liking for him, wished him to be his private secretary, and corresponded with him frequently, insisted on his producing something more, and in particular, wanted a hymn for his Secular Games in 737/17,[136] more mention of himself in poems like the *Satires* and

[135] *Epp.*, i, 108 : quod superest aeui, si quid superesse uolunt di. So in 14, 32 *sqq.*, he speaks of saying good-bye to all youthful frolics, dining lightly and sleeping much ; he looks ridiculous when he helps with the farm-work, *ibid.* All this suggests a man who was already old when he should have been in full vigour.

[136] For a recent and good discussion of the festival and the relation to it of Horace's poem, see J. Gagé, *Recherches sur les jeux séculaires*, Paris, Les Belles Lettres, 1934, especially chap. ii.

Epistles,[137] and further celebrations of the exploits of the Imperial house. Horace obeyed, though a little unwillingly.[138] The Secular Hymn is perhaps as good as such a work can be; it is dignified, long enough without being too long, and manages to introduce neatly mentions of some very unpoetical matters which it was necessary to speak of, as nearly as possible by their own names, in order to ask the divine blessing upon them. With it and the new loyal poems, also very good of their kind (two on the expected return of Augustus from Gaul and Germany in 741/13; one on the victory of Tiberius' younger brother Drusus over the Vindelici in 739/15; another on Tiberius' own campaign against the Raeti, at the same date; another, probably after Augustus' return, to the Emperor himself),[139] went enough shorter pieces, not his best but far better than anyone else could have written in those metres, to make up a fourth and last book of odes; the Carmen Saeculare itself seems never to have been included in any book, but published separately, as our editions print it.

Somewhere in the last twelve years of his life, the exact dates being highly uncertain, fall a series of short works, but longer than any we have so far discussed, which constitute Horace's final service to literature, and by no means his least. This is the group of literary epistles, whereof two constitute the second book of the *Epistles* proper, the third is the famous and much imitated *Ars Poetica*. In answer to Augustus' appeal, he wrote him a letter in verse, the first of the second book of *Epistles*, dealing with the state of literature. Horace begins with a protest against those who can see no good in the moderns (the quarrel between them and the ancients had already begun, in almost as absurd a form as it assumed in the seventeenth century), and involves an imaginary opponent in a pretty logical tangle. He himself would deal fairly by the older Latin writers (he assumes the greatness of the early Greeks), and, to show their real position in the history of letters, sketches the development of Roman literature

[137] Suet., *uita*: post sermones uero quosdam lectos nullam sui mentionem habitam ita sit questus; Irasci me tibi scito, quod non in plerisque eius modi scriptis mecum potissimum loquaris; an uereris ne apud posteros infame tibi sit quod uidearis familiaris nobis esse?

[138] Porphyrio on *carm.*, iv, 1, 1: hunc quartum (librum) scribere compulsus esse dicitur ab Augusto. In the *Life*, Suetonius says: scripta quidem eius usque adeo probauit (Augustus) . . . ut . . . eum . . . coegerit . . . tribus carminum libris ex longo interuallo quartum addere. The opening ode, a protest to Venus for bidding him love again, has a double sense, for Venus was the patron goddess of the Imperial family.

[139] *Carm.*, iv, 2 (for good comment on which see Fraenkel in *Heidelb. Sitz.* for Dec., 1932), 4, 5, 14, 15.

since 'Greece took captive her captor',[140] and even the rude beginnings which preceded that event. For the present, he has little hope that the drama will reach any great heights, for the popular taste is all for dumb-shows and too elaborate staging; non-dramatic poetry has a better chance, for Augustus is not an Alexander to be put off with tenth-rate verse, however much some inferior poets wish he were. Horace, good will notwithstanding, cannot be his epic poet; that he leaves to Vergil and Varius.[141]

The same collection has a second literary letter—both are of unusual size, and make up the second book by themselves—to Iulius Florus, a man of Horace's acquaintance who seems to have had poetical ambitions. Horace begins with a witty depreciation of himself as lazy and unreliable now that he has no need to write to keep himself from starving, as in the old days. Besides, he is growing old, and verse-making must sooner or later go the way of his other youthful follies. And how can any one write in the noise and distractions of Rome? The true poet loves quiet places; in town we have nothing but mutual admiration societies. If Horace will call some one else Kallimachos,[142] the other will agree that he is Alkaios come to life again, and so it goes. The real poet is critic also; but people hate to be criticized. Perhaps the happiest man is the harmless lunatic who writes very ill but thinks he writes very well; and in any case, at Horace's time of life it is seasonable to think of the way to true happiness, which lies through contentment, not riches.

This letter can be dated after a fashion. Horace writes to Florus, who some time ago went on a journey (20, proficiscenti tibi), and there is nothing to indicate that he has yet come back. But we know where he had gone from *epp.*, i, 3; he was on Tiberius' staff in the East. Augustus was back in October, 735/19; but Tiberius stayed some time longer. A date in the neighbourhood of 736/18 is therefore quite possible; that Horace professes to have said good-bye to poetry suits this period also, for, as we have already seen, no work of his (other than this epistle, if it was written then) can be put within the interval between the first book of the *Epistles* and the Secular Games. In the first epistle, Horace tells Augustus that he proved himself a great liar

140 Graecia capta ferum uictorem cepit, line 156.

141 This unfortunately does not help us to date the poem; both these masters have been rewarded, *munera tulerunt*, by Augustus, but this could be said with equal propriety whether they are alive to enjoy his further favours or not.

142 Possibly a hit at Propertius, cf. Prop., iv, 1, 64, Vmbria Romani patria Callimachi, also iii, 1, 1. But Kallimachos was so famous that it is unnecessary to suppose this in order to understand the passage; almost any writer not an epic or dramatic poet would take his name as a highly complimentary title.

(*Parthis mendacior*, 112), for after saying that he had given poetry up, he is composing again. This suggests that he is at work on some of the larger odes of Book IV, and thus that the epistle dates from about 739/15 to 741/13. Nearer than this it seems impossible to come, and even this is none too certain.

Horace's greatest work of literary criticism is again in letter form, and some prefer to call it the *Letter to the Pisones*, instead of by its traditional title *Ars Poetica*.[143] Under a mask of somewhat formless chat about poetry, it preserves the general outline of a Hellenistic treatise, that of Neoptolemos of Parion, as the ancient commentators observe and modern investigations, helped by the fragments of Philodemos, who makes considerable use of Neoptolemos, have confirmed.[144] As to who the Pisones were to whom Horace addresses himself, opinions differ and with them must differ our views concerning the date.

There are two families of Pisones which are of importance in this context, the households of L. and of Cn. Calpurnius Piso. The former, whom the ancient commentators name, had two sons, Lucius and Gaius. His dates, as we know from Tacitus (*ann.*, vi, 10, 3–4), were 705/49–785/32. Suppose that he was about twenty when he married, his eldest son might have been born about 726/28, and so been old enough to show some interest in literature in the last two or three years of Horace's life. The difficulty of this is that the *A.P.* mentions (55) Vergil as if he were still alive, along with Horace himself, as a modern who has the critics to reckon with, and Quintilius Varus, dead before the elder son of Piso was more than a baby, as if (438 ; cf. above, p. 275) he were fresh in their memories. Hence Gnaeus Piso has been suggested, and a date somewhere in the neighbourhood of 730/24 or not very much later. This man was born about the same time as Horace himself, and his son was a rising young politician, in attendance upon Tiberius, by whose orders or connivance it was afterwards alleged that he murdered Germanicus (Tacitus, *ann.*, ii, 69 *sqq.*). This was in 772/19, and Piso had been forty-five years in Tiberius' service, *ibid.*, iii, 16, 7 ; hence he might well have been addressed by Horace as *iuuenis* at the date suggested.[145] But we know nothing of any brother of his, nor of any special interest of the family in literature, whereas L. Piso was the owner of the Herculanean villa in which the writings of Philodemos were found, preserved, it would seem, in honour of the

[143] That this is its ancient title there need be no doubt ; Horace himself has no occasion to mention it (indeed it is probably his last work, see above), but every one from Quintilian (viii, 3, 60) to Priscian (vol. iii, p. 254, 16 Keil) who has occasion to quote it calls it either *ars poetica* or *de arte poetica*.

[144] See Rose, *H.G.L.*, p. 399 *sq.* ; more in Atkins, ii, p. 54 *sqq.* Cf. Porphyrio on *A.P.*, p. 344, 15 Meyer (the Teubner ed.).

[145] Pater et iuuenes patre digni, *A.P.*, 24.

family tradition. Since it is through Philodemos that we know of Neoptolemos, and since we have reason to believe that he was himself the centre of an active little group of poets and critics, including Vergil and Gallus, cogent reasons would have to be brought forward for rejecting this Piso in favour of the other. The mentions of Vergil and Quintilius are not unnatural in the mouth of one who had known them both well. We therefore must conclude that the *A.P.* was written late enough for it not to be absurd to attribute literary ambitions and interests to at least one of L. Piso's sons, and hence not earlier than 742/12 or even somewhat later.

The outline of the work may be thus given, introducing a little formality which is hidden under its easy style and careful avoidance of pedantic exactness, alien to the familiar epistolary manner. Part I (1–41), poetry in general (*poesis*)[146]; let the would-be author choose a subject self-consistent and capable of being handled by him as a whole; merely to have one or two good things in an otherwise unattractive or absurd work will not do. Part II (42–294), the form of the poem (*poema*); it will follow largely from the subject. Let the language be choice, not avoiding either neologisms or archaisms in strict moderation; the metre that which the practice of antiquity has shown suitable to the subject you have chosen, the tone befitting the type of composition, and before all things such as to give the impression of sincerity, especially in emotional passages. Let the characters be self-consistent, the beginning suitable and not too lofty; keep the story in agreement with itself; remember, in a drama, to let every character, young or old, together with the chorus, which should be treated as one of the actors, be given appropriate words and actions. Here follows a singularly long dissertation on the drama, including, what is very curious at that date and place and not yet satisfactorily explained, some precepts for the writing of satyr-plays, a thing which, so far as we know, no Roman ever seriously attempted. It is reasonable to suppose that one of the Pisos had some intention of reviving this long obsolete form of composition; certainly Horace himself had no inclination that way, for he never attempted drama at all. It is one of many reminders that we know little of the currents of literary opinion and discussion at that age, and can but judge as best we may from those works that have come down to us what tendencies lay behind not only them but those which have not survived or never were published. Finally, Part III (295–476) discusses the author himself (*poeta*), and of necessity touches on the old controversy

[146] *Poesis, poema, poeta* is the traditional division of the subject for Hellenistic critics; see further Atkins, *op. cit.*, p. 70 *sqq*.

whether native ability or training counted for more. Horace's opinion was that both are equally necessary [147]; assuming therefore sufficient genius (concerning which he is emphatic that it must be first-rate; a man of average abilities may cut a tolerable figure in other walks of life, but a poet, if not excellent, is intolerable),[148] he gives a series of precepts for training it. They reduce to three, wide reading of the best models, endless care in composition, and the conjunction of it all with the best available criticism.

This short analysis does no justice to the charm of the poem, the many shrewd observations by the way, the well-chosen illustrations, all in fact which makes it a work of literature and not merely a sensible little handbook. With it and the other literary epistles Horace establishes in permanent form the rules of classicism for the literature of his country. Whether they were the best possible it is hard to say; that they were abundantly misunderstood and misapplied in subsequent ages, both by Latins and others, is undoubted and cannot be laid to the poet's charge.

As already indicated, this is probably Horace's last work, and comes no great while before his death, which occurred near the end of his fifty-seventh year, on November 27, 746/8.

There remained an important field of poetry which Vergil had touched scarcely if at all, Horace never.[149] This was Elegy, for which it appears that the Italians of that day had a decided talent. The elegiac couplet (which may be, perhaps, most simply explained by saying that it is a hexameter followed by its own first half twice repeated) had for centuries in Greece been used for all manner of compositions in which neither the dignity of epic metre, the passion of lyric nor the rapidity of iambics was wanted. These included expressions of personal feeling, provided that the emotions were not at such a white heat that they could find vent only in song (though elegies were sung on occasion) or on such a scale that they needed a chorus to set them forth; the more every-day loves and hates, hopes and fears, found expression in this very adaptable metre. It is thus apparent that elegiacs covered a different field from what we understand by elegy, and

[147] *A.P.*, 409–10: ego nec studium sine diuite uena/nec rude quid prosit uideo ingenium.

[148] The famous dictum, *ibid.*, 372–3, mediocribus esse poetis non homines, non di, non concessere columnae (= booksellers' shops, with new works affixed to the pillars in front of them).

[149] Suetonius says that he has come across elegiacs supposed to be by Horace, but rejects them, because they are commonplace (*uulgares*), *uita, ad fin.* The general opinion seems to have confirmed him in this, for all trace of them is lost.

trespassed upon much ground which, for us, belongs to personal lyric. Sadness had never been a necessary concomitant of such a composition, there being no reason, from the first elegiac poem to the close of the great period of Alexandrian literature, why a poet should not use the couplet to set forth feelings wholly mirthful and joyous, or light, semi-philosophical reflections. Evidently, such a medium was especially well fitted for an amorous theme not too intensely passionate. Kallimachos and other Alexandrians had seen this, and two kinds of poem, so far as we know, resulted; one, the love-story in verse, whereof there were many written and a few examples survive to us in Greek; the other, the epigram, wherein the author set forth in a few lines his feelings towards another,—admiration, suspicion, jealousy, and so forth. But we have no positive evidence that any Alexandrian combined the two and told his own love-story, or what he feigned to be such, in an elegiac poem or series of poems. Here, however, the loss of the bulk of their writings must make us chary of saying positively that they did not do so.[150]

What we can say with certainty, for much of it survives, is that poetry of this kind was practised with great success by a little group of writers contemporary with or slightly younger than Horace. The main subject of all of them was love, and that particular kind which we call irregular, but Horace, voicing the normal sentiment of antiquity, *concessa Venus*,[151] allowable indulgence. All great cities, and Rome especially, had a large courtesan-class, or rather a whole series of such classes, from women who were almost the wives of their lovers, or at least entered into unions which lasted for years or might lead to that quasi-marriage known as concubinage,[152] down to the lowest prostitutes. For an unmarried man to amuse himself in this way, so long as he observed moderation and did not ruin his health or his estate, was considered at most a piece of levity, not becoming to the serious-minded. We have seen what a large part such affairs play in Comedy, and in this respect certainly it mirrored real life. Here, then, was an excellent subject for elegiac poetry; the feelings involved were, as a rule, but moderately intense, and their expression did not mean laying bare the intimacies of family life to the eyes of the reading public. We

[150] For Greek elegiac poetry, see Rose, *H.G.L.*, pp. 82 *sqq.*, 315 *sqq.*; for Catullus' poems in this vein, see above, p. 142.

[151] Horace, *sat.*, i, 4, 113.

[152] This was a perfectly legal relation; no stigma attached to the woman, and her children were not illegitimate; they could not, however, be the heirs of their father nor take his name as of right.

shall indeed find an occasional example of conjugal love forming the subject of such personal poems; but that is decidedly the exception.

The first of this series of writers, omitting Catullus, was Vergil's friend GAIVS CORNELIVS GALLVS. But his disgrace seems to have dragged down his poetry with it, unless, as already mentioned (p. 260), the *Ciris* is his. Of his life we know the main facts. He was born in Forum Iulii, the modern Fréjus, in 685/69, apparently of an obscure family.[153] In some way he attracted the notice of Octavian, and was promoted by him to responsible positions, being in command of a detachment during the campaign against Antony and afterwards governor of Egypt.[154] Here he seems to have lost his head completely after successfully putting down a rebellion in the Thebaid nome, and behaved with such utter lack of ordinary deference to Augustus that the latter was obliged, against his will, for he seems to have liked Gallus personally, to let an accusation against him come before the senate and, in consequence, to forbid him his house and, therefore, access to any of the Imperial provinces. Gallus saw that he was ruined, and killed himself.[155]

As to his poems, we know certainly that he wrote four books of elegies to a *mima* called Lycoris in his verses, really Cytheris, the mistress of Antony (see p. 150) among others,[156] and a poem in the manner of Euphorion on the grove of Apollo at Grynion

[153] Jerome, *an. Abr.* 1990 (727/27); Suet., *Aug.*, 66.

[154] Suet, *loc. cit.*; Jerome, *loc. cit.* and *an. Abr.* 1984; Cassius Dio, li, 9; liii, 23, 5 *sqq.*

[155] See the passages quoted in the last note from Suetonius and Dio. In addition, we have a trilingual inscription (published most recently in Dessau, *Inscriptiones Latinae selectae*, vol. iii, 2, p. xl *sq.*, who gives the Greek and Latin versions, with references to the publications of the very mutilated Egyptian text), which sets forth in Egyptian, Greek and Latin Gallus' exploits, taking all the credit to himself, which should by Roman practice go to Augustus, since Gallus fought under his *auspicia*. For a modern parallel, suppose that the governor of a Crown colony, having achieved some success with the troops under his charge, instead of reporting to the Colonial Secretary, issues a bulletin which is sent to all the principal newspapers of the world, in language implying that he has acted as an independent sovran in his own right. This, however, would not reproduce the atmosphere of the affair accurately, for Augustus' government, being new, was of necessity very jealous of its prestige, and Egypt was not properly a province, but an Imperial demesne.

[156] Servius on *ecl.*, x, 1; anon. *de uiris illustr.*, 82, 2. References to the Lycoris-elegies are fairly numerous, *e.g.*, Ovid, *amor.*, i, 15, 29–30. By the usual rule of such poetic names, Lȳcōrĭs and Cȳthērĭs have the same scansion, cf. Lēsbĭă—Clōdĭă, Plānĭă—Dēlĭă, Cȳnthĭă—Hōstĭă, and, in English, Atticus—Addison.

or Gryneia [157]; the obscure shrine and its little-known legend were themes to the Alexandrian taste. We have left part of one verse. What the contents of the poems on Lycoris were like we can guess with some accuracy from Vergil's tenth eclogue (see p. 244). Whether he wrote anything else which we can to any extent recover is a moot point.[158]

Gallus had at his side the grammarian and poet Parthenios, who compiled for his use the little collection of love-stories which still survives under the title of *Ἐρωτικὰ παθήματα*, 'adventures of lovers'.[159]

On the other hand, we are exactly informed concerning the poetical work of ALBIVS TIBVLLVS, to whom, as we have seen (p. 276), one of Horace's Epistles is addressed. He was one of a little circle of poets which was grouped, not around Maecenas, but around Messalla (see p. 305), and was evidently the best of them, for this time we are able directly to compare his work with that of his colleagues. His uneventful life is known in bare outline, mostly from his own allusions and references. He was of the equestrian order [160]; he possessed, whether from his own resources or from Messalla's liberality, a sufficient estate, consisting of or including some landed property at Pedum [161]; he had been better off, but had suffered losses, whether from the same cause as Vergil and Horace or some other we do not know [162]; he accompanied Messalla to the war against the Aquitani, in 726/23,[163]

[157] The form of the name varies, see Stephanos of Byzantion *s.u.* (p. 213, 10 Meineke) and Strabo, xiii, 3, 5; it was a town of the Aiolid, in Asia Minor, not far from the Troad.

[158] See above, n. 33.

[159] Cf. Rose, *H.G.L.*, p. 415.

[160] The chief external sources are, a very short life of him preserved in the MSS. of his poems, which is obviously a much damaged medieval excerpt from an ancient biography drawing upon good sources (it preserves an epigram of Domitius Marsus, giving the date of his death); Horace, *epp.*, i, 4; Ovid, *amores*, iii, 9. Of these, the first says he was *eques regalis*; I take this to be, not a scribe's blunder, but a medieval misinterpretation of an older original which said he was *eques R*(*omanus*).

[161] Horace, *loc. cit.*, 2. Pedum is between Tibur and Praeneste. *Ibid.*, 7, di tibi diuitias dederunt.

[162] Tib., i, 1, 19: uos quoque, felicis quondam, nunc pauperis agri/custodes . . . Lares. It is possible that he was really reduced to poverty by some misfortune and then given financial help by Messalla; it is to be remembered that Horace (see last note) says he was rich.

[163] The Life says: contubernalis Aquitanico bello (Messallae) militaribus donis donatus est. This agrees with his own words, i, 7, 9, non sine me est tibi partus honos.

and again to the East, on some imperfectly known occasion, when he fell ill and was left at Corcyra to recover.[164] He died in 735/19, apparently still comparatively young.[165]

His work, so far as we are concerned,[166] consists of two books of elegies and one poem which has strayed into another collection. The first of these consists very largely of addresses to a woman whom he calls Delia, her real name being Plania.[167] However, five of its ten poems have other subjects, Nos. 7 and 10 being concerned respectively with Messalla's triumph and his own disinclination to warlike exploits, while Nos. 4 and 8 tell of a boy called, at least by the poet, Marathus, and No. 9 is still on the subject of some boy-favourite, presumably the same, but not named. The second book has a different centre of interest; Tibullus says no more of Delia, but addresses himself to Nemesis, not the goddess, but a woman whose mythological name testifies to her low rank; we have no tradition that she ever went by any other, nor does Tibullus ever say anything concerning her that is inconsistent with the picture of a professional courtesan, extravagant and greedy, of whom he was, or poetically feigned to

[164] Since we do not know what the occasion was, we cannot say whether it was before or after the Aquitanian affair. The relevant passages are Tib., i, 7, 13 *sqq.*, where Tibullus speaks of the East and of Egypt in a context implying that Messalla had been there (the date of the poem is after the Aquitanian triumph of 727/27, which is spoken of in past tenses; possibly it was written on the first anniversary of it); 3, 1 *sqq.*, which mentions the illness and the stay at Corcyra.

[165] Ovid, *amor.*, iii, 9, compares him to a number of mythological personages, all of whom, with one exception, Aeneas, died young; 61–4, the shades of Catullus, Calvus and Gallus are invited to meet him; of these, only Gallus was over forty when he died. Horace, *loc. cit.*, 10, implies that his health was good; since this was written at the very most some four years and perhaps only one before his death, he presumably died of some acute illness. Marsus (see note 160) says: te quoque Vergilio comitem non aequa, Tibulle,/mors iuuenem campos misit ad Elysios.

[166] There is one quotation from him, Charisius, p. 87, 5 Keil, which is not to be found in our text. Confusion with some other poet and the occurrence of the words cited in a gap somewhere in the existing poems are equally possible with the existence of an elegy which we have lost.

[167] Apuleius, *apol.*, 10. This suits the feigned name, which is thus a sort of pun (*planus* = δῆλος). We learn therefore that she was a free woman, although of an obscure *gens*; and Tibullus indicates that she was watched (i, 2, 15), and was the wife of some one (*uiro*, i, 6, 8; *ibid.*, 22, she makes the rites of the Bona Dea an excuse for going out; this would seem to show that she was outwardly respectable). The same poem expresses the fear that she has another lover besides Tibullus; possibly a quarrel over this separated them (cf. 5, 47); she outlived him, Ovid, *loc. cit.*, 55–6.

be,[168] desperately enamoured. But here again, his loves are by no means his only subject; No. 1 is a description, particularly charming, of a country rite, the lustration of the fields; No. 2 is a birthday ode to Cornutus, who is also addressed in No. 3, though there he has not a little to say of Nemesis. No. 4 does but mention her in passing; the most part of the poem is taken up with a prophecy of the future greatness of Rome, addressed by the Sibyl to Aeneas, followed by a prayer that Apollo will now send peace and plenty. The occasion is the admission of Messalla's son Messallinus to the college of the *quindecimuiri*, in whose charge were the Sibylline oracles. This might give us an exact date if we knew when he attained this honour, but we do not. Finally, there is one little poem, an elegy of twenty-four lines, which has found its way into the third (or fourth) book of the collection. Its author says he is Tibullus,[169] and professes undying affection to some one, apparently a courtesan, for he says he would feel safe if only other men disliked her and that she will take advantage of him for declaring his love too openly; she may therefore be Nemesis.

All these poems, though not the work of a supreme poet, have a very distinct, quiet charm. The versification, while retaining a few licences not found in the highly polished work of Ovid, is smooth and melodious; the language is perspicuous, the passion expressed is just intense enough to be interesting, the tone of the addresses to Messalla, while respectful and admiring, is not that of a mere flatterer. The frequent references to and descriptions of country life ring true.

Following the two books of the elegies in our MSS. are two more, which some modern scholars would combine into one. It forms, or they form, a somewhat miscellaneous collection, the only bond of union being the relation of all but one of the authors to Messalla, which makes it likely that the remaining writer was likewise of his circle. This is the poet who calls himself LYGDAMVS [170] and writes to a certain Neaera six pretty, but slight poems. He wishes to marry her, and apparently her mother

[168] Horace, *loc. cit.*, speaks of Tibullus as probably engaged either in writing or in philosophical meditation (2–5), yet this was during the Nemesis-period (Ovid, *ibid.*, 58, says she was with him when he died).

[169] iii, 19 (= iv, 13), 13.

[170] As he also says he is a Roman citizen (iii, 1, 2, March 1 was New Year's day *nostris auis*; it begins the old Roman year), this is presumably a pseudonym, unless he was a freedman. Nothing whatever is known of him, except that he was not Tibullus, and that he was born in 711/43 (5, 18).

favours him [171]; but he lives in fear that her infidelity, the interference of some third person, or death may separate them. The sixth poem shows him trying to drink himself into forgetfulness of her, and so may be taken as meant for the position it occupies at the end of the series. After Lygdamus follows the work of a much inferior writer, 211 indifferent hexameters containing a silly and badly expressed laudation of Messalla.

The most remarkable poems, however, are also the shortest, and they were written by a woman, SVLPICIA, probably Messalla's niece. This would seem to follow from the mention of her name, against all poetic conventions and ordinary good manners if the poems are fictitious; but for naming herself in such a way she had Sappho's precedent, and hardly less than her passion. Her six little utterances, genuine in every line unless we assume that the hypothetical misuser of her name was also a poet of extraordinary dramatic power, are all addressed to some one she calls Cerinthus. The first is ten lines of sheer joy that she is his chosen, and a frank resolve to publish it to all the world; she 'cannot be troubled to compose her face for the sake of her reputation'; the real disgrace would be to keep it hidden that she has been 'worthily with a worthy love'. The next two are mere notes in verse; she must go into the country for her birthday, and hates the thought of leaving Rome; the plan has been changed and she is to stay after all. Then come six lines of hurt dignity from a woman who will not condescend to be jealous. Cerinthus has been with some vulgar light-o'-love; she leaves it to her friends to be troubled, and rather feels glad that he knows her well enough to take even that liberty. In the next, she is ill, but her only pain is the thought that perhaps Cerinthus may not care much whether she recovers or not. In the last, she has failed him at a rendezvous, being afraid to show how much she cared; and for this she asks his pardon.

These little gems of frank and real passion evidently came to be known, and some one wrote a kind of poetical commentary on them, very neat and pretty, and quite lacking the tone of real, first-hand experience. In the first, Sulpicia's beauty is described; she is dressed in her finery for the Kalends of March (the Matralia, one of the principal women's festivals of the year), but is lovely whatever she wears. The second of the series is supposed to be her prayer to Diana to protect Cerinthus while he hunts; the third, his prayer to Apollo to cure her sickness. In the last two, we have scenes of domestic cult; the former shows Sulpicia celebrating Cerinthus' birthday, henceforth to be her festival also,

[171] See 2, 13–14.

and in the latter, she is celebrating her own, secretly praying to her Iuno (the guardian spirit of a woman, corresponding to a man's Genius) to help her to her lover. As the poems are arranged in our MSS., the group which I have called the commentary comes first (iii, 8–12, or iv, 2–6), the really Sulpician poems next (iii, 13–18, or iv, 7–12).

There is but one more item in the collection, a four-line epigram on a mistress said to be unfaithful; who wrote it is as unknown as the authorship of the poems on Sulpicia.[172]

A bulkier poet than Tibullus, and on the whole a greater one, although opinions differed on that point in antiquity and may well continue to do so,[173] is SEXTVS PROPERTIVS.[174] We know concerning his life only what he tells us, mostly in an autobiographical poem, the first of his fourth book, by the usual numbering. He was an Umbrian, a native of Asisium (Assisi); his parents were well-to-do, and locally well known, but the confiscation of their estates impoverished them. His father died when he was a child, his mother sent him to Rome when he was old enough, intending him to become an advocate; but he rejected that career and took to poetry instead. Whether before or after this decision, he met the all-important experience of his life, and made the acquaintance of the woman he calls Cynthia; her real name was Hostia.[175] Concerning her we know a good

[172] Of course, conjectures are rife; Hosius, for example (Schanz-Hosius, ii, p. 190), is rather decidedly of opinion that the poems which I call the commentary are by Tibullus; I think them a little too artificial and a little too removed from his own concerns to be his.

[173] Quintilian, x, 1, 93: elegia quoque Graecos prouocamus, cuius mihi tersus atque elegans maxime uidetur auctor Tibullus; sunt qui Propertium malint; Ouidius utroque lasciuior, sicut durior Gallus.

[174] The *nomen* occurs several times in his poems; the *praenomen* is preserved as it were accidentally, in Donatus' *Life of Vergil*, 30 (45).

[175] The chronology of all this is not easy to determine exactly, but approximate dates can readily be got. He was a child when his father died and the estate was confiscated, *i.e.*, in or about 713/41 (iv, 1, 127–30). Some time after this (*mox*) he assumed the *toga uirilis* and came to Rome, *ibid.*, 131 *sqq*. He need not then have been more than about sixteen or seventeen years old. If we suppose that he was about ten when his father died (he was old enough to perform the rite of collecting the bones from the funeral pyre, if we take line 127 literally), this gives us a date in the neighbourhood of 719/35 or a little later, which fits well enough with the fact that he addresses Gallus in i, 5, 13, and 20. If this is Cornelius Gallus, and there is no real reason why it should not be, see Skutsch, *Gallus und Vergil*, p. 145 *sqq.*, we must suppose that it was before the campaign of Actium and Gallus' absence with Augustus' forces and in Egypt. He had been in Rome some three years when he became Cynthia's lover, iii, 15, 7, and so we might suppose the *Cynthia* to have been written not long before Actium, but still before it; this again fits the mention of

deal from his poems. She was a freedwoman,[176] a courtesan with many lovers besides himself; she was strikingly beautiful, accomplished, and, for her position, disinterested; she was at least capable of genuine affection for her gifted but poor adorer. Propertius seems, when he met her, to have been living what a later age would have called the life of a man about town; he had had one affair already, with a girl named (at least in his poetry) Lycinna.[177] But once in love with Cynthia, he was hers, despite quarrels and temporary separations, for some six years or more. He had plenty of learning, apparently was a fairly rapid composer, and had no lack of subject-matter; his *Cynthia*, a book of twenty-two elegies, made his name and hers. With very few exceptions, they treat of himself and his mistress,[178] describing the beginning of his affection for one against whom he had at first struggled for awhile, the well-meant endeavours of friends to distract or cure his passion, his jealousy when she left Rome for Baiae, and all the incidents of an irregular attachment between two self-willed people of strong character. The style of these poems has a power such as Tibullus never showed, though it lacks his sweetness and sanity; the learning is of the type made fashionable by Alexandrian poetry, including numerous, sometimes too numerous, mythological references and allusions; the metre, skilfully handled elegiac couplets, with a rhythm which Latin poetry, including most of Propertius' own, afterwards abandoned, for the pentameter, instead of ending with the dissyllabic word which is all but invariable in Ovid, rather seeks long words, those of

the battle in ii, 1, 34; 15, 44, as a past event, whereas there is nothing said of it or of any fighting in the East in *Cynthia*; indeed, in No. 6 of that book, Tullus is going to Greece and Asia Minor apparently as a tourist, certainly on no warlike errand, and invites Propertius to come with him.

That Cynthia is a poetical pseudonym for Hostia we are told by Apuleius, *Apol.*, 10; that the book which bears her name was published separately is clear from Prop., ii, 24, 1–2; Martial, xiv, 189.

[176] This follows from her name, which is Roman, combined with the implication in ii, 7, that Propertius cannot marry her; a Roman knight (that he was one is clear from iv, 1, 131; he took off a golden *bulla* when he assumed the *toga uirilis*; but only sons of knights and senators wore one, Livy, xxvi, 36, 5; Pliny, xxxiii, 10) could not marry a freedwoman. She need not, of course, have been a former slave herself (*liberta*), but she must have been of the class of *libertini*, which included *liberti* and their descendants. For the length of time the affair lasted, see iii, 25, 3: quinque tibi potui seruire fideliter annos. We do not know whether this includes the year during which she would not see him (iii, 16, 9).

[177] iii, 15, 6.

[178] Nos. 16, 20, 21 and 22 are not about her directly or indirectly, and the last two are not amatory.

four syllables or more.[179] Most striking of all, the passion is real.

One result of the publication of this book was that Propertius was introduced to Maecenas. In his private capacity, Maecenas would no doubt have been glad to welcome the poet for his own sake; but as the untitled Minister of Propaganda, he could not neglect his duties, and it is evident that Propertius was soon asked what he could do to forward and popularize the government's policy. Henceforth we find him seeking excuses and compromises, for propaganda was a thing he could not or would not write. In the second book of poems, which he published about three years after Augustus' triumphal return in 725/29,[180] this has already begun. No. 1 addresses Maecenas, explaining that Propertius would gladly celebrate Augustus' exploits if he could write in the heroic style at all, but he cannot; every man to his trade, and his is erotic poetry only. No. 10 is a resolution to turn to other subjects and sing of Augustus and his expected conquests. No. 31 combines the two interests very ingeniously; he is visiting Cynthia, who asks him why he has come so late, and excuses himself by telling her that he had been looking at the new temple of Apollo Palatinus (this dates the poem, for the temple was dedicated in October, 726/28).[181] But the rest of the book is practically pure Cynthia.

In this book we meet with a famous difficulty regarding the arrangement of the poems. In 13, 25, Propertius says that when he dies he wants no better funeral procession than *tres libelli* and no other mourner than Cynthia. But, by the usual numbering, he had so far written but two books; where is the third? The obvious answer is that of Lachmann, that our far from faultless MSS. have misdivided the books and Bk. III should begin with some earlier poem than this; he suggested No. 10, since it begins: sed tempus lustrare aliis Helicona choreis, which would make an excellent introductory line for a collection. This is very plausible, and is supported by the fact that Nonius, p. 159, 32, according to the best MS., quotes from our iii, 21, 14 as *Propertius elegiarum lib. IV*. But it has against it the fact that in ii, 24, 1 he represents some one as saying to him: tu loqueris, cum sis iam noto fabula libro/et tua sit toto Cynthia lecta foro? implying that the *Cynthia* is the only thing he has published, which is very odd if he had

[179] As: a dolor, ibat Hylas, ibat Hamadryasin (i, 20, 32); miles ab Etruscis saucius aggeribus (21, 2); Hypsipyle uacuo constitit in thalamo (15, 18).

[180] In ii, 34, 91, Gallus is recently (*modo*) dead, which fixes this poem about the end of 728/26; in 1, 31 *sqq*., the triumphs of 725/29 have been celebrated; No. 31 (see next note) falls between these.

[181] See Platner-Ashby, *s.u.* Apollo.

already put forth the nine excellent elegies comprised in Lachmann's Bk. II. To this again there has been found an answer. Propertius was much neglected in the Middle Ages, and our MSS. go back to one archetype ; now if we read the poems carefully, we find, apart from mere scribal blunders obscuring a word or two, a number of passages in which the connexion of thought is hardly, if at all, to be traced. But this is perfectly understandable if we suppose that what is known to have taken place in other authors (Lucretius for example) [182] has befallen Propertius ; the archetype was old and battered, it needed rebinding, and some leaves were put by the binder in the wrong places, or wrong side foremost. Hence not much can be proved from the order in which we now find two passages ; the later one in our tradition may be an earlier one mechanically displaced. For a highly ingenious, and extremely hazardous, reconstruction of the poems on these lines, see the edition of O. L. Richmond.[183] So far, however, transpositions based on such suppositions have failed to approve themselves to scholars in general, especially the more elaborate and far-reaching of them. It remains always possible to explain the matter much more simply ; we may suppose that Propertius had really written three books by the time ii, 13 appeared, in other words that Bks. II and III were published together. There is no unlikelihood in this ; we may compare the simultaneous publication of Horace, *Odes*, I–III (p. 273), and the lapse of time between the earliest and latest odes in the one collection is greater than that between the earliest and latest elegies in the other. For, as we saw, the Odes lie between 724/30 and about the middle of 731/23 ; while in the case of Propertius, his whole affair with Cynthia lasted at most six years (see note 177) ; he had already been her lover for a year when he published Bk. I (i, 1, 7) ; therefore, the poems relating to her in Bks. II and III were spread over not more than five years. The whole time taken in the composition of the three books is some eight years or more, from before Actium (see note 175) to the end of 731/23. It thus follows that about two years passed between the final separation of the lovers and the publication of Bk. III (and Bk. II, if that came out with it). I conjecture that Propertius spent much of that time in retirement, partly or wholly at Athens (iii, 21), and in study.

Book III opens with an appeal to the great Alexandrians, Kallimachos and Philitas,[184] to admit him of their company, for he will 'bring the rites of Italy among the choirs of Greece'. The next four poems are all skilful variants on his favourite theme, that he is the poet of love and nothing else. The next

[182] Lucretius, iv, 323, with Lachmann's note ; cf. also p. 7 of his commentary (ed. 2).

[183] Cambridge, University Press, 1928.

[184] The MSS. of Propertius spell the name Philetas, and this agrees with its form in late Greek authorities ; but the genuine name seems to have been Philitas, cf. Rose, *H.G.L.*, p. 341.

group have still Cynthia in the background, even in No. 7, when he is telling, with ingenuity and some real feeling, of the death of a friend, Paetus by name, who was drowned on a trading voyage to Egypt. The ninth is an apology to Maecenas, still justifying himself for writing no official poetry; the eleventh is chiefly a triumph-song for Actium, but curiously introduced by an amatory theme; it is no wonder that Propertius is under a woman's domination, when gods, heroes, and the great Antony have met the same fate. Then follow more love-poems still, erotic themes being blended in most ingenious fashion with others, as if he would show that his limitations are not so narrow as at first sight they would appear. In other words, he was showing himself a true Kallimacheian, adapting the elegy, as his model had done, to all manner of themes, and at the same time adding a touch of his own, for his adaptations are still amatory elegies. The end of this book records his final quarrel with Cynthia, his departure for Athens, and his parting message to her, that she will live to be old and despised. Included in this book, but assuredly later than its last Cynthia-poems, is a lament (No. 18) for the death of Marcellus, which fixes the publication of the whole as not earlier than the end of 731/23.

There follows a silence of some seven years, for the last book cannot be earlier than 738/16.[185] In the interval Propertius had developed a new interest, which he was to communicate to Ovid, the early history of Rome. The fourth book of his elegies begins with a quite unfamiliar theme to him, indeed one which he laughs at himself for attempting. He supposes himself acting as guide and antiquarian to an astrologer, Horus, who has come to visit Rome. He tells him something of the early history of the places he sees, and declares that he means to dedicate his talent, such as it is, to 'the holy rites and holy days, and the ancient names of places' (in Rome); in other words, he plans much the same work as Ovid afterwards partly accomplished in his *Fasti* (p. 335). The astrologer, however, is not enthusiastic; by way of giving Propertius a taste of his skill, he mentions some successful applications of his art, then sketches the poet's life for him, and tells him he will never make a success of any but amatory poetry, for he will never be out of love. Notwithstanding, Propertius, who had evidently been reading Varro or some other antiquarian, gives several samples of his new theme in the rest of the book.

[185] In iv, 11, 66, though the reading is doubtful, this much is certain, that mention is made of the consulship of P. Cornelius Scipio, which was in that year. In that year also, a success was won over the Sigambri, and allusion is made to this in 6, 77.

No. 2 is an account of the god Vertumnus, supposedly by himself; No. 3 is again a hint which Ovid took, for it is a poetical epistle from a wife, or mistress, to her absent man. No. 4 is antiquarian again, the story of Tarpeia; No. 5 (once more he led and Ovid followed) is a denunciation of a rascally old woman who bade his love scorn a poor, if poetical, suitor. No. 6 celebrates Actium once more. No. 7 is an example of his power over an uncanny theme; Cynthia's ghost visits him with a last message. No. 8 is one more Cynthia-poem, the tale of a quarrel between them. No. 9 is the story of Hercules and Cacus, No. 10 of the cult of Iuppiter Feretrius. The collection ends with perhaps the finest poem he ever wrote. His genius seems always to have had a morbid side, dwelling with a certain complacency on death and burial; here he has a theme suited to him. A noble lady, one of the Cornelii Scipiones, had just died [186]; Propertius represents her spirit as addressing her husband and children in a speech of deep and pathetic affection, ending with a word of hope for herself, *moribus et caelum patuit*, 'virtue can even inherit heaven'.

Here, suddenly, we take leave of Propertius, for we have absolutely no knowledge of what became of him after this date, no account of his death and no indication that he wrote anything else.

[186] It is commonly and naturally assumed that she was recently dead, or what point would there be in writing what is in effect a poem of consolation to her family?

Additional Note.—P. 240, n. 19. H. Wagenvoort, *Vergilius' Ecloga I en IX* (Meded. van de K. vlaamse Akademie, Kl. d. Letteren, XV, 3, Brussels 1953), p. 36, suggests that Tityrus is one of those who were spared because their holdings were smaller than the allotment given to each soldier, Dion Cassius, xlviii, 8, 5.

CHAPTER X

LIVY AND AUGUSTAN PROSE

WHILE no one name among the prose authors of Augustus' day is of such real importance as that of Cicero in the preceding generation, there is one which, for us, is as prominent among Vergil's contemporaries as the orator's among those of Lucretius. TITVS LIVIVS, familiar in English under the name of LIVY, is the greatest surviving example, perhaps absolutely the greatest, of that school of history to which attention has already been drawn (p. 111). There have been many who showed more diligence in searching for facts, although he did not neglect research; very many who have proved far greater sticklers for accuracy and better able to reconstruct the past by patient accumulation of data, political, economic and cultural; we have long perceived that when Dante speaks of 'Livy who errs not', he himself errs sadly. And yet, when all due allowance has been made for the faults of the man and the school, it remains true that very few, if any, have ever so completely succeeded in drawing an impressive picture of the past as they conceived it, or in extracting from it lessons for the moral needs of the present. We may rightly give the title of artist to one who, in the medium he chooses, achieves the result at which he aims. Livy shows us at the very beginning of his great work what his object was.

'This,' he tells his readers,[1] 'is the most wholesome and most fruitful outcome of historical knowledge, to have before one's eyes conspicuous and authentic examples of every type of conduct, whence the student may choose models for his own imitation and that of his country, and be warned against things ill begun which have likewise ended ill.'

We are at liberty to say that this is not the true end of history,

[1] Livy, *praefat.*, 10: hoc illud est praecipue in cognitione rerum salubre et frugiferum, omnis te exempli documenta in inlustri posita monumento intueri; inde tibi tuaeque rei publicae quod imitere capias, inde foedum inceptu foedum exitu quod uites.

but should be left for the moralist; in other words, that Livy and those who thought with him should not be called historians at all, but ethical teachers who drew their more or less well-attested examples from history and preferred the formula 'this and that befell Tarquin' to 'pride goeth before destruction'. But we must judge a writer, not by what we would have tried to do had we been he, but by what he attempted; if he has accomplished this, then we should beware lest our hostile criticisms of him turn out to be no more than subjective judgements amounting only to a personal preference for some other kind of artistry.

We may also, if we like, say that Livy was rather an epic poet in prose than a historian. It would not be wholly untrue, for there is much in him besides frequent poetical reminiscences in his language [2] which reminds us of Ennius and Vergil; indeed it is hardly unfair to say that, such is his skill in disposing of dry but necessary details, he is much less prosy than the former seems on occasion to have been. That his subject and treatment are alike of epic breadth he himself was manifestly conscious.

To quote again from the admirable preface to the history,[3] Livy says: 'Complaints cannot hope to be acceptable even when, as may happen, they are called for; at all events, let them not mark the beginning of my task, but rather would I commence, if that were the historians' custom as it is the poets', with the good omens of vows and prayers to the gods and goddesses to speed so vast an undertaking with their favour.' Again, his introduction to the second Punic War, one of the most dramatic narratives in all literature, might almost be the proem of an epic [4]: 'Never did mightier races or more potent states meet in arms; never had these states been so powerful and

[2] For instance, the opening chapters of Book ix, which tell the famous tale of the Caudine Forks, have the following distinctly unprosaic turns of phrase—i, 7: the Samnite general Pontius demands: quid ultra tibi, Romane, quid foederi, quid dis arbitris foederis debeo? ii, 7: ita natus locus est (meaning *ea est loci natura*); iii, 1: per obices uiarum. iii, 3: num montes moliri sede sua paramus?

[3] *Praefat.*, 12: sed querellae, ne tum quidem gratae futurae cum forsitan necessariae erunt, ab initio certe tantae oriendae rei absint: cum bonis potius ominibus uotisque et precationibus deorum dearumque, si, ut poetis, nobis quoque mos esset, libentius inciperemus, ut orsis tantum operis successus prosperos darent.

[4] Livy, xxi, 1, 2–3: nam neque ualidiores opibus ullae inter se ciuitates gentesque contulerunt arma neque his ipsis tantum unquam uirium aut roboris fuit; et haud ignotas belli artes inter sese sed expertas primo Punico conferebant bello, et adeo uaria fortuna belli ancepsque Mars fuit ut propius periculum fuerint qui uicerunt. odiis etiam prope maioribus certarunt quam uiribus, Romanis indignantibus quod uictoribus uicti ultro inferrent arma, Poenis quod superbe auareque crederent imperitatum uictis esse.

resistent. To this conflict they brought no unknown arts of war, for either had made trial of what the other could do in the former campaigns; and so uncertain was the fortune of the contest, so evenly balanced the favour of the god of battles, that it was the victors who underwent the direst peril. Moreover, the hatred they brought to the strife was wellnigh greater than their power; for the Romans were furious that the conquered should dare be the first to attack the conquerors, the Carthaginians chafed under the tyrannical and selfish rule of the victors.' Then follows the admirable and wholly poetical tale (no less poetical if it happens to be true) of how the child Hannibal at his father's bidding swore to be Rome's enemy from the first moment when he could.

This great artist was born in Patavium, the modern Padua, in 695/59.[5] He died there in 770/17.[6] At some time in his life he was at Rome, and there made the acquaintance of Augustus, who liked him well enough to make good-humoured fun of his partiality to Pompey,[7] and also of the future emperor Claudius, whom he encouraged to write history.[8] He had at least one son and one daughter.[9] This is practically all we know of his life; the little that we can guess of his character leads us to believe that he was an honest man, upright and patriotic; this not from the abundance of edifying sentiment in his work (Sallust outdoes him in that) but partly from the reputation of his native place, partly from the total absence of any charges of inconsistency between his life and his doctrine.[10] What set him to writing his History we do not know; that Augustus or Maecenas suggested it is of course possible, but his own reiterated expressions of delight in the work and particularly in the pictures of ancient virtue which it involves [11] make it clear that he needed little urging. His scope was ambitious enough, nothing less than the whole history

[5] Jerome, *an. Abr.* 1958 (= 695/59).

[6] Jerome, *an. Abr.* 2033 (= 770/17). A reason may be adduced for thinking at least the former date wrong. In it, Livy is coupled with Messalla Corvinus, who certainly was not born in that year, cf. p. 305. The latter date agrees well enough with the period at which Livy ended his history (see next page), for the last book mentioned the death of Drusus and the defeat of Varus, both A.D. 9.

[7] Tacitus, *ann.*, iv, 34, 4: Titus Liuius, eloquentiae ac fidei praeclarus in primis, Cn. Pompeium tantis laudibus tulit ut Pompeianum eum Augustus appellaret; neque id amicitiae eorum offecit.

[8] Sueton., *Claud.*, 41.

[9] Seneca rhetor, *contr.*, x, *prohoem.*, 2, L. Magius gener T. Liui. Quint., x, 1, 39: apud Liuium in epistula ad filium scripta.

[10] For the reputation of Patavium, see Pliny, *epp.*, i, 14, 6: for Livy's own, we may perhaps compare Tacitus, cited in n. 7, if *fidei* there refers to his personal honesty and not his trustworthiness as a historian.

[11] *E.g.*, *praefat.*, 5.

of Rome from its fabulous beginnings, which he makes no attempt to criticize,[12] down to his own day, the whole on a large scale, with increasing minuteness and detail as the materials became more abundant and trustworthy. The plan was as follows: Books I–V take the story from the foundation of the City to its rebuilding after the Gaulish disaster of 364/390. Books VI–X continue it to the triumph of Sp. Carvilius over the Samnites in 461/293; the lost books XI–XV came down to the eve of the first Punic War, XVI–XX to just before the second, the story of which is told in XXI–XXX. Then follow the Macedonian Wars and concomitant events; Book XL ends with the death of Philip V of Macedon, XLV with the triumph of L. Aemilius Paulus over Perseus in 587/167. Here the work, so far as we have it, breaks off, but it is clear that it falls into groups of five books, two of which are often combined into a larger unit, a decade as it is commonly called. And we know from the surviving epitome that the decades went on; thus, Book LXXI began the story of the Social and Civil Wars, while LXXX ended with the death of Marius, XC with that of Sulla. Up to that point, some called his work the *annales*,[13] perhaps; *historia* may have meant the remaining books, which apparently did not fall into decades. His own title for the whole seems to have been simply *ab urbe condita*.[14] When he had finished CXX, Augustus died,[15] and the work was continued under Tiberius, of whose relations to the historian nothing is known. It seems probable that after composing CXLII (death of Drusus) Livy himself died.

It is thus clear that the scale of the work varied very much,

[12] *Praefat.*, 6.

[13] Servius says (*ad Aen.*, i, 373): Liuius ex annalibus et historia constat. The natural interpretation of this would be that part of his work was called *annales*, part *historia*. We have, however, no definite evidence where any such division began, or even that it really existed; Servius himself explains that historia est eorum temporum quae uel uidimus uel uidere potuimus . . . annales uero sunt eorum temporum quae aetas nostra non nouit.

[14] Livy himself nowhere tells us what he wished his writings to be called; such expressions as vi, 1, 1 (quae ab condita urbe Roma ad captam eandem Romani . . . gessere . . . quinque libris exposui) and xliii, 13, 2 (in meos annales) prove nothing at all. But the best MSS. both of the surviving books and of the epitome give *ab urbe condita*, with or without some addition, such as *historiarum, antiquitatum, primae decadis*; while Pliny (*N.H.*, *praef.*, 16) has: Liuium . . . in historiarum suarum quas repetit ab origine urbis quodam uolumine, which sounds very like a sort of paraphrase of the briefer title *ab urbe condita*.

[15] *Epit. lib. cxxi* bears the title: ex lib. cxxi, qui editus post excessum Augusti dicitur.

several years being sometimes treated in one book, while elsewhere one year had several books devoted to it. The principal reason for this was simply the bulk of written sources which Livy had available. Thus, Polybios had dealt with the first Punic War in outline only, and there was no Latin author who treated it at any great length; we do not know what use Livy made of Naevius. But Polybios had handled the second Punic War fully and accurately, and Latin writers were available. Hence Livy devoted a good deal more space to it than to the first, although it was not so long and hardly more important. For his own day he had, of course, very abundant documents, and his readers' interest lay more in that direction than in antiquity,[16] though his own did not.

But for a writer like Livy, the most pertinent question to ask is, not at what length but in what manner he handled the subject. As already indicated, he made no very profound researches [17]; he had the earlier historians, one or another of whom he seems usually to have followed, occasionally adding the divergent account of a second author, or expressing doubt or incredulity, particularly in dealing with the remoter periods, or when confronted with a more than usually extravagant statement. Of the countries in which the action took place, he had often no clear idea; thus, the question of the route by which Hannibal crossed the Alps, left somewhat obscure by Polybios, is certainly brought no nearer solution by Livy, and remains a favourite theme of long and unprofitable discussion. Of his personal honesty and desire to tell the truth, where it was possible to come at it, there is not the least doubt. It is equally undeniable that all the great figures of his story were clear and real personalities to him. He may indeed have seen them a little schematically; Hannibal's character is not exhausted by the brilliant, if prejudiced, list of

[16] Livy, xliii, 13, 1: ceterum et mihi uetustas res scribenti nescio quo pacto anticus fit animus. *Praef.*, 4–5: et legentium plerisque haud dubito quin primae origines proximaque originibus minus praebitura uoluptatis sint festinantibus ad haec noua quibus iam pridem praeualentis populi uires se ipsae conficiunt; ego contra hoc quoque laboris praemium petam ut me a conspectu malorum quae nostra tot per annos uidit aetas, tantisper certe dum prisca illa mente repeto auertam.

[17] For some remarks on the often obscure question of his sources, see Schanz-Hosius, ii, pp. 306–10. In general, it may be said that he used written books, such as Polybios or Claudius Quadrigarius, preferring the writer nearest in time to the events, or, failing such a distinction, the one whose account seemed to him the more reasonable and probable. Of examination of ancient monuments, inscriptions and similar material which a modern historian would welcome almost above all other there is little trace.

military virtues and moral vices which Livy draws up [18]; we may perhaps even say that our author introduces us to a great historical portrait-gallery or museum of sculpture rather than to the society of living men. But they are speaking likenesses, statues which almost come down from their pedestals and move about; and that the craftsman to whom we owe them is of the first order cannot be questioned. Here Livy, as the defects of his method and school prevent him being so detailedly accurate as we should wish, is helped by the virtues of the tradition he represents to be vivid and persuasive. He has not our apparatus of footnotes and appendices, citations of authorities by page and line and references to the archives of a score of nations, discussions of the ethnological, economic and geographical background of events. But he has two means of making his heroes live, the character-sketch and the speech. The former need not detain us, and is not very common in Livy; but the latter is a great tool in the hands of so excellent a sculptor. It replaces all the dissertations on the situation, which often encumber a modern work, by a dramatic sketch of what the protagonist, or protagonists, at an important moment may be supposed to have thought. No one imagined that it was a verbatim record of what was actually said; the eloquence with which the Lex Canuleia is defended and attacked, at a date long before the beginnings of Roman oratory,[19] would rid any ancient of that notion, if he had for a moment entertained it. They are therefore not fictitious, but the recognized conventional way of explaining why this was done and that attempted. Like many ancient conventions, this one was tolerable in the hands only of a master; but, given a master to handle it, it may be doubted whether so good a means has been found since for instructing the reader without obtruding needlessly the person of the narrator.

Of Livy's style, which the ancients more than once called milky, *i.e.*, rich, smooth and free from turbulence,[20] no detailed account can be attempted. It is as good in its way as Cicero's, ultimately of the same tradition—it is to be remembered that Isokrates, the father of classical prose, taught historians as much as orators—and yet quite unlike it, especially in the somewhat poetical tone, already mentioned.[21] With Cicero, however, Livy

[18] Livy, xxi, 4, 3–9. [19] Livy, iv, 2 *sqq*.

[20] Quint., x, 1, 32, cf. 101; Jerome, *epp.*, liii, 1, 3, echoes Quintilian.

[21] It is an old question what Asinius Pollio meant (Quint., i, 5, 56; viii, 1, 3) by saying that Livy used the Paduan dialect (*Patauinitas*). This obviously jocular word, made up on the analogy of *Latinitas*, *urbanitas*, if it does not refer to indefinable nuances, not to be perceived by any but a native speaker of Latin as then spoken in Rome (cf. Hendrickson

has in common the great art of adapting his manner to his matter. He is not confined to one style, periodic or antithetical, plain or ornate, but varies from the most elaborate structures of words and clauses to almost arid plainness, according as he has to narrate great events, complicated intrigues, or a succession of minor matters, included simply because they come in the year of which he treats and must be mentioned by one who is trying to tell the whole truth so far as he knows it.

As already stated (p. 298), the greater part of Livy is lost to us. There survive Books I–X, XXI–XLV, the text, especially towards the end, being occasionally incomplete, while minor faults are inconveniently numerous in our MSS. Of the lost books we have a few fragments, an epitome of the whole work (generally called the *periochae*), a considerable fragment of a longer epitome, preserved on a papyrus from Oxyrhynchus,[22] and a number of later historical writers, to be mentioned in their place, who are known with more or less certainty to have used Livy.

Although Livy's principal work was the *ab urbe condita*, he is known to have been the author of other writings. One was a letter to his son, *i.e.*, an essay in epistolary form, containing his views on style and literary criticism [23]; the rest were philosophic works, 'dialogues which had quite as much historical as philosophical character, and other books professedly philosophical', says the younger Seneca.[24]

While Livy is the only prose author of that age who has come

in *Am. Journ. Phil.*, xxxvi, 1915, pp. 70–5), may refer to his vocabulary (so O. Rossbach in *Berl. Phil. Woch.*, 1916, col. 734, n. 2; cf. the whole article), but much more likely to peculiarities of pronunciation, occasionally shown by non-standard spellings long since smoothed away from our texts; see J. Whatmough in *Harv. Stud. Class. Phil.*, xliv (1933), pp. 95–130, who gives inscriptional evidence for their existence in North Italy.

[22] *Ox. Pap.*, vol. iv, no. 668. It is not the original of our epitome, but has features in common with it which suggest that both go back to an older work of the same kind; cf. Schanz-Hosius, ii, p. 304.

[23] Quint., x, 1, 39, cf. ii, 5, 20; viii, 2, 18, and a few other passages in which Livy is cited for a literary opinion or anecdote may refer to this work.

[24] Sen., *epp.*, 100, 9: nomina adhuc T. Liuium, scripsit enim et dialogos, quos non magis philosophiae adnumerare possis quam historiae, et ex professo philosophiam continentis libros. The point of the remark is not clear. We may perhaps conjecture that Livy wrote dialogues with a historical setting, like Cicero's *de oratore* and *de re publica* (see above, pp. 167, 185), in which his interest in the supposed characters led him to devote much space to their biography, or the like; and that he also produced works with a simpler setting, in which the discussion of philosophical views, or perhaps the recommendation of whatever system he favoured, formed the whole contents.

down to us sufficiently complete for proper appreciation of him, he was by no means the only good writer in that medium. The list of Augustan prosateurs is headed by the Emperor himself (IMPERATOR CAESAR AVGVSTVS DIVI FILIVS), who was a friend and patron of learning and a notable purist.[25] He put lucidity above all other virtues of style, waging war against those who affected archaisms, tried experiments with language, or otherwise sinned against the great principle that ' a writer should express with the utmost possible clearness just what he has in mind ',[26] and never hesitated to use a colloquial phrase if it would set forth his meaning vividly. It is to him, for instance, that we owe the famous saying ' to pay on the Greek kalends ', though that was in a private letter, not in a work intended for publication.[27] Himself a very well-educated man,[28] he seems to have taken great pleasure not only in reading and listening to all manner of works in both verse and prose,[29] but in composition of various kinds. When bathing, he would amuse himself by making epigrams in verse [30]; like other men in public positions, he had of course often to make speeches, and being busy, he departed from precedent and read them from a written copy.[31] He made one

[25] For his literary activities see especially Sueton., *Diu. Aug.*, 84–9. For his purism, see 86, which contains some sharp criticisms of those who ' stank of the dictionary ' (reconditorum uerborum, ut ipse dicit, foetoribus).

[26] *Ibid.*, praecipuamque curam duxit sensum animi quam apertissime exprimere.

[27] *Ibid.*, 87 : litterae ipsius autographae . . . in quibus identidem, cum aliquos numquam soluturos significare uult, ad kal. Graecas soluturos ait.

[28] An account of his teachers is given *ibid.*, 89. His knowledge of Greek was somewhat limited, for he never would compose in that language, but always employed a translator.

[29] *Ibid.*, 89 : ingenia saeculi sui omnibus modis fouit ; recitantis et benigne et patienter audiit, nec tantum carmina et historias, sed et orationes et dialogos.

[30] *Ibid.*, 85 : unus liber exstat, scriptus ab eo hexametris uersibus, cuius et argumentum et titulus est Sicilia (probably a poetical description of the island) ; exstat alter aeque modicus Epigrammatum, quae fere tempore balinei meditabatur. The ' bath ' is, of course, the means of cleansing which we now call ' Turkish ' ; buildings or apartments intended for this purpose were the ordinary lounge of a Roman, and often contained much besides the hot-rooms, plunges and so forth which were necessary, although the very elaborate structures like the surviving Baths of Caracalla were not yet built. Martial had read the epigrams, which, from the specimen he quotes (xi, 20) and praises for its plain and outspoken style (*Romana simplicitas*), were not always of the most chaste.

[31] Suet., 84 : ne periculum memoriae adiret aut in ediscendo tempus absumeret, instituit recitare omnia.

unsuccessful attempt at writing tragedy,[32] and some excursions into philosophy and kindred topics.[33] With his personal friends, and not least with Vergil and Horace, he kept up a lively and familiar correspondence.[34] But the most important work, and the greatest loss to us, was his autobiography,[35] in thirteen books, dedicated to his two great ministers, Maecenas and Agrippa. We have, however, an imperfect substitute for it. After his death, there were produced three volumes of his composition, the first containing full directions for his funeral; this, together with his will, was read to the Senate. The third, also made known in the same way, was an abstract of the resources of the Empire.[36] But the second survives to us, though in a damaged form. It was a brief account of his public life, composed by himself in his seventy-sixth year,[37] that is to say in 766/13, for he was born in 601/63 and died in 767/14. By his orders,[38] it was carved on bronze plaques and set up before the imperial tomb (Maussoleum Augusti, see Platner-Ashby *s.u.*), and, whether by his own instructions or those of Tiberius, copies were sent out to provincial towns. By great good fortune, the copy which the local authorities of Ankyra, the modern Angora, set up, in the Latin original and a not very admirable Greek translation, has been largely preserved, together with some useful fragments of another, from the Pisidian Antioch, and other fragments again from Apollonia in Galatia.[39] It is therefore generally called the *Monumentum*

[32] *Ibid.*, 85: nam tragoediam magno impetu exorsus, non succedenti stilo, aboleuit quaerentibusque amicis quidnam Aiax (obviously the name of his tragedy) ageret, respondit Aiacem suum in spongeam incubuisse (the traditional Aias fell on his sword, *in gladium incubuit*; Augustus meant that he had rubbed out, with a wet sponge on his parchment notebook, all that he had written).

[33] *Ibid.*, composuit. . . . *Rescripta Bruto de Catone* . . . item *Hortationes ad philosophiam*.

[34] Specimens are preserved in Suetonius' Life of Horace (above, p. 266, n. 109), and also in Donatus' life of Vergil, 31 (above, p. 237, n. 6).

[35] Suet., 85 (composuit) aliqua *De uita sua*, quam tredecim libris Cantabrico tenus bello (*i.e.*, to 729/25) nec ultra exposuit. We know it was addressed to Maecenas and Agrippa from Plut., *comp. Dem. et Cic.*, 3, 1; as the Greek authors frequently quote it under the title *ὑπομνήματα*, the Latins several times as *commentarii*, it is likely that the full title was *Commentarii de uita sua*, approximately 'notes for an autobiography'. The fragments are collected in *H.R.F.*, pp. 252–261.

[36] See, for these documents, Tacitus, *ann.*, i, 8, 1–3; 11, 5–6; Suet., *op. cit.*, 101.

[37] Suet., *loc. cit.*; *Mon. Anc.*, 35.

[38] Suet., *loc. cit.*; *Mon. Anc.*, title.

[39] This has been repeatedly edited; the fundamental edition is that of Th. Mommsen (*Res gestae diui Augusti ex monumento Ancyrano et Apolloniensi*, ed. 2, Berlin, 1883), on the very learned and acute com-

Ancyranum (Record from Angora) by moderns; Suetonius (see note 36) gives what was probably its ancient title, *Index rerum gestarum*.[40] The style is what it should be in such a document, perfectly simple and at the same time dignified.

Maecenas (GAIVS CILNIVS MAECENAS)[41] is one of the most paradoxical figures in history. One of the three men most really powerful in the whole state, he yet never held any of the traditional posts, but remained of equestrian rank only.[42] Of untiring energy in public affairs, he made his name a synonym for idler and fop.[43] A patron of literature as judicious as he was generous, he wrote in a very odd and very bad style, and we probably are but little the poorer for the loss, save for some fragments, of all his fairly numerous works in verse and prose. The surviving fifteen or twenty lines of the former[44] show that he

mentary of which every one since then has drawn. The latest, at the time of writing, are those of Concetta Barini, *Monumentum Ancyranum: res gestae diui Augusti: testo e commento storico*, Milan, 1930/viii, and of J. Gagé, Strasbourg, publ. de la faculté des lettres, 1935. Between these and that of Mommsen fall two important editions, that of E. G. Hardy, Oxford, 1923, and of Ramsay-Premerstein, *Klio*, Beiheft xix, Leipzig, 1927. A selection from the extensive literature will be found in Barini and in Schanz-Hosius, ii, p. 17.

[40] The heading of the *Mon. Anc.* itself is quaint: rerum gestarum diui Augusti quibus orbem terrarum imperio populi Rom. subiecit, et impensarum quas in rem publicam populumque Romanum fecit, incisarum in duabus aheneis pilis quae sunt Romae positae exemplar subiectum. Clearly, the worthy magistrates of Ankyra had copied out the last clause of the covering letter from Rome, 'we send you herewith a copy of the *Res gestae*', &c. See p. 322.

[41] The best collection of information concerning Maecenas' writings is P. Lunderstedt, *De C. Maecenatis fragmentis* (Commentationes philologae Ienenses, ix, 1), Leipzig, Teubner, 1911. For select literature concerning his life and activities, see Schanz-Hosius, ii, p. 18, and the various recent histories of the period. His name seems properly to have been simply C. Maecenas (so he is called on inscriptions); the Cilnii were related to him, for Augustus (*ap.* Macrob., *sat.*, ii, 4, 12) calls him *Cilniorum smaragde*. As he was of Etruscan origin, Augustus, *ibid.*, Horace, *sat.*, i, 6, 1, it is quite possible that he claimed descent from them on his mother's side and so added their name to his own after the well-known (matrilineal ?) fashion of his nation. He died in the same year as Horace (745/8), but a little earlier; his birthday was April 13, Hor., *carm.*, iv, 11, 14–20, but the year is unknown; it was between 680/74 and 690/64.

[42] Hence Horace, *carm.*, i, 20, 5, calls him *care Maecenas eques*, and, iii, 16, 20, *Maecenas, equitum decus*; cf. Velleius Paterculus, quoted in next note.

[43] Hence Juvenal, i, 66: multum referens de Maecenate supino, 'quite like Maecenas as he lolls'; cf. the character-sketch of him in Velleius Paterculus, ii, 88, 2.

[44] Frags. 1–9, Lund. No. 3, from Isidore, *etymol.*, xix, 32, 6, is attributed to him only by a conjecture, albeit a likely one. No. 1 is the famous

composed trifles in a variety of metres; of the latter, the elder Pliny makes some use as an authority on natural history,[45] and various writers cite fragments, mostly for rare uses of words or as examples of strange Latin.[46] Augustus parodied and laughed at the 'scent-soaked curls' of his writings,[47] and Seneca bluntly called his a drunken language.[48] Some at least of his prose pieces were named *Dialogi*[49]; their individual titles, if any, and subjects are quite obscure.[50] One, however, seems to have been called *The Banquet* (*Symposium*), the speakers being Vergil, Horace, Messalla, presumably the author himself, and possibly others.[51] In addition to his writings, he invented a shorthand.[52]

Messalla (M. VALERIVS MESSALLA CORVINVS) was a better writer, and a speaker of distinction. Cicero thought well of his earliest attempts,[53] and later ages confirmed his judgement; it would appear that his Latin was very pure and choice, his style on the whole Ciceronian, but softer and more obviously artistic,

passage (in Priapeans) cited and moralized upon by Seneca, *epp.*, 101, 11: debilem facito manu, debilem pede, coxo,/tuber adstrue gibberum, lubricos quate dentes,/uita dum superest, bene est; hanc mihi uel acuto/si sedeam cruce, sustine.

[45] He mentions him in the bibliographies of Books ix, xxxii and xxxvii; see Lund., pp. 35, 41.

[46] An account of the way in which such fragments as we have have come down to us in Lund., p. 6 *sqq*.

[47] Suet., *diu. Aug.*, 86, myrobrechis (*i.e.*, μυροβρεχεῖς) cincinnos.

[48] Sen., *epp.*, 19, 9: ebrius sermo. The fragments indicate an exaggerated Asianism (cf. p. 161).

[49] Maecenas in dialogo ii, Charisius, p. 146, 30 Keil.

[50] A work of some kind, in prose, was called *Prometheus*, Seneca, *loc. cit.* That one was called *de cultu suo* is a statement repeatedly made, with no justification. The MSS. of Seneca, *epp.*, 114, 4–5, have: uidebis itaque eloquentiam ebrii hominis inuolutam et errantem et licentiae plenam. Maecenas de cultu suo. quid turpius 'amne siluisque ripa comantibus', &c. The words *Maecenas . . . suo*, rightly bracketed by Hirzel and Hense, are of course a silly marginal heading. It is further stated by many moderns that he wrote, or had thoughts of writing, a history of Augustus. The supposed proof of this is Horace, *carm.*, ii, 12, 9–11: tuque pedestribus/dices historiis proelia Caesaris, /Maecenas, melius, which proves just nothing; there is no need to take *tu* as meaning Maecenas, for it is often used, like 'you' in English, as the indefinite pronoun; so Horace himself, *carm.*, ii, 18, 17; *sat.*, ii, 3, 139; *A.P.*, 128–9. The passage may therefore mean, 'Prose, Maecenas, is a better medium for one to use in writing about Augustus' campaigns than my kind of verse'.

[51] Servius on *Aen.*, viii, 310.

[52] Cassius Dio, lv, 7, 6.

[53] Cicero, *ad Brut.*, i, 15, 1. How old Messalla was then is uncertain; the dates arrived at by modern research are approximately 690/64 for his birth, 746/8 for his death; see Schanz-Hosius, ii, p. 21 *sqq*. Cicero wrote in 711/43.

his powers of oratory inferior to those of his great model, but far from despicable; it was a nobleman's manner, according to Quintilian.[54] We have already seen (p. 264) that he tried his hand at Greek verses. He also translated Greek speeches, including Hypereides' defence of Phryne.[55] He showed an interest in philology, and composed several essays on linguistic matters, including one on the pronunciation of a final *s* in Latin.[56] There was also a 'protest', dealing with a personal matter; he set out to prove that his own very distinguished family was not related to the Laevini, a much less noble line.[57]

In this department he had the precedent of an older kinsman, M. VALERIVS MESSALLA RVFVS, sometimes referred to as 'Messalla senior' (*senex*) to distinguish him from Corvinus. Rufus composed a work *de familiis*, occasioned, according to Pliny the Elder, by his noticing that the Pomponii were wrongfully claiming kin with the Scipiones.[58]

But one of his most important works was a history, or memoirs, of the civil war arising out of the death of Caesar, in which he had taken part under Cassius.[59] The few citations of this which we have show that Messalla was entirely free from any base flattery

[54] Quint., x, 1, 113, Messalla nitidus et candidus et quodammodo praeferens in dicendo nobilitatem suam, uiribus minor (than Pollio). Seneca rhetor, *contr.*, ii, 4 (12), 8: fuit autem Messalla exactissimi ingenii quidem in omnis studiorum partes, Latini utique sermonis obseruator diligentissimus. Tacitus, *dial.*, 18: Cicerone mitior Coruinus et dulcior et in uerbis magis elaboratus. His proems, Quint., iv, 1, 8; Tac., *ibid.*, 20.

[55] Quint., x, 5, 2: cum illa Hyperidis pro Phryne difficillima Romanis subtilitate (delicate style, so difficult to reproduce in Latin) contenderet.

[56] Quint., i, 7, 35: Messalla . . . quosdam totos libellos non uerbis modo singulis sed etiam litteris dedit. *Ibid.*, 23, a Messalla in libro de s littera positum; ix, 4, 38: quae fuit causa et Seruio . . . subtrahendae s litterae quotiens ultima esset aliaque consonante susciperetur; quod . . . Messalla defendit.

[57] Pliny, *N.H.*, xxxv, 8: exstat Messallae oratoris indignatio, quae prohibuit inseri genti suae Laeuinorum alienam imaginem. This may mean that the work was entitled *Indignatio*, or may be simply Pliny's way of saying 'Messalla's indignant protest'.

[58] Pliny, *loc. cit.*: similis causa Messallae seni expressit uolumina illa quae de familiis condidit, cum Scipionis Pomponiani transisset atrium uidissetque adoptione testamentaria Saluittonis (hoc enim fuerat cognomen Africanorum dedecori) inrepentes Scipionum nomini. *I.e.*, Scipio Africanus Salvitto, a degenerate member of that great family, having adopted a Pomponius by will, as he himself was childless, the latter assumed the position of a true-born Scipio and showed the *imagines*, or wax masks, of the family of his adoption in his hall. This was the ancient equivalent of bearing arms or wearing a tartan to which one has no right, and there was no King at Arms to see to it.

[59] Fragments and *testimonia* in *H.R.F.*, pp. 266–7.

of the victors, to whom he had become reconciled, serving Octavian well in the last campaign against Antony. He spoke of Cassius as 'my general' and claimed the first battle of Philippi as a victory for the party of Brutus, which indeed it seems to have been.[60] This was in accordance with his independent and upright character, worthy of a man of such high birth and contrasting sharply with the factious opposition, alternating with servility, which disgraced many members of good families under the early Empire. It was the same spirit which moved him, on being appointed city-prefect by Augustus in 728/26, to resign the post as being unconstitutional (*inciuilis potestas*), although he accepted and filled for many years the position of curator of the aqueducts,[61] an office too obviously for the public good for any one to have scruples regarding it, while at the same time it gave little chance for its holder to advertise himself by spectacular achievements, and therefore would hardly appeal to upstarts.

Augustus' most distinguished minister, especially in war, M. VIPSANIVS AGRIPPA, was a man of action and not of letters; he wrote, however, an autobiography in several books, of which two or three citations have come down to us.[62]

Much less important politically, though his services in this respect were considerable, but much more remarkable as a writer, was GAIVS ASINIVS POLLIO, the addressee of Vergil's fourth Eclogue (p. 241), 678/76–758/5. A personal friend of Antony, and so far as possible the mediator between him and Octavian, he took no further part in public life after the failure of the treaty of Brundisium,[63] but devoted himself to literature, criticism and

[60] Frags. 4 and 2 (Tac., *ann.*, iv, 34, 6, and Plut., *Brut.*, 42, respectively). Having joined Octavian, Messalla seems to have supported him in the quarrel with Antony with his pen as well as his sword, doubtless feeling that his was at least the more nearly constitutional of the two parties. Charisius (pp. 104, 18; 129, 7; 146, 34 Keil) cites him under titles which seem to bear on this, viz., *de Antonii statuis*, *contra Antonii litteras* and *de uectigalium Asiae constitutione*. These probably were pamphlets, perhaps in the form of speeches.

[61] Tac., *ann.*, vi, 11, 4, who says that Messalla resigned quasi nescius exercendi; Jerome, *an. Abr.* 1991 (= 728/26): Messalla Coruinus primus praefectus urbi factus sexto die magistratu se abdicauit, inciuilem potestatem esse contestans. We may suspect that Tacitus gives the official reason, Jerome (*i.e.*, Suetonius) the real one. Frontinus, *de aquis*, 99, (Augustus) curatorem fecit Messallam Coruinum. This was in 743/11; his successor was appointed in 766/13, *ibid.*, 102.

[62] See *H.R.F.*, pp. 261–2. Frag. 2, from Book ii, refers to an event of 717/37; Agrippa died in 742/12, but we do not know how far down he continued his memoirs. For his services to geography, see p. 439.

[63] See p. 241. Octavian asked him to accompany him to the campaign of Actium, to which he answered (Velleius Paterculus, ii, 86, 3):

forensic oratory. Of his speeches not much is known; Horace says he was a forceful advocate for the defence [64] and that he spoke on occasion in the Senate, also that he had written a tragedy, or tragedies. He was the founder of the first public library in Rome, in the *atrium Libertatis*,[65] a hall in the temple of Liberty, which he rebuilt with the spoils of his campaign against the Parthini of Dalmatia in 715/39. He also introduced, according to the elder Seneca,[66] the custom of public or semi-public recitations of his own works. This, from his time on, became the regular method of making a new book known to a select public, a sort of literary equivalent of the artist's 'private view' in our own day. The author would issue invitations, which it was bad manners not to accept, to a larger or smaller number, assemble them in a room of his own house, if spacious enough, or in a borrowed or hired hall, and there, in his best clothes and with his best voice and manner,[67] would delight or bore them by reading his performance. It is to be remembered that all ancient works of literature were meant primarily to be heard,[68] and that reading was a somewhat more laborious business than with us, for even the clearest ancient hand can hardly have been so quickly legible as a modern typed or printed page, with our elaborate systems of punctuation and capitalizing. Hence to be read to, by the author or by a servant whose business it was to do so,[69] was one of the commonest ways of making the acquaintance of a book, and references to it are extremely numerous in both Greek

mea in Antonium maiora merita sunt, illius in me beneficia notiora; itaque discrimine uestro me subtraham et ero praeda uictoris. This tactful answer and the freedom with which he generally expressed himself do not seem to have offended Augustus.

[64] Horace, *carm.*, ii, 1, 1 *sqq.*; motum ex Metello consule ciuicum (*i.e.*, the civil wars from 694/60 onwards) . . . tractas . . . paulum seuerae Musa tragoediae/desit theatris: mox ubi publicas/res ordinaris (have given a systematic account of the affairs of State), grande munus/ Cecropio repetes cothurno,/insigne maestis praesidium reis/et consulenti, Pollio, curiae. This is perhaps our most complete account of his literary and oratorical activities.

[65] See Platner-Ashby *s.u.* For the library, see Pliny, *N.H.*, vii, 115, xxxv, 10, xxxvi, 33; Ovid, *trist.*, iii, 1, 71–2.

[66] Seneca, *contr.*, iv, *praef.*, 2: primus enim omnium Romanorum (Pollio) aduocatis hominibus scripta sua recitauit.

[67] For a brilliant satirical picture of this, see Persius, i, 15 *sqq.*

[68] Scientific and technical works may have formed an exception, since they often contained diagrams and other illustrations; also such trifles as the epigrams of Martial, who often assumes (as x, 1; xi, 1, 13; xi, 107, and a score of other passages) that his public will read his works to themselves.

[69] An *anagnostes*, see Nepos, *Att.*, 14, 1; cf. Juvenal, xi, 179–82.

and Latin. Thus it was, probably, that Pollio himself criticized Livy (see note 21); his objection was not so much, if at all, to what the historian wrote as to the accent with which he read it.

Of Pollio's poetry we can say little. Vergil speaks well of it,[70] but in very general terms; Tacitus[71] gives us to understand that its style was too old-fashioned for the taste of his day; from the younger Pliny we gather[72] that it included some erotic trifles. Much more important was his historical work. This covered the period from 694/60 to perhaps the battle of Philippi; the latest event which we definitely know that he narrated, in the only considerable fragment we have,[73] is the death of Cicero.

It is, of course, impossible to judge fully of a man's style by one short extract, not twenty lines of an ordinary Teubner text in length. But we can say that it is highly rhythmical, the Ciceronian clausulae (cf. p. 163) all appearing, although, again with allowance to be made for the shortness of the extract, the proportions seem to be different, the *licitae* being as numerous as the *uerae*. The vocabulary seems to be perfectly normal Latin of that age, with no eccentricities of syntax. This is precisely what we should expect of a man so insistent upon purity of diction and so critical of others' performances as we know him to have been.[74]

[70] Verg., *ecl.*, iii, 86.

[71] Tac., *dial.*, 21.

[72] Pliny, *epp.*, v, 3, 5. Nothing whatever is left of any poems of his, for the fragment given in *P.R.F.*, p. 337, and coaxed into a sort of scansion, is made poetical in language only by a needless emendation (Veneris antistita Cypris, for Cuprus) and in all probability is plain prose, having something to do with the taking over of Cyprus by the Roman government. Morel omits it.

[73] Preserved in Seneca rhetor, *suas.*, vi, 24. It is frag. 5 Peter.

[74] I can find no traces of archaism. When Tacitus (see note 71) and Quintilian (x, 1, 113: multa in Asinio Pollione inuentio, summa diligentia, adeo ut quibusdam etiam nimia uideatur, et consilii et animi satis: a nitore et iucunditate Ciceronis ita longe abest ut uideri possit saeculo prior) tax him with an old-fashioned style, they mean simply that he had neglected the grace and finish which Cicero had successfully cultivated and he should have attained. Elsewhere (x, 2, 17) Quintilian says: tristes ac ieiuni Pollionem aemulantur. Tacitus admits (*op. cit.*, 25) that he is *numerosior* than most, *i.e.*, more rhythmical, which we have seen is the case. Finally, the younger Seneca (*epp.*, 100, 7) says that, in contrast to Cicero's gracious uniformity, Pollio's style is salebrosa et exsiliens et ubi minime exspectes relictura, *i.e.*, jerky, inclined to flare up suddenly and then disappoint the reader by failing him at the most unexpected places. All this is carelessness or lack of ability in composition, not archaism. But it is generally agreed that he was a very respectable writer; Seneca, *ibid.*, 9, puts him between Cicero and Livy, and says (8) that the total effect was good: totum corpus, uideris quam sit comptum, honestum est. As to his rhythms, Quintilian finds (ix, 4, 76) that he rather frequently makes an accidental verse. Seneca (*ibid.*,

There is a minor puzzle in connexion with his historical work. Plutarch, after quoting a remark of Julius Caesar, adds, 'These words, Pollio Asinius says, Caesar uttered in Latin, but he has turned them into Greek.'[75] The only natural interpretation is that Plutarch believed Pollio to have written his history in Greek, and not in Latin, which certainly is not the fact. It has further been noticed that Plutarch and Appian often agree in matter and to some extent in expression when speaking of the war between Caesar and Pompey and the events subsequent to it, and that the agreement sometimes extends to common mistakes. It is therefore a reasonable conclusion that both used some Greek work which in turn had used Pollio, and that Plutarch was somehow deceived into imagining that he was reading Pollio himself.[76]

Of his speeches again we do not know much; seven titles have survived, and little besides. The rest of his work, which Horace does not mention, consisted of critical writings, whereof we can name one or two. There was an essay directed against Sallust, for his affectation of archaic words.[77] Apparently different from this was a letter, no doubt an open one, which again touched on Sallust's faults.[78] In some work or works he found much fault with Cicero,[79] and we hear of adverse criticisms which he made on various writers, but little of any praise which he bestowed upon them, though in his account of Cicero's death, already mentioned, he allows him an immortal fame in literature and directs his attacks on his character, not his writings. The fact appears to be that Pollio was a man of respectable, but not first-rate abilities as soldier, statesman and writer, and that he was possessed by a vanity as marked as Cicero's, which made it intolerable for him to occupy any less than the first place in the sphere which he had chosen for the last years of his life. So long as he was the prominent friend of Antony, the peace-maker between him and Octavian, or the recent holder of the consulship and winner of

7) says epigrammatically: denique omnia apud Ciceronem desinunt, apud Pollionem cadunt exceptis paucissimis, quae ad certum modum et ad unum exemplar adstricta sunt; but this I take to refer to monotonous or careless arrangement of words and not to the clausulae.

[75] Plut., *Caes.*, 46, 2.

[76] For an account of the various explanations, see Schanz-Hosius, ii p. 28 *sq.*

[77] Sueton., *de gramm.*, 10; Asinius Pollio in libro quo Sallustii scripta reprehendit ut nimia priscorum uerborum affectatione oblita.

[78] Gellius, x, 26, 1: Asinio Pollioni in quadam epistula quam ad Plancum scripsit, &c.

[79] Quint., xii, 1, 22: quanquam neque ipsi Ciceroni Demosthenes uideatur satis esse perfectus . . . nec Cicero Bruto Caluoque . . . nec Asinio utrique qui uitia orationis eius etiam inimice pluribus locis insecuntur. By *utrique* he means Pollio and Asinius Gallus; see next page.

a triumph which Horace tactfully assured him would be ever memorable,[80] it might be sufficient if he had no more than a fairly high place among authors; but now that he had renounced all such activities and was become a writer only, he must be a leading writer, the foremost of his day, not overshadowed by the great memory of Cicero. Therefore we find him continually carping at his brother authors, and not least at the greatest of them,[81] and those who had excelled or were excelling in his own chosen fields of oratory and history.

His son, ASINIVS GALLVS, seems to have inherited alike his tastes and something of his self-conceit. Of the latter it is surely proof enough that he claimed to be the wonder-child of the Fourth Eclogue (see chap. ix, n. 27). Of the former, the chief indication is that he published a book comparing his father favourably to Cicero.[82] There is also a stupid little epigram by him.[83] He was consul in 761/8 and, being impeached under Tiberius, came to his end in 786/33.[84]

Besides Livy, there is one other Augustan historian of whose work we are able to form something like an adequate conception, although we have lost his writings and are dependent on an epitome. This is POMPEIVS TROGVS, whose second name is Gaulish,[85] while his *nomen* (his *praenomen* is unknown) is due to the fact that his grandfather was given citizenship by Pompey, apparently in return for good services in the war against Sertorius. His father served under Caesar as a kind of confidential secretary. We know nothing of his life, beyond the facts that he plainly was well acquainted with Greek and wrote something on natural history, including a work *de animalibus* extending to

[80] Cui laurus aeternos honores/Delmatico peperit triumpho, Hor., *carm.*, ii, 1, 15–16.

[81] For Cicero, see notes 73, 79; Livy, n. 21; Sallust, n. 77. That he found fault with Catullus, who had been polite to him in his youth (Cat., 12, 8), appears from Charisius, p. 97, 11 Keil. A collection of his attacks on minor speakers will be found in the index to Kiessling's Teubner edition of Seneca Rhetor, *s.u. Asinius Pollio.*

[82] Pliny, *epp.*, vii, 4, 3 and 6; Gellius, xvii, 1, 1.

[83] Preserved in Suet., *de gramm.*, 22.

[84] Tac., *ann.*, vi, 23, 1; Cassius Dio, lviii, 3, 1–7.

[85] See Justin, xliii, 5, 11: in postremo libro Trogus ait maiores suos originem a Vocontiis (a people of Gallia Narbonensis) ducere; auum suum Trogum Pompeium Sertoriano bello ciuitatem a Cn. Pompeio percepisse, patrem Mithridatico bello turmas equitum sub eodem Pompeio duxisse; patrem quoque sub C. Caesare militasse epistularumque ac legationum, simul et anuli curam habuisse. The actual name Trogus has not been found in the region named, but Trogius, which is clearly a derivative from it, is known to exist.

at least ten books.[86] For some reason, conceivably because he knew of Livy's work and thought that a companion history on a comparable scale, dealing with the peoples outside Italy, would be acceptable, he set himself to produce the *Historiae Philippicae*, which told in forty-four books the tale of the rest of the world, so far as it was accessible in Greek authors, for Trogus seems to have used no others,[87] from the days of Ninus king of Assyria to the absorption of the other nations, save the Parthians, into the Roman empire and the establishment of peace under Augustus. The title is Greek, first used by Theopompos and after him by Anaximenes of Lampsakos [88] for histories of Philip II of Macedon, and it is not inappropriate, for Trogus began with Book VII the account of Philip's rise to power, and the repercussions of that great event can hardly be said to cease until he reaches the Parthian empire, traced, in xli, 4, 1, to its beginnings *post mortem Alexandri Magni*. The early history of Italy is touched upon with curious brevity, ' so as not to outrun the limits of the task he has set before himself nor to pass over in silence the genesis of the city which is the queen of all the world ',[89] in the last book.

As Trogus was apparently a diligent excerptor of other men's works, not without intelligence in his arrangement of good second-hand materials, and a very passable stylist with some original views on how to write a history,[90] it is a great pity that his work is lost except for some fragments and that we have to depend on the epitome of it by an unknown M. IVNIANVS IVSTINVS, commonly called JUSTIN, of quite uncertain date. Even in this diminished condition, the history is interesting reading, often containing facts not to be met with elsewhere, and one of our

[86] Trogum de animalibus libro X, Charisius, p. 137, 9 Keil. Pliny, *N.H.*, xvii, 58, reproves him for believing that palms can be propagated from palm-leaves ; he must therefore have written something about trees.

[87] It is a very extraordinary thing that next to no use was made, save by Jews and, later, by Christians, of so interesting a collection of works as the historical books of the Old Testament, by this time rendered into the odd but intelligible Greek of the so-called Septuagint. Though meant primarily for Jews who did not understand Hebrew, it does not appear to have been kept in any way secret, especially as at this time proselytizing was going on vigorously.

[88] See Rose, *H.G.L.*, p. 310. Precisely what authors Trogus followed is uncertain ; see Schanz-Hosius, ii, pp. 323–4.

[89] Justin, xliii, 1, 2 : breuiter igitur initia Romani imperii perstringit, ut nec modum propositi operis excedat nec utique originem urbis quae est caput totius orbis silentio praetermittat.

[90] He disliked speeches, save in *oratio obliqua*, in a history : xxxviii, 3, 11 : in Liuio et in Sallustio reprehendit quod contiones directas prosa (*pro sua*, the MSS. ; he means that such things are all very well in epics) oratione operi suo inserendo historiae modum excesserint.

much too scanty sources for the history of the eastern Mediterranean and the adjacent countries after the time when mainland Greece ceases to be politically important, the so-called Hellenistic period.

Livy and Trogus, or rather Justin, practically make up the historiography of this period for us ; but there were other writers in that field, whose works we have lost completely save for some few references and fragments. The most important seems to have been FENESTELLA, also perhaps the latest in date, or at all events the longest lived, for he died under Tiberius, in 773/20.[91] His life is so completely unknown that we cannot even say what his full name was or to what class he belonged. Of the poems which St. Jerome says he wrote not a word has survived ; of his *annales* we have fairly numerous fragments (*H.R.F.*, pp. 272–8), all interesting. He is seldom or never cited for information about important political events, but regularly for laws, customs, the date at which this or that luxury was introduced, now and then for an anecdote of some well-known person. It would seem therefore that he wrote a kind of history of Roman civilization, interspersed with interesting stories and referring to public events just sufficiently to give the necessary chronological framework. As he was clearly a learned, well-informed and fairly accurate writer, the loss of his work, and even of the epitome which Diomedes the grammarian used, is much to be regretted.[92] Of other historians we know that they existed and wrote, but not always what they wrote. Q. DELLIVS had some reputation as a wit, and Horace addressed one of his finest odes to him ; he also was called by Messalla Corvinus *desultor bellorum ciuilium* (a *desultor* was an equestrian acrobat who could leap at full gallop from the back of one horse to another) because he successively deserted Dolabella for Cassius, Cassius for Antony and Antony for Octavian. He wrote, besides some *epistulae lasciuae* to Kleopatra, a history of Antony's operations in Parthia, of which he was qualified to speak, having served there under him.[93] Suetonius mentions four writers as his authorities for matters concerning Augustus, IVLIVS MARATHVS, who was the emperor's secretary, C. DRVSVS, of whom nothing further is known, IVLIVS SATVRNINVS and AQVILIVS NIGER.[94] Servius adds the name of a fifth, BAEBIVS MACER, who seems to have written on the principate of Augustus,[95] while another writer is a shade better known.

[91] Jerome, *an. Abr.* 2036 (= 773/20) ; Fenestella historiarum scriptor et carminum septuagenarius moritur sepeliturque Cumis. He was born, therefore, in 703/51 or the following year.

[92] Diomedes, p. 365, 7 Keil : apud Fenestellam . . . in libro epitomarum secundo. That Fenestella was not always perfectly accurate appears from Pliny, who, *N.H.*, ix, 123, finds a *manifestus error* in him, which he corrects out of Aelius Stilo (see p. 442).

[93] Horace, *carm.*, ii, 3, 4 ; Seneca rhetor, *suas.*, i, 7 ; fragments (two only, neither verbatim) in *H.R.F.*, p. 250 *sq.*

[94] Suet., *diu. Aug.*, 11, 27, 79, 94.

[95] Servius auctus on Verg., *ecl.*, ix, 44 ; Servius on *Aen.*, v, 556.

We hear of C. CLODIVS LICINUS as *consul suffectus* in 757/4, and as the friend of Hyginus the librarian (see p. 446); Livy and Nonius quote from his *res Romanae*, the former for an event of 560/194, from which it appears that he wrote a history of the Republic, or at least one which covered some part of that period; Livy's citation is from his third book, those in Nonius from the twelfth and twenty-first. Possibly he may have begun with the beginning of the second Punic War.[96]

It remains to speak of a very remarkable feature, to moderns at least, of both Augustan and subsequent literature, the prevalence of rhetorical exercises. It has already been more than once pointed out that to make the rustic Latin speech into a literary language a modicum of artistic, even artificial handling, in other words of rhetoric, was necessary; and it has been suggested that the study of rhetoric for its own sake was a not unlikely consequence of the disappearance of popular government and the resultant lessening of the practical value of oratory. But even these considerations hardly explain the craze for artificially ornate speaking on unreal themes which henceforth possessed Rome.

[96] Livy, xxix, 22, 10; Nonius, 221, 13; 535, 20. Cf. Suet., *de gramm.*, 20. We also know of the existence of three or four more historians. The younger Seneca (*epp.*, 114, 17) speaks of L. ARRVNTIVS, who was *uir rarae frugalitatis*, and wrote a history of the Punic War, apparently the first, in a very ridiculous style, a bad imitation of Sallust. Velleius (ii, 86, 2) has something to say of the *prisca grauitas* and the *fides* of a L. Arruntius, probably the one who was consul in 732/22. Pliny cites an Arruntius as an authority for his Natural History (bibliographies to Books iii, v, vi; as these deal with geography, it is not at all unlikely that the work in question was historical, since that would naturally contain some mention of topography also). It seems likely that all three authors mean the same man. The Vergilian *catalepton*, 11 (p. 263), mourns the loss to *Romana historia* of the Octavius whom it celebrates; he is usually identified with the OCTAVIVS MVSA who was a magistrate at Mantua in Vergil's time (schol. Bern., on Verg., *ecl.*, viii, 6, and Serv. auctus on *ecl.*, ix, 7), and he may be the M. Octavius who is mentioned as an authority in the anonymous *origo gentis Romanae*, 12, 2. Horace, *sat.*, 1, 10, 86, mentions a certain Furnius among his literary friends. This may be the younger of the two Furnii, father and son, who are mentioned as famous orators by Jerome, *an. Abr.* 1980 (= 717/37); the so-called Acro on Horace, *loc. cit.*, says he was a historian, and we have no reason to doubt either of them. His full name was LVCIVS FVRNIVS. But we may doubt the existence of OCTAVIVS RVSO. Horace, *sat.*, i, 3, 86 *sqq.*, speaks of some one called Ruso whom his debtor must satisfy or else *amaras porrecto iugulo historias captiuus ut audit*, which need mean no more than that he will be treated to a long sermon on commercial obligations; but the scholiast known as Porphyrio says there was a money-lender called Octavius Ruso who used to get an audience for certain histories he had written by summoning his debtors to his recitations. This tale sounds very like an invention, helped out perhaps by a reminiscence of Octavius Musa.

One of the most curious circumstances is that it grew out of perfectly practical and reasonable methods of teaching boys and young men to feel confident and express themselves coherently and effectively before an audience. There are two principal reasons for speaking in public, other than a simple desire to instruct or amuse: one is to recommend some course of action, such as the passing of a proposed law, to a legislative or other deliberative body; the other is to persuade a jury in a court of law. Given a southern European audience, it would be advisable in either case, even more than if dealing with northerners, to try to gain support by an appeal to strong emotions, such as hate or pity, especially in a judicial oration. It was therefore very natural and reasonable that teachers of rhetoric, besides giving rules and exercises for epideictic speeches, *i.e.*, such things as funeral orations, addresses of welcome or praise to some distinguished person and the like, together with eloquent and effective discussions of commonplaces or expositions of philosophic themes, should practise their students in imaginary cases or imaginary deliberations. It was equally reasonable that they should look for themes belonging to one of two classes, either those in which the probabilities or the reasons for and against a proposed course of conduct were nicely balanced, or else those which at first sight appeared totally one-sided, for there a promising pupil might gain an aptitude for making the best of a very bad case which would stand him in good stead as an advocate or a politician. It followed from this that a favourite rhetorical exercise of the kind called in Latin *suasoriae* was to bid the student imagine himself present at some notable event in history or legend, and called upon to give advice to one of the chief actors. Thus, he is to suppose he is one of Hannibal's officers the day after Cannae; Hannibal asks him whether he should at once advance on Rome or go elsewhere. Or, to take a judicial instance from the oldest known rhetorical exercises, the *Tetralogies* attributed to Antiphon the orator,[97] A has accidentally killed B; should the court follow the ancient rule which demands a life for a life, or the modern one which takes *animus* into account and allows for mitigating circumstances? Such cases as this might actually come before a court at certain times and places, while another of Antiphon's puzzles might even now confront, perhaps not a court of law, but a police force. A has been found dead, with B, his personal attendant, dying beside him; B lives long enough to accuse C, known to be A's enemy, of the murder; is C guilty? But as time went on, the *controuersiae*, as the Latin

[97] See Rose, *H.G.L.*, p. 280.

rhetoricians called them, tended to become more and more fantastic and unlike anything which any court on earth would ever have to hear. The most absurd laws are assumed, and the most unlikely situations arising out of them are the subjects of the debates. Thus: a husband may lawfully kill his wife's lover, provided he kills her also. Ingratitude is an actionable offence. Thus far, we have a kind of parody of Attic law.[98] But the case to be debated is the wildest romance. Kimon, son of Miltiades, has undertaken the obligations of his dead father to the state.[99] Kallias secures his release by paying the money owed to the treasury and marries his daughter to him. She plays Kimon false, and he exercises his right to kill her, despite her father's plea for mercy. Kallias sues Kimon for ingratitude. Again: a thief may not address the assembly.[100] A certain man has accused another of treason, and has proved his case by stealing from the defendant's house papers which show him to be in correspondence with the enemy. Later, he wishes to address the assembly, but is forbidden to do so by a magistrate. He now accuses him of *iniuriae*, conduct unlawfully prejudicial to himself.[101] Even if a more or less real situation is supposed, as in a *suasoria* whose theme is a debate among the Three Hundred whether they should remain at their posts at Thermopylai or not, the language and sentiments tended to be the most extravagant possible.[102]

There were still practical orators who looked upon this sort of thing as a useful exercise; we may suspect that it was not they who were guilty of the wilder language and more absurd suppositions (for the speaker had abundant licence to invent subsidiary facts) of which we hear. Doubtless also a man like Livy could derive from such artificialities a facility and a mastery of telling phrase which his unusual abilities could transmute into the splendidly effective speeches of his historical characters. But the extraordinary thing is the number of people who seem to have practised these declamations, as they were called,[103] for

[98] By Attic and indeed most ancient law the husband might do as he pleased with the man if he caught him in the act.

[99] The relations of Kimon and Kallias are real, save that Kallias is made a man of low birth, instead of the noble he actually was; the rest of the story is pure invention.

[100] Such a prohibition was actually imposed in most states upon certain persons guilty of disgraceful conduct of various kinds.

[101] These two examples are the first of Seneca's ninth book and the last of his tenth respectively.

[102] The second of Seneca's *suasoriae*.

[103] *Declamare*, to declaim, practise rhetoric, properly to shout; *declamator*, one who practises in this manner; *declamatio*, the exercise itself.

their own sake, and to have attained no other repute than as purveyors of such sham arguments and appeals to phantom emotions.

We are well informed concerning the rhetorical schools in the time of Augustus by the survival in considerable part of a most curious book of literary reminiscences. LVCIVS ANNAEVS SENECA the elder, generally called Seneca Rhetor to distinguish him from his better-known son and namesake, Seneca the Younger or Seneca Philosophus, was born probably about 699/55 [104] at Corduba, the modern Cordova, in Spain,[105] came to Rome at some unknown date, but apparently early in life, and there studied rhetoric zealously, though he had too much natural good taste and too much admiration for Cicero to approve all the extravagances of his contemporaries in the schools. It does not appear that he had any ambitions other than literary; philosophy he disliked [106] his manner of life was old-fashionedly honest and strict,[107] he held no public post. Of his formal published works next to nothing remains; they comprised certainly a history of Rome from the infancy of the state,[108] possibly a treatise on some matters connected with judicial eloquence.[109] But in his old age, to please his sons, he put together from memory [110] his recollections of the rhetoricians he had known, adding here and there, especially in the prefaces to the books into which his work was

[104] He says, *contr.*, i, *praef.*, 11, that so far as age goes he might have been with Cicero in illo atriolo in quo duos grandes praetextatos ait secum declamare. This is a joke of Cicero's, preserved in Suet., *de gram.*, 1; he meant the consuls Hirtius and Pansa, who were *praetextati* in the sense of being magistrates. Boys also wore the *praetexta*, or purple-edged toga, and so Seneca means that his boyhood coincided with Cicero's old age; *i.e.*, he was already old enough to study rhetoric, a subject which was begun about the twelfth year, in 711/43. When he died is not exactly known, but he survived Tiberius, for Suetonius quotes his account of the emperor's death, *Tib.*, 73, was not alive when his son was banished, and so must have died between 790/37 and 794/41.

[105] Martial, *epigr.*, i, 61, 7–8: duosque Senecas unicumque Lucanum/ facunda loquitur Corduba (in a list of birthplaces of literary men).

[106] Seneca phil., *epp.*, 108, 22: patre meo . . . qui . . . philosophiam oderat.

[107] *Idem, ad Heluiam matrem*, 17, 3: patris mei antiquus rigor.

[108] This is his own metaphor: frag. 1 (in Lactantius, *diu. inst.*, vii, 15, 14) divides the history of Rome into infancy (Romulus), childhood (Numa-Servius), adolescence (Tarquinius Superbus-end of Punic wars), adult vigour (to end of conquests), old age (from beginning of civil wars), decrepitude (Empire). Florus afterwards borrowed the figure, cf. p. 512.

[109] Quintilian quotes him, ix, 2, 98, on the propriety of oaths; but even assuming that this is not the younger Seneca, he may be citing some lost part of the *controuersiae*.

[110] *Contr.*, i, *praef.*, 2 sq.

divided, a number of good stories, mostly literary, about persons more or less well known whom he had met or heard of. Originally there were ten books of *controuersiae*, one of *suasoriae* [111]; the latter is preserved save for the loss of an unknown amount at the beginning, the former are represented by Books I, II, VII, IX and X and an epitome of the whole, by some unknown hand. It is amusing reading, partly because of the many well-told anecdotes, partly for the shrewd criticisms the author makes from time to time, and not least for the unconsciously funny phrases which the *declamatores* he quotes continually use. Yet mixed with their absurdities are abundant examples of cleverness, even of real oratorical ability, such as one regrets to see used in so futile a sphere. Seneca purports to record their *sententiae*, or epigrammatic and pithy turns of phrase, their *diuisiones*, or headings under which they handled their themes (the 'firstly, secondly, thirdly' and so forth of the old-fashioned sermon is in the direct line of descent from the classical rhetoricians) and their *colores*, the light in which they represented the alleged facts.[112] The second of these is a necessity for any orderly presentation of material in speech or writing; the first haunts Latin oratory and poetry from that time on, till it becomes utterly wearisome [113]; the third, used judiciously, is of course the foundation of all good advocacy, but some of these speakers misuse it and merely make themselves ridiculous instead of putting a favourable construction on the matter with which they deal and so forwarding their cases.

To these rhetorical exercises and the taste for over-spiced speaking and writing which they inevitably produced is due, far more than to the attitude of Pollio, the formation of what might be described as an anti-Ciceronian style. Cicero had been content to set forth his contentions clearly and with dignity and elegance; he was proving a case, not seeking applause every other minute. Hence critics of the Silver Age found him dull,

[111] That the *suasoriae* were written last is clear from *contr.*, ii, 4, 8: cum ad suasorias uenero. They are commonly printed first in our editions.

[112] Perhaps the best explanation of the meaning of *color* is given implicitly by Juvenal, vi, 279. A woman is caught in adultery, and he invites the best of rhetoricians to invent some favourable construction to put on her conduct: dic,/dic aliquem sodes hic, Quintiliane, colorem

[113] A somewhat exaggerated example, rightly criticized by Fronto (*ad M. Antoninum*, p. 157 Naber), is Lucan, *Phars.*, i, 1–7; I italicize the *sententiae*: *Bella* per Emathios *plus quam ciuilia* campos/*iusque datum sceleri* canimus, populumque potentem/*in sua uictrici conuersum uiscera dextra,/cognatasque acies* et rupto foedere regni/certatum totis concussi uiribus orbis/*in commune nefas*, infestisque *obuia signis/signa, pares aquilas et pila minantia pilis*.

containing few attempts at bright and exciting or amusing phrases and those but poor.[114] What kind of diction found favour with their audiences we may see most easily if we take a short example from Seneca's memoirs. The situation is supposed to be, Alexander the Great, having come in his conquests to the Ocean, debates whether he shall cross it to find new lands to subdue.[115] Albucius Silus addresses him in the following mixture of philosophy and epigram:

'The earth also has her bounds; the very stars of heaven have their setting; nothing is infinite. Since fortune has set no limit to your greatness, you must set one. Moderation in success belongs to a great soul. Fortune has set the same limit to your conquests as to the earth; the frontier of your rule is the Ocean. How far has your greatness exceeded nature's self! The world counts Alexander great, Alexander finds the world narrow. There is some limit even to greatness; the sky does not pass outside its appointed course, the sea rages within its confines. Whatever has reached its perfection has no room left for further growth. As we know nothing beyond the Ocean, so we know nothing beyond Alexander.'

As we read this, we can almost see the orator pausing to give his audience time to clap or cheer, as no doubt it did, for such utterances, by famous practitioners of the art, were commonly given before large crowds; it was somewhat unusual conduct on the part of Pollio [116] that he would not declaim in public. But also we are not surprised to learn that a practical and busy jury with a real case to try would not hesitate to stop such eloquence and request the advocate to get to the point.[117]

Thanks to Seneca, we know the names of a number of the *declamatores*, famous in their own time though now forgotten; the specimens of their work which he gives do not make us greatly regret the loss of the rest. One of them, TITVS LABIENVS (possibly the son of Caesar's officer, afterwards his enemy in the Civil War), was a totally unreconciled republican, who passed his life in poverty and great unpopularity, but admired for his eloquence as much as he was detested for his bitter tongue. He wrote a history, part of which even he dared not read in public, but said it should be read after his death. This hope was

[114] Tac., *dial.*, 23.

[115] Seneca, *suas.*, 1, 3.

[116] Sen., *contr.*, iv, *praef.*, 2. Labienus also refused to do so, as he considered it a piece of newfangled vanity, *ibid.*, x, *praef.*, 4.

[117] Tac., *dial.*, 19: saepe ultro admonent atque alio transgredientem reuocant et festinare se testantur. Even they, however, liked plenty of modernism, *ibid.*, 29: praecurrit hoc tempore iudex dicentem, et nisi aut cursu argumentorum aut colore sententiarum aut nitore et cultu descriptionum inuitatus et correptus est, auersatur.

frustrated, for his works were burned by order of the government. He refused to survive this, and had himself taken to his family vault, thus, says Seneca, not only killing but burying himself.[118] CASSIVS SEVERVS was a kindred spirit to Labienus. He was rather an orator than a declaimer, and by no means at his best in these artificial exercises. Indeed, in conversation with Seneca, he expressed a good deal of contempt for them. In or about 760/7 his bitter tongue and pen led to his banishment to Crete, in which country he died, miserably poor, twenty-five years later. While in Rome, he had distinguished himself in the courts, especially when he was himself sued; he was diligent in the preparation of his speeches, but always at his best when interrupted or forced for any reason to improvise.[119] Both these men had in them much of the older school of oratory, mixed with the new; MARCVS PORCIVS LATRO, a fellow-countryman of Seneca and a teacher of rhetoric of enormous popularity and equally enormous, if erratic, capacity for work, was a declaimer pure and simple. He killed himself in 750/4, being wearied with an incurable ague.[120] Another suicide, who began as an orator and continued as a declaimer with a school of his own, was C. ALBVCIVS SILVS, an Italian from Novaria.[121] ARELLIVS FVSCVS was a bilingual Asianic Greek, in nationality as in style; his chief claim to be remembered is perhaps that he taught Ovid rhetoric.[122] QVINTVS HATERIVS was a senator and accustomed to serious debate; but he excelled also in declamations, showing such fluency that Augustus was of opinion that he needed a brake. He died, nearly ninety years old, in 779/26.[123] LVCIVS CESTIVS PIVS was celebrated not least for his prodigiously good opinion of himself. He specialized in writing answers to Cicero's best-known speeches, and could not be persuaded or frightened by Cassius Severus into swearing that Cicero

[118] Sen., *contr.*, x, *praef.*, 4 *sqq.*

[119] Sen., *contr.*, iii, *praef.*, 1 sqq.; Jerome, *an. Abr.* 2048 (= 785/32): Cassius Seuerus orator egregius . . . xxv exilii sui anno in summa inopia moritur uix panno uerenda contectus; Tac., *ann.*, iv, 21, 5, cf. i, 72, 4, and Sen., *op. cit.*, x, *praef.*, 8; Tac., *dial.*, 19.

[120] He was a Spaniard, Sen., *contr.*, i, *praef.*, 16, cf. the whole passage for his habits and abilities. ii, 4, 8, Messalla said of him: sua lingua disertus est, *i.e.*, he spoke with a very strong provincial accent and had mannerisms, perhaps a choice of words also, which were not of the capital. His death, Jerome, *an. Abr.* 2013 (= 750/4): M. Porcius Latro Latinus declamator taedio duplicis quaternae semet interficit.

[121] Sen., *op. cit.*, vii, *praef.*, 1 *sqq.*; Suet., *de rhet.*, 6. Both authors give amusing anecdotes of his unfortunate attempts to introduce the methods of the lecture-room into actual trials.

[122] Sen., *contr.*, ii, *praef.*, 1 *sqq.*; ix, 6, 16, where for the *ex Asia* of the MSS. Schultingh and Kiessling unnecessarily read *ex Asianis* (of the Asianic school); ii, 2, 8 (Ovid Arellius' pupil). He had a son of the same name and it is not always certain which is referred to.

[123] Sen., *contr.*, iv, *praef.*, 6 *sqq.*; Tac., *ann.*, iv, 61, 1; Jerome, *an. Abr.* 2040 (= 767/14, 12 years too early): Q. Haterius promptus et popularis orator usque ad xc prope annum in summo honore consenescit.

was more eloquent than himself.[124] Of Asinius Pollio we have already spoken; Seneca mentions the names of over a score of others, most of whom would, but for him, be totally forgotten; one of them, CORNELIVS SEVERVS, we shall have occasion later (p. 343) to mention as a poet.[125]

In conclusion, it should be noted that we have from this epoch two specimens of eloquence which are not wholly of the schools and whereof one at least has the force which comes from its author's sincerity. These are two funeral orations (*laudationes*), evidently delivered, according to Roman custom, during the interment and then set up, presumably over or near the graves of the ladies concerned, as a permanent record of their virtues. The former of these, which is very largely preserved to us,[126] is conventionally known as the *Laudatio Turiae*, although, as we shall see, that title is doubtful. But that it commemorates a noble woman there is not the least doubt. Her husband, who delivers the speech, was a good enough orator to avoid rhetorical flourishes and let the facts speak for themselves. His wife had begun by defeating certain plots of her relatives which would have resulted in financial loss to her husband and herself; not long afterwards, she had to face a greater crisis, for her husband was among those proscribed by the triumvirs. Brutally repulsed by Lepidus, she in the end gained his pardon and recall from Octavian, and in the meanwhile found means to secure not only his safety but his comfort by secretly sending him supplies of money and other necessaries. After this, she and he had lived together happily, except that they had no children. She had thereupon offered to be divorced, promising to help him choose a new wife and to take a benevolent interest in any children he might have, at the same time reclaiming none of her dowry from him. Her husband rejected this proposal with horror, and their long union was brought to a close only by her death.

The names of the husband and wife are not preserved on the mutilated inscription. Mommsen in 1863 [127] suggested that he

[124] This is put together from several passages of Seneca, see Kiessling's index *s.u.*

[125] Sen., *suas*, 6, 25–7. It may be mentioned that L. IVNIVS GALLIO, adopted father of Seneca's son M. Annaeus Novatus, henceforth known as L. Annaeus Iunius Gallio, the 'Gallio' of the Book of Acts, was one of this group of rhetoricians and also wrote on rhetoric (Quint., iii, 1, 21).

[126] The inscription is *C.I.L.*, vi, 1527, 31670; Dessau, *Inscr. Lat. Sel.*, 8393, cf. addenda, p. cxc.

[127] Mommsen in *Abhand. d. berlin. Akad.*, 1863, p. 455 *sqq.*, republished in his *Juristische Schriften*, vol. i, p. 395 *sqq.* The story of Vespilio and his wife is told in Valerius Maximus, vi, 7, 2; Appian, *bell. ciu.*, iv,

was Q. Lucretius Vespilio, who was proscribed by the triumvirs and saved by his wife Turia. But the text of the *laudatio*, fuller now than the one which lay before Mommsen, states distinctly that the husband fled,[128] whereas Vespilio was hidden by Turia in their house.

The other inscription is much shorter (thirteen long lines of text) and, although it has suffered the loss of a considerable amount at the beginning, presents no difficulties. A son recounts the virtues, amiable but not extraordinary, of his mother Murdia. We know nothing of him or her, and can only say that the Latin seems to be Augustan in style, spelling and grammar.[129]

44. He was consul in 735/19, which would fit the date of the inscription well enough, for its author was married forty-one years, his wife saved him in 711/43, therefore its latest possible date is 752/2, and it is probably earlier.

[128] A fragment has been found since Mommsen wrote. It begins (2, 1) (*subsi*)dia fugae meae. W. Warde Fowler, however (*Roman Essays*, Clar. Press, 1920, pp. 126–38), suggests that this refers to an earlier event.

[129] Published most conveniently in *C.I.L.*, vi, 10230; Dessau, 8394. For it and the other *laudatio*, see Schanz-Hosius, ii, pp. 337–8.

Additional Note.—P. 304, n. 40. For the styl, see Annemarie Lauton in *Wiener Studien* lxiv (1949), pp. 107–23.

CHAPTER XI

OVID AND AFTERWARDS

WE have seen (p. 318) that in Augustus' days the style of prose moved away from Cicero. While Vergil was still a young man there was born a poet who, without the least hostility to him, led his art away from the manner and technique of the *Aeneid* and its companion works. PVBLIVS OVIDIVS NASO, usually called in English simply OVID, was born in Sulmo, a town of the Paeligni, ninety Roman miles from Rome, on March 20, 711/43.[1] His father, who was of the equestrian order, meant him to enter the service of the state, and so, after an elaborate education which included a visit to Athens, perhaps also to the near East, he settled in Rome and began a political career. But after holding some minor office, perhaps that of a *triumuir capitalis*,[2] he abandoned all thoughts of going further and devoted himself to literary activities, for which he had a natural ability, having possessed from childhood an extraordinary knack of writing smooth verse.[3] His earliest works, erotic elegies of a kind made popular by Tibullus and Propertius (pp. 285, 289), but written in a manner wholly his own, quickly won favour, and he became known, not only as an admirer of the older poets, most of whom he knew personally

[1] Ovid, *trist.*, x, 4, is the chief authority for his life, being an autobiography in verse. Birthplace, 3; year of birth, 6 (cum cecidit fato consul uterque pari, *i.e.*, the year of Mutina; the line is borrowed from Lygdamus, 5, 18, cf. chap. ix, n. 166); day, 13–14: haec est armiferae festis de quinque Mineruae/quae fieri pugna prima cruenta solet, *i.e.*, the second day of the Quinquatrus, Mar. 20, cf. Wissowa, *R.K.R.*[2], p. 253; Ovid, *fast.*, iii, 813.

[2] Ovid, *trist.*, iv, 16–36. He says (34): eque uiris quondam pars tribus una fui. The most likely board of this kind for him to have served on, of the minor magistracies known collectively as the vigintivirate, was the *iiiuiri capitales*, a sort of police magistrates. Athens, *trist.*, i, 2, 77.

[3] Ovid, *trist.*, iv, 25–6: sponte sua carmen numeros ueniebat ad aptos/et quod temptabam dicere (compose in prose, compose as a speech; the reading is somewhat uncertain, see the critical eds.), uersus erat. This is the origin of Pope's equally famous line ' I lisped in numbers, for the numbers came ', *Ep. to Arbuthnot*, 128.

save Tibullus and Vergil,[4] but as a leading poet himself. While always maintaining a decorous loyalty of language and sentiment, he was not a propagandist, but a man of letters pure and simple; and, having apparently sufficient means of his own, he never took either Maecenas or Messalla as his patron. He continued to produce amatory poems for a score or so of years, and then turned his attention to something on a larger scale, a quasi-epic. His was not a genius suited to long flights of the type of the *Aeneid*; he was a thorough Alexandrian in that respect, as in his learning and his high polish. But of ingenuity he had enough and to spare, and there never was a more finished metrician or a more excellent teller of stories. He therefore, following Alexandrian precedent,[5] collected a great number (some 250) of legends concerning the supernatural change of some one or some thing into a different form (Aktaion into a stag, Keyx and Alkyone into birds, and so forth) and fitted them into an ingenious framework which gave a sort of unity to the whole. Beginning with the greatest of all changes, that from chaos to the ordered universe, he continued in a series of narratives approximately chronological in their arrangement down to historical times, ending with the latest transformation, that of Julius Caesar into a god. In this way he, like Kallimachos in his *Aitia*, combined the ideal of neat and learned brevity (for no one story is told at any great length) with the opposed principle of writing a considerable work, since the entire poem, the *Metamorphoses*, extends to fifteen books.[6] The legends are introduced in the most unexpected ways, often in the form of a story within a story; thus, the daughters of Minyas, before their transformation into bats by the power of Dionysos, are impiously spinning and weaving instead of celebrating his rites, and beguile their labour by telling each other tales,[7] all turning on a wonderful transformation of some kind. But, as he was finishing this work and had it nearly ready for publication, the disaster of his life befell him. Hitherto he had lived quietly in Rome, popular, respected for his talent, happily married after two unsuccessful ventures,[8] and now a grandfather by his daughter's two marriages.[9] Then, in or about his fiftieth year,[10] he was

[4] Ovid, *ibid.*, 41–52.

[5] For instance, that of Nikandros, cf. Rose, *H.G.L.*, p. 329.

[6] For Kallimachos' *Aitia*, see Rose, *op. cit.*, p. 320.

[7] Ovid, *Met.*, iv, 32 *sqq.* [8] *Trist.*, iv, 10, 69–74. [9] *Ibid.*, 75–6.

[10] *Ibid.*, 95–6, he says he was ten Olympiads old when he was banished. He has clearly taken the Olympic *pentaeteris* as a period of five years, instead of the four which it really is (each celebration is in the fifth year, not five years, after the next), and therefore means that he was fifty years

suddenly relegated to Tomis,[11] on the extreme and half-savage north-eastern frontier of the Empire, probably the modern Constanza. He burned his unrevised *Metamorphoses* and other papers, including perhaps poems; fortunately the epic had already got about in copies among his acquaintances, and so was given to the world lacking only the final touches of its author.[12] To this day the cause of his banishment is unknown, but it may be guessed at with some probability. He himself says it was due to an *error*,[13] in other words to a mistaken or imprudent action of his. Elsewhere he laments [14] that he had seen what he ought not and complains [15] of the wickedness (treachery?) of certain slaves. The ostensible cause was the immorality of his masterpiece, the *ars amatoria*, a reason utterly and ridiculously inadequate, as Ovid himself [16] demonstrates at needless length. This alone is enough to prove that the real reason was something which might not be made known, and this consideration excludes all possibility of a treasonable plot, for instance, against Augustus' person; this would have been made known, punished otherwise than with relegation, and its discovery celebrated with public thanksgivings. Besides, nothing in Ovid's character or writings indicates the slightest interest in politics or discontent with the existing government. There remains something which closely affected the Emperor's private life, and here we have no difficulty in suggesting what it was. The licentiousness of his granddaughter Iulia was perhaps his bitterest grief, especially as it was the worst of hindrances to his honest attempts to reform public morals.[17] That Ovid had

old, for he certainly was not banished till well after 751/3. The date, then, was in or not long after 761/8. Again, *ex Pont.*, iv, 6, 5, he says he has been in exile five years and is beginning on the next five; he also mentions, *ibid.*, 16, the death of Augustus. Of this he could hardly have heard before the autumn of 767/14, for it took place on August 19 of that year. This would make his stay in Tomis begin in the autumn or summer of 762/9. His journey thither was in winter, *trist.*, 1, 4, 1, and he was in Ilva (Elba) when he heard the news, *ex Pont.*, ii, 3, 83–4. This makes the early autumn or late summer of 761/8 the probable time when the decree was issued.

[11] Relegation was the mildest form of banishment, for it consisted simply of an order to live henceforth in some named place outside Italy, and involved no loss of status or confiscation of goods. See p. 533.

[12] *Trist.*, i, 7, 13 *sqq.*, 23 *sqq.*; iii, 14, 19–24.

[13] *Trist.*, iv, 10, 90 and elsewhere, as ii, 109.

[14] *Trist.*, ii, 103: cur aliquid uidi? cur noxia lumina feci?

[15] *Trist.*, iv, 10, 101: quid referam comitumque nefas famulosque nocentes?

[16] *Trist.*, ii, 345 *sqq.*

[17] See Suet., *Aug.*, 65.

himself been Iulia's lover is an old idea,[18] but a ridiculous one; an amorous princess is not likely to be attracted by a man of fifty, not of high social standing, and, so far as we know, of perfectly respectable private life.[19] But that she, or her agent, somehow employed him in an intrigue is possible, that he accidentally became aware of one and was too good-natured or too frightened to report it until after some one else, slave or friend, anticipated him, is both likely and consonant with his own hints.

It was most fortunate for him that, although easily moved, he was not a man of deep feeling. Propertius or Vergil would probably have died broken-hearted and by his own hand on receipt of the imperial order to betake himself to Tomis. Ovid, though sorely hurt and most anxious to return, if not to Rome, at least to some more civilized and pleasant place than the Black Sea coast, survived the blow some ten years. Scarcely had he begun his long journey eastwards than he was recording his impressions of the voyage; and from then on he poured forth a series of poems on his hardships, the horrible nature of the savage country and its rude inhabitants, his own utter misery and longing for return, the virtues and clemency of the Emperor, from whom he continued to hope for pardon, and his relations, friendly and otherwise, with every one of any prominence whom he had ever known and one or two persons never seen in the flesh by himself or any other mortal man. Towards the end of his life he changed his theme and began to revise his most ambitious effort in elegiacs, the *Fasti*. On this he was engaged when death overtook him in 771/18.[20]

If now we look a little more closely at the individual poems, we must begin once more with those on amatory themes, which occupied him up to about 755/2.[21] Ovid first won his reputation

[18] Apollinaris Sidonius, *carm.*, xxiii, 160–1; adopted by Ben Jonson, *Poetaster*, iv, 7. Julia was banished the same year, see Tac., *ann.*, iv, 71, 7 (uiginti annos exilium tolerauit, *i.e.*, 761/8–781/28).

[19] See below, on the amatory poems.

[20] Jerome says he died *an. Abr.* 2033, which is 770/17; but *Fast.*, i, 223 *sqq.*, mentions the new temple of Ianus, dedicated October 18 of that year; we must allow some time for Ovid to hear of this in Tomis, and thus prolong his life to at least the early months of 771/18.

[21] *Amores*, ii, 18, 19–20, mentions the *A.A.* (quod licet, aut artes teneri profitemur Amoris,/ei mihi, praeceptis urgeor ipse meis), also, *ibid.*, 21 *sqq.*, the *Heroides* as being already completed and published. The former poem cannot have been completed before 752/2, for (i, 171, 177 *sqq.*) it mentions the *naumachia* (a variation of the usual gladiatorial shows; a miniature sea-fight was produced on a large artificial pond) and the start of the Parthian expedition, both of that year, see Vell. Pat., ii, 100, 1–2. *R.A.*, 155–6, mentions the end of the Parthian affair, four years later.

with those elegies which purport to record his own experiences in love,[22] and continued to work at them for some years, recasting and rearranging them, apparently rejecting a certain amount.[23] The existing poems form three books, containing in all forty-nine poems, none very long (they vary from 18 to 114 lines, not counting the prefatory epigram of two couplets), and most of them tell the story of the poet's relations to a certain Corinna. No one has ever succeeded in identifying her, and a careful reading of these most charming and daintily phrased trifles will lead any unprejudiced person to the conclusion that Ovid never had a serious affair with any woman in his life and Corinna was a lay-figure on whom to hang all that his taste (generally impeccable, if we make a little allowance for differences between one age and another in the standards of propriety in expression), his ingenuity, which was naturally great and quickened by rhetorical training, and his excellent knowledge of Greek literature (even we, who have lost most of the Alexandrians, can often trace in him themes known from such remains of them and their imitators as we have) could suggest. He has enjoyed Corinna's favours; he has sent a letter to her and got an unfavourable reply; he has had an intrigue with her maid and afterwards brazenly denies it; he is trying to visit her, but a swollen river stops him; she is ill; she is unfaithful.[24] In short, everything which Propertius passionately felt, Ovid feigns most prettily, in metre of perfect and exquisite smoothness and language which, although artificial to the last degree, is never once obscure, indeed, after a few pages, seems natural, from the absolute mastery with which it is handled. Occasionally he leaves Corinna and her entourage, and his other, yet more phantasmal, ephemeral loves, and shows his versatility on a different theme, as the death of Tibullus (iii, 9), or the immortality of the poet (i, 15). But love is the chief subject, and the title *Amores* which he himself gave the work is therefore justified.[25]

[22] *Trist.*, iv, 10, 57 *sqq.* The earliest datable poem is *amor.*, iii, 9. the lament for Tibullus, who died (see above, p. 286) in 735/19, when Ovid was about twenty-four. Ovid himself says, *trist.*, iv, 10, 60, that Corinna was a feigned name; but this in itself proves nothing, for the same may be said of Lesbia and Cynthia.

[23] The introductory epigram to Bk. i says there were formerly five books, but now only three. As five books with but eight or nine poems in each would be unusually small, it is probable that Ovid suppressed or else greatly shortened some pieces.

[24] *Amor.*, i, 5; 11 and 12; ii, 7 and 8; iii, 6; ii, 13; iii, 14. But the variety of themes can be judged only by the pleasant method of reading the entire work through.

[25] He calls it *Amores*, by implication, *amor.*, iii, 15, 1; *trist.*, iv, 10, 1.

These short poems were probably composed in the intervals of somewhat more ambitious work on similar themes.[26] An early work, though its exact date is not known, is the *Heroides*, a series of letters supposed to be written by famous women of mythology to their husbands or lovers. Of these, fourteen are beyond all doubt Ovid's own, the authenticity of the rest has been at one time or another disputed with more or less reason. The certainly genuine ones (Nos. I–XIV) are, in order: Penelope to Odysseus; Phyllis to Demophon; Briseis to Achilles; Phaidra to Hippolytos; Oinone to Paris; Hypsipyle to Jason; Dido to Aeneas; Hermione to Orestes (begging him to rescue her from Pyrrhos)[27]; Deianeira to Herakles (the situation is that of Sophokles' *Trachiniae*)[28]; Ariadne to Theseus (supposed to be written from Naxos); Kanake to Makareus; Medeia to Jason (supposedly just after she discovers his marriage to Kreon's daughter)[29]; Laodameia to Protesilaos (she has not yet heard of his death); Hypermestra to Lynkeus (after his flight). All these are most Ovidian versified *suasoriae*; the ladies plead their cases with the arts of the rhetoricians, made charming, though a little cloying if the reader goes through too many at a sitting, by the same methods which make the *Amores* so. The fifteenth epistle is Sappho to Phaon. Here the writer is not a mythological heroine, but a historical poetess; but around her there had grown a thick crop of legend, part of which was the story of her love for the wholly unreal Phaon.[30] That Ovid wrote an epistle of Sappho he himself testifies[31]; that it was by some accident lost and the one we have is by another hand is arguable, but to be proved will need stronger grounds than the fact that some MSS. do not contain it or the subjective objections which several readers have raised against it. A more complex problem is presented by the remaining epistles, XVI–XXI. Ovid's testimony is that he wrote letters of heroines only, and that Sabinus (p. 343) wrote answers to some of them.[32] But these six fall into pairs; XVI–XVII, Paris to Helen and Helen to Paris; XVIII–XIX, Leandros to Hero and her reply to him;

[26] Cf. note 21. The relevant legends will be easily found in Rose, *H.G.M.*

[27] A variant of the situation in Euripides, *Andromache*, cf. Rose, *H.G.L.*, p. 185.

[28] *Ibid.*, p. 167 *sq.*

[29] Cf. Eurip., *Medea*, Rose, *op. cit.*, p. 181.

[30] See Rose, *op. cit.*, p. 93 *sqq.* The epistle draws upon a life of Sappho, now lost, which was current in antiquity.

[31] *Amor.*, ii, 18, 26 and 34.

[32] *Amor.*, ii, 18, 27–34.

XX–XXI, Akontios to Kydippe and Kydippe's answer.[33] It is clear that these poems do not form part of the original *Heroides*, then; it is perhaps worth noting that they tend to be longer than the first fifteen epistles (XV, the longest of the single letters, has 220 lines; this is exceeded by XVI with 376, XVII with 268, XX with 242 and XXI with 248). Once or twice, a rule strictly kept in Ovid's best elegiacs is broken and the pentameter ends with a long word[34]; but this rule is less strictly adhered to in his later work. Neither these facts, nor the very weak MS. tradition of some considerable sections of the poems[35] nor certain small peculiarities of language which have been found here and there in them[36] are sufficient to counterbalance the Ovidian excellence of all six, especially the admirable reply of Helen to Paris, in which the remnants of her respectability fight a losing battle with her desire. The reasonable solution of the difficulty is that Ovid, some time after the first issue of the *Heroides*, very likely while in exile, prepared a new edition, adding the new pairs of letters and so avoiding (for he was evidently a most good-natured man) any rivalry with Sabinus.

Didactic poetry had already been tried often enough, and sometimes it had been mildly humorous; Ovid hit on the brilliant plan of making it amatory, and thus achieved a masterpiece, never equalled in its own kind. He began with a little poem whereof we have a hundred lines left, dealing with cosmetics (*de medicamine faciei*, or *medicamina faciei femineae*), the rest being lost.[37] But he passed on to something much better. Although, as already said (p. 326), he was not a man capable of strong and deep passion, he was amorous and easily moved to passing affection[38]; and, with no exacting employment and means which, while not large,[39] were evidently enough to keep

[33] For the first and last pairs, see Rose, *H.G.M.*, pp. 231, 277; Leandros swam the Hellespont from Abydos to Sestos to visit Hero (a feat physically impossible, owing to the strength of the current which would have swept him miles out of his course; the story was invented by some one who did not know the region) until he was drowned on a stormy night.

[34] As xix, 202, unda simul miserum uitaque deseruit.

[35] xvi, 39–142; xxi, 13–248.

[36] See, for details, the critical edition of the *Heroides* by Palmer (Oxford, 1898), and the literature cited by Schanz-Hosius, ii, p. 215 *sqq*.

[37] It is earlier than the *A.A.*, for that mentions it, iii, 205 *sqq*. Ovid there calls it *medicamina formae*; the titles given above seem to be medieval.

[38] See *trist.*, iv, 10, 65 *sqq.*; *am.*, ii, 4, 31, 39–48. He adds (*trist.*, ii, 353 *sqq.*) that much of his love-making was pure invention and he never was immoderate; I see no reason to doubt this.

[39] He says (*A.A.*, ii, 165): pauperibus uates ego sum, quia pauper amaui. But *paupertas* is a long way from *egestas*.

him very comfortably, there is no doubt that he had numerous temporary *liaisons* with the Roman courtesans of his day; in his opinion, it was not a city in which the coldest could remain chaste for long.[40] We have seen (p. 283) that public opinion and popular morals did not seriously disapprove of such levities; there was therefore no reason for any outcry against a work which half-seriously instructed the novice how to choose, woo and enjoy the available light-o'-loves; Ovid is very careful to explain that his instructions apply to these only, and that he disapproves of all attempts on the virtue of respectable women.[41] Therefore in his three books (*Ars amatoria*, or *Ars amandi*),[42] we move in a totally non-moral world, but not an unrefined one nor a stranger to good manners or to artistic and literary culture. Books I and II instruct men; Book III, as Ovid phrases it, provides the Amazons with arms,[43] and shows the intending courtesan how to make the most out of her lovers. It need not be doubted that Ovid got his information mostly from his own experience and keen observation; these are the most original poems he ever wrote, though it is highly likely that he took many hints for details from Hellenistic poetry. To complete the set, he added a fourth book, the *Remedium Amoris*, a series of instructions, as frank as they are ingenious and brilliantly expressed, on falling out of love; for in such relations, the same public opinion which allowed them prescribed their not going so far as to ruin the lover in reputation, purse or health.[44] The zealous frequenter of even the most attractive and reasonable courtesan must one day settle down and marry, as the heroes of New Comedy do and as Augustus expected every citizen to do. Hence to be able to conceive an indifference, even a repugnance for these irregular unions, if not before marriage at least some time after it,[45] is a very useful accomplishment. When, besides the art which can make the most intimate physical details as little repulsive as they are when the most subtle Parisian handles them, Ovid adds most amusing illustra-

[40] *Amor.*, ii, 4, 31: illic (in Rome) Hippolytum pone, Priapus erit.

[41] *A.A.*, i, 31 *sqq.*; cf. *trist.*, ii, 239 *sqq.*, 349 *sqq.*

[42] The latter is what Ovid calls it, *A.A.*, i, 1; when he speaks (*R.A.*, 487) of *artes*, the plural is used because there are three books.

[43] *A.A.*, iii, 1–2.

[44] See, for example, Horace, *sat.*, i, 2, 47 *sqq.*

[45] Ovid is very liberal here; he allows (*R.A.*, 565–6; 571) for the cases of a man who is married and even of one whose children are old enough to marry. For one who became a husband, like himself, when *paene puer* (*trist.*, iv, 10, 69), this need mean no more than the age of about thirty-five.

tions and digressions, taken indifferently from his stores of ancient mythology and modern life,[46] the result is a work of never-failing interest, which will continue to be thoroughly readable as long as urban human nature remains what it was then and is now.

If it were necessary to add that Ovid, having reached this climax, began to decline and never wrote anything so good again, he would still be a writer of vast merit. But his endless ingenuity found scope in a poem totally different from and yet resembling his earlier work, the *Metamorphoses*. Of its scope something has already been said (p. 324); it remains to point out that in it Ovid makes the best possible use of stock poetical material. The ancient legends were, of course, no more believed then by the educated classes than they are now; they were also too familiar for a poet to interest his audience by simply telling them straightforwardly. But to retell them briefly, allusively, with every rhetorical device skilfully employed to heighten the colour at the right moments, was still a fitting task for a man of supreme literary ability. The figures of Herakles, Acheloos the river-god, Erysichthon the violator of Demeter's grove whom she punished with insatiable hunger, had become puppets or decorations on a tapestry; Ovid made them speaking puppets, and put into their mouths speeches such as the cleverest declaimer he had ever listened to might have envied. Thus, Erysichthon [47] sells his daughter to buy food for his supernatural hunger; she prays to Poseidon to help her, and he turns her into a fisher-lad. Straightway the purchaser accosts her, or him, with a most dainty little speech of polite inquiry, asking whether 'he' has seen the missing slave-girl; the supposed boy answers that no man or woman 'except myself' [48] has come that way. Acheloos tells the story, and adds, with a sigh, 'I too can change my shape; one of my forms used to be that of a horned bull'. On

[46] It can hardly be too strongly insisted that Ovid is a modern, far nearer to us in all essentials than Dante or even Chaucer. If we add to his Rome quicker means of movement and communication, we shall have something very like a modern capital; our machines have replaced their slaves.

[47] These illustrations are taken from one passage of the *Met.*, viii, 843–ix, 98. A hundred as good could easily be found.

[48] *Met.*, viii, 867–8: nemo iamdudum litore in isto,/me tamen excepto, nec femina constitit ulla. The masculine participle (*excepto*) is the only direct lie in the whole speech, which thus forms an excellent example of the ambiguity dear to tellers of folk-tales in such situations. This is originally a folk-tale of a pan-European type, the story of the wizard's apprentice who learns the art of shape-changing and makes great profit by taking the forms of various beasts, being sold in these disguises, and then resuming his own form and coming home again.

being pressed for an explanation of this, he gives an account of his and Herakles' courtship of Deianeira, quoting in full his own speech in support of his claims and Herakles' blunt answer ; he describes their battle, and how Herakles broke off one of his horns when he was in bull-shape. Here at last the artificialities of the rhetorical school found their proper scope. The too clever utterances, the extraordinary and desperate acts begun for the most inadequate reasons, the exaggerated expressions of emotion, as they are ridiculous if attributed to real men and women, or as a preparation for dealing with actual flesh and blood in the affairs of life under the sunbeams, become piquant and entertaining when ascribed to beings a degree less substantial than Titania and Oberon and incomparably less so than Bottom or Peter Quince. Ovid's fancy is of the moonlight, and all crude colours and oversharp outlines are softened by it into a half-real harmony of fantastic beauty.

That the poem is unfinished we have little evidence ; the framework and all the episodes are complete, and it is unlikely that Ovid's revision would have extended to more than the finishing of an occasional line [49] and other minor modifications of detail. That he would have brought himself 'to govern his talent rather than give it its head', as Quintilian afterwards desired,[50] is not likely ; it is much more probable that he would have injured the poem in trying to improve it, for as the elder Seneca says,[51] he never could leave well enough alone, and yet could not bring himself to correct even what really needed correction, if the original expression happened to strike his fancy.

[49] See *Met.*, xiii, 333 : te tamen adgrediar (so all MSS.), longa formidine pulsa, *or* mecumque reducere nitar. Neither of these is a possible miswriting of the other, therefore it looks as if the line was left incomplete by Ovid and variously filled in.

[50] Quint., x, 1, 98 : Ouidii Medea uidetur mihi ostendere quantum ille uir praestare potuerit si ingenio suo imperare quam indulgere maluisset. Elsewhere (iv, 1, 77) he has an interesting criticism of the *Met.*, the point of which is that the ingenuity with which the transitions from one story to another are made is somewhat childish and lacks seriousness : quem tamen (Ovid) excusare necessitas potest, res diuersissimas in speciem unius corporis colligentem.

[51] Sen., *contr.*, ix, 5, 17 : nam et Ouidius nescit quod bene cessit relinquere. *Ibid.*, ii, 2, 12, he tells a good story on the authority of Albinovanus Pedo. Ovid and his friends agreed that they might strike out three lines of his poems if he might write down three which were not to be touched. When his choice and theirs were disclosed, it was found that they had both hit on the same verses. Two of them were *A.A.*, ii, 24 : semibouemque uirum semiuirumque bouem ; and *amor.*, ii, 11, 10 : et gelidum Borean egelidumque Notum.

The poetry of Ovid's exile is, as he himself [52] repeatedly says, not so good as what he had written in Rome, and certainly it is much less interesting, for the subject, his own misery in exile and desire to return, is too uniform and the tone too servilely suppliant. Yet even in the five books of 'mournful poems' (*tristia, sc. carmina*) as they are commonly called, his ingenuity is almost as great as ever, and the speed with which he composed such polished verses extraordinary. The first book was complete before he arrived in Tomis; it consists of eleven poems, totalling 738 lines; the second, one long address (578 lines) to Augustus, does not describe the winter, which the third [53] does; it is not likely that Ovid would have omitted so effective a theme if he had experienced what, to an Italian, must have been intolerable cold, and therefore Book II was very likely completed during his first summer in exile. All five books of the *tristia* are written and the *epistulae ex Ponto,* which continue them, have reached their fourth and last book (see note 10) by the year 767/14. He wrote, then, about a book and a half a year, and this without counting the other work in which he was then engaged or the time it must have taken him to become tolerably expert in the local speech [54] and make himself as comfortable as might be in his new quarters. Equal readiness is shown to adapt his theme, whatever it nominally is, to his own needs; descriptions of the seasons, mentions of mythological figures, the praises of true friends, especially his wife, or attacks on false ones, all come back to the same *motif*, the hardness of his lot and his urgent desire to be allowed to live in some more tolerable place before he dies of grief and misery. He almost succeeded, or thought he had done so,[55] in softening Augustus' heart; but the Emperor died without pardoning him, and Tiberius made no move to recall him.

Besides these works, Ovid while in exile wrote the *Ibis*, an

[52] As *trist.*, i, 1, 35 *sqq.*, iii, 14, 39, *et saep.*; sometimes, as *ex Pont.*, iv, 2, 33 *sqq.*, he assigns a good reason, that there was no literary society in Tomis, or even, *trist.*, v, 2, 67 *sqq.*, 7, 11–12, 51–60, any one with whom he could speak Latin, the local dialect being a barbarous patois, a mixture of Getic and Greek.

[53] *Trist.*, iii, 10, 9 *sqq.*

[54] He even claims to have written a poem in it, *ex Pont.*, iv, 13, 19; if this is true, it would be linguistically most interesting if it had survived, but he probably made no copy of it.

[55] *Ex Ponto*, iv, 6, 15: coeperat Augustus deceptae ignoscere culpae. That Tiberius did not recall him was most characteristic; he held pedantically to the precedent of his great predecessor and was unlikely to reverse a sentence of his.

amusing masterpiece of learned vituperation; like all his best work, it is unreal, Ibis being a purely imaginary figure,[56] with a name taken from Kallimachos' famous attack on Apollonios of Rhodes,[57] all the curses in which are hurled at Ovid's phantom foe as a mere makeweight. Written soon after its author's arrival at Tomis,[58] it satisfied a psychological need, as well as being most ingenious literature. Ovid knew perfectly well that his misfortune was largely his own fault; he also knew, as his other poems from exile show,[59] that he had enemies who were making themselves objectionable to his wife and other friends. To attack any of them by name would have been impolitic, if not illegal; of blaming himself he soon grew tired. Therefore he gave himself the satisfaction of thoroughly abusing a lay figure, credited with all the evil qualities which he, or any one else, could wish his worst enemy to have, and therefore offering a proper target for all the maledictions which his great mythological knowledge and considerable acquaintance with ritual could produce. After an introduction in which he recounts the wrongs done him by Ibis and threatens him with lampoons in the style of Archilochos (which he must have known very well he could not write), vows eternal enmity to him and makes one or two general comminations, he describes an imaginary rite of ill omens, in which everything is done the wrong way about and Ibis is thoroughly cursed, and at considerable length, with the hostility of the four elements and with ill luck lasting to his death and

[56] Since this does not seem generally recognized, I quote A. E. Housman's witty and trenchant statement (*Journ. of Phil.*, xxxv, 1920, p. 316): 'Who was Ibis? Nobody. He is much too good to be true. If one's enemies are of flesh and blood, they do not carry complaisance so far as to choose the *dies Alliensis* for their birthday and the most ineligible spot in Africa for their birthplace. Such order and harmony exist only in worlds of our own creation, not in the jerry-built edifice of the demiurge. Nor does man assail a real enemy, the object of his sincere and lively hatred, with an interminable and inconsistent series of execrations which could neither be read nor written seriously. [Ovid's curses invoke] calamities too awful to be probable and too improbable to be awful. And when I say that Ibis was nobody I am repeating Ovid's own words. In the last book he wrote, several years after the *Ibis*, he said (*ex Ponto*, iv, 14, 44), extat adhuc nemo saucius ore meo.'

[57] See Rose, *H.G.L.*, p. 325.

[58] He had completed ten *lustra* when he began it, *Ib.* 1, *i.e.*, he had passed his fiftieth birthday, but not his fifty-fifth. Therefore the poem was written between 760/7 and 765/12. The impression given by Ovid's words is that he was but little over fifty, *i.e.*, that the date is about 761/8, or not much after.

[59] *Trist.*, iii, 11; iv, 9. His wife seems to have failed him, *trist.*, iv, 3 (written in 763/10, see 6, 19).

beyond. Then, after a description of the circumstances of his birth, which were of the most horrible possible, Ovid proceeds to invoke on his enemy's head every kind of ill fortune known to legend. The catalogue is in the obscure style of Alexandrian riddle-poetry,[60] though the puzzles are less hard to solve than those of some of the more learned scholars of the Museion; it lasts for nearly 400 lines (251–638), and Ovid then apologizes for its brevity and promises more later, with Ibis' real name attached. Thus he at once vented his spleen against the world at large, showed his learning, and gave the public a thoroughly amusing poem, provided that the reader is himself fairly well seen in the legendary lore of antiquity and knows some of the more sensational historical facts as well.

A small poem of this period is the *Halieutica*, as Pliny, who quotes it,[61] rather curiously styles it, for in its present form it has little to say of fishing but something of fish. The Black Sea was a famous fishing-ground, and it would appear that Ovid set out to describe the inhabitants of its waters; probably, had he finished the poem, he would have spoken also of the methods of catching them, but either he grew tired of the subject or he died before finishing. We have 132 lines, presenting many gaps in the sense, as if they came from a rough draft.

The much more important *Fasti* have already been mentioned in passing. That the poem was worked on while Ovid was in exile is clear, for it mentions events contemporary with the poet's last years; thus, Augustus is dead,[62] Tiberius is emperor, Germanicus is addressed in the dedication.[63] But all these indications of date are in Book I; the rest address Augustus as still alive, and Ovid himself [64] says that he was dedicating the half-finished poem to him. What happened is obvious enough; the six books we have were composed before the exile, then neglected for some years, finally a new edition of them begun, doubtless in hopes that the new recipient of the dedication would use his influence for the restoration of the poet. But Ovid died with this task no more than commenced, and some one published new

[60] See Rose, *op. cit.*, p. 335 *sqq.* The most useful edition of the *Ibis*, because of its full commentary, is still that of Robinson Ellis, Oxford, 1881; more literature in Schanz-Hosius, ii, p. 251.

[61] Pliny, *N.H.*, xxxii, 11; 152. The former passage gives the name (=matters connected with fishing), both testify to its being by Ovid, the latter says he began it *supremis suis temporibus*. Some doubts of its genuineness have been raised.

[62] *Fast.*, i, 533.

[63] *Ibid.*, and 1 *sqq.*

[64] *Trist.*, ii, 549 *sqq.*

and old together from his papers [65]; apparently the poem had not seen the light before. We have cause to be grateful to him, whoever he was; for while it is not the poet's best work, it is good, and in addition, it contains a large amount of antiquarian information of excellent quality. It is a versified Roman calendar [66] for the first six months of the year. The dates are given with the ingenuity which we expect from Ovid, however prosaic his subject; but more important to us is the information regarding the history, rites and customs which attach to the various days. This, says Ovid, is 'dug up from ancient records',[67] which is doubtless true, but he was not himself an antiquarian. It is therefore highly probable that he used an existing treatise, and the one which suggests itself is that of Verrius Flaccus which lies behind the Fasti Praenestini (see p. 445). This being lost, we have Ovid as a substitute, apart from the poetical and literary value of the *Fasti* in themselves.[68]

The antiquarianism is lightened by much play of fancy. When a name, the origin of a custom, a ceremony or a public monument needs explanation, Ovid is ready with one, often with three or four. The more learned of these he no doubt owes to Verrius; the more fanciful and amusing we may strongly suspect of being his own. Naturally, where Greek mythology will serve his turn, he uses it; thus, on April 12, when the games in honour of Ceres (*ludi Ceriales*) begin, leading up to her festival on the 19th, he simply tells the story of Demeter and Persephone, for Ceres had long been identified with Demeter, whom indeed she much resembled. But on reaching the 15th, the Fordicidia, or sacrifice of cows in calf, after Ovid has given the etymology of the name, we may well suppose that the little tale he tells of how Numa, warned by a dream which Egeria interpreted for him, instituted the festival, goes no further back than the poet himself; it is such an episode as any versifier could invent, much more a man of his imagination.[69] But generally the antiquarian

[65] Despite his complaints (note 52) that he had no one to talk Latin with, he clearly had some sort of amanuensis or secretary, *trist.*, iii, 3, 1–2; this man may have saved the *Fasti* and brought them to Rome for publication.

[66] For Roman calendars and our knowledge of them, see Wissowa, *R.K.R.*², p. 2 *sqq.*

[67] *Fast.*, i, 7: annalibus eruta priscis.

[68] That it is an imperfect substitute is obvious; for some remarks on this head, see W. Warde Fowler, *Roman Festivals* (Macmillan, second ed., 1908), p. 13; he there supposes Varro to be the source, which is not a serious error, since Verrius drew largely upon Varro.

[69] Here, as so often, Kallimachos was his model (see *amor.*, ii, 4, 19; a girl who wants to be very complimentary to Ovid assures him that his

learning and the poetical inventions are easily enough distinguished, and the reader is therefore entertained without being misled.

There is a problem connected with the *Fasti* which we have not the materials to solve satisfactorily. Ovid says (*trist.*, ii, 549) that he had written twelve books; we have but six, and there is no sign that any one in antiquity had read the rest. Whether they were among the poems which Ovid burned when he was leaving Rome (*trist.*, i, 7, 15–16), or were merely drafted and not ready for publication, we do not know.

As a metrician, Ovid combines the highest dexterity and smoothness with a lack of that harmonious variation of rhythms which marks the very greatest poets; he resembles Pope, not Milton, in this respect. His elegiac couplets were henceforth the models for all aspirants in that medium; his hexameters have much less elision than Vergil's, and very seldom allow themselves those small irregularities and departures from the usual Latin norm which are common in the older poet. It may be noted that they tend to scan by accent more than those of the *Aeneid*; *i.e.*, the proportion is greater of feet which begin with a syllable bearing a natural stress. Such regularity can be acquired by diligence, and it is easier to master it, being a matter of rules and practice, than to echo Vergil's more complex and subtle music. Hence all subsequent hexameter poets are more or less Ovidian in this respect, even those who, like Statius, admire and imitate Vergil.

We know of several poems which Ovid wrote, but are lost to us by one chance or another. Besides his Getic poem (note 54), he composed a tragedy, *Medea*, no doubt a piece of rhetorical closet-drama, like those of Seneca; but good judges speak so highly of it that we conclude it was excellent rhetoric, and may well regret that only two or three short fragments remain.[70] He also made an attempt at mythological epic, on the Battle of the Gods and Giants (*Gigantomachia*), which he never finished.[71] These were composed in his early period; to the same stage in his life probably belonged an epithalamium which he composed for Fabius Maximus, as Fabius was consul in 743/11,

poems are much more polished than those of Kallimachos); in particular, no doubt, the *Aitia*. But there is no reason to suppose Ovid imitated the older poet so exactly as never to tell any story which had no warrant in literature (ἀμάρτυρον οὐδὲν ἀείδω, Kall., frag. 612, Pfeiffer). That it does not sufficiently distinguish between fancies, whether of Ovid himself or some other writer on whom he drew, and real traditions, is the most serious fault of the sumptuous and learned edition of the *Fasti* by Sir J. G. Frazer, Macmillan, 1929, *q.u.*, for further information on all matters connected with the poem.

[70] Ovid, *amor.*, ii, 18, 13–14; *trist.*, ii, 553–4; Quint., cited in n. 50; Tac., *dial.*, 12. That Ovid never wrote for the stage he himself informs us, *trist.*, v, 7, 27. The fragments of the *Medea* are in Ribbeck, p. 267; they come from Seneca, *suas.*, 3, 7, and Quint., viii, 5, 6.

[71] Ovid, *amor.*, ii, 1, 11 *sqq.*

and doubtless had married earlier than that.[72] It may well be that a number of trifles attributed to him, supposing them to be genuine, were written at various dates; they were in several metres.[73] Loss of much Latin poetry besides Ovid's prevents us from knowing exactly how he made a poem *in malos poetas* out of the tetrastichs of (the younger) Macer (see p. 341), or when he made it.[74] Since Messalla died some sixteen years before Ovid was banished, we can date the poem in commemoration of his death exactly enough.[75] In like manner we can place the poems celebrating the triumph of Tiberius in 766/13 [76] and mourning the death of Augustus in the next year.[77] But we have no information when he composed his *Phaenomena*, a poem, it would seem, which imitated or even freely translated Aratos.[78] That such works imply no knowledge of astronomy is clear from the elementary blunders in that subject which he makes in the *Fasti*.

Ovid was clearly imitated early, and sometimes well. Quite a happy essay in his manner is the lament of the Nut-Tree (*Nux*, or *Liber Nucis*).[79] The tree pitifully complains that for no crime save fertility it is perpetually being pelted and otherwise abused, till, like Klytaimestra, it feels that it would have been better to be barren. Opinions have differed as to whether this is not a genuine, perhaps early, Ovidian attempt; on the whole it is perhaps more probable that it is by some one coming not long after him and familiar with his poems and those of the other Augustans.

A Roman knight, whose name is unknown, produced in the years 746/8 and 747/7, or thereabouts, a little group of consolatory poems.[80] The year before the earlier of these dates, the

[72] Ovid, *ex Pont.*, i, 2, 131 *sq.*

[73] Remains in *F.P.R.*, p. 349 *sq.*/112 *sqq.*, along with the other fragments except the *Medea*; all fragments at the end of several editions of Ovid, *e.g.*, that in Postgate, *Corpus poetarum Latinorum.*

[74] Quint., vi, 3, 96.

[75] Ovid, *ex Pont.*, i, 7, 30.

[76] Ovid, *ex Pont.*, iii, 4, 5 *sqq.*

[77] *Ibid.*, iv, 6, 17 *sq.*

[78] Fragments, see n. 73.

[79] The MSS. fall into two families, which have respectively the former and the latter title. The poem is published in many editions of Ovid, also in Vollmer, *poetae Latini minores*, II, 2, p. 1 *sqq.* (Teubner, 1923). For literature on it, see Schanz-Hosius, ii, p. 254.

[80] That they are all by the same author is probable, though not certain. (1) The *Cons.* was written by a Roman knight, 202, who had served in Germany, *ibid.*, 85. The first elegy on Maecenas was written by some one who was on friendly terms with Lollius, and had seen service, 10 *sqq.* (2) The first elegy on Maecenas begins: defleram iuuenis tristi modo carmine fata, which fits the *Cons.* excellently. (3) Style and versification are much alike in all three poems.

elder Drusus died on campaign in Germany. A loyal address of commiseration and comfort to his mother, the empress Livia, was plainly in order. Our author, whose work has been preserved to us because some one, probably much later, mistook him for Ovid, wrote a poem of 474 lines, in elegiac couplets, which we know as the *Consolatio ad Liuiam.*[81] He was a very fair versifier and knew the correct topics (the dead man had already accomplished much ; he died universally mourned and beloved ; his spirit is in a better world ; he would not have his mother grieve too deeply, &c.), and handles them adequately. Where the rules fail him, he shows his own absence of native taste. It is probably he who wrote two little elegies on the death of Maecenas (746/8), perhaps presented to Terentia his widow. They are much poorer than the *Consolatio*, indeed parts of them are intolerably silly.[82] Ovid knew these works and borrows a hint or two from them in matters of phraseology.

Nothing whatever is known of GRATTIVS, not even the rest of his name, except that he was a Faliscan and an acquaintance of Ovid.[83] He wrote a poem on hunting, *Cynegetica*, whereof a MS. of about A.D. 800, not impeccably copied and much

[81] It is an almost incredible fact that several scholars (see for literature Schanz-Hosius, ii, p. 255 *sqq.*) would put the poem much later, *i.e.*, suppose the author such a fool as to write and publish a lament for something which had happened an indefinite number of years before, and so insensible to the disasters of Varus and of his own commander Lollius that he never mentions either when foretelling (271 *sqq.*) that vengeance will overtake the Germans. The only shadow of ground for this supposition is the undoubted resemblance (see the footnotes in Vollmer) between passages in the *Cons.* and in Ovid, *trist.* and *ex Pont.*, which is easily accounted for as above in the text. The title is better *Consolatio* than, as the earlier editors gave it, *Epicedion Drusi*, for it belongs to the type of composition known technically as consolations, for which there were regular rhetorical rules, see above, p. 189. The latest text is in Vollmer's *P.L.M.* (see n. 79), *ibid.*, p. 15 *sqq.*

[82] One can hardly, for instance, read with patience the elaborate defence of Maecenas' luxurious life and fine clothes, *eleg.*, i, 21 *sqq.*, which compares him at length with Dionysos. The MSS. write the poems as one elegy ; it is on the whole more likely that there are two, the second beginning after line 144 of the first and the subjects being respectively the life and character of Maecenas and his supposed dying words. An amusing fact is that the verses have come to us under the name of Vergil, dead a dozen years when they were written. Hence they are commonly included (*e.g.*, by both Ellis and Vollmer) in the *appendix Vergiliana*.

[83] Grattius, *Cyn.*, i, 40 : nostris . . . Faliscis. Hence he is sometimes called Grattius Faliscus, which is misleading, for we have no authority for saying that Faliscus was his *cognomen*. Ovid, *ex Pont.*, iv, 16, 36 (the poem is mostly a versified list of the poets whom he knew).

damaged,[84] has preserved us a large part of the first book. The metre, as regularly with didactic poems, is the hexameter, which Grattius manages well enough; his language is for the most part clear and his Latinity such as we should expect from his date; the difficulties principally arise either from the accidents of copying and the losses which the MS. has suffered or from our own imperfect acquaintance with hunters' vocabulary in antiquity.

Of lost poets we know the names of many and have fragments of some; with few exceptions, Ovid knew them and he is one of our best sources for information, since at least he generally gives some idea of their subjects and styles and, by implication, of their dates also. The oldest is L. VARIVS RVFVS, famous in his own day, forgotten now. While Vergil speaks of him as a much better poet than himself,[85] Horace couples him with Vergil and praises his epic,[86] and his tragedy, *Thyestes*, was richly rewarded by Augustus and highly regarded by Quintilian and Tacitus,[87] to us he is hardly more than the editor, together with Tucca, of the *Aeneid* (see p. 248). Concerning PLOTIVS TVCCA himself we know that he was Varius' fellow-editor, and there is some slight reason to suppose that he wrote verse.[88] Another of the older poets, who however lived long enough to be acquainted with the young Ovid, was AEMILIVS MACER. Two poems of his are mentioned and some insignificant fragments preserved, the *Ornithogonia* and the *Theriaca*.[89] The former doubtless dealt

[84] For the MS. tradition and the editions (which are numerous; two recent ones are those in Postgate, *C.P.L.*, and Vollmer, *P.L.M.*, II, I, p. 20 *sqq.*; there are also commentaries by P. J. Enk, Zutphen, 1918, and E. Raynaud, Paris, 1932), see Schanz-Hosius, ii, p. 265.

[85] Verg., *ecl.*, ix, 35. Some fourteen lines of various poems by him survive (*F.P.R.*, pp. 337–8/100–1).

[86] Horace, *A.P.*, 55 and elsewhere; *carm.*, i, 6, 1; *sat.*, i, 10, 43–4.

[87] Two MSS., Paris Lat. 7530, p. viii, and Casanatensis 1086 (see Lindsay in *Class. Quart.*, xvi, 1922, p. 180), preserve the following notice: Lucius Varius cognomento Rufus Thyesten tragoediam magna cura absolutam post Actiacam uictoriam Augusto ludis eius (*i.e.*, in 725/29) in scaena edidit, pro qua fabula sestertium deciens accepit. See Quint., x, 1, 98, cf. iii, 8, 45, which preserves the only fragment known to be from this famous play: (Atreus speaks) iam fero infandissima,/iam facere cogor: Tac., *dial.*, 12.

[88] Jerome, *an. Abr.* 2000 (= 737/17): Varius et Tucca Vergilii et Horatii contubernales poetae habentur inlustres; which may be merely a corollary to the fact that they edited the *Aeneid*, as he goes on to say.

[89] Ovid, *trist.*, iv, 10, 43–4: saepe suas uolucres legit mihi grandior aeuo,/quaeque nocet serpens, quae iuuat herba, Macer. This does not mean that he wrote three poems, but two, whereof the second was on

with legends of persons who had been transformed into birds and other stories of the way in which birds originated, the latter with snake-bites and the cures for them. We can name his models; Nikandros for the second poem, perhaps Boios for the first. He died, an old man, in 738/16; his native place was Verona, the scene of his death Asia Minor.[90]

This man is not to be confused with Licinius Macer the historian, see p. 203, nor with (POMPEIVS ?) MACER, a friend of Ovid, who wrote a poem on some of those parts of the Trojan saga which are not in Homer, also certain 'quatrains' (*tetrasticha*), upon which Ovid (see p. 338) based a poem; they were perhaps epigrams. It is also possible that he wrote Greek poems.[91]

The Ovidian poem mentioned in note 83 is almost a versified literary history of the times which succeeded the deaths of the greatest poets. It names the following writers, in order.

1. (DOMITIVS) MARSVS. This man was an epigrammatist, mentioned many times by Martial as one of the classical writers in that kind. His epigram on the deaths of Vergil and Tibullus has already been cited (chapter ix, note 160). We have another, directed against Bavius (p. 345) and his brother; it seems that they lived in perfect unity and had all things in common, until the wife of one took to loving the other

snake-bites and their remedies. The titles are given by the grammarians who quote him, see the fragments in *F.P.L.*, pp. 344 *sqq.*/107 *sqq.*

That the *Theriaca* was in two books (corresponding to the *Theriaca* and *Alexipharmaca* of Nikandros ?) is stated by the Berne scholiast on Lucan, ix, 701 (ed. H. Usener, Teubner, 1869). His name continued to be more or less famous as an authority on herbs, and one of the most famous medieval herbals is the (metrical) Macer Floridus, really by Odo Magdunensis.

[90] For Nikandros, see Rose, *H.G.L.*, p. 329 *sq.*; Boios is cited by Antoninus Liberalis the mythographer as an authority for stories of transformation into birds. For Macer's death, see Jerome, *an. Abr.* 2001: Aemilius Macer Veronensis poeta in Asia moritur.

[91] The whole matter is very obscure; the facts are as follows. (1) There was a Pompeius Macer who lived under Augustus and Tiberius, see Suet., *diu. Iul.*, 56, cf. Tac., *ann.*, vi, 18, 3–4. (2) Ovid knew a Macer who wrote a poem on the events leading up to the Iliad, *am.*, ii, 18, 1–2, cf. *ex Pont.*, ii, 10, 13, and who was his companion on a journey to Sicily and Asia Minor, *ex Pont.*, *ibid.*, 21 *sqq.*; the whole poem is addressed to him, but Ovid nowhere gives any more of his name. (3) In the Palatine Anthology, vii, 219 and ix, 28, also in Stobaeus, *floril.*, lxxviii, 7 (vol. iv, p. 617, No. 52 Hense), are respectively epigrams and a tragic fragment headed either *Πομπηΐου Μάκρου* or with some corruption which can be easily restored to that name. That all these references are to the same man seems not unlikely, but cannot be either proved or disproved. Finally, Tibullus, ii, 6, 1, speaks of a Macer who was apparently an erotic poet: castra Macer sequitur; tenero quid fiet Amori? which does not fit the little we know of either Aemilius Macer or the other.

too well. The 'brother' is apparently Mevius. A Marsus wrote an epic, apparently bulky and worthless, called *Amazonis*, but whether dealing with the exploits of Penthesileia before Troy or the war of the Amazons with Theseus, or both, we do not know; nor is it certain that this was the epigrammatist.[92]

2. 'Great-voiced' RABIRIVS, the rest of whose name we do not know. As he wrote an epic poem on the defeat of Antony, *i.e.*, on the campaign which ended in the capture of Alexandria, it may be that he is the author of one of the rare Herculanean fragments which are in Latin, a few score hexameters, good enough to have been written by an Augustan, which deal with that same subject; but the author's name is not preserved and probably many tried their hands at loyal effusions on so promising a topic. Apart from this, we have but the most meagre scraps of work of his.[93]

3. Omitting the younger Macer, the next name is (ALBINOVANVS) PEDO, of whom we know that he was an officer under Germanicus in 769/16. As the fleet and army had most unpleasant experiences on the unfamiliar coast of the North Sea, it is not surprising that Pedo, who was fairly well known as a poet, both for a *Theseid* and epigrams, was able to give a lively description in verse of the darkness and terror of the situation.[94]

4. CARVS, whose poem on the adventures of Herakles is mentioned in lines 7–8; another address of Ovid to him shows that he was the teacher of Germanicus' children.[95]

[92] See Martial, i, prefatory epistle: lasciuam uerborum ueritatem, id est epigrammaton linguam, excusarem, si meum esset exemplum; sic scribit Catullus, sic Marsus, sic Pedo, sic Gaetulicus, sic quicunque perlegitur. From vii, 29, 5, it would appear that some of Marsus' poems, epigrams or others, were erotic: nota tamen Marsi fusca Melaenis erat. Philargyrius on Verg., *ecl.*, 3, 90, cites the epigram mentioned above and says the collection was called *Cicuta* (hemlock; *i.e.*, it was 'poisonous', presumably to those whom it attacked). For this and other fragments, see *F.P.L.*, pp. 346 *sqq.*/110–11. Of the *fabellae* from the ninth book of which Charisius quotes part of a line (p. 72, 4 Keil) we know no more than what he tells us there. Quintilian, vi, 3, 102, says that he de urbanitate diligentissime scripsit, and quotes enough of it to show that it was in prose and meant by its subject more than simply wit or humour; the definition of *urbanitas* given was: uirtus quaedam in breue dictum coacta et apta ad delectandos mouendosque homines in omnem adfectum animi. For the epic, see Mart., iv, 29, 7: saepius in libro memoratur Persius uno/ quam leuis in tota Marsus Amazonide.

[93] The Herculanean fragment is in Baehrens, *P.L.M.*, i, p. 214 *sqq.*; for other publications before and since, see Schanz-Hosius, ii, p. 267. The certain fragments of Rabirius are in *F.P.L.*, pp. 356/120–1.

[94] See Tacitus, *ann.*, i, 60, 2, ii, 23–4; and cf. Furneaux' appendix to Book ii in his larger ed. vol. i (Oxford, Clar. Press, ed. 2, 1896), p. 386. The fragment is preserved by Seneca rhetor, *suas.*, 1, 15. The *Theseid*, Ovid, *ex Pont.*, iv, 10, 71; epigrams, Martial, first quotation in n. 92, and elsewhere.

[95] Ovid, *ex Pont.*, iv, 13, 47–8.

5. (CORNELIVS) SEVERVS, whom Ovid mentions as having written a ' poem of kings ' (*carmen regale*), whatever its exact subject may have been. He composed also an epic on the war in Sicily (presumably that of Octavian against Sextus Pompeius), of which Quintilian says that if the rest of it were as good as the first book, he might take second place to Vergil. That he could write well is clear from a fragment, probably of his *Res Romanae*, which laments the death of Cicero in language worthy almost of Lucan.[96]

6. By ' the one and the other PRISCVS ' Ovid perhaps means CLVTORIVS PRISCVS and some relation of his; he was rewarded by Tiberius for a poem on the death of Germanicus (772/19) and then ruined by its becoming known that when the younger Drusus was ill he had a poem on his death ready for use if needed.[97] Omitting ' the subtle NVMA ', of whom we know nothing whatever, we may name

7. (IVLIVS) MONTANVS, of whom Ovid tells us that he was good in elegiacs and hexameters alike, Seneca the younger that he was ' equally renowned for his friendship with Tiberius and his affected style ' and particularly fond of describing sunrises and sunsets.[98]

8. SABINVS we have already mentioned (p. 328); besides his replies to the *Heroides*, Ovid tells us that he wrote a poem whose name has been corrupted past certain restoration and another on ' days ', probably on much the same subject as his own *Fasti*, but that his death left them unfinished.

9. LARGVS (VALERIVS, the accuser of Gallus ?) wrote on the arrival of Antenor in Italy.[99]

10. There follows a group of unknown names, CAMARINVS, who composed a continuation of the Iliad, TVSCVS, whose subject was Phyllis and Demophoon, and so perhaps used elegiacs, MARIVS, who could ' turn his hand to any kind of writing ', TRINACRIVS, who wrote a *Perseis* (adventures of Perseus, or Persian wars ?), LVPVS, whose theme was the return of Menelaos and Helen; then

11. The unscannable TVTICANVS, who seems to have written a Latin adaptation of part of the Odyssey.[100]

12. (C. VALGIVS) RVFVS is rather better known. Ovid says he was a harper on Pindar's lyre, in other words a lyric poet; we have other

[96] Ovid addresses him also (*ex Pont.*, iv, 2, 1) as uates magnorum maxime regum. See Quintilian, x, 1, 89; Valerius Probus, vol. iv, p. 208, 16 Keil; Seneca rhetor, *suas.*, 6, 26. The *Bellum Siculum* was perhaps a part of the *Res Romanae*.

[97] Tacitus, *ann.*, iii, 49.

[98] Seneca, *epp.*, 122, 11–13.

[99] For the subject, see Verg., *Aen.*, i, 242–4; Largus may have written epic or a *κτίσις* or foundation-legend in elegiacs in the manner of Kallimachos. For Gallus, cf. p. 284.

[100] Ovid here (line 27) says: qui Maeoniam Phaeacida (Homer's Phaiakian episode) uertit; elsewhere (*ex Pont.*, iv, 12, 9 *sqq.*), he humorously complains that he cannot praise his friend without mispronouncing Tūtĭcānus as Tūtĭcănus or Tŭtĭcānus, and again mentions the Homeric poem.

evidence that he wrote elegiacs, and here he comes into contact with Vergil, for it appears that both had a common admiration for some one whom they both call Codrus; his real name remains unknown. Vergil makes one of his shepherds say that he is the next-best singer after Apollo, while Valgius more modestly declares that his poems resemble Cinna's.[101] Another testimony again is that Valgius composed a poem in hexameters, while we also know that he wrote on rhetoric, grammar and natural history; these works were in prose.[102]

13. TVRRANIVS, who wrote tragedies of which we know nothing, is followed by

14. (GAIVS) MELISSVS. We would gladly know more of him, for Suetonius gives us the curious information that he introduced a new sort of *fabulae togatae* and called them *trabeatae*. As the *trabea* was the full-dress uniform of the knights when on parade, we should expect this to mean a serious kind of play, perhaps concerned with military exploits; but Ovid assures us that Melissus was a comedian and his Muse was not heavy-handed.[103] It would therefore appear that he wrote comedies in which the characters were supposed to belong to the upper classes of Roman society. He also compiled 150 volumes of what he modestly called nonsense (*libelli ineptiarum*), apparently a collection of good stories and witty sayings of well-known people. This was the amusement of his old age; he was a learned man, a *grammaticus*, of the household of Maecenas, who set him free,[104] and he seems to have written something about bees, very appropriately, since that is what his name means.

15. VARVS and (SEMPRONIVS) GRACCHVS were tragedians. Of the latter we know a certain amount, not to his credit; he was a lover of the elder Iulia, and for that reason was exiled under Augustus and promptly executed by Tiberius on his accession. A few scraps of his works remain.[105] If by Varus Ovid means Quintilius Varus[106]

[101] See Vergil, *ecl.*, vii, 22, and the Veronese scholiast there. The fragments of Valgius are in *F.P.L.*, pp. 342 *sq.*/105 *sq.*

[102] Rhetoric, Quint., iii, 5, 17, and elsewhere; grammatical matters, Gellius, xii, 3, 1, and several quotations in the grammarians; natural history, Pliny, *N.H.*, xxv, 4.

[103] Ovid, *loc. cit.*, 30: et tua cum socco Musa, Melisse, leuis; Suet., *de gramm.*, 21.

[104] All this is from Suet., *loc. cit.* His story is extraordinary. As the result of some quarrel between his parents, he was exposed; some one found him, had him brought up and educated, and gave him to Maecenas. Later, when his mother tried to reclaim him, he would not accept the status of a free-born man. A more eloquent testimony to Maecenas' kindness to dependents could hardly be imagined.

[105] Tacitus, *ann.*, i, 53, 4–9; Velleius, ii, 100, 5; Ribbeck, *trag. Rom. frag.* 2, p. 230 (ed. mai., Teubner, 1871), p. 266 (ed. min.).

[106] If we could suppose that the division of the various kinds of poetry, &c., among the Muses is as early as this (see Rose, *H.G.M.*, p. 174), it might be thought appropriate to the death of a tragedian that Horace, *carm.*, i, 24, 3, bids Melpomene, who is often the Muse of Tragedy, sing a dirge for Quintilius.

(chapter ix, note 133) he can scarcely have known him, being but twenty years old when he died.

16. There follows a group of practically unknown names, PROCVLVS, who imitated Kallimachos, FONTANVS, who sang of the loves of Naiads and Satyrs, CAPELLA, who wrote elegiacs; finally the less obscure (M. AVRELIVS) COTTA MAXIMVS, son of the Messalla already discussed (p. 305), by adoption one of the Aurelii. He was both poet and orator; of his activities in the former direction we know practically nothing, in the latter he produced something which Ovid professes to have read with the greatest eagerness and admiration.[107]

Elsewhere in Ovid a few more are mentioned.

17. SERVIVS SVLPICIVS, apparently the grandson of the jurist (p. 177); it would seem that he wrote amatory verse [108]; PERILLA, a friend of Ovid's, who praises her verses [109]; PONTICVS, mentioned by both Ovid and Propertius; the latter tells us that he wrote, or at least began, a *Thebaid* [110]; BASSVS, who composed iambics.[111]

A little less obscure, for they have a kind of fame because they attacked Vergil, are the pair of poetasters BAVIVS and MEVIVS (less correctly MAEVIVS). The epigram on them by Domitius Marsus has already been mentioned (p. 341). We know from sundry passages in the commentators on Vergil and Horace that they worked together and put forth what was meant to be a satirical criticism of the *Georgics* [112]; Jerome says that Bavius died in 719/35, in Kappadokia [113]; lastly, each of the masters deigns to mention them, Vergil in a single line, Horace in one of the Epodes.[114]

There remains a curious and not very pleasant little collection of verses which seems to date from this epoch, the *Priapea*. From Hellenistic times onwards, the god of fertility worshipped at Lampsakos, Priapos, had become popular first in the Greek-speaking world and later in Italy.[115] His cult was, to begin with,

[107] Ovid, *ex Pont.*, iii, 5, 7 *sqq.*

[108] Ovid, *trist.*, ii, 441; Plin., *epp.*, v, 3, 5.

[109] Ovid, *trist.*, iii, 7, is addressed to her and is our only document.

[110] Ovid, *trist.*, iv, 10, 47; Prop., i, 7, 1 *sqq.*, 9, 9 *sq.*

[111] Ovid, *ibid.*

[112] Besides the passage from Philargyrius cited in n. 92, see Servius on *Georg.*, i, 210, and *ecl.*, iii, 90; Porphyrion on Hor., *sat.*, ii, 3, 239, and *epod.*, 10, 1. For the spelling of Mevius' name, see O. Keller, *Epilegomena zu Horaz*, Leipzig, 1879–80, p. 383; Heraeus in *Wochenschrift für klassische Philologie*, 1916, p. 785. The fact that Domitius calls them brothers has led to some misapprehension; they probably were not relatives (hence the different *nomina*), but close friends or literary partners.

[113] Jerome, *an. Abr.* 1982 (= 719/35). This looks as if they were, or at least Bavius was, considerably older than Vergil, whose youth and success may have been outstanding offences from their point of view.

[114] Verg., *ecl.*, iii, 90; Horace, *epod.*, 10.

[115] See H. Herter, *De Priapo*, Giessen, Töpelmann, 1932 (Religionsgeschichtliche Versuche und Vorarbeiten, 23).

of a sort too frank to be indecent ; he was represented as a grotesque little man, with the sexual organ exaggeratedly large and erect. This figure became a usual adornment of gardens, often of houses also. It was the fashion, Greek as well as Roman, to write comic tributes to him in verse, which doubtless were inscribed on walls, hung from his statue, or otherwise brought near him. Of Latin trifles of this kind we have in all eighty-six, counting those ascribed to Vergil (see p. 262). Some are witty, if *risqués* ; some are quite inoffensive, but these are in a small minority ; most are unmitigated filth, in cleverly phrased verse, which shows the influence of Ovid ; indeed he is said on good authority [116] to be the author of one of them, the third of our collection.

[116] Seneca rhetor, *contr.*, i, 2, 22. For the collection, see Buecheler at the end of his ed. of Petronius ; Vollmer, *P.L.M.*, ii, pp. 36–73.

CHAPTER XII

THE SILVER AGE TO THE DEATH OF NERO

HITHERTO we have been able to separate prose and poetry fairly well, although several authors have been dealt with who used both mediums. From now on the distinction between the two forms is less marked, both showing the strong influence of the all-pervading study of too elaborate rhetoric, until a rising tide of artificiality swallows both and leaves them equally unlike any human speech. The craze—it cannot be given a milder name—for striking, epigrammatic utterance, high colour, and collocations of words in which everything else is sacrificed to effect of necessity produced prose styles which tended towards poetical diction. At the same time, it made verse prosy, in the sense that poets paid far more attention to the rhetorical skill with which they expressed such ideas as they had than to the living presentation of emotion or reflection. Whether, under such circumstances, poetry of the highest kinds could have been produced, even if a second Vergil had arisen, is doubtful; certain it is that it never was produced, though much was composed in verse which had very considerable, if not characteristically poetical merit. Prose seems to have been less hampered, for one or two authors, notably Tacitus, made the artificialities of rhetoric their servants and not their masters and wrote such magnificent pages as have never been excelled since.

In one sense, Roman literature at this age ran parallel to that of the Greeks, for both languages were in the hands of rhetoricians; but in another, the Latin writers went their own way. For the best Greeks of that time were Atticists, busied in trying to revive the manner and the very dialect of classical authors dead four hundred years or more; the Romans were more nearly Asianic in their manner, Seneca being a remarkable example of that style.[1] But even so, Greece was in no position to correct the faulty taste of the masters of the world by recalling them to nature and the artistic adaptation of daily speech to

[1] For Atticists and Asianists, see above, p. 161.

literature; instead of this, we find movements towards or away from Cicero, in other words a struggle between complete artificiality and that classicizing which never produces a classic, while the verse writers show similar tendencies towards or away from Vergil. Therefore, as all alike were rhetoricians, and the art of saying what one had to say simply and as clearly as might be seemed to have taken refuge with the technical writers to be dealt with in a later chapter, it will be convenient to treat all the authors together in chronological order. The general name which moderns have given to this period of second-rate work, though often good second-rate, is the Silver Age, in contrast to the Golden period of Cicero and the Augustans. Since, with the exception of a few of the earliest, all the writers to be dealt with lived and died within the Christian era, the double dating hitherto adopted will now for the most part be dropped.

Literature in this epoch underwent a further restriction which was beginning to make itself felt even in the time of Augustus. We have seen that the writings of Gallus disappeared, those of Labienus were burned, and Ovid's works were excluded from the official public library on his banishment.[2] After Augustus we hear several times of suppression of a writer who had given offence to the reigning emperor; and consequently those who had occasion to speak of the existing government either expressed themselves with extreme caution or indulged in flatteries often so gross as to turn the stomach of a modern. Since this naturally meant a reaction in the direction of abuse of a fallen power, it is extremely difficult for the historian to form a clear conception of the real and often complex characters of men who are represented, in the surviving mentions of them, most commonly as either gods or devils.

Apart from this, the Emperors of the Julio-Claudian house for the most part favoured literature and were writers themselves. TIBERIVS (IMPERATOR CAESAR TI. CLAVDIVS NERO),[3] 14–37, was a zealous student of Greek literature and style, learned rhetoric under a celebrated master, Theodoros of Gadara, or, as he preferred to style himself, of Rhodes,[4] had an unusual mastery

[2] See above, pp. 284, 320; Ovid, *trist.*, iii, 1, 71–2; below, pp. 349, 350.

[3] Since every emperor took the *praenomen imperatoris*, *i.e.*, used *imperator* (general, commander-in-chief) as his first name after his accession, and also adopted the name Caesar even though he was in no way related to the *gens Iulia*, these additions are henceforth dropped in giving imperial names, also the invariable *Augustus* and, as a rule, the complimentary titles *pater patriae*, *Germanicus*, &c. See p. 387.

[4] Suet., *Tib.*, 70 (who mentions that in Latin his model was Messalla), 57; Quint., iii, 1, 17; Seneca rhetor, *suas.*, 3, 7.

of the language and himself composed poems in it.[5] In Latin his purism was combined with an archaizing fondness for old and unknown words; he was fond of the by-ways of philology and archaeology and always had men of learning about him, whom he loved to puzzle with strange questions.[6] He composed a poem on the death of Lucius Caesar,[7] an autobiography and some letters and speeches,[8] all of which are lost.

As a suppressor of literature which did not please him he had a bad name, at all events with posterity. It is recorded that he put to death two minor poets, AELIVS SATVRNINVS and SEXTIVS PACONIANVS, for alleged attacks on him in their poems; a third, MAMERCVS AEMILIVS SCAVRVS, was accused before him of inserting in a tragedy certain verses in which, apparently, Agamemnon was abused in words which could be taken to signify Tiberius. Whether for this or other and more substantial charges, he found it necessary to anticipate sentence by suicide, his brave wife accompanying him in death.[9] More famous is the historian CREMVTIVS CORDVS. If we may believe our authorities, he had done no more than to call Cassius the last of the Romans, in a history of the civil wars which he wrote. The work was publicly burned, and Cremutius ended his days by the rather fashionable method of starvation; his writings, despite the action of the government, survived him, though they have not come down to us[10]; one of Caligula's freaks was to restore them to favour.[11] Their title was probably *annales*. Tiberius also quarrelled with actors, who were capable, on occasion, of interpreting their parts by intonation and gesture to convey a meaning which the author had never thought of and was not welcome to a soured and suspicious man like the Emperor.[12]

[5] Suet., *Tib.*, 70. His models in Greek were Euphorion, Rhianos and Parthenios (see Rose, *H.G.L.*, pp. 343, 344, 415; Parthenios, besides the mythological handbook mentioned there, wrote learned poems in the Alexandrian manner).

[6] Suet., *ibid.*, 70; 71.

[7] Suet., *ibid.*, 70.

[8] Fragments of the latter in *O.R.F.*, p. 551 *sqq.*

[9] Tacitus, *ann.*, vi, 39, 1; 29, 4–7; Cassius Dio, lvii, 22, 5; lviii, 24, 3. Four lines probably by this Paconianus survive, *F.P.L.*, pp. 360 *sq.*, 123. Scaurus had also some repute as an advocate (fragments in *O.R.F.*, p. 558 *sqq.*); cf. Schanz-Hosius, ii, p. 673.

[10] Tac., *ann.*, iv, 34–5, cf. Suet., *Tib.*, 61; Dio, lvii, 24, 2–3. Suetonius says Cremutius used the words of both Cassius and Brutus, but Plutarch, *Brut.*, 44, 2, and Appian, *bell. ciu.*, iv 114, agree that Brutus used them concerning Cassius; it may well be that both draw on Cremutius. Fragments, *H.R.F.*, p. 286 *sqq.*, with more passages concerning him.

[11] Suet., *Cal.*, 16. One motive was doubtless to show himself unlike his unpopular predecessor. He did the same for T. Labienus and Cassius Severus (see p. 320).

[12] Cf. the story in Suet., *Nero*, 39; Datus, an actor of Atellanae, managed to allude by gestures to the murders of Claudius and Agrippina while pronouncing the perfectly innocent words 'good-bye, father, good-bye, mother'.

He therefore banished them all from Italy in 23[13]; six years earlier he had done the same to the astrologers, making an exception in favour of his own expert, Thrasyllos.[14]

His successor, GAIVS (37–41), better known by his nickname CALIGVLA ('foot-slogger'; *caliga* is an army boot), was himself a ready and effective speaker, while his opinions on literary matters, despite his madness, were not always as wild as might have been expected; it was he who called the younger Seneca 'sand without lime'.[15] Besides his restorations to the libraries of proscribed authors (see note 11), he was minded to remove Homer, Vergil and Livy, the first because Plato had objected to him, the others because they did not suit his own taste. He is said to have banished CARRINAS SECVNDVS for declaiming against tyrants and burned a writer of Atellanae alive for a line which might be taken as a joke against himself.[16]

CLAVDIVS (41–54), though somewhat slow of wit, was learned himself and a friend to learning; it is a well-worn commonplace to compare him to James I. He was fairly able to express himself in public, though no great orator[17]; he early turned to the composition of histories (cf. p. 297), and produced, in Latin, two attempts in this kind, one, in two books, from the death of Julius Caesar, the other, in forty-one, from the end of the civil wars, besides eight books of autobiography. These, while he was still a private individual, were composed amid difficulties, including very sharp criticism from his own relations of his outspokenness; as Emperor he might, of course, say what he liked.[18] In Greek, he produced a history of Etruria and another of Carthage, the former in twenty books and the latter in eight.[19] He also wrote some lighter pieces, a treatise on dice,

[13] Tac., *ann.*, iv, 14, 4.

[14] Tac., *ann.*, ii, 32, 5; Cassius Dio, lvii, 15, 7; Ulpian in *leg. Mos. et Rom. collat.*, 15, 2, 1, who fixes the date at *Pomponio et Rufo coss.*, *i.e.*, 17. For Thrasyllos (the same who edited Plato and Demokritos), see Suet., *Tib.*, 14; 62; *Cal.*, 19.

[15] Suet., *Cal.*, 53, cf. Tac., *ann.*, xiii, 3, 6. See *O.R.F.*, pp. 572–4.

[16] Suet., *ibid.*, 34; 27; Dio, lix, 20, 6. For this Carrinas, see Stein in Pauly-Wissowa, vi, col. 1612, 66 *sqq*.

[17] This is clearly shown from his oration, delivered in 48, on the citizenship of the Gauls, preserved in the famous inscription at Lyons, *C.I.L.*, xiii, 1668; a good separate edition is Ph. Fabia, *La table claudienne de Lyon*, Lyons, 1929. See further, *O.R.F.*, pp. 574–8. Edicts and letters bearing his name also survive, see Schanz-Hosius, ii, p. 426, but it is somewhat rash to assume that these are his own composition.

[18] Suet., *Claud.*, 41.

[19] *Ibid.*, 42. See further *H.R.F.*, pp. 294–6. It may be mentioned in passing that the empress AGRIPPINA, mother of Nero, wrote memoirs which are cited by Tacitus, *ann.*, iv, 53, also by Pliny, *N.H.*, vii, 46.

of which he was very fond,[20] and a reply to Asinius Gallus on the relative merits of Cicero and Pollio.[21] His proposed reform of the alphabet shows an interest in phonetics which, if a little pedantic, was not unintelligent.

NERO (54–68) had a showy and superficial education, which, combined with much flattery, could but increase his morbidly high opinion of his own talents.[22] He was shallowly clever, and could make a fair showing at acting, singing, harp-playing, poetry and, with Seneca to help him, oratory,[23] besides his favourite exercise of chariot-driving. Under him, several noteworthy writers arose, though here and there his jealousy checked them. The four complete lines of his verse which have come down to us are all good, and one is very pretty.[24] That the abilities which could suffice to produce them would enable their possessor to be interesting, or even tolerable, throughout so long a poem as his *Troica* must have been, to say nothing of the portentous epic on Roman history, in 400 books, with which he is alleged to have threatened the world,[25] is at least unproved. He also wrote some short pieces, erotic [26] and satirical.[27] He instituted a new festival, the Neronia, one event in which was a contest in eloquence; in other words, prize compositions were called for.[28] No doubt they were little better or worse than such things usually are.

But apparently the best poet of the imperial family was GERMANICVS IVLIVS CAESAR, usually called Germanicus simply,

[20] Suet., *ibid.*, 33.

[21] Suet., *ibid.*, 41.

[22] Suet., *Nero*, 52.

[23] Tac., *ann.*, xiii, 3, 5; xiv, 11, 4.

[24] Colla Cytheriacae splendent agitata columbae, cited by Seneca, *N.Q.*, i, 5, 6. Cf. *F.P.R.*, pp. 368 *sq.*/131 *sq.*; most of the fragments there attributed to Nero are not his, but Persius' parodies of the current style.

[25] *Troica,* Juvenal, viii, 220–1 (Orestes was not such a criminal as Nero, for though it is true he murdered his mother) in scaena numquam cantauit Orestes, Troica non scripsit; schol. *ad loc.*, hoc ideo quia Nero Troados libros scripsit. Cf. Cassius Dio, lxii, 29, 1–3; schol. on Persius, i, 121; frags. in *F.P.R.*, cf. n. 24. Presumably the poem on the fall of Troy which he declaimed or chanted while Rome was burning (Tac., *ann.*, xv, 39, 3; Suet., *Nero*, 38; Dio, lxii, 18, 1) was part of his own epic, supposing, which is a large assumption, that the story is true at all.

[26] Mart., ix, 26, 9–10; Pliny, *N.H.*, xxxvii, 50, says he called Poppaea's hair *sucinus* (amber-coloured). This, like the fragment cited in n. 24, suggests that he had a good eye for colour, perhaps the most artistic thing about him.

[27] Tac., *ann.*, xv, 49, 5; Suet., *Nero*, 24; *Domit.*, 1. Tacitus, *ann.*, xv, 34, 2, seems to indicate that he also wrote hymns on occasion.

[28] Tac., *ann.*, xiv, 20, 1; 21, 5; xvi, 2, 4; Suet., *Nero*, 12.

adopted son of Tiberius. Besides a few trifles,[29] he is the author[30] of a translation, or rather a free paraphrase, with corrections of the mistakes of fact in the original, of the poem of Aratos already rendered by Cicero (see p. 145). There is no doubt that Germanicus is a better poet than Cicero as well as a better astronomer. This work, although the only considerable monument we have of his abilities, was by no means the only thing he wrote. He was famous as an orator,[31] and, being evidently an excellent Greek scholar, he wrote comedies in that language, one of which Claudius staged after its author's death.[32]

Coming now to untitled writers, we have again to notice a poem dealing with the heavens, this time, however, astrological. Late in the principate of Augustus and early in that of Tiberius a certain M. MANILIVS, otherwise totally unknown,[33] set him-

[29] For epigrams, Greek and Latin, attributed with more or less certainty to him (a possible claimant for some at least is Domitian, who took the title of Germanicus), see Schanz-Hosius, ii, p. 438; cf. Rose, *H.G.L.*, p. 349.

[30] The MSS. (see, for particulars, the standard edition, that of A. Breysig, Berlin, 1867, with scholia, p. xiii *sqq.*) attribute the poem to 'Claudius Caesar', but Germanicus' name before his adoption was probably Nero Claudius Drusus Germanicus; the *editio princeps* calls the author Germanicus, presumably on some authority. Besides, the opening of the poem addresses a *genitor* who is emperor and has pacified the world, which fits Tiberius well enough; Lactantius, *diu. inst.*, i, 21, 38, names a Germanicus as the author, and the only other Germanicus with a real or adopted father who was emperor was Domitian, who did not assume that title until after his father Vespasian was dead and he was emperor himself. The astronomical improvements in the poem may well come from intelligent use of a commentary resembling the work of Hipparchos (see Rose, *op. cit.*, p. 379) which corrected Aratos' mistakes.

[31] See *O.R.F.*, p. 560 *sq.*

[32] Suet., *Cal.*, 3 (this gives also an account of Germanicus' learning and accomplishments in general), *Claud.*, 11.

[33] The name is given in the MSS. as above, with various curious additions, all apparently due to blunders of one kind or another. See A. E. Housman's larger ed., vol. i, p. lxix (Cambridge, 1903; this, in five vols., is by far the most useful modern edition, by reason of its very full commentary and introductions; there is a smaller edition, text and critical notes only, by the same editor, Cambridge, 1932). The date is determined thus. Book i ends: sit pater inuictus patriae, sit Roma sub illo, cumque deum caelo dederit, non quaerat in orbe. Augustus, but not Tiberius, accepted the title of *pater patriae*, and the god Rome has given to heaven is manifestly Julius; she is 'not to feel the lack of' one on earth (a favourite Manilian use of *quaero*), in other words, he hopes Augustus will live for ever. But, iv, 764, Rhodes is hospitium recturi principis orbem; Tiberius notoriously retired thither for a considerable time, and that during Augustus' lifetime his successor should be so clearly named as this is unthinkable; and two lines farther on, it is verily the home of the Sun, cum caperet lumen magni sub (in the person of) Caesare mundi.

self to explain the whole theory of astrology in Latin verse. His qualifications were, a very indifferent knowledge of the subject, a certain enthusiasm for the doctrines it taught, at all events in their Stoic form, and hence an occasional flight into poetry for a line or two, considerable facility in verse-making, and especially a knack of turning arithmetical calculations, in which he seems to have delighted, and other unpromising material into hexameters nearly as smooth as Ovid's. He composed five books, whereof he seems to have intended the fifth to be the last [34]; but he had by no means exhausted his topic when he got to the end of the poem as it stands. That he died leaving it unfinished is not certain, but probable; for not only does Book V break off suddenly, almost in the middle of a sentence, and the poem contain references to passages which do not occur,[35] but so many single lines or groups of lines make no sense where they stand and yet seem to be genuine compositions of Manilius that scribal errors will not explain their present position [36]; it is much more likely that they were inserted from the margins of the author's rough draft, where he had jotted them down as they occurred to him, to put in their proper places later, by some not over-acute editor or literary executor. As it stands, Book I treats of the origins of astrology and goes on to describe the appearance of the heavens and the different zones and circles, visible and theoretical, into which astronomy divides them; in conclusion, comets are discussed. Book II, after a long preface, discusses the sexes, nature, &c., of the signs of the zodiac, their aspects, relations to the gods and to the parts of the human body, their loves and hatreds, and finally the various methods of subdividing them. Book III, after a shorter proem, gives a

Finally, *ibid.*, 776, the reigning Caesar was born under Libra. The moon was in Libra on Nov. 16, 712/42, the future emperor's birthday. Augustus might have regarded it as his birth-sign, for it was his horoscope (*i.e.*, on the eastern horizon at his birth), but he preferred Capricorn, the sign under which he was conceived, cf. Man., ii, 509; evidence from coins shows that Libra was associated with Tiberius, Capricorn with Augustus. See Housman on the passages quoted. The first three books therefore were written not later than 14 (after 9, for i, 899, mentions the defeat of Quintilius Varus), the fourth and fifth after that date.

[34] Man., v, 1: hic (*i.e.*, with the end of iv) alius finisset iter. He therefore adds Book v as a sort of appendix.

[35] *E.g.*, ii, 750 promises a future discussion of the modifications of the influence of the signs caused by the presence of planets in various parts of them; but this never comes.

[36] This does not mean that there are no accidentally displaced lines; but a scribe, having omitted a line and noticed it later, would write it in on the margin somewhere within a page or two of its proper place, not a book or more away.

list of the twelve *athla* which correspond to the twelve signs,[37] adds rules for discovering the position of the most important points in a nativity, mentions the signs which rule the year, month and day (chronocrators) and the number of years of life which each sign can give, and ends with the four 'tropic' (solstitial and equinoctial) signs. The fourth book, again after a proem, informs the reader what characters are given by each sign, and then goes on to discuss the various fractions of the signs and the effects of each. Next follows an excursus on geography, leading to a discussion of the parts of the earth which the various signs govern. Then comes a curious section on what Manilius calls the ecliptic signs. It appears that according to the teaching of 'the ancients', if the moon is eclipsed, the constellation in which she is at the time is weakened and does not exert its normal influence, while the same effect is produced on the one diametrically opposite.[38] He concludes with a defence of the proposition that it is possible to foretell the future; man is akin to the heavens and can read them if he will.[39] Book V, which is adorned with a good deal of digression on star-myths, gives an account of the *paranatellonta*, *i.e.*, those signs which rise simultaneously with each of the twelve zodiacal constellations, but outside the zodiac; they also have their influence on the characters of mankind. He is speaking of the number and different magnitudes of the stars when the poem comes to an abrupt end.

In view of the popularity of astrology, it is curious that Manilius was so little read, for he is a tolerable writer and, considering the complicated subject, not obscure.[40] A few resemblances between him and Lucan have been detected, none enough to prove that the younger

[37] A sign (which, depends on the time of the birth) determines the fortune (wealth, position, &c.) of the person born; the next, his adventures abroad, and so on. It is a sort of artificial zodiac which the astrologer must apply to the real one, to learn, *e.g.*, whether the subject will be rich, whether it will be safe for him to join the army, and so forth.

[38] Who the ancients in question are (*antiqui*, iv, 849) is a puzzle, since no one else seems to hold this theory concerning eclipses.

[39] This is one of the passages in which Manilius achieves, if not quite poetry, at least good rhetoric in good verse: iv, 901 *sqq.*, unus in inspectus rerum uiresque loquendi/ingeniumque capax uariasque educitur artes/hic partus (*i.e.*, man) qui cuncta regit; secessit in urbes,/edomuit terram ad fruges, animalia cepit/imposuitque uiam ponto, stetit unus in arcem/erectus capitis uictorque ad sidera mittit/sidereos oculos propiusque adspectat Olympum/inquiritque Iouem. It is a fine expansion of Ovid, *Met.*, i, 83 *sqq.*, with a reminiscence of Sophokles, *Antig.*, 332 *sqq.*

[40] He is often very difficult for us, because he has been ill-copied and our knowledge of ancient astrology is not perfect. See p. 533.

poet had read the elder, but enough to make it not unlikely.[41] After that we hear no more of him till Firmicus Maternus (see p. 507), who uses him for part of his *Mathesis*. The moderns have been kinder to him, and the list of those who have emended and commented on his text includes Scaliger, Bentley and Housman.

In the year 29 a Campanian gentleman, M. Vinicius, was consul-designate. He had a fellow-countryman, a retired officer with a good though not particularly brilliant record, by name MARCVS (?) [42] VELLEIVS PATERCVLVS. This man, who had served under Tiberius in many of his most important campaigns, seems to have conceived an unbounded admiration for him and the whole Imperial family, in whose men he could see nothing but sublime virtues, while their enemies were compact of every possible vice. With this attitude of mind and some knowledge of history and rhetoric, Velleius had the idea of presenting Vinicius with a memorial of his consulship in the shape of a little work on the history of Greece and Rome. He completed his task in two books, the first taking the story down to about the middle of the second century B.C., while the second reaches the appearance of Caesar in public life by the forty-first chapter and then spends the rest of its space, to the 131st and last, in a comparatively detailed account of events since then. The first part of his work is naturally of little value, and his accuracy is not unimpeachable; he is at times of use, however, when the fuller and better historians fail us. But for the Augustan age and the

[41] Some are listed in Schanz-Hosius, ii, p. 446. One of the best is Lucan, x, 152–3: Fabricios Curiosque graues, hic ille recumbat/sordidus Etruscis abductis consul aratris, cf. Man., i, 787, Fabricius Curiusque pares; iv, 148–9: Serranos Curiosque tulit fascesque per arua/tradidit, eque suo dictator uenit aratro. With both of them, cf. Persius, i, 73–5. Not too much should be made of these stock examples, especially when so much literature of that time has been lost and a common model, unknown to us, may explain the resemblance.

[42] Velleius was very little read in antiquity, to judge by the extreme rarity of quotations from him, and but one MS. reached modern times, only to be lost again, as often happened, when it had been printed from. We have the *editio princeps* and a sixteenth-century MS. copied from the lost codex (see the preface of any critical ed., *e.g.*, that of R. Ellis, in the Oxford Class. Texts). The printed edition gives his praenomen as C., at the beginning and end of Bk. i; Priscian, ii, p. 248, 4 Keil, has M., which I see no cogent reason to reject. Of his life he himself tells us that he held various posts, ending apparently with the praetorship in 14 (see ii, 104, 3; 111, 3; 113, 3; 114, 2; 121, 3; 124, 4). We know nothing of him from any other source. He has been mistakenly called a flatterer; his tone is simply that of an honest soldier who, knowing that his old general was an efficient and considerate leader, attributes all other good qualities to him as well without much examination of the facts.

earlier exploits of Tiberius he is often either the only authority or the fullest, and even the extreme laudation of his hero in which he indulges has its merits as a corrective to the attacks on the latter's character made by Tacitus and Suetonius. The style is not bad, though less good than one would expect of a younger contemporary of Livy; it is to be remembered that Velleius had spent much more time in the camp than the study.

The principate of Tiberius produced no great historians; the only other surviving author of that period and *genre* is little better than a collector of anecdotes. His name is VALERIVS MAXIMVS, and the title of his nine books is *facta ac dicta memorabilia*, 'noteworthy doings and sayings'.[43] Of his life we know very little; he tells us himself that he was poor,[44] but found a kind patron in Sextus Pompeius, not the formidable half-pirate, half-patriot who so long troubled Octavian and his helpers, but a more peaceable bearer of the name, consul in 14, friend of Ovid and of Germanicus, and well-disposed to literature.[45] His work is a long series of tales grouped under appropriate headings,[46] as 'military discipline', 'modesty', 'self-confidence', 'chastity', 'cruelty' and so forth; in each section he begins by telling stories of Romans, generally well-known men, occasionally women, and then passes on to similar narratives about foreigners, principally Greeks. These are set forth in a most atrocious style, bombastic, would-be clever, full of artificial and at the same time clumsy and obscure phraseology. He intended evidently to produce a handbook for rhetoricians and orators, who liked to point their arguments with illustrative parallels; it is a pity that he was himself a rhetorician and a very bad one, for although he is inaccurate and cares nothing for historical truth if by neglecting it he can make a story more pointed, or flatter Tiberius, which he does most fulsomely, he had access to good histories now lost, such as the missing parts of Livy; hence under his irritating manner are hidden useful scraps of

[43] So at least our MSS., perhaps from the opening words, urbis Romae exterarumque gentium facta simul ac dicta memoratu digna.

[44] Not in iv, 4, 11, where *paruulos census nostros* is a piece of general moralizing, but in iv, 7, *ext.* 2, which gives us to understand that he owed a great deal to Pompeius' generosity. In ii, 6, 8 he relates a curious incident which he witnessed while with Pompeius on a journey to Asia Minor, presumably while his patron was on his way to his governorship there, about 27.

[45] Ovid, *ex Pont.*, iv, Nos. 1, 4, 5 and 15 are all addressed to Pompeius.

[46] Those which we find in our MSS. may not be his own, but they correspond well enough to the contents, and that he himself added headings of some kind is very likely.

information, while some of the events of which he speaks are so full of interest or so moving that even he cannot spoil them entirely. The date of publication is about 31 or not long after, for he attacks Seianus with the utmost fury, proving clearly that he was dead and suggesting that he had not been dead long and Valerius, like the men in Juvenal, is eager to show his loyalty by stamping on Caesar's fallen enemy.[47]

Valerius Maximus no doubt esteemed himself a finished product of the rhetorical schools; there was a humbler graduate of a lower form of instruction whose works have survived in a mutilated form to us. His name was PHAEDRVS; he was a Thracian by birth, and his father was apparently a teacher, probably a *litterator* (see p. 131). How and where he mastered Latin is not known; perhaps his father moved to Rome, or to some Italian town, and set up a school there. We have no indication that he ever became a Roman citizen, and some evidence that he was not, for we find him the hanger-on of freedmen, no doubt belonging to some important family, it may be even the Imperial household.[48] One of the commonest exer-

[47] In ix, 11 *ext.*, 4. The reference to Juvenal is *sat.*, x, 86. Ill-written though it is, Valerius' collection of anecdotes was apparently popular, and we have two epitomes of it, occasionally useful to correct a corrupt reading and also serving as substitutes for the considerable parts of the original work which are lost. Their authors are named IVLIVS PARIS and IANVARIVS NEPOTIANVS; nothing certain is known of them, except that they are manifestly of late date; see Schanz-Hosius, ii, p. 593.

By some accident, apparently because it happened to be in the same MS. as a copy of Paris' epitome, a little work *de praenominibus* is ascribed to Valerius Maximus by our MS. tradition. It assuredly is not his, and one copy ascribes it to a certain C. TITIVS PROBVS, and describes it as an epitome. Its table of contents shows that it went on to discuss other matters of nomenclature; it clearly goes back to a well-informed treatise, perhaps of the early Empire.

[48] *Name*; perhaps Phaeder in Latin, a form attested by inscriptions, cf. Ἀλέξανδρος—Alexander, Μένανδρος—Menander. *Birthplace and parentage*: iii, prol., 17 *sqq.*, ego, quem Pierio mater enixa est iugo,/in quo Tonanti sancta Mnemosyne Ioui/fecunda nouies artium peperit chorum,/quamuis in ipsa paene natus sim schola (this line, which makes perfect sense, has been wantonly altered by some editors), /curamque habendi penitus corde eraserim,/nec Pallade hanc inuita in uitam incubuerim,/fastidiose tamen in coetum recipior. A comparison with *ibid.*, 55 *sqq.*, cur somno inerti deseram patriae decus,/Threissa cum gens numeret auctores deos, &c., shows that 17–19 are to be taken literally; he was born in Pieria. The plain meaning of 20 is that he was born somewhere near a school (or lecture-room); therefore his mother was the wife or perhaps the servant of a school-teacher or lecturer; we do not know whether he was legitimate or illegitimate. *Relations to freedmen*: Book iii is dedicated to Eutychus, iv to Particulo, v to Philetus (addressed in

cises for little boys was to set them to write, in their own words, fables of the kind attributed by tradition to Aesop,[49] and in consequence of this there was a certain demand for models of such compositions. Phaedrus had undoubtedly a knack of composing verses—his chosen metre was the iambic trimeter [50]—and could express himself briefly and pithily, telling a short story not badly. This little talent he seems to have taken seriously,[51] while at the same time suffering from a sense of inferiority and nursing a grievance (possibly a suit at law had gone against him) which he laid to the charge of Seianus.[52] He produced five books of little stories in verse, which he seems to have called *fabellae Aesopiae*, or 'anecdotes in the manner of Aesop'.[53] Of these we have the skeleton only,[54] and must reconstruct the rest as best we may from a series of extracts made by Niccolò Perotti in the fifteenth century from a fuller MS. than any that has survived, together with the numerous

the last surviving line; the prologue is imperfect). Who these were we do not know, but their names are not those of Romans. Eutychus Phaedrus describes (iii, *prol.*, 1–14) as a busy man, married, with a household to look after, who might possibly find time on holidays (*feriae*) to read him. He was therefore not Eutychus the famous charioteer, favoured by Caligula (Suet., *Cal.*, 55), for the races were on holidays and charioteers would be especially busy then, like modern jockeys in our racing seasons. He perhaps was a civil servant, since the posts corresponding to those of our permanent under-secretaries and their subordinates were then filled from the freedman class or by slaves; but he may have been the factor of some wealthy private individual. Of the other two Phaedrus tells us even less.

[49] See Quintilian, i, 9, 2. For Aesop, who is nearly as fabulous as his own talking beasts, see Rose, *H.G.L.*, pp. 91, 356.

[50] Phaedrus' trimeter is an interesting compromise between the pure Greek form and that used by the Latin dramatists.

[51] For instance, iv, epil., 4 *sqq.*, he promises Particulo immortality as long as Latin literature exists because he mentions him in his fables. This is the conventional way of claiming to be a serious author, not a mere dabbler in literature.

[52] See iii, prol., 41 *sqq.* This helps to date the work; the lines would certainly not have been published, probably not even written, until after 31. In ii, 5, a story is told concerning Tiberius which it is more likely Phaedrus would wait till after the Emperor's death to give to the public, though it is not derogatory to him.

[53] See iv, prol., 10–11: quare, Particulo, quoniam caperis fabulis,/ quas Aesopias, non Aesopi, nomino. But elsewhere he calls them *fabellae*, contrasting them, iv, 22, with the *fabulae* of more ambitious poets.

[54] No book has more than 425 lines (the exact number is uncertain, owing to lacunae and spurious additions) and two have well below 200 each. For the prose fables and Perotti's extracts, see the prefaces of the critical editions (*e.g.*, Havet, Paris, 1895; Postgate, Oxford, 1919) and Schanz-Hosius, ii, p. 449 *sqq.*

prose fables of medieval date, whereof many (notably a number included in the collection of the so-called Romulus, a shadowy person of very uncertain age, perhaps somewhere between the fourth and sixth centuries) show plainly that they are paraphrased from verse, not a few are from surviving fables of Phaedrus and others well may be from lost ones. Probably Phaedrus, while almost entirely ignored by the better-known men of letters,[55] was popular in elementary schools as a reading-book, or as a model for very young students of rhetoric, and consequently circulated much in extracts and other shortened forms.

We now come to a writer, the most famous of the principate of Claudius and the emperors on either side of him, LVCIVS ANNAEVS SENECA. Of his works the writer finds it hard to judge fairly, owing to the loathing which his personality excites. That a man in exile should flatter basely those who have power to recall him is understandable ; Ovid did as much. That a prime minister in difficult times should show himself neither heroic nor self-consistent is no more than is to be expected of the vast majority of statesmen. That the influential adviser of an impressionable and unbalanced young prince should allow his master's favours to take the form of making him prodigiously wealthy is not remarkable ; we may discount the tales [56] of Seneca using extortion to add to his riches. That, having flattered, he should bespatter with abuse the object of his sometime adoration is certainly not commendable, but shows no deep depravity, merely a desire to swim with the current. That, being the most popular author of the day and master of an eloquence calculated to make the worst case appear passable, he should frame an elaborate justification of a matricide,[57] may be passed over as one of the hard necessities of his position ; but when the man who has done

[55] Seneca says (*dial.*, xi, 8, 3) that no one has written Aesopic fables in Latin ; Quintilian (quoted in n. 49) does not mention Phaedrus ; Martial (iii, 20, 5) asks whether Canius Rufus aemulatur improbi iocos Phaedri. A few of the surviving pieces might deserve to be called ' naughty ', so probably our Phaedrus is meant. This is then the earliest reference ; Avianus, *ep. ad Theod.*, mentions the five books (p. 1, 13–14 Ellis ; see below, p. 532).

[56] When Cassius Dio (lxii, 2, 1) knows a story that he irritated the Iceni to revolt by his merciless exaction of debts due to him, we may be sure that there were a hundred such rumours afloat in Seneca's own day. But since similar attacks are made on practically every one who becomes rich conspicuously and rapidly, we may in fairness set them down to nothing better than envious and ill-natured gossip from those who were less wealthy than he.

[57] Cf. Tacitus, cited in n. 23.

and is doing all this takes the tone of a rigid moralist and a seeker after uncompromising virtue, preaching, from his palace, simplicity and the plainest living with almost the unction of a St. Francis praising Holy Poverty, refusing all knowledge that does not tend to edification, and proclaiming, in verse worthy of a better man than Nero's hack, that the true king is he who fears nothing and desires nothing, the gorge of the reader rises and he turns for relief to some one who either made his life fit his doctrine or, if he behaved unworthily of the best that was in him, at least laid no claim to be a spiritual guide.

This eloquent moral weakling, the adviser, through his works, of thousands of men better than himself, was born at Corduba (Cordova) shortly before the beginning of the Christian era.[58] His father, Seneca the rhetorician, has already (p. 317 *sqq.*) been discussed; his mother's name was Helvia. Of his two brothers, something has been said of the elder, M. Annaeus Novatus, later, by adoption, L. Iunius Gallio; the youngest of the family was M. Annaeus Mela, father of Lucan the poet (p. 379). Seneca was always of delicate health, indeed he escaped Caligula's jealousy of his eloquence by a report that he was sure to die soon in any case and so was not worth the trouble of executing. Under Claudius he was banished to Corsica on a charge, engineered by Messalina, of being the lover of Iulia Livilla, sister of Caligula; Agrippina procured his recall in 49 and made him Nero's tutor. His influence lasted until the death of his partner in power, Burrus, commander of the Praetorian Guard, in 62; in 65, being allegedly one of the conspirators against Nero under Piso's incompetent leadership, he was forced to commit suicide.[59] He was quaestor under Tiberius, praetor after his recall from Corsica, consul under Nero; save for his exile, his childhood in Spain

[58] The place of his birth is certain, see Mart., i, 61, 7, the date somewhat vague; estimates vary from 8 to 1 B.C.

[59] His mother, named for instance in the title of *dial.*, xii (*ad Heluiam matrem de consolatione*); his brothers, Tac., *ann.*, xv, 73, 4; xvi, 17, 3–4. His aunt (step-sister by another father of Helvia) was very attentive to him in his youth and nursed him through a serious illness. Her husband was governor of Egypt for sixteen years; Seneca seems to have been with them, for he was a witness of the stormy return voyage in which her husband died and she was barely able to get his body ashore for burial. This was in 31–2. She used her influence to get him the quaestorship, presumably before the death of Tiberius. For these facts, see *dial.*, xii, 19. His danger under Caligula, Cassius Dio, lix, 19, 8; for his health, cf. also Sen., *epp.*, 78, 1 *sqq.* His banishment, Dio, lx, 8, 5, cf. Tac., *ann.*, xiii, 42, 3, and the writings from exile, see below. His return and position at court, Tac., *ann.*, xii, 8, 3; the sequel is well known from all histories of the times, ancient and modern. Death, Tac., *ann.*, xv, 60, 3 *sqq.*

and a visit to Egypt,[60] he seems to have spent his life in Italy, and chiefly in or near Rome. Of his rhetorical education something has been said in speaking of his father; he studied philosophy under Sotion of Alexandria, a Stoic, who, possibly by a side-wind from the revived Pythagoreanism of the times, was a vegetarian and for a while persuaded his pupil to become one likewise, Attalos, also a Stoic, and Papirius Fabianus, a Sextian (see p. 422).[61] He married twice; the first wife, the date of whose death is uncertain, left him two sons, one of whom died soon after Seneca left for Corsica[62]; the second wife, Pompeia Paullina, unwillingly survived him.[63]

His prose works fall into three main groups, at least in our MS. tradition; the dates are in many cases doubtful.

(A) There has come down to us a collection of twelve books, making in all ten treatises, under the odd title of *dialogi*, which certainly is not the author's own, for dialogues they are not. Their separate titles, which again we have no right to suppose in all cases Seneca's, and their contents, are as follows:

1. *De prouidentia*. This is the usual title; the MSS. give it a more explicit, but clumsy heading, *Quare aliqua incommoda bonis uiris accidant, cum prouidentia sit*, 'Why some misfortunes befall good men, seeing that there is a Providence.' This in turn is but a re-wording in worse Latin of the opening sentence, which puts that question as having been addressed to Seneca by his

[60] Quaestorship and visit to Egypt, see last note; praetorship, Tac., *ann.*, xii, 8, 3; consulship, he was *suffectus* in 56 (Klein, *Fasti consulares*, Teubner, 1881, p. 36).

[61] Sotion, see Sen., *epp.*, 49, 2, cf. 108, 17–22; Jerome, *an. Abr.* 2029 (= 13); id., *de uir. ill.*, 12; Attalus, Sen., *epp.*, 108, 3; 13 *sqq.*; 23; *N.Q.*, ii, 48, 2. Fabianus, *epp.*, 100 (the whole letter concerns F., 12 testifies that S. had attended his lectures).

[62] In *dial.*, vii, 17, 1 he supposes an opponent of philosophy to say to him: quare ergo tu fortius loqueris quam uiuis . . . et lacrimas audita coniugis aut amici morte demittis? This may refer to the loss of his own wife; if so, it is clearly not Paullina, to whom he refers later in the same chapter and who survived him some time, see below. But the whole passage is such a mass of rhetorical generalities that it is perilous to extract autobiography from it. At any rate, no writing datable after the exile of S. speaks of any wife but Paullina in terms which imply that she is alive, and if he merely heard of his wife's death (supposing the above passage really to allude to her) presumably he was in Corsica at the time, but not long there, or he would surely mention her in writing to his mother, as he does other members of the family, *dial.*, xii, 18–19. Death of his little son, *dial.*, xii, 2, 5; the surviving one, *ibid.*, 18, 4 (Marcum blandissimum puerum ad cuius conspectum nulla potest durare tristitia).

[63] Tac., *ann.*, xv, 64, 2.

friend Lucilius (see p. 384). Seneca replies that he can give a better answer in a longer work which he has in mind, explaining that the whole universe is governed by Providence and our own natures have divinity in them. However, he will plead the cause of the gods [64] in this particular also. No ill can befall the good, for contraries will not mix. Apparent ills are nothing but tests of true manhood, to be welcomed as such. God saves the good from the only real evils, wicked deeds and thoughts.

It is not known when this was written; the dedication to Lucilius, the recipient of the *Epistulae* (see p. 369) and the reference to the large philosophical work (cf. p. 376) which Seneca seems to have written late in life suggest that it is not early.

2. *De constantia sapientis.* The fuller title is, *Nec iniuriam nec contumeliam accipere sapientem,* 'The (Stoic) sage can receive neither wrong nor insult.' He can receive no wrong, for he cannot be harmed; the only harm that can be done any one is to make him evil, which is impossible in the case of the sage. As to insult, his magnanimity and consciousness of his own worth make him as superior to it as grown men, persons of high position, doctors are above receiving any insult from an ill-mannered child, a licensed jester, or a madman.

Caligula was dead when Seneca wrote this, since he uses him as an example of the insulting man (18, 1–5). It is generally supposed to have been written early in Nero's reign.

3–5. *De ira,* in three books, addressed to Novatus, in answer to his request for advice as to how anger might be restrained. The first book describes anger, proving it to be neither necessary, useful nor noble. The second shows that it is not an uncontrollable impulse, for although it may be first excited by a cause outside ourselves, it is in our own power to allow that cause to affect us to anger or not. There follow a discussion on the difference between anger and cruelty, and a reconsideration of a question raised in the first book, whether the sage will ever be angry; indeed, a good part of the material of the first book reappears in new wording. Towards the end of the book Seneca begins to discuss measures for restraining anger, and this topic, interspersed with examples of angry and patient men, occupies the third. The whole work is thus ill-arranged, different parts of the subject being curiously tangled one with another.

Caligula is again used more than once as an example, and is said (iii, 18, 3) to have committed one of his atrocities 'lately' (*modo*).

[64] Causam deorum agam, i, 1; the source, perhaps, of Milton's 'justify the ways of God to man'. Annotated ed. (Dutch) by W. Klei, Zwolle 1950.

Probably therefore the book was written early in the reign of Claudius, which fits with the use of the name Novatus, not Gallio, for Seneca's brother and the absence of any allusion to his exile. It is possible that Claudius, who had fits of anger on occasion, read this work and actually alluded to it in a public notice.[65]

6. *Ad Marciam de consolatione.* This lady was Cremutius Cordus' daughter (cf. p. 349); she had lost her son three years before Seneca wrote his address to her,[66] and still felt her bereavement very deeply. Seneca begins with examples of heavy losses which have befallen others, contrasting the excessive grief of Octavia for the death of Marcellus with the self-restraint of Livia when Drusus died. Then follows a large selection of the stock topics of consolation (cf. p. 339), with more examples of fortitude; here and there, partly because they both follow the same models and partly because Seneca has reminiscences of Cicero, the work reads almost like a paraphrase of the first book of the *Tusculans* (see p. 189).

There is no clear indication of date.

7. *De uita beata.* This work is preserved only in part; the twenty-eight chapters which we have show clearly enough that its plan was to define happiness on Stoic lines, defend this against the objections of other schools and, presumably, to end by elaborating the subject with eloquently urged examples.

The work being addressed to Gallio, not Novatus, *i.e.*, to his brother after his adoption, it must be later than the *de ira*; beyond this we know nothing certain of the time when it was written.

8. Another imperfect treatise is the *de otio*, of which we have but eight chapters. The MSS., obviously following an older copy which had lost several pages, attach it with no indication of a break to the end of the *de uita beata*, and Lipsius [67] was the first to separate it. It is a justification of the retirement of a Stoic from public affairs, which generally they took part in as a matter of principle. Explicitly the Stoic in question is Seneca himself,

[65] Seneca (*de ira*, i, 4, 1) differentiates *ira*, anger, from *iracundia*, hot temper. Suetonius says (*Claud.*, 38) that Claudius irae atque iracundiae conscius sibi utramque excusauit edicto distinxitque, pollicitus alteram quidem breuem et innoxiam, alteram non iniustam fore. It is perfectly possible that the well-meaning Imperial pedant had read Seneca's work and taken his warnings to heart; but the distinction itself is introduced by S. as something well known, hence the resemblance may be accidental.

[66] *Ad Marciam*, i, 7: tertius iam praeterit annus.

[67] Justus Lipsius, textual critic, exegete and historian, 1547–1606. See Sandys, ii, pp. 301–5. His work on Seneca is the foundation of organized knowledge concerning his writings.

and therefore the work was written after 62, when he withdrew from a court whose vileness was too much for even his wide tolerance, and his own position was daily becoming more insecure.

9. The *de otio* is apparently addressed to a friend, Serenus or Lucilius [68]; the next essay, *de tranquillitate animi*, begins with a dialogue between Serenus and the author, if that can be called a dialogue in which one speaker states his difficulties at considerable length and the other then treats him to a philosophic lecture of over thirty Teubner pages. The question and answer have singularly little to do with each other, for Serenus asks how, having devoted himself to a life of severe virtue, he may be rid of passing moods of envy of luxury and occasional debates with himself as to whether the particular form of virtuous living he has adopted is the best, while Seneca replies by detailing the various forms of inquietude which afflict idle and even vicious livers and some of the vulgar fears, as that of death, from which so nearly perfect a Stoic as his friend should *ex hypothesi* have long ago freed himself.

Again we have no clear indication as to date; it would seem not to be an early work, for Seneca is appealed to as an expert in the cure of souls (1, 2, quare enim non uerum ut medico fatear? 17, rogo itaque, si quod habes remedium quo hanc fluctuationem meam sistas, dignum me putes qui tibi tranquillitatem debeam).

10. The tractate *de breuitate uitae* is addressed to Paulinus. Seneca's answer to that complaint is that life is quite long enough if we do not waste it. His own mentality, or at least the attitude which he thought proper to feign, is best shown by the thirteenth chapter, in which practically all disinterested search after knowledge, including historical studies, is listed among the things whereby the foolish waste their time.

In 13, 8, Seneca remarks that historians state Sullam ultimum Romanorum protulisse pomerium. This ancient ceremony of enlarging the sacred boundary of Rome, in commemoration of a corresponding enlargement of her territories by conquest, was performed by Claudius some time between Jan. 25, 49 and Jan. 24, 50; Seneca could hardly have failed to know this if it had been done (he is apparently ignorant

[68] Annaeus Serenus, to whom also the *de constantia* is addressed, according to the MS. heading. He was commander of the Vigiles after Tigellinus, and died some time before Seneca. Lucilius, the addressee of the Letters and according to some the author of the *Aetna*, will be discussed on p. 384. That he is addressed in the *de otio* is suggested by Pichon, see Schanz-Hosius, ii, p. 690; the only authoritative MS. gives in the table of contents, as a separate work, *ad Serenum de otio*, but erases the first two words.

that Augustus had done it), therefore he wrote before the later of these two dates if not the earlier. See Tac., *ann.*, xii, 23, 4.

11. Nowhere else does Seneca descend quite so low as in the *Consolatio ad Polybium*. The person addressed is Claudius' powerful freedman, who had recently lost his brother. That Seneca, then in exile, should try to win the good graces of an official who had charge of petitions addressed to the Emperor was natural, and to comfort the bereaved is a charitable action. But it was not necessary to attribute to the survivor (whom, being himself a free-born man, Seneca no doubt heartily despised as a low upstart) every virtue in the Stoic manuals; he might have reminded him that his duty to his master forbade him indulging too much in grief without saying that the sight of Claudius' divine and effulgent person was an instant cure for every sorrow[69]; and, it might be added, a writer who certainly laid claim to originality of style need not so patently have imitated the least dignified parts of the poems of the exiled Ovid.[70]

Seneca writes some time after arriving in Corsica, *i.e.*, some time after 41, see note 70; but he has not been there as much as four years, for 13, 2 expresses the hope that Claudius will enjoy a triumph over the Britons; in 44 this actually took place.

That desperate attempts should have been made to prove this disgusting work spurious is but natural, see Schanz-Hosius, ii, pp. 693–4; it is, however, clearly genuine. The beginning is missing in our MS. tradition.

12. Much better than this deplorable production is the essay *ad Heluiam matrem de consolatione*. It is pleasant to record that Seneca in private life seems to have been amiable and a good son. For her sake he takes a manly tone and proves to her that his exile is not a thing to be mourned for. His material is, of course, the current commonplaces on exile, the theme of a hundred essays in an age when such sentences were frequent and banishment was perhaps especially often the lot of philosophers, or those who claimed to be such and on the strength of their studies indulged in opposition generally as futile as it was factious. His advice

[69] *Cons. ad Pol.*, 2; 12, 3.

[70] *Cons.*, 18, 9: haec, utcunque potui, longo iam situ obsoleto et hebetato animo composui. quae si aut parum respondere ingenio tuo aut parum mederi dolori uidebuntur, cogita quam non possit is alienae uacare consolationi quem sua mala occupatum tenent, et quam non facile Latina ei homini uerba succurrant quem barbarorum inconditus et barbaris quoque humanioribus grauis fremitus circumsonat. Cf. Ovid, *trist.*, iii, 1, 17–18; 10, 5–6; 14, 43 *sqq.*; iv, 1, 1–2, &c. It may be mentioned in passing that imitations of Ovid's verse are very common in Seneca's prose.

to her, to study philosophy for herself and in the meantime to take comfort in the affection of her sister and grandchild, if somewhat pedantic, is at least very well meant.

The work was, of course, written from Corsica ; he had been there some little time (1, 2), but how long there is nothing to show.

(B) Four prose works, of very different lengths, survive outside the above collection and the long series of letters (p. 369).

1. The first in date is infinitely the best Seneca ever wrote ; it is also one which no honourable man would have written. Claudius, to whom Seneca had professed that he owed his life [71] and who certainly had recalled him from banishment and given him a position of high influence, was dead, perhaps murdered. Ordinary decency would have seemed to dictate that Seneca should confine himself to congratulations and good wishes to his pupil, the young Nero, and leave the memory of his dead master in peace. Instead of this, he wrote an extremely funny account of how the old Emperor, having died in the most undignified manner possible, knocked at the gate of heaven and claimed admittance among the other gods. There ensued a brisk debate, ending, on the motion of the deified Augustus, in an order to Claudius to quit the precincts of heaven within thirty days. On this, Mercury took him to the lower world, where Aiakos sentenced him to play for ever at dice (an allusion to his weakness for gambling) with a dice-box which had no bottom. However, he was rescued from this by the ghost of Caligula, who claimed him as his slave and produced witnesses to prove that in life he had treated him as one. This reasonable plea being allowed, Caligula presented him to Aiakos, who in turn handed him over to Menander his freedman. The title of this witty libel is *Apocolocyntosis*.

The evidence for the title is external. Cassius Dio says [72] : συνέθηκε . . . ὁ Σενέκας σύγγραμμα ἀποκολοκύντωσιν αὐτὸ ὥσπερ τινὰ ἀπαθανάτισιν ὀνομάσας. From this we may correct the St. Gall MS., our chief authority, *diui Claudii ΑΠΟΘΗΟΣΙΣ* (*sic*) *Annaei Senecae per saturam*. The word is a parody of ἀποθέωσις, evidently ; the point of the second member, which is somewhat indecent, has at last been seen by H. Wagenvoort, in *Mnemosyne*, tert. ser., 1 (1934), p. 4 *sqq*.

Besides the matter, the form is interesting, for it is that of a Menippean satire (cf. p. 228). For the most part it is easy, colloquial prose, full of highly idiomatic phrases and catchwords, not always readily intelligible to moderns, with frequent tags of Greek ; but passages of verse are scattered up and down it pro-

[71] *Cons. ad Pol.*, 13, 2.

[72] Dio, *epit.*, lx, 35, 3.

fusely, the most important being a description of the Fates spinning a golden thread for Nero, while Apollo prophesies the golden age which is opening under his beneficent government.

2. Seneca was more suitably employed in recommending a practically absolute monarch to rule mercifully. The treatise *de clementia*, whereof we have one book complete and a part of the second, was evidently presented to Nero shortly after his accession. It sometimes attains real eloquence in presenting so good a case; perhaps its best recommendation is that Shakespere took hints from it for Portia's great speech in the *Merchant of Venice*. Book I keeps mainly to practical advice, seasoned with well-told stories of the clemency of great princes, especially of Augustus; Book II runs into hair-splitting distinctions between *clementia*, which is a virtue, and *misericordia*, which is a weakness, especially common among women, of whom Seneca was usually very contemptuous, at least on paper.

3. A longer and more elaborate work, extending to seven books, is the *de beneficiis*, addressed to Aebutius Liberalis, a man otherwise almost unknown, evidently a friend of Seneca. The best things in this treatise, which is for the most part a dry and casuistical discussion of what constitutes a benefit, who can and should receive it, and so forth, are the occasional examples of great and heroic actions for the good of another, as those in Book III [73] of the devotion of slaves. These, incidentally, are introduced by one of Seneca's best epigrams, whereof he has many. 'Can a master receive a benefit from his slave, then? No, but one human being can from another.'

It is clear from *de benef.*, i, 15, 5–6, that this book was written after the death of Claudius; how long after, and at what intervals the remaining books were produced, we have no certain indication. The title is Seneca's own, as *epp.*, 81, 3 testifies.

4. Late in life, Seneca addressed to Lucilius a work on physical science, the *Naturales quaestiones*.[74] This seems to have been enormously popular and to have suffered from its popularity; it has come down to us in a multitude of MSS.,[75] which disagree among themselves as to the order of the books, but agree in

[73] *De benef.*, iii, 23 *sqq*. The words translated in the text are *ibid.*, 22, 3: quid ergo? beneficium dominus a seruo accipit? immo homo ab homine.

[74] The proper form of the title is probably *Naturalium quaestionum libri octo*.

[75] See the preface to A. Gercke's critical edition, vol. ii of the Teubner Seneca, and for a conspectus of works dealing with the *N.Q.*, Schanz-Hosius, ii, p. 700 *sqq*.

omitting, clearly by some accidental loss of leaves at an unknown date in the history of the text, a great part of what they variously style the fourth, seventh, eighth or even tenth book [76] and of the one next following. The original number of books seems to have been eight. After a preface on the glories of the subject he is to treat, Seneca proceeds to deal with 'celestial fires', *i.e.*, meteors and the like; next with thunder and lightning, a section very interesting to students of ancient, especially of Etruscan religion, since he incorporates in it a large amount of the theory of Etruscan divination from those phenomena, taken from the work of a certain CAECINA, 'an eloquent man', says Seneca,[77] 'who would have made a name for himself sooner or later in oratory if he had not been overshadowed by Cicero'. As his name implies, he was of Etruscan descent, and therefore no bad witness for the traditional lore of his own people. Seneca next treats of the hydrosphere (*de aquis terrestribus*), going on to discuss that stock problem, never settled till modern times, the causes of the inundation of the Nile. This leads him to clouds, rain and hail, after which come wind, then earthquakes and finally comets. The whole work contains many references to the opinions of Greek physicists whose writings are lost to us and known to Seneca, probably not directly but in compendia and handbooks of philosophy. There are not a few good descriptions of striking natural phenomena in the work; of course, its independent scientific value is *nil*, and it is made wearisome at times by the author's incurable habit of moralizing. Thus, he concludes his account of thunder and lightning by saying [78] that he knows Lucilius had rather not be afraid of such things than understand them, and proceeding to draw edifying lessons from the facts and theories he has just given.

The date of Book VI, at all events, is determined by its opening chapter, an interesting description of the earthquake which damaged Pompeii in 63.[79] There seems no reason to suppose that the whole

[76] See Gercke's critical note to the title of his Book IV*a*. I follow his order for convenience' sake.

[77] *N.Q.*, ii, 56, 2: hoc apud Caecinam inuenio, facundum uirum; habuisset aliquando in eloquentia nomen nisi illum Ciceronis umbra pressisset. For a collection of his fragments, see G. Zimmermann, *de A. Caecina scriptore*, dissert., Berlin, 1852. For Etruscan fulgural divination, see especially C. O. Thulin, *Die etruskische Disciplin*, 1, Göteborg, 1906.

[78] *N.Q.*, ii, 59.

[79] *N.Q.*, vi, 1, 2: nonis Februariis hic (terrae motus) fuit, Regulo et Verginio consulibus, *i.e.*, Feb. 5, 63.

work took very long to compose or was written at different times; we may therefore think of Seneca as writing it about 64.

(C.) Last of the prose works we may put the bulky *epistulae morales*, addressed to Lucilius and numbering in all 124 as we have them.[80] That they, or at least some of them, are real letters, written in answer to questions on matters of conduct or other points of interest to the two friends, is very likely; it is, however, certain that what we have is a collection intended by the author to be published. The order of the letters is much too good to be accidental. Also, most of them, though they may pretend to be letters and have been really sent as such, are short essays; *e.g.*, the eightieth, written or supposed to be written on a day when Seneca is alone and at ease because most of his acquaintance are at a kind of boxing-match (*sphaeromachia*), is a short meditation on the theme of the neglect of mental and spiritual exercises, when the more arduous and less important training of the body is assiduously practised. Taken all together, they are perhaps Seneca's most pleasing philosophic work, because his least pretentious.

It has generally been held, since the time of Lipsius (see note 67) that Seneca wrote the Epistles in or about 63 and 64. This view is recommended by the plain references to his withdrawal from public life, *e.g.*, 8, 2: secessi non tantum ab hominibus sed a rebus, and to his advanced age, as 12, 1–3 (the house he built, the trees he planted, the little slave-boy who was his pet, are all very old now).

The style in which all these works are composed may be roughly described as a somewhat disconnected series of short, effectively constructed sentences, many of which contain or end in a pointed, epigrammatic remark or *sententia*. The period is used little. A rough rendering of a few lines from an epistle[81] will perhaps give a clearer idea of his manner than an abstract discussion. Seneca sees a ship come in which is bringing him letters from Alexandria concerning his property there. He feels in no hurry to meet it, for he knows that he cannot have gained or lost much.

'So I ought to feel, even if I were not an old man; much more so, since I am one. However small my means, I should now have more

[80] There were more in antiquity, for Aulus Gellius (xii, 2, 3–11) quotes from Book xxii epistularum moralium quas ad Lucilium composuit, whereas our MSS. divide the letters into but twenty books and the passage Gellius cites is nowhere in them. For other references to letters now lost, see Schanz-Hosius, ii, p. 707, 2.

[81] *Epp.*, 77, 3 *sqq.*

journey-money than journey left, especially as we are set out on a journey which there is no need to finish. Travel is incomplete if you stop half-way or before reaching the place you are bound for; life is not, if well spent. Wherever you stop, if you stop well, life is complete. And sometimes one must stop bravely, and that not for very important reasons.' He then goes on to tell of a suicide and the deliberations which took place before it. A Stoic thus advises the person in question. 'My dear Marcellinus, do not torment yourself, as if you were taking counsel on some great matter. Living is not a great matter; all your slaves are living, so are all animals. It is a great matter to die honourably, wisely and valiantly. Consider how long you will go on doing the same thing; food, sleep, desire, that is the circle in which we move. To wish to die is not only for a wise or brave or wretched man; even a bored man may wish it.'

One outstanding feature is that this sort of writing is far easier to represent in a modern language than Cicero's, for in the latter case, the elaborate structure of the sentences often has to be broken up into smaller units before it can be adequately translated into our idioms, with the exception of somewhat old-fashioned and ponderous German. English and French have on the whole elected for the short sentence, or if they use longer ones, they construct them loosely, and not as periods whose sense is not complete till the last word is reached, indeed sometimes can hardly be guessed till then. But the soundest opinion in both Greece and Italy was that the periodic structure, varied by an occasional shorter sentence or group of them, was that best suited to the genius of their tongues for serious prose; everyday chat or light compositions which imitated it were another matter. Seneca, in this as in several more technical points, less easily to be brought out in a translation, represents the influence of the Asianic school.

We may well believe Tacitus when he says that Seneca had a pleasant talent and well fitted to the taste of those times.[82] He has indeed all those qualities which at once strike a reader, happy, if not impressive, choice of words and phrases, a certain flexibility, euphonious collocation of sounds, highly elaborate rhythm, and withal perspicuity. It is not until after reading him for some time that it becomes apparent how wearisome a writer grows who has nothing else, neither depth of thought, real originality, nor the power to become perfectly plain and simple, with no epigrams and no rhetorical drawing of morals, when the matter calls for it. He is to a really great stylist what a bright popular air, set to sentimentally pretty words, is to a musical masterpiece.

[82] Tac., *ann.*, xiii, 3, 2.

Besides his achievements in prose, he is conspicuous in the poetry of that day.[83] A curious chance has preserved his dramatic works complete, while robbing us of the whole of Republican tragedy and of the productions of Varius and Ovid (pp. 340, 337); and therefore we are able to form some opinion of the kind of closet-drama which that age admired. We have ten tragedies bearing his name, whereof one is certainly not his, the others for the most part certainly are. That they were ever acted or meant to be acted is neither likely nor supported by testimonies of any sort; it is very probable that they were publicly recited, whether by the author or some one else, on occasion, since their merits are such as would be made most conspicuous by being read not only, as was the invariable custom, aloud, but with proper emphasis and intonation.

There being no indication of the relative date of these works, it is convenient to take them in the order of the best MS. This begins with the *Hercules*, usually called *Hercules furens* to distinguish it from the other play of the same name, though the traditional evidence for the adjective is weak. In general, the plot is that of Euripides' play[84]; Herakles, returning from the underworld, kills the tyrant Lykos who is persecuting his supposed father and his wife, and then, maddened by the Furies sent against him by Iuno, kills his children and their mother. Regaining his senses, he is dissuaded from suicide by Amphitryon and offered a refuge in Athens by Theseus. Thus far Seneca's model; but, besides minor changes,[85] the subtle characterization of the

[83] 'Vtinam', says Porson in his inaugural lecture on Euripides (*R. Porsoni Aduersaria*, ed. Monk and Blomfield, Cambridge, 1812, p. 30), 'uel istam (Ennius' *Hecuba*) uel aliam quampiam eius generis integram fabulam ex uetustatis situ aliquando erueremus; ipse quidem talem thesaurum libenter omnium Senecae, quae feruntur, tragoediarum iactura redimerem.' This expresses at once the opinion of the most competent critics as to the merits of the plays and the passing doubts which have been held concerning their authorship. Apart from the general resemblance in style and sentiment to the prose works, we have the following external evidence: Quintilian (ix, 2, 8; Medea apud Senecam, the name Seneca in Quint., with one doubtful exception, meaning the younger); [Probus] (iv, 224, 22, and 246, 19 Keil) and Tertullian (*de anima*, 42, 2; *de resurr. carn.*, 1), both for the *Troades*; the commentator upon Stat., *Theb.*, iv, 530 (*Thyestes*); Terentianus Maurus (vi, p. 404 Keil, line 2672; *Hercules furens*); Priscian (ii, p. 253, 7 Keil, *ibid.*, 9; *Phaedra, Agamemnon*), all for the Senecan authorship, while against there is only Apollinaris Sidonius, *carm.*, ix, 232 *sqq.* See further, p. 387.

[84] See Rose, *H.G.L.*, pp. 187–8.

[85] Iuno, not Amphitryon, speaks the prologue; the figure of Madness does not appear; Theseus enters early, to give him an opportunity to describe Hell while Herakles is away killing Lykos.

original, which makes his Herakles human and understandable in the most terrible surroundings, is replaced by rhetoric and epigram, both good of their kind, and both as a rule out of place where they stand. Thus, Herakles, having killed Lykos, will not wash his hands before bringing a sacrifice of thanksgiving, because a tyrant's blood is the most acceptable of all offerings.[86] Old Amphitryon, no less eloquent than his putative son, has already assured Lykos that the chief proof of Herakles' divine origin is Iuno's hatred of him and sustained against the king a learned mythological debate to show that gods may be subject to all manner of misfortunes and labours.[87] Not infrequently the tone rises from merely rhetorical to eloquent or even noble,[88] but of genuine drama there is little, only sensationalism.[89]

The *Troades* seems to have been suggested partly by Euripides' play of the same name and partly by his *Hecuba*.[90] The plot turns on the sacrifice of Polyxena to the ghost of Achilles and the slaying of young Astyanax, Hektor's son, after the taking of Troy. Here the resemblance to the Greek ends, for the deaths are delayed and much occasion given for school-eloquence by a debate between Pyrrhos and Agamemnon concerning the sacrifice, an attempt by Andromache to hide her child in his father's tomb, and the introduction of Helen, who tries to persuade Polyxena that she is being led off to marry Pyrrhos.

The so-called *Phoenissae* (again the title is Euripidean) [91] is nothing more than three disjointed scenes, one between Oidipus

[86] *H.F.*, 920–4.

[87] *Ibid.*, 439 *sqq.*

[88] One passage has the honour of being the bridge between Sophokles and Shakespere. The former makes one of the characters in the *Oedipus Tyrannus* cry out in horror at the ills of the house, *οἶμαι γὰρ οὔτ' ἂν Ἴστρον οὔτε Φᾶσιν ἂν | νίψαι καθαρμῷ τήνδε τὴν στέγην* (*O.T.*, 1227–8): Seneca expands this too learnedly when Herakles is in the depths of remorse, *H.F.*, 1323 *sqq.*: quis Tanais aut quis Nilus aut quis Persica/uiolentus unda Tigris aut Rhenus ferox/Tagusue Hibera turbidus gaza fluens/abluere dextram poterit? Arctoum licet/Maeotis in me gelida transfundat mare/et tota Tethys per meas currat manus,/haerebit altum facinus. Shakespere was not a good Grecian, but every Elizabethan knew his Seneca, and he caught at the best of this passage and improved it beyond easy recognition, *Macb.*, ii, 2, 76–9: Will all great *Neptunes* Ocean wash this blood Cleane from my Hand? no: this my Hand will rather The multitudinous Seas incarnadine, Making the Greene one, Red.

[89] In justice to Seneca, it should be pointed out that those critics are wrong who think that he makes Herakles murder his wife on the stage; Amphitryon (*H.F.*, 1002 *sqq.*) sees and horrifiedly comments on the murders through the door of the house, which Herakles has broken down.

[90] Rose, *op. cit.*, pp. 184, 187.

[91] *Ibid.*, p. 192 *sq.*

and his daughter Antigone, another between Oidipus and a messenger, who brings word that his two sons are going to war with each other, the third between Iokaste, Antigone, certain attendants, and the two sons, between whom their mother vainly tries to make peace.

The *Medea* is an exaggeration of Euripides' play.[92] In the Greek, Medeia, maddened by the desertion of her husband Jason, first contrives a safe retreat for herself and a day's delay in which to mature her plans before leaving Corinth; she then murders Jason's new bride and her own two sons, these in order to leave Jason quite bereft. Throughout, she remains a woman in the grip of a horrible fury of revenge, but still a woman. In Seneca, she is little but witch and murderess. He, whether on his own initiative or following some intervening model, removes the Euripidean scene in which she asks Aigeus, king of Athens, to receive her when she leaves Corinth and substitutes for it one in which she is busied with her incantations.

The *Phaedra* shows none of the psychological subtleties of Euripides' surviving *Hippolytus*, though it may owe something to his lost play of the same title.[93] Seneca's Phaidra is not a woman naturally chaste, afflicted with an overpowering illicit desire against which she struggles, but a wanton, who being hotly in love with her stepson tries, despite all advice to the contrary, to tempt him. He is not a coldly chaste man, but a woman-hater, who is rather glad that his mother is dead, because there is no other whom he must not detest. The divine interventions which occur at the beginning and end of the Euripidean play are not in Seneca, who makes little use of gods, though he likes ghosts and other horrors; Phaidra, having brought about the death of Hippolytos by false accusations, is struck with remorse, tells all and then stabs herself; in the Greek she was already dead when he died.

The plot of the *Oedipus* is in its main outlines derived from Sophokles' masterpiece.[94] Oidipus, trying to save the city of Thebes from the pestilence which has been sent upon it, decrees the expulsion of the murderer of his predecessor Laios; it transpires that he is himself the slayer, and also that his wife Iokaste is his own mother. He thereupon blinds himself in horror at his unwitting parricide and incest. Sophokles lets the unfolding of such moving events work their own effect on the audience by his

[92] See Rose, *op. cit.*, p. 181 *sq.*

[93] See *ibid.*, p. 182 *sq.*

[94] *Ibid.*, p. 165 *sq.* How much the changes may owe to the rhetorical closet drama of the fourth century B.C. (Rose, *ibid.*, p. 211) is a question which we lack the material to answer.

matchless telling of them ; Seneca must try to make the situation more impressive by introducing a long scene of necromancy in which the truth is told by the ghost of the murdered Laios, and further makes Iokaste stab herself on the stage, instead of following the example of his model and letting the suicide occur behind the scenes. This, however, is perhaps largely the result of the play never having been meant to be actually performed.

For the *Agamemnon* it can hardly be said that Seneca goes to Aeschylus,[95] though the main events, the murder of the returning Agamemnon by his wife Klytaimestra and her lover Aigisthos, together with the slaying of the Trojan princess Kassandra who is the king's paramour, are necessarily the same. But the prologue is spoken by the ghost of Thyestes, an epigrammatic phantom who finally, realizing that the sun will not rise in his hateful presence, courteously retires to allow day to dawn ; Klytaimestra hesitates between her passion for Aigisthos and her duty to Agamemnon in a scene which is a very poor imitation of Helen's letter to Paris [96] ; the most nearly impressive figure is Kassandra, the distant ancestress of Shakespere's Queen Margaret and Chettle's Lucibella.[97]

We cannot name with certainty any Greek original for the *Thyestes* ; though there were tragedies written on that theme, none has come down to us. The horrible story of how Atreus, pretending to be reconciled to his brother Thyestes, entertained the latter at a banquet and fed him with the flesh of his own sons would attract Seneca, who loves gory details and provides them in great abundance. The hideously bereaved father does not lose his power to speak pointedly ; when asked by Atreus, ' Knowest thou thy sons ? ' he looks at the children's heads displayed on the table before him and replies, ' I know my brother '.[98]

Seneca's name is attached to the portentously long *Hercules* which bears commonly the additional title of *Oetaeus*. The death of Herakles and his pyre on Mount Oite is one of Sophokles' most admirably used subjects [99] ; the Latin play is so absurd that

[95] See Rose, *H.G.L.*, pp. 154–5.

[96] See above, p. 329.

[97] See, for a good recent treatment of these somewhat Senecan figures, P. Simpson, *The Theme of Revenge in Elizabethan Tragedy*, Proc. Brit. Acad., 1935, annual Shakespeare Lecture, pp. 5, 30.

[98] For the legend, see Rose, *H.G.M.*, p. 247 (where correct, in ed. 1, the miswriting, Aithra for Aerope). The passage quoted is 1005–6 : gnatos ecquid agnoscis tuos ?—agnosco fratrem.

[99] In the *Trachiniae*, for which see Rose, *H.G.L.*, pp. 167–8 ; for the legend, Rose, *H.G.M.*, p. 219. Herakles had long become a model for the virtues of the Cynic-Stoic ideal, owing to his traditional simplicity of life and unending toils.

several scholars, with whom the writer is inclined to agree, have refused to credit the Senecan authorship. The puppet-figures of his undoubted plays have a sort of semblance of humanity about them ; one could imagine a real dramatist taking them and their situations, toning down their exaggerations, and making them fairly credible. But the Herakles of the *Hercules Oetaeus* never approaches reality of any sort, but divides his speeches between rants concerning his own divinity [100] and elaborate exhibitions of his superiority to the pain which is killing him. That the language and metre resemble Seneca's is not questioned.

Certainly spurious, on the other hand, is the *Octavia*, the one example we have, and not a contemptible specimen, of the *fabula praetexta* (cf. p. 35). The author is influenced by Seneca, and actually introduces him and Nero as characters. The subject, which is adorned with some of the usual machinery of that age, including the appearance of Agrippina's ghost, is the divorce of Octavia by Nero, in 62. The author was well acquainted with the events of the time, down to the death of Nero, which the ghost foretells in some detail, if we may judge from a corrupt text. The natural conclusion, since nothing points to his being as late as Tacitus, for instance, is that he wrote of what had happened within his own memory, perhaps in the days of Vespasian.[101]

The great influence of Seneca not only upon his contemporaries but in later times, although his style went out of fashion with the Ciceronian and archaizing movements of the following generations (cf. pp. 399, 518), was partly due to the respect which the Christians felt for him. At once too honest and too ill acquainted with history to perceive the deep gulf between his precepts and his practice, they felt that one who wrote so edifyingly and so eloquently must have been, if not exactly a Christian himself, at all events not far from the truth.[102] There even survives a forged correspondence between him and St. Paul, which was known to St. Jerome, but not to any one earlier.[103] In view of all this, it is somewhat remarkable that a large part of his

[100] As *Herc. Oet.*, 1709–10, and the whole passage. There is a resemblance between some of this and what the genuinely Senecan Herakles says (*H.F.*, 957 *sqq.*) when he begins to rave.

[101] See Schanz-Hosius, ii, p. 473 *sq.* I confess I cannot understand the attitude of some excellent scholars who have tried to prove Seneca the author.

[102] He is *saepe noster*, Tert., *de anim.*, 20 ; potuit esse uerus dei cultor si quis illi monstrasset, Lactant., *inst. diu.*, vi, 24, 14. There is of course a real resemblance between popular Stoic ethics and those of Christianity, cf. Jerome *in Isai.* 4, 10 (iv, p. 159e Vall.).

[103] Jerome, *de uir. illust.*, 12.

works is missing. We are told in general that he wrote poetry, *poemata*, which would seem to imply that his tragedies were not his only verse ; but only a few epigrams survive, and the authorship of these is not certain.[104] Of his prose works, we know of several which have disappeared.

His speeches, including his forensic orations, which had a considerable reputation, have all vanished ; the fragments are in *O.R.F.*, pp. 578–84, and comprise almost no verbatim quotations. For his missing epistles, see note 79. A palimpsest (Vaticanus Palatinus 24) of about the year 500 contains remnants of a biography of his father (*de uita patris*) and of a work *quomodo amicitia continenda sit* ; they are best edited by W. Studemund in the Breslau *Philologische Abhandlungen*, ii, 3 (1888). Dio says that he wrote in exile a work full of praises of Messalina and of Claudius' freedmen, which he afterwards was ashamed of and suppressed ; either this is an inaccurate reference to the *Consolatio ad Polybium* or the suppression was effective.[105] Pliny and others name two works apparently geographical, one on Egypt, the other on India.[106] He himself more than once speaks of a large work discussing the whole of ethics and casuistry (*moralem philosophiam . . . et omnes ad eam pertinentes quaestiones*)[107] ; if this was ever completed and published, we have quite lost it. A shorter treatise, *de officiis*, is cited by Diomedes and was apparently known in the Middle Ages ; it seems to have been used by Martin of Bracara.[108] Lactantius had read certain *exhortationes* and a work *de immatura morte* ;[109] Augustine, an essay *de superstitione* or *contra superstitiones*,[110] Jerome, one *de matrimonio*.[111] Seneca himself tells us that in his young days he wrote on earthquakes ; Pliny used writings of his concerning fish and stones ; Cassiodorus recommends his work *de forma mundi*. The fairly obvious suggestion that some of these are from the missing parts of the *Natural Questions* has been made, but there is no proof.[112]

[104] We have three headed with his name, a number of others which are grouped with them (as by Baehrens and Buecheler-Riese in their editions of the *Anthologia Latina*) because of a similarity in content and style. If they, or any of them, are really by Seneca, they are early works (before and during the exile, to which some of them refer), for the technique of the verse lacks the polish which the tragedies, especially their choral parts, regularly show.

[105] Dio Cassius, lxi, 10, 2.

[106] Servius on *Aen.*, vi, 154, and ix, 30 ; Pliny, *N.H.*, vi, 60, and the index to that book.

[107] Seneca, *epp.*, 106, 2, and elsewhere.

[108] Diomedes, i, p. 366, 14 Keil ; for Martin, see Schanz-Hosius, ii, p. 718.

[109] Lact., *diu. inst.*, i, 7, 13 ; iii, 12, 11.

[110] Aug., *de ciu. dei*, vi, 10 ; Diomedes, i, p. 379, 19 Keil.

[111] Jerome, *adu. Iouianum*, i, 49.

[112] Seneca, *N.Q.*, vi, 4, 2 ; Pliny, *N.H.*, ix, 167, and index ; xxxvi, index ; Cassiodorus, *inst. diuin.* ii, p. 153, 3 Mynors.

During Seneca's lifetime there wrote two highly interesting men, one a better Stoic and a better poet than he, the other a man of the world who ended a life of pleasure, frivolity and wit by a death not only brave but humorous. The former was AVLVS PERSIVS FLACCVS, a well-born and wealthy young man, a native of Volaterrae in Etruria, whose short life [113] (Dec. 4, 34–Nov. 24, 62) was yet long enough to enable him to produce one remarkable little book. Of singularly gentle and modest character, Persius was further encouraged to a virtuous life by coming, while still very young,[114] under the influence of Cornutus, a Stoic teacher of some importance. To his instructions the young man listened eagerly, and seems to have sought some means of spreading the ethics of the school himself. A reading of Lucilius gave him the medium which he, having had the usual rhetorical training, could use. He produced six satires, the first on the decay of literary taste in his own time and the neglect of the manly Republican authors, the second on the vanity of wealth and luxury, the third on idleness, the fourth on self-knowledge, the fifth on true liberty, the sixth on the proper use of riches. The style is one of the most extraordinary in all Latin, obscure, contorted, crammed with allusions, especially to Lucilius and Horace; the verses are purposely rough,[115] as befits the *genre*; yet these little works show not only intense earnestness of purpose but, here and there, an eloquence which would recommend a far weaker cause than the one he has at heart. The collection, revised and published posthumously by Caesius Bassus and Cornutus, quickly won and always kept a high place in the esteem of discerning readers.[116]

A fellow-member with Seneca of the court of Nero, GAIVS PETRONIVS, is commonly known to moderns as Petronius Arbiter, because Tacitus says he was *elegantiae arbiter*, almost a semi-official Master of the Revels, to the Emperor.[117] He was a man of

[113] Our chief source of information, besides what he tells us, is a short biography, said to come *de commentario Probi Valeri*; it is generally prefixed to modern editions of him.

[114] Persius, v, 30. For L. ANNAEVS CORNVTVS, see Rose, *H.G.L.*, p. 411; his only surviving work is in Greek. The *Life* says that Persius knew Seneca sero . . . sed non ut caperetur eius ingenio. Indeed Cornutus and Seneca were unfriendly; Sen., *epp.*, 88, is, in all probability, an attack on Cornutus' combination of philosophic and philological studies.

[115] He shows, in laughing at the over-refined technique of contemporaries, that he was himself master of it, i, 93 *sqq*.

[116] See Quintilian, x, 1, 94; Martial, iv, 29, 7–8.

[117] Tacitus, *ann.*, xvi, 17, 1; 18–20. Tacitus does not mention the *Saturae*; that they are identical with Petronius' message to Nero is a silly and long-exploded error. The date was 66.

pleasure, capable on occasion of vigour and certainly not lacking either courage or wit. He showed both when the enmity of Tigellinus caused an indictment of treason to be trumped up against him. He killed himself in a leisurely and painless fashion, by bleeding slowly to death, talking, joking, even eating and sleeping the while, and sent Nero, not the usual document of flattering homage and large legacies, but a full account, under proper headings, of all his most private debaucheries.[118] He had previously destroyed his signet-ring, to prevent compromising documents being forged with it, the seal and not the written signature being the ancient method of accrediting a writing.

In Petronius' time the Greek romance was apparently gaining popularity.[119] In these productions, a virtuous hero and heroine go through all manner of hair-raising adventures, generally in distant lands, and finally are re-united in the concluding chapters. Petronius writes a parody on this kind of thing, whether of his own invention or following some unknown model; the former is, on such evidence as we have, the more likely supposition. The hero and heroine are replaced by a wandering rascal, by name Encolpius, and an impudent boy called Giton; the strange lands are no farther off than Southern Italy; the high-flown amorousness of the Greek novels is represented by the most elaborate scenes of complicated lust; these parts are disgusting enough, but can hardly be called immoral, for it is doubtful if they are capable of inspiring any one with other than aversion from the practices described or hinted at. We have left only extracts from what are stated to be the fifteenth and sixteenth books of the work; in these we can trace a loose plot. Encolpius has contrived to offend Priapos, whose divine revenge on him takes the most embarrassing of forms in delicate moments, and whom he is trying to appease. He has a companion, Ascyltos, with whom he quarrels violently; he and Giton have offended a married couple, as they appear to be, Lichas and Tryphaena, and are for a while in danger from them till a reconciliation is arrived at. Outstanding characters are Agamemnon, a rhetorician, Eumolpus, a minor poet who recites his own verses in season and out of season[120] till he is silenced by stone-throwing and other forms of vigorous criticism, and most noteworthy of all,

[118] Tac., *ann.*, xvi, 19, 5: flagitia principis sub nominibus (under the headings of, in sections headed by the names of) exoletorum feminarumque et nouitatem cuiusque stupri perscripsit atque obsignata misit Neroni.

[119] See Rose, *H.G.L.*, pp. 414–17.

[120] He pretty clearly represents the literary views which Petronius, a supporter of the modern school, opposes. His most notable utterance is

the immortal Trimalchio, the local multi-millionaire of some country town in Magna Graecia, a self-made man at whose house Encolpius and his friends dine. The female characters are, if possible, more disreputable than the male; they include Quartilla, who is a sort of priestess of Priapos, Circe, a wealthy woman apparently of Kroton (Cortona), and Fortunata, Trimalchio's wife. The style of the work is admirable, the persons speaking in character, with the natural varieties of language, from inflated rhetoric to slang and street-Latin, often hard for us to interpret after so many centuries; the descriptive passages are clear and unaffected, full of witty turns. The title appears to be *Saturae, i.e., The Medley.*[121]

Closely connected with Seneca was his nephew, the son of his brother Mela, MARCVS ANNAEVS LVCANVS, generally known in English as LUCAN. He was born in 39,[122] brought to Rome when but seven months old, and early distinguished himself by his abilities as a rhetorician and a composer of verses. Among his acquaintance were Cornutus and Persius. After going to Athens to complete his education, he was summoned to court by Nero, given the post of quaestor, and for a while continued in high favour. But jealousies soon broke out between the lesser and greater poet; Lucan was slighted, and consequently was drawn into the conspiracy of Piso. Here, so long as it was a question of eloquent denunciations of tyranny, he proved a leading spirit; on being detected, he was offered pardon if he denounced his confederates, when allegedly he accused his own mother. The promise was not kept, and he died by the popular method of bleeding, reciting with his last breath some verses ot his own concerning a similar death.[123]

His fame rests entirely, for his other and apparently slighter works have all perished, on his epic poem concerning the Civil

sat., 119–24, in which he delivers himself of a poem on the Civil Wars, by way of showing how Lucan (not named, but unmistakably alluded to, 118, 6) should have done it.

[121] The MSS. vary widely between various spellings of this and the impossible *satyricon*. For a forged supplement to the fragments, see Farrer, pp. 21–4.

[122] Our chief authorities are a life prefixed to one set of scholia, the *annotationes super Lucanum*, and a second, badly mutilated, which is ultimately from Suetonius. The former, which is ascribed to a certain VACCA, also contains Suetonian material. Both are in Hosius' (Teubner) edition of Lucan. There are also mentions of him in Tacitus, *ann.*, xv, 49, 2–3; 56, 4; 57, 4; Cassius Dio, lxii, 29, 4.

[123] Tac., xv, 56, 4. Her name was Acilia. The Suetonian life supports Tacitus' statement. The lines he recited were probably *Phars.*, ix, 808–14.

War, the *Pharsalia*.[124] The title, of course, signifies that the battle of Pharsalos is the climax of the story, which is in effect a versified history of the conflict between Caesar and Pompey from the beginning to some unknown point (for the work was never finished) after the death of the latter. Naturally, historical accuracy is not to be looked for, and the action is diversified with a number of episodes, the most weird being the consultation of a witch, in Book VI, who reanimates a dead soldier to tell what he may of the future course of events, with speeches, fanciful and often horrible descriptions of battle-scenes, philosophical and other digressions—Lucan is perhaps rather especially fond of geographic excursuses—and all the usual adornments of a conventional epic except divine machinery, which is not used at all, no gods intervening anywhere. It will be remembered that a tendency in the same direction, although not so consistently carried out, is to be found in the plays of his uncle Seneca. Whether the result is poetry or not has been hotly debated since ancient times [125]; that the *Pharsalia* contains some of the finest rhetoric ever written in verse is not likely to be disputed by any who can appreciate that form of mastery of language. That it has also many faults and a number of glaringly bad passages is true; but such errors, in themselves pardonable in the work of an immature man in an age of false taste, are atoned for, and a large balance left to the credit of the author, by the macabre power of his witch-scene, the eloquence, rising at times almost to sublimity, of some of the best speeches, and perhaps most of all by the moving episode at the beginning of the seventh book in which Pompey, on the eve of the decisive battle, sees in a dream the happiness of his early triumphs. The philosophy of the poem is, of course, popular Stoicism, with the rant about freedom, *i.e.*, a republican form of government, which was part of that doctrine as understood in Senecan circles. The versification is of the smooth, somewhat monotonous kind which follows upon Ovid. The language is typical verse-Latin of the Silver Age, that is to say highly artificial but not often obscure.

Lucan's smaller works, which were numerous, for he was a prolific and rapid composer, have all perished, save for insignificant fragments, to be found in *F.P.L.*, p. 365 *sqq.*/128 *sqq.*, also in some editions of the *Pharsalia*, best in that of Hosius (Teubner, ed. 3, 1913). The *Life* by Vacca (see note 122) gives the following list, which is partly attested also by

[124] Lucan's own title, *Phars.*, ix, 986; the MSS. call it *de bello ciuili*.

[125] Lucanus . . . magis oratoribus quam poetis imitandus, Quint., x, 1, 90: sunt quidam qui me dicunt non esse poetam;/sed qui me uendit bibliopola putat, Mart., xiv, 194; *i.e.*, the *Pharsalia* was highly popular.

Statius [126]: *Iliaca*, dealing with the death and ransoming of Hektor, perhaps other episodes also. This was a juvenile work. *Saturnalia*, of which nothing certain is known. *Catachthonia*, from its title and Statius' account of it [127] a description of Hades. *Siluae* (*i.e.*, 'rough drafts') in ten books; this work may well have included the address to his wife Polla Argentaria which Statius mentions.[128] *Medea*, a tragedy, which was left unfinished. Fourteen *salticae fabulae*, in other words libretti (such as Statius also wrote, see p. 393) for the use of dramatic dancers (*pantomimi*). Vacca and Statius also mention an encomium of Nero, publicly recited at the Neronia (cf. p. 351), and an extempore poem, also composed for a competition, on *Orpheus*. He seems also to have written epigrams, and three speeches attributed to him were in circulation, one on the burning of Rome and two an imaginary accusation and defence of a certain Octavius Sagitta,[129] found guilty in 58 of murdering a woman who had been his paramour.

It will be convenient to mention here several minor poems of the Neronian age. We have a collection of eleven pastorals bearing, in the surviving MSS., the name of T. CALPVRNIVS SICVLVS. But we have also a collation of a MS. now lost which attributed the last four of them to Nemesianus (see p. 525). That this separation is correct is indicated by the difference in style between the two groups. Calpurnius, of whom nothing at all is known, lived under Nero, for there are definite allusions to that emperor such as would naturally come from a flattering contemporary, but no one else. The first, fourth and seventh of his poems are all courtly, with a thin veneer of the bucolic; in No. I, Faunus prophesies the glories of the Golden Age which is just beginning under a ruler who shall bring back law and order, not persecute the Senate,[130] and emulate the peaceful piety of the days of Numa. Further, he has successfully pled the cause of 'his mother's line, the Iuli', which exactly fits Nero, a Iulius through his mother, who had spoken on behalf of the people of Ilion, with special reference to their legendary con-

126 Statius, *sil.*, ii, 7, 55 *sqq.*, part of a prophecy by Kalliope supposed to have been delivered the day Lucan was born. See Vollmer, *ad loc.*

127 Stat., 57, sedes reserabis inferorum.

128 Stat., 62–3: hinc castae titulum decusque Pollae/iucunda dabis allocutione.

129 See Tacitus, *ann.*, xiii, 44; the Vaccan life mentions also *epistulae ex Campania*, of which nothing is known, and the Suetonian says: sed et famoso carmine cum ipsum (Neronem) tum potentissimos amicorum grauissime proscidit. Of this lampoon we have no traces at all. More on the lost works in Schanz-Hosius, ii, p. 494 *sq*.

130 Calp., i, 60 *sqq*. The allusion seems to be to the execution of senators under Claudius, see Seneca, *apocol.*, 14, 1.

nexion, through Aeneas and his son, with that family.[131] Finally, a comet has appeared in the sky,[132] which points to the year 54. This oracle two shepherds find written on the bark of a tree and proceed to set to music, hoping that Meliboeus will bring it to the ears of the Emperor. Who Meliboeus was appears more clearly in the fourth poem ; he is a kind patron who has rescued the shepherd Corydon from poverty, wherefore Corydon and his brother Amyntas, a promising young poet, sing a duet in honour, not of Meliboeus himself, but of Caesar, and the theme inspires them to rise, like Tityrus of old (*i.e.* Vergil), to something more than pastoral strains. In No. VII, Corydon, who is manifestly Calpurnius himself, has been to Rome and brings back a glowing description of a show he had seen and of the beauty and majesty of the 'godhead'[133] who presided. The other pieces are on themes less far removed from real country life, although they give little indication that Calpurnius knew more about it than he could have got from reading Vergil[134] and perhaps spending a holiday or two out of town. The second is a singing contest, resulting in a draw ; the third, a dialogue between two shepherds, one of whom asks the advice of the other how to win back the favour of his offended sweetheart and submits to his approval a song which he means to sing in her hearing. No. V introduces an old goatherd giving his flock to a young one, with instructions on how to care for it ; No. VI is a curious production, in which two shepherds quarrel violently as to the relative merits of two rustic poets ; one challenges the other to a contest of song, but neither can keep his temper enough for the matter to be decided in proper form.

Meliboeus, though obviously a contemporary man of letters, has never been clearly identified. The Senecas naturally suggest themselves, but it is not known that any of them wrote on weather-signs, on a theme connected with Dionysos (unless the allusion is to plays, which would fit the younger Seneca) and on some undefined theme which involves the good graces of Apollo (a composition which won a prize at one of Nero's contests ?).[135]

[131] Calp., *ibid.*, 45 : maternis causam qui uicit Iulis. See Tacitus, *ann.*, xii, 58, 1 ; Sueton., *Nero*, 7, who says the speech was in Greek. The date was 53, and the result was that the people of Ilion were freed from all public burdens.

[132] Calp., *ibid.*, 77–9.

[133] *Mea numina*, vii, 80 ; so far as the shepherd could see from one of the more distant seats in the Circus, the deity in question looked like a combination of Mars and Apollo.

[134] The imitations of Vergil throughout the poems are innumerable.

[135] Calpurn., iv, 53–7 : nam tibi non tantum uenturos dicere uentos/ agricolis qualemque ferat sol aureus ortum/attribuere dei, sed dulcia carmina saepe/concinis, et modo te Baccheis Musa corymbis/munerat et

There is another specimen of pastoral poetry from the same age, for it is loud in its praise of a divine harp-player, so excellent a poet that Vergil will hardly be worth reading again, and of an era of such perfect peace that sons will look at their fathers' swords and wonder what they are. The reference to Nero's accomplishments and to his generally peaceful reign is patent enough, and the Latinity sufficiently like that of Calpurnius for it to be from a contemporary. Perhaps it is fanciful to suggest that we have here a specimen of the verse of 'Amyntas', *i.e.*, Calpurnius' brother or friend (see above).[136] Be that as it may, the work is very slight, consisting of two poems, both imperfect, whether the author left them so or, which is perhaps more probable, they have been damaged in copying. We have but one MS., preserved at Einsiedel, hence the name *Carmina Einsidlensia* given to them.

Yet another anonymous writer of this age is the author of the poem known as the *Laus Pisonis*, a panegyric on the virtues and accomplishments of that singularly inefficient conspirator against Nero who came to his end in 65. The poet spends 261 quite passable hexameters in explaining that Piso's nobility, eloquence, literary, musical and athletic achievements, and skill at the *ludus latrunculorum*, a game which seems to have resembled draughts, also his disinterested kindness and judicious choice of friends, have so impressed him that he wishes this paragon to be his patron, not from any base desire of gain, for although poor he is of a respectable family, but because he realizes that even Vergil would not have become famous but for Maecenas. Who he was and whether his suit was successful we have no idea.[137]

We do, on the other hand, know the name of the author of the *Ilias Latina*,[138] which is not a translation of the Iliad but a sort of compendium of it. The author begins and ends with acrostics which proclaim (with a break at one point where his ingenuity has failed to find the proper initial letter or bad copying

lauro modo pulcher obumbrat Apollo. Seneca's generosity was well known, see Juvenal, v, 109, though it does not appear that it was specially directed to literary men. That Meliboeus is connected with Nero's entourage is clear enough from i, 94: forsitan Augustas feret haec Meliboeus ad auris. It cannot be determined whether any of the characters except Corydon and Meliboeus are real persons.

[136] For more guesses as to the authorship, see Schanz-Hosius, ii, p. 491 *sq*. A handy text is that at the end of C. Giarratano's second edition of Calpurnius and Nemesianus, Turin, 1924.

[137] Conjectures, ancient and modern, *ibid*., p. 490. The poem is published in some of the older editions of Ovid and is perhaps most accessible in *P.L.M.*, i, pp. 225–36 (Baehrens).

[138] Text in *P.L.M.* (Vollmer), ii, 3, with good critical notes.

has lost it again) that *Italicus scripsit*; while one MS. has preserved his full name, BAEBIVS ITALICVS; the rest ascribe the work to Homer, which is natural enough, or to Pindar, which is a vagary hardly to be explained.[139] The date is roughly determined by the statement that if Poseidon had not saved Aeneas 'there would not have remained to us the fountainhead of the famed line', *i.e.*, the Julio-Claudian dynasty, which suggests that it was still ruling when the verses were written,[140] in other words, that they are not later than Nero, while the technique shows that they cannot be much earlier. Apart from an ability to make his lines scan neatly enough, the writer had little poetic gift and no sense of proportion. He uses 1,070 lines in all (the original number was perhaps slightly larger, for a few seem to be lost). Of these about 175 correspond to nothing in Homer. Of the remaining 900 or so he should therefore give about thirty-seven or thirty-eight to each of the twenty-four books; as a matter of fact, he is at line 110 before he finishes Book I, more than half-way through by the end of Book V, and, as he assigns well over 200 verses to the last three, the rest have to be crowded into fewer than 400.

Both date and authorship are uncertain in the case of the *Aetna*, a poem which for some extraordinary reason was ascribed to Vergil as early as the time of Suetonius; anything more unlike his style can hardly be imagined. It was for a while fashionable to assign it to Lucilius, the friend of Seneca, but there is no sufficient proof of his having written it.[141]

These are the ascertained facts. 1. The poem was written before the eruption of Vesuvius (79), for it says that the region between Naples and Cumae, though it must once have been volcanic, has long been inactive (*frigidus*, 432). 2. Style, metre and language, though all somewhat peculiar and original, are of the Silver Age. 3. It does not resemble the work of any other poet between 14 and 79. 4. Seneca, *epp.*, 79, 5, says he is sure Lucilius will not be able to resist the temptation of describing Aetna in his poem, for although Vergil had done so (*Aen.*, iii, 571–87), Ovid had also attempted it (*Met.* v, 352–8), and Cornelius Severus (p. 343; no doubt it was in his poem on the Sicilian War, and there is no ground for supposing, as some unknown humanist and after him Scaliger did, that the *Aetna* is his work) described it yet again. That Lucilius dealt with Sicily and was interested in science is

[139] See Schanz-Hosius, ii, p. 507 *sq.*

[140] *Il. Lat.*, 899–902.

[141] See, for relevant literature, editions, &c. (that of Ellis, Oxford, 1901, is the fullest in English and contains a discussion of the authorship), Schanz-Hosius, ii, pp. 80–2. Add E. Köstermann in *Gnomon*, 1935, pp. 31–3, who argues for Lucilius' authorship.

clear from many passages of Seneca. Therefore he may be the author, but there is no reason for saying positively that he is.

But whoever the author was, he was not a contemptible poet. The little work, unfortunately much obscured by the errors of copyists and, in many editions, by the emendations of unskilful editors, is not unworthy of the inspiration which it clearly draws from Lucretius. After a proem on the freshness and truth of science as a theme, it sets forth a current theory of the cause of eruptions, which is, briefly,[142] that subterranean winds under high pressure produce intense heat by friction, especially in a kind of stone the poet calls *lapis molaris*, which is capable of being liquefied and burning if the temperature is high enough; the force of these winds causes them and the hot matter which they carry to break out through the surrounding obstacles, and so an eruption occurs. The poem concludes by telling effectively the beautiful local legend, how the two good sons, abandoning all their property, carried away their aged parents from the lava-stream, and how the very volcano reverenced their piety and the fire gave way to them wherever they went till they came to a place of safety.

A great many poetical works of this period have no doubt been utterly lost to us, for verse-writing was very popular. Two names less obscure than the rest deserve mention. PVBLIVS POMPONIVS SECVNDVS, a friend of the elder Pliny, consul at some unknown date, was in danger of his life after the fall of Seianus, lived to produce tragedies under Claudius, became *legatus* in Upper Germany in 50, and there by good handling of his troops destroyed a raiding party of the Chatti, for which service he was granted the nearest approach to a triumph allowed by Imperial practice to a subject, the *ornamenta triumphalia*. Of his tragedies, which Tacitus valued highly, practically nothing is left.[143] CAESIVS BASSVS was a friend of Persius, and, according to Quintilian, the only Latin lyricist except Horace whom it is worth while for any one to read who desires to form an oratorical style. Persius says that his lyre gives forth manly and truly Latin strains; the scraps which are left are in a number of metres and suggest ingenious trifles. He was also an authority on the theory of metre, and quotations from him occur in the surviving writers on that subject.[144]

[142] The author himself sums it up in three lines, 566–8.

[143] See Tacitus, *ann.*, v, 8 (vi, 3); xi, 13, 1; xii, 27, 3–4. He probably got his information from a biography of Pomponius which the elder Pliny wrote, see Pliny the Younger, *epp.*, iii, 5, 3. See, for certain details concerning him and the references for the few fragments, Schanz-Hosius, ii, p. 476.

[144] Persius, 6, 1 *sqq.*; the judgement above quoted forms the motto on the title-page of this book. Quintilian, x, 1, 96; he adds that there

For lack of any exactly determinable date, we may discuss here a very entertaining writer, who deserves the popularity he enjoys so long as he is read for what he can give, and not for historical information. Alexander the Great was a favourite subject for rhetoric and imaginative embroidery generally, in antiquity as in later times; Greece produced a number of more or less reliable histories of his exploits and, later, an Alexander-romance which grew more and more fantastic as time went on and spread to medieval Europe to be yet further distorted, while Kleitarchos was a sort of compromise, history with an infusion of romance.[145] QVINTVS CVRTIVS RVFVS wrote in ten books, whereof there survive the last eight, with some gaps, a work after Kleitarchos' manner, not unlike those half-fictional biographies of famous persons which are now popular. As a stylist, he is good, pleasant in narrative, eloquent in the numerous speeches, skilled in omitting the drier parts of his subject and setting forth the most interesting; as a historian, he is a kind of parody of Livy, for while the latter is often uncritical in handling his material, Curtius cheerfully tells us that he sets down much more than he believes so as not to omit anything his authorities tell him.[146] A historian, therefore, must exercise the utmost caution in looking for information in him; a reader who wishes to be entertained with a good story founded upon fact will be well satisfied.

Except that his Latin is too good to be very late, we have no real evidence when this author lived and wrote. Resemblances to Livy probably, indeed certainly, indicate that Curtius is the borrower. As his whole manner suggests the post-Augustan period, this tells us little. In vii, 1, 19 *sqq.*, he puts into the mouth of Amyntas, accused of treason against Alexander, a speech whose principal arguments (26 *sqq.*) are practically identical with those which M. Terentius, in Tacitus (*ann.*, vi, 8) and Cassius Dio (lviii, 19, 3–4) uses when similarly accused before the Senate. Amyntas had been the friend of the traitor Philotas, Terentius of the recently disgraced and executed Seianus; the situation is thus so much alike that the same speech, with the change of a few names, would do for either of the accused. We do not know what Curtius' model was, but it seems reasonable to suppose that what Terentius actually said was recorded and all three writers used it, directly or indirectly. Therefore this tells us no more than that Curtius wrote after the year 32. Finally, he himself says (x, 9, 1 *sqq.*)

were contemporaries of his own who were far better, but we know nothing of them. For his prose work on metres, see Schanz-Hosius, ii, p. 485–6. Verse fragments, *F.P.R.*, pp. 364–5/126–7.

[145] See Rose, *H.G.L.*, pp. 364–5, 413.

[146] Curtius, ix, 1, 34, cf. x, 10, 11.

that the civil wars after Alexander's death resulted in the downfall of his empire, and goes on to comment : proinde iure populus Romanus salutem se principi suo debere profitetur, qui noctis quam paene supremam habuimus nouum sidus inluxit. huius hercule, non solis, ortus lucem caliganti reddidit mundo, cum sine suo capite discordia membra trepidarent. quot ille tum extinxit faces, quot condidit gladios, quantam tempestatem subita serenitate discussit ! non ergo reuirescit solum sed etiam floret imperium ; absit modo inuidia, excipiet huius saeculi tempora eiusdem domus utinam perpetua, certe diuturna posteritas (3–6).

It has repeatedly been suggested that this ruler who has brought sunshine back to a darkling universe is the Emperor Claudius, and that there is a pun, in *cālīganti*, on the name of Călĭgula. But apart from the facts that Tiberius' successor was officially called Gaius and that the difference of quantity in the first two syllables makes the pun an extremely bad one, too bad for an author of Curtius' ability,[147] there was no ' tempest ' and no threat of widespread civil strife for Claudius to check ; his predecessor fell a victim to his own unpopularity and an intrigue among members of the bodyguard, and the household troops put him on the throne within a few hours. A much more likely person to be alluded to is Vespasian, who did indeed find the Empire without a head, not at the beginning of his rebellion but shortly after, and by establishing himself firmly on the throne ended all commotion. I would therefore, with reserve, adopt the view of Stroux [148] and put the composition at all events of the last book about the year 69 or not much later.

[147] The parallels adduced by Schanz-Hosius, ii, p. 597, note 3, seem to me unconvincing.

[148] J. Stroux in *Philologus*, N.F., xxxviii (1928), pp. 232–51. Curtius' concluding sentence with its plain reference to the expected successors of the new ruler seems to me especially applicable to Vespasian, with his two sons ; *eiusdem domus* might, of course, mean ' the same dynasty as before ', *i.e.*, the Julio-Claudians, if we suppose Claudius to be meant, but is at least as applicable to a new dynasty which it is hoped will continue and thus avoid all quarrels regarding succession.

Additional Note.—1. Pp. 371–5. For some interesting recent criticism of Seneca's plays, see W. H. Friedrich, *Untersuchungen zu Senecas dramatischer Technik*, Leipzig, Noske, 1933.

2. P. 348, n. 3. Considerable doubt has been cast on the *praenomen imperatoris*, see H. Wagenvoort, *Roman Dynamism* (Oxford, Blackwell, 1947), p. 63, but that *imperator* formed part of the Imperial titulature is undisputed.

3. P. 358, n. 49. The fullest information concerning Aesop and his alleged sayings and doings is now contained in B. E. Perry, *Aesopica*, I, Urbana, Ill., U.S.A., 1952.

CHAPTER XIII

THE SILVER AGE TO THE DEATH OF TRAJAN

AFTER the deaths of Nero and his three short-lived successors, the accession of VESPASIAN (FLAVIVS VESPASIANVS, 69–79) ushered in a series of Emperors all of whom at least posed as friends of learning and literature, while some showed themselves to be so in fact. Vespasian seems to have been a tolerable orator [1] and to have ventured so far at least into authorship as to leave behind some memoirs.[2] He was a patron of poets and artists, and was the first to found regular professoriates of rhetoric, both Latin and Greek, which were paid by the State.[3] Being fond of a joke, he was indulgent to the same liking in his subjects, even when their wit was directed against himself.[4] His son TITVS (79–81) had certainly some talent for both oratory and poetry, though we need not take too literally the praises bestowed on it, in view of his popularity both before and after death.[5] DOMITIAN (FLAVIVS DOMITIANVS, 81–96) was known, before his accession, as a poet, and of course declared to be a master of that art.[6] On becoming Emperor, he seems to have given up all such pursuits and

[1] Aurelius Victor, *Caes.*, 9, 1: Vespasianus . . . facundiae haud egens promendis quae senserat. Tacitus, *hist.*, ii, 80: satis decorus etiam Graeca facundia.

[2] Used by Josephus, *uita*, 65, 342 (iv, p. 317 Niese); see *H.R.F.*, p. 306 *sq*.

[3] Sueton., *Vesp.*, 17–19: Jerome, *an. Abr.* 2104, says Quintilian was the first holder of the chair (presumably) of Latin rhetoric: primus Romae publicam scholam et salarium e fisco accepit.

[4] See Cassius Dio, lvi, 11, 1: if lampoons against him were found posted up, he was not annoyed but merely added replies.

[5] See Pliny, *N.H.*, praef., 5, 11; ii, 89: Suet., *Tit.*, 3.

[6] As by Quintilian, x, 1, 91–2; Statius, *Achil.*, i, 15; Valerius Flaccus, i, 12–14, which indicates that Domitian wrote on the Jewish war. He also composed a little work on hair (he was bald himself and very sensitive about it), Suet., *Domit.*, 18 (*de cura capillorum*). This was in prose, as is shown by a sentence which Suet. quotes from it.

devoted himself entirely to statecraft,[7] but was not without some interest in learning, for he was at pains to restore libraries destroyed by a fire and to get from Alexandria the most accurate copies possible of the books they were to contain.[8] But throughout this dynasty we find an undercurrent of opposition between letters and the throne, the blame for which does not rest wholly on the government. The Flavians had no prestige of ancient nobility behind them, and the factious theoretical republicanism of the Senate came to a head as early as Vespasian's time in the outrageous conduct of the fanatic Helvidius Priscus, who publicly affected to treat his sovran as a private individual. Vespasian found himself obliged to banish this disturber of the peace and at length half-heartedly to give orders for his execution.[9] Following upon this came a decree banishing philosophers generally, or at least Stoics, and with them astrologers,[10] for a good enough reason in both cases; for Stoicism meant the continual glorification of 'free' government, and therefore potential danger (since the mildest ruler could not be sure that some hot-head would not take the denunciations of tyrants and praises of their slayers seriously and proceed to put them into practice against himself), while astrologers might encourage an ambitious man by assuring him that he had a royal nativity, *i.e.*, was born under a combination of stars which would inevitably make him a king, or strengthen a doubtful conspirator by proving to him, on like authority, that the reigning Emperor was destined to die shortly. Under Domitian, who was suspicious, easily frightened, and full of his own superhuman importance, this led to a positive reign of terror, in which all free speech came to an

[7] Quint., *loc. cit.*; Suet., *op. cit.*, 2, 20. The statement there that he never read anything henceforth except the records of Tiberius' reign is gossip, associating the two morose and unpopular Emperors. Domitian seems to have been, despite his hateful private character, an able administrator. Both Pliny and Trajan, neither of whom, certainly, was prejudiced in his favour, refer to edicts of his as respectable authorities (Pliny, *ad Trai.*, 58, 5; 60; 66; 72).

[8] Suet., *op. cit.*, 20.

[9] Suet., *Vesp.*, 15; Cassius Dio, lxvi, 12. Both authors (Suet., *ibid.*, 13; Dio, *ibid.*, 13, 2–3) agree as to the contemptuous leniency he showed to Demetrios the Cynic, to whom he sent word that he would not kill a dog for barking at him.

[10] Dio, *ibid.*, 13, 1, who says he banished, at the advice of Mucianus, πάντας τοὺς τοιούτους, whether this is philosophers generally or Stoics and Cynics, with the exception of Musonius Rufus (see Rose, *H.G.L.*, p. 410). Astrologers, Dio, *ibid.*, 9, 2. Cf. Jerome, *an. Abr.* 2105 and 2111 (= 89 and 95; the Armenian version puts the second event in 92) for similar edicts of Domitian.

end, one writer after another was impeached and put to death for merely expressing admiration of such men as Helvidius Priscus and other members of the quasi-philosophical opposition, and even private conversations were spied on and reported in a way which has unhappily come to be once more familiar in some modern states.[11] Although he re-enacted his father's edict against philosophers and astrologers, however, Domitian had no objection to literature in general, provided it satisfied his exacting standard of loyalty; indeed, he founded a quadrennial contest, the Agon Capitolinus, which included competitions in music and literature,[12] evidently on the model of Nero's similar institution (p. 351). The accession of COCCEIVS NERVA (96–8) put an end to the restrictions on speech, and his adopted son and successor TRAJAN (M. VLPIVS TRAIANVS, 98–117) continued his policy in this respect. Nerva was something of a poet,[13] Trajan wrote an account of his own Dacian wars, unhappily lost, and could certainly express himself clearly and concisely, as his surviving correspondence with the younger Pliny proves.[14] Trajan was also the founder of a library, the Bibliotheca Vlpia in the Forum Traiani, and his relations to literary men, including Dion of Prusa, surnamed Chrysostomos,[15] were friendly, even warm. Under such Emperors any talent there might be had a clear field; under Domitian there was room for some kinds of literature, if not for the best.

We may begin with a writer who lived through a considerable part of the earlier period described in the last chapter, for he was consul in the last year of Nero, 68, and on to about the end of the first century, when an incurable ailment induced him to end his own life, after he had survived all the other

[11] See, for a catalogue of his victims, Suetonius, *Domit.*, 10; Tacitus, *Agric.*, 2; Cassius Dio, lxvii, 13, 2–4.

[12] Expulsion of philosophers, Dio, *loc. cit.*; Jerome, *an. Abr.* 2105 (= 89), who also mentions astrologers. Agon Capitolinus, Suet., *Domit.*, 4, besides numerous mentions in other authors. The quality of the judges of these competitions may be estimated when we remember that Statius never won a prize but a wretched little infant prodigy of 11½ years did, see *C.I.L.*, vi, 33976.

[13] The Tibullus of his day, according to Nero, *ap.* Martial, viii, 70, 7–8 (Nero himself, of course, being the Vergil, cf. *carm. Einsidl.*, i, 49).

[14] He was no great speaker and generally had his speeches composed by L. LICINIVS SVRA (Julian, *Caesares*, p. 327 B, Spanheim), a Spaniard like himself, who apparently used a rather archaic style (Martial, vii, 47, 1–2); for his public career, see Schanz-Hosius, ii, p. 435. For the correspondence with Pliny, see p. 418; for his history, Priscian, ii, p. 205, 6 Keil.

[15] See Pliny, *Paneg.*, 47, 1. For Dion, see Rose, *H.G.L.*, p. 406.

Neronian consulars. This was TIBERIVS CATIVS ASCONIVS SILIVS ITALICVS, the most tedious writer of the whole Silver Age. Having led an active and not altogether well-reputed life under Nero, shown moderation as an associate of Vitellius and governed Asia Minor laudably, he spent the rest of his days in elegant retirement, which his wealth made easily possible, first in Rome and later in Campania. He was a great collector of books and objects of art, and had a religious reverence for Vergil.[16] Unhappily, he felt moved to imitate him by writing an epic poem. The result was his wholly intolerable *Punica*, seventeen books of quite correct, even melodious hexameters, which recount the events of the second Punic War with all the epic machinery, divine interventions, battles in which the generals engage each other hand to hand like Homeric heroes, a visit to the other world, funeral games. Even the younger Pliny, who was indulgent towards every writer, could find nothing better to say of him than that he showed more diligence than talent in his poetry.[17] The unfortunate fact is that he had absolutely no talent and no taste (as the stupid unreality of those episodes which he invents indicates), but a good rhetorical and literary education, which had taught him how to arrange material and turn anything he had to say into verse. But to write an epic on a grand scale requires genius; even good rhetorical history in verse, like Lucan's poem, demands very considerable gifts. Anything short of this produces nothing but flat boredom.

A writer of very different calibre was PVBLIVS PAPINIVS STATIVS, of Naples.[18] This man's father kept what the snobbery of a different age and country would have called an academy for the sons of gentlemen, and the poet gives a glowing account of its curriculum and popularity.[19] Brought up in such an atmosphere, it is no wonder that Statius was learned and had poetical leanings; we do not know whether he owed it to his

[16] His life is known mostly from Pliny, *epp.*, iii, 7, from which the above facts are taken. Martial mentions him frequently and with praise. Cornutus (above, p. 377) dedicated to him a work *de Vergilio*, Charisius, i, p. 125, 16 Keil. Cf. *Class Rev.*, 1936, pp. 56–8.

[17] Pliny, *loc. cit.*, 5. See further Schanz-Hosius, ii, pp. 526–31.

[18] This we know from his own words, *silu.*, v, 3, 129 *sqq.*, which shows that his father spent the greater part of his life there, though born in Velia; iii, 5, 10 and 81–2. That Chaucer calls the poet 'the Tholosan that highte Stace' and that he is styled Sursulus or, later, Surculus in MSS. arises from a confusion of him with STATIVS VRSVLVS TOLOSENSIS who celeberrime in Gallia rhetoricam docet (Jerome, *an. Abr.* 2092 = 56).

[19] Statius, *loc. cit.*, 146 *sqq.* The elder Statius was himself a poet and won several prizes at competitions, *ibid.*, 133–45.

father or himself that he was also one of the most perfect specimens of the tuft-hunter that have ever lived. This shows itself in his works, not only in flattery of Domitian, under whom he seems to have written his poems,[20] but in one versified address after another to men socially prominent, many of them giving the reader to understand, what was probably quite true, that he had been a guest in their houses,[21] and therefore moved in the best circles. It was not poverty which impelled him to this, for he seems to have been fairly well off [22]; probably his father had left him a not inconsiderable estate. Apart from this weakness, Statius was to all appearances an amiable man, certainly a good son (his poem in memory of his father shows real affection through all the pedantry). He had, moreover, a gift for verse composition, combining great readiness [23] with great ingenuity. His taste was far from impeccable, but when it did not fail him, he is often eloquent, and at times, though never for long at a stretch, genuinely poetical, as in the lovely address to Sleep,[24] the sudden gloomy magnificence of some of his images,[25] and the proud humility of his tribute to the great memory of Vergil.[26]

Little is known of his private life, which indeed was probably of no great interest to any one but his immediate circle. He married, apparently not very early, a widow named Claudia, who had one daughter by her former husband. She was, by his own account, a good wife to him, but they had no children, and a little boy whom Statius adopted died young.[27] He seems

[20] References to Domitian are frequent in Statius, indications of his having lived into the times of Nerva or Trajan entirely wanting.

[21] As *silu.*, i, 5; ii, 2, &c.

[22] He had an estate near Alba to which Domitian permitted him to lead water from the public aqueducts, *silu.*, iii, 1, 61–4.

[23] He composed *silu.*, i, 1,—107 good hexameters full of ingenious flattery—in some twenty-four hours, see the prefaratory epistle to that book.

[24] *Silu.*, v, 4.

[25] As *Theb.*, vii, 474–8; xi, 422–3; 443–6.

[26] *Theb.*, xii, 816 (his address to his poem; grandly imitated by Chaucer, Bk. v, 1789–92 of *Troilus and Criseyde*): uiue, precor; nec tu diuinam Aeneida tempta,/sed longe sequere et uestigia semper adora.

[27] His wife is addressed and some particulars of her given in *silu.*, iii, 5; he says he married her florentibus annis, 23, cf. 25, adhuc iuuenile uagantem, but this need mean no more than that he was not yet old; *iuuenis* is a man in his prime. *Silu.*, v, 5, is a lament for the boy's death; he is described as *infans*, 9, and as crawling about the house and just beginning to talk, 83, 86. Apparently he was the son of a slave, 73, which passage makes it clear that Statius adopted him, and also (79–80) that he had no child of his own.

to have come to Rome early or at all events not late in life, and to have made money there by writing libretti for *pantomimi* (cf. p. 381),[28] rather than by his more literary works. Some of these, however, it is not unreasonable to regard as a sort of payment for social favours, Imperial or private, a more exalted equivalent of the ' bread-and-butter letter '. Growing older and feeling the burden of his years, he retired to Naples about 94 and seems to have died there.[29]

Statius' poems, which were well liked, may be divided into three classes, omitting the libretti already mentioned. First come some prize compositions, none of which won the Capitoline wreath, although one of them, a glorification of Domitian's German and Dacian campaigns, received the crown at the minor competition at Alba. Since we have but four lines of this last effort [30] and nothing left of the rest, they need not detain us. The *Siluae*, or Miscellanies, fill five books, the last having apparently lost its concluding lines.[31] These are *vers d'occasion*, mostly in hexameters, but four in hendecasyllables [32] and two in lyric metres borrowed from Horace. Their subjects vary; some have already been cited for information concerning Statius himself

[28] This fact is derived from a famous passage of Juvenal (vii, 82 *sqq.*): curritur ad uocem iucundam et carmen amicae/Thebaidos, laetam cum fecit Statius urbem/promisitque diem (a parody of the indecent phrase *promittere noctem*; this and the punning use of *amicae* mean that Statius, as we should say, prostitutes his talent); tanta dulcedine captos/adficit ille animos tantaque libidine uolgi/(again an ambiguous phrase) auditur; sed cum fregit subsellia uersu,/esurit, intactam Paridi nisi uendit Agauen (obviously the libretto of a ballet; Paris is the famous pantomime, a great favourite of Domitian; again there is an indecent *double entente*). It probably is largely on the strength of these words, which are pure spite, that the common idea arises of Statius being miserably poor (' Statius flattering a tyrant, and the minion of a tyrant, for a morsel of bread ', Macaulay, *Essay on Montgomery*, with an allusion to *silu.*, iii, 4, an address to Domitian's boy favourite Earinon).

[29] See, for this and other personal matters concerning Statius, the useful collection of facts in the preface of Vollmer's edition of the *Siluae* (Teubner, 1898), pp. 1–21.

[30] See *silu.*, iii, 5, 28–33. The fragment of the poem *de bello Germanico* is preserved in Valla's scholia on Juv., iv, 94, and published in the ordinary editions of Statius and in *F.P.R.*, p. 370.

[31] Or it may be that Statius never lived to complete the poem; the death of the child, whom he seems genuinely to have loved, possibly hastened his own. The fifth book of the *siluae* is manifestly unfinished, for it lacks a preface; the epistle to Abascantus which precedes it is an introduction only to the first piece, not, as with the other books, a sort of table of contents to the whole.

[32] The English reader will most easily understand this metre from Tennyson's experiment in it, ' O you chorus of indolent reviewers '.

and his family, the others are addressed, occasionally to Domitian, but usually to prominent men of lower status than his, in commemoration of events great and small, as the building of a new house, the dedication of a statue, the death of a favourite slave, and so forth. They use, especially when the Emperor is the subject, a most elaborate and developed technique of flattery, in which the divinity and amazing virtues of Domitian, the extraordinary merits and amiability of the other persons named, are put in the best light.[33] It need hardly be said that neither sincerity nor great self-respect is to be looked for in such works (though it does not follow that Statius never means what he says, or that he was any more degraded than the vast majority of his contemporaries in their relations to a monarch who insisted on being called 'Lord and God' and was intolerant of the least breath of opposition); their merits are the neatness and ingenuity with which they belaud their addressees and the good style and very considerable, indeed too great, learning which they show.

Third and by far the most important come his two epic poems, the second a fragment. The *Thebaid*, Statius himself tells us, occupied him for twelve years.[34] To appreciate it, the reader must rid himself of the prejudice which many moderns have against highly artificial works; it is artificial from start to finish, but the artificiality is of a kind which only an able writer could produce. After a proem composed partly of mythological learning and partly of praises of Domitian,[35] he occupies the first of his twelve books with the events leading to the Theban War,[36] the quarrel of the two brothers, the exile of Polyneikes, his arrival in Argos, meeting with Tydeus and marriage to a daughter of Adrastos. In Book II, the ghost of Laios is sent to warn Eteokles that his brother will attack him; Tydeus arrives at Thebes with a demand that he yield up his throne to Polyneikes; this is refused, and on the way back Tydeus is attacked by fifty Thebans, all but one of whom he kills. The third book narrates the deliberations and preparations leading to the attack on Thebes; the fourth, the assembly of the seven

[33] For the technique of his and Martial's flattery, see F. Sauter, *Der römische Kaiserkult bei Martial und Statius*, Stuttgart and Berlin, Kohlhammer, 1934 (Tübinger Beiträge zur Altertumswissenschaft, xxi).

[34] *Theb.*, xii, 811.

[35] The mythology is introduced by a well-known rhetorical figure; he gives a list of the various Theban legends of which he is not going to write.

[36] For the stories, see Rose, *H.G.M.*, pp. 189–93; cf. also *H.G.L.*, p. 200.

champions, and the beginning of their march. It also contains two interesting episodes, one in which Teiresias calls up the ghost of Laios to learn the issue of the war, the other, the story of the founding of the Nemean Games, which continues throughout Book V. The Argive army being in want of water, for Dionysos has caused all the streams but one to hide themselves, Hypsipyle shows them where to find this one; while she is guiding them, her nursling Opheltes is killed by a dragon. The Argives, to console the child's parents, institute the games, and the sixth book is occupied by a long description of them. In Book VII, the army, being aroused by Iuppiter, finally arrives at Thebes, and fighting begins in earnest. Iokaste vainly tries to make peace; the town is assaulted, and Amphiaraos, retreating, is swallowed up in the earth; his reception in the lower world is described in Book VIII, which continues the story to the death of Tydeus. Book IX ends with the death of Parthenopaios,[37] Book X, after sundry episodes, with that of Kapaneus. The eleventh book describes the concluding episodes of the war, the duel of the two brothers, their deaths at each other's hand, and the retreat of the remaining Argives. Kreon succeeds to the throne. The last book contains the famous story of how the Argive widows implored Theseus of Athens to intervene and force Kreon to allow the burial of their dead.[38] He consents, assembles his army, and arrives just in time to save the lives of Antigone and Argeia, who have been caught by Kreon's men as the former was trying to bury her brother, the latter her husband, Polyneikes. Kreon is killed, peace made and the dead buried.

In this poem, as in much which the Silver Age produced, we find what may well be described as romanticism.[39] Strange events of all kinds, unnatural loves and hatreds, exaggerated passions, the more horrible kinds of supernatural happenings, slaughter and cruelty, and side by side with these appeals to a

[37] This passage is one in which Statius' sentimentality rises to something at least approaching real pathos. Parthenopaios, who is little more than a boy, is sympathetically drawn, for the poet seems to have liked young people. Being mortally wounded (877 *sqq.*) sociis in deuia campi/ tollitur (heu simplex aetas) moriensque iacentem/flebat equom.

[38] The story is in Rose, *H.G.M.*, 193, so far as it concerns Antigone; where Statius got the episode of Argeia, or if he invented it, is not known.

[39] It is a somewhat gross blunder to think of romanticism as a product of modern times. Being the natural reaction from classicism, it may occur whenever that has run its course and is dwindling into monotony and dullness; authors of any talent naturally then turn to whatever is not regular and normal to find subjects which still have life and vigour in them.

somewhat sentimental pity, are very frequent. Statius is by no means alone in his emphasis on such things, for they are as common in Seneca and Lucan. He also liked romanticism of another kind, whereof something appears in his unfinished epic, the *Achilleis*. The story of how the young and handsome hero was hidden by his mother among the maidens of Skyros, because she knew that if he went to Troy he should never return, was of a kind to interest any one who followed the Hellenistic traditions in literature, partly because it offered piquant contrasts between Achilles' real strength and boldness and his affected femininity, partly because Thetis, though a goddess, was a fitting subject, in her maternal anxiety, for one of the characteristically Alexandrian humanizations of a deity; she could remain a Nereid in name and become in all essentials a mortal mother afraid for her offspring. Statius handled the story well enough, with a good deal of Ovidian prettiness, for 1127 lines, but wrote no more.[40]

Besides the prize compositions already mentioned there is another lost work of Statius, a letter, whether in verse or prose we do not know, but probably the former, as it was plainly meant to be read by others than the nominal recipient, to Maximus Vibius, *de editione Thebaidos*. He promises also to write Plotius Grypus something worthier of his position than the jocular copy of hendecasyllables addressed to him, but we do not know if he kept his word in this respect.[41]

A less important but very pleasant poet was contemporary with Statius; we can trace his activities between about A.D. 70 and 90.[42] This was GAIVS VALERIVS FLACCVS SETINVS BALBVS, clearly a man of good social standing, being a member of the priestly college of the Quindecimuiri.[43] In him the romanticism of the age takes another turn, for he resorted to the perennially fascinating story of the Argonauts for his theme,[44] and his treat-

[40] The best MS. tradition divides the poem into two books, the second beginning at line 961; an inferior division is after 674. The work was begun after the *Thebaid*, i, 10–13.

[41] See *silu.*, iv, praef.; for the little that is known about these two men, cf. Vollmer, *op. cit.*, pp. 483–4, 491.

[42] He knows of Titus' campaign in Judea, i, 12–14 (cf. note 6), therefore he wrote that part of the poem not earlier than 70; he was dead *nuper* when Quintilian wrote the mention of him, x, 1, 90, which was about 92, see below, p. 399. His name is given in full only in the MSS. of his poem.

[43] See Val. Flacc., *ibid.*, 5–6: si Cymaeae mihi conscia uatis/stat casta cortina domo. Only the quindecimuiri had access to the supposed oracles of the Cumaean Sibyl.

[44] For the legend, see Rose, *H.G.M.*, pp. 196–205.

ment of it shows features which may remind the reader of William Morris, especially of his *Life and Death of Jason*. For the first four books he keeps pretty closely, though by no means slavishly, to his principal model, Apollonios of Rhodes (see p. 146). Having brought his heroes to Kolchis, however, he introduces a new element into the story. King Aietes is at war with his brother Perses, and the Argonauts agree to help him if they may have the Golden Fleece. This has at least the advantage over the ordinary form of the story that it gives Medeia something to admire in Jason, who fights valiantly. But Aietes will not keep his word, and the tale then proceeds in the usual way, Medeia falling in love with Jason (after the usual amount of intervention by an unconvincing Iuno), helping him by her magic to get the Fleece, and then eloping with him. Apsyrtos pursues them, and at the end of the poem as its author left it the suggestion that Medeia be surrendered to him is being hotly debated. Thus far, Apollonios is once more Valerius' model; but there are indications that he would have continued differently. Doubtless the murder of Apsyrtos and the flight of the Argonauts would have come next, but it is very probable[45] that he would then have proceeded to make them go up the Danube, overland to the Rhine, and so to the North Sea and the British Isles, thence home by the Straits of Gibraltar, instead of down a non-existent Eridanos to somewhere near Marseilles and so back to Greece via Kyrene, as in Apollonios. Such a route would have had the double advantage of giving him plenty of opportunities to praise Vespasian, under whom he began the poem, or Domitian, in whose time he continued it, and also of introducing scenes in strange countries and among savage peoples, upon whom he might have employed his far from contemptible powers of description and invention. That he would have written twelve books, like Vergil and Statius, is a reasonable supposition; as we have it, the *Argonautica* fills but eight, the last being only 467 lines long.

Some lost poets of this period may be mentioned here. Tacitus, in his *Dialogus* (see p. 411), gives a leading part to CVRIATIVS MATERNVS, who, though gifted with considerable abilities for oratory, had turned his attention to writing tragedies. We know four of his subjects, two Greek (*Medea, Thyestes*), two Roman (*Cato, Domitius*; the latter was probably that Domitius Ahenobarbus who served Brutus and Cassius

[45] He refers somewhat pointedly to Vespasian's services in Britain, *ibid.*, 7–9, cf. Sueton., *Vesp.*, 4. Agrippa's exploits would have given him a good excuse for praising Domitian.

till after Philippi, went over to Antony, and just before Actium left him for Octavian)[46]; he therefore wrote *praetextae* as well as plays with Greek themes. Other tragedians of that time are hardly even names to us. Martial, Tacitus and the younger Pliny also mention several men who seem to have written epics, but nothing more is known of their work.[47]

A central figure of the literature and criticism of this time is QUINTILIAN (MARCVS FABIVS QVINTILIANVS). This man was the son and apparently the grandson of rhetoricians. He was born at Calagurris in Spain, came to Rome to be educated, returned to his own country, was brought back to Rome by Galba when he became for a few months Emperor, remained after the fall and death of his patron, and prospered, occasionally speaking before the courts but making his reputation as a professor of rhetoric (see note 3) and afterwards as tutor to the younger members of the Imperial household under Domitian. He was married, but had the misfortune to lose both his wife and his two sons. His dates are not exactly known, save for his arrival in Rome under Galba, *i.e.*, in 68; if we suppose him to have been born about 30 and died about 96, these years will fit all the facts well enough.[48]

At an unknown date, but not very early, he wrote a small treatise *On the Reasons for the Corruption of Oratory* (*de causis corruptae eloquentiae*). This has been lost, although it was for a time suggested that we had it in the *Dialogus* now universally attributed to Tacitus (see p. 411). To judge by what its author says of it, the theme was that rhetoric as generally taught was to blame, because it occupied students in unreal exercises, lack-

[46] Our information is derived from Tacitus, *dial.*, 2–3; there was a Maternus put to death under Domitian, Cassius Dio, lxvii, 12, 5, but Dio says he was a σοφιστής, *i.e.*, a rhetorician. He may, however, have been the same man.

[47] For these shadowy figures, see Schanz-Hosius, ii, pp. 525, 545–6, 561–4.

[48] His birthplace is mentioned by Jerome, *an. Abr.* 2104 (= 88) and others. His father was a rhetorician, as appears from *inst. orat.*, ix, 3, 73; Seneca rhetor, *contr.*, x, praef., 2, says: quomodo . . . Quintilianus senex declamauerit. This can hardly mean our Quintilian's father, who would not be *senex* to Seneca, and so is more probably his grandfather. His education in Rome follows from his mention of Domitius Afer (see p. 401) as one of his teachers, x, 1, 86. His coming to Rome under Galba is attested by Jerome, *an. Abr.* 2084 (= 68); therefore he must have gone back, presumably to Spain, in the meantime. He taught oratory for twenty years, i, prooem., 1. His post in the Imperial household, iv, prooem., 2 (cum uero mihi Domitianus Augustus sororis suae nepotum delegauerit curam). His marriage and bereavements, vi, prooem., 1–14. Speeches, see n. 50.

ing all force and virility and seeking only to please for the moment; Quintilian hoped that a manlier teaching, which should keep in as close touch as possible with reality, would bring back the ancient glories of Cicero and his contemporaries.[49] In addition to this, he himself published one of his forensic speeches, while others again got abroad without his knowledge from shorthand reports.[50] Two of his lecture courses also were published, without authorization, from the notes of his pupils.[51] Nothing is left of the text of any of these works.

We therefore come to his most celebrated composition, the only one which is both certainly genuine and preserved to us, the twelve books of the *Institutio oratoria*, *i.e.*, *The Education of an Orator* (about 92–96). Since Quintilian was in the sound tradition of the best orators from Cato to Cicero, and held that a public speaker was to be not only skilled in eloquence but a good man (*uir bonus dicendi peritus*, cf. p. 94), he begins at the beginning and discusses the training of the future orator from infancy. The early education occupies the first book, and it is not too much to say that any one who knows that thoroughly and can make the necessary slight adjustment to apply its principles to subjects not in a Roman curriculum [52] may safely leave all that has been written on education from Rousseau to the latest pseudo-psychologist to gather dust on library shelves. Moral training, learning through play, instruction in spoken languages, discipline, the relative advantage of school and private tuition are all there; the moderns have done no more than

[49] Title of the work, vi, prooem., 3. He wrote it just after the death of one of his sons; now both sons survived their mother, *ibid.*, 6, and she was eighteen years old when she died, *ibid.*, 4, and much younger than Quintilian, more like a daughter than a wife, *ibid.*, 5. The boy was five years old at his death, *ibid.*, 6, and was the younger son. All this suggests that Quintilian was at least middle-aged when he wrote the work, probably had been teaching in Rome long enough to have a considerable reputation. On the other hand, it was not written very late, for he quotes it in the earlier parts of the *institutio*, see below. If we suppose that it was written in the eighties of the century, we probably shall not be far wrong. Contents, *instit.*, v, 12, 17–23 (attack on declamations); ii, 10, 4, has some very similar remarks; 4, 41–2, he has elsewhere discussed the origin of such exercises (alio libro; this is not another book of the *inst.*, therefore presumably the *de causis*); viii, 3, 58, he has discussed affectation in alio opere; 6, 76, he has spoken of hyperbole in the *de causis*.

[50] Quint., vii, 2, 24. The unauthorized editions, he says, minimam partem mei habent. See, for what little is known, *O.R.F.*, pp. 594–6.

[51] Quint., i, prooem., 7.

[52] Notably the physical sciences, together with mathematics.

express in many words what Quintilian expresses in few, apart from aberrations which they may justly claim as their own, for Quintilian would never have so far departed from his native good sense as to be guilty of them. As to the duty of the teacher towards his pupil, no one has ever improved on his statement, for it is the best possible wording of the highest possible principle of conduct.[53] The second book continues the subject for a while, and contains the admirable principle that the best and most experienced teachers, not the poorer ones, should handle beginners.[54] The following sections of this and the next books are of less general interest, for they deal with literary education directed to the acquisition of oratorical skill, not with education in general. Even so, they teem not only with information interesting to the historian or the student of rhetoric but with practical and shrewd observations on the formation of style, the use of the various types of argument, the employment of appeals to the hearers' emotions and their sense of the ridiculous, in short on all that distinguishes the orator from the mere 'spellbinder' and the work of literature from the transiently attractive imitation. The tenth book has a most interesting section on the literature which the orator should read, both in his own language and in Greek.[55] Quintilian never posed as a literary critic, and his primary object is to choose those writers who will be useful in forming a good style, especially a forensic style, for a public speaker; these limitations are to be kept in view in reading his chapter. They make it, however, all the more interesting, for they result in our having before us, not an individual's judgement, however good, but the consensus of the best opinion of Hellenistic criticism for the Greeks, of the soundest Roman for the Latins. In this as in all parts of his work, Quintilian is a Ciceronian; the changes in style since Cicero have been for the worse, so far as oratory is concerned (the historical and poetical styles are another matter), and a return to his methods the only way of salvation. Naturally, his attitude

[53] Quint., i, 1, 24 (Aristotle did not think it beneath him to teach the young Alexander): fingamus igitur Alexandrum dari nobis, inpositum gremio dignum tanta cura infantem; quamquam suus cuique dignus est. There is a good annotated edition of this book by F. H. Colson, Cambridge, 1924.

[54] Quint., ii, 3, which chapter also considers the extent to which children can learn from one another.

[55] Quint., x, 1, 27–131. There is a full and good edition of this book by Sir Wm. Peterson, Oxford, 1891, also a smaller edition, published a year later. See also Atkins, vol. ii, pp. 254–98, and for more literature on Quintilian, Schanz-Hosius, ii, pp. 752–5.

towards Seneca is one of hostility, though he does justice, and is even generous, to his cleverness.[56]

These being his principles, it is hard to accept as really his the rhetorical exercises which have come down to us under his name. There are two collections, one larger, containing originally 388 pieces, whereof 145 survive, the other, generally known as the greater declamations, consisting of nineteen only. The latter give the declamations, which are on the usual fantastic themes such as we have learned to know in dealing with the elder Seneca, in full; the former give outlines only, accompanied with a *sermo* in each case, *i.e.*, a discussion of how the theme may best be handled. It is perfectly clear that they represent lecture notes; but considering Quintilian's outspoken opposition to such methods as those of the teacher to whom they are due, we have but two possible theories, the style being such that it might quite well be of his age. Either his views on the subject modified greatly as he grew older, and in his earlier years as a teacher he was still using the conventional methods, or else these declamations are not his at all, but those of another, perhaps contemporary rhetorician.[57]

Of other orators and teachers of the subject there was no lack, in and about the time of Quintilian. Most of them are the merest shadows, known to us only because Quintilian cites their views on this or that point or refers his readers to books of their composition, or from their occurring in Suetonius' work *de rhetoribus* (p. 511). The following, however, stand out a little from the darkness. CN. DOMITIVS AFER, one of the chief speakers in Tacitus' *Dialogus* (p. 411), was active under the earlier Emperors as an advocate, especially famous for his eloquence in prosecution, and also had a career in the service of the state, being praetor in 26, consul suffectus in 39, superintendent of the water system 49–59, in which year he died, having outlived his eloquence. He was a native of Nemausus (Nîmes) in Gaul.[58] IVLIVS AFRICANVS, according

56 Quint., *ibid.*, 125–31. He disclaims any personal animus; the quarrel between them is one of principle, and rather with those who imitated his faults than with his own works: non equidem omnino conabar excutere (sc., e manibus adulescentium), sed potioribus praeferri non sinebam, 126.

57 The lesser declamations are in the Teubner series, edited by C. Ritter; the greater have been edited by G. Lehnart, Leipzig, 1905, besides various earlier publications of both.

58 Birthplace, Jerome, *an. Abr.* 2060 (= 44): Domitius Afer Nemausensis clarus habetur. His activities, Tacitus, *ann.*, iv, 52, and elsewhere; Quint., x, 1, 118; xii, 11, 3; more in the article on him in Pauly-Wissowa, v, 1318. Quintilian was a great admirer of him and in some sense his pupil, cf. Pliny, *epp.*, ii, 14, 10. For his fragments, see *O.R.F.*, pp. 563–70.

to Quintilian, was comparable to him, but not so good.[59] POMPEIVS SATVRNINVS was a friend of the younger Pliny, who praises his eloquence and his merits in various styles of composition, verse and prose.[60] PVBLIVS RVTILIVS RVFVS rendered into Latin a work of Gorgias, not the great rhetorician of the fifth century B.C.,[61] but a later author, who numbered among his pupils M. Cicero the younger. About half of this little treatise survives; Quintilian read and used the whole of it; the subject of the remaining part is figures of language, while the lost section dealt with figures of thought.[62] VERGINIVS FLAVVS is doubly distinguished, for he was the teacher of Persius and was banished, along with Musonius Rufus the philosopher, by Nero in 65. He also was the author of a rhetorical handbook which Quintilian used.[63]

In 64 there arrived in Rome a needy but clever young Spaniard, a native of Bilbilis (a small town in Hispania Tarraconensis), where his father and mother, Valerius Fronto and Flaccilla, had given him a good education of the usual type. His name, MARCVS VALERIVS MARTIALIS, is curtailed to MARTIAL in our mouths. The next year, he found himself deprived of his natural patrons, the Senecas, and probably counted himself lucky not to have been implicated in the conspiracy of Piso. He therefore set himself to earning a living by miscellaneous writings in verse.[64] Had he lived in our days, his very considerable talents would have assured him a tolerably good living as a free-lance journalist, or attached him to the staff of some important paper as what is called in America a columnist, with the task assigned him of making daily comments in a humorous vein on passing events. This he would have done well, and added to his salary by publishing the best of his remarks in little volumes of light verse, or perhaps essays. But antiquity had nothing corresponding at all closely to our journalism, so far, that is, as the methods of publication went; the reading public remained comparatively

[59] Quint., x, 1, 118. Fragments, *O.R.F.*, pp. 570–2.

[60] Pliny, *epp.*, i, 16, is a brief laudation of him.

[61] For this Gorgias, see Rose, *H.G.L.*, p. 279.

[62] The work is published in Halm, *Rhetores minores Latini*, iii (Leipzig, 1863). That it is incomplete appears from Quintilian, ix, 2, 102 *sqq.*

[63] Tac., *ann.*, xv, 71, 9; Quint., vii, 4, 40 and elsewhere; *Vita Persi Flacci*.

[64] For a full discussion of Martial's life and works, see the introduction to Friedländer's edition, Leipzig, 1886, also his *Sittengeschichte*, ed. 9 (edited after his death by Wissowa), iv, pp. 290–6. Birthplace, Mart., i, 61, 12. Date of arrival in Rome, calculated from x, 103, 7: he had been away from Bilbilis thirty-four years; this poem can be dated in 98, therefore he came to Rome in 64. He was then not much over twenty, for *ibid.*, 24, 4, he mentions his fifty-seventh birthday. Lucan's widow remained a patroness of his (x, 64), hence his praises of Lucan (*e.g.*, i, 61, 7) and of heroes and heroines of the Opposition, as i, 13; 42.

small, and the patron was the one means of getting more than the barest pittance from literature. Martial was ready to write verses on anything that could be briefly expressed, down to labels for the presents or favours (*xenia* and *apophoreta*) [65] given to guests at dinners; he seems to have had no scruples of conscience, no politics and no pride. Hence in his fifteen books of verse we find all manner of things.[66] There is a collection of epigrams addressed to Titus on the completion of the Flavian Amphitheatre and its formal opening, attended by a multitude of ingenious and elaborate shows, in 80. There are addresses, varying from highly complimentary to downright abusive, to every actual or potential patron he could think of. There are pretty sketches of the peace and quiet of country life. There are a few little poems on a slave-child, by name Erotion, of whom Martial seems to have made a pet and for whose death he evidently was really grieved, for it was one of his amiable qualities that he loved children. There are witty comments on what we may suppose to be pieces of current gossip, with names belonging to persons insignificant or wholly fictitious; indeed, the amusing scandals which form the subject of such epigrams may well be, in many cases, Martial's own invention. Running through it all, up to the death of Domitian, is endless and endlessly clever flattery of him. Most of them were written in Rome, though for a while Martial left the city and moved to Forum Cornelii (Imola) in Cisalpine Gaul.[67] Unfortunately, as generally happens when free speech, in the political sense, is completely departed, Martial found the society for which he wrote tickled by the grossest libertinism of expression, and in consequence, for he was always ready to please his public, he often descended to obscenities so foul that even his abundant wit does not excuse them; nothing quite so vile as some of his worst offences in this regard is to be found elsewhere. The death of Domitian did not check his activities, for he was perfectly willing to flatter the new Emperor; but the tone of the

[65] These comprise two books of our collection, Nos. xiii and xiv.

[66] As we have them, the epigrams consist of (*a*) the *liber epigrammaton*, often called *liber spectaculorum*, apparently a selection from the epigrams to Titus, for there is no mention of several interesting numbers which we know to have been on the programme of the shows; (*b*) twelve books, often revised and enlarged editions, which he published from time to time. The earliest of them represents the author as already well known, i, 1, 2–3 (toto notus in orbe Martialis/argutis epigrammaton libellis; he would seem therefore already to have published more than one collection); (*c*) the two books mentioned in n. 65.

[67] From there he wrote the third book, see iii, 1 and 4.

court changed very decidedly under Nerva and Trajan, from whom he apparently could not win much favour even by the subtle compliment of declaring that compliments were not wanted under their free and just rule [68]; it is also reasonable to suppose that the society he was accustomed to, the 'smart set' of Domitian's time, largely vanished with the death of its leader. He therefore retired, and, it would seem, gladly, to Spain, and he spent the remainder of his days on an estate given him by a Spanish lady named Marcella, to whom he addresses a charming little epigram of gratitude.[69] From Spain he sent one last book to Rome, and probably died after but a few years of the peace and quiet for which he had professed to long, though when away from Rome he speaks with regret of what it had to offer.[70]

Martial is our one surviving example of Roman epigram at its best; from other sources we have either much inferior specimens or so few that we cannot form a complete judgement of the authors' skill. Martial has all the virtues of the best Greeks in this department, save one; he cannot, because he writes in Latin, be at once perfectly simple, elegant and impressive on a serious theme. This is clear, for example, when he tries to put into verse the death-scene of Arria and her husband,[71] which he merely makes far less touching than it is in the plainest prose. But he can be simple, elegant and funny,[72] or pungent,[73] or neatly abusive [74]; he can thank an admirer in the most graceful manner possible,[75] or address one who has disappointed him with apparent compliments that bear a sting in their tail [76];

[68] Book x, 72, from which it is easy to judge how much sincerity his praises of Domitian had contained.

[69] Book xii, 31; cf. also 21.

[70] Pliny, *epp.*, iii, 21 (date uncertain, conjectured by Mommsen to be 104), mentions his death as a recent piece of news. For Martial's mixture of pleasure in his quiet and independent life in Spain and regret for the capital, see xii, 18, and 21, 9–10 (tu desiderium dominae mihi mitius urbis/esse iubes; Romam tu mihi sola facis).

[71] One of the most famous martyrdoms of the philosophizing Opposition. Arria was the wife of Caecina Paetus, who was condemned for taking part in a rebellion against Claudius. Being allowed to end his own life, he was encouraged by Arria, who stabbed herself and then handed him the dagger, telling as she did so such a lie as only a wholly devoted woman would be capable of: *Paete, non dolet.* See Pliny, *epp.*, iii, 16, 6 *sqq*. Martial, i, 13, makes one of his few bad blunders by expanding her dying words to a whole couplet.

[72] As ii, 78 and a thousand more, to be found by simply turning the pages of a Martial.

[73] For instance, iii, 15; 28; 29, besides many hardly quotable.

[74] For example, iii, 34; 61; iv, 21.

[75] As iv, 29.

[76] One of the best examples is iv, 40.

while the resources of his flattery know no bounds,[77] and even his puns are of the most varied and subtle.[78] Also, he is not limited to amusing tales, jokes and scandal, nor to the arts of a courtier, for he was capable of what seems to have been real affection, both for friends and, as already mentioned, for children.[79] The one requisite was that the subject should be capable of being given a clever, if possible an unexpected turn. Under such circumstances he was capable of real poetry. Despite the unpleasant features, which were due more to his public than to himself, he deserves his lasting popularity, which continues through the late antique and medieval periods [80] down to our own day.

To pick up a living, by means more or less honest, from the fringes of a corrupt society is a disheartening business, unless one has an unusually tough skin. Martial was insensitive to any but very decided slights, and those he could avenge by an epigram over which Rome would chuckle, doubtless seeing easily through the fictitious name. Hence he enjoyed, not exactly prosperity, but a fair amount of success.[81] He had an acquaintance of whose early life we know but little; his character, however, is tolerably apparent from his works. This was JUVENAL (DECIMVS IVNIVS IVVENALIS) of Aquinum, the last classical Latin poet of importance and the best-known of all satirists.[82] He

[77] For the variations he can make on the one theme 'Domitian is a god', see the work quoted in n. 33.

[78] There are good ones, for example, in iv, 47; 53.

[79] Hence the altogether charming epigram on the death of Erotion, v, 34. It is a letter of recommendation addressed to the shades of his own parents, who will be her *patroni* in the other world (being dead, she is no longer a slave) and are to be careful lest the darkness and monsters of Hades should frighten her, little as she is.

[80] An account of his influence and the form in which his works have been preserved is given in Schanz-Hosius, ii, pp. 557–60.

[81] Though he always speaks of himself as very poor, and continually asks for presents, small and great, he incidentally admits that he had a little estate near Rome and a small house in the capital (ix, 18, 2; whether or not this was the estate of which he speaks very slightingly in xi, 18, is uncertain). Domitian gave him the *ius trium liberorum*, or confirmed a grant made by Titus (ix, 97, 5–6, he says *Caesar uterque* gave it), *i.e.*, the privileges enjoyed by men who had at least three legitimate children. By way of showing his appreciation of this, he expresses his resolve never to marry, ii, 92, and kept his word. But as regarded money or anything which would cost money, the Emperor was stingy to a degree towards Martial, see vi, 10.

[82] His life is recorded in a very poor, short and untrustworthy biography from late antiquity, prefixed to most modern editions of his works; Martial mentions him several times, *e.g.*, vii, 24, which expresses warm affection for him (provided that this is the same Iuuenalis); 91, 1, which calls him *facundus*. Birthplace, iii, 319 (tuo . . . Aquino; Juvenal is addressed).

seems to have been a rhetorician and the hanger-on of wealthy families for the greater part of his life,[83] during which time he conceived the natural bitterness of a poor and unsuccessful man against the rich and fortunate, and could comfort himself by giving his ill-feeling a moral tone; for we may in fairness credit him with a real hatred of vice and preference for simplicity and honesty, though this was not strong enough to draw him away from Rome to the quiet and inexpensive country towns which he recommends.[84] Criticism of the age was not safe under Domitian, but once he was dead, Juvenal seems to have turned his attention seriously to indicting contemporary wickedness in a series of powerful sketches in verse, the sixteen satires [85] which

[83] That he was a rhetorician is stated in the *Life* (ad mediam fere aetatem declamauit), and with this Martial's *facundus* (see last note) agrees, though the word is not used only of those who are eloquent in prose. He evidently knows the miseries of a client's position from within, see for instance the fifth satire.

[84] For example, in iii, 165 *sqq.*

[85] He would appear to have published them in five books; so, at least, they are arranged in our MSS., and the order, so far as the dates can be determined, is chronological. No. i mentions, 49, the condemnation of Marius Priscus for extortion, as if it were a recent event; it took place in 99/100. There is nothing to suggest that the other four which, with this one, make up the first book contain anything earlier. No. vi, which constitutes Book ii, speaks (407–8; 411) of a gossiping woman who has news of a comet (there was one in 115, visible from Rome) and an earthquake (probably on Dec. 13 of that year, at Antioch). No. vii, which with viii and ix makes up Book iii, speaks of a Caesar who is the only hope for letters (1 *sqq.*). The natural interpretation is that Hadrian is meant, and therefore this book was published in 117, his first year, or not long after. Nos. x–xii form Book iv; in this there is no clear mark of date, but presumably it comes after Book iii and before Book v. This comprises Nos. xiii–xvi, whereof the latter is incomplete, probably through early loss of its concluding verses. In xiii, 16, the person addressed, Juvenal's friend Calvinus, has completed his sixtieth year and was born *Fonteio consule, i.e.*, in 67; the date is therefore 127, and this agrees with xv, 27, nuper consule Iunco; Iuncus was consul in 127, hence this satire can hardly be later than 128. The dates of Juvenal's life are unknown; a certain loss of vigour in the last few satires suggests that he was then aging. If he was about seventy when he died and his death was not far from 130, *i.e.*, within some two years of his last datable work, he would have been born about 60, and therefore the end of Domitian's reign, the earliest time when he can be supposed to have left declamations for satire, would bring him to about middle life (thirty-six years old or so), thus agreeing with the biography. There is an inscription, C.I.L., x, 5382, Dessau 2926, set up by a . . . *nius Iuuenalis*, an officer in the army; if we could confidently restore *D. Iu—* for the lost letters, we should gain the information that he had seen some service, which would agree approximately with an absurd anecdote in the *Life*, but not with his expressed detestation of military ways in sat. xvi.

have come down to us. He is careful, as he explains, to name no living offenders,[86] but it may very well be that contemporaries are masked under the names of the dead, or otherwise alluded to. The series of proofs that Rome was wicked to the highest possible degree was as popular as such things, if well done, usually are, and all the more so as they abound in piquant descriptions of the vices they lash. Juvenal was, like most moralists of his age, a Stoic, if he can be reckoned as of any philosophical school, and made free use of the convenient dictum of his teachers that all sins are of equal magnitude. Hence, though not without traces of somewhat heavy-handed humour, he was able to denounce Nero [87] for assassinating his mother and wife and for writing bad poems and appearing on the stage, and to include among notable sinners of high rank the amateur charioteer Lateranus, who has so far forgotten what was due to his position as consul as to drive himself up and down the public roads after dark, while, once his term of office is expired, he will fall into blacker vice yet, driving in the daytime and afterwards refreshing himself in a common tavern kept by foreigners. In dealing with greater sins, such as meanness to dependents, gross and infamous sexual irregularities, forgery, theft, perjury, murder and their like (if these indeed are worse than an ex-consul giving a coachman's salute with his whip), Juvenal sometimes leaves a sceptical reader a little in doubt whether he is more angered at the wickedness of the world or obliged to it for giving him such admirable subjects for his great eloquence and extraordinary power of composing vigorous hexameters, easily the best of their kind since Lucan, whereof every one is a lash.

The subjects of the individual satires are as follows. No. i, the sins of the age and the impossibility of refraining from writing satire [88]; a series of vignettes of the principal types of offenders. No. ii, the prevalence of unnatural vice, especially among those who make high pretences to morality.[89] No. iii, the miseries of life in Rome; this is the original of Johnson's *London*. No. iv, a meeting of Domitian's privy council to decide what is to be done about a huge fish which its captor, knowing better than to try to sell it, has presented to him. No. v, the

[86] See i, 170–1.

[87] Sat. viii, 220–1; 146–82.

[88] Difficile est saturam non scribere, 30; the same poem contains the equally famous phrases probitas laudatur et alget, 74, and si natura negat, facit indignatio uersum, 79.

[89] Again a famous line, 3, qui Curios simulant et Bacchanalia uiuunt.

wretchedness of hangers-on of the stingy and mannerless rich.[90] No. vi is Juvenal's masterpiece, for he seems to have disliked women only one degree less than Jews, who were his especial aversion, even as compared to other Easterners.[91] A friend who thinks of marrying is adjured to do no such thing, for there are no virtuous women left, or, if any, they are so proud of their virtue as to be intolerable to live with. This thesis is sustained by a series of brilliant descriptions of various kinds of female offenders, the adultress of high or low degree, the wife who makes her dowry or her beauty a lever to get her own way with her husband, the too perfect woman who is much too proud of her virtue and her breeding, the smatterer of Greek on all occasions, the masterful type, with her mother as her ally, the litigious, the athletic, and the jealous (with a digression on the monstrous impurity of some of the higher circles), the extravagant (again an excursus on vice and its teachers),[92] the music-lover, the gossip, the mannish and ill-tempered sort, the blue-stocking, the rich woman, who is worst of all, the prevalence of cruelty and superstition, magic and poisoning. No. vii, which has a preface in praise of Hadrian (see note 85), pretty obviously an addition to the original work, deals with the woes of students and teachers of arts and letters. No. viii treats of the vanity of rank ; No. ix returns to the subject of No. ii from a different angle. No. x, the original of Johnson's *Vanity of Human Wishes*, deserves the attention he paid it, for it is one of the noblest pieces of solemn moralizing in all Latin verse, especially in its magnificent closing paragraph on wise prayer.[93] No. xi attacks gluttony and luxurious living. No. xii treats of a feast of thanksgiving in honour of a friend's safe return from a dangerous voyage. No. xiii consoles a friend who has been robbed ;

[90] For the whole question of the relations of men of letters to the new nobility of the Flavian times, see Friedlaender, *Sittengeschichte*, ed. 9, vol. ii, ch. x.

[91] For examples of his detestation of them, see iii, 13–16 ; vi, 542–7 ; xiv, 96–106. Their chief offences in his eyes seem to have been that they were mostly poor, that some of them practised as diviners, especially as dream interpreters, and that they proselytized.

[92] This (between 365 and 366 of the old numbering of the lines) is the passage containing the famous 'new fragment', preserved in one MS., cod. Canonicianus class. Lat. 41, in the Bodleian Library. Its loss at some unknown but early date is a curious chapter in the history of Juvenal's text, which, owing to his great popularity, is full of the errors which arise from copying an author too familiar and therefore apt to be written down from memory instead of closely following the archetype.

[93] Lines 357–62 (after the too much quoted mens sana in corpore sano).

the chief topic is the torment which a guilty conscience inflicts. No. xiv [94] has for its main topic parents' duty of setting their children a good example; it is loosely constructed and wanders off at the end into a discussion of avarice. No. xv describes an alleged case of cannibalism in Egypt, and No. xvi speaks of the ill-treatment of civilians by soldiers.

In all of these satires, Juvenal's tone is the same; he is dealing with a very vile world which is at the same time very interesting. It is his business as a satirist to point out the evils and make them as hateful as he can, not to suggest remedies. It is equally his business to make out his case; he is not a judge, but an advocate for the prosecution. These considerations are alone enough to explain why he draws so very different a picture from that presented to us by the good-natured and tolerant Pliny, who likewise had the advantage of being in very easy circumstances, while Juvenal in all probability was often at his wits' end to get the ordinary necessaries of life, certainly never well off. Moreover, Pliny (see p. 417) shows us the society in which he moved under Nerva and Trajan, principally the latter; when he tells a story of the times of Domitian, it is generally by way of contrast with the better days that have come.

Though the only surviving satirist, and probably the best, of his times, Juvenal had not the field to himself. There was a certain TVRNVS, of whose verses we have one short sample,[95] not enough to tell us anything about him; Martial assures us that he had great powers (*ingentia pectora*), and contented himself with writing satires, not tragedies, because his brother MEMOR was a tragic poet and he did not wish to rival him. There is also in existence a copy of verse, 70 hexameters in all, complaining of the expulsion of the philosophers under Domitian. This is headed with the name of SVLPICIA,[96] but in the first place we

[94] Again containing a very familiar dictum, 47, maxima debetur puero reuerentia, si quid/turpe paras (usually misquoted *pueris*, and without the concluding words). A little less famous and hackneyed is 321, numquam aliud natura, aliud sapientia dicit.

[95] Preserved in the scholiast on Juvenal, i, 71; it consists of two hexameters, the second badly corrupted. See *F.P.L.*, p. 371/134. For Martial's mention of him, see xi, 10, cf. vii, 97, 7–8. Valla's scholiast on Juv., i, 20, says the magnus Auruncae alumnus mentioned there (undoubtedly Lucilius, cf. p. 82) is either Turnus or one of two other quite unknown satirists, all alleged to be natives of the same place.

[96] The verses are in *P.L.M.*, v, pp. 91–7, Jahn and Leo's edition of Juvenal and Peiper's ed. of Ausonius. Of the real Sulpicia (not the poetess mentioned, p. 288 above) Martial says (x, 13, 10–13): cuius carmina qui bene aestimarit,/nullam dixerit esse nequiorem,/nullam dixerit esse sanctiorem. The apparent contradiction is explained by her having written with the greatest frankness of her own relations to her husband Calenus. There is one short fragment of her (*F.P.L.*, p. 370/134)

know enough of her to say that it is unlikely she should have written this kind of work, in the second the lines are not good enough nor in sufficiently classical Latin to be the production of anyone of that age.

Undoubtedly the greatest writer of this period was CORNELIVS TACITVS.[97] As he, like Juvenal, came too late to have his biography written by Suetonius (p. 511) we know little of the external facts of his life; but his own works tell us all that is necessary. He was evidently associated closely with the senatorial Opposition and was a theoretical republican, though not so fanatical as to refuse to serve the Imperial government. He held public office under all three of the Flavians,[98] married, in or about 78, the daughter of Cn. Iulius Agricola, the most distinguished of the governors of Britain under Domitian, and was away from Rome, clearly on public business of some sort, when his father-in-law died in 93.[99] Returning to the capital later in that year, he lived through the reign of terror which marked Domitian's last days, was consul in 97 under Nerva, and, while still holding that office, pronounced the funeral oration over one of the most admirable characters of the day, Verginius Rufus.[100] Three years later, he and Pliny successfully pled the cause of the African provincials against Marius Priscus.[101] Under Trajan, about 112, he was governor of Asia,[102] and may well have outlived him, since he mentions a state of things which existed

which bears this out. The author of the hexameters clearly meant to pass for Sulpicia, see his lines 62, 65. The poem is certainly late, Baehrens thinks later than Ausonius (see p. 527), as its miserably clumsy phraseology and versification show.

[97] His *praenomen* is uncertain, authorities, none very reliable, varying between Publius and Gaius; see Schanz-Hosius, ii, p. 603.

[98] Tacitus, *hist.*, i, 1: dignitatem nostram a Vespasiano incohatam, a Tito auctam, a Domitiano longius prouectam non abnuerim. Precisely what the offices in question were is not known, but probably a minor magistracy (Vespasian) and the quaestorship (Titus), followed by the position of aedile or tribune (Domitian). In 88, still under Domitian, he was praetor and *quindecimuir sacris faciundis*, by his own testimony, *ann.*, xi, 11, 3.

[99] Tac., *Agr.*, 45.

[100] Pliny, *epp.*, ii, 1, 6. This is the Verginius who put down the revolt of Vindex towards the end of Nero's principate and asked to have inscribed on his grave the famous epitaph: Hic situs est Rufus, pulso qui Vindice quondam/imperium adseruit non sibi sed patriae (Pliny, *epp.*, vi, x, 4).

[101] Pliny, *epp.*, ii, 11, 2.

[102] This is known from an inscription, best published in *Jahreshefte des österreichishen archäologischen Instituts*, xxvii (1932), p. 234. By the usual practice of those times, the governorship would come about fifteen years after the consulship.

only at the end of his principate in an early book of the *Annals.*[103] Throughout a great part of his life he enjoyed the high reputation as a writer which he deserved.

What is usually considered his first work is the *Dialogus de oratoribus*. In answer, as Tacitus says in the opening chapter, to repeated inquiries from a friend, Fabius Iustus (*consul suffectus* in 102), he discusses the question why there are no moderns worth calling orators at all, whereas in the old days that art flourished. When much younger, he heard some eminent men discuss that very question, and will set down his recollections of their arguments.[104] Curiatius Maternus (see p. 397) was visited by Domitius Afer (p. 401) and Iulius Secundus, with the young Tacitus in attendance. Domitius asks Maternus why, with his natural gifts for oratory, he neglects that art for poetry, and exalts the busy and successful life of an eloquent advocate. Maternus replies that there is more quiet and safety and quite as much real fame to be had from poetry, and he does not care for the dangerous and uncertain rewards which eloquence may bring, at the cost of a life of continual dispute and turmoil. At this moment Vipstanus Messalla arrives [105] and, on learning what the conversation is about, raises the question why the ancient orators were so much better than the moderns. Afer at once replies that, so far as the word ' ancient ' has any meaning when applied to men who lived but a century or so ago, the ancients were bunglers who did not yet know how to construct a telling speech ; only a few of them, including Cicero, realized that such an art was possible and made efforts, very creditable for that period, to attain to it. Messalla, at Maternus' suggestion, dismisses all this as clever paradox and gives his opinion at length ; the speakers of to-day learn nothing but a little false rhetoric, and have neither a moral, a philosophic, nor a literary education, nor even a knowledge of law. The ancients

[103] *Ann.*, ii, 61, 2, Roman sovranty reaches rubrum ad mare, *i.e.*, to the Persian Gulf ; this was true in 116, not earlier, and the Empire receded from Trajan's new Eastern provinces at the beginning of Hadrian's reign.

[104] All this is not to be taken seriously, being a mere literary device to introduce the representatives of different points of view. The dramatic date is the sixth year of Vespasian, 17, *i.e.*, A.D. 74, and Tacitus was iuuenis admodum, perhaps about 20 or so.

[105] This Messalla was, according to Tacitus, a man of high birth (*hist.*, iii, 9) and noble character, which showed itself particularly in his defence of his brother (*ibid.*, iv, 42), Aquilius Regulus, the notorious *delator*, against the vengeance of the Senate in 70. From the part he takes in the dialogue it would appear that he was something of an antiquarian, not only in his studies but in his style.

were properly brought up at home, thoroughly educated in all liberal studies, and learned to plead causes, not among children in a class-room, but among men in the actual courts. They thus learned how to use the many and widely different manners which are necessary before different audiences. After some remarks of Secundus,[106] Maternus again speaks. The reason, according to him, why eloquence was so characteristic of the close of the Republic was that the times were turbulent and oratory a most necessary weapon. Nowadays, in a quiet and orderly state, there are no longer the great and sensational public trials, the vast juries and the excited public opinion which roused the contemporaries of Cicero to such prodigious feats of expression; it is the price we pay for better government and fewer rascals.

While no one now seriously doubts that Tacitus wrote this excellent work, there is no absolutely cogent argument in favour of his authorship. That the style is very different from that of the historical works is irrelevant; it differs in matters of rhythm and sentence-structure, of which the author would be conscious and which he could change at will. The vocabulary, the grammar and the flashes of epigram are all Tacitean. Of external evidence there is a little; Pliny, writing to Tacitus (*epp.*, ix, 10, 2), speaks of poems, quae tu inter nemora et lucos commodissime perfici putas, which is a fairly plain allusion to *dial.*, 9, in nemora et lucos, id est in solitudinem secedendum est (poetis), and 12, nemora uero et luci et secretum . . . mihi adferunt uoluptatem. There is therefore no reason to identify the book with the lost *de causis* of Quintilian (p. 398), still less to attribute it to Pliny, who never produced anything so good.[107] The date cannot be exactly determined; Tacitus implies (*dial.*, 1) that he is now no longer a young man, and he speaks of Vibius Crispus, who was prominent under Domitian, in a more contemptuous way (13) than would be likely if he were still alive when Tacitus wrote. I would gladly see in the mention of Vespasian as uenerabilis senex et patientissimus ueri (8) a sidelong compliment to the old and mild Nerva, suggesting that the book, or that part of it, was produced in his time, 96–98, but it may be later than that. For

[106] Between chaps. 35 and 36 of our texts there is clearly something lost. The former ends, the latter begins with a broken sentence; in the former, Messalla is speaking, but 42 begins with *finierat Maternus*, showing that the preceding remarks, 36–41, have been from him. Also, in 16, it is said that Secundus will speak, but in the *dialogus* as we have it there is nothing more than an occasional short remark from him. The great lacuna, therefore, as it is called, contained his speech, the end of Messalla's and the beginning of that of Maternus. For Tacitus' literary views in general, see Atkins, vol. ii, pp. 175–96.

[107] The only Plinian thing is the general tone of acquiescence with the Imperial government.

the whole question of date and authorship, see Schanz-Hosius, ii, pp. 610–11, and the editions.[108]

Concerning the remaining works there has never been any doubt that Tacitus wrote them.[109] The earliest of them seems to be the biography of his father-in-law, the *Agricola*. This short and eloquent sketch, full of a very understandable partiality for a man who seems to have been both able and patriotic, is rendered all the more interesting to us because its subject performed his most important services in Britain, where he served under Suetonius Paulinus in Nero's time and returned under Domitian to govern the province. In consequence, Tacitus devotes comparatively much space to describing the island itself and Agricola's operations in it. His deficiencies as a geographer and strategist, which are perhaps his worst fault, make his narrative less clear than we could wish, but any document from that age and based on the good information available to him is precious, and the book in consequence is one of the chief treasures of historians who study this difficult chapter of British history.[110]

Another most valuable work, shorter than the *Agricola* by some five Teubner pages but consisting almost wholly of description and therefore fuller when fulness is most wanted, is the famous *Germania*, a sketch. probably somewhat later in date than the biography, of the Central European peoples, so far as any knowledge of them had reached the Romans through war,

[108] The most elaborate is that of A. Gudemann, 2nd ed., Teubner, 1914; handy English editions are those of Sir Wm. Peterson, Oxford, 1893, and in the Loeb series.

[109] Doubt of the authenticity of a writing implies sufficient knowledge and critical sagacity to entitle one to judge; these do not appear in the shallow works of M. Ross, *Tacitus and Bracciolini*, London, Deeprose and Bateman, 1878, and his French ape, P. Hochart, *De l'authenticité des Annales et des Histoires de Tacite*, Paris, Thorin, 1910, who imagine the *Annals* (and *Histories*) forged.

[110] As an example of the difficulties which surround it may be instanced the crowning battle of Agrippa's campaigns, at Mons Graupius (29 *sqq*.). One of the few certain things about this is that it was not fought at the Grampians, which owe their modern name to a false reading, *Grampium* for *Graupium*, and a false location of the conflict. The book has been edited again and again, best in the revision, by H. Furneaux and J. G. C. Anderson, Oxford, 1923, of the standard work of the late Professor Haverfield. A selection from the mass of literature concerning it in Schanz-Hosius, ii, p. 616 *sq*. Translations in all the principal European languages and small school editions are very numerous. The date is shown pretty clearly by the wording of ch. 3 to be early in Trajan's principate, probably 98; Tacitus emphasizes the long silence which has preceded his writing, hence this may be the earliest of all his works.

trade or other sources. That some legend is mixed with the fact is inevitable; that the knowledge is imperfect goes without saying; the reader has also to be on his guard occasionally against Tacitus' weakness for idealizing the German as the noble savage and contrasting him favourably with the vices of over-civilized Rome; but with all allowances made, we have in this little book a document of first-rate importance, the only one in Latin, save a few chapters of Caesar, which tells us anything at all about this highly important people at so early a date; for Velleius Paterculus describes Germany and the Germans hardly at all, being too occupied with his account of Tiberius' battles against them, and the parts of Livy and other historians which would be relevant are lost. Hence the *Germania* has been most eagerly studied for centuries, and may now be considered critically and thoroughly known, which is not to say that no future discovery will ever throw further light on it.[111]

The date is roughly determined by ch. 37, which mentions the second consulship of Trajan, 98. The book therefore was not written earlier than that year, and there is nothing to indicate that it is much later. One reason at least for its composition was in all probability to familiarize future readers of the larger historical works Tacitus was planning with the scene of many of the events. In studying it, the conventions of ancient ethnography have to be borne in mind; some of these are admirably explained by E. Norden in his charming work *Altgermanien*, Teubner, 1934.

Tacitus by this time had fully made up his mind to write this history of his own times, taking advantage of the 'uncommon good fortune of our day, in which one may think what he will and say what he thinks'.[112] He began by writing the events which led up to the coming of the Flavian dynasty, and the principates of that house.[113] This work, the *Historiae*, is unhappily preserved only in part, breaking off part way through the fifth book, which describes the beginning of the siege of Jerusalem in 70, with a curious and ill-informed excursus on the early history of the Jews, and then goes on to the revolt

[111] Perhaps the most useful edition is that of W. Reeb and H. Volkmann (Teubner, 1934), with text, notes, and essays on the problems of German archaeology and proto-history involved; several Germanists have furnished these from their own specialist knowledge. Smaller, but good, is the edition (with German translation) of E. Fehrle, Munich, Lehmann, 1929.

[112] *Hist.*, i, 1: rara temporum felicitate, ubi sentire quae uelis et quae sentias dicere liceat.

[113] This is certain from *ann.*, xi, 11, 2: libris quibus res imperatoris Domitiani composui.

of Civilis in Gaul. It begins with the so-called year of the three Emperors, 68–69, and describes in the first four books the struggles between Galba and Otho, Otho and Vitellius, Vitellius and the generals of Vespasian, with the concomitant events in other parts of the Empire. The arrangement is annalistic, each year's happenings being finished before the next is begun; the disadvantage of this, which is a fault of many ancient histories, is that the thread of the narrative is often broken, as for instance at iv, 86, which leaves Civilis, to return to him at v, 14. It is much to be regretted that the books dealing with the later events have perished; Domitian's times especially would have afforded the historian the best possible field for his peculiar powers of describing horrors. Conjectures as to how many books are lost have been made, but in the nature of things are futile.[114]

The exact time in which the *Histories* were written is not known, but Tacitus was in correspondence with Pliny while busy with them, and the letters from the latter which deal with the subject (Tacitus' own are not preserved) seem to fall between the years 104 and 109.

His greatest work, however, so far as we can now judge, for it also survives in a mutilated form,[115] is that generally known as the *Annals*, though the best MS. tradition entitles it *ab excessu diui Augusti*. It is a treatment, as the title implies, of the period before that recorded in the *Histories*, and has therefore a most rich and varied theme, containing abundant illustrations of what Tacitus, with his republican traditions and his total lack of any personal acquaintance with the Republic, honestly believed, that that Imperial system was bad in itself, though mitigated by the occasional appearance of a good ruler who had something of the democrat in him. It is to be remembered that the last years of Domitian, through which he had passed, were not of a nature to prejudice him in favour of the existing type of government, for that Emperor's suspicious cruelty had borne hardest upon the Senate and upon the writers and thinkers of whose creed Stoicism formed part. Tacitus tried hard to be impartial, and probably thought that he was; but his eyes were apt to see everywhere the form of Domitian under different names. Had the third of the Flavians been as reasonable and as popular as the first two, it is not likely that we should have

[114] Of the many editions, perhaps the best-known English one is that of W. A. Spooner, London, 1891; see further Schanz-Hosius, ii, pp. 625–6.

[115] We lack most of Book v, the beginning of vi, the whole of vii–x, about the first half of xi, and everything after xvi, 35, *i.e.*, part of the year 66 and the whole of 67 and 68.

had so gloomy a portrait of Tiberius as exists in the *Annals*, for the constant insinuation, often, it would seem, made unconsciously, that his only genuine qualities were his most unlovely ones, the rest being the product of deep cunning, again and again sets in a wrong light the facts which the author is much too honest to falsify. Of a soured and cynical man, thrust into supreme power when his abilities fitted rather to be a thoroughly reliable and intelligent second in command, he has made a hypocritical tyrant, while Claudius, in his portrait of him, exposes to our view all his least admirable features. Tacitus probably did not spare Caligula, in whose defence indeed there was nothing to be said save that he was mad,[116] and certainly he was at no pains to palliate the many and undoubted vices of Nero. But this bias, for which it is not difficult to make allowance, while it somewhat lessens the merit of this great work as history, is one of its virtues as literature. Tacitus has superb powers of description; but he excels even his own high standard when he has to move the reader to terror and indignation. He nowhere describes a victory with such vividness as he does the desperate plight of Caecina's army when in danger of annihilation in one of Germanicus' campaigns,[117] and the few glimpses of happier things in Rome are pale beside the gloomy majesty of his numerous death-scenes and the concentrated grimness of those passages in which he lets hideous facts speak for themselves.[118]

That Tacitus has a philosophy of history, or that he was a philosopher at all, can hardly be maintained. Indeed, he himself confesses that of the various views he has heard concerning the destiny of mankind he does not know which to adopt[119]; while as to political theory, he hardly goes beyond a rooted dislike of absolutism. His interest in religion seems to be simply antiquarian; certainly he never expresses the least sympathy for any of the various faiths, including Judaism and Christianity, which were then becoming well known in the Empire. What he does believe in is the traditional Roman virtues, especially in their popular Stoic dress, and of these the one he seems most to admire is fortitude in adversity.

His style is perfectly inimitable, though it can be seen that he had learned something from earlier authors, not least, perhaps, from Sallust. It is very definitely of the modern school,

[116] I do not trouble to examine the paradoxes of one or two moderns who seem to discover virtues in this criminal lunatic.

[117] *Ann.*, i, 65.

[118] As *ann.*, vi, 4 (v, 9).

[119] *Ann.*, vi, 22.

as unlike Cicero or Livy as good Latin of any age could be. Force, epigrammatic point,[120] extreme conciseness of phraseology, often amounting to obscurity, deliberate avoidance alike of the Ciceronian period and the Ciceronian rhythms; all these characterize his developed manner as seen in the *Annals*. Handled by a master, this style can be impressive as few others have ever succeeded in being; yet it contains in itself the seed of the corruption by which classical Latinity was to perish within the next few centuries. It is such Latin as no one ever spoke. Cicero indeed did not write in the tone of his familiar talk, nor construct his speeches with the vocabulary and word-order of his hurried notes to Atticus; yet the resemblance between his most casual and his most elaborate expression is closer than that between either of these and the manner of another author, and the nearest parallel to both is to be found in the letters of his acquaintance. Tacitus uses a Latinity not much nearer to what we may suppose to have been the ordinary speech of educated men in his time than the Latin preface of one of the Paravia editions is to the daily Italian conversation of the scholar who writes it. It was but a step to the style of such men as Apuleius, for whom there exists neither usage nor difference of date, but only a store of Latin words, from which the writer may select such as appeal to his individual taste as appropriate to the effect he wishes to produce.

Tacitus had intended to write the history of Nerva and Trajan,[121] that is to continue his narrative down to his own old age; but we have no indication (cf. note 103) that he long survived Trajan, and probably these works never were begun. Certainly we have no trace of them.

A close friend of this modernist genius was a very worthy third-rate classicizer, GAIVS PLINIVS CAECILIVS SECVNDVS, nephew of the encyclopaedist (see p. 435). The name Plinius he owed to his adoption by the older man, who was his mother's brother. Of his life we are well informed, for he tells us a good deal about himself and was, moreover, enough of a public character for some inscriptional mentions of him to have survived. He was born in 61 or 62,[122] at Comum, and inherited a considerable fortune. He was married several times, but died childless. He

[120] Some of his epigrams have passed into proverbs, as 'conspicuous by their absence' (*ann.*, iii, 76, 5); capax imperii nisi imperasset (*hist.*, i, 49); odisse quem laeseris (*Agric.*, 42); ubi solitudinem faciunt, pacem appellant (*ibid.*, 30); omne ignotum pro magnifico est (*ibid.*).

[121] *Hist.*, i, 1: quod si uita suppeditet, principatum diui Neruae et imperium Traiani . . . senectuti seposui.

[122] *Epp.*, vi, 20, 5; he was in his eighteenth year in 79.

was educated in Rome, where Quintilian was his most celebrated teacher,[123] and from his enthusiasm for Cicero Pliny (so he is usually called in English) seems to have acquired, not only a model for his writings but an example for his life. He had indeed all the vanity of his hero, an amiability like his, a small fraction of his talents and, apparently, little or none of his moral and political uncertainties. Indeed, the circumstances of his political career left far less room for them. Like Cicero, Pliny was a patriotic and honest man, quite willing to serve the State under the guidance of a worthy leader; and, after suffering under the last years of Domitian, whose death came in time to prevent his own accusation, with the result determined in advance,[124] he found in Trajan one whom he could serve with a clear conscience. He had held a number of magistracies, at dates not exactly determinable,[125] under the Flavians; in 100 he was *consul suffectus*, thus enjoying a faint shadow of the power which Cicero had held a hundred and sixty-three years earlier, and in 111 or 112 he became governor of Bithynia, where, in constant correspondence with the Emperor, he carried out with uprightness and good sense a number of ordinary duties. Here there occurred an event which was probably of no great importance to him, but of vast interest to modern historians; he came into contact with a Christian community, and succeeded in suppressing activities of theirs which were not compatible with the fixed routine of Roman procedure and, in particular, were interfering with the State cult. As an honest magistrate should, he made first-hand inquiries into the nature of the new organization, its rites and beliefs, and transmitted to Trajan a short account of them, which still survives, to the effect that they seemed to be doing nothing criminal or immoral, save in so far as any sort of secret association was illegal, and that their worship was of the simplest and they themselves merely 'superstitious beyond all reason'.[126] A brief answer also survives, which directs him not to seek them out, nor to pay any

[123] Pliny, *epp.*, ii, 14, 10: ita certa ex Quintiliano, praeceptore meo, audisse memini.

[124] *Epp.*, vii, 27, 14.

[125] Pliny's dates are almost all doubtful. The fundamental work (for more literature, see Schanz-Hosius, ii, p. 658) is Mommsen in *Hermes*, iii (1869), 31 *sqq.* = *Gesammelte Schriften*, iv, p. 366 *sqq.*, but his conclusions, as must be the case where the data are insufficient, contain a large amount of hypothesis.

[126] *Ep. ad Trai.*, 96 (97), 8: nihil aliud inueni quam superstitionem prauam immodicam. The numerous difficulties of this letter cannot be gone into here.

attention to anonymous accusations, but if any are proved to belong to the forbidden sect and will not renounce it, to let the law take its course.

Pliny was, like his model, a pleader, and had considerable success; we have already seen that he was associated with Tacitus in the prosecution of Marius Priscus (p. 410), and mentions of speeches which he had delivered, or published after delivery, are frequent in the correspondence. He also wrote a little light verse [127] and was in touch with the literary men and movements of the day; Martial, for example, addressed one of his most respectful and delicately flattering poems to him, and Pliny in return paid the expenses of his journey to Spain.[128] Of his eloquence we have one specimen, and few readers will greatly regret the loss of the rest. It is his formal and loyal address on the occasion of his entry on the position of *consul suffectus*; it was then obligatory for the newly-made magistrate to thank the Emperor, and Pliny, at all events in the published version of the speech, took occasion to pass in review all the admirable actions and good qualities of Trajan. The praise is quite sincere, the object of it deserving to an unusual degree, and the style about what might be expected from an imitator of Cicero who had been born when Seneca was predominant; a certain amount of interesting information is incidentally to be had from it; and the total effect is wearisome in the extreme. This well-meant piece of oratory is generally known as the *Panegyricus*.

A great deal better is the collection of letters, in nine books, or ten if we count the separate volume of correspondence with Trajan. The style is pleasant, varied, and generally light and graceful; Pliny had evidently studied Cicero's epistolary manner with intelligent diligence. The subjects include such interesting matters as important trials, the lives and deaths of prominent men whom he had known, the eruption of Vesuvius, which he had witnessed in 79,[129] and, for Pliny was genuinely charitable and good-hearted, but too fond of mentioning the fact, instances of his gifts to various deserving recipients. The sharp contrast between his pictures of the age and those of Juvenal has already (above, p. 409) been touched upon. The weakest point of the collection is that we have the letters as revised for publication by their author, and while they doubtless gain in elegance they

[127] *Epp.*, vii, 4.

[128] *Epp.*, iii, 21; the poem is Martial, x, 20 (13).

[129] *Epp.*, vi, 16; 20, to Tacitus, who had asked for particulars to insert in his *Histories*.

lose in vitality and the abundance of detail which would for many reasons be interesting. In the correspondence with Trajan, it is probable that at least the Emperor's brief and business-like replies are given to us as Pliny received them.

An account of several speeches, now lost, which Pliny is known to have delivered on various occasions will be found in *O.R.F.*, pp. 598–604, and in Schanz-Hosius, ii, p. 659 *sq.*

Contemporary with Tacitus and Pliny, or a little before them in date, come a number of historical and rhetorical writers whose works have vanished. The following were of some importance. AVFIDIVS BASSVS seems to have written under Tiberius and Claudius, and to have been the author of two works, one *de bello Germanico*, conjectured to have dealt with the campaigns of Drusus, Tiberius and Germanicus, the other of wider scope, beginning somewhere towards the end of the Republic and coming down to an unknown date under the Empire.[130] The elder Pliny (cf. p. 436) continued his work. CLVVIVS RVFVS played a part under Nero and in the confusions immediately following him which does not entirely redound to his credit, but at least gave him abundant opportunity to get first-hand knowledge of the facts. He acted as announcer for Nero when the latter was giving his theatrical performances, served under Galba in Spain, then after his death joined Otho, left him for Vitellius, and seems finally to have made his peace with Vespasian's party. He wrote a history of his own times, coming down at least to the death of Nero, if not to that of Otho.[131] FABIVS RVSTICVS is quoted by Tacitus for information concerning Britain and one or two other matters[132]; ANTONIVS IVLIANVS also was possibly used by Tacitus for Book V of the *Histories*; he certainly wrote something on the Jews or the Jewish War.[133] Biographies and memoirs were written in abundance; thus, PVBLIVS CLODIVS THRASEA PAETVS, whose death under Nero is the last surviving incident in Tacitus' *Annals*, composed a life of the younger Cato which Plutarch seems to have used for his own work on that subject,[134] and similar works were common among members of the Senate. GNAEVS DOMITIVS CORBVLO, Nero's general in the Eastern campaigns of 54 and the following years,

[130] A few facts about him (he was a valetudinarian, of the Epicurean sect in philosophy, mentally active despite his poor health) are preserved in Seneca, *epp.*, 30, 1 *sqq.*; his works, Quint., x, 1, 103, who praises his historical style, utique in libris belli Germanici. His fragments are in *H.R.F.*, pp. 298–300.

[131] Fragments and *testimonia*, *H.R.F.*, pp. 311–14. The resemblances which have often been noticed between Plutarch's lives of Galba and Otho and the corresponding parts of Tacitus' *Histories* are perhaps more naturally to be explained by supposing Plutarch to have read Tacitus than that both had used Cluvius.

[132] Tacitus, *Agric.*, 10; *ann.*, xiii, 20, 2; xiv, 2, 3; xv, 61, 6. Very little more is known of him.

[133] Fragments in *H.R.F.*, p. 307.

[134] Plut., *Cat. min.*, 25, 2; 37, 1.

wrote an account of his operations.[135] GAIVS SVETONIVS PAVLINVS, who put down the revolt of the Iceni in Britain, was also active in Africa and wrote something concerning his experiences there.[136] VIPSTANVS MESSALLA, the speaker in Tacitus' *Dialogus*, is cited in the *Histories* for facts of the year 69.[137]

[135] See *H.R.F.*, p. 303.
[136] Pliny, *N.H.*, v, 14–16.
[137] Tac., *hist.*, iii, 25; 28; cf. n. 105.

CHAPTER XIV

PHILOSOPHY, SCIENCE AND SCHOLARSHIP

HAVING now come to the last of the great classical authors, we may pause a moment to consider what Rome had done and was doing for other than purely literary forms of production. We shall find that, save in literature and literary and grammatic criticism, she had contributed nothing and at most showed herself a useful propagandist. It is an extraordinary fact that in all the centuries between Livius Andronicus and the breakdown of the Western Empire so great and, in many ways, so intelligent a people produced not one original scientist, no metaphysical or ethical thinker whose abilities would fit him for a junior lectureship in those subjects at any modern University, and, despite the great feats of engineering which they performed, no mathematician whom either we or the Greeks would set to teach children of twelve; but fact it is.

Philosophy, therefore, save in so far as men like Seneca and Cicero may be considered philosophers, we may dismiss in a few words. There was one short-lived and unimportant attempt at a Roman school of philosophy, that of the Sextians. It is noteworthy that the language of their founder, QVINTVS SEXTIVS, a Roman by birth and thoroughly Roman in spirit, according to our reports of him, was nevertheless Greek, and his thought Stoic.[1] His originality, such as it was, showed itself in a refusal to follow the generally received Stoic principle of taking part in public affairs; he declined Julius Caesar's offer of a place in the Senate [2] and spent a retired life in study and writing. Though his chief interest was ethics, he wrote likewise on other subjects, or at all events his followers did, for there gathered around him a few men of earnest mind and philosophic or scientific interests. These included L. Crassicius (see p. 137); PAPIRIVS FABIANVS, who passed from rhetoric to Sextian philosophy and wrote, says

[1] Most of our information comes from the younger Seneca, whose teacher Sotion seems to have been influenced by the Sextians. The chief sources are *epp.*, 59, 7; 64, 2 *sqq.*; 73, 12 *sqq.*; 108, 17.

[2] Seneca, *epp.*, 98, 13, cf. Plut., *de profic. in uirt.*, 77e.

Seneca, about as much as Cicero on philosophic subjects [3]; and two men who, to judge from what we know of their writings, were more nearly scientists than philosophers. One of these was apparently the son of Quintus Sextius, SEXTIVS NIGER. His work is lost, but we know from many references to it that it dealt with materia medica; in other words, it was a kind of herbal, like the surviving treatise of Dioskurides, which uses it as a source. As, however, it was written in Greek, its place is rather in a history of Greek literature, or of the rise and progress of botany in ancient and modern times, than in this book.[4]

The other was the first surviving medical writer whose work is in Latin, AVLVS CORNELIVS CELSVS. Whether he was ever in practice is a somewhat vexed question, the fashion just now being to deny it. But it is certain that he lived and wrote about the time of Tiberius, and that what we have of him is not a separate work, though as a treatise on medicine it is a tolerably complete account of the knowledge then in existence, but part of a kind of encyclopaedia having the general title of *artes*.[5] It handled, besides medicine, philosophy, jurisprudence, rhetoric, strategy and agriculture, and seems to have been regarded as a valuable compendium of most if not all of these.[6] That the first five books

[3] Seneca rhet., *contr.*, ii, praef., 2–5; Seneca phil., *epp.*, 40, 12; 52, 11; *dial.*, x, 10, 1: Fabianus, non ex his cathedrariis philosophis sed ex ueris et antiquis 'not one of these modern professors of philosophy, but a real philosopher of the old school', *i.e.*, one who lived his doctrine and did not merely lecture about it. See also Pliny, *N.H.*, ii, 121 (wind); xxxvi, 125 (geology), and the bibliographies of Bks. ii, vii, ix, xi–xv, xvii, xxiii, xxv, xxviii, xxxvi. Clearly he had fairly wide knowledge and interests.

[4] Fragments in vol. iii, pp. 146–8, of M. Wellmann's edition of Dioskurides, Berlin, 1914; Pliny cites him repeatedly. As Quintus Sextius is spoken of as *Sextius pater* (Seneca, *epp.*, 98, 13; 64, 2), this implies a *Sextius filius* who was also notable in some way, probably as a writer, and what we can gather of the date of Sextius Niger fits excellently.

[5] The title of the first book in our MSS. is *liber vi artium*; this fits very well with Columella, i, 1, 14: Cornelius totum corpus disciplinae (*i.e.*, agriculture) quinque libris complexus est; ix, 2, 1, the subject cannot be treated ornatius quam Vergilio nec elegantius quam Celso. Finally, it suits Celsus' own quotation (v, 28, 16) of the books on agriculture, and the absence of any self-quotation from the other parts of the encyclopaedia.

[6] Philosophy: Quintilian, xii, 11, 24, it is not too much to expect an orator to understand philosophy and jurisprudence, since not only have the greatest geniuses known all arts but Cornelius Celsus, mediocri uir ingenio, non solum de his omnibus conscripserit artibus sed amplius rei militaris et rusticae et medicinae praecepta reliquerit. The section on jurisprudence is deduced only from this passage compared with *ibid.*, 9; Augustine, *de haeres.*, praef., says: qui sectas uarias condiderunt

treated of agriculture and medicine came next we know from what we have left and from Columella's reference; apparently there were six books on philosophy, in which the author contented himself with a review of existing opinions, in other words, with the history of the subject; the size of the other sections is not known. Though Quintilian (see note 6) thought none too well of his abilities, and naturally, with the progress of medicine, he has long ceased to be a venerated authority among moderns, the fact remains that he was a man of good sense, who had digested his wide reading and could express himself as a scientist should, in clear, pleasant language, free from all rhetorical flourishes and with lucid explanations of the technical terms which necessarily abound. He himself, in his preface,[7] deprecates mere verbal cleverness, remarking pointedly that it is treatment and not eloquence which will cure the sick; he dislikes extreme theories and extreme practice of all kinds.

His work as we have it falls into eight books.[8] The first, after an introduction which sketches the history of medicine hitherto (a most valuable document, since Celsus had access to numerous writings now lost), gives regimens for those in health and those who are ill; it proceeds with a few remarks on differences of constitution, age and season as affecting health. Now follow various affections of the head, of the stomach and intestines, and of the sinews. The second book again has a preface, explaining what seasons of the year, times of life and so on are healthy or otherwise; it proceeds with a series of chapters on symptoms and on methods of treatment in general, including, what the best of the ancients stressed, diet and exercise. The third, after a brief explanation of the traditional division of diseases into acute and chronic, treats of those ailments

usque ad tempora sua . . . sex non paruis uoluminibus quidam Celsus absoluit, which, if it refers to our Celsus and to the philosophical part of the encyclopaedia (neither proposition being certain) confirms Quintilian. Rhetoric: Quint., iii, 1, 21, and elsewhere. Juvenal, vi, 245, names a Celsus as an authority on rhetoric, and probably means this one. Strategy: Vegetius, *de re milit.*, i, 8, confirms Quintilian, above. Agriculture: see last note.

Celsus' approximate date is thus determined. (1) Pliny, *N.H.*, xiv, 33, says Graecinus (father of Agricola, died 38) copies Celsus. (2) Columella, i, 1, 14, counts Celsus among the writers nostrorum temporum. (3) Celsus mentions *Tryphon pater*, vi, 5, thus implying that he knew of a *Tryphon filius*; the latter was Scribonius' teacher. All this fixes him in the time of Tiberius.

[7] 1, praef., p. 7, 11 Daremberg. The aphorism is itself Empiric, but Celsus clearly relishes it.

[8] *I.e.*, Books vi–xiii of the whole encyclopaedia.

which affect the whole body, as fevers, dropsy and paralysis. The fourth treats of ailments which affect a part only, and handles them in order, from the head to the extremities. The fifth discusses remedies, for the compounding of which a multitude of prescriptions is given, and passes to a consideration of the different sorts of wounds and sores in general. The sixth treats those which affect some one part of the body only, as ulcers in the ears, and mentions the approved methods of treatment. The seventh discusses surgery, and the eighth the various types of fractures and dislocations.

We have another medical writer of slightly later date,[9] SCRIBONIVS LARGVS. He was certainly a practitioner, and of empirical tendencies, not to say a quack. The little work which has alone survived out of his treatises [10] is nothing but a collection of prescriptions, addressed to Gaius Iulius Callistus, one of Claudius' influential freedmen, who apparently dabbled in medicine to the extent at least of wishing to be able to doctor himself on occasion, and had recommended Scribonius' writings to the Imperial favour. It begins, after a fashion which seems to have grown as increasingly popular as it is grossly unscientific, with the ailments of the head, and so down to those of the extremities, with especial attention to gout. Why any of the remedies advised should be efficacious Scribonius does not attempt to explain, though some of his other writings may have faced this question. They vary from simples to highly complex mixtures, include some which are pure folklore,[11] often are recommended as having been used by past and present members of the Imperial household,[12] and might sometimes be described as proprietary, for several originated with persons of varying

[9] Besides the dedication to Callistus, we have the following indications. He was with Claudius on the expedition to Britain, 163 (he says cum deo nostro Caesare, which so far as that goes might be Caligula, but 60, Messalina dei nostri Caesaris, shows whom he means). Therefore he wrote his book after 43, but before Messalina's death in 48. Possibly the date is 47, for Polybius, who had been Claudius' secretary, died in that year, and if Callistus succeeded him, as he probably did, that would be a natural occasion for a token of regard ; but it is by no means necessary to suppose this. See Schanz-Hosius, ii, pp. 793–5.

[10] Callistus (introductory letter, p. 5, 22–3 of Helmreich's Teubner ed. of Scribonius) had recommended Scribonius' scripta Latina medicinalia to Claudius, and it is partly in return for this favour that he hurriedly, while on a journey and away from most of his library (p. 6, 5–6), prepares this little treatise.

[11] For instance, 152 (avoidance of iron ; but he characterizes this as a superstitio, not part of the original prescription) ; 16 and 17 (strange cures for epilepsy, which are extra medicinae professionem).

[12] As 16, 31, 60, 70, 175, 177, 268, 274.

qualifications, from celebrated physicians to a woman from Africa who had a wonderful cure for colic.[13]

It is worth while here briefly to review the short history of Latin medical works, other than those which form parts of larger surviving treatises, as in the case of Pliny the Elder. After Scribonius we have another collection of prescriptions, the fullest title of which in the MSS. is *liber medicinalis Q. Sereni*. Who the author was we do not directly know, but a conjecture is possible and has been made.[14] Under the Severi there lived a polymath, by name SERENVS SAMMONICVS, who possessed a library of 62,000 volumes, is cited several times (principally by Macrobius, see p. 459) for curious and interesting antiquarian facts, and was killed by Caracallus.[15] We are not told that he wrote any verse, but his son and namesake was a friend of that short-lived ruler Gordian II, and also of Alexander Severus, who liked his poetry.[16] This, then, may be our author, for the collection is in verse, quite workmanlike hexameters, to the number of 1107. He certainly was a man of literary knowledge, as his many reminiscences of earlier and better poets indicate; indeed, he relieves his versifications of Pliny and medical writers (for it does not appear that he was a physician himself, though he occasionally [17] mentions that he knows at first hand of the efficacy of a certain remedy) by citing the classical authors whenever he can.[18] The arrangement is practically the same as that of Scribonius, and a fair proportion of magical remedies is included.

Magic forms a small proportion of the *Veterinaria* which has come down to us under the name of a certain PELAGONIVS.[19] His date is roughly determinable, for apart from the fact that Vegetius (see below)

[13] See 94 (Scribonius' teacher, Apuleius Celsus, would not reveal in his lifetime the nostrum which is here given), 97 (Paccius Antiochus made a great secret of a remedy for pleurisy, but at his death left a written account of it which Tiberius sent to the public libraries), 122 (the African woman's remedy, which cures colic so thoroughly that the patient never after is capable of feeling anything worse than a sort of numbness in that region).

[14] See Schanz-Hosius-Krüger, iii, pp. 28–30; the text is best edited by F. Vollmer in *Corpus medicorum Latinorum*, ii, 3 (Teubner, 1916).

[15] *Hist. Aug.*, xiii, 4, 4; xiv, 5, 6; xx, 18, 2.

[16] *Ibid.*, xx, 18, 2; xviii, 30, 2. It is to be remembered that all theories based on the *Hist. Aug.* stand on slippery ground, but in this case the statements are reasonable enough and the conclusions drawn from them follow unforcedly.

[17] As 401, 486, 621; but these may be taken over from his authorities. In 785 he admits that he knows of the cure described only from reading.

[18] He cites by name Plautus (425), Titinius the comedian (1037), Lucretius (606), Horace (529) and Livy (721), besides authors more or less medical (Varro, Pliny) and innumerable tacit quotations and imitations.

[19] See in general Schanz, iv, 192–4. The best edition is that of Ihm, Leipzig, 1892.

cites him as a fairly recent author,[20] he dedicates his work generally to Arzygius, probably the consular of Tuscia and Umbria,[21] a post which did not exist before 366, and a chapter of it to Astyrius, or Asterius, possibly the L. Turcius Apronianus Asterius who was city prefect in 363.[22] The work seems to be a compilation from sources which, while largely Greek, include Columella and Celsus. Most of the prescriptions are of a rational or quasi-rational kind. Pelagonius again was used by VEGETIVS, the author of the military textbook to be noticed presently. He wrote a manual on the cure of diseases of mules, *Mulomedicina*, which still survives. It extends to four books, whereof the last treats of diseases of cattle. The author professes to have got together all the Latin authors on the subject, his real sources being Columella, Pelagonius, and a Latin version, the vulgarity of whose style he complains of, of a Greek compilation known as the *Hippiatrika*, which Pelagonius used in the original. This version also survives, with an imposing list of alleged authors, beginning with Cheiron the Centaur, and is a valuable monument of the non-literary speech of that day. It would seem therefore that it was made between Pelagonius' and Vegetius' time.[23] Along with Vegetius there has come down to us a fragment, on the treatment of cattle, described as *ex corpore Gargili Martialis*; *corpus* is evidently 'collection', GARGILIVS MARTIALIS is dealt with below.[24]

At some unknown date, but probably between 300 and 350 or thereabout, the collection of medical passages from Pliny known as the *Medicina Plinii* was made by some unknown hand. The author supplies little but a preface on the rapacity of physicians, a subject of which many of these collectors of prescriptions seem fond.[25]

There survive a few fragments of VINDICIANVS, a celebrated medical

[20] Veget., prolog., 2, licet proxima aetate et Pelagonio non defuerit et Columellae abundauerit dicendi facultas. His *proxima aetas*, however, must be a fairly long period if it includes both Columella and Pelagonius. See p. 468.

[21] *C.I.L.*, vi, 1702. The identification is not certain.

[22] Mentioned by Ammianus Marcellinus, xxiii, 1, 4 and elsewhere.

[23] The *praenomen* of Vegetius is given as Publius in the MSS.; it is, however, the general opinion that he is identical with the author of the *epitome rei militaris*; see Schanz, iv, p. 199. His full title is *digestorum artis mulomedicinae libri*, and this describes his book well enough, for he adds practically nothing save prefaces and some bettering of language. His work has been carefully edited by E. Lommatzsch (Teubner, 1903). The Hippiatrika in its Latin form is edited by E. Oder (Teubner, 1901), under the title *Claudii Hermeri mulomedicina Chironis*, and is often cited simply as 'Chiron'.

[24] This fragment is to be found at the end of Lommatzsch's edition of Vegetius, see last note.

[25] See Schanz, iv, p. 201 *sqq*. The book is edited by V. Rose, Teubner, 1875, along with Gargilius Martialis *de medicina*, a series of medieval excerpts, probably from his work on agriculture (see p. 431), dealing with the uses of herbs, fruits, &c., in medicine.

contemporary of Augustine.[26] His pupil, THEODORVS PRISCIANVS, wrote, first in Greek and then in Latin, a work on *Cheap Remedies* (*Euporista*), which has a good deal, but by no means all, in common with a treatise of like title which goes falsely under the name of Galen. Three books, dealing with outward diseases, inward ailments, and diseases of women respectively, have come down to us, together with two chapters of a fourth. The work, which ekes out more or less scientific medicine with a little magic, was popular, to judge by the various enlargements which sundry MSS. of it give.[27]

But all such works are scientific and reliable by the side of MARCELLVS, often surnamed EMPIRICVS, or BVRDIGALENSIS, by moderns. This amateur of medicine, a Gaul, was *magister officiorum* under Theodosius I and apparently survived into the reign of Theodosius II (408–450). He set himself to collect all he could find in such works as those of Pliny, Scribonius Largus, whom he nearly copies out entirely, and other accessible writers; in addition, a fact which justly endears him to folklorists, he assembled all the popular remedies he could hear of. His own contribution is a number of mistakes in excerpting and some Gaulish names for plants. All this treasure-house of charms and herbal lore is sandwiched in between some apocryphal letters of great physicians and a copy of verses, whether his own or not, describing the contents of the work and ending with the hope that the reader will live a year for each line,—they number 78.[28]

Later still seem to be a number of writers on medicine who lead up to the medieval physicians. Greek was passing out of use in the West, and Latin replacing it, though a strange Latin, mixed with many Greek words, as the medical language; it was destined to hold that position till modern times, when it has yielded, not rapidly nor without retaining vestiges of its old pre-eminence, to the more convenient modern tongues.

It should be mentioned also that, besides the many medieval herbals in Latin, there are a few which fall within our period. Of these the chief is the collection falsely labelled with the name of APVLEIVS (cf. p. 523). It may have originated in the fourth century, and so is earlier than the Latin version of Dioskurides, which is apparently of the sixth. After a preface on the wickedness and greed of doctors, it proceeds to list numerous herbs in order, each section being headed with a drawing of the plant in question and going on to give a list of its virtues. As might be expected, the illustrations have been variously miscopied and the text greatly interpolated, chiefly from Dioskurides, in our

[26] See Augustine, *conf.*, iv, 3, 5; vii, 6, 8; *epp.*, 138, 3; his fragments are at the end of Rose's Priscianus (see next note).

[27] See Schanz-Hosius-Krüger, iv, pp. 275–8; the principal edition is that of Valentine Rose, Teubner, 1894.

[28] See *ibid.*, pp. 278–82; a full and good edition is that which constitutes vol. v of the *Corpus medicorum Latinorum* (Teubner, 1916).

MSS.[29] Associated with it is a brief treatise on the medical uses of betony (*herba uettonica*), attributed to ANTONIVS MVSA, Augustus' physician, who certainly had been long dead before it was written. This is one of several trifles of quasi-medical content, all bearing the name of Musa and none genuine. Mention may be made also of a collection, by one SEXTVS PLACITVS PAPYRIENSIS, entitled *de medicamentis ex animalibus pecoribus et bestiis uel auibus*, whereof we have two recensions, differing not a little from each other. The date may be about the same as that of Marcellus, *i.e.*, early fifth century, and the contents are about on the same level of intelligence.

Mention has been made in the preceding paragraphs of a very respectable writer of early Imperial date, LVCIVS IVNIVS MODERATVS COLVMELLA. He seems to have been read, not by literary men for his style, though that is good, but by country people for his advice, which appears to have been in accordance with the best information to be had in his time. His subject was agriculture and he was a practical farmer on a large scale. Born in Gades (Cadiz),[30] he came to Italy and served for a while in the army as a tribune, or legionary staff officer.[31] He soon had enough of this, however, and as neither trade, the bar, nor the life of a hanger-on of great men had the least attraction for him, he followed in the footsteps of his paternal uncle, a diligent and successful landowner in Spain, and apparently invested his fortune in Italian estates, which he then proceeded to cultivate, employing his spare time in writing about them.[32] We have altogether thirteen books of his, twelve *de re rustica*, covering the whole subject, including the management of arable land, viticulture, the care of all kinds of stock, the rearing of poultry and birds of various sorts, the making and maintenance of fish-ponds and enclosures for edible wild beasts, bee-keeping, gardening (at this point his enthusiasm breaks the bounds of prose, and his tenth book is in very respectable hexameters), the care of the farmhouse itself and the assignment of duties to its staff, with

[29] Edited in vol. iv of the same series (1927), along with pseudo-Musa, Sextus Placitus, and a most curious work *de taxone*, dealing with the medical or magical uses of the various parts of a badger (*taxo*) and the proper formulae to utter in cutting off each part. See Schanz-Hosius-Krüger, iv, p. 130–1, for pseudo-Apuleius.

[30] Columella, *de r.r.*, viii, 16, 9.

[31] *C.I.L.*, ix, 235 (= Dessau, 2923), L. Iunio L.f. Gal. Moderato Columellae trib. mil. leg. VI Ferratae.

[32] Columella, *de r.r.*, v, 5, 15: M. quidem Columella patruus meus . . . diligentissimus agricola Baeticae prouinciae. Columella's distaste for other careers, *de r.r.*, i, *praef.*, 7–10. His estates are mentioned in a number of passages, and seem all to have been Italian.

directions for preparing the contents of its store-rooms; and, finally, a separate book on arboriculture. This, however, is but a part of a longer work, for its opening words refer to a previous book [33]; external evidence suggests that it is the second of three books, and also that there was another monograph on viticulture and arboriculture.[34] This, however, is completely lost, and with it a treatise *Against astrologers* and another *Concerning the lustrations and other rites on behalf of the fruits of the earth.*[35] The style of the surviving books is straightforward and pleasant, the writing of a sensible man who had had a rhetorical training but knew better than to try to be eloquent in the wrong place. The date of the larger work is in the neighbourhood of 60.[36]

[33] Colum., *de arbor.*, i, 1: quoniam de cultu agrorum abunde primo uolumine praecepisse uidemur. The MSS. put this book between Bks. ii and iii of the *de r.r.*; but this would require *prioribus uoluminibus*, and besides this, what the MSS. call Bk. xi says in its first sentence: superioribus nouem libris, and several other references confirm this.

[34] A note at the end of Bk. xi runs: praeter hos duodecim libros singularis est liber ad Epirum Marcellum de cultura uinearum et arborum. This is not the book on arboriculture which we have, for that is not dedicated to any one. It might, however, be argued that an introductory paragraph of address to Marcellus has been lost, for the contents fit the description well enough. But we learn from Cassiodorus, *inst. diuin.* i, 28, 6 (p. 72, 7, R.A.B. Mynors, Oxford, Clar. Press, 1937), that Columella sedecim libris per diuersas agriculturae species . . . illabitur, which number could be made up thus: the twelve books of the larger work; the existing single book on arboriculture; the 'first volume' to which that refers; a third book to complete the treatise (judging by the order in which Columella handles his subject in the *de r.r.*, Bk. i would deal with cereal crops, &c., Bk. iii with the farmhouse, its surroundings, and the minor sources of revenue such as the poultry-run and kitchen-garden; there is hardly room for a fourth book in a work on that scale); and the book *ad Epirum Marcellum*. Columella repeatedly mentions criticisms of his opinions, thus indicating that the three-book treatise was published before the *de r.r.*

[35] *De r.r.*, xi, 1, 31: in iis libris quos aduersus astrologos composueram. ii, 22, 5–6: hoc loco certum habeo quosdam cum solemnia festorum percensuerim desideraturos lustrationum ceterorumque sacrificiorum quae pro frugibus fiunt morem priscis usurpatum. nec ego abnuo docendi curam, sed differo in eum librum quem componere in animo est cum agri colationis totam disciplinam praescripsero. It is not, therefore, certain that he lived to write it.

[36] *De r.r.*, iii, 3, 3: Seneca owns an estate near Nomentum which produces wine at the rate of 8 *cullei* for each *iugerum*. It so happens that we know something of that estate, for it was famous. It was bought, says Pliny, *N.H.*, xiv, 49, within the last twenty years by Remnius Palaemon (see p. 447), who in less than ten years sold it, for four times the price he had paid, to Seneca. As Pliny writes under Vespasian, the dates in question cannot be earlier than about 50 and 60 respectively, and probably are later; Columella therefore was writing his third book

Columella has been much neglected by modern editors. The only complete editions accessible are those of C. Gesner (*Scriptores rei rusticae*, vol. i, Leipzig, second ed., 1773), of J. G. Schneider (Leipzig, 1794, little more than a reprint of Gesner), and that by J. H. Ress, Flensburg 1795, of Columella alone. The tenth book has been repeatedly published separately, *e.g.*, by J. P. Postgate, *Corpus poetarum Latinorum* (London, 1905), Vol. ii, p. 206 *sqq.* A new edition, by V. Lundström, has been in progress since 1897, and so far there have appeared the *liber de arboribus*, also several books of the larger work (Uppsala, various dates). This, when complete, will supersede the older ones, but in the meantime, this interesting author is exceedingly hard for the average student to get, save in a large library.

In discussing the medical writers, mention has been made of Gargilius Martialis. His works are lost, although a mutilated Florentine MS. seems once to have contained them, save for the series of extracts, *de medicina* and *cura boum* (see p. 427 and note 25). But Palladius (see below) makes some, perhaps much, use of him, and we thus learn that he was a writer on agriculture; that he should be cited for prescriptions and the like is natural, for all the authors of this class give them, since the ancient farmer was often his own veterinary surgeon and not seldom called upon to deal with his own ailments and those of his labourers as best he might. To judge by the respect in which these later writers appear to hold him, his work was considerable. His date is determined conjecturally, but with fair probability. An inscription [37] gives us the distinguished military career of a QVINTVS GARGILIVS MARTIALIS, who fell in action on March 25, 260. As the name Gargilius is very rare, there is a reasonable likelihood that this man and the writer are the same; if so, we know at least his century.

PALLADIVS RVTILIVS TAVRVS AEMILIANVS, as his MSS. call him, is a very indeterminate figure as regards date, and it is not even certain that he falls within our chronological limits. We have from him a work on agriculture in fourteen books. The first is introductory, the next twelve give advice as to the tasks for each month of the year, the last is a not very inspired poem in elegiacs on grafting (*de insitione*). The style of the prose books is plain to baldness; despite his one attempt to be literary he was a practical man, who evidently knew what he was talking about, but had also read some of the standard writers; he cites Columella often, Gargilius not seldom, and has made use, for his remarks on farm-buildings, of an epitome of Vitruvius (see p. 432). The interest of his work lies wholly in its matter, which includes some information

not earlier than 60, and obviously not so late as the death of Seneca in 65. He probably was no longer young at the time, for his concluding sentence (xii, 57, 6) apologizes for any omissions and adds nec tamen canis natura dedit cunctarum rerum prudentiam, implying that his own hair was white.

[37] *C.I.L.*, viii, 9047; Dessau, 2767. Cf. also *C.I.L.*, viii, 20751. He cannot be much earlier than this, for he cites Galen, who died about 201. See Schanz-Hosius-Krüger, iii, pp. 222–4.

not to be had elsewhere on farming conditions and other things under the later Empire. In an introductory epistle to his verses, he addresses a Pasiphilus, whom he describes as *uir doctissimus*. Thus far fact; all else is deduction based on scanty material. He clearly is later than Gargilius, and we have seen that the latter probably was killed in 260. He is earlier than Cassiodorus, who mentions him in a passage written about 540.[38] We know three men called Pasiphilus, all of whom may have been learned, while one certainly was. They are, Fabius Felix Pasiphilus Paulinus, *praefectus urbi* in 355; a philosopher Pasiphilus, of whose heroism Ammianus Marcellinus tells us in describing the events of 371[39]; and a third Pasiphilus, otherwise unknown, who is mentioned in the Codex Theodosianus.[40] Of these, the philosopher is perhaps the most likely to be Palladius' learned acquaintance, if any of them was; in that case we may put him in the fourth century, which accords with the absence of any very marked signs of degeneracy in his Latin, and also of any indication that he was a Christian.

The Romans were good farmers, and also good, if rough and ready, engineers. But, while we have a considerable bulk of treatises on agriculture, from Cato onwards, engineering, the theory of structure and its cognate art of architecture have left us but one work, of moderate length, and an epitome of it. The ten books of VITRVVIVS POLLIO *de architectura* date from the times of Augustus, to whom he dedicated the treatise.[41] By *architectura* he means not simply what we understand by that term, though in this sphere he is one of our chief authorities and has much that is interesting and accurate to say about the proper proportions of temples and other buildings, the different orders (Dorian, Ionian and so forth) and other things that an architect should know. But he includes such matters as we think of in connexion with contractors or even experts on the theory of structure; the different sorts of stone, cement and so forth take up not a little of his space, and he evidently writes from sound knowledge, theoretical and practical. In addition, as it was a common ancient custom to name a work after its

[38] Cassiod., *de inst. diuin.*, 28, 6. See also p. 533.

[39] Ammianus, xxix, 1, 36.

[40] Cod. Theod., ii, 1, 8 (Impp. Arcad(ius) et Honor(ius) AA. Pasifilo suo, Dec. 25, 395). The first of these Pasiphili had a contemporary named Taurus, *praefectus Italiae* in 357, consul in 361; but to identify him with Palladius is rash (see Schanz, iv, p. 191). That Palladius is very largely dependent upon Gargilius, indeed is a sort of watered-down reproduction of him, is argued by Wellmann, *Hermes*, xliii, 1908, p. 1 *sqq*.

[41] The Emperor is addressed simply as *Caesar*, but mentions occur of *diuus Iulius*, under whom Vitruvius seems to have served (collection of relevant passages in Schanz-Hosius, ii, p. 387), and to have received some kind of salary or pension from Augustus (i, praef., 3). He was old when he wrote (ii, praef., 4), perhaps in retirement.

first subject, he goes on in his eighth, ninth and tenth books to discuss matters which could be brought under no definition of architecture, water supply (Book VIII), clockwork, as then understood [42] (Book IX), and machines of all sorts, including engines of war (Book X). Originally, the text was illustrated,[43] but the diagrams have not come down to us. This is the more to be deplored because the style is very obscure, the half-Greek jargon of technicians. Vitruvius honestly acknowledges that he is no stylist,[44] though a lover of reading as well as of his own speciality [45]; it is unfortunate that he tried to be rhetorical in his prefaratory remarks, for the result is wretched. Apart from this, he is a man to respect, as one must respect a master of a craft which he exalts and delights in.[46]

The exact date at which Vitruvius wrote is hard to determine, for the indications he gives are ambiguous. He mentions, besides several buildings which cannot be dated by our present knowledge, the temple of Ceres (iii, 3, 5), which was destroyed by a fire in 723/31; but it was at once rebuilt, see Pliny, *N.H.*, xxxv, 154, and it may be to the restored temple that he refers. Again, he mentions the temple of Quirinus, which he says was dipteros octastylus et pronao et postico, sed circa aedem duplices habet ordines columnarum, iii, 2, 7. This temple, which had been burned in 705/49, was not restored till 738/16, when Augustus rebuilt it apparently from the ground up (ἐκ καινῆς οἰκοδομήσας, Dio, liv, 19, 4; it had in the meantime been patched temporarily). But all the details Vitruvius gives could have been easily made out by any architect from the ruins or the temporary restoration. He once speaks of Augustus by that title (v, 1, 7), though he always addresses him as *Caesar* or *imperator*, as was customary; therefore he writes after 727/27, when the title was conferred upon him; and he implies (iii, 3, 2) that there is but one permanent stone theatre in Rome, viz., that of Pompey, and therefore that the

[42] The water supply he was well qualified to speak of, for he took some part in building the aqueducts (Frontinus, *de aquis*, 25). The clocks he knew were not driven by a compressed spring, like ours, but by water-power. Incidentally, the striking clock in Shakespere's *Julius Caesar* is no anachronism; Vitruvius' Greek sources, some centuries older than Brutus, describe more than one type.

[43] See Vitruvius, iii, 5, 8; ix, praef., 5; 8.

[44] Vitr., i, 1, 17, cf. x, 8, 6: quantum potui, niti ut obscura res per scripturam dilucide pronuntiaretur contendi, sed haec non est facilis ratio neque omnibus expedita ad intellegendum praeter eos qui in his generibus habeant exercitationem.

[45] Vitr., vi, praef., 4: philologis et philotechnis rebus commentariorumque scripturis me delectans.

[46] Qualifications of an architect, i, 1, 4 (literature, painting, mathematics, mythology, philosophy, music, medicine, law and astronomy, besides his technical attainments). High standard of professional etiquette, vi, praef., 5.

theatre of Marcellus (741/13, see Platner-Ashby *s.u.*) and that of Cornelius Balbus (same year, Dio, liv, 25, 2) were not yet erected. Nearer than this it does not seem possible to come.

His sources, as might be expected, are principally Greek, for as he says, there were but few works in Latin, and those of small extent.[47] The names of those who can be identified with certainty or probability are in Schanz-Hosius, ii, pp. 390–2.

Like all standard treatises, his was epitomized, and we have a little work, written, according to two of its MSS., by an otherwise unknown architect, Marcvs Cetivs Faventinvs, of very uncertain date; Palladius seems to have used him, but perhaps through Gargilius Martialis (cf. p. 431); if this is so, he must have lived before 260. He has excerpted from Vitruvius what he thinks useful for domestic architecture, and added a chapter on sundials (*de horologii institutione*), from some other source.[48]

There is another work dealing with a subject akin to that of Vitruvius, which may be mentioned here. Sextvs Ivlivs Frontinvs, a man of very considerable ability, several times consul, governor of Britain after Cerialis, where he conquered the Silures of South Wales, was appointed *curator aquarum*, or commissioner for the water-supply of Rome, in 97, and continued to hold that post till his death. While in office, he wrote, primarily for his own guidance, an essay *de aquis*, which he published later, in hopes that it would be of use to others interested in the matter. It certainly is of much interest to modern students of the subject, for it is a plain and well-informed account of the aqueducts, their history, mode of construction, and other particulars, with sections on the laws regarding the conservation of the water-supply and the method of measuring the flow.[49]

[47] Vitruvius, vii, praef., 14.

[48] It is from this epitome only that we have his full name; the MSS. of his own work and the two or three literary references to him call him simply Vitruvius. The standard edition (including the epitome) is that of V. Rose, Teubner, 1899 (ed. 2), but several have appeared since (including one in the Loeb series), with and without translations and other helps.

Since Vitruvius reckons painting among the things an architect should know (see n. 46), mention may be made here of a Latin writer, Fabivs Vestalis, who may have dealt with that subject at a date unknown but earlier than Pliny the Elder, who says (index to Bk. xxxv): ex auctoribus . . . Fabio Vestale qui de pictura scripsit. But as Fabius is cited (*N.H.*, vii, 213) only for the date of the first Roman sundial, Mayhoff (ed. of Pliny, Teubner, 1906) may be right in supposing that we should read *scripserunt*, taking the verb to refer to the Greek writers whose names follow.

[49] The facts of Frontinus' life, with the dates so far as they are exactly known, are in the introduction to the Loeb edition (C. E. Bennett) of the *Strategemata* and *de aquis*. See also Schanz-Hosius, ii, pp. 795–9.

Frontinus also wrote several other works. There exists a not uninteresting little treatise in four books, the *Strategemata, i.e., Les ruses de guerre,* being a selection of anecdotes of the manner in which commanders, Roman and other, have deceived their opponents. It is, however, now generally held that the fourth book is an addition by an unknown hand, and also that the three genuine books contain interpolations.[50] He himself informs us that he had written a treatise, apparently of a more theoretical nature, on the art of war,[51] but this is lost, as is also another work on land-surveying, whereof some fragments survive embedded in the *Gromatici* (see p. 465).

One of the most influential books ever written in Latin, and to this day one of the most interesting, is the *Naturalis Historia* of the elder PLINY. GAIVS PLINIVS SECVNDVS, maternal uncle of the writer already discussed (p. 417), was born, either in 23 or 24, at Novum Comum, in the territory north of the Po, and thus could claim Catullus as his fellow-countryman (*conterraneus*). He came early to Rome, served in the army for a time, going to Germany with a cavalry unit, was back again not later than 52, and at various dates was absent, on official business under Vespasian, in more than one province; we know of Africa and Spain as having been visited by him. While not thus engaged, he was occasionally active as a pleader. But his great occupations, from which he never desisted, were reading and writing. Although uncritical and often hasty, he had a boundless thirst for knowledge of all kinds, and was diligent in reporting and spreading it.[52] Of the 102 volumes he wrote, we have thirty-seven, and they are a treasure-house of bookish learning. His

[50] See Bennett, *ibid.*, pp. xviii–xxxii; Schanz-Hosius, *loc. cit.* The order of composition is (1) the military handbook, see *strat.*, i, praef., *ad init.*, (2) the *strat.*, which often mentions Domitian as Germanicus (which title he assumed in 83), and never implies that he is dead, (3) the *de aquis*. The date of the work on land-surveying is unknown, save that it was under Domitian, whom a fragment of it mentions as *praestantissimus*.

[51] *Strat.*, i, praef., *init.*

[52] The authorities for his life are (1) his own incidental references, (2) two letters of the younger Pliny, iii, 5 (writings), vi, 20 (death), (3) a fragmentary biography by Suetonius. Birth; he was in his fifty-sixth year when he died, Pliny, *epp.*, iii, 5, 7, therefore born in 23 or 24. Birthplace; Suet. calls him *Nouocomensis*. Mention of Catullus, *N.H.*, i, praef., 1. In Rome early, *N.H.*, xxxvii, 81, he saw Servilius Nonianus during his consulship (35). Services in Germany, Pliny, *epp.*, *ibid.*, 4. Return to Rome, *N.H.*, xxxiii, 63, he saw Agrippina sitting beside Claudius at the *naualis proelii spectaculum*, which was in 52. Provinces besides Germany; Spain, Pliny, *epp.*, *ibid.*, 17. Africa, *N.H.*, vii, 36: ipse in Africa uidi. Activity as a pleader, Pliny, *epp.*, *ibid.*, 7.

end was characteristic of his curiosity and his humanity alike. When the great eruption of Vesuvius occurred in 79, he was in command of the naval base at Misenum. The smoke-cloud from the volcano having been pointed out to him, he wished to see it from nearer at hand; as he was setting out in one of the smaller cruisers (*liburnicae*), an urgent message reached him from a lady of his acquaintance, telling him that she was in danger from the eruption. Ordering out some of the larger units of the fleet (*quadriremes*), he proceeded to combine a rescue expedition with his scientific exploration. On landing, however, at a point much nearer Vesuvius, he was overcome with the hot and ash-laden air, lay down on the ground, and never rose again.

Pliny's literary activities began in his youth, with a treatise *On the use of the javelin in the cavalry* (*de iaculatione equestri*), written while he was himself in command of a troop or squadron (*ala*) of horse. Next followed a biography, in two books, of his friend Pomponius Secundus. While serving in Germany he was visited in a dream by the ghost of Drusus, who asked that his memory should not be allowed to die. In obedience to this, he began his work *On the German Wars*, a complete history of the subject up to his own time, comprising twenty books. This he followed with a treatise, in three volumes, on *The Student* (*studiosus*), in which, says his nephew, he began and completed the orator from the cradle onwards. In other words, he covered much the same ground as Quintilian (see p. 399), but on a smaller scale. Late in the reign of Nero, when historical research was not the safest of occupations, he confined himself to grammar, and wrote, in eight books, a treatise on *Doubtful Speech* (*dubii sermonis octo*, sc., *libri*). Later still, when tongues and pens were once more free, he wrote his continuation (cf. p. 420) of Aufidius Bassus, *a fine Aufidii Bassii* (*libri*) *triginta unus*. From the respect which Tacitus shows him, it would seem that he was a far from contemptible historian [53]; his nephew says that he wrote with the most scrupulous accuracy (*religiosissime*).[54] However, all these works are lost, and we have no trace of any speech he may have delivered while practising in the courts.

There remains, therefore, the great *Enquiry into Nature*

[53] All these details as to Pliny's works are from the younger Pliny, *epp.*, iii, 5. For Tacitus' use of the historical books, see, *e.g.*, *ann.*, xiii, 20, 3; xv, 53, 4–5, where he criticizes him. Fragments in *H.R.F.*, pp. 308–11.

[54] Pliny, *epp.*, v, 8, 5.

(*Naturalis historia*) in thirty-seven books, forming a compendium of ancient observational science. It was his last work, perhaps never really finished,[55] and contains the cream of his 160 closely-written book-rolls of excerpts from authors.[56] He himself reckons the facts included in the work at 20,000, the reading involved at 2,000 volumes.[57] The first book is introductory, a preface to Titus, in whose time the work was completed, so far as it ever was complete, followed by the indexes of the remaining books. Books II–VI describe, first the universe, as understood by ancient astronomy, then the surface of the earth ; VII deals with man ; VIII–XI are zoological, man being mentioned every here and there to compare and contrast him with the other animals. Next comes a long dissertation on botany, XII–XIX, which leads up to the section on the use of plants in medicine, XX–XXVII. Here the regular succession of subjects is interrupted, for the medicines derived from the animal kingdom come next, filling Books XXVIII–XXXII. The last five books, XXXIII–XXXVII, deal with the mineral kingdom, including an account of the uses to which the minerals have been put in the arts, and therefore a sort of history of painting and sculpture, very valuable for later students of these departments of ancient activity.

All this is book-knowledge, with little or no evidence of any original observation on Pliny's part, frequent uncritical use of the material and not a few blunders in translating from the Greek authors. Indeed, Pliny's worst faults are haste and credulity ; perpetually reading and writing, he seems but seldom to have reflected on what he read. Most of his comments are moralizings, of the popular Stoic sort with which we are already familiar. But when all allowances are made for his undoubted faults, Pliny remains one of our principal authorities for information of the most diverse types, from lost works of art to popular or learned magic, including history, literature, Roman ritual and customs, and much else.

[55] For the signs of incompleteness and perhaps of revision, see Schanz-Hosius, ii, p. 771. The most noteworthy is that whereas the author several times refers to the bibliographies as prefixed to the separate books, we have them all together in the first book, at the ends of the epitomes, thus : l(ibro) xix continentur lini natura et miracula (&c.), ex auctoribus (follows a list of 19 Latin names) ; externis (a list of 6 Greek names).

[56] Pliny, *epp.*, iii, 5, 17.

[57] Pliny, *N.H.*, i, praef., 17 ; he speaks also of exquisiti auctores centum, presumably his principal sources.

It was inevitable that this great compiler should be used by lesser men. Besides numerous series of extracts from him, we have a work largely made up of unacknowledged borrowings.[58] A certain GAIVS IVLIVS SOLINVS has come down from antiquity as the author of a 'collection of remarkable facts' (*collectanea rerum memorabiliorum*), whereof part is stolen from Pliny without acknowledgement, part is from Mela, part from some unknown author or authors. Solinus' plan was to describe the earth and its wonders, a type of work which grew increasingly popular in late antiquity. He has the merit of brevity, the demerit of being capable of atrocious blunders in reading his own language.[59]

That geography should be studied by the Romans would seem inevitable; nevertheless, they never produced a writer of much merit in that department. There survives the work of POMPONIVS MELA, a man of somewhat uncertain date, but probably contemporary with Claudius.[60] It is practically what the Greeks called a *periplus*, for it describes chiefly the shores of the various seas, with the cities and other noteworthy features given in the order in which a traveller would come to them if he started from the Straits of Gibraltar, sailed along the north coast of Africa, went on to Asia, and so back to Europe, where he begins with Scythia and ends with the British Isles. Excursuses on islands off the coasts and on the various seas complete the second and third of his three books respectively. Although he had planned a larger work on the subject,[61] whether he ever wrote it or not, he was no geographer, but a rhetorician, ignorant of the science as it was known in his day to the extent of omitting facts which one would suppose familiar to every intelligent

[58] The *Medicina Plinii* has already been dealt with, p. 427. The most important, though no longer the latest, edition of Solinus is that of Th. Mommsen (ed. 2, Berlin, Weidmann, 1895). His date must be after Pliny, probably after Suetonius, whom he seems to have used, certainly before Ammianus Marcellinus, who uses him.

[59] Thus, Pliny says (iv, 67, in a list of the islands of the Aegean): Paros cum oppido, ab Delo xxxviii, *i.e.*, Paros (island and town), thirty-eight miles from Delos. In Solinus (11, 26) this becomes: Paros . . . Abdelo oppido frequentissima! See further Schanz-Hosius-Krüger, iii, pp. 224–7.

[60] He lived under a 'very great emperor' (principum maximus) who had opened up Britain and conquered tribes there not even heard of before (iii, 49). The least likely identification is Julius Caesar, somewhat more likely Caligula, much the most probable Claudius. The affected style would also suit that age very well. See further Schanz-Hosius, ii, pp. 654–6.

[61] Mela, i, 1, 2: dicam autem alias plura et exactius, nunc ut quaeque erunt clarissima et strictim.

subject of the Empire.[62] He must have depended on books, and old ones at that.[63]

Concerning his life nothing more is known than what he himself mentions, that he was born at Tingentera in Spain.[64]

A very much greater contribution to geography was made by AGRIPPA (cf. p. 307). In the midst of his many occupations, he found time to plan a map on a large scale of the whole known world, to be depicted on the walls of a portico in the Campus Martius. He died before this was done, but Augustus took over and finished the work.[65] It was an immense task, for although there were good Greek works on geography to be had, also attempts at maps of various dates, nothing like a survey of the Empire, much less of the lands beyond its borders, was in existence. The chief guide to distances was the lengths of roads, whereof no doubt the Imperial archives had full accounts. But of the width of the country between the roads, or of districts which the road-makers had not yet penetrated, there can have been no trustworthy records. We may therefore suspect that Agrippa's map, and the various copies of it which seem to have existed in antiquity,[66] bore a certain resemblance to that famous medieval chart, the Tabula Peutingeriana,[67] in which the known world appears as a sort of broad ribbon, with the distances from east to west (the direction of the majority of the longest and most important roads) given with some accuracy, while the whole space from north to south is ridiculously compressed. Even if the original was as distorted as this, however, it repre-

[62] A glaring example is iii, 2, 25, where he bounds Germany by the Rhine, the North Sea, the Sarmaticarum confinium gentium, and the Alps. In other words, he ignores or has never heard of the Danubian frontier of the Empire and all the territories on it. This might be taken as an indication that he wrote under Julius Caesar, before the Augustan rectifications of this much disputed line, were it not that the style is so unlike that of the Golden Age.

[63] He actually cites no one later than Nepos (see p. 208) and Hanno (cf. Rose, *H.G.L.*, p. 312).

[64] Mela, ii, 96.

[65] See Pliny, *N.H.*, iii, 17. *Ibid.*, 16, he complains of the difficulty of finding exact dimensions, even for one province. That the Empire was ever exactly surveyed seems to be a mere fable, see Schanz-Hosius, ii, p. 331.

[66] Besides being credible in itself, this has some literary and epigraphical support, see Schanz-Hosius, *ibid.*, where also mentions of maps earlier than Agrippa and existing in Italy are collected.

[67] A useful edition of this most interesting document is that of K. Müller, *Weltkarte des Castorius, genannt die peutingersche Tafel*, Ravensburg, Maier, 1888, reprinted, with a pamphlet of comment, in 1916, by Strecker & Schröder, Stuttgart.

sented a very great advance on anything of the kind that had been produced before. Its value was increased by a written description which accompanied it and seems to have been Agrippa's own, or at least composed under his orders and intended for use with his map. This in turn, we may reasonably suppose, is the predecessor, if not the actual ancestor, of the various Itineraries, all of late date,[68] which still survive. It is used by Pliny for his geographical books, as was to be expected, and treated with the utmost respect.[69]

Before leaving this part of the subject, we may mention that one of the latest authors capable of composing correct Latin verse was interested in geography. RVFIVS FESTVS AVIENVS [70] seems to have written at least part of his works between Lactantius and Jerome (see pp. 481, 489), for the latter mentions his translation of Aratos, while the former quotes only from Cicero and Germanicus (pp. 145, 352). We learn from his own testimony that he was a native of Volsinii and descended from Musonius the Stoic philosopher; that he was twice proconsul, wrote many poems, was married and had a large family. Of his poems there survive three of some importance, besides one or two trifles attributed to him. One is a translation of Aratos into Latin hexameters, which is 724 lines longer than the original, much of the extra matter being versified scholia. Another, also in hexameters and longer, by about 200 lines, than the original, is a version of the poem of Dionysios Periegetes,[71] in

[68] We have the *Itinerarium prouinciarum Antonini Augusti*, which in its present form dates from Diocletian's time; if the title is authentic the Antoninus in question is perhaps Caracallus; also the *Itinerarium Hierosolymitanum*, or *Burdigalense*, which gives the route from Bordeaux to Jerusalem, returning by Rome and Milan, and is the composition of a Christian, of the year 333. The MSS. of the Antonine itinerary also preserve, in an incomplete form, an *Itinerarium maritimum*, in other words a *periplus*. There is a work known as the *Itinerarium Alexandri*, but this is really a compendium of the eastern campaigns of Alexander the Great and also of Trajan, written for and presented to Constantius, son of Constantine the Great, on his departure for a Persian expedition. The sources are Arrian and the so-called Kallisthenes, the author of the Alexander Romance in its earliest Greek form; the writer is possibly that IVLIVS VALERIVS who also made a Latin rendering of pseudo-Kallisthenes. See, for more details of these and a few other records of road-distances, Schanz, iv, pp. 112–16.

[69] See especially the indexes to Bks. iii–vi.

[70] Life, *C.I.L.*, vi, 537 Dessau, 2944. It is an inscription put up by him to the Etruscan goddess Nortia; hence we learn that he was one of the surviving pagans of his time. Jerome mentions him, *comm. in epist. ad Titum*, ch. i, 12 (vol. iii, p. 706 E. Vall.) as having rendered Aratos *nuper*.

[71] For this Dionysios, see Rose, *H.G.L.*, p. 384.

other words a compendium of geography. The third, called *ora maritima*, is the most interesting; it is later than the translation of Dionysios, for it cites it[72]; the metre is iambic trimeters, which therefore was presumably that of the Greek original. This was a somewhat extraordinary work, apparently put together by its unknown author from a *periplus* of the fourth century B.C. and another of about 200–150. Why Avienus chose this antiquated document instead of something which would have given a trustworthy account of western Europe (for he sets out to describe the world from the Atlantic coast to the Black Sea) is not known; he does us the service of preserving a monument of Hellenistic geographical knowledge which is of interest for the history of the subject. About half of his poem survives, amounting to 713 lines, many of them much damaged in the imperfect MS. to which our tradition goes back.

Avienus is said also to have versified Livy and written some sort of a paraphrase of Vergil, or of selected stories from him; but these works are totally lost.[73]

But the branch of study in which the Romans did best was literary and historical. *Grammatici*, in other words philologists, and antiquarians flourished from before the days of Varro. We have seen that Accius and Lucilius (see pp. 69, 84) were interested in such things, to say nothing of the great philological and archaeological knowledge of a number of authors as different from one another as Vergil and the elder Pliny; but there was in addition a succession of scholars who had no other activity, or none of importance, from about the time of Ennius' death onwards.[74]

Suetonius assures us that the first beginnings of this movement were due to an accident. Krates, the Homeric scholar,[75] being in Rome on an errand for his master, king Attalos of Pergamon, fell and broke his leg, and beguiled his convalescence by giving lectures, which were popular and found imitators. This is, of course, folklore, although the accident may be historical; by the time Ennius was old, it was inevitable that some interest in philology and history should have sprung up among the

[72] *Ora marit.*, 71–3.

[73] Servius on Verg., *Aen.*, x, 272 and 388.

[74] Krates (see below) came to Rome sub ipsam Ennii mortem, according to Suetonius, *de grammaticis*, our chief ancient authority, par. 2. The fragments and notices of these early scholars, up to and including the time of Augustus, are conveniently collected in Funaioli (see Bibliography).

[75] Suet., *ibid.* This would be about 584/170, cf. p. 34.

more cultured members of a community which had already a long past and more than the rudiments of a literature. Passing to fact, we find recorded as the first name of a Latin *grammaticus* known to Suetonius that of C. OCTAVIVS LAMPADIO, whose exact date is not known (it might be about the age of the Gracchi),[76] and whose claims on the interest of posterity are based on his having edited Naevius (cf. p. 26) and divided his *bellum Punicum* into the traditional seven books, also doing something for Ennius, whose *Annals* were extant in A. Gellius' day in a venerable MS. corrected by Lampadio himself.[77] Apparently, however, a regular edition of Ennius was not produced till the time of Q. VARGVNTEIVS, of whom we know only that he came later than Lampadio.[78] Later still, and concerned with Lucilius, whom they knew personally, were Q. LAELIVS ARCHELAVS and VETTIVS PHILOCOMVS.[79] A far greater name, however, is that of LVCIVS AELIVS STILO, or PRAECONINVS (cf. p. 104), of whom, from the many respectful mentions of him in a variety of authors, we gather that he was interested in textual criticism (he appears to have introduced the conventional signs of the Alexandrian critics),[80] in the interpretation of the hymn of the Salii (cf. p. 4), in the plays of Plautus and in etymology and lexicography. His dates would be about 600/154 to somewhere after 664/90, to judge by the dates of his known acquaintances.[81] His son-in-law, SERVIVS CLODIVS, with whom he afterwards quarrelled, was also a man of learning.[82] These two were Roman knights, and took some part in public life; but learning was by no means confined to free men, since to teach a clever slave thoroughly might be a good investment; he could earn money for his master by giving lessons, or he might be sold outright at a handsome profit, as was LVTATIVS DAPHNIS, to give him his freedman's name, for whom Q. Catulus paid 700,000 sestertii (about £7,000 or $35,000) and shortly afterwards manumitted him.[83] Another freedman, of uncertain but fairly early date, was SEVIVS NICANOR, whose former master was an obscure man, M. Sevius by name.[84] Yet

[76] Suet., *ibid.*; Funaioli, p. 21 *sq.* [77] Gellius, xviii, 5, 11.
[78] Suet., *ibid.*; Funaioli, p. 50. [79] Suet., *ibid.*; Funaioli, pp. 50–1.
[80] Suet., *ibid.*, 2–3; Funaioli, pp. 51–76. [81] Funaioli, p. 52.
[82] Suet., *ibid.*; Funaioli, pp. 95–8; the fragments deal with etymology and lexicography.
[83] Suet., *ibid.*, 3; Funaioli, p. xiii. There are no fragments of him, nor proof that he wrote anything; he was active as a teacher.
[84] Suet., *ibid.*, 5; Funaioli, pp. xiv, 86; he was certainly of Republican date and not the end of the Republic, for in a verse which survives from a *satura* of his writing he twice drops a final *s*; also Suet. mentions him before Opillus and says he was the first regular teacher (*professor*) to win fame by his teaching.

another was AVRELIVS OPILLVS, author of nine volumes of miscellaneous learning (*uaria eruditio*), the number being that of the Muses. These he wrote in Asia, whither he had left his school to follow Rutilius Rufus (cf. p. 108).[85] M. ANTONIVS GNIPHO was free-born, exposed by his parents, and set free by some one who had picked him up and reared him. He was contemporary with the youth of Julius Caesar, had no fixed fees but let his scholars pay whatever they thought fit, and is known to have written a commentary on Ennius.[86] Of M. POMPILIVS ANDRONICVS we know only what Suetonius tells us,[87] that he was a contemporary of Gnipho, but too lazy to take very high rank. L. ORBILIVS PVPILLVS, of Beneventum, had an unusual career. He was a soldier in his prime, though always interested in learning, began to teach in the year of Cicero's consulship (691/63), when he was forty-nine, and was celebrated for his vigorous methods of maintaining discipline (Horace, who was one of his pupils, calls him *plagosus*, and Domitius Marsus agrees.)[88] He lived for some fifty years longer, though towards the end he lost his memory. His son was also a *grammaticus*. He must have been about contemporary with CORNELIVS EPICADVS, a freedman of Sulla the dictator, who completed his old master's memoirs for publication.[89] L. ATEIVS PRAETEXTATVS, or, as he called himself, PHILOLOGVS, was acquainted with Sallust and, after his death, with Asinius Pollio, both of whom he helped in their historical work. It is significant that he wrote a sketch of Roman history for the former, an essay on historical style (*praecepta de ratione scribendi*) for the latter. But these works, and also his 800 volumes of 'raw materials' (*hyle, i.e.*, ὕλη, cf. the title of Statius' *Siluae*, p. 393) and one or two other books which he is known to have written are lost save about a dozen fragments.[90] Almost nothing is left of the works of STABERIVS EROS, but he deserves mention because he numbered Brutus and Cassius among his pupils and, in the days of Sulla, would take no fee for teaching the children of the proscribed.[91] CVRTIVS NICIAS, after being on familiar terms with Pompey and Memmius

[85] He was therefore alive and vigorous enough to undertake a long journey in 662/92 or about that time, but no longer young, for Suet. says he *consenuit* with Rufus, who died about 676/78.

[86] Suet., *ibid.*, 7; Funaioli, pp. xiv; 98–100.

[87] Suet., *ibid.*, 8. He was a Syrian and an Epicurean.

[88] Suet., *ibid.*, 9, who cites Horace (*epp.*, ii, i, 69) and Domitius (*F.P.L.*, p. 347/111).

[89] Suet., *ibid.*, 12; Funaioli, pp. 103–5.

[90] Suet., *ibid.*, 10; Funaioli, pp. xx, 136–41.

[91] Suet., *ibid.*, 13.

(Lucretius' patron), was forbidden the house by the former, who discovered that he had brought in a love-letter from Memmius to his wife. Cicero also knew him and several times mentions him in his surviving correspondence.[92] POMPEIVS LENAEVS, a freedman of Pompey the Great, defended the memory of his patron in a satire against Sallust, who had attacked him, and, being left without any member of the family to whom he might attach himself, earned his living by setting up a school. He has a small place in the history of medicine, for by Pompey's directions he translated into Latin the captured medical library of Mithridates.[93] Q. CAECILIVS EPIROTA, Atticus' freedman, is the earliest known commentator on Vergil and other Augustans He was expelled from Atticus' house owing to his suspicious conduct towards the latter's daughter, who was his pupil, and betook himself to Gallus the poet (see p. 284), after whose disgrace and death he also set up a school.[94]

He was thus a contemporary, probably somewhat older, of M. VERRIVS FLACCVS, the greatest of Augustan scholars. He was a native of Praeneste, a member of the freedman class (*libertini*), and was the first to institute prizes for proficiency among his pupils. He became tutor to the Imperial children under Augustus, but was allowed to continue his school on condition of receiving no new pupils, and to use a room in the Palatine for his classes. His salary from the Emperor was 100,000 sestertii (approximately £1,000, or $5,000), and his life was prolonged into the next reign.[95]

Of the elaborate and learned works which he produced, not one survives intact. He wrote a treatise *de obscuris Catonis* (*On some Difficulties in Cato*), extending to not fewer than two books; another on orthography, a third entitled *Saturnus*, presumably dealing with the cult of that god and his festival, the Saturnalia, a history of Etruria (*res Etruscae*), a miscellany (*res memoria dignae*), and some letters, probably essays on philological and

[92] Suet., *ibid.*, 14; Funaioli, pp. 382–3.

[93] Suet., *ibid.*, 15; Pliny, *N.H.*, xxv, 5–7. The king's interest in medicine was in all probability practical; he wished to guard himself against poisoners. The tale, which Pliny evidently believed, that he made himself immune by a mixed diet of poisons and antidotes, doubtless arises from this. See also Funaioli, pp. 403–4.

[94] Suet., *ibid.*, 16; Funaioli, p. xxiii *sq.*

[95] What is left of Verrius, apart from the Fasti and Festus, is assembled in Funaioli, pp. 511–23. See also Suet., *op. cit.*, 17. The purchasing power of Verrius' salary would be many times that of a sum of the same face value to-day; it made him, if not exactly rich, at least very comfortably off.

other matters in epistolary form. All these are lost, save for some fragments and references; as regards two other works, we are somewhat more fortunate.

We have several references to a sort of encyclopaedia, *de uerborum significatu*, in which he assembled a great store of words from old writers and explained them fully, going into innumerable points of historical, antiquarian and philological interest. This has not survived, but an epitome of it was made by a man of unknown but much later date, POMPEIVS FESTVS, and of this we have a sorely battered copy. Festus in his turn was epitomized by Paulus Diaconus, in the time of Karl the Great, and his miserably skeletonic production has come down to us in full. We are thus able to reconstruct a good deal of Verrius, the more so as he was used by many later authors, as Ovid, Plutarch and Pliny the Elder, and material from Festus has found its way into glossaries.[96]

In addition, Verrius was much interested in the religion of his country, and above all, it would appear, in the calendar. He erected in his native town a permanent stone calendar, with annotations explaining why each feast day or other anniversary was kept; and this, though in a damaged and imperfect condition, has survived, either in the original or in a copy set up elsewhere in the town.[97] Known generally as the Fasti Praenestini, it is one of our principal documents for that part of the study of antiquity; whether its annotations were composed solely for the purpose they served or were extracts from a longer work on the subject is an undecided question, but the second hypothesis is the more plausible.

Another erudite subject of Augustus was C. IVLIVS HYGINVS, whom he appointed librarian of the Palatine Library. This man was a Spaniard by birth, or, according to some, an Alexandrian, and a pupil of the very learned Cornelius Alexander, surnamed Polyhistor.[98] Originally a slave, perhaps a prisoner of war, he was set free by the Emperor, and, besides his functions as librarian,

[96] After various earlier editions, the best-known that of Otfried Müller, Leipzig, 1839, by the pages of which Festus was long quoted, the sadly damaged and incomplete text has been put in as good order as possible by W. M. Lindsay, ed. minor, Teubner, 1913, by the pages and lines of which quotations are now made; ed. maior, Paris, 1930 (*Glossaria Latina*, vol. IV). For more particulars, see Schanz-Hosius, ii, pp. 362–6.

[97] It is *C.I.L.*, i (ed. 2), 230. That it is by Verrius is clear from its many agreements with Festus; the only reason for supposing that it is not the one which Suet., *loc. cit.*, says he erected is that that was in the forum of Praeneste, the fragments we have were found some distance from that spot. See Schanz-Hosius, ii, p. 362.

[98] Suet., *ibid.*, 20; Funaioli, pp. 525–37. For Polyhistor, see Rose, *H.G.L.*, p. 405.

was active as a teacher, and became the personal friend of Ovid and of Clodius Licinus (see p. 314). His works are all lost, but we know they included a treatise on agriculture, another, apparently separate, on bees, a commentary on the *Propempticon* of Cinna (cf. p. 137), another on Vergil, supplemented perhaps by a series of essays on particular points in his poems, and several historical, geographical and antiquarian writings.[99] These comprised one entitled *de uita rebusque inlustrium uirorum,* which would seem to have been a compilation something like the surviving work of Nepos (see p. 208), another called *exempla,* literally 'precedents', perhaps remarkable sayings and doings of noted people, after the manner of Valerius Maximus; a book, or books, *de familiis Troianis,* giving an account of those houses which claimed descent from companions of Aeneas; another treatise *On the origin and topography of Italian cities*; and finally, two theological works, in the ancient sense of 'theology', which includes mythology and the history of religion. Of these, one was called *de proprietatibus deorum* (*On the characteristics of the gods*; it dealt among other things with the proper sacrifices to make to them, and included stars among the deities to be worshipped),[100] the other *de dis Penatibus.*[101]

It is thus apparent that Iulius Hyginus was a man of wide learning, well versed in the literature of both Latin and Greek, whichever of them was really his native speech. This should have been enough to prevent his ever being identified with a miserable sciolist, of about the age of the Antonines, whose little book, entitled *Genealogiae* or *Fabulae,* has attached to it the name Hyginus, probably on the authority of the now lost MS. from which the *editio princeps* was printed. It consists, as we have it, of 243 chapters (originally 277) of content mostly mythological and going back to a tolerably good Greek handbook of the subject. We have not Hyginus' own work, however, but some unknown excerptors' selections from it; had we the complete book, it still would show a vast number of absurdities, the fruit of Hyginus' extremely imperfect knowledge of Greek and incredible stupidity.[102]

[99] The works on farming and bees are cited as *de agri cultura* and *de apibus* respectively; if the latter were part of the former, we should expect the title to be *de re rustica.* Gellius in one passage (i, 21, 2) cites his *commentarii* on Vergil, in another (xvi, 6, 14) his *libri,* which suggests two works rather than two names for one.

[100] The only certain fragment, preserved by Macrobius, *sat.*, iii, 8, 4, says: Hyginus de proprietatibus deorum, cum de astris ac de stellis loqueretur, ait oportere his uolucres immolari.

[101] For ancient theories on this matter, see G. Wissowa, *Gesammelte Abhandlungen* (Munich, Beck, 1904), pp. 95–128 (reprinted from *Hermes,* xxii, 1886, p. 29 *sqq.*).

[102] For discussion of the various difficulties, and a critical text of the work, see Rose, *Hygini Fabulae,* Leiden, Sijthoff, 1934.

Perhaps by the same author is a work generally called *Poetica astronomica*, a title which lacks all ancient authority, as does the conventional division into four books. Certainly it shares some characteristics with the *Genealogiae*, and seems to refer to it as by the same writer; it is based upon some Greek work which had made use of Eratosthenes, a commentary on Aratos and a star-map, or, less likely, its compiler went to these sources for himself. Blunders due to poor knowledge of Greek are not uncommon, and the style is bad, though, since it has not come down to us in excerpts but directly, it is better Latin than the *Genealogiae*. If both works are from the same hand, they are not later than the second century, for the former is quoted in 207 by an unknown grammarian who renders part of it into Greek; neither is at all likely to be earlier than that century.[103]

Suetonius also gives an account of a slightly later *grammaticus*, REMMIVS PALAEMON.[104] If his story is true, this man picked up his first knowledge of reading and writing by listening to the lessons his mistress' son was given in the school to which he accompanied him as personal attendant or *paedagogus*, and so improved his opportunities that he became learned and, being afterwards set free, became a teacher, despite his extremely immoral character, which moved both Tiberius and Claudius to warn parents against him. In taste he was a modern, in whose opinion Varro was 'a pig' (as we should say, an old ass), while he himself was the only authority on literature, which would die with him; for his conceit was his most outstanding characteristic. He was also a clever versifier, able to compose extempore poems on all manner of metres. But his chief renown rested upon his Latin grammar, which, though now lost, was so celebrated in antiquity that its traces are to be found in all or nearly all subsequent writers on that subject.[105]

About the same time lived IVLIVS MODESTVS,[106] a freedman of Iulius Hyginus, who followed in the footsteps of his patron as regards his studies, and POMPONIVS MARCELLVS, a word-hunting pedant, of

[103] There is no critical edition of the *Astronomica*, that of Bunte, Leipzig, 1875, being quite inadequate, while van Staveren's (in his *Mythographi Latini*, Leiden, 1742), though good for its time, is now badly out of date. See further Schanz-Hosius, ii, pp. 372–9. For Eratosthenes, see Rose, *H.G.L.*, p. 379.

[104] Suet., *op. cit.*, 23; Schanz-Hosius, ii, pp. 728–30.

[105] The learned lady in Juvenal, vi, 452, has his grammar constantly in her hands, repetit uoluitque Palaemonis artem. For traces of its influence, also works falsely ascribed to Remmius, see Schanz-Hosius, ii, p. 729 *sq*.

[106] Suet., *op. cit.*, 20. He wrote a philological miscellany, *quaestiones confusae*, Gellius, iii, 9, 1, also a work *de feriis*, several times cited by Charisius and Diomedes. See Schanz-Hosius, ii, p. 730.

whose preoccupation with precise speech Suetonius has some good stories to tell, one being to the credit of his honesty; when Tiberius used some doubtful Latinity and was assured that it was correct, or would in future be counted so, Pomponius frankly said that the Emperor could confer citizen rights on men, but not on words.[107] A man of some interest, because of his preserving some extremely doubtful statements concerning Vergil, was NISVS, who also wrote on grammar and composed a commentary on the calendar.[108]

A very good scholar of early Imperial date (he seems to have written about the beginning of Nero's principate) was Q. ASCONIVS PEDIANVS, who, besides some lost works,[109] wrote a commentary on Cicero's speeches, part of which survives and forms one of our best helps to understanding their historical background; purely linguistic matters are not touched upon. He seems to have been a Paduan, and his commentary was intended primarily for the use of his sons.[110]

Falsely ascribed to Asconius is another commentary, by no means worthless, on part of the Verrine Orations of Cicero.

A very celebrated scholar was M. VALERIVS PROBVS, of Berytus (Beirut), who is important as marking the beginning of a return to the study of Republican authors. He had read, says Suetonius, some ancient works in his province, at an elementary school, for the memory of the older writers was not completely dead there, as it was in Rome. When, giving up all thoughts of a career in the army, for he had not influence enough to obtain a centurion's post, he took to scholarship instead, he persisted in the taste thus formed, despite the general contempt for his favourites. He never became a teacher, at most allowing some three or four persons to visit him in the afternoons, when he would chat with them on general topics and now and then favour them with an informal lecture.[111] He published little that was

[107] Suet., *ibid.*, 22. Pomponius' words to Tiberius were: tu enim, Caesar, ciuitatem dare potes hominibus, uerbo non potes. See Schanz-Hosius, *ibid.*

[108] Donatus, *uit. Vergil.*, 42, says he reported that he had heard from older men that Vergil wrote the lines *ille ego*, &c., but Varius cut them out. See chap. ix, n. 54.

[109] A *liber contra obtrectatores Vergilii*, Donatus, *uit. Verg.*, 46; a life of Sallust, Acro on Horace, *sat.*, i, 2, 41; one or two others are conjectural only, see Schanz-Hosius, ii, p. 733.

[110] He calls Livy *noster*, p. 77, 5 Clark; 60, 15 Stangl (*Ciceronis orationum scholiastae*, Vienna and Leipzig, 1912; A. C. Clark's edition is in the Oxford Classical Texts, 1907). His sons, p. 43, 28 Clark, 38, 22 Stangl. Pseudasconius, Stangl, *ibid.*, p. 185 *sqq.*

[111] Suet., *de gramm.*, 24. See, in general, Schanz-Hosius, ii, pp. 734–41.

original, but we have more or less cogent proofs that he edited Vergil, Horace, Lucretius and Terence, perhaps Persius, possibly Plautus and Sallust.[112] Of his date we are ill-informed. Suetonius includes no living scholars in his *de grammaticis*, therefore Probus was dead early in the second century, say about 105; but he mentions him after Remmius Palaemon, who was at the height of his repute about 48 and probably dead before the seventies of the century.[113] If, therefore, we suppose that he was busy with his learned researches about the time of Domitian, we shall not be far wrong. By that time Vergil and Horace were fast becoming *antiqui*, or had already achieved that position.

Several surviving works are allegedly by Probus. Of these one, a little treatise on abbreviations,[114] has nothing in it to suggest that it is later than his day, and a scholar who was interested in cryptograms (see note 112) may have studied abbreviations also.

Valla's scholiast on Juvenal, published in his edition of that poet and since reprinted (most recently in the Teubner edition of the scholia) bears the name of Probus, but is certainly very much later and cannot claim to go back to anything he wrote, for we do not hear of his commenting on contemporary poets and it is very unlikely that he was alive when Juvenal's satires were published.

[112] Suet. definitely says: nimis pauca et exigua de quibusdam minutis quaestiunculis edidit. The following works must therefore have been short: *epistula ad Marcellum* (possibly the Vitorius Marcellus to whom Quintilian's *Institutio* is addressed), Gellius, iv, 7, 1; *commentarius de occulta litterarum significatione in epistularum C. Caesaris scriptura, ibid.*, xvii, 9, 5; *de inaequalitate consuetudinis*, Charisius, i, p. 212, 7 Keil; *de temporum conexione*, Servius on Aen., vii, 421 (if that was by the same Probus); *de genetiuo Graeco*, Pomponius, v, p. 182, 30 Keil (with the same qualification). The 'many volumes' of Probus which Gellius says he had (xv, 30, 5) perhaps included the non mediocris *silua obseruationum sermonis antiqui* of which Suet. speaks. As regards the editions, those of Vergil, Horace and Lucretius (possibly a miswriting for Lucilius) are attested by the anonymous grammarian, vii, 534, 5–6 Keil, the first also by several mentions in the extant commentators; Terence, by mentions in the commentary of Donatus; the others only by more or less plausible conclusions from scraps of ancient evidence, see Schanz-Hosius, ii, p. 735 *sq*. He certainly had studied Plautus, Gellius, vi, 7, 3.

[113] Jerome says, *an. Abr.* 2072 (= 56) that Probus *agnoscitur* then, but what authority, if any, he has for this is unknown. He puts the *floruit* of Remmius at *an. Abr.* 2064 (= 48), again on unknown authority; Pliny, *N.H.*, xiv, 49, mentions him in a context which suggests he was then dead. Martial, iii, 2, 12, speaks of Probus as if he were alive (illo iudice nec Probum timeto; but possibly he means only 'the sternest critic', 'the most implacable Aristarchos').

[114] Published in Keil, iv, p. 271 *sqq.*; its traditional title, which is not original, for it does not fit the contents, is (*de*) *iuris notarum*.

Four little grammatical works, the *catholica Probi* and *appendix Probi*, both on accidence, the *instituta artium* on the parts of speech, and the *de nomine excerpta*, on the inflections of the noun, are of various dates and unknown authorship, certainly not by the grammarian of Berytus, though someone of the same name may conceivably have had a hand in them.[115]

There is a commentary on the *Eclogues* and *Georgics* of Vergil which also bears the name of Probus. It again is manifestly not so early as his time, and moreover does not contain the views which are elsewhere ascribed to him, besides being marred by blunders he certainly would not have made. Nevertheless, it is not devoid of value and that its author made some use of the real Probus here and there is not impossible.[116]

The Life of Persius, on the other hand (cf. p. 377, n. 113) may really go back to his commentary, as it professses to do.

As we have already mentioned Gellius often and shall have occasion to do so again, it is convenient to deal with him here. There has come down to us a work originally in twenty books, whereof the eighth is lost except for the headings of the chapters. Its author is a certain AVLVS GELLIVS, of whom we know what he tells us, and little more. To judge by the names he cites as known to him in his youth and early maturity, he must have been born between 130 and 140.[117] After a studious boyhood, during which he was taught literature by Sulpicius Apollinaris (p. 452) and rhetoric by Antonius Iulianus (p. 420), he became a judge in one of the minor courts, and seems to have discharged his office with the most painful conscientiousness.[118] Later in life, he spent some time, perhaps a year, in Athens and the neighbourhood, and, in memory of that happy and busy stay, named his work *Noctes Atticae*. It is a collection of anecdotes of people he had known, grammarians, rhetoricians and philosophers, and of the great ones of the past, together with extracts from all manner of learned works, Greek and Latin, dealing with literature and antiquities ; for, as was natural in that age when Fronto was the leading spirit (see p. 518), Gellius was an enthusiast for the older Latin literature, down to the Augustan poets at latest. He

[115] Published respectively in Keil, vol. iv, p. 3 *sqq*., p. 193 *sqq*., 47 *sqq*., 207 *sqq*.

[116] Published in the third volume of Thilo-Hagen's Servius, pp. 323–90.

[117] See especially Gellius, vii, 6, 12 : adulescens ego Romae, cum etiam tum ad grammaticos itarem, audiui Apollinarem Sulpicium. . . . Erucio Claro praefecto urbi dicere, &c. Erucius was consul in 146 and *praefectus urbi* till about 157 ; an *adulescens* would not be more than eighteen or nineteen ; hence a birth-date somewhere in the thirties of the century is indicated.

[118] Gellius, xiv, 2.

often combines the two fashions of writing, beginning with his conversation with a scholar and continuing with a quotation from some book out of which the great man produced a solution for his problem. It does not, of course, follow either that all these occasions are historical or that Gellius had himself read all the Republican writers upon whom he draws; extracts from them would be common in the later philological treatises which he undoubtedly had studied. But, be his quotations first-hand or not, they are from good sources, and we have every reason to be grateful to him for his habit of excerpting what he read. For he must have had access to very respectable libraries, and probably owned many books himself; of these, the majority are lost to us, and the facts about them which he preserves most welcome. Personally, he gives the impression of having been an amiable man, modest and of a tender conscience, whose one great delight was learning and who therefore paid the utmost deference to all who could and would teach him. He and Chaucer's Clerk of Oxenford would have understood and respected each other.

He states his intention of compiling more material, but we have no indication that he ever wrote anything but the *Noctes Atticae*.[119]

Among the *grammatici* known to Gellius we may name L. CAESELLIVS VINDEX. No complete work of his has survived, but there are extracts from him in a collection from various authors by Cassiodorus [120] known as the *de orthographia*, and Gellius, Terentianus Scaurus and Sulpicius Apollinaris all attack him for errors of one sort or another.[121] We know that he wrote treatises entitled *lectiones antiquae* and *Stromateus*, *i.e.*, *Readings in ancient authors* and *Miscellany*, or more likely, one work which had a double title. Since writers of the second century criticize him freely, it is not unreasonable to suppose that he was an earlier contemporary of theirs, and lived about the time of Hadrian.

One of his critics was Q. TERENTIANVS SCAVRVS, who seems to have been the leading philologist of Hadrian's time. He wrote

[119] Gellius, i, *praef.*, 24.

[120] The work is best published in vol. vii, p. 129 *sqq.*, Keil; the excerpts are in the tenth and eleventh sections, Cassiodorus being clearly under the impression that he was excerpting two authors, one called L. Caecilius Vindex and the other Caesellius. This corruption of the grammarian's somewhat unusual name occurs elsewhere, see Schanz-Hosius-Krüger, iii, p. 155.

[121] Gellius, vi, 2, 1 *sqq.*, catches him in a bad blunder which shows that he had read his authors carelessly. For Scaurus and Sulpicius, see below. As all the quotations from him, whether attributed to the *lectiones* or the *Stromateus* or without any title, are of much the same kind, the conclusion that they are all from the same work is plausible.

on orthography, and we still have two little essays of his on that subject.[122] His Latin grammar, his commentary on Horace and his polemical work on the errors of Caesellius Vindex are known to us only by citations in Gellius and later writers. His chief source, so far as it is known, was apparently Varro. Another and apparently a contemporary writer on the same subject was VELIVS LONGVS,[123] whose treatise on spelling we still have, though his remaining works, including a commentary on the *Aeneid*, are lost. Of Gellius' own teacher, GAIVS SVLPICIVS APOLLINARIS of Carthage, we have very little left; there survive metrical synopses (*argumenta*) of the comedies of Terence, prefixed to the text of the plays in the MSS., and Gellius reports his views on various philological matters. He probably died about the middle of the second century.[124] AEMILIVS ASPER is mentioned neither by Gellius nor by Suetonius, but is used by Iulius Romanus (see below), and therefore may not unreasonably be placed about the late second or early third century. He wrote commentaries on Vergil, Terence and Sallust; other works ascribed by ancients or moderns to him rest on imperfect evidence or are certainly spurious.[125] The name of FLAVIVS CAPER is attached to two surviving works,[126] the *orthographia Capri* and the treatise *de uerbis dubiis*, which in all probability have been much modified by subsequent writers but are based on compositions of his, for we know he wrote *de Latinitate* or *de lingua Latina* and also *de dubiis generibus*. Between Gellius and Iulius Romanus we may put STATILIVS MAXIMVS,[127] whose work on the rare words (*singularia, i.e.,* ἅπαξ εἰρημένα) which are to be found *apud Ciceronem quoque*, meaning apparently that they are not confined to Cato, on whom also he commented, is several times cited. It is possible that this is the T. Statilius Maximus Severus who in 136 visited the so-called statue of Memnon in Egypt and scribbled four verses on it. In the work of Charisius (see below) we have numerous excerpts from IVLIVS ROMANVS, probably all from a treatise entitled ἀφορμαί, *i.e., Startingpoints* (for a knowledge of grammar), in other words the fundamentals of language. This seems to have been a compilation from the earlier writers; it cites no

[122] See Keil, vii, p. 3 *sqq.*; Schanz-Hosius-Krüger, iii, pp. 156–8.

[123] See Keil, *ibid.*, p. 39 *sqq.*; Schanz-Hosius-Krüger, *ibid.*, pp. 158–9.

[124] The *Hist. Aug.*, viii, 1, 4, says Pertinax was a pupil of Sulpicius Apollinaris and for a while succeeded him as a teacher. Pertinax became an officer in the army not later than 161; before this therefore must come his career as a teacher and the death of his predecessor. See Schanz-Hosius-Krüger, *ibid.*, pp. 159–61.

[125] *Ibid.*, pp. 161–2.

[126] *Ibid.*, pp. 163–4.

[127] *Ibid.*, 164–5; Bücheler, *carmina epigraphica* (Teubner, 1888), No. 227.

one later than Apuleius (see p. 520), and must of course come before Charisius, that is to say before the middle of the fourth century; it seems reasonable to put it in the third. Two works, a grammar (*de institutis artis grammaticae*) and a treatise on metre (*de metris*) seem both to be the work of a man called MARIVS PLOTIVS CLAVDIVS SACERDOS, perhaps late third century; the so-called *Catholica Probi* (see p. 450) is practically the same as the second book of his *de institutis*. Sundry quotations dealing with metre can be referred to a certain IVBA, not the famous Juba of Mauretania, who was a contemporary of Augustus, but a much later writer, probably also a Mauretanian; the year 200 is about the date when he flourished.[128] Somewhere about this time also lived a writer very important for our knowledge of the pronunciation of Latin, TERENTIANVS MAVRVS. He was a skilled metrician, and wrote three books in verse, *de litteris*, *de syllabis*, *de metris*. In the first of these he discusses the phonetics of the language, explaining clearly how the mouth should be held to produce the sounds which the letters signify.[129] The other two are of less importance to us. Terentianus had probably used Caesius Bassus (cf. p. 385), who was also a source for ATILIVS FORTVNATIANVS, a man of unknown life and date, whose treatise on metre, especially on the metres of Horace, still survives. A more important writer in every way was C. MARIVS VICTORINVS AFER (the last name merely signifies that he was from the province of Africa). From him we have a so-called *ars grammatica*, really a treatise on metre, whereof one book, the fourth, is testified by a MS. subscription to be taken from a lost metrician, by name AELIVS FESTVS APHTHONIVS.[130] But he was also a rhetorician,

[128] For Romanus, Sacerdos and Iuba, see Schanz-Hosius-Krüger, iii, pp. 168–75; Keil, vol. vi, p. 427 *sqq*.

[129] The cognomen Maurus rests on the authority of a mention of him in S. Augustine, *de util. cred.*, 17; it may not be part of his name but mean simply 'of Mauretania'. His work has been several times published, most recently in vol. vi of Keil, p. 313 *sqq*.; an older imprint is that in the second edition of Gaisford's Hephaestion, Oxford, 1855, p. 215 *sqq*.

[130] See Schanz, iv, p. 149 *sqq*.; the work is published in Keil, vol. vi, p. 3 *sqq*. For the date and some incidents in the life of Victorinus, who seems to have been a man of engaging character, see Jerome, *de uir. ill.*, 101 (who gives his rhetorical activity as being sub Constantio principe, i.e., 337–61, his conversion as in extrema senectute, which is manifestly an exaggeration); Augustine, *confess.*, viii, 2, 3, 5; 5, 10. He should not be confused with MAXIMVS (MAXIMINVS, MAXIMIANVS) VICTORINVS, a contemporary grammarian, apparently also a Christian, for he mentions Lactantius, who wrote a little treatise *de ratione metrorum* and probably another *de finalibus metrorum*, to be found in Keil, *ibid*., pp. 216 *sqq*., 229 *sqq*.

a philosopher after the fashion of his time, and, after his conversion, some time between 353 and 357, to Christianity, a theologian. Or rather, he had always been theologically inclined, and his conversion brought him new material and a new point of view. Therefore we have also from his pen a commentary on Cicero's *de inuentione* (see p. 165),[131] a work *de definitionibus*, falsely ascribed to Boethius,[132] and mentions survive of a number of other works, translated from the Greek, with philosophical content. There are also commentaries on the Epistles to the Philippians, Galatians and Ephesians, in which it is noteworthy that he contents himself with explaining and does not allegorize at every turn, as was then the fashion, and theological tractates on the Arian controversy,[133] to say nothing of an array of pieces in prose and verse doubtfully or falsely ascribed to him.

Deserving of separate mention is a treatise which may be called the first Latin dictionary to survive almost complete, the *De compendiosa doctrine* of NONIVS MARCELLVS, an unknown man of unknown date, but probably living about the beginning of the fourth century.[134] His work falls into twenty books or chapters, whereof the sixteenth is missing; it dealt with names of shoes. The first twelve treat of the meanings, inflexions, genders and so forth of words; the rest group them into classes (XIII, names for different kinds of ships, XIV, those of clothing, and so on). Nonius was a fool; but he was industrious, and excerpted for his lexicon a number of annotated editions, works on grammar and so forth, from which he compiled a considerable mass of quotations from books and authors now lost, including several of the great republicans. This only makes him valuable.[135]

It was an age of compilers and epitomizers in which Nonius lived; there have come down to us many works of men not unlearned but without originality. In the field of philology, these include AELIVS DONATVS, who was a contemporary of

[131] Published in Halm, *Rhetores Latini minores*, Leipzig, 1863, p. 155 *sqq*.

[132] The only critical edition is in Stangl, *Tulliana et Mario-Victoriana* (Programm d. K. Luitpold-Gymnasiums, Munich, 1888), pp. 12–48.

[133] See Schanz, *ibid.*, p. 156 *sqq*.

[134] It may be, though there is nothing to prove it, that this is the Nonius Marcellus Herculius who is mentioned in an inscription of the year 324, *C.I.L.*, viii, 4878 = Dessau 2943.

[135] The best edition is that of W. M. Lindsay, Teubner, 1903; for some account of the vast amount of writing which has gone to tracing Nonius' learning to its sources, see Schanz, iv, p. 145 *sq*.

Victorinus,[136] and left such a reputation for his learning that a *donet* means, in medieval English, a Latin grammar. Besides two grammars, a larger and a smaller, this man wrote commentaries on Terence and Vergil. The former survives in a damaged shape, the notes on the *Heautontimorumenos* being lost and the rest represented by extracts often stupidly bad; the latter is generally supposed (but see below) to be lost except for the Life of Vergil and the introduction to the *Eclogues*.[137] After him come a number of grammarians, CHARISIVS,[138] DIOMEDES,[139] and others, who are to be found, so far as they survive, in Keil's *Grammatici Latini*, down to the famous PRISCIAN [140] More interesting than any of them, however, is SERVIVS (the rest of his name is uncertain). This scholar is introduced by Macrobius as one of the speakers in his *Saturnalia*, and a series of learned remarks concerning Vergil are put into his mouth. That he commented on the poet is beyond doubt; that he is the author of the commentary which goes under his name (though some MSS. call him Sergius) is hardly a view which any one would now defend. Nevertheless, the commentary itself is of high value, not only for the interpretation of the poems but for the vast amount of miscellaneous information which it contains; that some of it goes back to Servius himself is, of course, likely enough. We have it in two forms, whereof the longer is generally known as Daniel's Servius, from the scholar, Pierre Daniel, who in 1600 published it for the first time, or simply *Seruius auctus*. It is a better work than the shorter, especially in that it is far more learned and fuller of interesting antiquarian material; that it is not by the same hand as the shorter notes is clear from the fact that the latter often oppose a view which the former adopts. Whether or not the attractive suggestion of Professor Rand is

[136] Jerome says, *an. Abr.* 2370 = A.D. 354: Victorinus rhetor et Donatus grammaticus praeceptor meus Romae insignes habentur.

[137] The grammars are in Keil, vol. iv, pp. 355 *sqq.*, 367 *sqq.*; the commentary on Terence is published in the Teubner series, edited by P. Wessner, besides sundry earlier editions; the scholia in the codex Bembinus of Terence, which contain Donatian material, have recently been edited by J. F. Mountford, London, Hodder and Stoughton, 1934. For the *Life* of Vergil, to which the introduction to the *Eclogues* is attached, see Chap. ix, n. 6. Its value is due to its lack of originality; all that is material in it goes back to Suetonius.

[138] FLAVIVS SOSIPATER CHARISIVS; in Keil, vol. i. See p. 533.

[139] The rest of his name is unknown; his work is published after Charisius in Keil.

[140] End of the fifth and beginning of the sixth century; in full, PRISCIANVS CAESARIENSIS (*i.e.*, of Caesarea in Mauretania); see Keil, vols. ii and iii, and Schanz-Hosius-Krüger, iv, pp. 221–38.

right,[141] that Daniel's Servius represents large extracts from the lost commentary of Donatus, we may be certain that it contains good Roman learning, such as Donatus would know and have the scholarship to value and excerpt. The shorter and poorer notes may in like manner be extracts from the commentary, intended rather for learners than the learned, of the real Servius.

There are other commentaries on Vergil extant. The best known is that of TIBERIVS CLAVDIVS DONATVS, formerly confused with Aelius Donatus, with whom he has nothing to do. His work is intended to enable his son, apparently a schoolboy, to appreciate the rhetorical beauties of Vergil; hence it discusses punctuation often and continually and lengthily paraphrases the text, but has nothing to say of grammatical difficulties, historical allusions, &c. Its best edition is that of H. Georgi, Teubner, 1905–6 (2 vols.).

Still dealing with Vergil are several short commentaries. (1) The so-called Probus on the *Bucolics* and *Georgics*, cf. p. 450. (2) The badly damaged Veronese scholia, on all three poems, containing, where they can be made out, very good material. (3) IVNII FILARGIRII (*i.e.*, PHILARGYRII) *grammatici explanatio in Bucolica Vergilii*. We know nothing about this man, nor about several other writers whose notes are found along with his in a collection, with a somewhat bewildering MS. tradition, seemingly due to Adamnanus, abbot of Iona. (4) The Berne scholia, which belong to the same group as (3). They are published by Hagen in Supplement IV (1861–7) of Fleckeisen's *Jahrbuch*. (5) *Anonymi breuis expositio Vergilii Georgicorum*. All these, save (4), are in the *Appendix Seruiana* which forms the last volume of Thilo-Hagen (see note 141); for some account of them and their interrelations (on which the last word has by no means been said), see Schanz-Hosius, ii, pp. 107–10.

Several grammatical works are ascribed by tradition or conjecture to Servius, with more or less cogency; see Schanz, vol. iv, pp. 175–7. His date can be roughly determined as follows. He is represented in Macrobius as a young man, and the supposed date of the *Saturnalia* must be before 384, the year of the death of Symmachus (p. 524), who takes part in it. Therefore, Servius, at some date earlier than this, was, at most, in his twenties. Hence his birth would fall about the middle of the fourth century.[142]

Horace also had his commentators, and the collections of scholia on him which we have are associated with respectable names. One miscellaneous mass, published, among others, by O. Keller, Teubner, two volumes, 1902 and 1904, is usually referred to as pseudo-Acro. HELENIVS ACRO probably lived after Gellius, who never cites him, and

[141] *Class. Quart.*, vol. x (1916), pp. 158–64. A new edition of Servius, planned by Rand to supersede that of Thilo and Hagen (3 vols., Leipzig, 1887 and following years), is now being published by the Lancaster Press (Lancaster, Pa., U.S.A.) for the American Philological Association.

[142] Macrob., *Sat.*, vii, 11, 2.

before Porphyrio, who does; it would therefore seem that his date is about the late second or early third century. Sundry mentions of him indicate that he wrote commentaries on Terence, Persius and Horace, but all these are lost, and the scholia we have are by many hands; the name Acro is attached to them in a MS. of the early thirteenth century (Keller, vol. i, p. vi), but apparently not before that.

POMPONIVS PORPHYRIO is cited by Charisius (p. 455), who at that point (p. 220, 27) is drawing upon Iulius Romanus (p. 452). We gather, therefore, that he lived not very late in the third century. There is a collection of Horatian scholia bearing his name, but a glance at the preface of a good edition (there is one by W. Meyer, Teubner, 1874), or better, at the notes themselves, shows very plainly that we have not what the original commentator wrote, but a damaged and deformed series of excerpts. Porphyrio himself would appear to have been a respectable, if not very profound, expositor, a man of some learning.

There exist further scholia on Horace, whereof a number have been collected and published by H. J. Botschuyver, Amsterdam, Bottenburg, 1935. They are of interest chiefly as illustrating the degeneracy of ancient learning, even of the modest sort required to explain a school author, in its passage through the Middle Ages.

We now discuss three writers of some interest in themselves and very considerable importance for the material they preserve. The first is unfortunately lost, but later writers quote him often, thus in their turn saving not a little that is of value. CORNELIVS LABEO may have lived in the time of Arnobius or not much earlier, that is to say (cf. p. 480) at the end of the third or the beginning of the fourth century [143]; but the evidence is of the most doubtful kind. Certain it is, however, that he was interested in Roman religion as a subject for historical study and likewise, it would appear, in its philosophical justification. He wrote, so far as we know, at least three and at most five works. The treatise *de oraculo Apollinis Clarii* manifestly philosophized,[144] for it would seem to have identified Apollo, Dionysos and Yahweh with each other and with the Sun. The *Fasti* was no doubt a work on the Roman calendar and its festivals, and no doubt also it owed much to Verrius Flaccus.[145] That he wrote something

[143] The evidence, such as it is, is this. Arnobius, ii, 15, takes objection to the views of certain *noui* concerning the immortality of the soul. The views in question appear to have been held by Labeo; therefore Labeo may have been, when he wrote, a recent author.

[144] Macrob., *ibid.*, i, 18, 21: huius oraculi . . . interpretationem qua Liber patet et sol Ἰαὼ significatur exsecutus est Cornelius Labeo in libro cui titulus est de oraculo Apollinis Clarii. The oracle itself is of a late type, and declares Hades, Zeus, the Sun and Yahweh to be the same god at different seasons.

[145] Macrob., *sat.*, i, 16, 29.

about the Penates is certain, but that it was a separate treatise is not so sure.[146] The late and totally unreliable Fulgentius says he composed fifteen books *de disciplina Etrusca*, and this may happen to be true. That he had something to say about Etruscan belief and ritual is highly likely.[147] Finally, there was a treatise of which we have tantalizing glimpses in quotations ; it was called *de dis animalibus*, consisted of more than one book, and described the rites by which a human soul might become a god. As the Penates were assigned by him to the category of these ' soul-gods ' (*di animales*), this may be the work referred to above in which he treated of them.[148] By the frequency with which the Christians quote and controvert him, it is not an unreasonable supposition that he definitely set out to check their growing influence and oppose another theology to theirs. That we have only some thirty fragments of him, including one or two whose authenticity is anything but undoubted,[149] is much to be deplored, for he obviously was a learned and interesting writer.

A man of misty personality and very uncertain date is MARTIANVS CAPELLA, once widely studied, now remembered chiefly for a single passage. His book reads almost like a product of the Middle Ages, for it is an allegory of the Seven Liberal Arts. Mercury is to marry Learning (*Philologia*), hence the title of the work, *de nuptiis Philologiae* [150] ; Iuppiter makes great preparations for the festival, and the Liberal Arts attend with the other deities, each of them making a long speech explaining her scope. It is the dullest and poorest stuff imaginable, but for a long time was used as a handbook of the subjects. In the first book, however, we come upon a sudden gleam of real and out-of-the-way learning. The invitations from Iuppiter are sent to all parts of the heavens, and these number sixteen, the Etruscan division

[146] *Ibid.*, iii, 4, 6 : Nigidius enim de dis libro nono decimo requirit . . . . Cornelius quoque Labeo de dis Penatibus eadem existimat. This might mean equally well ' in his treatise entitled *de dis Penatibus* ' or simply ' when discussing the Penates '. From the care taken in the rest of the passage to indicate books as being such, *e.g.*, 13, addit Hyginus in libro quem de dis Penatibus scripsit, the latter interpretation seems more likely.

[147] Fulgentius, *expos. sermon. ant.*, 4, p. 112 Helm (in the Teubner series). This Fulgentius wrote perhaps towards the end of the fifth century, see Schanz-Hosius-Krüger, iv, 2, p. 205–6.

[148] Servius on *Aen.*, iii, 168.

[149] Collection and discussion in J. Muelleneisen, *de Cornelii Labeonis fragmentis, studiis, adsectatoribus*, Marburg, 1889 ; see further Schanz-Hosius-Krüger, iii, p. 182.

[150] So the one MS. subscription ; *d. n. Mercurii et Philologiae* Fulgentius, *d. n. Philologiae et Mercurii* many moderns, with no authority.

for sundry sacral purposes. Moreover, the division of the gods among these regions agrees pretty well with that on one of the few intelligible Etruscan monuments, the famous bronze model of a liver from Piacenza.[151] Thus we seem to have in him a genuine bit of Etruscan lore, perhaps from Labeo.

Thirdly, we may mention AMBROSIVS THEODOSIVS MACROBIVS, a miscellaneous writer of date around the year 400.[152] Besides a grammatical treatise on the Greek and Latin verb whereof extracts survive,[153] he wrote two works of some importance, both of which have come down to us. The shorter is the commentary on Scipio's dream (see p. 186), the longer is the *Saturnalia*, in seven books, which we have nearly complete. This interesting compilation, whether or not it is modelled directly upon the *Deipnosophistai* of Athenaios,[154] is of the same kind as that famous production of late Greek erudition. Several men of rank and learning meet at a dinner, during the Saturnalia (Dec. 17–23 at that date) [155]; there they fall to discussing the festival itself, and pass from that to numerous matters of history, philology (including Vergilian criticism) and antiquities. Thus we have preserved to us a great deal of scholarly material, for Macrobius regularly cites his authors, though we are not to imagine that he had read them all for himself, it being the fashion of that age (as indeed it still is, in semi-learned works) to quote, not from the later book the writer has actually before him, but from the earlier ones which that in its turn quotes. Incidentally, he throws a welcome light on educated society in his own day.

This is not a treatise on Roman law; but brief mention must here be made of the legal writers, who were numerous and important. Most of their writings are known to us only by refer-

[151] On this see C. Thulin, *Die Götter des Martianus Capella und der Bronzeleber von Piacenza*, Giessen, Töpelmann, 1906. Martianus' date seems to be after the capture of Rome by Alaric, for he speaks of her greatness as past, vi, 637, but before the fall of Carthage to Geiseric, for he was a proconsul, ix, 999, and there were none in Carthage after that time. Hence he wrote between 410 and 439. . His name is uncertain, but the MSS. call him Martianus Min(n)eus Felix Capella. See p. 533.

[152] As his MSS. call him *uir clarissimus et illustris*, a title belonging only to men of very high rank, it is likely that he is that Macrobius who was praefectus praetorio Hispaniarum in 399, proconsul Africae in 410 and praepositus sacri cubiculi in 422, according to sundry passages of the Codex Theodosianus.

[153] They are in Keil, vol. v, p. 599 *sqq.*; the title was *de differentiis et societatibus Graeci Latinique uerbi*.

[154] Wissowa denies, Kaibel asserts that it is, see Schanz-Hosius-Krüger, iv, p. 195. For Athenaios, see Rose, *H.G.L.*, p. 404 *sq.*

[155] Macrob., *sat.*, i, 10, 2–3.

ences and citations, for naturally they were superseded by later legislation, especially when the great collections made by order of Justinian became the only standard works on the subject. However, both Justinian's lawyers and the earlier writers whom they consulted in making the *Digest* are full of references to the opinions and writings of famous jurisconsults, at least from about the time of Cicero on. Hence we know that Q. MVCIVS SCAEVOLA (born about 614/140, killed 672/82; cf. p. 107) wrote eighteen books on the civil law and a book of ὅροι, or legal definitions, and considerable fragments of the former work are preserved.[156] We have also some knowledge of his pupil, SEXTVS PAPIRIVS, who collected the old laws alleged to date from the kings,[157] and we have a mass of references to the greatest of the lawyers whom he trained, SERVIVS SVLPICIVS RVFVS (649/105–711/43).[158] Besides a number of lesser names, we can give some account of PVBLIVS ALFENVS VARVS, a pupil of Sulpicius, a man of low birth, a native probably of Cremona, who by sheer force of his learning rose to be *consul suffectus* in 715/39 and left behind him a Digest of the law of that day.[159] His fellow-pupil AVLVS OFILIVS was a friend of Cicero and Caesar and appears to have outlived them both; his writings were extensive and we have several quotations, if not of his exact words, at least of his opinions.[160] Another lawyer of Cicero's acquaintance was GAIVS TREBATIVS TESTA, whose exact dates are unknown, but he was with Caesar in Gaul in and after 700/54.[161]

All these men are of the Republic; with the Empire we come to a series of great names. MARCVS ANTISTIVS LABEO was one of the foremost lawyers of the time of Augustus, and there still remain some 200 Teubner pages of citations and discussions of his views, which were expressed in a long series of writings, including another Digest.[162] Students of Roman religion would wel-

[156] Bremer, i, pp. 48–104, see Bibliography.

[157] *Ibid.*, pp. 132–8; cf. p. 29.

[158] *Ibid.*, pp. 139–242.

[159] *Ibid.*, pp. 280–330. This is traditionally the Alfenus whom Horace, *sat.*, i, 3, 130, mentions and calls a shoemaker, which need mean no more than that he had invested his money in a shoemaking establishment, probably buying slaves to do the actual making.

[160] *Ibid.*, pp. 330–57.

[161] *Ibid.*, pp. 376–424.

[162] *Ibid.*, ii, pp. 9–261. The coming of the Empire meant three great changes in legislation and its enforcement and interpretation. (1) The Senate, hitherto an executive body (in effect; in theory it was merely consultative) became also legislative. (2) The rescripts and edicts of the Emperor, *i.e.*, his written answers to questions in dispute which were submitted to him, whether immediately, by way of appeal, or simply by

come the recovery of some of the works of C. ATEIVS CAPITO, who was employed by Augustus to draw up the regulations for his secular games in 737/17, for his specialty seems to have been the sacral law, *ius pontificium*, although he is cited on other matters as well.[163] MASVRIVS SABINVS was perhaps a native of Verona—at least, there is evidence of the existence there of a man bearing that somewhat unusual name[164]—attained to equestrian rank in middle life and seems to have been the first member of that order to be given the right to respond *ex auctoritate principis* (see note 162). This was under Tiberius; Masurius survived him and lived on into the reign of Nero, leaving behind him a great name not only as a lawyer but as a man of general culture and learning.[165] After him the school of the Sabinians was named; for, as early as Labeo and Capito, jurisconsults had become divided into two factions, some following one of these authorities and some the other; the differences in principle are hard to see, though we are informed of particular points at issue between them. Curiously enough, the two schools were not called after the men from whom the division began. The Sabinians were also known as Cassians, after C. CASSIVS LONGINVS, who came of a legal family, being the grandson, on his mother's side, of Q. Aelius Tubero (cf. p. 203) and, through her also, the great-grandson of Servius Sulpicius Rufus. Being relegated by Nero for making too much of the memory of his ancestor, Cassius the conspirator against Caesar, he was recalled by Vespasian and died in old age.[166] The other school got the name of Proculans, from

magistrates and others in need of advice, and his published notices of the principles on which the law was to be administered, obtained the force of law. Theoretically, this could be considered as simply an extension of the pretorian edict, see below. (3) Whereas *responsa prudentium*, *i.e.*, replies to questions on matters of law given by those best qualified to do so, had always been taken into account, it was now possible for a jurisconsult of good standing to be given permission *respondere ex auctoritate principis*, thus giving his responses something like the legal force of a pronouncement from the bench in our courts, while the earlier ones had been rather of the nature of counsel's opinion.

[163] *Ibid.*, pp. 261–87.

[164] *C.I.L.*, v, 3924 = Dessau, 6704. See Bremer, ii, pp. 313–582.

[165] So at least Athenaios represents him, *Dipnosoph.*, I c, 623 e, if this is to be taken seriously as an account of our Masurius; cf. Bremer, *ibid.*, p. 315.

[166] Bremer, ii, 2, pp. 9–99. The most authentic account of the matter is in Tacitus, *ann.*, xvi, 7, 1–9, 1. The recall is mentioned by Pomponius in the *Digest*, i, 2, 2, 52, a valuable section of that great compilation, since it contains a history of Roman jurisprudence, brief but well informed, at least for Imperial times. Testimonies to his vast knowledge and skill are plentiful, see Schanz-Hosius, ii, p. 765.

PROCVLVS (the rest of his name is uncertain), a man of whom very little is known, except that he lived under the later Julio-Claudians; fairly numerous quotations from him support the conclusion which would be naturally drawn from his position as head of the school that he was reckoned an outstanding authority.[167] His predecessor was M. COCCEIVS NERVA, grandfather of the Emperor of that name, who was a personal friend of Tiberius [168] and ended his days in 33, out of sheer despair at the state of the commonwealth. Later members of this school were PEGASVS, mentioned by Juvenal as *praefectus urbi* in Vespasian's days,[169] IVVENTIVS CELSVS and his son of the same name, whereof the latter is the better known and was obviously a great lawyer and conscious of his own powers,[170] and L. NERATIVS PRISCVS, whom Trajan is said to have had thoughts of nominating to succeed himself [171]; if this is true, it is to the credit of Hadrian that he continued to use Priscus' services and showed no jealousy.[172] To the Cassians, on the other hand, belonged CN. ARVLENVS CAELIVS SABINVS, whose activities seem to have been chiefly under Vespasian [173]; TITIVS ARISTO, who appears to have been a pupil of Longinus and was certainly a friend of the younger Pliny and often mentioned by him [174]; perhaps VRSEIVS FEROX, a man of rather uncertain date, known to us because Salvius Iulianus (see below) wrote a commentary on his works which is often cited in the *Digest* [175]; and the eccentric

[167] Bremer, ii, 2, pp. 99–170.

[168] *Ibid.*, ii, 1, pp. 300–11. The account of his death is in Tac., *ann.*, vi, 26, 1–3.

[169] Juvenal, iv, 77–81; Bremer, ii, 2, p. 541, emends a doubtful passage of the *Digest* to bring in a mention of the *ius Pegasianum* which the scholiast on Juvenal, *loc. cit.*, says was called after him. See Schanz-Hosius, ii, p. 761.

[170] See Bremer, ii, 2, pp. 494–504. His full name was P. Iuventius Celsus Titus Aufidius Hoenius Severianus. His public life was exciting and eventful, including a conspiracy against Domitian, from which he escaped with his fortunes intact by befooling the Emperor with promises which he never fulfilled, see Cassius Dio, lxvi, 13, 3–4. His most celebrated response, frag., 1, Bremer, is to a certain Domitius Labeo and begins: aut non intellego quid sit de quo me consulas aut ualide stulta est consultatio tua (*Dig.*, xxviii, 1, 27).

[171] Bremer, *ibid.*, pp. 286–359. For the alleged relations between him and Trajan, see *Hist. Aug.*, i, 4, 8.

[172] *Hist. Aug.*, i, 18, 1: cum iudicaret (Hadrianus), in consilio habuit non amicos suos aut comites solum sed iuris consultos et praecique Iuuentium Celsum, Saluium Iulianum, Neratium Priscum aliosque, quos tamen senatus omnis probasset.

[173] Bremer, ii, 2, pp. 249–56.

[174] *Ibid.*, pp. 359–94.

[175] *Ibid.*, pp. 170–85.

IAVOLENVS PRISCVS, whose oddities do not seem to have affected his knowledge of law nor his utility in a number of provincial posts, including the governorship of Britain.[176]

These men take us down to the end of Trajan's principate; under Hadrian, a new order of things began, in law as in much else. It had been customary for many centuries for a praetor, since he had to deal with cases involving foreigners who might not use the forms of native Roman law, to promulgate by public notice (*edictum*) the principles on which he meant to decide cases. It was usual and, after the Lex Cornelia of 687/67, obligatory for him to adhere to these principles throughout his term of office; hence the notice was called his 'standing edict', *edictum perpetuum*. It was also very natural that his successor should take it over, with such changes in detail as might suggest themselves. This and similar edicts by other magistrates in time grew into a considerable body of usage and precedent, known collectively as *ius honorarium*, or magistrates' law. Hadrian put a stop to its further growth by ordering L. OCTAVIVS CORNELIVS SALVIVS IVLIANVS AEMILIANVS to edit it, together with the edict of the aediles, once and for all.[177] Iulianus was, apart from this task and his commentary on Urseius Ferox (see above) a man of much literary activity, and a number of works by him are mentioned in the *Digest*. Contemporary with him was POMPONIVS (we know no more of his name), who, besides a number of legal treatises lost to us save for the references in Justinian's compilation, wrote an *enchiridion* or handbook of the subject, apparently in two forms, one in a single volume, the other in two. From the former comes the long extract in *Digest*, i, 2, 2 (cf. note 166) to which reference has already been made as throwing light on the history of the subject. It is characteristic that none of these men seems to have had very much acquaintance with the old laws of the Republic; they were lawyers, not historians of law, in the first instance.[178] Acquainted with Iulianus, but apparently somewhat younger, was L. VOLVSIVS MAECIANVS, the tutor in law of the future Emperor Marcus Aurelius. From his pen we have one small pamphlet, not dealing with law but with weights and

[176] *Ibid.*, pp. 394–494. The chief evidence of his eccentricity is Pliny, *epp.*, vi, 15. It seems to have consisted mostly in rather untimely outspokenness; Pliny says that he is *dubiae sanitatis*, but still goes about in society (interest tamen officiis).

[177] See Schanz-Hosius-Krüger, iii, pp. 186–90. The portentous length of this man's name (usually shortened to Salvius Iulianus) is characteristic of the age. Cf. n. 170.

[178] See Schanz-Hosius-Krüger, iii, pp. 190–1.

measures [179]; his legal treatises are known from numerous citations, and his public career lasted through the principates of Antoninus Pius and of his own pupil.

The one man of this age from whom we have a considerable work was for long so obscure and so little quoted that we do not even know his name, but are obliged to call him GAIVS, since that alone has come down to us; it is much as if we were reduced to referring to Lord Verulam as Francis. In a very battered but still intelligible form there is preserved this writer's *Institutiones*, or elementary text-book of law, an admirably written manual, well-informed and interesting, which much later served as a basis and model for the famous *Institutes* of Justinian.[180] It is clear from his own references and allusions that he lived under the first two Antonines and that he was interested in and had written concerning provincial law; all beyond this is conjecture.

Now begins the series of the greatest Latin jurists. The first name is that of Q. CERVIDIVS SCAEVOLA, one of Marcus Aurelius' advisers, and author, among other works, of a *Digest* in forty books, a great collection of case-law, followed by a shorter treatise, *Responsa*, in six, probably written in the time of Septimius Severus (193–211).[181] Under Septimius also, with whom he is said to have been connected by marriage, lived that jurisconsult who, by common consent, was the greatest of all, AEMILIVS PAPINIANVS (PAPINIAN), so many fragments of whose work, the *Quaestiones et Responsa*, have been preserved by the admiration of later lawyers that moderns are able to appreciate his merits.[182] He became, to later generations, a sort of incarnation of law, as Cicero was of eloquence, and the fact that he fell a victim to the cruelty of Caracallus has been remoulded into a martyrdom; he is credited with having preferred death to justifying the crime of Caracallus in murdering his brother Geta.[183] After him follow

[179] Schanz-Hosius-Krüger, iii, pp. 191–2; the little work (*assis distributio*) has been several times published, among others by F. Hultsch, in *Scriptores metrologici* (Teubner, 1866), ii, p. 61 *sqq*.

[180] It is mostly preserved in a palimpsest in the library at Verona. The recent discovery (see F. de Zulueta in *Journ. Rom. Stud.*, xxiv, 1934, pp. 168–86) of considerable new fragments has put all editions out of date (including that of Poste and Whittuck, with translation and commentary, Oxford, Clar. Press, 1904), save the latest (seventh) impression of B. Kuebler's, Teubner, 1935. In restoring illegible passages, the *Institutes* of Justinian are the chief help. See p. 468.

[181] See Schanz-Hosius-Krüger, iii, pp. 198–201.

[182] *Ibid*., pp. 201–3, especially p. 202, which cites a few expressions of good modern juristic opinion concerning Papinian.

[183] He was iuris asylum et doctrinae legalis thesaurus, *Hist. Aug*., x, 21, 8; xiii, 8, 1 *sqq*., gives an account of his death, criticizing the stories

three writers of high rank in the science, though without his supreme ability, DOMITIVS VLPIANVS (ULPIAN), IVLIVS PAVLVS and HERENNIVS MODESTINVS, all extremely learned and of vast industry. With these, and some minor authors of about their time, the great days of Roman jurisprudence pass; the latest of them is of the age of Alexander Severus (222–235).[184] The rest of the history of the subject is little but a list of collections and epitomes, often showing diligence and intelligence, but not juristic talent of high order.[185]

The Romans were by tradition and of necessity land-surveyors. From ancient times there had existed in their country the institution known as the *templum*, which, at any rate as applied to land, signified this. The operator, wishing to parcel off a piece of ground, large or small, for practical uses or purely sacral purposes, *i.e.*, to divide it among farmers, found a city or lay out a camp on it, trace out regions within which he proposed to look for omens, or finally to build on it what we call a temple and Romans an *aedes sacra* or consecrated room, began by choosing a central point at which to stand. From that he traced two real or imaginary lines at right angles to each other, the *cardo* and *decumanus*; one of these ran north and south, the other east and west, though which should run in which direction was a controversial point. To obtain a rectangle, which seems, though the matter is not certain, to have been the normal shape of the *templum*, it was necessary only to draw lines at right angles to these two, from their extremities. Having thus obtained a square or oblong with a cross inscribed in it, the operator might subdivide as often as he chose, by repeating the process in each of the smaller figures into which the larger one fell. Thus a given territory could be split up into 4, 16, 64, &c., smaller units with tolerable accuracy, and without requiring either mathematical knowledge or any more complicated apparatus than a

of his refusal to justify the murder of Geta, which even this author finds mere fables, containing impossibilities of detail. According to him, the real excuse for putting him to death was that he allegedly had favoured Geta. That he was amicissimum imperatori Seuero, ut aliqui loquuntur adfinem etiam per secundam uxorem, is stated *ibid.*, 2.

[184] See Schanz-Hosius-Krüger, ii, pp. 203–13, for the long list of the known writings of these three, also the names of the lesser men.

[185] There were two collections of *constitutiones principum*, *i.e.*, decisions of various emperors on points laid before them. The earlier, which came down to about 295, was the *codex Gregorianus*; the later, including documents of the period 291–365, the *codex Hermogenianus*. Both were presumably named after their compilers, and obviously were useful works of reference; but the abilities needed to make them were simply those of a good law-reporter.

few stakes and cords.[186] A natural development of this was that in time some considerable body of practical experience and knowledge, a very little very elementary plane geometry, some acquaintance with the laws governing land-holding, and finally a simple instrument, the *groma*,[187] for laying out the necessary lines, were added to the surveyor's technical equipment, and the matter became one of secular rather than religious importance. We have a collection, dating as it stands from the fifth century and bristling with corruptions, interpolations and changes of all sorts, of technical writers, known either as *agrimensores*, from their function, or *gromatici*, from their instrument. Besides the scraps of Frontinus already mentioned (p. 435), they consist of the following treatises.[188] HYGINVS, of whom we know only that he cannot be either the librarian or the author of the *Genealogiae* or the *Astronomica* (p. 446). He deals with boundaries (*de limitibus*), with the status of holdings (*de condicionibus agrorum*) and with the disputes which arise (*de generibus controuersiarum*). He is probably not the author of another little work, *de limitibus constituendis* or *constitutio limitum*. Nor did he write the treatise on camps (*de munitionibus castrorum*) which is commonly, and for no reason, attributed to him.[189] BALBVS lived under a ' very great Emperor ' who won a victory in Dacia; it is perhaps a little more likely that this was Trajan, who did conquer Dacia, than Domitian, whose campaigns there were only official successes. SICVLVS FLACCVS also wrote *de condicionibus agrorum*, and lived some time after Domitian. M. IVNIVS NIPSVS is of the second century. Much later than these are AGENNIVS VRBICVS and INNOCENTIVS, of whose writings something survives, alongside of and blended with much late interpolation. The latter wrote an odd and, in its present form, hardly intelligible little treatise on conventional uses of letters on maps to indicate buildings of different types.

In conclusion, there are three works of some interest. The

[186] The origin (alleged to be Etruscan), age and much else concerning the *templum* are highly controversial matters, which need not be discussed here; the text gives known facts only.

[187] This apparently is nothing but Greek γνώμων badly corrupted on Italian lips.

[188] The standard edition of these is still that of Blume, Lachmann and Rudorff, *Die Schriften der römischen Feldmesser* (2 vols., the former containing the texts, Berlin, 1848 and 1852). C. Thulin began a new edition in 1913 (Teubner), but so far only one part of it has appeared.

[189] This is published separately, in the Teubner series, edited by W. Gemoll, 1879; also by A. v. Domaszewski, Leipzig, 1887, with translation and notes in German. It was probably written in the third century.

first of them is the treatise of CENSORINVS, addressed, by way of a birthday gift, to a rich acquaintance, Q. Caerellius, in 238. Entitling his book *de die natali*, he includes in it some interesting information, often from good sources, on various topics more or less connected with the occasion, such as the Genius and the sacrifice made to him on birthdays; embryology and birth, and so to the significance of numbers, climacteric years, astrology, and other matters bearing on man's life; from that he passes to time in general, where he preserves some very interesting information on chronology, the *saeculum*[190] and so forth. The end of his work is lost, our MS. tradition going on to another book of miscellaneous information which has lost its beginning. Clearly the archetype of our copies had lost some pages in the middle. This nameless work is commonly called the *fragmentum Censorini*; its authorship is unknown and the only guide to its date is that that part of it which deals with metre cites no poet later than Lucan.

Mention has already been made of FLAVIVS VEGETIVS RENATVS. Besides the work on veterinary medicine which is supposedly his (p. 427), he compiled a handbook of tactics, *de re militari*. The first book, on the training of recruits, was issued separately and addressed to the then reigning Emperor; his effort was favourably received and he was encouraged to go on, which he did, composing three more books on various branches of the military art. He calls Gratian *diuus*, and therefore wrote after that emperor's death in 383; Flavius Eutropius, in 450, made a critical recension of his work, traces of which are to be seen in a note at the end of some MSS.[191]; therefore Vegetius finished his treatise before that year, probably some considerable time before. Which emperor he addresses, however, is a disputed point. His knowledge is throughout theoretical and second-hand, for he was never himself a soldier and frankly acknowledges that he has merely arranged the material from older writers, from Cato onwards.

190 Properly, the time elapsing between a given day and the death of the longest-lived person born on that day; its length was variously calculated and it was an important unit, especially in Etruria. For Censorinus, see further Schanz-Hosius-Krüger, pp. 219–24. The first critical edition is that of O. Jahn, Berlin, 1845; he has since then been re-edited by F. Hultsch (Teubner, 1867) and J. Cholodniak (Petersburg, 1889).

191 The note, technically called a *subscriptio*, runs: Fl. Eutropius emendaui sine exemplari Constantinopolim (*sic*), consul. Valentiniano Augusto vii et Auieno (*i.e.*, 450). This, as often happens, has been copied into later MSS., and its presence forms the distinguishing mark of a whole group of those which we have. The work is edited by C. Lang, Teubner, 1885 (2nd impression). See further. Schanz, iv, pp. 194–7.

We may end this chapter with APICIVS. There was a rich and luxurious man of that name in the time of Tiberius; he was really called M. Gavius, but the name of Apicius, which had belonged to a famous *bon vivant* of some hundred and fifty years earlier, had attached itself to him.[192] We possess a cookery-book, apparently called originally *Caelii Apicius de re coquinaria*, *i.e.*, 'Apicius, or the Art of Cookery; by Caelius.' Who Caelius was there is nothing to tell us; the very late language of the little work would put it far below Tiberius' time even if the mention of dishes named after the Emperors Vitellius and Commodus did not. It is commonly but incorrectly cited as *Apicii de re coquinaria*. Both matter and style are interesting.

[192] See Tacitus, *ann.*, iv, 1, 3; Cassius Dio, lvii, 19, 5; Athenaios, pp. 168 d, 294 f. The real M. Gavius Apicius seems to have written on cookery, cf. Seneca, *dial.*, xii, 10, 8; schol. on Juv., iv, 23; and on erotic matters, *hist. Aug.*, ii, 5, 9, if the MS. text is sound there, a very doubtful matter. There is a good edition of the existing book in the Teubner series, by Giarratano and Vollmer, 1922.

Additional Notes.—1. P. 427, n. 20. I now think the passage slightly corrupt, and that Vegetius meant, 'Pelagonius in recent times, Columella in his day, were respectable stylists.'

2. P. 464, n. 180. Add now the critical edition of M. David in *Studia Gaiana* i (Leiden, Brill, 1948).

CHAPTER XV

CHRISTIANS AND PAGANS

CHRISTIANITY, so far as the West was concerned, had begun as a sect spreading among the lower orders, who for the most part were not Italians and spoke Greek, or some jargon based on Greek, rather than any kind of Latin. Hence, for about two centuries after the visit of St. Paul to the nascent Roman Church, Latin was not that Church's language to any great extent, and all the early documents relating to its activities are Greek. But gradually both the linguistic and the social conditions modified. Christianity began to attract some converts from higher ranks of society, and therefore from the educated users of Latin. At the same time, the number of Latin speakers was increasing, with the completion of the Romanizing of the western provinces, though the local idioms were not extinct; the triumphant progress of Greek was being arrested, and not merely at the frontiers of the official and ruling classes. In Africa, a province in which Latin was the language of culture rather than Greek (for Punic, though resistant, was gradually dying out and no native speech became anything better than a barbarous dialect), a new Latin style was developing, which found itself pressed into the service of Christian apologists. These, by this time, were ceasing to be the boorish, half-educated men whose opposition to cultural interests is so conspicuous in the case, for example, of Tatian. Several of them, while as zealous as any for their religion, sought to clothe its doctrines in choice and eloquent language, and to reinforce the arguments in its favour with such learning as was available in an age rapidly losing all sense of literary and historical criticism and preferring to make acquaintance with the scholarship of the past through the medium of compendia. Hence it is that some are properly included in a book like this, which excludes from its scope all consideration of the history of dogmatics, apologetics and the religious movements of the eventful opening centuries of the present era.

Perhaps the earliest [1] is a slight but very pleasing writer, MINVCIVS FELIX. He was probably an African,[2] certainly had some connexion with that region, but lived, at least for some considerable part of his life, in Rome. The dialogue, *Octavius*, which is all we have of him and all that we can be sure he wrote,[3] recounts the conversion to Christianity of his friend Caecilius, who like himself was a lawyer. Octavius and Minucius had been converted some time before the work begins; they are lifelong friends, and the former comes to visit the latter. A day or two later, they go for a walk on the beach near Ostia, in company with Caecilius, who salutes in passing a statue of Serapis. Octavius deplores this sign of ignorant superstition, and after some indifferent conversation, Caecilius professes himself hurt and distressed by Octavius' adhesion to any system so absurd as Christianity. The three sit down to argue the matter out. Caecilius urges that everything concerning the supernatural is extremely uncertain, philosophers having arrived at no satisfactory conclusion and only Academic skepticism being any fit position for an intelligent man. It is therefore best to adhere to the traditional cults, which have made Rome great. Octavius replies at somewhat greater length, declaring that philosophers do agree regarding some of the most fundamental truths of Christianity, that paganism is demonstrably false, and that the virtuous lives of the Christians (he refutes the usual fables [4] of their immoral rites, which Caecilius had mentioned)

[1] Between his work and that of Tertullian, especially the *Apologeticum*, there is a closer resemblance than can be accounted for by a common source or the use of both of the stock arguments of apologetics. Therefore one copied the other, but which is the original and which the copy has never been determined. See, for recent discussion, Hoppe in *Gnomon*, May, 1934, review of J. Schmidt, *Minucius Felix oder Tertullian?* A. Souter in *Class. Rev.*, l (1936), p. 39 (review of I. I. de Jong, *Apologetiek en Christendom*). The former leaves the matter undecided, the latter, with the reviewer's agreement, makes Tertullian earlier. Cf. n. 5.

[2] *I.e.*, a European living in the province of Africa. Fronto is referred to as *Cirtensis noster*, 9, 6, cf. 31, 2, suggesting that the speaker, Caecilius, is of African domicile or birth; Octavius has to come some distance by sea to visit Minucius, 3, 4, which fits well with his residing in Africa; all three are old friends.

[3] He seems, 36, 2, to be planning a treatise on fate. Jerome, *de uir. ill.*, 58, knows of a work *de fato uel contra mathematicos* which he says is well written (diserti hominis), but not in the style of the *Octavius*.

[4] The chief ones were, (*a*) that the killing and eating of an infant was a central rite of initiation into Christianity, (*b*) that various sexual abominations formed part of the Christian services. The second of these is merely common form in slandering any sect or community which keeps its proceedings private; the first appears to be a malignant distortion

together with their grasp of great and incontrovertible truths shows the superiority of their faith over the other systems. After pondering for a while, Caecilius declares himself convinced, and the three friends part for the night.

A much more important and bulky mass of writings, a stronger character, and at the same time a far less agreeable personality and a style so peculiar and affected as often to be nearly unintelligible, belong to Tertullian (Q. SEPTIMIVS FLORENS TERTVLLIANVS). Of his life something is known. He was born about 160, in Carthage, his father being a centurion. He studied law and rhetoric, went to Rome, probably appeared there as a pleader, was converted at some unknown date to Christianity, and returned to Carthage, in the neighbourhood of 195, where for about a decade he was prominent as a vigorous defender of his new faith.[5] Then, probably at some date between 202 and 207, he left the Catholic communion and betook himself to the fanatical Phrygian sect known as the Montanists, from the name of their founder, Montanus. Despite his bitter tongue and his repeated emphasis on martyrdom as a duty in times of persecution, he seems to have lived to a good old age and died a natural death.[6]

His mind was that of an advocate, and not an advocate of the highest type, but rather an unscrupulous pleader. Of scholarship, second-hand as was usual in his age, he had no small share, and we get a good deal of information, distorted but intelligible, about the various systems which he attacks from his accounts of them. His style is like no other; every device of rhetoric, epigram, assonance, rime, paradox, antithesis, plays on words, but never naturalness, simplicity, nor harmonious beauty of phraseology or thought, is at his command. His attempts at philosophizing are contemptibly bad, and he seems always to be in a rage. Yet his powers of analysis and of seizing upon

of the Eucharist. One of the puzzles of the history of religion is why this same story, with a few alterations in detail, should be told against the Jews at various dates down to the present day, seeing that nothing in their ritual remotely suggests the devouring of human flesh or the swallowing of blood.

[5] Jerome, *de uir. ill.*, 53, sketches his life, but gives no dates; it can but be supposed, from the order in which he names the various writers, that he thought him earlier than Minucius Felix, with whom he deals, *ibid.*, 58; elsewhere (*epp.*, 70, 5; 60, 10; *in Isaiam*, viii, *init.* (vol. iv, p. 330, Vall.) when mentioning several Latin Christian writers together, his order is always Tertullian, Cyprian (if mentioned at all), Minucius. *Id.*, *an. Abr.* 2224 = 228, says Tertullian was very well known (omnium ecclesiarum sermone celebratur) then, whether for his eloquence or his Montanistic leanings we are not told.

[6] He lived usque ad decrepitam aetatem, Jerome, *de uir. ill.*, *loc. cit.*

the salient points of his case to set them in the most effective light indicate that he must have been a formidable opponent at the Bar; while the range of his theological interests was so wide that he is to be credited with a considerable part in forming that rigidly dogmatic system into which Western Christianity hardened.

The surviving works of Tertullian can be dated exactly enough for most purposes by their attitude towards Catholicism and Montanism.[7] Before he left the former for the latter system, he wrote a number of works in defence of Christianity against paganism. The two books *ad nationes* (*i.e.*, *To the Gentiles*, those who do not belong to the spiritual Israel, in other words the pagans) have an additional interest for us because they make use of the lost *Antiquitates* of Varro (p. 223), and thus preserve us a good deal of his learning. The argument is, firstly, that the pagans know nothing of Christianity, judge it with ignorant partiality, and ascribe to its adherents all manner of wickednesses whereof they are perfectly innocent. Secondly, these same wickednesses are commonly to be found among the pagans and their gods. The *Apologeticum*, addressed to the government of his province, provides Tertullian with opportunity to handle a somewhat similar theme from a different point of view. He refutes the allegations of immoral rites; he defends the neglect of the traditional worship and of sacrifices and prayers to the state gods on behalf of the Emperor on the ground that false gods deserve no worship. He then goes on with a powerful rebuttal of the charge that Christians are bad citizens. On the contrary, their strict moral code, sanctioned by the fear of Divine wrath, makes them carefully refrain from the very things which the law most sternly forbids. A third treatise, the *Testimonium animae*, approaches apologetics from yet another point of view. The fundamental doctrines of Christianity, such as the existence of God, are to be found everywhere; they are a part of natural religion. Hence the soul of man is by nature Christian (*naturaliter Christiana*). It is the old Stoic argument of the *consensus gentium* given a new turn, and an ingenious one.

Tertullian also composed during this period a number of works intended for a Christian public. These include the tractate *ad martyras*, addressed to certain Christians who had been

[7] See Schanz-Hosius-Krüger, iii, p. 274 *sqq*. The *ad nat.* alludes (i, 17) to the battle of Lugudunum (Lyons), Feb. 19, 197. The *Apol.*, 35, refers to the detection of partisans of the fallen Pescennius Niger, and therefore to 197 also. The *test. anim.* is a sort of appendix to the *apol.*, see 5 and cf. *apol.*, 17, end. The *apol.* has recently been edited by J. Martin (Bonn, Haustein).

arrested and were awaiting trial and consequent execution, during one of the numerous outbursts of persecution. It is possible that the author is thinking especially of SS. Perpetua and Felicitas, who were put to death in 203.[8] The curious book *de spectaculis* denounces stage shows as heathenish, on account of their origin in religious rites. The *de idololatria* is fanaticism gone mad; Tertullian finds idolatry in such things as the business of a statuary, the occupation of a teacher of literature, the trade in frankincense, and of course astrology. The two books *de cultu feminarum* remind women that, since they are descended from Eve, gay attire does not become them, and informs them that the tendency to decoration was first suggested to them by the fallen angels who made love to the daughters of men.

Another group discusses a series of doctrinal points. The pamphlet *de baptismo*, occasioned by the opinion of an otherwise unknown Gaius that baptism was not really necessary, deals with a number of controversial points, the most notable being the question (decided, of course, in the negative) whether baptism by a heretic is valid.[9] The *de oratione* deals with a number of matters regarding the correct costume, posture and so forth of a person engaged in prayer. The *de paenitentia* shows its author taking a step towards Montanism. That sect denied the possibility of salvation for any one who sinned after baptism; Tertullian here allows him one repentance. In the *de patientia*, he frankly admits that he is praising a virtue for which he himself is not conspicuous. It is specifically Christian and Godlike, and by no means to be confused with the pagan virtue of endurance. The two books *ad uxorem* discuss the question whether a Christian widow should remarry if so inclined; in the first, he gives his decided opinion that she should not, for a variety of reasons, while in the second he stresses the duty of a widow, if she must remarry, choosing a Christian husband. The work concludes with a sketch of a Christian pair.

[8] See Schanz-Hosius-Krüger, iii, p. 283, for various views on this matter. The other writings of this group can be dated with tolerable accuracy; the *de spectaculis* was written in a time of persecution, 27, which fits the year 197, though not that year only; it is earlier than the *de idol.* and *de cult. fem.*, for they both refer to it.

[9] There is a critical edition of the *de bapt.*, *Mnemosyne*, 1931, No. 1, by J. G. P. Borleffs, who has also edited the *de paen.*, *Mnem.*, 1932, p. 254 *sqq.* It is usually considered an early work; the *de orat.*, probably of about the same date. The *de paenit.* refers, 12, to an eruption which can only be that of Vesuvius in 203; the *de pat.* may have been written about the same time. Of the *ad uxorem* hardly more can be said than that it is not Montanistic.

Heresy was always an especial bugbear of Tertullian, and he set out fairly early (about 200)[10] to define it. Like a true lawyer, he laid down a *praescriptio*, otherwise known as an *exceptio*, an objection to be raised which, if sustained, would save the controversialist the trouble of any further inquiry into the merits of his opponent's case. Can the propounder of the new doctrine trace it back to the Apostles? If so, it is Catholic teaching; if not, it is heresy, and there the matter ends. Hence the title of his work, *de praescriptione haereticorum*. The work *aduersus Iudaeos*, despite its title, is of this group. It begins indeed with the usual arguments against the Jews, viz., that their Law has been replaced by the new one to which it looks forward; Jesus is the promised Messiah of the Hebrew prophets. But here the discussion turns sharply off. Marcion had also denied that the prophecies of the Old Testament had been fulfilled; he thus is to some extent on the side of the Jews. The rest of the work is therefore an anti-Marcionite treatise (see below), clumsily joined to the anti-Judaic one; that such careless work is due to Tertullian himself, who constructs his arguments skilfully, is very doubtful.

Having turned Montanist, Tertullian showed, if anything, more zeal than in his Catholic days for the cause of orthodoxy. He may quite possibly have written against the communion he had left; Jerome[11] knows of works lost even in his own day, and certainly if these were anti-Catholic their chances of preservation would not be great. But his strongest attacks, so far as we know, were against two dangerous enemies, the Gnostics and the Marcionites. The series begins with a skirmish against Hermogenes, painter and metaphysician, who accounted for the evil in the world by supposing that God created it out of eternal matter, which in itself is erratic in motion. This work, *aduersus Hermogenem*, must come before the anti-Valentinian treatise, which quotes it, and itself seems to refer to the *de praescriptione*. Whereas Hermogenes has traces in his doctrine of that extraordinary and complicated system known as Gnosticism, Valentinus, who flourished about 150, left behind him an important Gnostic sect, against whose mystery-mongering and intricate theology Tertullian wrote the *aduersus Valentinianos*, which

[10] This date may be roughly assigned to the work, because (*a*) it seems to imply that the persecution of 197 is over, (*b*) it contains teaching inconsistent with Montanism, the promise of the coming of the Holy Ghost being interpreted as referring to Pentecost, not to the activities of prophets contemporary with Tertullian.

[11] *De uir. ill.*, 53.

professedly sets out to make the subject ridiculous and does not go into any deep analysis of the matter; indeed, a large part is merely borrowed from the Greek treatise of St. Eirenaios *Against Heresies*. With the doctrines of Marcion, however,[12] Tertullian dealt more seriously, and we have a long work in five books which attacks them section by section. Precisely when he wrote it is uncertain, and it is not known at what intervals the various books were composed; he may have finished it by about 211. Praxeas was not a Marcionite, but a patripassionist,[13] and, moreover, an enemy of Montanism; hence the book *aduersus Praxeam*, one of the early monuments of the long series of controversies concerning the Trinity, probably owes some of its excellence as a piece of polemic to the personal feeling of its author against his opponent. Perhaps it is in the *de anima*[14] that Tertullian shows how far from a metaphysician he was. The fundamental doctrine for him is that the soul is material, which thesis he proves in the most crassly Epicurean way. The manner in which this is brought into line with Christian eschatology is interesting, however, and the treatise does not lack evidence of his unfailing sharpness of wit and powers of presenting a clever case. It is a kind of sequel, apparently, to a work *de censu animae*, which he had directed against Hermogenes, but which is now lost; it deals only incidentally with the Gnostics and their doctrines. Gnostic again are some of the heretical views opposed in the tract *de carne Christi*, the object of which is to show that the body of Christ was fully human. The work *de carnis resurrectione* is a vigorous defence of the resurrection of the body.

During this period also, he strove with paganism. A soldier having refused to put a garland on his head during a festival,[15]

[12] No full account of Marcion can be given here; there is a short one in Hastings, *Encyclopaedia of Religion and Ethics*, viii, 407–9, which gives references to the standard works on the subject. Marcion declared the God of the Old Testament to be a comparatively inferior being, entrusted with the mean task of creating the material world and given to representing himself as the supreme Deity; he had succeeded in deceiving the Old Testament writers and most of the Apostles, and therefore the only inspired Scriptures were a much-expurgated edition, which Marcion prepared, of the Pauline and Lucan writings.

[13] *I.e.*, he held that the First Person of the Trinity shared in the sufferings of the Second.

[14] Latest ed. by J. H. Wazink, Amsterdam, Meulenhoff, 1947.

[15] The Christians had no objection to flowers, loose or in wreaths, in general, but took exception to the custom of crowning one's self with them, in which they correctly saw a piece of pagan ritual (it is originally a means of magical protection against hostile influences). They were fond of saying (see, *e.g.*, Minucius Felix, 28, 2) that they smelt with their noses, not the tops of their heads.

it became known that he was a Christian and his imprisonment followed. Tertullian was of that zealous faction who held that his action was fully justified by his creed, and accordingly wrote the monograph *de corona militis*. Out of the incident arose a persecution, and during it Tertullian composed his address to the then governor of Africa, *ad Scapulam*,[16] warning him of the supernatural penalties which awaited his action. Following this came a discussion of the casuistic question whether it was allowable to avoid persecution by flight; Tertullian voiced the emphatic opinion that it was not in the work *de fuga in persecutione*, and followed it up by the *Scorpiace* or *Antidote for scorpion stings*, the scorpions in question being those weak brethren who did not regard martyrdom as a positive duty and thought that outward conformity might be allowed. These persons being Gnostics, he had all the more reason for opposing them.

All these works were negative in tone more or less decidedly, for their chief object was to explain what must not be done or thought. A positive doctrine is to be found in the tractate *de uirginibus uelandis*, on the immorality of allowing marriageable girls to go about with their faces uncovered.[17] Both the *de exhortatione castitatis* and the *de monogamia* preach the sinfulness of a second marriage with right Montanist fervour. The *de ieiunio aduersus psychicos* reveals itself as Montanist by its very title, for the followers of that sect claimed to be spiritual (*pneumatici*) and gave the title of *psychicus* ('natural man' in the English version of the Pauline writings) to the more moderate Catholic. Its contents are quite in accord, for the Montanists were very ascetic, and long and elaborate fasts formed part of their regular programme.[18] More respectable than this practice was their high standard of chastity; hence Tertullian's wrath was aroused by a certain Pope, whose name we do not know, but who suggested that adultery, while a grievous sin, was not unpardonable. Tertullian, in the *de pudicitia*, vehemently assails this thesis, and claims for that offence its rightful place with the other two unpardonables, idolatry and murder.[19]

[16] This shows itself later than the *de corona* by an allusion to the event which gave rise to the latter work (*ad Scap*. 4: nam et nunc a praeside legionis . . . uexatur hoc nomen).

[17] To do the Montanists justice, neither they nor the Christians generally were responsible for this piece of prudery, which was one of many pieces of Oriental custom that had made their way westward under the Empire.

[18] This was written after the *de monogamia*, for it refers to it, sect. 1.

[19] To call the Bishop of Rome the Pope, at that date, is a slight anachronism, for the word *papa* was not specialized to that meaning but

Finally, we have to notice one of this writer's most curious, difficult and interesting works, the famous *de pallio*. It may have been written about 210[20]; the occasion of it was that Tertullian had ceased to use the characteristic Roman dress, the toga, and adopted the traditional cloak of Greeks (especially Greek philosophers), the *pallium*, which was then the nearest approach to academic dress; for, as he correctly states, not philosophers only but teachers and various professional men commonly wore it. He justifies his change of attire by a series of arguments which show him the true contemporary and spiritual kinsman of the endlessly ingenious sophists of his epoch.[21]

Of less literary interest is ST. CYPRIAN (CAECILIVS CYPRIANVS), bishop and martyr. He was an African,[22] perhaps a Carthaginian, who was converted when already a mature man and ordained priest, became bishop of Carthage about 249, and at once found himself in the midst of a series of stormy and trying events. The persecution under Decius broke out soon after he was made bishop; he left Carthage and hid himself, maintaining connexion with his see by correspondence. Though some of the more zealous blamed him for this prudence, he seems to have held the

employed in addressing any bishop. But Tertullian indicates that he is addressing an occupant of that see and that its claims were already high by referring to him in his first chapter as pontifex scilicet maximus, quod est episcopus episcoporum. It is usually supposed that it was Callistus; if so, the work, which is certainly one of Tertullian's later writings, is not earlier than 217. See Schanz-Hosius-Krüger, iii, p. 304.

[20] The Empire is governed by a triplex uirtus, 2, and the evil weeds of hostility and treachery have been uprooted, *ibid*. This suggests that the enemies of Septimius Severus are defeated and he has given his two sons a share in the government, a state of things which existed in 209–211.

[21] A number of other works by Tertullian are known to us by title. For a list of them, see Schanz-Hosius-Krüger, iii, pp. 322–6. There exist also a few which are falsely attributed to him, some being much later and none in his peculiar and original style. These include the pamphlet *de execrandis gentium diis*, a not uninteresting little work of unknown authorship, critically edited in *Rheinisches Museum*, 1927, p. 404 *sqq*., by E. Bickel; a short tract *aduersus omnes haereses*, by some contemporary of Tertullian, though not by himself; two works really by Novatian, *de trinitate* and *de cibis Iudaicis*; and some copies of verse on scriptural subjects (Jonah, Sodom, &c.), also one *aduersus Marcionem*.

[22] The main source of information about his life, apart from his own works, is a biography by one Pontius, who claims personal acquaintance with the saint. It has been often published; the standard edition is that in the *Corpus scriptorum ecclesiasticorum Latinorum* (Vienna, various dates), vol. iii, 3, p. xc *sqq*. The bishop is always called Caecilius Cyprianus in the MSS., but says himself (heading of *ep*. 66) that he is *Cyprianus qui et Thascius*, a form of double name not uncommon in late antiquity. He would seem then to have been called Caecilius Cyprianus or Caecilius Thascius, but generally referred to as Cyprianus. See p. 533.

affection of his own flock. Soon after, he was involved in a dispute at Rome between Cornelius, the newly elected occupant of the see, and Novatianus, who may be described as the antipope. Later, between 254 and 257, he was engaged in a controversy with Stephanus, bishop of Rome, concerning the efficacy of heretic baptism, which he denied and Stephanus affirmed. In 257, another persecution broke out, and Cyprian was arrested, banished, and afterwards (Sept. 14, 258) beheaded.

Cyprian was a warm admirer of Tertullian, whom he constantly read and called his teacher[23]; it is therefore not remarkable that his writings are for the most part on very similar subjects.[24] We have from him a series of pamphlets on questions of the day. The little treatise *ad Donatum*, with a not unpleasing, if too florid style, reminding us that Cyprian was a rhetorician in his unsanctified days, has something of the form of a dialogue. Cyprian invites his friend Donatus to sit with him in a pleasant arbour; he then addresses him at length on the blessedness of a Christian life and the wickedness and unrest of the pagan world; the latter subject is dwelt upon with much emphasis. Donatus himself says nothing. Probably this is a very early work, written shortly after his conversion and before the Decian persecution. After the persecution come a number of tractates which are somewhat of the nature of encyclicals. The *de habitu uirginum* deals especially with the proper dress (he recommends a Quakerish plainness) of those who had vowed to remain virgin. The *de lapsis* discusses the proper attitude of the faithful towards those who had 'fallen', *i.e.*, conformed outwardly to paganism, during the recent troubles. Cyprian recommends widely different degrees of severity according as the *lapsi* in question had or had not actually been tortured, also in proportion to the degree of their conformity; he sternly reproves those who had bought false certificates of conformity,[25] or had merely contrived to escape notice, with the intention of renouncing their faith if necessary, but show no signs of deep penitence. The prevalence of heresies produced the *de catholicae ecclesiae unitate*, an urgent appeal for unity. A commentary on the Lord's Prayer, *de dominica oratione*, is of quite uncertain date. The work *ad*

[23] Jerome, *de uir. ill.*, 53.

[24] Some difficulty is caused here by uncertainty as to the exact number of Cyprian's works; see Schanz-Hosius-Krüger, iii, pp. 337–40, for ancient lists and some account of the criticism thereof.

[25] *Libelli*; *libellus* is the general name for a document of almost any kind, because it would be contained in a small book-roll. The holders of these products of official venality were nicknamed *libellatici*, or certificate-men.

Demetrianum was provoked by an opponent who had brought up a charge, apparently already well worn, that the misfortunes of the times were due to the Christians. Cyprian answers that they are partly due to the weaknesses of an aging world,[26] partly righteous punishment for the flagrant sins of mankind. But one misfortune was arousing doubt and backsliding in Cyprian's own community; an epidemic had been raging in Carthage for some years. The bishop, in addition to arguments, Christian and general, against the fear of death, appeals to visions of his own which bear the same message; the title of the work is *de mortalitate*,[27] *Concerning the pestilence*. Two short works, *de opere et eleemosynis* and *de bono patientiae*, need little explanation; the former is one of many calls to generosity in almsgiving, the latter owes much to Tertullian's treatise on the same virtue; a sort of appendix to it is the work *de zelo et liuore*, as much sermon as pamphlet, urging the wickedness of envy and ill-will, which breed among other evils schism and dissension.[28]

Proof-texts were the order of the day then as for many centuries afterwards, and Cyprian prepared two sets of them; one, *ad Fortunatum de exhortatione martyrii*, was called forth by a sufficiently real need. At the request of the addressee, the bishop collects passages of Scripture in support of the propositions that idols are naught and their worship a sin, that the true faith must be kept, persecution is not to be feared, and so forth. Probably the immediate occasion was the persecution under Valerian, in 257; who Fortunatus was is a controversial and unimportant point. A larger work, in three books,[29] was composed at the request of one Quirinius, presumably a member of his own diocese, since he addresses him as 'son' (*fili carissime*).[30] It contains a large selection of texts from the Old and New Testaments, arranged under appropriate headings, as 'that Christ will come in judgement', 'that we should not indulge too

[26] This idea, the *senescens mundus*, while much earlier than the Christian doctors (it appears, for example, in Lucretius), is particularly common among them. The date of the work may be about 251 or 252, if the remarks on Divine vengeance in sect. 17 allude, as they may, to the death of Decius.

[27] This work and the next two are discussed in the order in which they come in one of the ancient lists, that of Pontius, which seems meant to be chronological.

[28] The allusion is to the controversy with Stephanus, hence the date is about 256 or the following year.

[29] Originally two; the genuineness of the third has been doubted, see Schanz-Hosius-Krüger, iii, p. 354.

[30] The books are variously called *ad Quirinium* or *testimonia*; the words quoted above are from the first sentence.

great desire for food', and various other dicta, theological and ethical.

There survive eighty-one letters, of various dates from about the beginning of his episcopate to shortly before his martyrdom, dealing with matters of ecclesiastical interest, and also a long document, attached to his works because he was one of the signatories and the question interested him greatly, containing the opinions of the African bishops on the validity of heretical baptisms. The literary interest of these writings is not high, their value being chiefly for the ecclesiastical historian.

Since Cyprian was a valiant defender of orthodoxy and had in addition the prestige deservedly attaching to a martyr, it was only to be expected that a number of works of doubtful authorship should have come down to us headed with his name. A commonplace little attack on the pagan deities, entitled *quod idola dii non sunt*, is printed with his writings, but hardly is by him ; of his time it may be.[31] Certainly not his are fifteen miscellaneous pieces, theological, moral and controversial, which are collected in the appendix to the Vienna edition.[32] There are likewise four letters, two purporting to have been written to and the others from him, which are not in his style, and six very indifferent poems on Scriptural subjects, a form of composition which we have no reason to suppose he engaged in.

Another African writer of some interest had the courage to turn Christian in the days of Diocletian.[33] This was ARNOBIVS of Sicca, who is said to have been converted by dreams from paganism. The bishop to whom he applied for admission was naturally suspicious, for Arnobius, who was a rhetorician of some note, had previously been a vehement opponent of the newer creed. By way of reassuring him, the convert wrote, manifestly in haste, the work *aduersus nationes* which survives in a somewhat damaged copy. It is in seven books, and of importance, not so much for its highly coloured style as for the considerable mass of information it preserves to us concerning ancient cult (here, presumably, the ultimate source is Varro, derived through some such writer as Cornelius Labeo,

[31] Jerome, *ep.*, 70 (84), 5, says it is Cyprian's ; if so, it is hardly on the stylistic level of most of his work. See Schanz-Hosius-Krüger, iii, p. 355.

[32] *Corpus scriptorum ecclesiasticorum Latinorum*, iii, 3 (the third volume of W. Hartel's edition of Cyprian, the best collected recension). The poems are really the work of another and later Cyprian, a Gaul who wrote between 397 and 425, see Schanz, iv, pp. 212–14.

[33] So Jerome, *de uir. ill.*, 79 ; in the Chronicle he mentions Arnobius as 'famous' in *an. Abr.* 2343 (= 327), and tells the story of his conversion.

see p. 457) and also theological speculations, together with valuable side-lights on contemporary worship.[34]

Arnobius had a pupil much more famous and a much better writer than himself, LVCIVS CAECILIVS FIRMIANVS LACTANTIVS, sometimes called the Christian Cicero. His dates are uncertain, but as he lived to see the peace of the Church and in his old age was tutor to Crispus, son of Constantine the Great,[35] we must not put his birth too early in the third century. Presumably he was born in Africa, and his early studies were purely literary; indeed, he may have been a pagan, though there is nothing to prove this definitely. From Africa he went, apparently by invitation, to Bithynia, where he lived in Nikomedia for some years, teaching Latin rhetoric to such pupils as he could get in that Greek-speaking city. Later, he left the East for Gaul, and would seem to have continued for a good many years to put forth treatises as distinguished for their comparative purity of style (when we consider their date) as for their generally moderate and reasonable tone, if allowance is made, as is but fair, for their author having lived through the last and worst of the persecutions, that of Diocletian.

According to Jerome, Lactantius wrote in his youth a work called *Symposium*. We may conjecture that this was a miscellany of the type of Macrobius' *Saturnalia* (p. 459), but know nothing else about it. A quaint episode in the history of literature is its identification with a collection of 100 riddles in verse, the production of a totally unknown, but late, SYMPHOSIACVS,[36] the resemblance of whose name to the word *symposium* has led to his being called Lactantius, both before and after the Revival of Letters, by too ingenious readers. Lost also is a versified account of his journey to Nikomedia, the *Hodoeporicon* or log-book; Jerome says it was in hexameters. Probably he used prose for his *Grammaticus*, but we have no nearer information.

Probably the earliest of his surviving works is the little treatise *de opificio Dei* (*On the Craftsmanship of God*), in which

[34] There are so far two usable editions of his treatise, that of Reifferscheid in the *Corpus scriptorum ecclesiasticorum Latinorum* (Vienna, 1875), and that of C. Marchesi (Turin, Paravia, 1934), see A. Souter in *Class. Rev.*, xlix (1935), p. 209.

[35] Our information concerning Lactantius comes largely from St. Jerome, *de uir. illust.*, 80. There is a good article on him by Lietzmann, with references to a selection of the enormous literature, in Pauly-Wissowa, xii, 351–6. Crispus was born about 307, proclaimed Caesar 317, put to death 326. Jerome says Lactantius was Crispus' tutor extrema senectute, and in Gaul.

[36] See Schanz, iv, pp. 74–6. One genuine work of Lactantius (or at least considered to be so by Jerome), a collection of epistles in two books, addressed to Demetrianus, is wholly lost.

he works out with some elaboration the thesis that the human body shows by its admirable structure the existence of a wise and beneficent Creator. There is nothing peculiarly Christian in this argument, nor does he say in so many words that the addressee, a prosperous man named Demetrianus, who had formerly been his pupil, was a Christian, though it is easy enough for us to see that he was.[37] Probably the persecution of Diocletian was begun or at least threatening, and neither pupil nor teacher was of the fanatical type that would wantonly seek martyrdom.

His principal work probably occupied him for several years. It is entitled, on the analogy of legal handbooks, *Institutiones*, with the significant addition *diuinae*.[38] It runs to seven books, and differs from the earlier apologetic works in Latin by its more positive contents. It does indeed begin with the arguments, already well worn, against paganism (Book I treats *Of false religion*, Book II, *Of the Origin of Error*, which Lactantius traces to the Devil's machinations, Book III, *Of the false wisdom of the Philosophers*), but the remainder sets out to give a full and eloquent statement of what Christian doctrine is, with the incidental result that we get a most interesting and very readable account of what an intelligent Christian believed in an age so uncritical that the forged Sibylline oracles were accepted without hesitation as genuine early documents, on the strength of which a detailed picture could be drawn in the last book of the approaching end of the age.[39] Under Constantine, Lactantius was requested by some one named Pentadius to epitomize his work, and did so; both forms survive complete.[40]

[37] Lactantius says to him, *de opif.*, 1, 9: memento et ueri parentis tui et in qua ciuitate nomen dederis et cuius ordinis fueris. This could easily be explained away to any one not used to Christian symbolism and discipline; such crypto-Christian utterances were, of course, common in disturbed times.

[38] This is the author's own explanation of the title, *inst.*, i, 1, 2. As to the date, on the one hand he several times speaks of the persecution as existing, on the other he refers in so many words to Constantine's edicts in favour of the Christians, including that of Milan, 313, and to the deaths of the persecutors, over whom he triumphs in the last chapter but one of Bk. vii. The natural conclusion is that he began to write under Diocletian—indeed, the concluding chapter of the *de opif.* shows that he already had the work in mind—but finished and revised the treatise in Constantine's time, being himself then presumably in Gaul.

[39] For the pseudo-Sibylline literature, see Rose, *H.G.L.*, p. 74; the complicated history of the eschatological doctrines involved cannot be gone into here.

[40] It is an interesting fact that Jerome, *loc. cit.*, says the epitome is 'headless', in libro uno acephalo. So it is in all but one of our MSS.; Jerome's copy must be an ancestor, direct or collateral, of our inferior codices.

Lactantius wrote one more theological work, the pamphlet *de ira Dei*, which discusses the question in what sense anger can be attributed to a perfect Being.[41] He is probably the composer of a quasi-historical monograph, that entitled *de mortibus persecutorum*. The style certainly resembles his; the author was some one who knew Nikomedia well; the most serious objection is that the tone lacks the moderation which this gentle and amiable writer generally shows, but to expect him never to be bitter against the deadliest enemies of his Church is rather too much to ask of any one.[42] There is also no convincing reason for denying his authorship of a poem, *de aue phoenice*, which is attributed to him on tolerable authority and handles the legend of the phoenix.[43]

We need not linger over two little copies of verse, *de Pascha* and *de passione Domini*, to which his name has by some chance been attached, for it is long since any competent scholar imagined them to be his. More interesting is the confusion between this Lactantius and a scholar of unknown date, certainly not early, who declares himself to be the author of some notes on Statius and that his name is LACTANTIVS PLACIDVS.[44] On the strength, apparently, of this indication, some of the scribes of the existing Statian scholia have added the names Caelius Firmianus to our author's signature and ascribed to him the whole collection which we have. It seems in reality to be the work of several hands.

The now triumphant Church, although still torn by heresies and schisms of all kinds, went rapidly on with the work of defining her doctrines and propagating them in a world by no means

[41] Since he cites the *institutiones* in *de ira*, 2, 6, he must have written it after that work, or at least its first four books (the citation is from Bk. iv) were composed and published; there is no guide to the exact date.

[42] The sole MS. calls the author Lucius Cecilius, the latter being a not uncommon corruption of Caelius. Jerome says that Lactantius wrote a work *de persecutione*, probably meaning this one. For some account of the relevant literature, see Lietzmann, 355, 8 *sqq*.

[43] Jerome does not mention the poem, but Gregory of Tours names it as by Lactantius, to whom the existing MSS. attribute it; there is nothing in the style or versification which cannot be his, but the absence of any specifically Christian reference suggests that it is an early work.

[44] On *Theb.*, vi, 342 (364), he says: ex libris ineffabilis doctrinae Persei praeceptoris seorsum libellum composui Caelius Firmianus Lactantius Placidus, or so the MSS. make him say. If we could date this unknown Perseus, some little light would perhaps be thrown on Placidus; as it is, we can but note that Jerome, *adu. Ruf.*, i, 16, mentions a number of authors on whom commentaries had been written, but Statius is not one of them, suggesting that in his time either the scholia we have were not composed or at least he had not heard of them. See further Wessner in Pauly-Wissowa, xii, 356–61.

wholly Christian even in name, as yet, throughout the fourth and fifth centuries. In this period we meet three of the greatest names in ecclesiastical history, those of men whose striking personalities were bound to make them conspicuous in some form of activity in any age or nation.

First in time is AMBROSIVS (S. AMBROSE OF MILAN, Bishop and Doctor).[45] He was the son of an official, prefect of Gaul at the time of the saint's birth, and at first followed his father's career, studied rhetoric, practised at the Bar, and was appointed to a judicial post. In this capacity he found himself at Milan during a time of some turbulence. The Arian bishop Auxentius had died, and the populace was anything but quiet in choosing a new occupant of the see; they appear to have been Catholics for the most part, but the Arian faction was noisy and had friends at court. Ambrose went to the cathedral to harangue them into order, when some one (Paulinus says it was a child) shouted *Ambrosius episcopus*, the cry was taken up by all present, and Ambrose found himself, despite all attempts to decline the honour, forced to accept the see, with the approval of his official superior, Probus the *praefectus praetorio*. Once bishop, he took his duties seriously (his seems to have been a pious family; his sister was a nun), acquired very great influence and found himself involved in two notable struggles with the civil power. The first of these occasions was in 385–386. The then Empress, Iustina, was herself an Arian, and tried to get possession of the cathedral for the use of her faction. Ambrose countered her by the simple means of entering the church with his congregation and refusing to leave it. The Empress dared not use force against so popular a man, and after two years of strife, was obliged to yield. The next was more important. In 390, Theodosius the Great had avenged the murder of certain officials in Thessalonike by a massacre; Ambrose forbade him to enter the church and excommunicated him till he did penance for his cruelties. Beside this braving of the highest authorities of the land in the cause of his doctrines, it is a small matter that he persuaded Valentinian II to refuse the request, voiced by Symmachus (p. 524) to restore the altar of Victory to the senate-chamber. His life came to an end on April 4, 397.

As might be expected from such a man of action, the works

[45] Ambrose's works contain many references to his own affairs and contemporary events; we have also a biography, very laudatory and containing marvels in the taste of that age, but based upon personal knowledge, by his secretary Paulinus. Some further information can be had from St. Augustine.

which he left behind him were mostly connected with the questions of the day; he was rather an eloquent and impressive expositor of the doctrine of his party than a creator of it. We have ninety-one letters bearing his name and for the most part clearly genuine; they consist, with but few exceptions, of expositions of matters of ecclesiastical polity or doctrine, in other words, they are rather official communications of Ambrose the bishop than the private utterances of Ambrose the man. A number of hymns also are credited to him, but certainly the collection includes some which he never wrote. Four are assuredly his, for St. Augustine, his convert and friend, vouches for their authenticity, viz., *Deus creator omnium*; *Aeterne rerum conditor*; *Iam surgit hora tertia*; *Veni, redemptor gentium.*[46] All are in a perfectly simple metre, the iambic dimeter, and the language is correspondingly simple, but dignified and not without a certain beauty; they are admirably adapted for congregational singing, and for this their author intended them. The fashion of congregational singing was of Eastern origin, and the first to use it in the West was Hilary of Poitiers, whose attempts met with but indifferent success. Ambrosius found in it a means of counter-propaganda against the Arians and also a heartening employment for his congregation when they occupied the cathedral in the time of Iustina.[47] He has therefore the right to be considered the true father of Western hymnody. But his style, though good, was not inimitable, while the fame of his sanctity and eloquence naturally led to hymns by other authors being credited to him if they were at all in his manner; it is therefore quite doubtful what other hymns than the above four, of the many which are ascribed to him in various sources, he really wrote.

The *Te Deum*, however, is not by Ambrose but probably by Niketas (Niceta) of Remisiana (near the modern Nish), about 380–390. See A. E. Burn, *Niceta of Remisiana*, in the Cambridge Patristic Series.

As might have been expected of a very busy and energetic man, in charge of an important diocese and on occasion the

[46] See August., *confess.*, ix, 32; *retract.*, i, 21, 1; *de nat. et grat.*, 74; *serm.*, 372, 3. The value of this last testimony, however, is doubtful, as the authenticity of the sermon is by no means above suspicion. But it would appear at all events to be early work, by some well-informed divine.

[47] Ambros., *sermo contra Auxentium*, 34, a passage which might also be taken to mean that the hymn *O lux beata Trinitas* is Ambrose's; Paulinus, *uit. Ambr.*, 13; August., *confess.*, ix, 15. See further Schanz, iv, pp. 228–33. The metre of the hymns is familiar to moderns from the *Veni, Creator Spiritus*.

spiritual adviser of his sovran, Ambrose devoted much time to preaching, and his works are mostly sermons, doubtless revised for publication to some extent, together with handbooks of divinity. In all, the style is good, although without the striking originality and vigour of Jerome and Augustine, and sometimes so elaborate as to make the reader wonder if it was not over the heads of the less learned brethren in his congregation. In matter, he gives much space to Biblical exegesis, and therein follows the vicious fashion of that time in extracting most extraordinary allegories from the text at every turn. Here, as in so much else, his models are the great Greek fathers. Often he shows an admirable liveliness and lightness of touch, however, as in the long digression on the sins of money-lenders which occupies most of the sermon on the Book of Tobit and is worthy of a first-rate satirist. His rhetoric is often really eloquent, and he can on occasion be perfectly simple and plain.

We have the following works which are undoubtedly his. The series of discourses on the Creation collected under the general title of *Exameron* (this seems to be his Latinization of *ἑξαήμερον*, doubtless in accordance with contemporary usage; editors often print closer approximations to the Greek, but without sufficient support from the MSS.) has for its model the work of like title by Basil the Great; like its original, it consists of nine discourses, which are divided into six books, one for each day. After this come treatments of the succeeding parts of Genesis; the *de Paradiso*, *de Cain et Abel* and *de Noe* consist of one book each, the *de Abraham* of two. The *de Isaac et anima*, despite its title, has little to say of the patriarch and much of the Song of Songs, in which the bride is allegorized into the human soul. He then proceeds to discuss the relations of man to death, in the discourse *de bono mortis*. The contents of the sermon to the newly baptized entitled *de fuga saeculi* are naturally an exhortation to avoid the vanities of this world; it is equally natural, considering the date, that authority for this should be sought in the institution of the cities of refuge, and that use should be made, by no means for the only time, of Philon of Alexandria (Philo Iudaeus). Like many of the fathers Ambrose was concerned to present a Christian philosophy to his hearers or readers, as a counterpoise to the older systems which had long dominated the minds of the more thoughtful; hence his two books *de Iacob et uita beata* are his answer to the old question what constitutes the happy or perfect life. Chastity is the principal virtue held up for imitation in the *de Ioseph patriarcha*; allegories have full play in the *de patriarchis*, since its theme is the blessings bestowed by the aged Jacob on his sons, the obscure and allusive language of which invited such attempts at finding a meaning. Lent was the natural and appropriate season for a discourse on fasting, and Elijah furnished an example; hence the little work *de Elia et ieiunio*. The sin of covetousness is the theme of the moralization of the story of Naboth's vineyard, *de Nabuthae*. In the *de Tobia*, besides the long and vehement attack on money-lenders already mentioned, there is sounded the praise of piety and generosity. Four sermons make up the work (often printed in four books, but without ancient authority) on the evils of human life which goes by the name *de interpellatione* (*i.e.*, protest) *Iob et Dauid*; 'David's' contribution to the discussion is the forty-first, forty-second and seventy-second Psalms.[48] The moral character of David had given rise to much heart-searching; Ambrose defends him in the *apologia Dauid*, on the ground that although he undoubtedly sinned, his penitence, as expressed especially in Psalm 50, did much to atone for this.[49] But the Psalter received separate treatment also, in the *enarrationes* on twelve of the hymns it contains, and the series of sermons on the long 118th. Against this mass of exposition of the Old Testament, Ambrose left little on the New; there is, however, an *expositio* of the Gospel of St. Luke, consisting of a number of sermons collected into ten books.

Ethics always interested Ambrose very greatly, and it is not surprising to find that he wrote a sort of elaborate adaptation of Cicero's *de officiis* (cf. p. 192), for the guidance of the young priests of his diocese. It is the first systematic work on Christian ethics that has come down to us, and bears the title *de officiis ministrorum*. Like its original, it is in three books. Special problems of conduct, especially sexual, also claimed his attention, witness the three books *de uirginibus* addressed to his sister Marcellina. These warmly commend to her and to all readers the life of vowed virginity which she had embraced, and hold up as shining examples, besides the Virgin Mary herself, Saints Agnes and Thekla and an unnamed virgin of Antioch, whose adventures and final martyrdom form a considerable portion of the second book. Companion pieces are the two shorter works *de uiduis* and *de uirginitate*, while the tractates *de institutione uirginis* and *exhortatio uirginitatis* still harp on the same theme in

[48] Those numbered respectively 42, 43 and 73 in the Hebrew (and English) versions. It is to be remembered that the composite authorship of the Psalter and its collection at a date long after David's death were not suspected until modern times.

[49] A second work with the same subject and title is apparently some later writer's imitation of the genuine Ambrosian piece.

various forms. Whether Ambrose wrote the book *de lapsu uirginis* is not certain; it is a rhetorical account of a nun who had broken her vow of chastity.

The feeble Emperor Gratian (Flavius Gratianus Augustus, 367–383), who had more taste for letters, theology and his favourite amusement of javelin-throwing than for government, was entirely under the domination of Ambrose's strong character in religious matters. In 377 or the beginning of 378 he was on the eve of marching eastwards to help Valens, his co-Emperor (Flavius Valens Augustus, 364–378) against the Goths, and found that a suitable moment to ask his spiritual adviser for a treatise on the Christian faith. The bishop therefore composed for him the first two books of the work *de fide*. Coming back alive from the disastrous campaign, in which Valens had been killed, the Emperor asked for more, and Ambrose wrote another two books, and finally a fifth.[50] The main purpose of the argument is the refutation of Arianism; the manner in which the subject is handled shows very clearly that Ambrose was an orator and a man of affairs, not a dialectician. His other theological works are not important; a treatise *de paenitentia*, in two books, deals as much with discipline as with doctrine. The *de mysteriis* is a part of the instruction given by the bishop to his catechumens, and consists of an explanation of baptism and the Eucharist. Two similar treatises, both dealing with the Creed, the *explanatio symboli ad initiandos* and the *exhortatio ad neophytos de symbolo*, are in the former case doubtfully genuine, in the latter certainly spurious. A larger work of much the same kind is the collection of sermons known as the *de sacramentis*, in six books; while more Arian controversies, and Gratian's thirst for doctrinal instruction, produced the three books *de spiritu sancto*, a kind of supplement to the *de fide*, completed in 381.[51] A debate between Ambrose and two Arians was arranged some time after this; the bishop's opponents not appearing, Ambrose delivered a sermon on the Incarnation instead, which survives under the title *de incarnationis dominicae sacramentis*.[52]

[50] Besides references in the work itself to the time and manner of its composition, for instance *de fide*, i, 1; iii, 1; v, 6, we have the correspondence relating to it in the first of Ambrose's letters in the Benedictine collection.

[51] Athanric, king of the Goths, died in 381, and Peter, bishop of Alexandria, in June at latest of the same year; *de spir. sanc.*, i, prol. 17–18, mentions the death of the former but implies that the latter is living.

[52] *De incarn.*, 1, mentions the proposed debate; *ibid.*, 62, speaks of the quinque illi quos scripsisti libri de fide, and so must have been written after 379, but *ibid.*, 80, is evidently addressed to Gratian, and so is earlier

Some theological works which he is known to have written are lost (a fragment of one, an *expositio fidei*, is preserved in a Greek version in Book II of the *Eranistes* or *Polymorphus* of Theodoretos of Cyprus), and some are attributed to him which he certainly never wrote, the most remarkable being the so-called Athanasian Creed, or *Quicunque uult*.

As was to be expected, Ambrose was called upon to deliver addresses on various occasions, and there survive his funeral sermons over Valentinian II (murdered in 392) and Theodosius the Great (died 395). Of more personal interest are his two orations over his dead brother Satyrus, the former instinct with a warm and genuine affection which glows through the rhetorical trappings, the second an expression, cast in the form of a classical *consolatio*, of faith in an after-life; hence it is often called *de fide resurrectionis*. Finally, there is the attack on the Arian Auxentius, already referred to; it is appended to *ep*. 21 (Ambrose to Valentinian II).

Undoubtedly the greatest scholar among the Western Christians was EVSEBIVS HIERONYMVS (generally known in English as ST. JEROME). This man was a native of Stridon, an unimportant town in Dalmatia, and was born in or about 348, the exact date being uncertain; he died at Bethlehem in 420, on Sept. 30. His education was received in Rome, where he was a pupil of Donatus in literature; who taught him rhetoric we do not know, but he must have been a very apt pupil. In Rome also he was baptized.[53] After finishing his studies, he went to Gaul, and there decided to give himself up wholly to a religious life. For a while he and his old schoolfellow Rufinus were members of a little community at Aquileia; then, about 373, this group broke up and its members departed, mostly for the East. Jerome himself started for Jerusalem, was detained by sickness at Antioch, and there began a course of theological studies under one after another of the Eastern divines. For three years (375–8) he retired into the wilderness and while there learned Hebrew; Greek he already knew well. This hermit life

than 383. For the complete works of Ambrose there is nothing later or more critical than the Benedictine edition and its reprint in Migne; some few pieces have been re-edited. See further Schanz, iv, pp. 315–65.

[53] Biographies of St. Jerome exist, but they are without exception medieval and of no historical value, being full of the pious folklore which regularly floods the legend of any saint, Christian or other. The only reliable source is contemporary literature, especially his own bulky writings. These are not to be had complete in any later edition than that of Vallarsi (Verona, 1734–42; 11 vols.), except the Migne reprint; but large portions have been edited in recent years, *e.g.*, the letters, the Chronicle and much of the translation of the Bible.

he felt obliged to abandon in order to play his part in controversies which were breaking out at Antioch ; in that city he was ordained priest, and soon after left it for Constantinople, which in turn he quitted for Rome, spending the years 382–5 there and making the close acquaintance of the then Pope, Damasus. To him he seems to have owed the idea of making a revised version of the whole Bible in Latin, to replace the unsatisfactory texts then current, in which the Old Testament had been rendered from the Greek version and not from the original. At the same time he made the acquaintance of several noble ladies, notably Paulla and her daughter Eustochium, who looked to him as their spiritual guide. But after the death of Damasus, he found it impossible to stay longer in Rome. His was a strange and somewhat morbid character, with its natural eccentricities aggravated by the repressions and hardships of his ascetic life ; those with whom he came in contact seem almost without exception to have revered and admired or else bitterly hated him, and spiteful gossip found a handle in his perfectly innocent relations with the women who sought his advice. After a leisurely journey eastwards and a stay in Egypt, he and his companions made their way to Bethlehem, and there, on that holy ground, formed two monastic communities, Jerome founding one for men, Paulla and Eustochium one for women. Always a diligent writer, Jerome entered into a stage of continuous productivity, occasionally interrupted by ill-health, and marked by its stormy tone, for he was engaged in one controversy after another, not the least bitter being that with Rufinus. This activity lasted to the time of his death.

Of Jerome's services to the translation of the Bible this is not the place to speak in detail, for the criticism of the Vulgate is a specialist's subject. This much may be said, that he began his labours in Rome, making a new edition of the Latin Gospels with a minimum of alteration from the familiar text then in use in the churches.[54] At Bethlehem he set about a similar revision of the Old Testament, using as his guide the Hexapla of Origen, the most original theologian and greatest Biblical scholar whom the Eastern churches ever produced.[55] Finally, he undertook a

[54] This we know from Jerome's own preface to the Gospels, addressed to Damasus, vol. x, p. 658 *sqq.*, Vallarsi.

[55] Jerome, *praef. ad lib. psal.* (vol. ix, pp. 1155–6 Vallarsi) and the preface to his second revision, vol. x, p. 105 *sqq.*, Vallarsi. He revised the Psalter twice on the basis of the Greek, once in Rome, once at Bethlehem ; the third attempt was a new translation from the original. The Hexapla was a Hebrew text of the Old Testament, followed by a transliteration into Greek characters and four Greek translations.

complete new translation from the Hebrew.[56] It need hardly be pointed out that the various copies of these versions which got about, blending as they inevitably did with the existing translations, have in time given rise to all manner of mixed texts, which the criticism of our day is slowly disentangling in hopes of restoring what Jerome actually wrote.

Like Origen, Jerome gave much time and energy to the exegesis of the Scriptures. To begin with he contented himself with translating Origen's own works, fairly literally it would seem. Their total bulk was enormous, and the hopes he entertained of rendering most of them into Latin [57] were never fulfilled. However, he completed, before his arrival in Rome, versions of the twenty-eight homilies on Jeremiah and Ezekiel and two of those on the Song of Songs. Much later, at Bethlehem, he turned into Latin the thirty-nine homilies on the Gospel of St. Luke, for the use of Paulla and Eustochium. Later still [58] he gave nine of the homilies on Isaiah a Latin dress.

His next step was to write exegetical works of his own, in the allegorical manner popularized by Origen especially. He began with the Minor Prophets, commenting first on five of them, then on two more, finally on the remaining five.[59] The last of this long work was not complete till 406. Shortly after this he

[56] This was not decided upon all at once, nor without much hesitation and many solicitations from his friends, for he exposed himself to the malignant attacks of all the ignorance of the day. Those readers who are old enough to remember them may fruitfully compare the virulent assaults to which the Revisers, both English and American, of the King James version were subjected in their time. Some part of the story may be read in the extremely interesting prefaces to the various sections of Jerome's translation (vol. ix, pp. 1, 355, 453, 683, 781, 901, 1097, 1153, 1293, 1405, 1521, 1565, Vallarsi). It is noticeable that when rebuking these shallow pretenders to criticism, Jerome loses the irritable tone which mars much of his controversial work, and takes on the dignity of a scholar stopping the mouths of the presumptuous and foolish.

[57] See the opening sentence of his prefaratory epistle to the translation of Origen's Homilies on Ezekiel (vol. v, p. 741, Vallarsi): magnum est quidem, amice, quod postulas, ut Origenem faciam Latinum. He goes on to explain that he is hampered by sore eyes and lack of competent secretaries, and so must for the present content himself with the fourteen homilies which follow, having dictated them from time to time.

[58] This seems a reasonable conclusion from his not mentioning them in his list of his own works (see below, p. 493); they therefore come after 392.

[59] This can be gathered from Jerome's prefaces to the commentaries, for which see the sixth volume of Vallarsi's edition.

began on the Major Prophets, in the order Daniel, Isaiah, Ezekiel, Jeremiah.[60] He had already, while in Rome, expounded Ecclesiastes to Blaesilla, daughter of Paulla, who requested him to write down his interpretation. This he ultimately did, after her death, while at Bethlehem, some time between 387 and 390.[61] Of the New Testament, he dealt with the Epistles to the Galatians, Ephesians, Philemon and Titus. But his indefatigable zeal produced other expository works also, whereof several survive, more or less as he wrote them.[62]

He was, however, not only a translator and exegete but something of a historian, and several works in this field survive and are of value and interest. In the long line of those who have written legends of the saints he has a prominent place, for he is the author of laudatory biographies of three ascetics, Paullus, Hilarion and Malachi, all hermits except the last. To these he added, late in his career,[63] a Latin version of the rule of Abbot Pachomios of the Thebaid, together with a rendering of the epistles of that extraordinary person, which are crammed with mystical groups of letters presumably having some esoteric meaning for the writer, if for no one else. Not a few of his own letters are really short historical works, being obituary notices in epistolary form of certain of his friends.[64] In addition, he performed two great services to literary history especially. The ecclesiastical historian Eusebios had composed a chronicle of events from the Creation to his own day; Jerome made a Latin version of this, to which he added much from his own reading, especially valuable being extracts from Suetonius on Latin literature. He also continued the work down to the year 378, the original having ended at 325. Jerome's compilation is all the more useful to us because Eusebios is lost and cannot be entirely restored in his

[60] Daniel, vol. v, p. 617 *sqq.*, Vallarsi; Isaiah, vol. iii, p. 1 *sqq.*; the opening sentence of the introductory address to Eustochium mentions the commentaries on the Minor Prophets and Daniel. Ezekiel, vol. v, p. 1 *sqq.*; a similar preface mentions all the above commentaries. Jeremiah, vol. iv, p. 833 *sqq.*, again mentioning in its preface all the earlier commentaries.

[61] See Vallarsi, vol. iii, pp. 381–498; the history of the commentary is given in the preface.

[62] The commentaries on the New Testament are in Vallarsi's vol. vii; for a fuller account of Jerome's activities in this direction, see Schanz, vol. iv, pp. 457–73.

[63] See Vallarsi, vol. ii, p. 53 (the preface to the translations from Pachomios), which states that it is written after the death of Paulla, that is to say, later than January 404.

[64] Nos. 60, 66, 77, 108, 127.

original form.[65] Finally, Jerome compiled a short history of Christian literature, from the time of the Apostles to his own day, including a list of his own works. The resulting 135 chapters, whereof the first 78 are simply taken from Eusebios' Ecclesiastical History with the addition of some careless errors of Jerome's own, go under the general name of *de uiris illustribus*, title and scheme being alike due to Suetonius (cf. p. 511). The rest consists apparently of a list of such writers as the author happened to remember, with brief comments. Yet with all its faults, the work is a valuable document, Jerome's wide learning and evidently tenacious memory making even his hurried scribbles contributions to our knowledge.

For the Martyrologium Hieronymianum, a compilation which as we have it dates from about 600, but which goes back ultimately to a work of Jerome himself, see Schanz, vol. iv, pp. 441–3.

Nothing that he wrote is of more interest than his correspondence, to equal which in liveliness and revelation of personality we must go back to Cicero ; a greater contrast could not be imagined than between this and the lifeless elegances of Symmachus (see p. 524). As already indicated, some items are letters in outward form only, being really short, and not always even short, treatises. Enough are left after subtracting these to gain him a place as one of the great letter-writers of the world. The subjects are naturally doctrinal for the most part, but many letters deal with matters as interesting now as then, namely pictures, anything but flattering, of the society of the day, which Jerome handles at times in almost Juvenalian fashion.[66] The style yields nothing in vigour to any writer ; elegance and moderation it cannot always claim, for Jerome could seldom forget that he was learned man and a rhetorician. However, his correspondents probably expected of him just such a manner as he used.

Between the letters and the controversial works there is a certain resemblance, for both reveal the character of their author in clear, even glaring colours. Jerome never could discuss calmly any question, were it the most abstract possible, in which he was interested ; his theological opponents are one and all treated as

[65] Perhaps the most convenient edition of Jerome's chronicle is that of J. K. Fotheringham, London, Milford, 1923. The standard edition of Eusebios is that of Schoene, Berlin, 1875.

[66] A very noteworthy example is the long twenty-second letter, to Eustochium, encouraging her in her resolution of virginity. In telling her what company she should avoid, he does not mince his words, and is as unsparing of the clergy as of the laity. The correspondence is to be found in vols. 54 and 56 of the Vienna corpus.

personal enemies, and indeed those who criticize his textual remarks on the Scriptures are not handled more gently; scarcely a preface to his commentaries or translations lacks a sneering reference to 'my friends' who do not agree with his dicta. Even the greatest receive on occasion a most irritating meed of faint praise.[67] But had he been the most even-tempered of men, a certain heat would have been almost inevitable in one so constantly and bitterly assailed as he was during a great part of his career. Not an original theologian, he was early attracted to the greatest of all the Fathers, Origen, and learned from him, not only his allegorical method of Biblical interpretation, but also something of his boldly speculative attitude in metaphysical things. But Origen, though he retained a great repute as an exegete, was a much too independent thinker to escape a reputation for heresy in a Church busily engaged in forming a scheme of orthodox belief, and Jerome, while often and truthfully protesting that he did not share the great Alexandrian's views on many things, found himself labelled an Origenist. As early as his sojourn in Rome this began. Damasus asked him to write something on the Holy Ghost; he answered this request by translating the Greek treatise of Didymos, one of Origen's warmest admirers. Promptly the hunt was up, and accusations of heresy were rife against Jerome, Didymos and Origen alike. He stopped his work for a while, only to finish it later at Bethlehem,[68] and the completed translation was provided with a preface not of the most conciliatory nature, seeing that the Roman clergy are called a senate of Pharisees and their city a heathen place. However, this did not prevent him thundering against heretics himself; this congenial occupation also began while he was in Rome, with the short treatise *aduersus Heluidium*.[69] This Helvidius, if we will believe Jerome, was a man of no education and a heretic to boot, for he had put forward the proposition that St. Mary was not virgin all her life, and, what was almost worse, that virginity itself was not a higher state than matrimony. Jovianus put forward similar ideas, adding another, that to eat with thankfulness is as meritorious as fasting, and certain other propositions which

[67] As a glaring example, see the reference to Ambrose, *de uir. ill.*, 124: he will not criticize him ne . . . aut adulatio in me reprehendatur aut ueritas. Again, in the preface to his translation of Origen's Homilies on St. Luke, he speaks of a certain commentary which in uerbis luderet, in sententiis dormiret; we know from Rufinus, *inuect.*, ii, 21, that he means that of St. Ambrose, cf. p. 487.

[68] All this is clear from the preface itself, vol. ii, p. 105, Vallarsi, cf. ep. 33 (to Paulla).

[69] Vol. ii, pp. 205–30, Vallarsi.

were condemned by the ascetically minded orthodox, but most vigorously of all by Jerome in his two books *aduersus Iouianum*,[70] where again he finds yet another fault in his opponent, a very bad Latin style. While at Bethlehem, he was naturally in close touch with the ecclesiastical life of Jerusalem, and a friendship which he had formed with John, the bishop of that see, was ended by a fierce theological debate. John had defended the orthodoxy of Origen; Jerome, by this time a vehement opponent of the latter's views, assailed him in the book *contra Ioannem Ierosolymitanum*.[71] Yet more violent was his quarrel with an old schoolfellow, Rufinus. This man was an industrious translator, and having put forth a rendering of Origen's work *περὶ ἀρχῶν*, or *Concerning first principles*, he was assailed for it, and defended himself by a counter-attack in two books, generally known as the *Invectives*; Jerome replied with three books *contra Rufinum*, which left little unsaid that a bitter temper and great powers of vituperation could suggest.[72] Yet another attack of the same nature came from a Gaulish priest, one Vigilantius, who had been hospitably received in Jerome's monastery on the strength of a letter of introduction which he brought. He then had the execrable taste to find fault with his host's orthodoxy, and at the same time put forth his own opinion, that the relics of the martyrs were receiving too much veneration. A letter and a short treatise [73] from Jerome can have left him in little doubt of the latter's feelings with regard to his personal habits, his style of writing and his theological opinions.

Less personal in tone are two dialogues which Jerome composed on theological topics. A sect, called after its founder [74] the Luciferians, was raising difficulties about the position of converts from Arianism who had held office on their own sect; Jerome represents two nameless persons, a Catholic and a Luciferian, meeting by chance in Antioch [75] and passing from railing to serious controversy, in which the former converts the latter. A longer treatise, in three books, assails the Pelagians, whose champion, Critobulus, is staunchly opposed by a Catholic repre-

[70] *Ibid.*, pp. 237–384.

[71] *Ibid.*, pp. 407–54.

[72] *Ibid.*, pp. 583–674 (Rufinus' treatise), 457–572 (Jerome's reply).

[73] The treatise, *ibid.*, pp. 387–402; the letter is No. 61; cf. 58, 11, to Paulinus, mentioning Vigilantius in laudatory terms.

[74] Bishop Lucifer of Caralis (Cagliari), the chief city of Sardinia. The dialogue is in Vallarsi, vol. ii, pp. 171–202.

[75] This is clear from the mention in sect. 1 (171 B Vallarsi) of the street-lamps being lit; Antioch was the only ancient city which had a regular system of street-lighting.

sentative, Atticus, who is evidently meant to have the better of the argument, though in the end he merely opposes quotations from authorities to the pertinent questions of his antagonist.[76]

The above works, together with a few homilies,[77] comprise the known literary activities of this most interesting, if somewhat unattractive figure of the fourth-century Church.

We now pass to one of the most outstanding men in the whole history of Christianity and of literature, AVRELIVS AVGVSTINVS, Bishop of Hippo (ST. AUGUSTINE). Of the most significant events of this great man's life we have the best possible testimony, his own, set forth in the very remarkable autobiography generally styled the *Confessions*. There is also a critical review of his literary activity, by himself, the *Retractationes*. The former work does not pretend, however, to be a complete history of his life, even up to the date, about 400, when it was apparently finished [78]; the latter must have been written in 427, about three years before his death; his dates are Nov. 13, 354–Aug. 28, 430. We can supplement these testimonies by various references in his other works to his life and activities, and there is also a biography of him by Bishop Possidius, his personal friend and disciple. The facts are briefly as follows. His father Patricius did not join the Church till late in life, and apparently was not much interested in religious matters; his mother, St. Monnica, was a fervently devout Catholic, whose great aim in life was the spiritual welfare of her son. The young Augustine was well educated, in Latin

[76] In Vallarsi, *ibid.*, pp. 679–792. The names of the interlocutors are imaginary, as appears from the preface to the first book, p. 682 A Vallarsi.

[77] Jerome was never a parish priest, and his activities in this direction were confined to addresses given in his monastery. For an account of the discourses, lost or surviving, which are known to be his, see Schanz, vol. iv, pp. 483–6.

[78] We have no exact indication of its date, but Augustine's own catalogue of his works, *Retr.*, ii, 6/32, places it between the *contra partem Donati*, which is lost but apparently was written in or about 400, and the *contra Faustum*, which is also of about that year. In reading this work, or rather the first ten books of it, which are properly autobiographical, it is to be remembered that, while any imputation of deliberate deceit on its author's part is merely absurd, we are dealing, not with a diary, but with the facts as seen through the medium of a very sensitive man's retrospection, and therefore cannot always assume the objective accuracy which a historian would look for. Precisely the same caution has to be observed in reading that English work which perhaps most resembles the *Confessions*, despite innumerable differences of outlook, education and environment, Bunyan's *Grace Abounding to the chief of Sinners*.

at least, for he never fully mastered Greek,[79] first in his native town of Thagaste in Numidia, then at Madaura, later, from about his sixteenth year, at Carthage; by this time his father was dead, the family circumstances, never brilliant, were decidedly straitened, and his expenses were paid by a well-to-do fellow-citizen, Romanianus.[80] In Carthage he led what he afterwards declared to be a most wicked and irregular life. If, however, we look for concrete facts, we find merely that he lived from about 371 to 385 with a woman who bore him a son, Adeodatus (372–about 390); she was plainly not of loose life, but simply his *concubina*, and the union of a sort sanctioned by practically all but Christian moralists of the day as only less respectable than marriage.[81] He was studious and earnest, and before long began experimenting with the available religions. For a considerable time Manichaeism attracted him, and he became a member of its outer circle of adherents, the *auditores*.[82] Meanwhile his rhetorical studies were advancing, and Cicero's *Hortensius* (cf. p. 189) awaked in him a zeal for philosophy which never quitted him. In 383 he went to Rome, in 384 to Milan, where he accepted a post as professor of rhetoric. By this time he was tired of Manichaeism, and troubled rather with a sceptical attitude of mind, the fruit of what he could understand of Academic philosophy. Now two new influences were brought to bear upon him, that of St. Ambrose, whose expositions of the Scriptures pleased him, and, perhaps even more important, that of Platonism, which was made known to him through the writings of Marius Victorinus (cf. p. 454). In 386 came what is usually regarded (it was certainly so regarded by him) as his conversion.[83] A child's

[79] That he was badly taught in this subject and found it extraordinarily difficult appears from *conf.*, i, 14; that he was not quite ignorant of it, at least of Biblical Greek, is clear from fairly numerous references to it in his many exegetical passages especially. He seems to have had neither the interest nor the talent of Jerome for linguistics.

[80] Romanianus is often mentioned by Augustine, *e.g.*, *conf.*, vi, 14, and his assistance acknowledged, *c. Acad.*, ii, 3 (p. 262 E).

[81] For his laments over his former life, see especially *conf.*, iii, 1 *sqq.* The length of his association with the woman (she was still with him at Milan, *conf.*, vi, 15), and her declaration on quitting him (*ibid.*) that she would know no other man, show clearly enough that it was a semi-regular union.

[82] See *c. Fortunatum*, 3 (vol. viii, p. 94 B, ed. Bened.): nostis autem me non electum uestrum sed auditorem fuisse. Cf. *de mor. Manich.*, ii, 68: nouem annos totos magna cura et diligentia uos audiui.

[83] See *conf.*, viii, 12/29: et ecce audio uocem de uicina domo cum cantu dicentis et crebro repetentis quasi pueri, an puellae nescio, Tolle lege, tolle lege. Characteristically, although he knew it to be a human voice and asked himself whether there was any game in which children

voice bade him 'take up and read', and opening a copy of the Pauline epistles at random, he hit upon what he regarded as an authoritative and Divine message, Romans 13, 13–14. Henceforth he was, not only a Catholic, but dedicated to a semi-monastic life. He was baptized at Easter, 387, by Ambrose, left Milan for Rome, and at Ostia that autumn lost his mother, who had accompanied him to Italy. A year later he returned to Africa, spent some time at Thagaste with a group of friends, immersed in philosophic and theological studies, was persuaded, about 390, to go to Hippo and accept priest's orders, became coadjutor bishop of the diocese in 395, and shortly afterwards, by the death of the senior bishop, found himself in sole charge. He continued to exercise his functions till the time of his death.

His activity as a writer was so enormous, and so large a part of it purely theological, that no complete analysis can be attempted here. It may, however, be conveniently divided into groups.

I. The earliest works were mostly philosophical, but include a few of grammatical content. The latter were, Augustine says, a series of treatises which he wrote in connexion with his teaching activities and afterwards mislaid, save for the six books *de musica* which we still have.[84] These deal with rhythm and metre. He had already, while in Carthage, tried his hand at a philosophical essay, *de pulchro et apto*, which also he lost, and no trace of it has ever been found; it was probably of no great worth. We have, however, the fruits of his studies in 386, while he was living in retirement near Milan. They are the three books *contra Academicos*, one *de beata uita* and two *de ordine*. They may fairly be regarded as a record, in the comparatively finished literary form natural to one of his rhetorical antecedents, of his own problems; the speakers, for they are all dialogues, are himself and members of his actual circle of friends, while the subjects (the arguments against skepticism, the attainment of true happi-

used such words, he took it for an omen; a Greek would have said it was a κληδών, or utterance charged with a meaning not intended by the speaker but sent as a divine message to the accidental hearer. See, for a good and recent discussion, Geffcken in *Archiv für Religionswissenschaft*, xxxi, p. 1 *sqq.*; for a brief exposition of Augustine's religious life, A. D. Nock, *Conversion* (Oxford, Clar. Press, 1933), p. 259 *sqq.*

[84] See *retract.*, i, 6. He says there that he began works on dialectic, rhetoric, geometry, arithmetic and philosophy, and that the general title of the series was *disciplinarum libri*, its purpose per corporalia ad incorporalia quibusdam quasi passibus certis uel peruenire uel ducere, in other words he meant to lead up through the liberal arts to metaphysics and theology.

ness by knowledge of God and the questions involved in the doctrine of a Providence) are just such as he was certainly occupied with at that time. In this matter, as in many others, Augustine was a Ciceronian in the best sense, not slavishly imitating his model in language or anything else but adopting his methods of arguing out such matters as most concerned him, not only orally but pen in hand, and at the same time catching more than a little of his literary principles. Throughout his work, Augustine is the best stylist of all the Christians, not even excepting Lactantius, and proves himself able to combine ornateness and simplicity, dignity and a feeling for the colloquial language of the day, to an extent which makes his writings interesting even for the least theologically inclined of moderns and those most out of sympathy with the doctrines which he taught.[85]

A little later, but still of the same group, come the *Soliloquia*, two books in which the author represents himself as replying to his own questions concerning the characteristics which any one desirous of attaining to knowledge of truth must have and the immortality of really existent things, especially the soul. This work he never completed.[86] Two somewhat unsatisfactory tractates are the *de immortalitate animae*, which was not finally revised nor intended for publication, and the curiously named dialogue *de quantitate animae*.[87] A better product of his dialectical and philological skill is the dialogue *de magistro*, in which he discusses with Adeodatus (represented as being about fifteen years old, which fixes at least its dramatic date at 387) the significance of words; the title alludes to the text around which the final paragraph is built, Matt. 23, 8.[88]

II. Polemical divinity attracted Augustine's attention early and held it late. While in Rome in 387–388 he began the long series of such works with the dialogue on freewill (*de libero arbitrio*) and the discourse *de uera religione*, neither of which was finished, however, till he had returned to Africa.[89] Both of these books incidentally attack Manichaean dogmas; the subject is more fully dealt with in the two books entitled respectively *de moribus Manichaeorum* and *de moribus ecclesiae Catholicae*, to which may be added the two books on the exegesis of Genesis, *de Genesi contra Manichaeos*. All these works would appear to

[85] The dates of the works here mentioned may be easily gathered from *retract.*, i, 1–3, except the first, which is mentioned *conf.*, iv, 13/20, 15/27; the latter gives his age when he wrote it as twenty-six or twenty-seven.

[86] *Retr.*, i, 4.

[87] *Retr.*, i, 5, 1; 8, 1.

[88] *Retr.*, i, 12; *conf.*, ix, 6/14.

[89] *Ibid.*, i, 8, 1; 13, 1.

have been commenced in Rome but finished at Hippo.[90] In 391 he wrote the *de utilitate credendi*, to his old friend Honoratus, who had induced him to join the Manichaeans years before; naturally the belief which he now recommends to him is that which he had himself adopted.[91] In or about 391 he contended, in the tractate *de duabus animabus*, against one of the fundamental Manichaean dogmas, that man has both a good and a bad soul.[92] In 392 he held a public disputation against a prominent Manichee, by name Fortunatus, the official report of which is preserved under the title *acta seu disputatio contra Fortunatum*.[93] Two or three years later, he assailed Adimantus, a disciple of Mani himself, in the *contra Adimantum*[94]; in 397 he came to even closer grips with the sect by publishing an attack on Mani's own writing; the work is entitled *contra epistulam quam uocant fundamenti*. Augustine must, of course, have used a translation of the heresiarch's work, from which he quotes, for Mani wrote in Aramaic; it is, however, not likely that his African followers were any better off in this respect.[95] The work was never completed; Augustine perhaps left it to write his long refutation

[90] *Retr.*, i, 7, 1; 10, 1. The former passage states that he wrote the first two works in Rome after his baptism; the latter, that he composed the *de Genesi* in Africa. But the opening words of the *de mor. eccl.* plainly allude to the publication of the *de Gen.* Either, therefore, Augustine made a blunder of a kind hardly likely or he refers to the place where the bulk of each work was written, neglecting revisions and small additions.

[91] *Retract.*, i, 14, 1, which states that he wrote it apud Hipponem Regium presbyter constitutus.

[92] *Ibid.*, 15, 1: scripsi adhuc presbyter.

[93] *Ibid.*, 16, 1: eodem tempore presbyterii mei contra Fortunatum quendam Manichaeorum presbyterum disputaui . . . quae disputatio nobis altercantibus excepta est a notariis (taken down by shorthand reporters) ueluti gesta conficerentur, nam et diem habet et consulem. The opening words of this record (in vol. viii, p. 93 A of the Benedictine ed.) are: quinto kalendas Septembris, Arcadio Augusto II et Rufino u. c. consulibus, *i.e.*, Aug. 28, 392. All the anti-Manichaean treatises are in the same volume.

[94] *Ibid.*, i, 22, 1; Adimantus had written certain works to prove that the doctrines of the Old and New Testaments were irreconcilable, a favourite tenet of several of the contemporary sects. It is, of course, quite correct in a sense, the two sets of documents belonging to different stages of religious development and the older one being the product of a period of some centuries. Hence, in the main stream of Christian exegesis, the older doctrine that the Old Testament must be allegorized and the later one of a process of progressive revelation, which has also ancient parallels.

[95] See, for example, A. A. Bevan in Hastings, *Enc. Rel. Eth.*, viii, p. 395b; for a sketch of Manichaeism, see the whole article. The date of the work may be gathered approximately from *retr.*, ii, 2, 1; it is the second work he mentions as written after his consecration as bishop.

of Faustus, one of the prominent local members of the sect, the thirty-two books *contra Faustum Manichaeum.*[96] Another disputation, this time with a Manichee named Felix, is preserved to us, under the title *contra Felicem* or *de actis cum Felice Manichaeo*; the date is given exactly, Dec. 7 and 12, 404. He followed it up with another writing, *de natura boni contra Manichaeos* (about 405), and shortly after that was himself confronted with an attempt to convert him back to the doctrine he had abandoned. The Manichaean missionary, Secundinus, was answered in what Augustine himself considered his best work of this class, the book *contra Secundinum Manichaeum.*[97] The much later works *contra aduersarium legis et prophetarum* and *ad Orosium contra Priscillianistas et Origenistas* touch only incidentally on Manichaeism.[98]

The Donatist heresy gave Augustine much trouble, the more so as its differences from Catholicism were minute and rather matters of church discipline than doctrine. His first contribution to the long and painful quarrel between them and his own party was also a remarkable product from the point of view of metre; it is the so-called *Psalmus contra partem Donati*, or *Abecedarium*, intended to be sung by his congregation, for he wrote it before he became bishop.[99] It consists of twenty stanzas, each of twelve verses, with the refrain *omnes qui gaudetis pace, modo uerum iudicate*; 'all ye that delight in peace, give now true judgement'. The interesting thing about the work is that it is in accentual metre, thus marking a further concession to the popular loss of sense for quantity than the hymns of St. Ambrose, for these are still quantitative, although most lines could be scanned by accent as well. The contents are of no special interest, being merely a popular statement of the objections to Donatism, which are set forth at great length in his prose treatises.

It may be mentioned here that he wrote at least one piece of quantitative verse. In the *de ciuit. Dei*, xv, 22, he quotes three hexa-

[96] *Ibid.*, 7, 1; as Augustine had also the Donatist controversy on his hands at the time, it is a great tribute to his industry that he could embark on anything so elaborate.

[97] *Ibid.*, 8–10.

[98] The former work is mentioned, *ibid.*, 58; the latter, *ibid.*, 44. The dates are respectively 420 and 415. In the opening paragraph of each he remarks that his anti-Manichaean works contain refutations of several of the propositions advanced by the new adversaries.

[99] *Retr.*, i, 20; Augustine there says that he wrote non aliquo carminis genere, meaning no sort of quantitative metre. See Schanz-Hosius-Krüger, iv, 2, p. 461; Rose in *Journ. Theol. Stud.*, xxviii (1927), pp. 383–92.

meters from what he calls *laus quaedam cerei*, meaning apparently 'the praise of the candle'. We may conjecture that it was a sophistic exercise in verse, a laudation of an unpromising subject, given a religious turn, for the surviving lines deal with the goodness of all things created by God. Their quality is not such as to make us anxious for more of this author's poetry. A few other short pieces are more or less plausibly attributed to him.[100]

The *Psalmus* was accompanied by a work in prose, *contra epistulam Donati*, which is lost [101]; but after becoming bishop, Augustine wrote much on this theme. We have the three books *contra epistulam Parmeniani* and the seven *de baptismo contra Donatistas*, both of about the year 400 [102]; a little later come the three books *contra litteras Petiliani* and the *epistula ad Catholicos*, otherwise the *de unitate ecclesiae*, if this last is really Augustine's.[103] Still belonging to the same part of the controversy are the four books *contra Cresconium* (Cresconius was a Donatist writer who had taken up the cudgels on behalf of Petilianus) and the work *de unico baptismo*.[104] A conference between representatives of the two parties is recorded in the *breuiculus collationis cum Donatistis*; it is dated towards the end of May (the year is known to have been 411) and is not the official shorthand report, but Augustine's own summary of what took place.[105] He followed it up by an address to his opponents, variously known as *ad Donatistas post collationem* or *contra partem Donati post gesta*, which appeared in 412. A pause of some four years now followed, but besides a lost work directed against the Donatist bishop Emeritus, we still have a sermon, *ad Caesariensis ecclesiae plebem*, and the report of a controversy with Emeritus (*gesta cum Emerito*), respectively of Sept. 18 and Sept. 20, 418.[106] Several other works are missing, references to the controversy are common in Augustine's correspondence and elsewhere, and it need hardly be said that several anti-Donatist works by other hands have at one time or another been falsely attributed to him.

[100] Particulars in Schanz-Hosius-Krüger, iv, 2, p. 461 *sq.*

[101] See *Retr.*, i, 21, 1.

[102] *Ibid.*, ii, 17; 18.

[103] The former, *retr.*, ii, 25; the latter is not mentioned by Augustine, perhaps because he considered it a letter, not a treatise; it is, however, spoken of as his by Possidius in the index of works with which he concludes his *Life* of the saint; see vol. x, p. 284 of the Benedictine ed.

[104] *Retr.*, ii, 26; 34.

[105] *Ibid.*, 39.

[106] *Ibid.*, 46; 51. The sermon he does not mention, but it is published separately from the other sermons, vol. ix, p. 617 *sqq.* of the Benedictine, vol. liii, p. 179 *sqq.* of the Vienna edition.

Yet another long and complicated controversy was that with the Pelagians, in which Augustine began to be engaged in 412, Pelagius himself having by that time visited Africa and found there a vigorous supporter, by name Caelestius. Neglecting sermons and other such utterances, we have left to us the three books *de peccatorum meritis et remissione et de baptismo paruulorum* (it is Augustine who was first to state fully and explicitly the doctrine of original sin, with its corollary, the absolute necessity of infant baptism); the book *de spiritu et littera*, and the long letter, which its author exceptionally regards as a separate treatise, to his friend Honoratus, *de gratia noui testamenti*. These are of the first period of this controversy[107]; in 415 comes another series, first the two works *de natura et gratia* and *de perfectione iustitiae hominis*[108]; next, as Pelagius' activities continued and he won more or less support in various districts of the Empire, sundry letters and a longer communication, *de gestis Pelagii*,[109] sent to the Bishop of Carthage in 417; in the next year, two books *contra Pelagium et Caelestium*.[110] The next opponent to be met was a certain Iulianus of Aeclanum, who raised the objection that Augustine was implicitly denying the admitted holiness of marriage by some developments of his doctrine; two books *de nuptiis et concupiscentia* countered his attacks, while in 419 Augustine had found objections to the views on the soul expressed by yet another Pelagian, Vincentius Victor of Caesarea, with whom he dealt in his four books *de natura et origine animae*.[111] Four more books, in 420, were produced on the suggestion of the then Bishop of Rome, Boniface, who had sent Augustine some letters written by Italian bishops in support of Pelagianism; hence the title, *contra duas epistulas Pelagianorum*.[112] Six more books against Iulianus (*contra Iulianum*), composed about the same time, were not enough to dispose of that stubborn opponent, who it seems had not heard of them when he brought out a new work of his own. For some reason Augustine did not at once reply to this, and when, in 428, he set about doing so, he never lived to finish his treatise, which remains a fragment, six books long, the *opus imperfectum*

[107] *Retr.*, ii, 33; 36; 37; *ep.*, 140. The text of the anti-Pelagian treatises is in vol. x of the Benedictine ed.; vol. lx of the Vienna corpus contains some of them.

[108] *Ibid.*, 42; the *de perf.* he does not mention.

[109] *Ibid.*, 47.

[110] *Ibid.*, 50.

[111] *Ibid.*, 53; 56.

[112] *Ibid.*, 61; see further the opening sections of the treatise itself (vol. x, p. 411, ed. Bened.).

contra secundam Iuliani responsionem.[113] Augustine, however, followed up his earlier anti-Pelagian works by a series of writings emphasizing his own doctrine, *de gratia et libero arbitrio* and *de correptione et gratia*, both in 426 and the following year, then, about a year later, *de praedestinatione sanctorum* and de *dono perseuerantiae.*[114]

With the Arians Augustine came comparatively little in conflict; there remain two works, *contra sermonem Arianorum*, of 415, and *collatio cum Maximino haeretico, Arianorum episcopo*, some twelve years later; the latter is Augustine's expansion of an actual debate with the Arian bishop, Maximinus.[115]

The brief handbook of the whole subject, *aduersus haereses*, or *de haeresibus*, which he wrote late in life, contains little that is original, only the last four of its eighty-eight sections being more than an epitome of the information given by earlier and fuller writers, such as Epiphanios.[116]

III. The care of his flock and especially their training in virtuous living was almost as important to him as the defence of their orthodoxy. Hence a number of moral treatises. The *de mendacio* is an early production, a more uncompromising view of the unjustifiability of lying being reached in the much later *contra mendacium.*[117] On the question of sexual ethics, which was a veritable obsession to the Church of that day, Augustine took up a more reasonable position than Jerome; while setting the same exaggerated value on virginity as his colleagues (witness the *de sancta uirginitate*, written near the beginning of the fifth century) and holding, like the rest, that a widow was much more to be commended if she did not remarry than if she did (*de bono uiduitatis*, 414), he nevertheless warmly acknowledged the worth of the married state (*de bono coniugali*, about the same date as the treatise on virginity).[118] One of his latest works was a long selection of Biblical passages bearing upon conduct, known as the *Mirror* (*Speculum*), as comprising the best possible

[113] For the former work, see *retr.*, ii, 62; for the latter, *ep.* 224, 2.

[114] The first two are mentioned in the last two sections of the *retr.*; the others are nowhere mentioned either by their author or by Possidius, but are attributed to Augustine by several other writers, and the internal evidence for their genuineness is perfectly plain.

[115] *Retr.*, ii, 52; Possidius, *uit.*, 17. The text of both is in vol. viii of the Benedictine edition.

[116] Not in the *retr.*; see *epp.*, 222–4, the correspondence between the deacon Quodvultdeus and Augustine on the subject.

[117] See *retr.*, i, 27.

[118] *Ibid*, ii, 22, 23; the *de bono uid.* he seems to have regarded as a letter, not a treatise; it is in vol. xli, p. 303 *sqq.*, of the Vienna corpus, vi, 369–386 of the Benedictine.

guide for the faithful to follow.[119] He was always willing to give his opinion on cases of conscience, as many of his letters show, and to prescribe, if called upon, for other communities than his own, as is clear from the work *de opere monachorum*, maintaining the wholesome doctrine that the monks of Carthage, about whom he had been consulted, were not to make their sanctity an excuse for living idly on the alms of the laity.[120] Theory was joined to practice, witness the very interesting tractate *de catechizandis rudibus*,[121] composed about 400. As a preacher he was indefatigable; his known sermons run into hundreds. A great body of what we have from him consists of series dealing with one book or another of the Bible, a common practice among the Fathers, notably frequent, for instance, in St. Chrysostom. These we may consider under

IV. Although Augustine was at home in neither of the languages used by the Biblical writers (we have seen that his Greek was poor, and he knew no Hebrew at all), and therefore was compelled for the most part to rely on translations, he was by no means indifferent to scholarship. After some hesitation, he introduced Jerome's revised Latin Bible into his diocese,[122] and his commentaries are full of references to matters of interpretation and the correct rendering of the original, the fruit of second-hand information most diligently gathered. His own repute as an exegete was enormous and grew after his death. Either in the form of courses of sermons or in treatises meant only to be read, we have from him two commentaries on Genesis, with a third unfinished, two more dealing with chosen passages from the Heptateuch (*quaestiones in Heptateuchum* and *locutiones in Heptateuchum*, each running to seven books), one on Job, a very long series on the Psalter, and, from the New Testament, an elaborate exposition of the Sermon on the Mount (*de sermone Domini in monte*), two books of *quaestiones euangeliorum*, or discussions of difficulties in the Gospels of Matthew and Luke, the long series of *tractatus* on his favourite Fourth Gospel, supplemented by ten more *tractatus* on the First Epistle of St. John, an exposition of the Epistle of St. James and commentaries, complete or unfinished, on Romans and Galatians. It is to be noted that those of his expositions which are originally sermons

[119] Written after *retr.*, as that does not mention it; vol. xii (Vienna), iii, 681–818 (Bened.).

[120] *Retr.*, ii, 21.

[121] *Ibid.*, 14.

[122] Though not without doubts and difficulties; see the extremely interesting *ep.* 71 (Augustine to Jerome).

are quite clearly marked by their style, full as that is of popular turns of phrase, language and rhythm; for Augustine knew how to adapt himself to his audience and write in learned or unlearned fashion as might be required. Some account of his principles on this matter is to be gathered from the four books *de doctrina Christiana* (*i.e.*, 'Learning in the service of Christianity'), which among other admirable instances of its author's good taste justifies this use of the common speech to make oneself better understood and analyses two Biblical passages from the point of view of their stylistic and rhetorical excellence.[123] It is a very remarkable instance of ability to penetrate through the superficial inelegancies, caused by the rendering of a foreign idiom into Latin with too great fidelity, to the broader stylistic features which a translation, if it will but give the sense and arrangement of the original, does not obscure. A work at once exegetic and controversial is the four books *de consensu euangelistarum*, upholding the negative in the debate, which was already growing threadbare, as to whether or not the four Gospels contradict each other at times.[124]

V. A great part of Augustine's works are dogmatic and apologetic. Apart from letters—people seem to have resorted to him for theology as regularly as they did for exegesis to Jerome, and his patience and good sense were alike admirable—miscellaneous works (*de diuersis quaestionibus ad Simplicianum* and *de diuersis quaestionibus lxxxiii*; *de octo Dulcitii quaestionibus*) and short handbooks (*de fide, spe et caritate enchiridion*), he wrote on the Creed, on faith, on the indissolubility of marriage, on demonology and what we should call psychical research,[125] had a brief skirmish with the Jews,[126] and, what is much more important, spent the leisure of several years (412–426) on a long and elaborate statement of his philosophy of history, the *de*

[123] *De doctr. Christ.*, iv, 24 (cf. *enarr. in Psal.* cxxxviii, 20); 11–20; the passages analysed are 2 Cor. 11, 16 *sqq.*, Amos 6, 1 *sqq.*

[124] *Retr.*, ii, 16.

[125] *De diuinatione daemonum* and still more *de cura pro mortuis gerenda*, besides numerous references to such things as ghosts, visions, clairvoyance and so forth, scattered up and down his other works. I am inclined to agree with Professor E. R. Dodds (*Greek Poetry and Life*, Clar. Press, 1936, p. 382) that 'Augustine deserves a more honourable place in the history of psychical research than any other thinker between Aristotle and Kant'.

[126] *Aduersus Iudaeos*, a sermon which apparently was published separately. The author does not mention it in *Retr.*; the text is in vol. viii, p. 29 *sqq.*, of the Benedictine ed. The chief matter in dispute is, of course, the Messianic passages of the Old Testament.

ciuitate Dei.[127] The original occasion of this was the sack of Rome by the Goths in 410, which had galvanized into life the old complaint that nothing had gone well since the Christians came. The first ten books uphold the theory that the pagan deities are of no avail for this life or any other. This is familiar ground enough, though he handles it freshly, not the least interesting parts being the digressions into discussion of subordinate problems. The rest of the twenty-two develop the concept of a Divine social order, of the next world rather than this, and its final goal, including the expected last conflict between the earthly and heavenly realms which is to lead through the Millennium, the appearance of Antichrist and the Second Coming to the Last Judgement. The last book closes with a description of the peace of the eternal Sabbath.

Of less general interest than this, but always worth reading, even by those uninterested in theology and Church history, if only for the digressions they contain and the constant realization the author shows of the life and thought of his time,[128] are the various other theological treatises, such as the *de baptismo, de Trinitate* and others, which he composed from time to time. A detailed description of them, however, would be out of place in such a manual as this.

To conclude this section, mention may be made of two interesting figures, a converted astrologer and a Christian poet. IVLIVS FIRMICVS MATERNVS seems to have been something of an authority on the pseudo-science which he practised for many years; at all events, he wrote a long treatise on it, the eight books of which were eagerly read, official denunciations notwithstanding, for centuries after the author's death, to judge by the many MSS. which survive.[129] To a modern, it is exceedingly dry reading, remarkable partly for its preserving information which is not elsewhere accessible, partly because it is one of the very few works which make any use of Manilius (cf. p. 355). The date is towards the end of Constantine's reign.[130] But about

[127] This is perhaps his most famous work and one of the few which have been well edited. Texts are to be found both in the Teubner series (Dombart) and the Vienna corpus (vol. xl, a, b).

[128] See Rose in *Proc. Camb. Phil. Soc.*, 1926, pp. 5–21, for one aspect of this.

[129] See the preface to vol. ii of the Teubner edition, the only modern one (ed. Kroll-Skutsch-Ziegler, 1897 and 1913). The title of the work is *Mathesis*, a not uncommon name for astrology, as the learning *par excellence*.

[130] The eclipse of the sun on July 17, 334, is recent, *Math.*, i, 4, 10; Constantine is several times mentioned, always as being still alive; he died on May 22, 337. See further Schanz, iv, 1, p. 131.

ten years later, we find Firmicus a zealous Christian, writing a treatise *On the Error of Profane Religions*, which certainly has the advantage of being more lively than his longer work. It is unfortunately much battered and has lost several passages, this being the more deplorable because its author seems to have known a good deal about the pagan cults and gives many interesting details.[131]

An anonymous work, entitled *consultationes Zacchaei et Apollonii*, is also by Firmicus, according to Dom G. Morin, who has recently published a critical edition of it (Bonn, Hanstein, 1934). Its interest is mainly for students of the history of Christian dogma and specialists in the text of the Latin Bible. See p. 533.

AVLVS PRVDENTIVS CLEMENS was roughly a generation younger than Firmicus, since he reached his fifty-seventh birthday in 405. He was a native of Spain, apparently a fairly prominent member of the civil service, until, feeling the approach of old age, he retired and devoted himself to pious works. These, by his own account,[132] consisted of hymns for day and night hours, attacks upon heresies and defences of Catholicism, overthrowings of paganism, especially Roman, and the praises of the martyrs and apostles. So far as is known, his hope that such occupations should be his only ones for the remainder of his days was realized.

He is best known to the moderns as a hymn-writer, for some of his performances keep a place in our collections.[133] In this sort of composition he shows facility, a knowledge of classical metre which, for his date, is very fair,[134] and a certain prettiness

[131] The approximate date is given by the address to Constantius II and Constans, *de errore*, 20, 7. This must be not later than Jan., 350 (death of Constans). 28, 6, speaks of the British expedition of 343, thus narrowing the possible dates to those seven years.

[132] Our information is derived from Prudentius himself, who prefixed to a collection of most of his poems a short autobiography. In this he says he was born in the consulship of Salia, *i.e.*, Flavius Salia, consul, with Flavius Philippus, in 348 (line 24) and goes on to mention (37–42) the poems, as cited above. The opening lines give his age and therefore the year, 405, of this publication.

[133] Thus the not unfamiliar hymn, 'Of the Father's love begotten', is an adaptation of part of No. 9, the long *hymnus omnis horae*, in honour of Christ. The hymn for cock-crow, No. 1, *ales diei nuntius*, or rather some part of its hundred lines, is also in occasional use.

[134] He uses a great variety of lyric lines, also iambics, trochees and hexameters. His prosody is far from impeccable, though some of his many false quantities are doubtless to be accounted for by contemporary pronunciation, a few by metrical necessity. The word *catholicus* can be got into most of his metres only by lengthening the first syllable, as he regularly does, using a licence as old as Homer. His fondness for making

of fancy. His chief defect is that he is interminably long, his grace before meat, for instance, extending to 205 lines. The title of the collection, *Cathemerinon, i.e., Hymns for daily use,* is not quite appropriate, for it includes a hymn for a funeral, also others for Christmas and Epiphany.

His controversial works are the *Apotheosis*, which deals with the human and divine natures of Christ, and therefore has much to say of heretical teachings, and the poem on the *Origin of Sin* (*Harmartigenia*), in which he opposes the doctrines of Marcion. These are in hexameters, with introductions in iambic metres; the same is true of the *Conflict for the Soul* (*Psychomachia*), interesting as being the first allegorical poem in Europe. Successive pairs of abstractions (True Faith and Idolatry, Pride and Humility, and so forth) contend for possession of the soul of man. Prudentius must be credited here with a certain ingenuity, though he had not the rare power to make personifications live. This work is not on the author's own list, and therefore must have been composed later than the collection to which his autobiographical verses form the preface. His attack upon idolatry is his reply, in two books of hexameters, to Symmachus (cf. p. 524), a versification, sometimes vigorous, of the stock arguments of Christian controversialists. The prefaces are in glyconics and the title, for once deserting Greek, is simply *contra Symmachum*.

As for the martyrs and apostles, it may be said that Prudentius is worst on this, his most promising subject. Such legends as that of S. Romanus, who by miracle continued to testify when his tongue was cut out, or of the virgin martyr Agnes, might in the hands of a good poet have been made moving and thrilling. Prudentius is often disgusting, from his morbid insistence on the details of torture, generally puerile and always tedious; martyrs always and persecutors sometimes orate volubly and have no idea when to stop. The most elaborate piece and probably the earliest, or one of the earliest,[135] the martyrdom of

the first syllable of *haeresis* short is in accordance with the pronunciation of his day, in which Greek *αι* and Latin *ae* alike had become a short *e*; sometimes he lengthens a short syllable because it is accented, as *Asclepiādes, utrāque* (neut. plur.).

[135] The arguments for the date of this work will be found briefly stated on p. xii of the best edition of Prudentius, that of J. Bergmann, Vienna and Leipzig, 1926 (Corpus script. ecc. Lat., vol. 61). Prudentius, in the versified preface already quoted (lines 40–41) says: conculcet sacra gentium, labem, Roma, tuis inferat idolis. This suggests two poems; if one is the *contra Symmachum*, it is hard to see what other he can mean except the *sancti Romani martyris contra gentiles dicta*, as *perist.* 10 (the numbering is due to modern editors) is called in the best MS. A large part of it consists of Romanus' lengthy discourses against paganism.

Romanus, runs to over 1,100 iambic lines and ends with the silliest possible conceit; Prudentius hopes that at the last day he may be among the reprobate, for the pleasure of owing his salvation to Romanus' intercession. The general title of this collection, whether its author's own or not, is *Peristephanon, i.e., περὶ στεφάνων*, 'concerning the crowns' (of the martyrs).

A trifling work which goes under this author's name and may well be his is a series of epigrams on Biblical events, from Eve and the apple down. Each is in four hexameters. Some late authorities say he wrote a poem on the Creation, *Hexaemeron* or *de mundi exordio*. If this is true, it is completely lost to us.[136]

Having thus given a sketch of the Christian authors, omitting scores of the lesser names, it remains for us to glance in like manner at those pagans who came later than Juvenal. It will be seen that they rapidly diminish in importance and ability; clearly the better intellects of the third and later centuries were passing over to the newer faith, and all the more readily because the age was deeply religious, and it would seem that the great majority of thinking men and women were adherents of one or another of the several cults which were or had become transcendental in their teaching.

We begin with a very respectable author, to whom we owe much, C. SVETONIVS TRANQVILLVS. A friend of the younger Pliny and for some time in the service of Hadrian (117–138), he was one of the most learned men of that age. Of his quiet life not much is known. Pliny [137] gives him a thoroughly amiable character, and certainly would not have given his own intimacy to one who was undeserving, nor recommended him to the special favour of so clear-sighted an Emperor as Trajan. Suetonius was born about the beginning of Vespasian's principate, his father having served under Otho at Bedriacum. The family was of equestrian rank.[138] Being well educated and unambitious, he began to write at a fairly early age, though he was slow to publish;

[136] See Bergmann, p. xiii.

[137] Pliny, *epp.*, i, 18 (asks a small favour for Suetonius); i, 24 (gives his opinion about a dream Suetonius had had); iii, 8 (consents to transfer a commission in the army from Suetonius to a friend); v, 10 (urges Suetonius to publish); ix, 34 (consults him on a matter of literary etiquette); x, 94 (asks Trajan to grant Suetonius the *ius trium liberorum*); 95 (Trajan consents). These letters, Suetonius' own incidental mentions of his affairs, and the imperfect catalogue of his works in Suidas, *s.u.* *Τράγκυλλος* are almost our only biographical materials. See, for the latest study, the art. of Funaioli in Pauly-Wissowa, 2e Reihe, iv, 593–641.

[138] Suet., *Nero*, 57; he was *adulescens* twenty years after Nero's death, *i.e.*, in 87; *Otho*, 10 (Suetonius' father).

his interests were primarily literary and antiquarian, but on becoming secretary to Hadrian [139] he had access to Imperial records, including private letters of Augustus and other personal documents, of which he made good use for the only work which has survived entire. This is the famous series of biographies of the twelve Caesars (Julius to Domitian inclusive), in which the author shows a certain originality of form. Hitherto, the type of biography which he writes, little more than an orderly arrangement of facts, small and great, under rubrics of birth, early life, public career, private qualities, good and bad, death, had been used for literary men, apparently ever since the days of Aristotle's immediate followers.[140] Suetonius applies it to princes, whose lives had hitherto tended, if written at all, to be panegyrics or the reverse, illustrations of what prominent men should or should not be. The result is that he gives us, in a clear, unaffected style, a most precious storehouse of materials, of very unequal value it is true, since anecdote and folktale often jostle the most authentic documents and the writer's love of gossip is undisguised, and so leaves us to form our own conclusions, with the help of a few moral reflections introduced from time to time. Within his limits he is critical, some of his material at least is first-rate,[141] and his intention to tell nothing but the truth is admitted by every fair judge.

Of another important work we have considerable and useful fragments. Its title, which we have only in Greek, was something like *de uiris illustribus*, and it consisted of biographies of men celebrated in literature, including, apparently, all the branches represented in Rome. It was thus a kind of history, or rather collected materials for a history, of Latin literature. Reference has already been made to the lives of Terence, Vergil, Horace, and Lucan (pp. 73, 237, 266, 379), which we still have; all of these may with more or less certainty be traced to Suetonius' work. He was St. Jerome's source and model for literary history (pp. 492, 493). Finally, the sections on grammarians and rhetoricians still survive (cf. pp. 441, 511).[142]

Of his remaining works, which were many and important, we know less, and cannot exactly estimate the debt which later writers owe to him, though it is certainly not inconsiderable. He composed three books *de regibus*, including, it would seem, lives of many foreign and

[139] *Hist. Aug.*, i, 11, 3.
[140] See Rose, *H.G.L.*, pp. 354, 357.
[141] His sources, however, are very uncertain, see Funaioli, 615, 67 *sqq*.
[142] See, for particulars of this important work, Funaioli, 597, 54 *sqq*.

some exceedingly obscure monarchs.[143] Suidas (cf. note 137) and Ioannes Lydus give also the following titles: *Concerning notorious courtesans*, no doubt a collection of learned scandal, to which there are Alexandrian parallels[144]; *Concerning Cicero's 'Republic'*, which, Suidas explains, was a reply to Didymos, the famous and prolific Alexandrian scholar[145]; *Concerning the pastimes of the Greeks* (this was apparently written in Greek, included such things as children's games, and is often quoted by late Greek writers); *Concerning Roman spectacles and contests* (two books), which may be the work elsewhere heard of as *historia ludicra*[146]; *Concerning the Roman Year*; a work on clothing which seems to have been called *de genere uestium*[147]; *Concerning Rome and its customs and habits* (two books); *Concerning abusive language*[148]; *Concerning the signs used in books* (*i.e.*, the conventional marks used by Alexandrian critics to call attention to various things in the text); *The Book of Kinship* (Συγγενικόν), which may have dealt with the words used to express relationship. Finally, from Latin writers, we have quotations from a miscellany called *Prata* (*pratum*, a meadow, renders the Greek title Λειμών, often used for a work dealing with a variety of topics; the plural merely means that it was in several books). It would seem to have been of grammatical and lexicographical content.

Suetonius, if not exactly a historian, was a respectable antiquary and a collector of useful materials. No such praise can be given to ANNIVS FLORVS (the *praenomen* is uncertain, our authorities varying between P., L. and Iulius, whereof the last is, of course, impossible),[149] author of two books on the military history of Rome to the time of Augustus. He gets his facts largely from Livy, adding some blunders of his own, his arrangement from the elder Seneca (cf. ch. x, n. 108), and contributes

143 Mentioned by Ausonius, *ep.* 23; his old pupil, Pontius Paulinus, had been amusing himself by turning Suetonius' work into verse.

144 Ioannes Laurentius Lydus, *de magistrat.*, iii, 64 (p. 155, 22 Wuensch).

145 This becomes comprehensible when we compare Ammianus Marcellinus, xxii, 16, 16, who tells us that Didymos wrote six books against Cicero, which produce, iudicio doctarum aurium (does he mean those of Suetonius?), the effect of a puppy yapping at a lion. For this Didymos see Rose, *H.G.L.*, p. 390; besides the commentaries there mentioned, he composed a prodigious number of works on all manner of philological subjects.

146 Gellius, ix, 7, 3: Suetonius etiam Tranquillus in libro ludicrae historiae primo. This fits well enough with Suidas' περὶ τῶν παρὰ Ῥωμαίοις θεωριῶν καὶ ἀγώνων βιβλία β', except that Gellius' *primo*, if that, and not merely I (*i.e.*, *priore*) is what he really wrote, should mean that there were at least three books of the work. See Funaioli, 625, 45 *sqq.* for some theories on this matter.

147 See Servius on Verg., *Aen.*, vii, 612.

148 See, for what is known of this, Funaioli, 629, 22 *sqq.*

149 See Schanz-Hosius-Krüger, iii, p. 76.

some showy rhetoric often of a poetical flavour. It may therefore very well be that he is the poet Florus who exchanged jokes in verse with Hadrian and has left us a few trifling compositions preserved in the Latin Anthology.[150] There is also no serious objection to supposing that he is that Florus who wrote a dialogue on the stock school question whether Vergil should be called a poet or an orator. If this is so, our writer was growing old by Hadrian's time, for he says in the fragment of the dialogue which survives that he was an unsuccessful competitor in the Agon Capitolinus under Domitian.[151]

Here we may mention a very remarkable poem indeed, whose composition has been attributed, by little more than guesswork, to Florus. The *Vigil of Venus* (*Peruigilium Veneris*) is one of the most delightful monuments of Latin literature, preserved without the name of any author, uncertain, but not early, in date, and looking forward in a surprising manner to medieval and modern lyrics. The scene is Sicily; the time, spring; the morrow is a festival of Venus, and meanwhile she holds revel in the woods by night, and a refrain, which divides the poem into stanzas of unequal length, bids all who have or have not loved to love on the coming day. The poet hails her, in language almost as inspired as that of Lucretius' proem, as the great goddess of increase, and ends on a sudden note of sadness; his spring will not come, and, unlike the nightingale which sings to Venus and her followers, he will never break silence.[152] Whoever he was, this work shows such poetical ability and feeling as to constitute a decided objection to crediting Florus with it.

Somewhere about this time, for his historical section brings down the series of Roman wars no further than Trajan, lived an otherwise unknown LVCIVS AMPELIVS. This man had a friend, by name Macrinus, who thirsted for universal knowledge, and Ampelius wrote him a handbook (*liber memorialis*) concerning 'the universe, the elements, what the earth has to show and what mankind has done'.[153] It

[150] *Hist. Aug.*, i, 16, 3–4; *Anth. Lat.*, 87 and 245 Riese, P.L.M., iv, pp. 279 and 346 Baehrens.

[151] See Schanz-Hosius-Krüger, *ibid.*, p. 75. The historian lived at least to Trajan's day, for he several times alludes to him. The text of the dialogue, so far as it survives, was first published by Ritschl in *Rhein. Mus.*, i (1842), p. 302.

[152] Editions and outline of some critical difficulties, Schanz-Hosius-Krüger, *ibid.*, pp. 73–5.

[153] The opening sentence is: uolenti tibi omnia nosse scripsi hunc librum memorialem, ut noris quid sit mundus, quid elementa, quid orbis terrarum ferat, uel quid genus humanum peregerit. The work has been recently edited by E. Assmann (Teubner, 1935) and by N. Terzaghi, Turin, n.d. (1944 ?).

has at least the merit of brevity; for example, it devotes about 200 words to the entire history of the Punic Wars.

Also under Hadrian, perhaps,[154] lived GRANIVS LICINIANVS. We know from Macrobius and other authors that he was an antiquarian, but none of his works have survived, save a historical composition, whereof we have some badly damaged fragments on a palimpsest. It seems to have been an account, divided into many and probably short books, of the history of Rome. A principal source was Livy. This Granius plainly cannot be the same as GRANIVS FLACCVS, for we know that he dedicated a treatise to Julius Caesar.[155]

Here, since it claims to use sources of Hadrian's time and succeeding reigns, we may deal with a curious collection of Imperial lives, written in pitiably bad imitation of Suetonius and known under the general title of *Historia Augusta*. Taking it at its face value, it is the collected works of a whole group of writers, most remarkably alike in style, or absence thereof, and silliness. Their names are AELIVS SPARTIANVS, IVLIVS CAPITOLINVS, VVLCACIVS GALLICANVS, AELIVS LAMPRIDIVS, TREBELLIVS POLLIO and FLAVIVS VOPISCVS. They claim to derive their information from earlier authors, MARIVS MAXIMVS, who wrote the biographies of the Emperors from Nerva to Elagabalus, and IVNIVS CORDVS, whose specialty was the lives of the obscurer Emperors, beside a number of writers who are cited occasionally, certain documents and a chronicle. But the *Historia Augusta* is a work of so little credit that we cannot take at their face value any such indications. Certainly many of the documents alleged to be quoted are forgeries. However, some at least of the writers seem to be real; L. Marius Maximus Perpetuus Aurelianus was a public man of some prominence in the late second and early third centuries, the chronicle gives some of the best information we have in the whole collection, and Cordus is a credible figure if we suppose a silly gossip-writer turning his attention to past instead of present notorieties.[156] If the collection is what it purports to be, the date of it is between 284 and 337, for several of the lives are dedicated to Diocletian and Constantine, so presumably fall within their reigns. But it is

[154] The chief indication of date is the words, p. 6, 8 Flemisch (Teubner, 1904): aedes nobilissima Olympii Iouis Atheniensis diu imperfecta permanse— suggesting that Licinianus mentioned, or at all events knew of, Hadrian's completion of the temple; the last word should probably be *permansit* or *permanserat*.

[155] Censorinus, 3, 2: Granius Flaccus in libro quem ad Caesarem de indigitamentis scriptum reliquit. Cf. p. 29, n. 37.

[156] For what is known of these sources, see Schanz-Hosius-Krüger, iii, pp. 81–8.

now widely held that Capitolinus and the rest are phantoms and the whole work was written much later than its alleged date, either under Theodosius I (so Dessau) or at earliest under Julian (so Baynes).[157] But the whole question is very obscure, and nothing like general agreement has yet been reached, which is the more to be regretted as the *Historia*, wretched though it is, is often our only or principal continuous account of events in the later Empire.

In the degenerate state of historical writing and in view of the loss of a good deal of what was written, we are obliged to take notice of some very trifling compositions. Some unknown person, in or about the year 354, since that is the date at which he ends, wrote a chronicle, sometimes called that of Philocalus, since one FVRIVS DIONYSIVS PHILOCALVS informs us that he *titulauit* the work, which need not mean more than that he was a professional copyist and wrote out an ornamental title-page. It comprises a calendar, lists of consuls to 354 and of city prefects to the same date, also lists of the burials of the Bishops of Rome and of the martyrs. Associated with it, more or less loosely, are several similar documents.[158]

AVRELIVS VICTOR, an African,[159] wrote a sketch of the Empire under the title *Caesares*; it extends to 360. Perhaps its chief claim to remembrance is the delicious remark which concludes the history of the Julio-Claudian house, to the effect that a prince ought to be both virtuous and cultured, but if he finds that impossible, he should at all events be the latter. Some unknown hand enlarged this into what is sometimes called the *Historia Tripertita*, and used mistakenly to be credited to Victor also, by adding an *Origo gentis Romanae*, from Saturn to Romulus, in which he professes to make much use of the Republican authors, and no doubt has excerpted some respectable works to make his little pamphlet, though not so many as he would have us think, and furthermore an enumeration of famous individuals from Proca, king of Alba Longa, to Antony and Kleopatra (this

[157] Dessau, first in *Hermes*, xxiv (1889), p. 337 *sqq.*, after which the theory was followed up, elaborated and opposed by a number of writers, including Mommsen and Seeck, see Schanz, iv, p. 60; Baynes, *The Historia Augusta: its date and purpose*, Oxford, 1926.

[158] For the text of these chroniclers, who are much more important for history than for pure literature, see Mommsen, *Chronica minora*, Berlin, 1892, and his *Gesammelte Schriften*, vol. vii, p. 536.

[159] Victor Afer, *origo, init.* Hence, *Caes.*, 20, 6, he speaks of Septimius Severus as being *gentis nostrae*. His praenomen was apparently Sextus, see Pichlmayr's (Teubner) edition, *praef.*, p. iv (the same volume contains the *origo* and *de u. il.*).

is commonly called *de uiris illustribus urbis Romae*, a title which fits most of its contents accurately enough). In all three works we find scraps of information which are welcome. Evidently Victor was read, for there is an epitome of him made about the end of the century and bringing the narrative down to the death of Theodosius I in 395.

Contemporary with Victor was EVTROPIVS, an official at the court of Valens (Emperor 364–378). His sovran, wishing to know something of history and having no time, or no inclination, to study it, asked Eutropius to draw him up a short account, which he did. The work survives under the title of *Breuiarium ab urbe condita*; its ten books occupy but 75 Teubner pages, it carries the history of Rome down to the death of the Emperor Jovian in 364, and it is written clearly and simply. Of independent historical value it has of course none, but is occasionally useful where its sources are lost.

We may suppose that IVLIVS OBSEQVENS lived in the fourth century. His little work *de prodigiis*, derived from Livy,[160] gives an account of portentous happenings and the means taken to avert their ill-omened threats between the years 564/190 and 742/12. Since its moral is that only the correct rites can be trusted to stay disaster (and so, by implication, that the new-fashioned Christian ways are unreliable), it is reasonable enough to see in him, as most scholars do, a supporter of the last champions of paganism.

Much more famous is the work of LVCIVS SEPTIMIVS, which, to judge by its style, is likewise of the fourth century. He composed a free rendering in Latin of the Greek Diktys, allegedly a companion of Idomeneus of Crete in the War of Troy, really a fictionist of perhaps the second century A.D., possibly the first,[161] who wrote what purported to be an eye-witness's account of the war. The work is rubbish, save that it here and there preserves some interesting fragment of tradition not unrecognizably altered; Septimius' version is not bad in style, for the period. We know nothing about him.

Much later, about the beginning of the sixth century, Diktys' companion author, Dares the Phrygian, was given a Latin dress, for it seems likelier than not that this work also rests upon a Greek

[160] Probably not directly, but from some chronicle or epitome which in turn had used Livy. See Schanz, iv, pp. 84–5.

[161] Septimius in his prologue to the work says the original was found in the thirteenth year of Nero (66/67) and translated out of Phoenician into Greek; this may therefore be the date of its composition. For the surviving fragment of the Greek, see Rose, *H.G.L.*, p. 417.

foundation. Bedecked with an introductory epistle from Cornelius Nepos to Sallust, it was taken at its face value by the Middle Ages and formed, along with Diktys, the foundation of the Troy-saga for many centuries.[162]

From these and similar petty scribblers we turn to a real historian, the last of Latin antiquity. Curiously enough, he was not of Western origin nor a professional man of letters, but a Greek officer, by name AMMIANVS MARCELLINVS. He set himself the ambitious task of continuing Tacitus down to his own day. How well he succeeded in the earlier parts of the work, we do not know; our copies begin with his fourteenth book. But from that point onwards, that is to say, for part of the reign of Constantius II and the whole of the succeeding principates down to the death of Valens in 378, we have his trustworthy guidance. Despite his deplorable style, he not only speaks from first-hand knowledge of many events and other good information of the rest, but he understands the duties of a historian as no one since Tacitus had done. For a man whose life had been for the most part spent in active occupations, his purely literary knowledge is extraordinary, while his numerous digressions, on matters especially of ethnology and geography, show indeed second-hand learning, but by no means the worst of its kind. A great admirer of the most controversial personality of his day, Julian the Apostate, he nevertheless criticizes him on occasion; a pagan, he has no bitterness against Christianity, but merely a certain contempt for its internal squabbles.[163] Best of all, he brings to his task a virile understanding, and his comments are for the most part his own, not mere school-maxims and commonplaces.

We should like to know more of this man and of the means by which, in that age, he attained to such a combination of sanity, practical experience and literary knowledge; but, except for a mention or two of him in the correspondence of Libanios the sophist,[164] we have only the information which he gives us incidentally in his history. He was an officer under Ursicinus, commander of the eastern armies of the Empire from 350; this might mean that he was born about 332, for young men often received a commission when eighteen years old. He was a

[162] See, for these two authors, Schanz, iv, pp. 85–90; iv, 2, pp. 84–7.

[163] See his remarks, xxi, 16, 18; xxii, 5, 3–4. In the former, he describes Christianity as absoluta et simplex, 'a complete, straightforward system', and regrets that Constantius corrupted it with silly superstition and misplaced curiosities.

[164] Libanios' 983rd letter is addressed to Ammianus, who was evidently on friendly terms with him.

Greek of good family, and in the course of his service he travelled widely, visiting Greece, Egypt, various parts of Asia, the neighbourhood of the Black Sea, and some parts of the West, including what seems to have been a long stay at Rome. How long he took to write his history and how long he lived after completing it we do not know.[165] With him we may end the Latin historians.

An unknown writer, called, from his first editor, the Anonymus Valesii, is commonly printed along with Ammianus; his work, which is represented only by excerpts, concerns the Constantines and Theoderic. It is scrappy, but not worthless.

Rhetoric and *belles lettres* took, under the Good Emperors, a decided turn for the worse, guided by M. CORNELIVS FRONTO. This amiable man, the teacher of Marcus Aurelius Antoninus, inflicted upon his native language the final injury, from which it never fully recovered, despite the efforts of St. Augustine and a few others. It was already artificial, but so are all literary languages, more or less; he made it archaistic as well, and that in the very worst way. The Greek Atticizers[166] had striven, often very cleverly, to imitate an idiom no longer in living use, not because it was old but because it was good. Archaism in Fronto's writings, as with the artists of Hadrian's day and later, became an esteemed ornament. Now it is true that good exponents of any medium of expression, audible or visual, have a regard for usage in the past and for the tradition of their art, and on occasion revive forms (words or phrases in language, technical methods in sculpture, and so forth) which have for a while gone out of fashion. But Fronto employs his antiquarian spoils to adorn his style in such profusion and so intricately blended with the Latin of his own day that to get a modern equivalent one must imagine a writer of our date filling his sentences with a heterogeneous collection of words and phrases taken from all manner of authors from Chaucer to Addison and stitched on a fabric of ordinary modern English. Such barocco writing may, in the hands of a really skilful artist, be used now and again

[165] Ammianus, xxxi, 16, 9 (ego ut miles quondam et Graecus); xix, 8, 6 (he is ingenuus and unused to severe toil); xiv, 9, 1 and many other passages, his service under Ursicinus; xxvi, 10, 19, he has visited Lakonia; xxii, 15, 1, Egypt; 8, 1, the Pontic region; xiv, 6, 2 *sqq.*, Rome. It appears from Libanios that Antioch was his native town. The best edition of his work is that of Clark, Traube and Heraeus, Berlin, Weidmann, 1910–15 (to xxxi only); an older one is that of Eyssenhardt, Berlin, Vahlen, 1871. Brief account of further literature in Schanz, iv, pp. 94–107.

[166] Cf. Rose, *H.G.L.*, p. 396 *sqq.*

with effect; the prose romances of William Morris have more than a little of it. But it is a hopeless model for the less able to follow, and has in it no possibilities of growth in the one wholesome direction for a style, that which enables it still to keep in touch with living speech. Fronto himself is frankly tedious and irritating, except that the contents of his works are often interesting in themselves. What we have of him is chiefly his letters, together with some replies of his Imperial pupil, also of Antoninus Pius. These deal with a variety of matters, literary and personal; but some of them are covering letters to rhetorical exercises, mostly in Latin, as the *Encomium on Smoke and Dust* and the *Praise of Carelessness*, but occasionally in Greek, as the *Amatory Discourse*.[167] Many other works, referred to in the correspondence or mentioned by other writers, are now lost; these include a number of speeches, some forensic, others on special occasions, the latter being of the nature of loyal addresses. The one which it would be most interesting to recover is certainly the invective against the Christians, mentioned by Minucius Felix.[168]

We know the main facts of his life.[169] He was a native of Cirta in Numidia, and practised for a time as a pleader. Becoming interested in the antiquarian studies of Probus (cf. p. 448), he developed, under Hadrian, his own peculiar style, the *eloquentia nouella*, and, being in full accord with the corrupt taste of that

[167] Till 1815, practically nothing was known of Fronto, except that various late writers praise him highly. In that year, Cardinal Mai published what he could make out of a sixth-century palimpsest in the Vatican, containing the correspondence with Antoninus Pius, Marcus Aurelius, and some private friends, together with answers to certain of the letters and the enclosures mentioned in the text. Mai published more in 1823, from another fragmentary MS. Various scholars contributed to the deciphering and elucidation of the difficult text; the standard edition at present is that of Naber, 1867, but much work has been done since, especially by Hauler, some of which is incorporated in the Loeb edition, by C. R. Haines. Quotation is usually by Naber's pages; unfortunately Haines adopts a totally different arrangement, which makes his edition very difficult to use.

[168] Min. Fel., 9, 6; 31, 2.

[169] Birthplace, Min. Fel., *ll. cc.*, Fronto, *ep. ad amicos*, ii, 11 (p. 200 N., i, 292 H.); as pleader, Cass. Dio, lxix, 18, 3, *Φρόντων ὁ τὰ πρῶτα τῶν τότε* (in 136) *Ῥωμαίων ἐν δίκαις φερόμενος*. He was still orator insignis some thirty years later, Jerome, *an. Abr.* 2180 = 164. Did not study the older authors in early life, *ad M. Caesarem*, i, 8, 4 (i, p. 122 H.); that Probus in particular influenced him later is a reasonable conjecture without direct proof. His influence, see, *e.g.*, *ad Antoninum*, i, 2, 2 (ii, p. 36 H.), which passage also is one of the many mentions of his tutorship to the princes. His private life; most of the relevant passages are conveniently listed in H.'s index, under *Fronto*.

day, came to the front as a leading authority in literary matters. Hence his position at court, which he won by his style and kept largely by his real goodness of character. It is, indeed, hard to find any great fault with him except that he wrote affectedly and complained continually of his poor health. Materially, he was apparently very prosperous; his family life was most unhappy, at all events before the end, for he lost his wife and five daughters. His public career was marked with all the conventional honours, the consulship being granted him for two months in 143.[170] He probably exercised no very active functions; certainly he refused a province. How long he lived is not known; his own frequent mentions of his health make it plain that he suffered much from gout.

It has already been said that an able artist could produce fine effects with Fronto's barocco style. Such a one was LVCIVS AP(P)VLEIVS of Madaura in Africa (Mdaurusch, on the borders of the ancient Numidia and Gaetulia, now in Algeria). Born of a family of some local eminence and educated first in his native town, then at Carthage, later in Athens, he attained to great learning, as learning then went, in both the classical tongues, and added thereto a native genius for different kinds of composition. His dates are a matter of conjecture, but he must have been born in the neighbourhood of 125.[171] While still a young man, but with a considerable reputation as a rhetorician and pleader, he married a widow older than himself, by name Pudentilla, of Oea (Tripoli). Out of this marriage grew a lawsuit; her relations accused him of influencing her by magic, a

[170] This appears from *ad M. Caesarem*, i, 8, 4, written by Fronto while consul and mentioning that Marcus is twenty-two years old, which gives the date 143. *Ibid.*, ii, 7, Fronto cannot get away from Rome till Sept. 1; his term of office therefore will have expired then. Thus the months must have been July and August (vol. i, pp. 122, 146, Haines).

[171] Much about Apuleius is uncertain. That his praenomen was Lucius is stated by the inferior MSS. of his works, which may be simply confusing him with the hero of his own romance. That he came from Madaura is certain from *Met.*, xi, 27, confirmed by August., *de ciu. Dei*, viii, 14; cf. *Apol.*, 24; *ibid.*, 23, he and his brother between them inherited about 2,000,000 sestertii = approximately £20,000 or $100,000. Studies at Carthage and Athens, *Flor.*, 18. Age; he was a school-fellow of Aemilianus Strabo, *Flor.*, 16, so presumably about the same age; now Strabo was consul suffectus in 156, consequently would be then about thirty-three or older, see Mommsen, *Staatsrecht*, i (ed. 3), p. 574. This brings us to the neighbourhood of 123 for the births of both men, but a margin of a few years either way must be allowed. The other events mentioned in the text are all to be gathered from the *Apol.*, except the priesthood (*Flor.*, 16, August., *epp.*, 138, 19) and the retirement, which is conjectural, see below.

charge to which Apuleius' evident interest in all forms of mysticism gave some colour. We have the speech (*Apologia*, sometimes called *de magia*), in which he defended himself before the governor of proconsular Africa, Claudius Maximus; the exact date is unknown, but it was under Antoninus Pius and the result was certainly acquittal. After this, it would appear, he held the office of *sacerdos prouinciae* at Carthage. No more is known of his life, but it seems not impossible, at all events, that his last years were spent in religious retirement. He never held any secular office; Pudentilla's comfortable fortune no doubt made life easier for him, but apart from this he would seem to have supported himself, so far as the competence he inherited from his father needed supplementing, by his public exhibitions of rhetorical skill.

Besides the *Apologia*, a monument to artificial ingenuity in its style, which combines archaic Latin with the newest eccentricities of phrase, and in its contents almost a compendium of contemporary superstition,[172] we have left of his considerable writings several minor works and one very remarkable composition, the *Metamorphoses*, often called by moderns *The Golden Ass*, 'golden' referring to the excellence of the work. We may describe it briefly by saying that it is a picaresque romance enlisted in the service of mystical religion, a sort of *Pilgrim's Progress* whose Christian spends most of the book enjoying himself heartily at Vanity Fair. The plot is taken from a Greek tale, whereof we have a re-writing, due, as is generally supposed, to Lucian, but professing to be the work of Lucius of Patrai. This is much shorter than Apuleius' romance, 35 Teubner pages against 277, and it is the additions which are the most interesting parts.[173] In both stories, which are told in the first person, a young man of Greek nationality but Roman citizenship, by name Lucius, visits Thessaly, the traditional home of witchcraft, and there so misuses a magical process that he turns himself into an ass, retaining, however, his human mind and feelings. In his new shape he changes owners several times and meets a number of absurd and not over-edifying adventures, all the time seeking vainly for roses to eat, since by no other means can he regain his proper shape. At last he succeeds and is delivered. Here the story ends in Lucian. Apuleius, in the first place,

[172] There is a handy edition with English notes by H. E. Butler and A. S. Owen, Oxford, Clar. Press, 1914; pp. 181–3 give some idea of the chief works on Apuleius, including the most important of those on the many references to magic.

[173] See Rose, *H.G.L.*, p. 420.

introduces a most interesting episode; Lucius, being captured by brigands, hears an old woman try to divert a girl whom they have made prisoner by telling her the folktale of Cupid and Psyche, the one story of its kind which has come down as such from antiquity,[174] though the language is certainly not of the people, but Apuleius' own gorgeous barocco, and it is at least not unlikely that he meant to introduce an element of Platonic allegory, the salvation of the human soul (Psyche) by Love (Cupid). This is interesting enough; but even more so is the ending of the narrative. Apuleius' Lucius appeals for succour to Isis, and gets the necessary roses from the head of one of her priests. He then becomes a devotee of the goddess, being initiated into one mystery after another of the complicated Graeco-Egyptian ritual which had grown up around her. The tale concludes with his retirement from all worldly activities. It is hard to resist the impression that we have here more than a story. Apuleius, as appears plainly from the *Apologia*, was interested in mystical religion and an initiate into certain cults; there is nothing remarkable in his retirement to a contemplative life, especially in the service of so immensely popular a goddess as Isis. Monks and hermits, so far from being peculiarly Christian, were adopted by Christianity from other faiths, not least those of Egypt. But in any case the story is meant to convey a religious lesson; Isis saves Lucius from the vanities of this world, which make men of no more worth than beasts, to a life of blissful service, here and hereafter.

It is worth mentioning that there exists a Christian novel, the first of its kind, slightly resembling Apuleius' work, though vastly inferior to it, the so-called *Clementine Recognitions*. As we have it, it is in Latin, but translated from a Greek original by Rufinus, and evidently related, though exactly how is obscure, to a surviving Greek collection of discourses, known as the *Clementine Homilies*. Its author is quite unknown, but professes to be S. Clement of Rome, who certainly composed not one word of it. Clement, in search of the true religion, is directed to S. Peter, who preaches to him a remarkable doctrine, widely different from ordinary Catholicism, and then allows his convert to follow him in his journeys and witness his contests with Simon Magus. In the course of his wanderings, Clement finds and recognizes (hence the title) his long-lost parents.[175]

[174] See Rose, *H.G.M.*, pp. 286–8; *Cupid and Psyche* has several times been edited separately, for example by L. C. Purser, London, Bell, 1910, who gives an account of earlier editions, &c.

[175] See, for a brief account, Schanz, iv, p. 420. That Rufinus (for whom cf. p. 495) is the translator he himself testifies, see the concluding remarks of his translation of Origen's commentary on Romans. Though

The minor works include a collection of purple passages from Apuleius' speeches, known as the *Florida*, also several philosophical pamphlets, all of Platonic tone, as Platonism was then understood. They are, a sketch in two books of Plato's doctrine (*de Platone*) and a discourse on what was already called the daemon or god of Sokrates, *de deo Socratis*.[176] There is also a translation of the tractate *On the Universe* (*de mundo*), the original of which has come down to us under the name of Aristotle.[177]

Falsely ascribed to Apuleius is a work very interesting in itself, a Latin rendering of a Hermetic treatise, *Asclepius*, giving an account of certain doctrines of that curious little Graeco-Egyptian sect; it is of uncertain date and unknown authorship. A work *περὶ ἑρμηνείας*, with a title borrowed from Aristotle, is of doubtful authorship. Of the herbal fathered on Apuleius something has been said on p. 428. There is also a *Physiognomonica*, from a Greek source, which bears his name but is probably a good deal later than his day.

He was a prolific writer, and a great number of his works have been lost; their titles and what is known of their contents will be found in Schanz-Hosius-Krüger, iii, pp. 125–9.

After Apuleius we have no more pagan writers with any real claim to eloquence or ingenuity in prose composition; that only a few have survived is probably no loss to literature. Oratory is represented, so far as surviving works go, by sorry specimens of the stupidest of all its branches, the panegyric. Some admirer of this kind of composition has preserved for us a collection of twelve, beginning with that of Pliny the Younger, already mentioned (p. 419), and continuing with the performances of NAZARIVS, who addresses Constantine the Great, CLAVDIVS MAMERTINVS, who presents to Julian the usual speech of thanks for the consulship, and LATINVS PACATVS DREPANIVS, the target of whose eloquence was Theodosius. In addition there are eight speeches of unknown or doubtful authorship. Interest in late developments of Latin and in a few historical facts which can be wrung from this mass of words are the only rational motives for reading any of them.[178]

more work has been done on the *Recognitions* of recent years, the latest complete edition is still that of E. G. Gersdorf, Leipzig, Tauchnitz, 1838, and the Migne reprint thereof.

[176] S. himself merely said that a *δαιμόνιον*, a supernatural warning which he did not profess to explain, at times restrained him from an act.

[177] Cf. Rose, *H.G.L.*, p. 272; the work is really much later than Aristotle. For the *Asclepius*, see Scott-Ferguson, *Hermetica*, iv (Oxford, 1936), pp. x–xxxiii.

[178] There is an edition of the collection by Baehrens in the Teubner series.

Better, but still poor enough, are the performances of a noteworthy man, one of the last champions of Western paganism, the eloquent Q. AVRELIVS SYMMACHVS.[179] Born about 340, the son of a man of some distinction, L. Aurelius Avianus Symmachus, he became a prominent public servant and won fame as the leading orator of the day. We have some fragments of his speeches, which are no emptier than other productions of the same kind (they deal largely with the virtues of contemporary Emperors) and show in their style the after-effects of Fronto's antiquarianism and a good knowledge of the ordinary classical authors. Much bulkier is his correspondence, and of this a part, his official dispatches or *relationes*, is by no means without interest, for the contemporary events were sufficiently stirring. The most famous, and the most admired in those days for its eloquence, is the third, an unsuccessful plea addressed to Valentinian II for the restoration of the last remnants of official paganism, the altar of Victory in the senate-chamber and the public maintenance of the Vestals.[180] The other letters are the most perfect and unsurpassable models in any language of the art of saying nothing at all in a style of the most extreme artificiality. The fact is that classical Latin was no longer a spoken tongue, and these writings are exercises in the use of a dead language which pretends still to be alive. It comes almost as a shock to learn that this spinner of artificial phrases in which the vocabulary and syntax of several centuries mingle took an active part in affairs both civil and military and was at least once in real personal danger, after the fall of the usurper Maximus in 388, who had courted the pagan party and been addressed by Symmachus in a speech of compliment.

It will surprise no one to hear that during this age poetry was at a low ebb. With one exception, presently to be discussed, Juvenal is the last Latin poet ; after him there are but versifiers. That it was not technical skill that was lacking, at least at first, for even that went towards the end, is clear enough ; a group of poets, known collectively as the 'moderns' (*neoterici*), who

[179] The standard edition is that of Seeck, Berlin, Weidmann, 1883, in the *Monumenta Germaniae historica*.

[180] This was the work to which Ambrose (p. 484) and Prudentius (p. 509) wrote replies. Both praise its eloquence ; the former says : aurea enim, sicut scriptura diuina docet, est lingua sapientium litteratorum, quae phaleratis dotata sermonibus et quodam splendentis eloquii uelut coloris pretiosi corusco resultans, capit animorum oculos specie formosi, *epp.*, xviii, 2. The latter (*c. Symm.*, i, 632 *sqq.*) says Symmachus is more eloquent than Cicero, that if only he would turn Christian his words would deserve to be written in gold, &c., &c.

wrote about the time of Hadrian,[181] were capable of much variety of metre and various clever tricks such as writing lines which would scan and make sense whether one began with the first word or the last; they had a successor as late as the time of Constantine, PVBLILIVS OPTATIANVS PORFYRIVS, probably the city prefect of 329 and 333, certainly a man of high rank, who, falling into disgrace, wooed back the Imperial favour with a most extraordinary volume of complimentary verses, in which he does almost everything conceivable with language except making it into poetry. There are figure-poems, *i.e.*, those in which the lines, being of various lengths, trace pictures; square poems, in which every line has the same number of letters and the number of letters equals the number of lines, while the two perpendicular sides and even the diagonals of the square spell out words; anacyclic verses, in which each couplet is read forwards and then backwards.[182] Imperial patronage was not wanting, for again and again we hear of literary men in high office or otherwise favoured, and several of the Emperors were themselves poets of some repute; for example, Hadrian and Gordian I. The real lack was something to say which had not already been said a hundred times; it is symptomatic that Nemesianus, in rejecting hackneyed subjects, uses a formula which had become very hackneyed indeed since Vergil had employed it.[183]

This man, M. AVRELIVS OLYMPIVS NEMESIANVS, of Carthage, was such a pupil as might have satisfied the heart of any schoolmaster, and indeed he celebrates, under the name of Meliboeus, the man who had taught him. Nemesianus, presumably under 'Meliboeus'' tuition, acquired a very good acquaintance with the technique of the hexameter and with the older poets; thus equipped, he wrote four pastorals, which have come down to us in the same MSS. as those of Calpurnius (cf. p. 381), for which reason the two writers have often been confused. These poems have a sort of faded prettiness here and there, the result of an imitation of Vergil and Calpurnius so close as often to lead to

[181] They are cited by Diomedes and Terentianus Maurus; the fragments are in *F.P.R.*, p. 374 *sqq*. See Schanz-Hosius-Krüger, iii, pp. 21–5.

[182] The latest edition is in the Teubner series, by Kluge, 1926. As an example of anacyclic verses the following may suffice; it is the last four lines of his poem on Venus and Adonis: impatiens Venus est siluas dum lustrat Adonis,/carpit si matrem iam cui conueniat./conueniat cui iam matrem si carpit Adonis/lustrat dum siluas, est Venus impatiens. See further Schanz, iv, pp. 11–14.

[183] Namely, a list of stock themes about which he does not mean to write; used by Vergil, *Georg.*, iii, 3 *sqq.*, who possibly had it from Choirilos of Samos, and after him by Manilius, iii, 5–26, the *Aetna*, 9–28, Juvenal, i, 7 *sqq.*, to name no others, and now by Nemes., *Cyn.*, 15–47.

whole lines or even one or two short passages being borrowed entire.[184] They are the perfection of schoolboy diligence in the art of verse-making, and if he had had the power, he might have gone on to write poetry. However, he had not that gift, and so merely produced a versified treatise on hunting, thus following in the footsteps of Grattius (see p. 339), and apparently another on fowling, unless this was part of the same work. We have left 325 lines of the former poem, the *Cynegetica*, and some fragments of the other.[185] His date is exactly fixed by himself, for he praises the Emperors Carinus and Numerianus, both of whom took the title of Augustus in 283, and died, the former in 285 and the latter in September 284; 283–4 is therefore the time when he composed, or at all events finished, the *Cynegetica*. Like the *Bucolica*, it has occasionally some pretty lines, and its versification is competent.

A collection of moral verses, very popular in the Middle Ages, has come down to us under the name of CATO. Whether this was really the name of the author or has resulted from a tendency to ascribe all nameless moralizings to Cato the Elder (p. 91) is uncertain; it is generally supposed that the writer lived about the third century. His maxims are trite enough, but not ill expressed, each being set forth in two hexameters, whence the work is often called *Catonis disticha*. It has survived in a recension of the time of Karl the Great, by which the original arrangement has been disturbed and some prefaratory verses added to the four books into which it is now divided.[186]

There were numerous minor poets, for nearly every one of any education seems to have dabbled in verse. The efforts of many have been preserved, at least in part, in the collection known as the Latin Anthology [187] and sporadically in sundry

[184] The *Bucolica* are edited, *e.g.*, by C. Giarratano in the Paravia series, with Calpurnianus, also in *P.L.M.*, iii, p. 174 *sqq*. The passage referred to is i, 32–80. If I am right in supposing that the singer represents Nemesianus and Meliboeus is his old teacher, the Bucolics probably are an early effort, as the singer is called *puer* in 81 and urged to persevere.

[185] See *P.L.M.*, iii, p. 190 *sqq.*; cf. Schanz-Hosius-Krüger, iii, pp. 30–4.

[186] Latest publication in the Loeb series (*Minor Latin Poets*, J. Wight Duff and A. M. Duff). See Schanz-Hosius-Krüger, iii, pp. 39–41.

[187] This is a collection of poems made in Africa, under the Vandal monarchy, by some unknown person possessed of a certain amount of learning and no sense whatever, whose affected preface, written in riddling language taken from glossaries, is still extant. It, or smaller collections taken from it, is preserved in various MSS., and has been published, first by Salmasius, later by various scholars, including Baehrens (*P.L.M.*, iv) and, with supplements from other sources, chiefly epigraphical, by Buecheler, Lommatzsch and Riese, in the Teubner series.

MSS.; for example, some copies of Solinus (p. 438) give us the opening lines of a poem, *Pontica*, which set out to treat of the sea. Many of these authors are nameless, nearly all insignificant; mention may be made of one or two. HOSIDIVS GETA was one of a number of persons who apparently found nothing better to do than rearrange Vergil's lines into centos. He was a contemporary of Tertullian,[188] and patched together tags of his model, mostly half-lines, into the dialogue and choruses of a *Medea*. Later, for he was probably the 'eloquent' governor of Gaul whom Jerome mentions,[189] came TIBERIANVS, who is not unworthy of record for some tolerable little poems in different metres which are ascribed to him, but much more so if, as some have suggested, it was he who wrote the *Peruigilium Veneris* (p. 513).

Scarcely better than the rest of these triflers, but bulkier or at any rate better preserved, is a man who deserves some attention because he may be regarded as the first faint glimmer heralding the full day of French literature. DECIMVS MAGNVS AVSONIVS of Burdigala (Bordeaux) was born early in the fourth century, the exact date being unknown, as is the time of his death. He was educated partly in his native city, partly at Tolosa (Toulouse), and was for thirty years a teacher, first of grammar and then of rhetoric, at Burdigala, until he was summoned to court to become the tutor of Gratian, son of the then Emperor Valentinian, who was in residence at Trier. He must have acquitted himself well, for he was given several high offices, including the consulate (379), still a great honour, though it had long ceased to be of any political importance, and before that, under Gratian, the governorship first of Gaul and then of Italy, Illyria and Africa, these in conjunction with his own son, Hesperius. In 383 Gratian was murdered, and Ausonius retired into private life, still keeping up a correspondence, however, with some of the most noteworthy men of his time, including Symmachus (p. 524), Paulinus of Nola, the future Bishop of that place, and the Emperor Theodosius.[190] The mixture of pagan and Christian

[188] Tert., *de praesc. haer.*, 39: uides hodie ex Vergilio fabulam in totum aliam componi . . . denique Hosidius Geta Medeam tragoediam ex Vergilio plenissime exsuxit. Several such performances will be found along with Geta in *P.L.M.*, iv, p. 197 *sqq*.

[189] Jerome, *an. Abr.* 2352 = 336: Tiberianus uir disertus praefectus praetorio Gallias regit. The suggestion that he wrote the *Peruigilium* is due to Baehrens, see *P.L.M.*, iii, p. 264, and the literature there cited; it has since found some support.

[190] All this is mostly from his own versified preface to a collection of his works, which is the first poem in modern editions of him; these include that of R. Peiper, Teubner, 1886, now somewhat difficult to get, and that

names in his list of friends is an indication of his own position. Nominally, he was a Christian, as is shown by the orthodox tone of the prayers and hymns contained in his works here and there.[191] That he had any deep convictions is, however, most unlikely; he conformed decorously to the prevailing religion of the time, as he would, a century earlier, have respectfully taken part in the older one. His chief interest was the elegant handling of language, in which he showed, not indeed first-rate skill, for that was now hardly to be found, but very fair acquaintance with the classical models and some ingenuity. Higher than this we cannot justly praise him; he wrote trifles, sometimes pretty or clever, often merely tiresome in their emptiness.

Ausonius himself seems to have made a collected edition of his works, to which the poem cited in note 190 was the preface. This must have been before 383, since he says nothing of the death of Gratian. A later and fuller edition, possibly the work of Hesperius, seems also to have been published, and our MSS.[192] between them give us a fairly good idea of both. Naturally, a certain number of small pieces not by him have in time found their way among the genuine ones. We have, besides the preface to his own collection and a prose letter from Theodosius asking for Ausonius' works, to which is appended the poet's elegiac reply, the following groups: (1) The *Ephemeris*, a versified account of Ausonius' day from morning to night. (2) A group of six poems dealing with personal matters, his estate, his consulship, &c. (3) The *parentalia*, thirty epitaphs on dead members of his immediate circle. (4) The *commemoratio professorum Burdigalensium*, which performs the same office for the staff of Bordeaux in Ausonius' student days. (5) Thirty-five miscellaneous epitaphs, ranging from the heroes of the Trojan War to real or imaginary contemporaries; it would seem as if Ausonius was somewhat in demand for these little tributes. (6) The *eclogarum liber*, thirty-six miscellaneous pieces on a variety of topics. (7) *The crucifixion of Cupid*, a bad dream of the love-god

of H. G. E. White, 1919, in the Loeb series, which is much more accessible. The necessary additions to what Ausonius there tells us are: his summons to court must have been after 364 (accession of Valentinian) and was before 368, for he was then with the Emperor on his campaign against the Alemanni and was given a German girl, Bissula, as his share of the spoils (see the little poems on her, vol. i, pp. 216–22 White; he apparently freed her, taught her or had her taught Latin and made a great favourite of her); his consulate is dated by Prosper's Chronicle; his return to Burdigala is mentioned in a note prefixed to *epist.*, 1.

[191] As ii, 3; iii, 2 and 3. See White, vol. i, pp. xii–xiv.

[192] Some account of the tradition is given in White's preface; more in Schanz, iv, pp. 24–8.

in which all the unfortunate heroines of mythology, and his own mother, threaten him with most dire vengeance. (8) The epigrams, already mentioned, to Bissula. (9) His best poem, *Mosella*, a description, not without some merit and feeling for nature, of the river Moselle. (10) A series of rather feeble addresses to twenty famous cities, beginning with Rome and ending with Burdigala. (11) *Technopaegnion*, still more feeble, being nothing but a dozen copies of hexameters in which every line ends, and, in the first of the series, begins also, with a monosyllable. (12) A kind of pageant, in which each of the Seven Sages appears, gives a short account of himself and retires. (13) Verses on the Twelve Caesars, a sort of brief metrical commentary on Suetonius. (14) A few trifles in verse to be appended to a list of the consuls down to his own year which he had compiled. (15) A poem, expounding all the properties of the number three, with an introductory letter to Symmachus, explaining that he wrote the original draft in mess, while on active service. (16) The *cento nuptialis*, a poem written by order of Valentinian and consisting wholly of Vergilian tags, like Hosidius Geta's production (p. 525); the most ingenious part is also the most unpleasant, for by a process of collocation totally innocent phrases of the poet are twisted into indecent meanings. (17) A collection of thirty-four epistles, mostly in verse; some of them are not from but to Ausonius. Fragments of others remain. (18) A collection of epigrams, some from Greek originals. (19) A prose speech of gratitude to the Emperor for his consulship.

The senile degeneration of literature in Ausonius' circle is shown not merely by the feebleness of most of his writings but by the obvious fact that he was admired for them.

Towering above all these pygmies comes one figure, as mysterious as it is astonishing, which appears for nine years only and in that time wins a place in Latin literature worthy of better ages. CLAVDIVS CLAVDIANVS, whose name is usually shortened to CLAUDIAN in English, was perhaps born in Alexandria, had certainly lived there; we have even some lines of an extremely silly Greek poem on the battle of the gods and Giants which are ascribed to a Claudian, though if our poet wrote them it must have been in his school-days.[193] At all

[193] The full name of the poet is preserved in the headings of some of his MSS. For more particulars of him, see Schanz-Hosius-Krüger, iv, 2, pp. 3–32. The Greek fragment is in vol. i, p. lxxviii *sqq*. of L. Jeep's edition, Teubner, 1876–9, one of the principal modern recensions; the other is that of Th. Birt, Berlin, 1892 (vol. x of *Monumenta historiae*

events, his native language was Greek and he had written something in that tongue before he began to use Latin. This was not the handicap it would have been in Vergil's or Lucan's day; all the writers in verse were using a medium foreign to their daily speech, hardly less than to the language of modern Europeans, some of whom (Buchanan, Milton, Cowper and others) have been far better poets in Latin than the latest of the Latins. In this respect Terence (p. 72) is a more surprising phenomenon. But the really remarkable thing about Claudian is that in that age he recovered more than a little of the manliness of the best Latins, and even when flattering the feeble sons of Theodosius, does so with a vigour worthy a contemporary of Statius. But he is much better at invective, witness his poems against Eutropius. The guiding principle of his poetical activity, so far as it was concerned with contemporary events, was his zeal for the great Vandal general Stilicho, concerning whom there is no need to say anything so long as the twenty-ninth chapter of Gibbon's *Decline and Fall* is extant. The series of his works begins with a panegyric on the consuls of 395 (cf. note 193), a subject on which one would have thought it impossible to say more than worn-out nothings; but Claudian has the happy idea of making the goddess Rome in person visit Theodosius in the hour of victory, thus introducing a picture of the warlike deity and the warlike Emperor which Lucan could not greatly have bettered. There follow (Nos. 2, 3, 4 and 5 in our editions) two books of invective against Rufinus, the powerful favourite of Arcadius. The metre is the hexameter, each book having a prologue in elegiacs; mythological machinery is used with less creaking than might have been expected of so rusty a device (Claudian likes describing the powers of evil, who of course support Rufinus), and the favourite's murder is described and lauded with the utmost gusto. This is followed by loyal poems on the third and fourth consulates (396 and 398) of Stilicho's

Germanica). Jeep, *ibid.*, lxxx–lxxxi, gives the few other poems which have the name of Claudian (*Κλαυδιανὸς*) attached to them. Since there was another and later writer of that name, it may be that all are his; two certainly are, for they are distinctly Christian. That our Claudian had lived in Egypt (and therefore, since he was a man of letters, in Alexandria) is clear from his own words, *carm. min.*, 4, 3, nostro cognite Nilo, cf. Apollinaris Sidonius, *carm.*, ix, 274, Pelusiaco satus Canopo, which means simply 'Egyptian', cf. Lucan, viii, 543. Greek compositions, *carm. min.*, 3, 13–14, to Probinus: Romanos bibimus primum te consule fontes/et Latiae cessit Graia Thalia togae; this was in 395, the consuls being Sex. Anicius Hermogenianus Olybrius and Sex. Anicius Probinus.

nominal sovran Honorius [194] (Nos. 6–8), and a series (9–14) on the marriage of that feeble-minded youth to Stilicho's daughter Maria.[195] No. 15 deals with Stilicho's war against the African usurper Gildo; it is incomplete as we have it. No. 17 is another panegyric on a consul, this time Manlius Theodorus, who held that office in 399, the year after the affair of Gildo; it also has an elegiac introduction, No. 16. Nos. 18–20 contain some of the most eloquent abuse in Latin, which is particularly happy in that branch of rhetoric; they are an account of the rise and fall of Eutropius the eunuch, Rufinus' successor in the real mastery of the Eastern Empire, and they do not spare him. Nos. 21–24 are a long, though incomplete, paean of joy at Stilicho's consulship in 400; Eutropius had fallen during the previous year. After this the poems come less thickly; Nos. 25 and 26 are respectively the preface to a hexameter piece and the hexameters themselves, dealing with the battle of Pollentia, Easter Day, 402, which Claudian represents as a Roman victory. Nos. 27 and 28, again an elegiac prelude and hexameter poem, date themselves by their subject, the sixth consulate (404) of Honorius. Less exactly datable are the panegyric on Serena, Stilicho's wife, the niece and adopted daughter of Theodosius (No. 29), which merely states (verses 1–2) that Claudian has delayed a long while in giving her this tribute, and the marriage-poem (No. 31, with its short preface, No. 30) in honour of Palladius and his wife Celerina; the former was a high official of the court, and both he and the father of Celerina were personal friends of the poet.

Besides these occasional pieces, Claudian tried his hand at mythological epic on a small scale. There is a fragment (No. 37) of a *Gigantomachia* in Latin, certainly Claudian's, whether he wrote the Greek one or not; it is incomplete, perhaps never finished, but more of it existed in antiquity, to judge by a quotation in Jerome.[196] It is better than one would expect of that century, though not without absurdities; Claudian was not well advised to make Athena wound a giant with her spear in one

[194] There is some doubt where the poem conventionally numbered 4 should go in this series; Jeep puts it before No. 8 (Honorius' fourth consulship), instead of No. 5 (the second book against Rufinus).

[195] Of these, Nos. 11–13, *Fescennina*, are a series of three little poems in lyric metres, supposed apparently to be sung at the wedding.

[196] Cf. n. 193. The passage of Jerome is *comm. in Isaiam*, viii, 27 (vol. iv, p. 361 A Vall.): pulchre quidam poeta in Gigantomachia de Encelado lusit, 'quo fugis, Encelade? quascunque accesseris oras,/sub deo (Claudian of course wrote *sub Ioue*) semper eris'.

part of his body while turning the rest of him into stone with the Gorgon on her corslet.[197] More elaborate is the poem on the *Rape of Proserpina*, which is also unfinished, its fourth and last book (No. 36; the first three and the prefatory elegiacs are Nos. 32–35), ending as Demeter begins to search for her daughter. It is unfortunate that the last surviving lines are another very forced conceit [198]; there are other and better things in the work.

A number of short poems have come down bearing Claudian's name, though not all are genuinely his; to discuss their subjects and authorship would be too lengthy. As a sample of the mordant wit of which he was at times capable, we may instance the epigram to Iacobus, the *magister equitum*. This worthy is implored to be merciful to the poet's verses, and the conditional blessings of various Christian saints (Claudian remained impenitently pagan all his life) invoked upon him. But those especially asked to prosper his warfare are female, Susanna and Thekla, and the final grace that is to be his is never to stain his hand with the blood of a foe.[199]

What became of Claudian after the death of Stilicho we do not know, for he passes out of history as abruptly as he entered it.[200] His is the last name of any real importance among the pagans. We may mention that there was a certain AVIANVS (not to be confused with Avienus, for whom see p. 440), who wrote a book of Aesopic fables in bad elegiacs, about the end, as is generally supposed, of the fourth century.[201] Lastly, a Gaul, RVTILIVS CLAVDIVS NAMATIANVS, had occasion in 416 (or 417) to return from Rome to his native country. The elegiac poem [202] which he wrote to commemorate this event has come

[197] No. xxxvii, 111–13.

[198] At the sheen of Demeter's torches antra procul Scyllaea petit canibusque reductis/pars stupefacta silet, pars nondum exterrita latrat.

[199] The epigram is No. 9 of the *carmina minora* in Jeep's edition. For Claudian's paganism, see Augustine, *de ciuit. Dei*, v, 26; Orosius, *adu. pag.*, vii, 35, 21 (taken from Aug.).

[200] See W. H. Semple in *Class. Rev.*, xlviii, p. 232, and the book he there reviews, P. Fargues, *Claudien*.

[201] For date and other particulars of this poetaster, see Schanz-Hosius-Krüger, iv, 2, pp. 32–5. The fullest edition in English is that of R. Ellis, Oxford, 1887.

[202] There is a handy edition with translation and notes by C. H. Keene, London, Bell, 1907; more recent is that of J. Vessereau and F, Préhac, Paris, Les belles lettres, 1933. The passages in question are respectively Rutilius, ii, 41–60 (see O. Schissel-Fleschenberg in *Janus*, ii, 1920) and i, 47 *sqq*. More details in Schanz-Hosius-Krüger, iv, 2, pp. 38–41.

down to us and is noteworthy for two passages in particular, one an invective against Stilicho, the other an apostrophe to Rome surprisingly noble for that age:

exaudi, regina tui pulcherrima mundi,
  inter sidereos Roma recepta polos,
exaudi, genetrix hominum genetrixque deorum,
  non procul a caelo per tua templa sumus.
te canimus semperque, sinent dum fata, canemus;
  sospes nemo potest immemor esse tui.

With this we may fittingly end our survey.

ADDENDA

p. 173. Note 56.
Carsten Hoëg, in *Δράγμα* (Lund 1939), pp. 264–79, argues that these speeches were actually delivered.

p. 325. Note 11.
That this, not Tomi, is the correct form is shown by the MSS. of *trist.*, iii, 9, 33, *Pont.*, iv, 14, 15; see Owen in *Oxford Class. Dict.*, art. *Ovid*, 4.

p. 354. Note 40.
One line, iv, 16, nascentes morimur finisque ab origine pendet, is common on tombs, see A. Brelich, *Aspetti della morte* (Budapest, 1937), p. 30.

p. 432. Note 38.
A fourteenth book, *de ueterinaria medicina*, was discovered in a MS. of the Ambrosian Library by J. Svennung in 1926. It is probably by Palladius, but consists largely of extracts. See *Class Rev.*, li (1937), p. 19.

p. 455. Note 138.
There is a later edition by C. Barwick, Teubner 1925.

p. 459. Note 151.
For a recent discussion, see S. Weinstock in *Journ. Rom. Stud.* xxxvi (1946), pp. 101–29.

p. 477. Note 22.
For a critique of the documentary evidence regarding his martyrdom, see R. Reitzenstein in *Sitzungsber. Heidelb.*, 1913, Abhandlung 14.

p. 508. Note 12.
Dom Morin's views are criticized by B. Axelson in *Bull. de la Société royale des lettres de Lund*, 1936–37, p. 107 *sqq.*

BIBLIOGRAPHY

The writings about Latin writers are so many that to give a complete list of them would mean compiling another volume larger than this one. Consequently, nothing is attempted here beyond naming a few fundamental works from which detailed information may be had, together with some account of the chief series of texts. A number of annotated editions and other useful books of reference are mentioned in connexion with the authors of whom they treat.

TEXTS

(1) The Teubner series (Bibliotheca Teubneriana), published by B. G. Teubner, Leipzig and Berlin. The most nearly complete; usually good critical editions, embodying recent scholarship, and often the best or the only modern texts available. The same firm publishes several larger editions of authors or parts of authors, details of which may be found in its catalogues. (2) The Oxford series (Bibliotheca classica Oxoniensis, or Oxford classical texts, abbreviated O.C.T.). Contains hitherto a few authors only; generally well edited. Publishers, the University Press, Oxford. (3) The Paravia series, published by I. B. Paravia & Co., Turin. Contains handy editions, with critical notes and introductions, of a selection of authors. (4) The Loeb series, Heinemann, London, and Harvard University Press. Texts of varying degrees of accuracy with translations in English on the opposite page, also varying much in value. (5) The Budé series, published by Les Belles Lettres, Paris. Critical texts, generally good, with French translations opposite. Most of the authors mentioned will be found in one or another of these series, some of them in most or all.

The following are referred to by abbreviations in the course of this book:

Bremer. *Iurisprudentiae antehadrianae quae supersunt* edidit F. P. Bremer. Teubner, 2 vols., 1898 and 1901.

Capt., *see* Plautus.

Cato. Except for the *de agri cultura*, this author is cited from *M. Catonis praeter librum de re rustica quae exstant*. Henricus Iordan recensuit et prolegomena scripsit. Teubner, 1860.

C.I.L. *Corpus Inscriptionum Latinarum*, Berlin, various dates from 1862.

Dessau. H. Dessau, *Inscriptiones Latinae selectae*, 3 vols. in 5, 1892–1914.

F.I.R.A. *Fontes Iuris Romani Antiqui*; edidit C. G. Bruns. Editio septima, cura Ottonis Gradenwitz. Tübingen, Mohr, 4 vols., 1909–12.

F.P.L., *F.P.R.* (1) *Fragmenta poetarum Romanorum* collegit et emendauit Aemilius Baehrens. Teubner, 1886. (2) *Fragmenta poetarum Latinorum epicorum et lyricorum praeter Ennium et Lucilium* post Aemilium Baehrens iterum edidit Willy Morel, Teubner, 1927. References are given thus: *F.P.L.* (or *F.P.R.*) 42/15, meaning that the passage in question is on p. 42 of Baehrens', p. 15 of Morel's work.

Funaioli. *Grammaticae Romanae fragmenta* collegit recensuit Hyginus Funaioli. Teubner, 1907. (Vol. i only has appeared.)

H.R.F. *Historicorum Romanorum fragmenta* collegit disposuit recensuit Hermannus Peter. Teubner, 1883.

Keil. *Grammatici Latini ex recensione* Henrici Keil. 7 vols., Teubner, 1857–1880. All cited as 'Keil', although several volumes and parts of volumes are by other editors.

Klussmann. *Cn. Naeuii poetae Romani uitam descripsit, carminum reliquias collegit, poesis rationem exposuit* Ernestus Klussmann. Jena, Hochhausen, 1843.

O.R.F. *Oratorum Romanorum fragmenta ab Appio inde Caeco et M. Porcio Catone usque ad Q. Aurelium Symmachum.* Collegit atque illustrauit Henricus Meyerus. Turici, typis Orellii, Fuesslini et sociorum. Ed. 2, 1842.

Pease, *see* Vergil.

Plautus. *The Captini of Plautus, edited with introduction, &c.*, by W. M. Lindsay, London, Methuen, 1900, is cited as 'Capt.'.

Ribbeck. *Scaenicae Romanorum poesis fragmenta* tertiis curis recognouit Otto Ribbeck. Teubner, 2 vols., 1887 and 1888.

Vergil. The edition of Aen. iv, *P. Vergilii Maronis Aeneidos liber quartus*, edited by Arthur Stanley Pease, Harvard Univ. Press, Cambridge, Mass., 1935, is cited as 'Pease'.

WORKS OF REFERENCE

The principal treatise on Latin literature is that of the late Martin Schanz, *Geschichte der römischen Litteratur.* This is published by Beck, Munich, and is now undergoing revision. Vols. i and ii have been revised by C. Hosius and are cited as 'Schanz-Hosius'; vols. iii and iv, 2, by C. Hosius and G. Krüger (these are cited as 'Schanz-Hosius-Krüger), while vol. iv, 1, is still in Schanz' own latest revision. This elaborate work contains large select bibliographies in connexion with the treatment of each author. It is also to be understood that the reader is referred to the various classical dictionaries, especially, where available, to the great *Realencyclopädie des klassischen Altertums*, edited originally by Pauly, revised (since 1893) by G. Wissowa, W. Kroll and K. Mittelhaus, assisted by a number of scholars (Stuttgart, Metzler). The *Year's Work in Classical Studies* (Arrowsmith, Bristol, 1906–47) gave accounts of new work in this and other fields of classical study; in French, *L'Année Philologique* aims at complete information. More will be found, but at longer intervals, in the successive volumes of *Jahresberichte* issued by O. R. Reisland, Leipzig, which from time to time include studies of works produced in this field. Most periodicals dealing with classical scholarship contain reviews of recent books in English, these include *C.R.*, *J.H.S.*, *J.R.S.*, *Greece and Rome*, *C.Ph.* (Chicago).

The following are cited in this work by abbreviations not explained in the text or notes:

Altheim, R. R. Franz Altheim, *Römische Religionsgeschichte*, Leipzig and Berlin, de Gruyter, 3 vols., 1931–32–33.

Atkins. J. W. H. Atkins, *Literary Criticism in Antiquity, a sketch of its Development*, Cambridge, University Press, 2 vols., 1934.

Farrer. J. A. Farrer, *Literary Forgeries*, London, Longmans, Green & Co., 1907.

Friedländer, *Sitt.* Ludwig Friedländer, *Darstellungen aus der Sittengeschichte Roms*, ed. 9–10, revised by G. Wissowa, Leipzig, Hirtzel, 1919–21 (4 vols.).

Gagé. Jean Gagé, *Recherches sur les jeux séculaires.* Paris, Les belles lettres, 1934.

H.G.L., *see* Rose.

H.G.M., or Myth., *see* Rose.

P.C.I., *see* Rose.

Platner-Ashby. *A Topographical Dictionary of Ancient Rome*, by Samuel Ball Platner, completed and revised by Thomas Ashby. Oxford, Clar. Press, 1928.

Roscher, *Lex.* *Ausführliches Lexikon der griechischen und römischen Mythologie*, edited by W. H. Roscher and others. Teubner, 1884–1937.

Rose, H. J. *Handbook of Greek Literature*, Methuen, 3rd edn. 1948 (' H.G.L.') ; *Handbook of Greek Mythology* (' H.G.M.', or ' Myth.'), same, 4th edn. 1949 ; *Primitive Culture in Italy* (' P.C.I.'), same, 1926.

Sandys. J. E. Sandys, *A History of Classical Scholarship*, Cambridge, Univ. Press ; vol. i, ed. 3, 1921 ; vols. ii and iii, 1908.

Walde. Alois Walde, *Lateinisches etymologisches Wörterbuch*, Heidelberg, Winter, ed. 1, 1906, ed. 3, revised by J. B. Hoffmann, now being issued in parts.

Wissowa, *Ges. Abh.* G. Wissowa, *Gesammelte Abhandlungen zur römischen Religions- und Stadtgeschichte*, Munich, Beck, 1904.

Wissowa, *R. K. R.* Same author and publisher, *Religion und Kultus der Römer*, ed. 2, 1912.

Zielinski, *Clauselgesetz.* Th. Zielinski, *Das Clauselgesetz in Ciceros Reden*, Leipzig, Dieterich, 1904.

Zielinski, *Con. Ryth.* Same author and publisher, *Der constructive Rhythmus in Ciceros Reden*, 1914.

Pp. 470–510. While this edition was in preparation, a ' new, complete and critical edition ' of the Latin Christian writers was announced from the Abbey of St. Pierre, Steinbrugge. It will consist of 175 large volumes, to be published at the rate of about ten a year, and part of Vol. i (Tertullian) has now (1953) appeared.

INDEX

(In the following Index, for assistance in preparing which I have to thank Miss E. Söwy and my son P. H. P. Rose, the principal reference to each author is printed in bold-faced type. Pronunciation is indicated by an accent, as Cornu'tus, for all names of more than two syllables whose accent does not come on the third syllable from the end (antepenult). Some obvious abbreviations, such as s(on), d(aughter), w(ife), f(ather), m(other), are used.)